Toward the Common Good

Toward the Common Good

Perspectives in International Public Relations

Donn James Tilson

University of Miami

Emmanuel C. Alozie

Governors State University

Boston • New York • San Francisco
Mexico City • Montreal • Toronto • London • Madrid • Munich • Paris
Hong Kong • Singapore • Tokyo • Cape Town • Sydney

Series Editor: *Molly Taylor*
Editorial Assistant: *Michael Kish*
Marketing Manager: *Mandee Eckersley*
Editorial-Production Administrator: *Anna Socrates*
Editorial-Production Service: *Omegatype Typography, Inc.*
Manufacturing Buyer: *JoAnne Sweeney*
Composition and Prepress Buyer: *Linda Cox*
Cover Administrator: *Kristina Mose-Libon*
Electronic Composition: *Omegatype Typography, Inc.*

For related titles and support materials, visit our online catalog at www.ablongman.com.

Between the time Web site information is gathered and published, some sites may have closed. Also, the transcription of URLs can result in typographical errors. The publisher would appreciate notification where these errors occur so that they may be corrected in subsequent editions.

Many of the designations used by manufacturers and sellers to distinguish their products are claimed as trademarks. Where those designations appear in this book, and Allyn and Bacon was aware of a trademark claim, the designations have been printed in initial or all caps.

Library of Congress Cataloging-in-Publication Data

Toward the common good : perspectives in international public relations / edited by Donn
    James Tilson, Emmanuel C. Alozie.
        p. cm.
    ISBN 0-205-36138-2 (alk. paper)
        1. Public relations—Cross-cultural studies.   I. Tilson, Donn James.   II. Alozie, Emmanuel
C.

HM1221.T68 2004
659.2—dc21

2003052164

Printed in the United States of America

10   9   8   7   6   5   4   3   2   1   08   07   06   05   04   03

To our loving families and to our God

Bring me my Bow of burning gold:
Bring me my Arrows of desire:
Bring me my Spear: O clouds unfold!
Bring me my Chariot of fire.

I will not cease from Mental Fight,
Nor shall my Sword sleep in my hand
Till we have built Jerusalem,
In England's green & pleasant Land.
—William Blake, *Milton, a Poem in 2 Books*

Contents

Foreword

Tim Traverse-Healy

In this sound byte, cliché-ridden age, I ask for forgiveness for asserting that this book both "plugs a gap" and "fills a need." The gap: Scholars, who are shadowing the public relations field of human endeavor, have outlets available to them wherein the results of their studies and research projects can be published and shared with others. Where international, as opposed to domestic, topics are concerned the situation is dire enough, but when the amount of coverage accorded the affairs of developing countries is reviewed, it is even worse. The need: Practitioners want access to authoritative information describing the nature and the state of the craft in areas, territories, and countries with which they are not immediately professionally familiar but in which they can suddenly find themselves having to initiate operations. Under the political, economic, and commercial pressures of globalization, practitioners are fast entering the realms of developing countries.

This book—*Toward the Common Good: Perspectives in International Public Relations*—is overdue. The problem is that the canvas is so large, the space comparatively small, and the brushes of necessity broad. So like the movie *Star Wars* this should only be *Toward the Common Good One* and, it is hoped, *Toward the Common Good Two* is on the drawing board.

Only a few years ago, a well-known international statesman was publicly accused of having a secretive affair with a courtesan of beauty and note. To the media, his fellow citizens, and, presumably, his wife, he vehemently denied it. The courtesan's subsequent comment was the ultimate in "put downs" for corporate spokespersons who are economical with the truth—"Well, he would say that, wouldn't he?" Consider the credibility of the source. At the other end of the social spectrum, a famous Oxford University don carried the nickname of "BIM." This was because he was in the habit of introducing each and every one of his lectures with the same stricture: "Ladies and gentlemen, please Bear In Mind when analyzing the matter under discussion today that you should not only concern yourself with the writer's content but also ask yourself, 'Why is he saying it?' " In another word, the context. Always, it is a wise approach to consider the source and the context when assessing reports, particularly those from foreign parts. But in the case of *Toward the Common Good,* the reader can be assured that the contributions have been validated by academic and practitioner peers alike.

It is a historical fact that the professional practice of public relations "went international" in the immediate post–World War II years—the 1950s and 1960s. The driving forces were not diplomatic, but rather the commercial imperatives of the oil, arms, airline, automotive, and drug industries, followed closely by travel and tourism. In the capital cities of the nations of the developed world—war-torn or not—corporate public relations executives began to appear, and small consultancies emerged to serve them. Interestingly, they seemed to have known each other and an intriguing, indeed unique, network was formed. Currently, in the wake of such dominating brands as Nike, McDonald's, and Coca-Cola, the marketing fraternity has coined the mantra, "Think global and act local." But those early pioneer public relations managers, and the international institutions and multinationals they represented, learned the hard way—often to their dismay and chagrin—that, although centrally developed policies could be promulgated from afar, the activities involved in interpreting them successfully on a national level could not be designed and imposed from a distance. Furthermore, they learned that a capital city was not a country and that public relations activities could not end at the city limits.

In geographical terms, these pages examine what is happening in the so-called "developing countries"—presumably, Eastern Europe, the Middle East, Asia, Africa, and Latin America—as opposed to events in the arguably "developed countries" of North America and Western Europe. But all citizens everywhere are subject to their histories and cultures, to say little of the political, social, economic, and commercial structures, of not only the countries of their birth but also the countries of their adoption and their residency. And the pace at which and the way in which public relations practice develops is a direct reflection of the mores and structures of a particular society. I have never found it especially surprising, for instance, that the first organized public relations association to be formed in the world was in Finland, mirroring the plethora of state institutions there at that time— the ministries, boards, industries, and other government agencies all with their fully staffed information departments.

It should be understandable, therefore, that even today in some countries the professional bodies are closely linked with the apparatus of government or even with the dominant political party. In the industrial and commercial sector, too, professional practice reflects the degree to which that sector is controlled, the way state and private enterprise is balanced, and the extent to which enterprises are really competitive. Additionally, in some countries individual practitioners are subject to a discrete form of official registration or certification. But these matters are only milestones en route to professionalism— pathways that practitioners in many countries have had to travel. But perhaps their journeys will prove less calamitous than those in countries wherein the sudden winning of freedoms has been followed by unlimited license.

Essentially, public relations is a situational discipline and, regardless of how far individual countries have traveled toward embracing the concepts of democracy, it is, nevertheless, accurate to observe that the forces that have created and now provide the societal justification for the existence and practice of professional public relations are at work, and their effect on the process of acceptance will accelerate based on both internal and external political pressures. These forces are fivefold. First, information is the handmaiden of democracy, and with increasingly better educated and informed citizenry, the demand for more and, hopefully, better information will escalate. Second, there is increased recognition among leaders and managers that every initiative involves a degree of conflict, and the ideal is to ensure that the interests of all parties—not only those with vested interests—are considered and accommodated, if not totally reconciled. Third, we have come to understand that what John Donne said all those years ago is true—"No man is an island." In this age, every corporate action or reaction has a domino effect—positive or negative—on those associated with the particular institution. Appreciating the likely effect and complexities of this so-called "interdependence factor" has become a skilled occupation. Fourth, in part as a consequence of such greater awareness, there is increasing evidence that the social, as distinct from the political, impact of corporate plans and programs is being considered before action is taken. The signs indicate that the paradigm shift in human values away from institutionalism and toward individualism, as identified by the forecasters, is not confined to the developing countries or to the established democracies. And finally, but by no means least in effect, is the colossal impact of the information superhighway with its instant and individual accessibility.

Although attitudes about issues of freedom of information and expression are changing, it would be true to say that Western concerns and concepts regarding such matters as transparency, accountability, governance, and social responsibility have yet to take root. But it would also be true to report that in establishment circles there is increased recognition that publicity is not and cannot take the place of information, and that propaganda is not public relations. The more sophisticated leaders appreciate that government by consent depends on dialogue, and that although the currency of dialogue is information, the price that has to be paid is controversy.

In any country, opinion as to what is truthful and what is in the public interest in a given situation differs like beauty in the eye of the beholder. But in some countries and cultures, such opinions are more valuable than in others. The more often and the greater depth in which academics and practitioners can be encouraged to research and report—and the more widely their findings can be published—the better we professionals can hope to serve our communities in particular and society in general.

About the Authors

Emmanuel C. Alozie (Ph.D., University of Southern Mississippi) is professor of media communications at Governors State University, University Park, Illinois. He has taught at Shaw University, Lincoln (Missouri) University, and Edward Waters College. Alozie served as interim coordinator of marketing, public relations, and outreach at St. Mary's Health Center, Jefferson City, Missouri. He was an accounts and public relations/advertising official with the United Bank of Africa, Lagos, Nigeria. Alozie has worked for the *Columbus (Georgia) Ledger-Enquirer, Asbury Park Press, Kansas City Star, Topeka Capital-Journal,* and *Oakland Tribune.* A graduate of Rust College and Arkansas State University, he has received fellowships from the Freedom Forum, American Press Institute, Cap-Cities/ABC, Inland Press Association, Dow Jones Newspaper Fund, American Society of Newspaper Editors, and Poynter Institute. His areas of research interests are in development communication, international/cultural journalism, advertising, and public relations. Alozie has published articles and reviews in academic journals, conference proceedings, and has contributed book chapters. He has presented his scholarly works at national and international conferences. Alozie serves as assistant editor for *Democratic Communiqué.* Edwin Mellen Press, Haworth Press, and University Press of America have accepted his works on international/intercultural communication, advertising, and journalism for future publication.

Isaac Abeku Blankson (Ph.D., Ohio University) is assistant professor of international public relations and intercultural communication at Southern Illinois University, Edwardsville. He has studied in Ghana and Norway, where he developed a multidisciplinary academic and research background in international development, public relations, environmental policy, and communication technologies. He has served as public relations and media consultant to organizations in Ghana.

Hugh M. Culbertson (Ph.D., Michigan State University) is professor emeritus of journalism at Ohio University. Named Public Relations Society of America Educator of the Year in 1990, he also received the PRSA Pathfinder Award for excellence in public relations research in 1985. He is author or co-author of more than sixty refereed articles and ten books and monographs, including *Social and Political Economic Context in Public Relations: Theory and Cases* and *International Public Relations: A Comparative Analysis.* He served as head of the fundamentals section, PRSA Body of Knowledge project.

Arnold S. de Beer, APR (Ph.D., Potchefstroom University, South Africa), is professor emeritus in the Department of Journalism, University of Stellenbosch, South Africa. Formerly head of the Department of Communication at Potchefstroom University and also

Free State University, he serves as research director for Media Tenor SA–Institute for Media Analysis. Founding editor of *Ecquid Novi–SA,* a journal for journalism research, and board member of *Journalism Studies,* he is chair of the African Council on Communication Education—Media and Society Division. He is the first recipient of the SA Public Relations Institute's SA Communication Educator of the Year Award, and the first university professor in South Africa to become an accredited member of the Public Relations Society of America. An international council member of the International Association for Media and Communication Research and member of the Appeals Board of the SA Press Ombudsman, he is co-editor with John C. Merrill of *Global Journalism.*

Rachael E. Doksoz (M.A., University of Miami) is a communication studies graduate with research interests in international and cross-cultural mass media and intercultural communication. Her thesis, "The Portrayal of Muslims in American Newspapers," presents a qualitative content analysis of media coverage during the five-day period following the September 11, 2001, attacks. In 1998, as an undergraduate, she presented a paper, "Growth of the Television Medium in India," at an Indiana Academy of Social Sciences conference. She holds a B.A. in communication from Indiana University Southeast of New Albany and plans to begin work on her Ph.D. in 2004.

John Fobanjong (Ph.D., University of Arizona) is an associate professor of political science and director of the African/African American Studies program at the University of Massachusetts, Dartmouth. Prior to joining the University of Massachusetts, he taught at Alabama State University, Auburn University, the University of Maryland Eastern Shore, Wilberforce University, and the University of Arizona. He has authored articles in journals and a recent book, *Understanding the Backlash against Affirmative Action.*

Alan Freitag (Ph.D., Ohio University) is an assistant professor in the communication studies department at the University of North Carolina, Charlotte. He teaches graduate and undergraduate courses in public relations. A U.S. Air Force veteran, he retired in 1995 as a lieutenant colonel after more than twenty-two years of service, including twelve years overseas and four years at the Pentagon, primarily in public affairs. His work has been published in professional and academic journals, and he has presented papers and served on panels for regional, national, and international groups. He is frequently the subject of print and broadcast media interviews given his background in NATO, defense issues, crisis management, and international public relations.

Amiso George (Ph.D., Ohio University) is coordinator of the public relations program at the Donald W. Reynolds School of Journalism at the University of Nevada, Reno. Prior to joining the Reynolds School, she taught at the University of Texas at San Antonio and consulted for nonprofit organizations in Texas. A member of the Public Relations Society of America and the Association for Business Communication, George has published and presented papers on crisis communication at national and international conferences. She was a radio and television broadcaster and journalist in Nigeria and Ohio before embarking on an academic career.

James E. Grunig (Ph.D., University of Wisconsin) is a professor of public relations in the Department of Communication at the University of Maryland, College Park. He is the co-author of *Excellent Public Relations and Effective Organizations: A Study of Communication Management in Three Countries, Managing Public Relations, Public Relations Techniques,* and *Manager's Guide to Excellence in Public Relations and Communication Management.* He is editor of *Excellence in Public Relations and Communication Management.* He has published more than 215 articles, books, chapters, papers, and reports. He has won three major awards in public relations: The Pathfinder Award for excellence in public relations research of the Institute for Public Relations Research and Education, the Outstanding Educator Award of the Public Relations Society of America, and the Jackson, Jackson and Wagner Award for behavioral science research of the PRSA Foundation. He also won the most prestigious lifetime award of the Association for Education in Journalism and Mass Communication, the Paul J. Deutschmann Award for Excellence in Research.

Larissa A. Grunig (Ph.D., University of Maryland) is a professor of public relations in the Department of Communication at the University of Maryland. She has received the Pathfinder Award for excellence in public relations research sponsored by the U.S. Institute for Public Relations, the Outstanding Educator Award of the Public Relations Society of America, and the Jackson, Jackson and Wagner Award for behavioral science research of the PRSA Foundation. She is co-author of *Women in Public Relations: How Gender Influences Practice, Excellent Public Relations and Effective Organizations: A Study of Communication Management in Three Countries,* and *Manager's Guide to Excellence in Public Relations and Communication Management.* She has written more than 190 articles, book chapters, monographs, reviews, and conference papers on public relations, activism, science writing, feminist theory, and communication theory and research.

Mazharul Haque (Ph.D., Ohio University) teaches at the University of Southern Mississippi. His research interests include cultural critical studies, international communication, and new technologies. He has published book chapters, a book, a monograph, and articles in *Journalism Quarterly, Asian Journal of Communication, Odin, Media Asia,* and the *Gazette.* Prior to joining Ohio University, he worked as information officer to the president of Bangladesh and deputy principal information officer to the government of Bangladesh.

Dean Kruckeberg, APR, Fellow PRSA (Ph.D., University of Iowa, Iowa City), is coordinator of the mass communication division and full professor in the Department of Communication Studies at the University of Northern Iowa, Cedar Falls. A member of the Public Relations Society of America's College of Fellows, he is academic co-chair of the Commission on Public Relations Education. He received PRSA's national Outstanding Educator Award (1995) and the Institute for Public Relations's Pathfinder Award (1997). He served as part of the project team that developed the public relations degree at the United Arab Emirates University. He has addressed the Swedish Public Relations Association; communications faculty in the Baltic States and Russia; a USIA (United States Information Agency)-Soros Foundation-funded workshop in Riga, Latvia; and a USIS (United States Information Service)-Sofia program on media relations for Bulgarian media, government officials, nongovernmental organizations, and government ministry press secretaries. Co-author of *Public Relations and Community: A Reconstructed Theory* and *This Is PR: The Realities of Public Relations* (1996, 2000 editions), he also has authored book chapters, articles, and papers dealing with international public relations and ethics.

undergraduate program, advises the Public Relations Student Society of America chapter, and teaches graduate courses in ethics. Previously, she served as director of marketing and communications for Macomb Community College and as associate vice president for university advancement at Ferris State University. She has been active in PRSA for more than twenty years and currently serves as chair of the East Central District.

David Ritchey (Ph.D., Louisiana State University) is an associate professor in the School of Communication at The University of Akron. He has taught public relations at Renmin University in Beijing, China, and City University, Hong Kong, and led students on summer study abroad tours of England. In 1998, he visited St. Petersburg, Russia, on behalf of the Citizens for Democracy Corps, where he conducted research for the case study published in this volume. With the approval of the U.S. Department of the Treasury, he visited Cuba with a group of American writers in 1999. He has published in the *Public Relations Quarterly, International Educator, PR Tactics, The Cleveland Plain Dealer,* and *The West-Side Leader.* In the spring of 2003, Ritchey was a Fulbright Scholar at the University of Bucharest, Romania.

Melvin L. Sharpe, APR, Fellow PRSA (Ed.D., University of Florida), is a professor at Ball State University where he teaches undergraduate and graduate courses in public relations. He served in public relations posts with the United States Marketing Information Service, the U.S. Army, Oklahoma State University, and the University of Florida Institute for Food and Agricultural Sciences before being named assistant to the president of the University of Florida and assistant to the chancellor of the State University System of Florida. A recipient of the Public Relations Society of America's Outstanding Educator Award, he has chaired PRSA's College of Fellows, the Educators Academy, and the Continuing Education Board.

Amos Owen Thomas researches the globalization of television and advertising at the Australian Key Centre for Cultural and Media Policy, and lectures in marketing and international business at Griffith University. During the past twenty-five years he has worked at universities, transnational advertising agencies, government agencies, and nongovernmental organizations, mostly in the Asia-Pacific region.

Donn James Tilson, KHS, APR, Fellow PRSA (Ph.D., University of Stirling, Scotland), is an associate professor of public relations at the University of Miami's School of Communication. The first in Europe to graduate with a doctorate in public relations, he has published and lectured internationally on corporate public relations, including as a European University Public Relations Confederation Visiting Scholar at Complutense University in Madrid and Autónoma University in Barcelona. A member of the Public Relations Society of America's College of Fellows, he serves on the editorial board of *Ecquid Novi,* the research journal of the Southern African Communication Association, and is the former book review co-editor of *Journalism Studies.* He is a participating faculty member of the University of Miami's Institute for Cuban and Cuban-American Studies and Center for Latin American Studies and has led students on summer abroad programs to Spain. Prior to joining UM, he served as a public relations manager for BellSouth for sixteen years, directing the company's charitable contributions and educational relations programs in

Florida. In 1999 he was inducted as a Knight of the Equestrian Order of the Holy Sepulchre of Jerusalem, one of the oldest orders of chivalry in the world.

Tim Traverse-Healy is director of the Centre for Public Affairs Studies (United Kingdom). A Fellow of the Royal Society of Arts, he is a founder member and past president of both the International Public Relations Association and the (British) Institute of Public Relations, and a past vice president of the European Centre des Relations Publiques. He has received numerous honors in recognition of his lifetime achievements, including induction as a Hall of Fame member of the Arthur Page Society (United States) and reception of the Officer Order of the British Empire for services to the public relations profession.

Katerina Tsetsura (M.S., Fort Hays State University) is a doctoral candidate in the Department of Communication at Purdue University as well as a specialist with a diploma degree in journalism from Voronezh State University, Russia. Her research interests include the theoretical development of public relations in Eastern Europe and the countries of the CIS, international public relations ethics, and social construction of identity and public relations. She has presented papers at U.S. and international professional association conferences, including the ICA (International Communication Association), NCA (National Communication Association), PRSA Educators Academy, CSCA (Central States Communication Association), and OSCLG (Organization for the Study of Communication, Language and Gender) as well as research conferences in Russia.

Anuradha Venkateswaran (Ph.D., Virginia Polytechnic Institute and State University) is assistant professor of marketing at Wilberforce University, Ohio. A member of the American Marketing Association, her research interests in marketing include strategic marketing, Internet marketing, e-commerce, social and economic implications of technology, and consumer behavior with a focus on African American consumers. She has published in refereed journals and conference proceedings. Prior to her appointment at Wilberforce University, she held positions as design engineer at Media One (now Time-Warner), National Research Council associate at Wright Patterson Air Force Base, Dayton, Ohio, and postdoctoral fellow and instructor at Virginia Polytechnic Institute and State University.

Dejan Verčič (Ph.D., London School of Economics) is a founding partner in Pristop Communications, a communication management consultancy based in Ljubljana, Slovenia, and assistant professor for public relations and communication management at the University of Ljubljana. Among his clients are governments, domestic and international corporations, and associations. From 1991 to 1993, he led the foundation of the Slovenian News Agency—STA. In 2000 he received a special award from the Public Relations Society of Slovenia for his contributions to the development of public relations practice and research, and in 2001 he was awarded the Alan Campbell-Johnson Medal for outstanding service to international public relations by the UK Institute of Public Relations. Since 1994, he has organized annually the Lake Bled International Public Relations Research Symposia. He is president-elect of the Euprera (the European Public Relations Education and Research Association) for 2003.

Acknowledgments

The authors would like to thank the reviewers of this book: John R. Baldwin, Illinois State University; Josh Boyd, Purdue University; Jennifer Floto, University of Southern California; Liese L. Hutchison, St. Louis University; Corwin P. King, Central Washington University; Donald Panther-Yates, Georgia Southern University; Laurie J. Wilson, Brigham Young University; and Rhonda Zaharna, American University.

Toward the Common Good

Toward the Common Good

A Global Overview

Donn James Tilson

Emmanuel C. Alozie

The world has become a global village: Olympic athletes are natives of one country but represent another in the Winter Games; U.S. football players play on teams in NFL Europe; artists, such as British rocker Sting, play in Santiago de Compostela, Spain, to packed houses of concertgoers from across Europe, and Chinese Taipei pop star A-mei performs in mainland China; Fortune 500 companies commonly earn more than 50 percent of their earnings internationally; headquarter staffs reflect a global mix of talent; and packaged apple juice sold in the United States contains concentrate from Turkey, Poland, and Argentina.

And where there are international sporting events, rock concerts, and business deals, you'll find public relations professionals working as publicists, public information officers, and corporate managers. As the public and private sectors have globalized so has the public relations profession as practitioners follow employers, clients, and new opportunities. As Sandra L. Montenegro reports (Chapter 5), "today, the largest public relations firms, such as Fleishman-Hillard, Weber Shandwick Worldwide, Hill & Knowlton, and Burson-Marsteller earn about half of their fees abroad according to *PR Week*'s global rankings for 2001." As of 2000, there were eighty-two national public relations professional associations in sixty-one countries, according to Melvin L. Sharpe and Betty J. Pritchard (Chapter 1).

To prepare properly, then, for a career in public relations, it is essential to globalize your education. This book is intended to do just that. It introduces you to the latest research in the field from the best scholars in the profession. Many of the chapters offer an inside look into ongoing studies by researchers in regions such as Eastern Europe and sub-Saharan Africa. Other chapters review new and timely regions of interest that have been previously unexplored, for example, Ecuador, Peru, Indonesia, Kenya, South Africa, and Russia. Still other scholars provide extended discussions of strategic regions and nations

1

that have been underresearched, such as Romania, Malaysia, and Singapore. Some chapters present case studies—the Fujimori Administration's PromPeru (Chapter 4); a Citizens Democracy Corps (CDC)–sponsored project in St. Petersburg, Russia (Chapter 9); the Obasanjo Administration in Nigeria (Chapter 11); and Shell Petroleum in Nigeria (Chapter 12)—whereas others present an overview of a particular region, such as Latin America (Chapter 5) or Asia (Chapter 16). In all, a broad range of public relations practices and institutions—governments, public relations firms, corporations—are examined within a discussion of history, politics, economics, culture, and communication. Key points at the outset of each chapter guide you in focusing on the main ideas. And at the conclusion of each chapter, a series of discussion questions facilitate a review of those main points and, it is hoped, encourage consideration of their deeper implications. Most chapters also offer a list of appropriate Web sites for more information on the topic.

More importantly, however, this book offers thoughtful analysis and commentary from leading scholars and new, alternative voices who address issues of importance to the world community—the effects of privatization and globalization, emerging public opinion and democratic movements, corruption, professional ethics, and the role that public relations practitioners can and should play both locally and globally. Many of the contributors hail from the countries they examine and offer critical insights into challenges in their homelands. Moreover, the book's authors take a multicultural approach, offering both theoretical foundations and practical applications, with a view of fostering curiosity, creative thinking, problem solving, and an expanded multivision and heightened sense of social responsibility for our profession. Consider this a "next generation" book that will open the doors to a new dimension in your public relations education.

Some Common Themes

As you read the chapters in this book, you'll notice that they are organized by region, with each section introduced by a short essay that gives an overview of important points to consider. Some themes will seem to reoccur from one nation and from one region to the next throughout the book—the interplay of democratic movements and emerging free-market economies; press freedom; the empowerment of public opinion; and the conflict of an aroused, mediated citizenry with authoritarian regimes and entrenched special interests. The opening chapter by Melvin L. Sharpe and Betty J. Pritchard provides a good overview of these points; these authors observe that "the development of public relations as a profession globally correlates to historical developments in three areas: communication, democracy, and global social interdependence." The constant revisiting of these themes is neither accidental nor planned—these forces are emerging universally and simultaneously as societies, and public relations practitioners in particular, grapple with the enormous pressures of modernity on their institutions.

That is also why this book is different from others you may have read. In this book you will not find the usual chapters on public relations in Japan, Germany, or any other developed nation. Those societies already have been documented, and there is no need to review them again. We have chosen, instead, to present cutting-edge research on countries considered to be "emerging democracies" because that is where the next wave of public relations professionals are also "emerging." By "emerging democracies" we mean nation-states that are struggling to firmly establish those institutions and processes that we normally associate with a democratic form of government (some suggested that, given the interesting twists and turns in voting during the 2000 presidential election, we should include the United States on our list of "emerging democracies," but we declined). In some societies, democracy may be long-standing but in name only. Mexico, for example, won its independence from Spain in 1821 but was ruled by one dominant political party from 1930 to 2000. Ghana, which achieved independence from Britain in 1957, suffered a succession of authoritarian civilian and military governments until the mid-1990s when extensive democratic and liberal reforms were finally instituted. In Nigeria, during its more than forty years of independence, northerners have ruled the nation for more than three decades. Other nations, such as Romania, only recently have emerged officially as democratic states; the communist regime of Nicolae Ceausescu was overthrown in 1989, and a new constitution drawn up in 1991. South Africa dates its independence and democratic form of government from 1994, when Nelson Mandela was elected the nation's first president. Some nations, such as Ecuador, seem to be taking one step forward and two steps back with representative government—returning to civilian rule in 1979 after a long history of *caudillos,* Ecuador had three presidents in one week during February 1997, and a military coup in 2000 overthrew a democratically elected administration. In nation-states such as these, public relations professionals are dealing with fundamental issues that affect us all as a global society—freedom of expression, human rights, and social justice.

Democracy, Economic Development, and Public Relations

Various studies, including one by Freedom House in 2000 (Oppenheimer, 2000), indicate that the development of democratic institutions in a society is a catalyst to economic development. Totalitarian nation-states have some of the world's lowest per capita incomes, whereas those societies judged to be the most "free" are the most developed economically. Even when comparing poor nations, democratic states had higher economic growth rates (well more than double the annual growth rate between 1990 and 1998) than totalitarian ones. As the report notes, "economic growth is accelerated in an environment where the rule of law is respected, property rights are enforced, citizenry is actively engaged in the political process, and investigative media serve to expose and thus reduce corruption" (Oppenheimer, 2000, p. 6a). For example, as Cornelius Pratt and Charles Okigbo (Chapter 13) note, free elections and economic reforms in many African nations underscore "the continent's improving economic and political stability," which "is attracting foreign investment and stimulating new domestic economic ventures." Conversely, in nations that suffer from "economic mismanagement, political turmoil, and military dictatorship," as Emmanuel C. Alozie (Chapter 11) notes concerning Nigeria at the beginning of the Obasanjo Administration in 1976, citizens have little faith in government, the foreign image of the country is unfavorable, and foreign investment is discouraged. Chris W. Ogbondah and Amiso George (Chapter 12) observe that the image of Nigeria in the international community has been further damaged over the years as indigenous peoples of the Niger Delta have fought government troops and Shell Petroleum workers to protect their homeland from pollution and other serious environmental effects of oil drilling. The long-standing struggle, which often has turned violent and included a government-sanctioned execution of tribal leaders by the Abacha military dictatorship in 1994, dates from Shell's entry into the region in 1957. As Ogbondah and George reflect, "the situation in which the region that produces the bulk of the nation's wealth [and] . . . receives the least in socioeconomic development amounts to grave social injustice."

As nation-states implement free-market reforms, expanding business opportunities and the development of public relations, and its promotional cousins advertising and marketing, are enhanced. Many have argued, in fact, that economic expansion and promotion are intertwined variables in a nation-state's development, as evidenced in various capitalistic societies (Wernick, 1991). For example:

> public relations as an organized practice in the U.S. emerged as departments within companies and as outside counsel with industrial expansion and the concentration of corporate power following the Civil War. In the wake of the post–World War II economic boom, the number of U.S. practitioners increased 50% in 15 years, spawning the birth of the Public Relations Society of America in 1948, even as the number of colleges offering public relations courses grew from 30 in 1946 to more than 300 in 1970. (Simon, 1984, as cited in Tilson, 1996, p. 133)

Indeed, as many of the following chapters testify, public relations practitioners generally follow their employers or clients into new business opportunities. Public relations activities in Thailand, reports Mazharul Haque (Chapter 16), "have grown in concert with the growth of the economy" and are mostly corporate based. In Singapore, for example, Doug Newsom (Chapter 17) observes that "it wasn't until the late 1960s that international public relations firms began to appear to service their multinational clients." In Mexico, Richard K. Long (Chapter 2) notes that "in the early days of public relations . . . large agencies were nonexistent . . . this changed dramatically in 1994, when NAFTA went into effect. Most of the U.S.-based firms opened Mexico City offices . . . primarily to serve U.S. companies that were coming to Mexico." Generally speaking, in Latin America, as Sandra L. Montenegro (Chapter 5) observes:

> the profession of public relations developed in Latin America by the middle of the twentieth century as foreign companies started business in the region. Hill & Knowlton was among the first public relations firms to follow clients by opening offices in the countries where clients began operations . . . the development of public relations in the region has been directly linked to its economic growth.

Similarly, Katerina Tsetsura and Dean Kruckeberg (Chapter 8) observe that "with political and economic changes in Russia, public relations came to life. . . . Moreover, the need for public relations was accelerated because of Russia's emerging democracy and free-market economy." James E. Grunig, Larissa A. Grunig, and Dejan Verčič (Chapter 6) note that public relations developed rapidly after Slovenia gained its independence, changed its political system from socialism to democracy, and changed its planned economy to a free-market one. Political and economic stability often provide the necessary foundation for a growing national tourism sector—and for public relations support—as David Ritchey (Chapter 9) notes in his study of a business in St. Petersburg, which runs a successful tourism center "profitable enough to carry some of [the] less profitable areas."

And Rachael Doksoz (Chapter 7) reports that "while Romania was under the rule of Ceausescu, tourism was stunted" but now "the government is trying to improve the economy, in part, by boosting tourism." Many businesses, especially in Transylvania, are promoting the region as a tourist attraction, using the Dracula legend as a promotional hook.

In Kenya, Jacquie L'Etang and George Muruli (Chapter 10) note that "growth of private sector public relations was a postwar and largely postindependence phenomenon and took place first in organizations such as Kenya Power and Lighting, Kenya Shell, and the East African Harbours Corporation." Various consultancies—mostly foreign owned—emerged to service these corporations, themselves largely multinational firms, inasmuch as "most multinational corporations preferred foreign-based firms to Kenyan consultancies," and the firms "were more interested in global public relations than in developing local consultancy business. Nairobi was seen as the gateway to the continent." L'Etang and Muruli further explain that the birth of public relations in Kenya "followed the pattern of the colonial power, Britain, where private sector public relations was fairly limited until after World War II." Its development in the United Kingdom, in part, was "in response to the perceived threat of nationalization that emerged from the Labour Party's policy on state ownership."

Problems of Reform

Although free-market reforms and economic development can commercialize society and generalize promotion throughout a particular culture, further stimulating consumer demand, the confluence of such forces also can exacerbate unemployment, underemployment, and poverty in nation-states. According to the UN's *Human Development Report 2001,* 4.6 billion of the 6.1 billion people in the world live in developing nations, 87 percent of whom live on less than two dollars a day; moreover, the richest 1 percent receive as much income as the poorest 57 percent (Erickson, 2001). The International Monetary Fund reports in its *Scorecard on Globalization 1980–2000* that per capita income for nations in low- and medium-income groups actually "grew faster in the period 1960–1980 than in the era of globalization that began around 1980" (Bussey, 2001, p. 1E). The UN study notes that Latin America, which began privatizing state-run industries and implementing free-market reforms in Chile, Mexico, and Argentina in the mid-1980s, has the widest gap between rich and poor in the world, with the richest 20 percent having thirty times the income of the poorest 20 percent (Oppenheimer, 2001b). Moreover, the region's average per capita income declined from 50 to 30 percent of the average in the developed world since 1950 according to the Inter-American Development Bank's *Development Beyond Economics* 2000 study (Bussey, 2000). The number of poor has grown from 136 to 180 million since 1986 (Oppenheimer, 2001a). In Argentina and Peru, hundreds of thousands of workers lost their jobs when industries were privatized, but few provisions were made for workers' retraining, out-placement, or social welfare. Alan Freitag (Chapter 4) notes that unemployment and underemployment in Peru now stand at 61 percent of the population, and "90 percent of Peruvians spend 80 percent of their income on food." Richard K. Long (Chapter 2) reports that in Mexico 43 percent of the population lives in "intermediate" or "extreme" poverty. David Ritchey (Chapter 9) observes that St. Petersburg's fashionable Nevsky Prospekt street "is lined with fashionable stores and resembles U.S. streets with its two Pizza Huts, a Kentucky Fried Chicken outlet, a Baskin-Robbins and several McDonald's restaurants." However, as Montgomery (2001) reports, "much of the wealth is in the hands of a few . . . millions can barely afford food and clothes" (p. 5A). As for Romania, Rachael E. Doksoz (Chapter 7) notes that "after the fall of communism . . . marketing organizations relied heavily on advertising, especially television, to promote products. Such promotion pushed prices to the point where Romanians could not afford many of the items being advertised." A Stanford University study reported that the economy today is only 76 percent of what it was in 1989; inflation reached 40 percent, and the average worker earned less than one-third of a counterpart in Hungary (Dorschner, 2001, p. 1L). Anuradha Venkateswaran (Chapter 19) explains that, in Malaysia, that country's phenomenal economic progress has largely benefited only the Malay people (about 60 percent of the population) to the exclusion of other ethnic groups, including Chinese and Indian. Moreover, the Malay-dominated government—led by Prime Minister Mahathir bin Mohamad since 1961—"has been criticized for human rights violations and repression of Chinese and Indian minorities" according to Venkateswaran.

Given such extreme conditions, public relations, advertising, and marketing professionals must ask whether it is socially responsible to engage in promotional activities that seem to exacerbate the social and economic injustices in a society. Is it ethical for professionals to promote fast-food chains, for example, in countries where a majority live in poverty? How socially responsible is it to market televisions or other luxury consumer items in societies where the annual per capita income is barely more than $2,000? As Amos Owen Thomas (Chapter 18) notes, the "domination of public discourse by professional communications such as advertising, market research, and public relations . . . undermine[s] the authenticity of social and political discourse, which ought to be grounded in constituent groups of civil society rather than in artificial market segments purporting to represent views sympathetic to certain dominant corporations." Such challenges, according to Cornelius Pratt and Charles Okigbo (Chapter 13), "underscore the importance of Kruckeberg and Starck's 1988 and Starck and Kruckeberg's 2001 reconstructed theory and the relevance of organizational social responsibility. This means that practitioners need to engage in a balancing act that is responsive to overall national interests and to the importance of professional do's and don'ts that perpetuate such interests." Indeed, the hallmarks of a professional are professional autonomy or independence, moral accountability, and a sense of social justice.

On a hopeful note in that regard, Arnold S. de Beer and Gary Mersham (Chapter 15) report that South African practitioners are increasingly serving as "change agents" in redressing social imbalances in that nation. "Public relations in South Africa has become the face of the new democratic society," they observe, with "corporate and government social investment . . . two of the key driving forces in South African public relations." Early efforts began with black empowerment programs in corporate public relations departments and have since expanded to include social responsibility endeavors in housing assistance, educational subsidies, transportation, the environment, and other areas of community need. As de Beer and Mersham conclude, "the nature and success of social change in South Africa will depend on the business community's social vision and basic conception of humanity."

Corruption and Its Effects

As often has been the case in developing nations, corruption both within and without a particular society is further encouraged by the increase in business opportunities that a free-market economy offers, presenting multiple challenges to public relations practitioners. As Dean Klitgaard of the Rand Graduate School noted at an international forum on corruption, "privatization in many countries has been the foremost source of corrupt payments" (Bussey, 1998, as cited in Tilson, 1999, p. 70). In the case of Mexico, the number of billionaires in that country increased from two in 1991 to twenty-four in 1994, as many garnered the winning bids in the sale of government industries through their association with the Salinas presidential family and the ruling Institutional Revolutionary Party (Oppenheimer & Ellison, 1996). Such "crony capitalism," as a 1998 World Bank study noted, imposes "massive costs on countries, by, among other things, discouraging foreign and domestic investments," virtually assuring that the benefits of free-market reforms do not filter down to society (Oppenheimer, 1998, p. 6A). Moreover, corruption inhibits the flow of foreign capital into the general economy because government officials and economic oligarchies often monopolize such funds for their private interests. A 1998 Miliken Institute study of credit availability in thirty-one emerging nations (Fields, 1998) ranks Chile fifth among the top in liquidity and five other Latin American nations among the middle to bottom range—Peru (13), Brazil (14), Mexico (21), Ecuador (20), and Venezuela (25). These rankings seem to correlate with those in 1998 and 2002 Transparency International corruption indices. In 1998, Chile (20) ranked among the least corrupt of the eighty-five nations reviewed, whereas other Latin American nations ranked in the middle to bottom range: Peru (41), Brazil (46), Mexico (55), Ecuador (77), and Venezuela (77). In a 2002 study of one hundred nations, countries in Latin America maintained similar rankings, with Chile and Uruguay scoring above the norm in the region; Brazil (45), Mexico, and Colombia (57) emerging toward the middle; and Peru (45), Venezuela (81), and Ecuador (89) slipping farther toward the bottom; other nations at the lower end included Argentina (70), Guatemala and Nicaragua (81), Haiti (89), and Paraguay (98) (Bussey, 2002; Tamayo, 2002). A study in 2002 conducted by the International Budget Project, part of the Washington-based Center on Budget and Policy Priorities, noted that citizens in Brazil, Mexico, and Peru, among other countries, believe they know little about how the government spends their tax money. It should be noted that the issue of budget transparency, and massive government corruption in Indonesia, triggered, in part, the Asian financial collapse of 1997. And when that crisis adversely affected Indonesia, as Amos Owen Thomas (Chapter 18) reports, "student demonstrations over corruption, and violence against them by the military, compelled the handover of the government by Soeharto in 1998 to his deputy, Habibie." As financial analyst David Lloyd George noted on *Wall $treet Week with Louis Rukeyser,* emerging Asian nations and other emerging capitalist economies must demonstrate "integrity. . . . There has to be transparency to maintain investor confidence" (George, 1998). Such integrity is essential, whether it be a government administration, such as the Soeharto regime in Indonesia, or a corporation, such as Enron in the United States.

In Peru (Chapter 4), where corruption, as Alan Freitag observes, is "a recurring element in the political culture," President Alberto Fujimori—who considered himself the "Lee Iacocca of Latin America"—actively led an aggressive global public relations campaign to solicit foreign investment and present Peru as a nation of "economic stability and confidence." A "divestment blitz" privatizing many state-run industries generated billions of dollars—U.S.$2.8 billion in 1994 alone—but "beneath the surface, certainly during Fujimori's final years . . . the patterns of corruption, exploitation, and despotic control continued to infect Peru's political fabric." Following a "disgraceful resignation via fax from a hotel in Japan" in 2000, Fujimori remains in exile even as ongoing investigations of corruption in his administration have "been extended to include possible manipulation of public opinion through considerable financial incentives to media that supported the government." As Freitag sadly notes, Fujimori's "disgraceful departure . . . belied the optimism of the communication campaign that the world witnessed and betrayed the sinister duplicity of the nation's top leadership."

Ultimately, of greater importance for a society is the deflating effect that corruption can have on its citizenry and on the public relations profession itself. During the meltdown of the Argentine economy in 2001 and revelations of endemic public corruption, only 15 percent of the nation reported that it trusted Congress, down from 75 percent in 1983. A 2001 Latinobarometro poll reported that only 25 percent of Latin Americans were satisfied with democracy, down from 37 percent in the mid-1990s. Even when political reforms are implemented allowing public participation in government affairs, as was the case with the Rawlings Administration in Ghana in 1995, a society can be slow to respond and remain inactive given a history of popular mistrust of government. As Isaac Abeku Blankson (Chapter 14) notes, this "culture of silence" continued through 1999, a consequence "of decades of manipulation, suppression, and control by powerful forces in the society . . . to discourage and inhibit both lateral and upward communication." Even today, according to Blankson, "many practitioners pay financial or material incentives to government officials in order to gain access to state and national resources . . . [which] has contributed to the tainted image of Ghanian practitioners." In Russia, where the popular memory of "Soviet propaganda" is still fresh, Katerina Tsetsura and Dean Kruckeberg (Chapter 8) observe that "historically, public relations is associated with propaganda." Currently, they report that "the most popular discussion in modern Russian public relations theory is built around the problem of 'black PR' versus 'white PR.'" The first, they explain, "is associated with manipulative techniques that can be used mostly in election campaigns and advertising," whereas the second "represents the Western-type public relations practice that is based on the philosophy of 'excellent' public relations." In Romania, Rachael E. Doksoz (Chapter 7) explains, "there are democratic institutions . . . but corruption is also present . . . practitioners do not adhere to the generic principles that characterize excellence in public relations. . . . Romanians use the word 'publicate' to describe both propaganda and publicity. . . . Propaganda is a primal stage of public relations." Kruckeberg (1992) contends, however, that "any misuse or abuse of public relations is a question, not of 'bad' public relations . . . but . . . becomes a question of unethical professional practice which is of collective concern" (p. 34). Even in Slovenia (Chapter 6), where public relations has developed rapidly because of contact with scholars and practitioners from the United States and Europe, Grunig and colleagues report that most still practice public relations as a limited, technical support function, a far cry from the standard of excellence common in more developed nation-states.

Press Freedom and Public Opinion

As emerging democracies transform themselves politically and economically, the record shows that such reforms also have included an unleashing of the media, allowing for greater press freedom and an increasingly mediated citizenry. And in turn, as historically marginalized and disenfranchised peoples become increasingly politically conscious, governments and other special interests with authoritarian worldviews come into sharp conflict with such emerging, participative publics. *Caudillo*-style regimes, albeit ostensibly democratically elected administrations, accustomed to shaping public policy by command rather than by collaboration, encounter significant public opposition in such societies and, ultimately, face a governability crisis as they manage conflict with citizens less effectively and fail to establish organizational credibility. As Donn J. Tilson (Chapter 3) notes, the Duran-Ballen administration in Ecuador, not to mention subsequent administrations in that nation, is only one example. As Melvin L. Sharpe and Betty J. Pritchard note (Chapter 1):

> the most significant factor in the empowerment of public opinion has been global public access to information . . . motion pictures, telegraph, photography, radio . . . television . . . the steady . . . development of computer technology . . . uncontrolled by organizations or media gatekeepers . . . providing people throughout the world with a new and broader concept of the power of public opinion in influencing social change. The result is a growing social expectation that organizations and governments will perform responsible public relations.

Amos Owen Thomas (Chapter 18) reports that, in Indonesia, following the 1997 economic crisis and public outcry over government corruption as discussed earlier, the interim administration "set an agenda for reform, including democratic elections for the first time since 1955. Radical changes were made also to the laws governing both broadcast and print media to allow greater freedom." As a consequence, the television industry has been totally deregulated, the number of commercial stations has grown, and television has become "a medium for political discourse . . . [with] the prevalence of news, current affairs, political forums, [and] talk-back programs." Press licensing laws were relaxed for print media, with a new press law passed by Parliament guaranteeing noncensorship, and the ownership of such publications is now more diverse as are television and radio. More importantly, however:

> no longer is it taboo for journalists to criticize activities of conglomerates . . . or their powerful allies in government. Consequently, no longer can public relations executives take for granted that a positive spin automatically will be given to those firms, shareholders, and political leaders in these media. The corporate image of many a conglomerate in Indonesia is in dire need of repositioning as a responsible corporate citizen. . . . Certainly, practitioners and other officials in government . . . will be held far more accountable on human rights and freedom of information.

Similarly, in Ghana, as Isaac Abeku Blankson (Chapter 14) explains, political reforms after 1995 ushered in "an open, free, and independent media environment that began to expose problems and issues of societal concern and interest." This, in turn, created "a critical, discerning public and advocacy groups that demanded more information and accountability from organizations" which "is forcing Ghanian [public relations] practitioners to pay more attention to the importance of public opinion in their practices." The democratic elections in South Africa that ushered in Nelson Mandela as president in 1994 also initiated new political and social realities according to Arnold S. de Beer and Gary Mersham (Chapter 15). Whereas "in the recent past, political leaders . . . could exercise a great deal of control over domestic and foreign opinion through control of information and communication," today "the questioning by black people of all aspects of their social, political, and economic environment . . . requires the rapid dissemination of appropriate information." Moreover, such public reawakening, they contend, has required a "shift toward consensus seeking at a national level between the trade union movement, business, and government," and "the recognition of the voice of local communities."

Sadly, however, in many countries, such as Malaysia, the converse is still in effect. Anuradha Venkateswaran (Chapter 19) reports that "the current relationship between the government and any of the other constituents, such as the private sector, media, or consumers, still reflects a highly unequal status, inhibiting effective two-way symmetrical communication." According to Venkateswaran, "the government has the power to shut down newspapers, withdraw publishers' licenses indefinitely, and arrest anyone who violates the [government's press] act." As a result, newspaper content is largely progovernment and dominated by issues from the government's agenda. The private sector also "is expected to cooperate with the government" and to promote the government's developmental priorities. Corporate public relations practitioners, in particular, "always implicitly considered potential government response to organizational messages" and routinely keep government officials informed of organizational actions inasmuch as the government has "the power to rescind the sale of a privatized company and assume its daily operations." Similarly, public relations consultancies are expected to keep up-to-date on government initiatives and positions.

Even when such government "nation-building" communication campaigns are well intentioned, they face enormous problems. As Mazharul Haque (Chapter 16) explains, "communication/public relations policy makers in many Asian countries have to function within a resource-poor environment," often having to conduct social mobilization programs in societies with a multiplicity of languages and dialects, which leads to "linguistic conflicts and chauvinism"; in one state (Madhya Pradesh) within India, for example, Haque notes that there are more than 375 languages and dialects.

Even in some emerging democracies such as Singapore that still control the media, however, Internet access is proving to be problematic for governments endeavoring to control public opinion. For example, in Singapore, as Doug Newsom (Chapter 17) reports, "when the government began invading e-mail systems to test them to see if they could be accessed . . . unhappy citizens took their complaints to the government-owned newspapers. To their credit, the papers covered the story and the government ministry apologized. For some native Singaporeans, this was an indication that the new electronic society had indeed changed the way government responded to its citizens." In that society, which has "a history of top-down governance from its colonial experience," government efforts to elicit citizen recommendations on domestic and international affairs have prompted public demands for "a greater say in their national affairs and more of a stake in their government." Given a pragmatic administration that wants to position the nation as a global leader, Newsom observes that Singapore really has "no option but to advocate an open economy, one based not only on the free flow of trade and investment but, more crucially, on the free flow of information."

In Kenya, as Jacquie L'Etang and George Muruli (Chapter 10) note, "nation-building and public relations strategies were required to construct and promote the new Kenyan identity" following that nation's independence in 1963. Those "promotional efforts . . . led, in turn, to an opening up of debate among Kenyans as to their identity" and their role in society, especially when "[i]ndependence did not deliver all the hoped-for dreams." That debate included a professional development seminar of the International Public Relations Association in Nairobi in 1992—a "key turning point" for practitioners because the issues discussed there "encapsulated the zeitgeist of the times and looked toward increased democratization and transparency, values that would facilitate the growth of public relations."

Ultimately, unchaining both the media and citizens will require a greater "self-confidence" by administrations in emerging democracies, as Doug Newsom (Chapter 17) observes, trusting that people will collectively make the right decisions for their future and that of society. There are many hopeful signs that such divesting of authority is indeed occurring—Indonesia, Ghana, Singapore, and the other nation-states discussed in this book are only a few examples. Perhaps, in the case of Romania (Chapter 7), the drafting of the nation's new constitution illustrates the spirit that is moving across borders. That document, according to Rachael E. Doksoz, "affirms political pluralism as a right along with cultural and religious freedoms and also states that . . . citizens have the same rights as declared in the Universal Declaration of Human Rights—the right to privacy; confidentiality of correspondence; and freedom of conscience, expression, assembly, and association . . . rights of private property; judicial independence; and freedom of the press." Those rights, proclaimed by the UN General Assembly in 1948, underscore the individual worth of every person. Indeed, "a basic moral test of society is the welfare of its most vulnerable members," and, ultimately, "a community of conscience is required to orient public and private life toward the fundamental dignity of all human beings" (Tilson, 1999, p. 72).

In the long run, such an orientation will lead public relations practitioners into an Aristotelian-like professional ethic (Tilson, 1999) that encompasses *prudence* or practical wisdom that makes the right choice, *justice* that includes fairness and honesty, *fortitude* or courage in pursuing the right path despite great risks, and *temperance* that requires self-discipline in all things" (p. 73). Most importantly, however, "in embracing these virtues in our professional and personal lives, we will develop the moral character necessary to transform our society and our world into communities that are civil, ethical, and equitable for all peoples" (Tilson, 1999, p. 73). Such a path, ultimately, will not only best serve the international public relations profession but also the common good.

References

Bussey, J. (2000, May 21). Despite reforms, the Americas continue to lag much of the world. *The Miami Herald,* p. 1E.

Bussey, J. (2001, August 5). Promise and peril of globalization. *The Miami Herald,* p. 1E.

Bussey, J. (2002, August 29). Latin America low on corruption scale. *The Miami Herald,* p. 2C.

Dorschner, J. (2001, August 26). A Romanian journey. *The Miami Herald,* p. 1L.

Erickson, A. (2001, October). True justice: The challenge of economics. *Decision,* 18.

Fields, G. (1998, October 26). Group: To stay afloat, increase liquidity. *The Miami Herald Business Monday,* p. 11.

George, D. (1998, February 6). Interview on *Wall $treet Week with Louis Rukeyser,* WPBT-Channel 2, Miami.

Kruckeberg, D. (1992). Ethical decision-making in public relations. *International Public Relations Review, 15*(4), 32–37.

Kruckeberg, D., & Starck, K. (1988). *Public relations and community: A reconstructed theory.* New York: Praeger.

Montgomery, D. (2001, August 19). In Russia, capitalism's fruits a bounty for few. *The Miami Herald,* p. 5A.

Oppenheimer, A. (1998, July 13). Lenders weigh tougher rules. *The Miami Herald,* p. 6A.

Oppenheimer, A. (2000, December 24). Study sees relation between democracy, prosperous nations. *The Miami Herald,* p. 6A.

Oppenheimer, A. (2001a, June 17). Gloomy times: Latin Americans' view of the future no longer as shiny as in early '90s. *The Miami Herald,* p. 1L.

Oppenheimer, A. (2001b, July 12). Latin America leads world in inequality, U. N. study says. *The Miami Herald,* p. 14A.

Oppenheimer, A., & Ellison, K. (1996, August 17). Awaiting broader shift to private enterprise, Latin America frets over pitfalls of the past. *The Miami Herald,* p. 1A.

Starck, K., & Kruckeberg, D. (2001). Public relations and community: A reconstructed theory revised. In R. Heath (Ed.), *Handbook of public relations* (pp. 51–59). Thousand Oaks, CA: Sage.

Tamayo, J. (2002, October 13). As Latin America economies modernize, intolerance for corruption is spreading. *The Miami Herald: The Herald Americas Conference,* p. 9.

Tilson, D. (1996). The commodification of Latin America: A confluence of telecommunications, the media and promotion. *World Communication, 25,* 133–141.

Tilson, D. (1999). Against the common good: The commodification of Latin America. *Media Development, 46,* 69–74.

United Nations Development Programme. (2001). *Human development report 2001: Making new technologies work for human development.* New York: Oxford University Press.

Wernick, A. (1991). *Promotional culture: Advertising, ideology and symbolic expression.* London: Sage.

Part I

A Preodyssey View

1

The Historical Empowerment of Public Opinion and Its Relationship to the Emergence of Public Relations as a Profession

Melvin L. Sharpe

Betty J. Pritchard

Key Points _____

- Public relations has evolved historically as the result of social pressures on organizations rather than as the result of voluntary management action responding to the information needs of the public.

- Open record laws and restrictions on lobbying as well as the amount and kind of support that politicians may receive are empowering public opinion.

- Growing economic and environmental interdependence combined with global population growth are major factors contributing to global social interdependence.

- Advancements in electronic communication resulting in instantaneous uncensored communication are increasing the organizational need for proactive and reactive public relations performance.

- Public relations has emerged as a profession (with professional organizations, codes of ethics, and a body of knowledge) with the empowerment of public opinion locally and globally.

- The profession of public relations is the result of a social mandate brought about through the empowerment of public opinion demanding social responsibility and improved communication on the part of organizations.

Public relations textbooks frequently reach back in world history and identify communications and publicity activities as evidence of early recognition of the value of public relations performance. Even the Romans recognized the importance of positive public relations as revealed by the ancient proverb, "The voice of the people is the voice of God," as did many whom we now view historically as effective rulers (Baskin, Aronoff, & Lattimore, 1997, p. 26).

But if recognition of the value of public relations existed so early in human society, the following questions must be raised: "Why then did it take so long for public relations to emerge as a profession?" and "What had to occur or be in place before individuals would be identified as part of a new profession with an economic base for their services?"

A new theory is proposed in this chapter that increases an understanding of why a relationship-building function that is increasingly viewed as essential to organizational stability in modern society took so long to evolve into a recognized profession. Individuals who are now viewed as public relations pioneers began practice at the turn of the twentieth century. But the growth of practitioners sufficient for the development of professional organizations did not occur until nearly fifty years later. The development of an ethics code, a body of knowledge, and educational requirements for performance and academic status within educational institutions equal to other recognized professions are all important milestones in the development of any profession. A public mandate for the existence of a profession in society is also a critical milestone.

A convergence of three factors contributed to the emergence of public relations as a profession: a growth in the global acceptance of democratic principles, growing global social interdependence, and the emergence of direct instantaneous communication abilities. These factors have now empowered public opinion to a degree that public relations performance is no longer a choice on the part of organizations. Instead, the authors contend that the empowerment of public opinion has reached a level where a public mandate now exists globally for the public relations profession and that this mandate corresponds to the growth and development of public relations as a profession within modern society.

This chapter examines the convergence of these three social advancements, which appear to have been necessary before a major movement in world history could take place toward the development of public relations as a profession. It also examines the forces that are now driving the development of public relations as a strategic and necessary profession within societies globally.

In suggesting the evolution of the empowerment of public opinion, the authors rely heavily in their examination on developments within the United States, in part because of the documentation available from scholars and library resources but also because the democratic model is more closely identified with the United States than with any other country. In addition, the public relations profession in the United States is larger and more developed than in any other country. As a result, data on events and developments in the United States allow the evolution of advancements relating to the three factors to be examined more fully than they can be in other parts of the world.

The authors are aware that professional public relations performance appears now to be global. The rate of its holistic development within countries differs, but the growth continues. The authors suspect that the rate of the convergence of the three factors differs within countries. There is also a global effect of the convergence that is forcing countries and businesses seeking international trade to respond to the public opinion force factors external to their countries. Strong evidence indicates that the advancements in communication technology, and environmental and economic interdependence are the driving factors, even when advancements in democratic reform or acceptance lag behind the other two factors. In recent developments in the Middle East, it is also clear that the United States is being influenced through global public opinion with unprecedented force because of the worldwide convergence.

Scott Cutlip (1994), one of the leading authors of basic public relations textbooks commonly used in education, opened his public relations history book with the statement that public relations in the United States has had an impact on U.S. society that is largely unnoted. He pointed out that public relations strategies and tactics are increasingly used as weapons of power in our no-holds-barred competition in the public opinion marketplace. Cutlip made the point that "the social justification for public relations in a free society is to ethically and effectively plead the cause of a client or organization in the free wheeling forum of public debate" (1994, p. xi). The reason, he stated, is because it is a basic democratic right that every idea, individual, and institution have a full and fair hearing in the public forum.

Based on Cutlip's conclusion, the public relations profession in the United States could not evolve until democracy was in place. This would not, however, explain the rapid emergence of the public relations profession globally as an identifiable function in social systems in only the past hundred years. Although democracy is still young in terms of global acceptance, its implementation in the United States and in other countries throughout the world certainly predates 1900. Yet it can be clearly shown that the rapid growth of public relations as a profession occurred even more recently.

Public relations textbook authors universally recognize World War II as the turning point in the growth of the profession. This chapter examines some of the factors that accelerated the development of public relations and provides insight into the reasons why the profession did not emerge at least a century earlier with the establishment of democratic social systems.

The chapter also points out some of the reasons why the growth of public relations today is no longer limited to only democratic social systems. Its performance within other countries relates to factors that can now be identified. Lord Chadlington (1999), founder of Shandwick Public Relations in Great Britain, one of the world's largest international public relations counseling firms, provided a clue when he said that corporate reputations are a valuable asset to be protected, conserved, defended, nurtured, and enhanced at all times. His statement is as true when referring to governments and other organizations within the world's social systems as it is for corporations.

An Historical Overview

Public relations as a profession is usually described as corresponding to the twentieth century or with the fight for democracy in the United States. Baskin and colleagues (1997), for example, believe the public relations profession began with the American Revolution; they describe the developmental stages of the war as involving manipulation, information, and mutual influence and understanding. Cutlip, Center, and Broom (2000) trace the development in six eras starting with the early 1900s, which they refer to as the Seedbed Era.

All of the texts identify early practitioners and credit them with the identification of principles needed for ethical performance, the writing of the first books, the use of the term *public relations,* and the application of what we know today as public relations activities. But an examination of the way that public opinion has gradually empowered society in its ability to influence management decisions and performance is consistently understated.

Most textbook authors have recognized that the spread of global democracy and the increase in sophistication of communication technology have had major roles in historical change and that new policies of social responsibility exist for institutional managers today. However, the impact of communication, the reasons behind management recognition of the importance of social responsibility, and the relationship of these factors to the development of a new profession is frequently much less clear. This lack of emphasis may well contribute to the lack of understanding of the importance of public relations to society today.

Seitel (1998) stated, "In truth, institutions in the 1990s had little choice but to get along with their publics" (p. 8). An understanding of the reasons for this lack of choice, not only in U.S. society but globally as well, is also an objective of this chapter.

Social Conditions Shaping Public Opinion

Three social conditions can be identified as vital to the development and performance of public relations globally. All have had their impact on the continuous empowerment of public opinion. The social conditions are as follows:

1. *Global communication.* Instantaneous communication capable of transcending artificial barriers, made possible with the emergence of an international language and with nondependence on media gatekeepers for access or interpretation (Cutlip et al., 2000).
2. *Democracy.* A representative process that gives people voice in their governments and in what takes place within their social systems (Newsom, Scott, & VanSlyke Turk, 1992).
3. *Social interdependence.* Clear recognition of the need for global cooperation in maintaining the existence of life on earth and its quality, and for preserving our ability to learn what we yet do not know about ourselves and our planet (Cutlip et al., 2000).

Seitel (1998), in examining issues of the twenty-first century, points out that the three social conditions exist in a pressure-cooker environment brought about by economic globalization and an emerging "information highway" coupled with major political shifts toward democracy throughout the world.

Global Communication

Many factors have contributed to the increase in global communication: advancements in technology, literacy, the development of a common global language, and an increase in speed of travel between geographical points. But the most significant factor in the empowerment of public opinion has been global public access to information. The more unfiltered and instantaneous the communication, the more powerful public opinion has become in the political framework of global interaction (Turow, 1999).

To increase public access to information, public educational systems in countries around the world had to develop along with access to media uncontrolled by governments or organizations. Widespread literacy followed by awareness and understanding of issues are the bedrock of the development of public opinion. According to Wardhaugh (1987), global scientific and technological developments depended heavily on the spread of a common language. Such advancement could only be accomplished through widespread sharing of information. The adoption of English as the international language of commerce, scientific journals, diplomacy, and international conferences occurred after World War II. According to the history of English, this was first because of the outreach of the British Empire and second, because of the involvement of American, Canadian, Australian, and British troops during World War II in locations around the world.

Technological advancements in communication tools have also been recognized as a major factor in the development of public opinion. The printing of the Guttenberg Bible and the use of movable type are frequently cited by historians as milestones in the development of informed public opinion (Straubhaar & LaRose, 1997). In the United States, as in many nations around the world, the readership of newspapers and magazines increased as their cost declined because of improved printing presses, more efficient delivery services, and an increase in literacy that resulted in more readers and more advertising and circulation revenue.

The development of newspaper readership in the United States provides a good example: In 1870, there were about 4,500 U.S. newspapers in print; by 1880, more than 7,000 newspaper existed in the United States; and by 1890, 12,000. By 1914, however, there were only about 14,000 weekly newspapers (Mott, 1950). Americans were now getting their information from larger consolidated daily newspapers. The change allowed for better reporting from larger newspaper staffs supported by improved travel funds. Newspaper circulation reached 40 million subscribers in 1930, dipping only in the depression years, then reaching a new high of 41.5 million in 1937 (Mott, 1950).

One result of economic growth in the news media was the development of journalism as a profession, along with the growth of journalism education programs at the university level and an increased sense of recognition on the part of journalists to protect and advance the public's First Amendment rights in having access to information. The importance of the journalism profession's recognition of its responsibility for "investigative reporting" and for balanced and accurate news coverage can not be ignored (Payne, 1970). And it cannot be assumed that the profession's or the U.S. government's recognition of the importance of this role for democracy occurred with the establishment of the U.S. Constitution or a Bill of Rights. History shows that the development took time. The maturity of the journalistic profession, however, is critical in the empowerment of public opinion in the United States and globally, and the importance of the factor can be seen in new democracies where news media access has occurred but where full journalistic freedom and responsibility have not yet fully evolved.

As Payne (1970) has pointed out, good journalism, as we know it today, requires education, training, and, above all else, a commitment to a public responsibility to ferret out truth and serve as the public watchdog. But this recognition and its social acceptance have required time all over the world. Even today in the United States, the rights and degree of access remain a point of frequent debate. Still, the exercise of journalistic responsibility and the resulting empowerment of public opinion are related to the emergence of public relations as a profession.

Another historical turning point was the public's growing access to electronically delivered communication. By 1947, 48 percent of Americans reported that they "got most of their news" from newspapers, but 44 percent said they relied chiefly on radio (Payne, 1970). The development of radio resulted in increased competition for advertising and changed the way people got information. At the same time, it increased public access to information for those without reading skills. By 1950, television newscasts also began to impact the newspaper industry creating a visual medium for the transmission of news (Payne, 1970).

In spite of the dramatic impact that television would have in shaping public opinion, no one fully anticipated the impact electronic global communication would have in empowering public opinion, even with Marshall McLuhan's prediction that the twenty-first century would be a "global village" wired for immediate communications. With satellite communication advancements, and the development of CNN and other global and regional broadcast capabilities, millions of global citizens watched the Gulf War on cable and television sets serviced by satellite dishes. The World Trade Center terrorist attack again allowed a global public to witness events with their own eyes and ears as they happened. The era of waiting for reporters and photographers to provide information has been replaced by an era in which information and interpretation follow actual observance. Video cameras also allow public participation in the collection process and the recording of actions in buildings, on public transportation, and on street corners that can later have dramatic impacts on public opinion.

Internet communication abilities, including e-mail and the World Wide Web, became available to growing audiences beginning in the 1990s and have extended the public access to information without the control of traditional gatekeepers, such as news editors, public relations managers, or government officials. The AOL–Time Warner merger announced in January 2000, and other mergers in 2001, have given consumers the ability to get "whatever they want—books, movies, magazines, music—whenever they want it, whatever way they choose, whether on a television, a personal computer, a cell phone or any of the myriad wireless devices that are hurtling toward the marketplace" (Okrent, 2000, p. 43).

A global media is clearly rapidly emerging. In Europe, the television service Canal One has teamed up with Bertelsmann of Germany to create a formidable competitor for all European audiences. TVB in Hong Kong is seeking to dominate media delivery to China and Southeast Asia. MTV and ESPN are both building advanced production studios in Singapore. In 1995, Viacom launched its MTV service to Asia with local hosts. NBC bought the European Super Channel cable network in 1983 and has since added business news from the *Financial Times,* a London newspaper. It has also teamed up with TV Azteca in Mexico. Time Warner's HBO is in partnership with Omnivision, a Venezuelan cable company, for the HBO Ole pay-television service in Latin America (Vivian, 1999).

Wilhelm (1990) summarizes the field of influence on growing world communication as the influence of public relations, advertising, public administration, and business communication, together with the one-world English language. Ronald Reagan (1989) described the impact of world communication in a 1989 Churchill Lecture when he said, "The biggest of big brothers is increasingly helpless against communication technology. The peoples of the world have increasing access to this knowledge. It seeps through walls topped with barbed wire. It wafts across the electrified booby trapped borders" (p. 3).

The Impact of Electronic Advancements.   Advancements in communication technology can be identified as early as the 1400s, and increasing since then at an ever-faster pace. Table 1.1 shows that although the invention of electronic communication began at the turn of the twentieth century, broad public access did not occur until after World War II, some fifty years later. The first satellite communication allowing instantaneous global access to information occurred in the 1960s, and the first advancements in global news service began more than twenty years later in the 1980s. The 1990s, however, is the first decade for broad global public use of the Internet as a communication tool. Table 1.1 shows the reasons for the decrease in the ability of gatekeepers to censor and control information.

TABLE 1.1 *Key Achievements in the Historical Advancement of Instantaneous, Electronic Communication*

1876	Telephone invented by Alexander Graham Bell.	1948	CBS creates the first network evening news program.
1888	Radio invented by Guglialmo Marconi in Italy.		First cable TVs appear in rural U.S. areas.
1889	First motion picture camera invented by Thomas Edison and William Dickson.	1951	CBS makes first color TV broadcast.
			Mauchly and Eckert create UNIVAC, the first commercial computer.
1895	France's Lumiere brothers build a portable movie camera and open first movie theater in Paris.	1952	First use of TV for U.S. presidential elections.
1906	First voice broadcast experiment conducted.	1953	First IBM computer, the 701, introduced.
1923	Vladimir Zworykin patents design for iconoscope, a television transmission tube.		Standard color TV system introduced in United States.
1927	First sound motion picture.	1954	Radio sets in the world outnumber newspapers printed daily.
1936	First regular public television service—BBC London.		First transistor radio.
	Britain's Alan Turing publishes description of a universal computing machine.	1955	Music recorded on tape in stereo.
1941	NBC broadcasts the first TV commercial.	1957	First book entirely phototypeset is offset printed.
1945	ENIAC, built by John Mauchly and J. Presper Eckert, the first electronic digital computer, is put into service, weighing 30 tons and needing 1,500 square feet.	1958	Stereo recording introduced.
			Videotape delivers color.
			Microchip invented.
1946	First commercial advertisement for television in the United States.	1959	Eurovision network—first integrated global enterprise.
	Peak of U.S. movie attendance—90 million per week.	1960	Eighty-seven percent of U.S. households have at least one television.
1947	Transistor invented at Bell Telephone Laboratories.		Transistors first used in televisions.
			AT&T introduces touch-tone digital dialing.

TABLE 1.1   *Continued*

1961	Federal Communications Commission (FCC) authorizes FM stereo and first broadcast occurs.	1979	Inmarsat established in London with 48 member countries.
	Massachusetts Institute of Technology starts shared use of computer by multiple users.		Holland contributes the digital videodisk read by laser.
1962	Telstar, first communications satellite, launched.		Ericsson introduces first cellular phone.
			CompuServe launches on-line service.
1964	First worldwide satellite communications network launched.	1980	Ted Turner establishes TV's first 24-hour news network with introduction of CNN.
	Intelsat—11 countries.		Phototypesetting can be done by laser.
	Japan develops the videotape recorder for home use.	1981	IBM releases first PC.
		1982	*USA Today* type set in regional plants by satellite command.
	IBM launches the first commercial mainframe computer.		Johnson & Johnson uses satellite transmission to reach hundreds of reporters in 30 cities with information on Tylenol product tampering.
1967	Donald Davies develops way of routing electronic information through networks.		
1969	A network of university computers (ARPA Net) is installed at the University of California in Los Angeles (UCLA).	1983	Digital compact disk is introduced.
		1984	Television broadcast in stereo begins.
	First commercially viable VCR sold by Sony.		Apple releases the Macintosh.
		1985	Intersputnik signed cooperative agreement with Turner Broadcasting.
	Bell Labs creates Unix, an operating system that works across computer platforms.		ARPA Net renamed the Internet.
1970	First transmission of data into a computer network by radio waves.		CD-ROMs hold 270,000 pages of text on a CD.
1973	Four million ARPA Net users in 43 countries.	1986	3,500 satellites in orbit.
			Compact disk text publishing initiated.
1974	Vinton Cerf and Robert Kahn design Transmission Control Protocol for linking different computer networks.		IBM sells 3 millionth personal computer.
			European radio stations use the FM carrier wave to transmit data.
	The first personal-computer kit, the Altair 8800, goes on sale for $439.	1988	U.S. government brochure mailed to 107 million addresses.
1977	Interactive cable in use.		Japan conducts world's first large-scale analog-TV broadcast from the Seoul Olympics.
	First videocassette sales.		PanAmSat launches the first privately owned communications satellite.
	Steve Jobs and Steve Wozniak develop the Apple II.		
1978	First digitally coded laser videodisks appear on the market.	1989	Olympus: Western Europe's largest communication satellite launched by European Space Agency.
	Programmer Ward Christensen writes MODEM (modulator–demodulator) allowing PCs to talk over public telephone lines.	1990	Direct broadcast satellite PrimeStar launched.
			Tim Berners-Lee creates an Internet protocol called the World Wide Web.

(continued)

TABLE 1.1 *Continued*

1991 Laserdisk introduced.	CD-ROMs carry full-length feature films.
Three out of four U.S. homes own VCRs, fastest-selling appliance in history.	First live radio broadcast of a sports event over the Internet by Broadcast.com
1992 Cable Act forces TV programmers to sell services to direct satellite operators.	1996 Telecommunications Act of 1996 made sweeping changes in the way telephone, cable, and Internet companies do business.
1993 U.S. White House goes on-line.	Internet becomes available on cable through WebTV.
Internet talk radio premiers.	
First television show is distributed over the Internet in digital format.	1997 First Internet telephone-to-telephone service.
1994 Digital audio radio introduced.	1998 New Windows version introduced.
High-definition television transmission begins.	Digital HDTV broadcasts begin.
Sixty countries communicating with Internet with 150,000 new users every month.	An estimated 3.6 million Web sites exist to surf.
1995 Radio broadcast data system initiated, permitting sound, and later, pictures to be sent in real time over the Internet.	2000 AOL–Time Warner merger: first step in providing integrated technology services.
Convergence of communication technologies begins.	2001 Bill Gates, Teldesic Corporation, and Craig McCaw of McCaw Cellular Communications announce plans to launch 840 communication satellites "to wire world."
CNET is launched on television and Internet.	
Major U.S. dailies create national on-line newspaper network.	Average U.S. worker spends 3.1 hours per workday at a computer.

The development of public relations as a profession closely parallels the development and wide usage of electronic media. The calendar of electronic communications advancements is staggering in its rapidity of development from World War II to the present. However, only the past fifteen years has provided instant communication and the technology for global communication on the part of average citizens on a wide scale. A chronological examination of the advancements in communication indicate that it took much of the nineteenth and twentieth centuries for global communication to occur simply because of the distances to be breached, the illiteracy to be overcome, and the cost of each advancement in technology. Each advancement had to become accessible to the public and profitable before a more advanced technology could be developed and then emerge.

If there is any single factor that has empowered public opinion globally more than others, it appears to be the advancement of the pluralism of media. This began in the first half of the twentieth century with a combination of motion pictures, telegraph, photography, radio, and finally television. After World War II, the impact of television and the steady progression of the development of computer technology is evident as well as the increased frequency of new inventions. Each advancement can be recognized as contributing to the development of public opinion by allowing greater global access to media information sources uncontrolled by organizations or media gatekeepers. Each advancement increased the speed of communication exchange, but only the most recent have allowed individual participation and control and a full integration of the media for individual communication needs.

Democracy

It is difficult to separate a discussion of world democracy from its formation in the United States although the authors are fully cognizant of the many contributions to the advancement of democracy that have been made globally. In the discussion of advancements, therefore, the authors invite international students to analyze parallel developments in their own countries. Mexico, for example, implemented its first freedom of information law in the summer of 2002, exposing the government and its records to greater public scrutiny. The law required all branches of government to provide copies of public documents—from government employees' salaries to details about public relations and government contracts—within twenty days of any citizen's request. Similar advancements in democracy in the United States, some of which were first achieved in other countries, are identified because of the impact that each advancement could have in empowering public opinion. The intent is not to attempt to cite advancements throughout the world or to overlook or minimize global advancements. Instead, the intent is to show the progression as it occurred in one democracy and why each action advanced democracy globally by further empowering public opinion.

When U.S. public relations textbook writers consider the development of public relations, they recognize that the founding fathers of U.S. democracy learned to use the power of the press in winning public support for the Revolutionary War movement (Cutlip et al., 2000). Even the approval of the Constitution and Bill of Rights are viewed as the masterful use of public relations (Nevins, 1963). But the establishment of the Constitution and Bill of Rights and the resulting advancement of free expression did not result in the rapid emergence of public relations as a profession. Although both empowered public opinion, its full empowerment would emerge much more slowly in relation to advancements in the democratic process. Some of the reasons relate to the following facts about the United States:

1. At first, only property owners could vote.
2. Slavery was very much a part of U.S. society, disenfranchising a large segment of the population.
3. Women could not vote until 1920.
4. Industrialization and the large influx of immigrants into the country to serve the needs of industry resulted in a class of citizens that earlier immigrants failed to embrace with full equality (Wilcox, Ault, & Agee, 1992).

The general attitudes of business toward the rights of the common citizen and laborer are reflected in the "public be damned" statement by William Henry Vanderbilt and by George F. Baer, who issued the following statement in a Pennsylvania coal field strike in 1902:

> The rights and interest of the laboring man will be protected and cared for not by labor agitators, but by the Christian men to whom God in his wisdom has given control of the property interests of the country. (Cutlip, 1994, p. 46)

This attitude took time to change. According to Cutlip (1994), "J. P. Morgan was one of the first financial giants of this period to see that to win their way in Washington, they had to build a supportive public opinion and could no longer rely on pressure and bribery of legislators to gain the day" (p. 47).

Marvin Olasky (1987) contends that public relations in the late nineteenth and early twentieth centuries worked to restrict economic competition rather than to serve any altruistic public welfare notions. Corporations did not willingly support public relations programs. Instead, crisis situations, such as the Ludlow Massacre, allowed Ivy Lee and Edward Bernays to find a market for their services (Seitel, 1998).

Certainly, people were better informed as communications technology made the news media accessible, but the public had to learn how it could make its voice heard before the bureaucratic management systems within government and business would respond to public opinion pressure.

Six Major Developments.   Six major developments in democracy in the United States can be identified that have contributed substantially to the emergence of public opinion as a force in the U.S. social system. All of them relate to increased access to information by the public or an increase in the ability to influence management decisions.

Labor Union Development.   The first development was that of labor unions. From about 1890 to 1920 employees in large U.S. corporations began to realize that if their working conditions were to improve, they needed a collective voice (Galenson, 1986). Union organization movements, along with the exposure of worker conditions in society by the "muckraking" journalistic writers, forced business to begin communicating with the public. Big business learned it had an image problem it could not ignore. For the first time, businesses were forced to defend positions, decisions, and conditions to the public.

Access to Financial Information.   A second development occurred in economic protections with the stock market crash of 1929. The financial tragedy resulted in the demand by investors for improved information and protection for the small investor in particular. The result would be annual report requirements and stock exchange control improvements preventing insider trading. Antitrust laws were also a part of the public demand for consumer protection. All resulted from public opinion pressures and each protection, when achieved, resulted in a more informed public and more confident consumer (Cutlip et al., 2000).

Public Activism.   A third development, public activism, was most evident starting with the civil rights movement in the 1960s and continued through the 1970s. In this period, people in the United States learned that they could build public awareness and support through peaceful demonstrations. Special interest groups learned to use the media to acquaint others with their causes and found they could awaken the public conscience to social issues (Cashman, 1991). Successful demonstrations generating wide media coverage against nuclear power plants, the Vietnam War, and all types of environmental causes made the public recognize that the force of public opinion could change decisions, conditions, and laws.

Consumer movements emerged in the late 1960s and early 1970s with Ralph Nader and others who began to demand rights for consumers based on the successful techniques used in the 1960s by social movements. Consumer movements generated public concern for safety, quality, and nutritional value of products, resulting in the recall of hundreds of products to ensure that they met public expectations (Wilcox et al., 1992). The impact was to strengthen consumer protection laws and to increase the liability of manufacturers (Mayer, 1989). Their success taught consumers to build and use public opinion in achieving change.

Open Records Laws. The fourth development was the state-by-state approval of what have become known as "sunshine" or "open record" laws. These were new laws that opened state government records to the news media and general public (Turow, 1999). The laws ensured prompt access to information at a reasonable cost. By 1980 all states had passed laws that opened all types of state records to the review of the media and the public. A federal law also opened the records of 400 federal agencies at the national level, and this law was expanded in the 1990s to ensure even greater public access to information.

The ability of people to learn and form educated opinions has been emphasized by Wilhelm (1990) who related how quickly the Russian people learned to think for themselves following *glosnost.* The implication is that human beings now have the ability to observe other social systems and, as a result, the time required for global change has been reduced.

Leveling of Public versus Corporate Influence. The fifth development has been the movement toward leveling of corporate influence and public opinion. This leveling process is reflected in two ways: (1) court and jury decisions in favor of consumers and the willingness of consumers to join in class action suits and (2) the limitations of the degree to which corporations may financially influence congressional and legislative decisions. Laws implemented since the 1970s have limited the amount of money that corporations may donate to elected officials and required that lobbyists register. Financial gifts to political campaigns and to elected officials are now a part of the public record (Wilcox et al., 1992).

Corporations, however, have been creative in circumventing limitations. Political action committees (PACs) are an example. They allow a number of corporate officials in industrywide areas or special interest groups, including labor unions, to provide financial gifts of substantial influence. Political campaign laws have been similarly circumvented, causing continuing debate created by presidential candidate John McCain in the 2000 election in calling for campaign finance reform (Pooley, 2000; Simon, 2000).

Globalization of Democracy. The sixth development is the globalization of democracy itself. Culbertson and Chen (1996) state that "democratic advancements," for example, freedom of speech, public debate, and an informed populace, are Western ideas that are seeping into cultures with or without governmental consent. This may be a function of communication technology; the fall of the Berlin Wall is certainly symbolic of the futility of barriers.

The change is not always viewed as positive by governments or by fundamentalist religious groups. Livingston noted that even in the United States, "In recent years, observers of international affairs have raised the concern that the media have expanded their ability to affect the conduct of U.S. diplomacy and foreign policy. Dubbed the 'CNN effect,' the impact of these new global, real-time media is typically regarded as substantial, if not profound" (Livingston, 1997, p. 291). According to Norris (1997), "the techniques for monitoring the pulse of the public, including focus groups, daily tracking polls, and electronic town meetings, have gradually moved beyond [political campaign use] to become an integral part of governing" (p. 9). Therefore, all governments, regardless of whether they are democratic, are increasingly influenced by the power of global public opinion. This, in itself, is a movement toward democracy.

Somewhere in the mix of advancements in democracy and communication, public acceptance has developed for the principles that all men and women have the right to accurate information about pending decisions relating to them and their welfare, the right to voice their opinions in relation to proposed decisions, and the right to attempt to influence or change power structure decisions (Sharpe, 1996).

Advancements in Democracy.   Democracy, of course, is a critical part of the equation. Advancements in democracy have, more than any other factor, made public opinion a force to which organizations have had to respond. Although the freedoms allowing democracy were fought over for a period of at least six centuries, the struggle for the right to express opinions, to have access to information, and to influence and shape decisions with equality has spanned two centuries and continues to be an ongoing process throughout the world.

The emergence of labor unions resulted from the lack of ability by workers to influence management decisions. Both the civil rights movement and the consumer movement were responses to similar inabilities on the part of disenfranchised groups within society.

The Securities and Exchange Commission Acts, Investment Company Acts, open record laws, and federal Freedom of Information Acts opened records to the public to protect the public welfare. The most dramatic advancement of democracy in empowering public opinion may be the access to state and federal records. What is notable is that the access was not granted until nearly twenty years after the end of World War II, or nearly 200 years after the struggle for the creation of the United States as a democracy.

Another ongoing struggle for the empowerment of public opinion has also evolved since the end of World War II. Federal regulation of lobbying activities, limitations on political gifts, disclosure requirements, and the Consumer Bill of Rights have restricted the ability of organizational management to influence the political and judicial systems, while increasing the influence of consumers and citizens. Although the impact of the empowerment is difficult to measure, the changes can be noted in the tables throughout this chapter, and the time period can be related to additional growth in the public relations profession even in a period of corporate mergers and downsizing.

Table 1.2 indicates that before democracy can become fully functional, access to information (open records) must occur combined with the opportunity for involvement (leveling of the ability of the public to influence government). As access to information increases, the demand for involvement increases (consumer and activists movements) and, with involvement, public opinion achieves greater influence in its ability to affect organizational performance in a global social system. The result is increased opportunities for public relations performance on the part of organizations within the social system.

Social Interdependence

Isolation created the framework for humankind's identification of social self-interest as independence, superiority, and domination. According to Rothman and Wheeler (1981), social isolation also encouraged individuals to support management systems that gave these attributes to them. For centuries, this is the way the nations behaved. Although trade has continually increased social contact and the development of social relationships based on mutual benefit, trade in itself did not create a global recognition of the world's increasing economic social interdependence.

TABLE 1.2 *Historical Advancement of Democracy Using the United States as the Primary Model*

930	Iceland's parliament, the Althing, is established.
1215	Magna Carta—the "great charter" of English liberties.
1689	Bill of Rights confirming rights and liberties of British citizens.
1776	U.S. Declaration of Independence.
1789	Ratification of the U.S. Constitution.
1791	Bill of Rights; First Amendment added to the U.S. Constitution.
1862	Emancipation Proclamation freeing slaves in the United States.
1890	Sherman Antitrust Act becomes law, protecting consumers from monopolies in the United States.
1900	Labor unions begin to fight for rights of employees.
1914	The Clayton Act becomes law in the United States, and the Federal Trade Commission is created; both are intended to strengthen antitrust enforcement and protect consumers.
1918	Women given the right to vote in Great Britain.
1920	Women given the right to vote in the United States.
1929	Stock market crash initiates steps to protect investors.
1933	U.S. Securities Act requires organizations to provide information allowing investors to make purchases based on facts, restricts corporate communication before and during the period that new securities are being registered with the Securities and Exchange Commission (SEC), and requires filing with the SEC when securities are offered to the public.
1934	U.S. SEC requires companies to provide quarterly and annual reports and provides consumer protection from fraud.
1936	Consumers Union forms and produces *Consumer Reports*.
1946	Federal Regulation of Lobbying Act in the United States.
1947	Taft-Hartley Act in the United States prohibits corporations and unions from supporting political candidates for federal office.
1960s	Open record law movement begins in the United States.
1966	U.S. Freedom of Information Act opens records of 400 federal agencies.
1965	Consumer Federation of America is formed.
1970s	Consumer movements gain power resulting in hundreds of product recalls and enforcement of Truth in Lending Act and Product Safety Act in United States.
1971	U.S. Federal Election Campaigns Act creates limits on gifts. Consumer Federation of America and the Nader organization created.
1974	U.S. Freedom of Information Act opens records of all federal agencies with security exemptions.
1976	Government in the Sunshine Act requires 50 federal agencies to open governing board meetings to public.
1985	Intense consumer pressure forces Coca-Cola to sack new formula.
1986	Government fees reduced for news media and educational institutions in acquiring copies of government records.
1995	U.S. Lobbying Disclosure Act. Clinton administration issues new Freedom of Information Act. Guidelines provide greater public access and make it more difficult to classify records as exempt for security reasons.
1997	Consumer Bill of Rights provides protection and quality in the health care industry for consumers.

The development of holocaust weapons may be responsible for the first recognition of human social interdependence, but population growth and its consequences on the global environment have been the factors that are bringing the realization down to personal concern. It is now estimated that, short of major health or famine catastrophes, the world's population will be between eight and nine billion in twenty-five years. This is up from an estimated 760 million in 1750, 1.63 billion in 1900, and slightly more than 2.5 billion in 1990. Global population more than doubled in only forty years from 1950 to 1990, and it is estimated to double again in only twenty-five years (Cassel, 1994).

Nothing may be binding the world together more, however, than an awareness of the effect of global pollution and of the destruction of the earth's vegetation and wildlife. The depletion of natural resources, particularly those strategic to global economic and cultural stability, demonstrates just how socially interdependent global societies now are.

Van Gunsteran (1998) sees an increase in shared interests with the manifestation of global citizenship and the recognition of interdependence, the advancement of human rights, humanitarian and international interventions, a strengthening of the power of world opinion, and alliances among democracies. According to Galtung and Vincent (1992), the recognition of shared global interests and needs resulted in the post–World War II development of the International Monetary Fund, the World Bank, and the General Agreement on Tariffs and Trade. Cutlip and colleagues (2000) made the point that in order "to prosper and endure, all organizations must (1) accept the public responsibility imposed by an increasingly interdependent society, (2) communicate, despite multiplying barriers, with publics that are often distant and diverse, and (3) achieve integration into the communities that they were created to serve" (p. 122). In 1989, Dow Chemical Company president Frank Popoff said, "Once people talked about industrialization, about nations developing the machinery and the skills to manufacture and distribute products on a large scale at affordable cost. Now we talk about globalization, about the world as a global community where nations and people can share one economy, one environment, one technology and at least in commerce, one language" (Cutlip, 1994, p. 47).

Chadlington (1999), quoting from *The Lexus and the Olive Tree* by Thomas Friedman, identified what he sees as the true meaning of "globalization":

> the globalization system, unlike the Cold War system, is not static, but a dynamic ongoing process: globalization involves the inexorable integration of markets, nation-states and technologies to a degree never witnessed before—in a way that is enabling individuals, corporations and nation-states to reach around the world farther, faster, deeper and cheaper than ever before, and in a way this is also producing a powerful backlash from those brutalized or left behind by the new system. (pp. 7–8)

The Increase in Global Social Interdependence.   World population growth has obviously been essential in spurring the development of social interdependence because of the increasing burden it is placing on world resources and because of the pollution and environmental problems occurring from the growth. Global awareness of the problems, communicated instantly via satellite communication technology, fax, and e-mail, has heightened universal awareness of our global social interdependence.

Table 1.3 and the literature indicate that although World War II ended the isolation of countries and demonstrated social interdependence, its end also marked the development

TABLE 1.3   *Key Achievements and Events in the Historical Development of Global Social Interdependence*

1500s	Global trade begins.	1950	World population reaches 2.516 billion.
1750	World population reaches an estimated 760 million.	1951	UNESCO initiates global arid zone research.
1784	American trade begins with China.	1952	Britain develops nuclear bomb.
1810–1890	Slavery abolished; no longer condoned globally.	1953	United States Information Agency is created for international communication.
1802–1938	Child labor laws instituted: United Kingdom, Europe, United States.	1960	The Organization of Petroleum Exporting Countries (OPEC) is formed.
1895	International Red Cross founded.		France develops nuclear bomb.
1896	World Olympic Committee founded.		World Health Organization identifies air pollution as a serious global problem.
1900	World population reaches 1.63 billion.		
1914–1918	World War I creates a new level of social interaction.	1961	Rachel Carson's *Silent Spring* draws international attention to global chemical pollution.
1918	League of Nations proposed.		
1939–1945	World War II—Expands English-speaking troops from Great Britain, United States, Canada, Australia around the world and made global cooperation necessary.	1963	First limited Test Ban Treaty on nuclear weapons.
		1965	Global information age begins.
		1968	Nuclear Nonproliferation Treaty.
1941	End of U.S. isolationism with entry in World War II.	1969–1972	Strategic Arms Limitation Talks (SALT).
1944	World Bank created.	1970	Transnational codes emerge as a result of dramatic increase in international economic activities.
1945	United Nations (UN) inaugurated.		
	First atomic bomb used, creating first awareness of global consequences of holocaust weapons.		Foreign direct investment trade services begin.
	International Court of Justice established.	1971	Greenpeace is founded as international environmental citizen action group.
	World Federation of Trade Unions established.	1972–1979	SALT II.
	Awareness of German Jewish extermination creates new global human rights concerns.	1973	Arab oil embargo results in drastic increase in oil prices creating global recognition of dependence on oil producing countries for this natural resource.
1946	U.S. creates Office of International Information and Education Exchanges under the Fulbright Act.		
1948	UN Declaration of Human Rights approved.		First international agreement to protect endangered species reached with 80 countries participating.
	World Health Organization created.		
	UN General Agreement on Tariffs and Trade established.	1974	India develops nuclear bomb.
1949	Russia develops nuclear bomb.	1979	A serious reactor leak at Three Mile Island in the United States creates first public concerns about safety of nuclear power.
	International Confederation of Free Trade Unions founded.		

(continued)

TABLE 1.3   *Continued*

1980	Big three automakers in United States lost over $4 billion to stiff foreign competition.
	UN establishes multilaterally agreed-on equitable principles and rules for the control of business practices to forbid bribery.
1986	Effect of acid rain recognized.
1990	World population reaches nearly 5.3 billion.
1993	European Union (EU) establishes single market.
	North American Free Trade Alliance (NAFTA) established.
1998	Bank for International Settlements reports daily forex trading reached $1.5 trillion a day.
	Forrester Research reports world Internet commerce reached $80 billion in goods and services and predicts it will reach $3.2 trillion in 2003.
2025	World population predicted to reach more than 8.1 billion.

of growing international cooperation in addressing global issues and needs. All result from a global social interdependence related to protection of the environment, trade needs, and shared communication needs.

When the tables in this chapter are examined, a convergence can be identified of advancements in communication, democracy, and social interdependence that helps explain the growth of public relations globally. Global communication, global awareness of advancements in democracy, and an increased awareness of social interdependence are suggested by the advancements that have been simultaneously achieved in the past fifty years in particular. The events noted in the tables throughout this chapter appear to indicate that the convergence has been instrumental in the empowerment of public opinion globally, perhaps because of the global observation that may now take place. The impact is shown in the formation of international agreements and the creation of international bodies resulting from global public opinion pressures. Although cause and effect cannot be proven by this research method, the correlation is evident. The conjecture may also be drawn that the same increase in public opinion empowerment that spurred the need for public relations as a profession within world governments will also increasingly demand more of the profession ethically and in its performance of public service.

Development of Public Relations as a Profession

The initial years of activity by public relations pioneers can, at best, be described mainly as publicity and lobbying activities. In 1906, Ivy Lee defended International Harvester Company against possible antitrust action. By 1914, however, Lee was involved in defending the Rockefeller name following intense assault from the U.S. press and public for their brutal strike-breaking tactics in the Ludlow Massacre, the deadly result of a Colorado mining strike (Cutlip, 1994). In most cases, the use of public relations resulted from what Cutlip identifies as a growing awareness of the need to court public opinion. The activities reflect the end of a time period where big business "was committed to the doctrine that the less the public knew of its operations, the more efficient and profitable—even the more socially useful—operations would be" (Cutlip, 1995, p. 187).

Still, not until the 1960s would public relations practitioners be forced to rethink their approaches to their audiences. Although practitioners saw the need for two-way communication, the performance models used research as a tool to manipulate behaviors, not to serve the public interest (Turow, 1999).

By the 1970s and 1980s, however, public relations had turned to strategic planning. Public relations educators began to recognize that a "symmetrical" two-way relationship between an organization and its audience helps ensure organizational stability in ways that one-way communication cannot. In this new model of public relations performance, research would be used not only to position and shape messages but also to determine how the organization could position its policies and performance to most please its target audiences (Turow, 1999).

In the 1990s, reputation management became a critical issue, partly because of the development of the Internet and instant satellite communication (Chadlington, 1999). *Spin doctors* became a term identified with public relations performance (Traverse-Healy, 1998), and leading professionals, such as Paul Alvarez, former president of Ketchum Communications, saw the new public relations challenge as the management of the fragmentation of audiences and the delivery of understandable messages (Alvarez, 1995).

John Budd, a visionary ahead of his time, projected that corporations would have chief executive officers for external affairs and internal affairs, with senior officers responsible for information and communication and for public policy and issues (Budd, 1989). Lord Chadlington (1999) supported Budd's recognition a decade later and believes it to be the global challenge of the twenty-first century.

As noted in Table 1.4, although the first textbook was written by 1923 and some formation of professional organizations had been initiated prior to World War II, the formation of national and international professional organizations began near or in the second half of the twentieth century. Although the achievements of founders can be cited at the turn of the twentieth century, virtually all of the efforts toward the creation of professional organizations or advancement in educational requirements occurred after World War I, with the major professional advancements in creating national memberships and involvement following World War II.

In 1965, the Public Relations Society of America (PRSA) had only 1,500 members. Although 300 U.S. universities reported teaching courses in public relations as early as 1964, only 28 percent had full-time public relations educators on their faculties as late as 1970. In 1975, studies showed that the norm nationally for public relations educational programs was only two public relations courses per university.

By the 1990s, growth in the number of national and international organizations increased, student interest in public relations dramatically increased, and professional membership continued to steadily increase, including membership in specialized areas of public relations. PRSA became the largest public relations professional body in the world, and public relations educators organized themselves into an academy of public relations scholars who founded the first all-inclusive international, interdisciplinary public relations research conference open to scholars regardless of academic placement in communication, the behavioral sciences, or business.

TABLE 1.4 *Key Achievements in the Historical Development of Public Relations as a Profession*

1923	First textbook published: *Crystallizing Public Opinion* by Edward Bernays.
	First class taught at New York University (by Edward Bernays).
1929	Religious Public Relations Council founded.
1935	National School Public Relations Association founded.
1938	Wise Men begun in 1938 by John W. Hill.
1939	American Council on Public Relations founded by Rex Harlow.
1944	*Public Relations News* founded, first newsletter of the profession.
1945–1965	Boom period in growth and development of public relations practice.
1946	Twenty-six universities or colleges offer public relations instruction.
	Public relations firms and corporate public relations departments begin to proliferate.
1947	First master's degree in public relations established at Boston University.
1948	Public Relations Society of America (PRSA) founded and first president elected—Howard Chase.
	Gold Anvil Award created to honor distinguished achievement by PRSA.
	Canadian Public Relations Society founded.
	Institute of Public Relations in United Kingdom founded.
1950	PRSA assembly adopts Code of Ethics.
1951	First edition of *Effective Public Relations* by Scott Cutlip and Allen Center published; the first widely used textbook.
1953	Agricultural Relations Council founded.
1954	Code of Ethics revised by PRSA.
	Baptist Public Relations Association founded.
1955	International Public Relations Association (IPRA) founded and first president elected—Sir Tom Fife Clark of the United Kingdom.
1958	*PR Reporter* founded; first newsletter with behavioral focus.
1959	PRSA Code of Ethics revised.
1960	National Society of Fund Raising Executives founded.
1963	PRSA Code of Ethics revised.
1964	Some 300 universities offer courses in public relations and 14 provide programs for bachelor degrees.
	American Hospital Association forms a professional society for practitioners.
1965	Code of Athens adopted by IPRA.
	PRSA reaches 1,500 membership.
1968	Public Relations Student Society of America (PRSSA) is founded with chapters at 9 universities.
1969	National Investor Relations Institute founded in the United States.
	United Kingdom forms Public Relations Consultants Association; only its 160-member consultancies may use the title "registered public relations consultants."
1970	PRSA Outstanding Educator Award created and awarded.
	International Association of Business Communicators (IABC) founded.
	Twenty-eight percent of educational programs teaching public relations in the United States have full-time teachers; 4 percent have two or more full-time teachers.
1973	Black Public Relations Society chapters formed.
	PRSSA numbers 35 chapters with 1,000 student members.
	A PRSSA assembly is authorized by PRSA and formed.
	Bateman and Cutlip cochair first Commission on Public Relations Education.
	First national PRSSA president elected.

TABLE 1.4 *Continued*

1975	Council for Advancement and Support of Education founded (CASE).
	Thirty-seven percent of educational programs teaching public relations in the United States have full-time teachers; 12 percent have two or more, 5 percent have with three or more.
	Walker research study finds two courses with public relations in the title is the national public relations program norm.
	Bateman and Cutlip Commission on Public Relations Education report recommends four core courses for public relations study.
1976	Paul M. Lund Public Service Award created and awarded.
1977	IPRA President's Award established to recognize organizations or individuals "who have contributed to better world understanding."
	First recipient: The Nobel Foundation.
	PRSA Code of Ethics revised.
1980	First PRSA Task Force on Stature and Role of Public Relations provides report and recommendations.
1981	Friends of PRSSA created to support PRSSA programs.
1982	PRSA adopts official statement defining public relations.
	IPRA International Commission on Public Relations Education founded.
	Issue Management Council founded.
1983	PRSA Code of Ethics revised.
	Arthur W. Page Society formed.
	Ehling and Plank Commission on Undergraduate Public Relations formed.
1985	U.S. Commission on Graduate Study in Public Relations, cochaired by Hesse and Alvarez, recommends a curriculum with four courses with public relations in the title for a master's degree and several specialized seminars in public relations and dissertations applicable to the solution of public relations problems for doctoral study.
	Study finds 51 universities claim graduate-level programs in public relations.
1987	Ehling and Plank Commission on Undergraduate Public Relations Education recommends five courses for public relations study.
	PRSA Task Force on Demonstrating Professionalism.
1988	PRSA Code of Ethics revised.
	First formal *Public Relations Body of Knowledge* released by the Foundation for Public Relations Research and Education.
1990	PRSA Foundation created.
	PRSA College of Fellows created: first president is Chester Burger.
	First Golden World Awards given by IPRA for excellence in public relations practice.
1991	IPRA adopts Charter (code) on Environmental Communications.
1997	PRSA Educators Section becomes an Educators Academy with a new mission for interdisciplinary synthesization.
	155,000 people work full time in public relations.
1998	PRSA Educators Academy hosts first International Interdisciplinary Public Relations Research Conference founded by Dr. Mel Sharpe.
1999	Commission on Public Relations Education cochaired by Kruckeberg and Paluszek recommends seven public relations courses for undergraduate degree programs in public relations; five courses for master's program content combined with management science area content; and doctoral programs with several specialized seminars in public relations as well as research seminars in related social, behavioral, and business sciences.
	Largest public relations firms have offices throughout world and begin creation of their own educational programs for international staff.
	European Public Relations Body of Knowledge Project initiated.

(continued)

TABLE 1.4 *Continued*

2000 IPRA creates an educators membership category to encourage international public relations educator unity and identity.	PRSA provides 16 special interest sections for members each with own officers, conferences, and agendas.
Eighty-two national public relations organizations exist in 61 countries in the world; IPRA membership is in 70 countries.	PRSSA reaches 6,000 members in 211 chapters nationally.

Conclusion

The development of public relations as a profession globally correlates with historical developments in three areas: communication, democracy, and global social interdependence. Its emergence as a profession in the United States occurred at a time when employees and consumers began to demand rights through unionization, when journalistic "muckrakers" drew attention to industry and government abuse, and when a newborn sense of social responsibility defined by an evolving journalism profession made public opinion a force in society.

The greatest growth and development of public relations as a profession followed World War II, assisted by consumer and social movements, open record laws, and restrictions on lobbying and political gifts. Each new advancement in communication technology spurred development by adding to the complexity of achieving effective communication and of maintaining organizational understanding. New and improved methods of evaluating public opinion have also played a role in defining organizational needs and responses.

Advancements in global communication, creating instantaneous global awareness of issues and actions all over the world, is a major factor in the empowerment of global public opinion, causing even previously closed systems, such as the Eastern Block countries and China, to embrace public relations. Their embrace of the profession has been a defensive necessity in a period when public opinion has much greater global force than at any previous time in history.

It is important to recognize that the Declaration of Independence and the creation of a Constitution and of a Bill of Rights do not appear to have instantly created a social condition in the United States where public relations could emerge as a profession. The reason appears to be that the human society had to learn how to force the management structure of the social system and its internal parts to respond to its concerns. This did not occur until the 1960s. The learning process has been lengthy and complex.

The empowerment of public opinion is elevating recognition of the importance of the public relations profession in what has become an increasingly interdependent global social system. Each advancement in the empowerment of public opinion has increased the responsibility of the public relations profession to the public—in serving as a conduit that provides management with an understanding of public concerns and their intensity; in serving in a check-and-balance relationship with the journalism profession that ensures both organizational and media responsibility in the performance of professional responsibilities; and in establishing standards for ethical performance of public relations on the part of nations, organizations, special interest groups, and, of course, practitioners. Global communication is providing people throughout the world with a new and broader concept of the power of public opinion in influencing social change. The result is a growing social expectation that organizations and governments will perform responsible public relations.

Empowerment is creating greater social awareness of the important role that public opinion pressure and public relations responses will have in a social system where many organizations operate as international and multinational institutions without the national loyalties or controls that once existed. Both governing boards and investors are increasingly international, and many corporations are wealthier than some countries.

Although there is little doubt that a global society governed by public opinion has many risks and that the fragmentation and segmentation of an increasingly complex global society increases the problems organizations have in communicating, it is also clear that the empowerment is mandating the need for competent, educated, ethical public relations counsel. Furthermore, the mandate is coming from social systems rather than from the captains of industry. Public opinion, therefore, has become the means of forcing organizational response, requiring the public relations profession to become increasingly proficient in evaluating relationship needs. Ultimately, this may make public relations professionals worldwide the "peacemakers" and social stabilizers in world society (Black & Sharpe, 1983).

Discussion Questions _____

1. Select a developed country other than the U.S. or a Third World country where students in the class have familiarity and identify the degree of convergence of communication technological advancements, global social interdependence, and democratic advancements. How does the rate of convergence of the three factors compare to the development of public relations in that country?

2. List as many evidences of the empowerment of global public opinion as you can from your reading in the media. Relate the effect of public opinion as a power source in your own country and others around the world.

3. What do you think people all over the world have to learn before their collective voice becomes a force factor in their own society or on a global scale?

4. What do you believe organizational management teams throughout the world will need to recognize before they will be in a position to perform effective public relations?

5. As multinational and international corporations become more and more economically powerful and their governing boards and executive officers more and more international in composition, what changes do you believe will be required in the performance needs of public relations staffs of these organizations? Of governments? Of special interest groups?

6. Conduct research on any of these questions and bring your findings to class to share and discuss in the next class period.

References

Alvarez, P. (1995). *A house divided: Communicating to a fractured society.* Vernon C. Schranz Distinguished Lectureship Series. Muncie, IN: Ball State University.

Baskin, O., Aronoff, C., & Lattimore, D. (1997). *Public relations: The profession and practice.* Dubuque, IA: Brown & Benchmark.

Black, S., & Sharpe, M. (1983). *Practical public relations.* New York: Prentice Hall.

Budd, J. (1989). *When less is more: Public relation's paradox of growth.* Vernon C. Schranz Distinguished Lectureship Series. Muncie, IN: Ball State University.

Cashman, S. (1991). *African-Americans and the quest for civil rights.* New York: New York University Press.

Cassel, R. (Ed.). (1994). *Old debates, new conclusions.* Piscataway, NY: Transaction.

Chadlington, L. (1999). *Globalization, the Internet, and the future of public relations.* Vernon C. Schranz Distinguished Lectureship Series. Muncie, IN: Ball State University.

Culbertson, H., & Chen, N. (Eds.). (1996). *International public relations: A comparative analysis.* Mahwah, NJ: Lawrence Erlbaum Associates.

Cutlip, S. (1994). *The unseen power: Public relations, a history.* Mahwah, NJ: Lawrence Erlbaum Associates.

Cutlip, S. (1995). *Public relations history: From the seventeenth to the twentieth century.* Mahwah, NJ: Lawrence Erlbaum Associates.

Cutlip, S., Center, A., & Broom, G. (2000). *Effective public relations.* New York: Prentice Hall.

Galenson, W. (1986). The historical role of American trade unions. In S. Lipsert (Ed.), *Unions in transition* (pp. 39–73). San Francisco: ICS Press.

Galtung, J., & Vincent, R. (1992). *Global glasnost.* Cresskill, NJ: Hampton Press.

Livingston, S. (1997). Beyond the CNN effect: The media foreign policy dynamic. In P. Norris (Ed.), *Politics and the press: News media and their influences* (pp. 291–318). Boulder CO: Lynne Rienner.

Mayer, R. (1989). *The consumer movement: Guardians of the marketplace.* Boston: Twayne.

Mott, F. (1950). *American journalism, a history of newspapers in the United States through 260 years: 1690 to 1950.* New York: Macmillan.

Newsom, D., Scott, A., & VanSlyke Turk, J. (1992). *This is PR: The realities of public relations.* Boston: Wadsworth.

Nevins, A. (1963). *The constitution makers and the public: 1785–1790.* New York: Institute for Public Relations Research and Education.

Norris, P. (1997). Introduction: The rise of postmodern political communications? In P. Norris (Ed.), *Politics and the press: News media and their influences* (p. 9). Boulder, CO: Lynne Rienner.

Okrent, D. (2000, January 24). Happily ever after? The "most transformational event" turns Wall Street on its ear, two giants into one and the future into an alluring promise. *Time,* p. 43.

Olasky, M. (1987). The development of corporate public relations. *Journalism Monographs, 102.*

Payne, G. (1970). *History of journalism in the United States.* Westport, CT: Greenwood Press.

Pooley, E. (2000, February 28). Read my knuckles. *Time,* p. 31.

Reagan, R. (1989, June 13). The triumph of freedom. Speech presented as the Winston Churchill Lecture to the English Speaking Union, London.

Rothman, D., & Wheeler, S. (1981). *Social history and social policy.* San Diego: Academic Press.

Seitel, F. (1998). *Effective public relations.* New York: Prentice Hall.

Sharpe, M. (1996). What school administrators need to understand. In T. Kowalski (Ed.), *Public relations in educational organizations* (pp. 59–61). Englewood Cliffs, NJ: Prentice Hall.

Simon, R. (2000, January 17). Now it's put-up time. *U.S. News & World Report,* p. 19.

Straubhaar, J., & LaRose, R. (1997). *Communications media in the information society.* Boston: Wadsworth.

Traverse-Healy, T. (1998). *The spin doctors.* Vernon C. Schranz Distinguished Lectureship Series. Muncie, IN: Ball State University.

Turow, J. (1999). *Media today.* Boston: Houghton Mifflin.

Van Gunsteran, H. (1998). *A theory of citizenship: Organizing plurality in contemporary democracies.* Boulder, CO: Westview Press.

Vivian, J. (1999). *The media of mass communication.* Boston: Allyn & Bacon.

Wardhaugh, R. (1987). *Languages in competition.* Malden, MA: Basil Blackwell, Ltd.

Wilcox, D., Ault, P., & Agee, W. (1992). *Public relations strategies and tactics.* New York: HarperCollins.

Wilhelm, D. (1990). *Global communication and political power.* Piscataway, NJ: Transaction.

Part II

Around Latin America

Latin America: A Perpetual Land of the Future?

Donn James Tilson

We start our journey exploring the world of public relations with a visit to Latin America, a continent that John Gunther (1966) once described as a region "in the state of active flux, grasping for a future, with fundamental . . . impulses for change apparent almost everywhere" (p. xii). Today, that description still holds true as illustrated in the following chapters on Mexico, Ecuador, Peru, and a survey chapter on the region. In some respects there are hopeful signs, including the rise to power of new political voices in Mexico under the Fox administration and an increasingly politically active citizenry in Ecuador (yet with many age-old problems continuing to persist, including widespread poverty and unemployment, corruption, and *caudillo*-style government) (Tilson & Rockwell, 2004). It is indeed a region in transition (some say taking one step forward and two steps back), a region of great promise and of promises unkept. Hopefully, it will not remain, as Brazil has been characterized in a carioca proverb—"Brazil is the land of the future—and always will be" (Gunther, 1966, p. 1).

A review of the region suggests that privatization, free-market reforms, democratization, telecommunications, and globalization are transforming the economic, political, and cultural landscape. Such forces have spurred the development of business, the promotional sector (public relations, advertising, and marketing), and higher education communication curriculum. Indeed, as public relations consultancies have followed their clients into the hemisphere, these practices have expanded their reach to the extent that most multinational firms—Burson-Marsteller, Ketchum, and Edelman, among others—now have offices or affiliates in the major capitals of Latin America and regional headquarters in South Florida. In turn, growth in these sectors has facilitated, if not accelerated, the commodification of society (Wernick, 1991), ushering in a world of MTV,

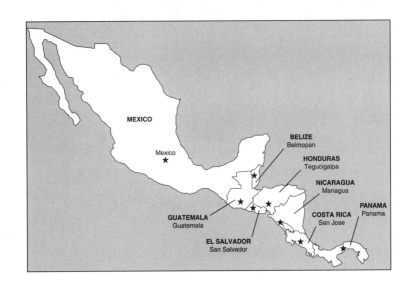

MEXICO

Mexico ★

BELIZE
Belmopan

HONDURAS
Tegucigalpa

NICARAGUA
Managua

PANAMA
Panama

GUATEMALA
Guatemala

COSTA RICA
San Jose

EL SALVADOR
San Salvador

GUYANA
Georgetown

SURINAME
Paramaribo

FRENCH GUIANA
Cayenne

Caracas

VENEZUELA

Bogotá ★

COLOMBIA

ECUADOR ★
Quito

PERU ★
Lima

BRAZIL

Brasília ★

BOLIVIA ★
La Paz

PARAGUAY
Asunción

CHILE

ARGENTINA

Santiago ★   Buenos Aires ★

URUGUAY
Montevídeo

Wal-Mart, Coca-Cola, and English-language television programming. Some argue that these changes have ushered in more open and democratic societies with greater economic opportunities, but others contend that the confluence of outside and indigenous special interests has only benefited ruling oligarchies and exacerbated unemployment and poverty (Tilson, 1996, 1999).

A closer look at the economies in the region reflects both sides of the argument. According to the World Bank, the number of poor has grown from 136 million in 1986 to 180 million but, as a percentage of overall population, it has declined since 1992 from 40 to 34 percent currently; moreover, projections suggest that poverty levels will fall to 24 percent by 2015, even as the total number of poor increases to 147 million (Oppenheimer, 2001a). Of further concern, however, is the increasing concentration of wealth in the region. A 2001 UN Development Fund study details severe disparities in income, with the richest 20 percent of the population earning a disproportionate share as compared with the poorest 20 percent; several countries top the list, not only in the hemisphere but in the world—Bolivia (income 38 times that of the poorest), Honduras (38), and Nicaragua (28). Moreover, argues the study, privileged classes that rule such societies do little to support public policies necessary to provide vital social services to the poor (Oppenheimer, 2001b). An Inter-American Development Bank (IDB) report corroborates the inequities in economic development and places the responsibility squarely on the shoulders of public institutions—government administrations, justice systems, and electoral bodies. As Ricardo Hausmann, IDB chief economist noted, "Latin American countries have problems with the rule of law, corruption and the ineffectiveness of government" (Bussey, 2000, p. E9).

Although no one country or region has a monopoly on corruption, it seems that privatization of state-run industries in developing nations "has been the foremost source of corrupt payments," according to Dean Klitgaard of the Rand Graduate School (Bussey, 1998; cited in Tilson, 1999, p. 70). As during the Salinas administration in Mexico, "corrupt government officials . . . have given privatization deals and other business contracts to associates," which discourages investors and inhibits the flow of free-market reform benefits to society (Tilson, 1999, p. 70).

A review of two studies issued almost simultaneously indicates that corruption inhibits the flow of foreign capital into the general economy with government officials and economic oligarchies often monopolizing such funds for their private interests. A Miliken Institute study of credit availability in thirty-one emerging nations (Fields, 1998) ranked Chile fifth among the top in liquidity and five other Latin American nations among the middle to bottom: Peru (13), Brazil (14), Mexico (21), Ecuador (20), and Venezuela (25). These rankings seem to correlate with those in a 1998 and a 2002 Transparency International corruption index based on residents' and nonresidents' perceptions of the level of corruption in each country. In 1998, Chile (20) ranked among the least corrupt of the eighty-five nations reviewed, whereas other Latin American nations ranked among the middle to bottom: Peru (41), Brazil (46), Mexico (55), Ecuador (77), and Venezuela (77) (Survey says Denmark least corrupt, 1998). In a 2002 study of one hundred nations, countries in Latin America maintained similar rankings, with Chile and Uruguay scoring above the norm in the region; Brazil (45) and Mexico and Colombia (57) emerging toward the middle; and Peru (45), Venezuela (81), and Ecuador (89) slipping farther toward the bottom. Other nations at the lower end included Argentina (70), Guatemala and Nicaragua (81),

Haiti (89), and Paraguay (98) (Bussey, 2002; Tamayo, 2002). As the following chapters illustrate, fighting corruption has been a top priority of the Fox administration in Mexico and "crony capitalism" is a major recurrent theme that has plagued a host of government administrations in Ecuador.

Most important for the future of the hemisphere, however, as noted by various Latin heads of state attending a Summit of the Americas in Miami in December 1994, "corruption in both the public and private sector weakens democracy and undermines the legitimacy of governments" (Declaration of Principles, 1994, p. 14). It was just such public fatigue with corruption that prompted a change in Mexico's presidency in 2000 after seventy-one years of rule by the Institutional Revolutionary Party, and that also climaxed in massive protests driving several administrations from office in Ecuador, and ousting five presidents in less than three weeks in Argentina in 2001, while also leaving twenty-eight dead and a nation in bankruptcy. By the time that the de la Rúa administration collapsed in Argentina, political expenditures were estimated at U.S.$2 to U.S.$4 billion for almost one million federal and provincial employees, many of whom were party loyalists who had been rewarded with lifetime "political spoils" jobs protected by law (Oppenheimer, 2001c). With the average public-sector worker making almost twice that of private-sector employees, and federal legislators earning two hundred times that amount, it is not surprising that only 15 percent of the public said they trusted Congress, down from 75 percent in 1983 when the nation returned to democracy (Oppenheimer, 2001a). In general, popular support for democracy has been eroding throughout Latin America as citizens are discouraged by political corruption, insufficient social services, and continuing poverty. A Latinobarometro 2001 poll revealed a drop from 60 to 48 percent in support for democracy across the region; in some countries, such as El Salvador and Brazil, only 25 percent and 30 percent polled thought that "democracy was preferable to any other kind of government," with the most trusted institutions being the Church (76 percent) and television (70 percent) (Oppenheimer, 2001d, e).

Public relations professionals share some of the blame as U.S. firms often have counseled some of the most violent and corrupt regimes in the hemisphere (Tilson, 1999), including Duvalier in Haiti (Hill & Knowlton), Somoza in Nicaragua (Norman, Lawrence, Patterson & Farrell), and Argentine leaders during the nation's "dirty war" against suspected dissidents in the 1970s (Burson-Marsteller). Such representation did little to endear Latin Americans to the United States or its interests in the region. Further, a report for the

Mexico

Government type	Federal republic
Capital	Mexico City
Language	Spanish, regional indigenous
Ethnic groups	Mestizo (Amerindian-Spanish), Amerindian or predominantly Amerindian, white
Religion	Roman Catholic, Protestant
Major industries	Food, beverage, tobacco, chemicals, iron and steel, petroleum, mining, textiles, clothing, motor vehicles, consumer durables, tourism

Sources: National Geographic Atlas of the World Seventh Edition, CIA The World Factbook 2002

Ecuador

Government type	Republic
Capital	Quito
Language	Spanish, Quechua
Ethnic groups	Mestizo (mixed Amerindian and white), Amerindian, Spanish, black
Religion	Roman Catholic
Major industries	Petroleum, food processing, textiles, metal work, paper products, wood products, chemicals, plastics, fishing, lumber

Sources: National Geographic Atlas of the World Seventh Edition, CIA The World Factbook 2002

Peru

Government type	Constitutional republic
Capital	Lima
Language	Spanish, Quechua (both official), Aymara
Ethnic groups	Amerindian, mestizo (mixed Amerindian and white), white, black, Japanese, Chinese
Religion	Roman Catholic
Major industries	Mining of metals, petroleum, fishing, textiles, clothing, food processing, cement, auto assembly, steel, shipbuilding, metal fabrication

Sources: National Geographic Atlas of the World Seventh Edition, CIA The World Factbook 2002

2001 Summit of the Americas in Quebec indicated that foreign and domestic corporations in Latin America do little to promote the welfare of employees or the local community. The report urges corporations to proactively work with host governments to institute private-sector initiatives to improve social conditions and to strengthen codes of conduct with anti-corruption measures. Such corporate responsibility should be a priority for public relations professionals who counsel top management, and good citizenship an integral part of every strategic public relations plan. In so doing, the profession not only can best serve its interests and those of its employers but also can help transform societies into ones that are civil, ethical, and equitable for all peoples.

References

Bussey, J. (1998, April 3). Anti-corruption summit seeks solutions. *The Miami Herald,* p. C3.

Bussey, J. (2000, May 21). Despite reforms, the Americas continue to lag much of the world. *The Miami Herald,* p. E1, E9.

Bussey, J. (2002, August 29). Latin America low on corruption scale. *The Miami Herald,* p. 2C.

Declaration of principles. (1994, December 11). Miami: Summit of the Americas.

Fields, G. (1998, October 26). Group: To stay afloat, increase liquidity. *The Miami Herald Business Monday,* p. 11.

Gunther, J. (1966). *Inside South America.* New York: Harper & Row.

Oppenheimer, A. (2001a, June 17). Gloomy times: Latin Americans' view of the future no longer shiny as in early '90s. *The Miami Herald,* p. L1.

Oppenheimer, A. (2001b, July 12). Latin America leads world in inequality, U.N. study says. *The Miami Herald,* p. A14.

Oppenheimer, A. (2001c, July 22). Argentines want politicians to tighten their belts, too. *The Miami Herald,* p. A6.

Oppenheimer, A. (2000d, August 5). Dear Mr. President: Latin America needs your attention. *The Miami Herald,* p. A8.

Oppenheimer, A. (2001e, October 18). Latin America suffering 'democratic fatigue.' *The Miami Herald,* p. A6.

Survey says Denmark least corrupt; U.S. tied for 17th. (1998, September 23). *The Miami Herald,* p. A8.

Tamayo, J. (2002, October 13). As Latin America economies modernize, intolerance for corruption is spreading. *The Miami Herald: The Herald Americas Conference,* p. 9.

Tilson, D. (1996). The commodification of Latin America: A confluence of telecommunications, the media and promotion. *World Communication, 25*(3), 133–141.

Tilson, D. (1999). Against the common good: The commodification of Latin America. *Media Development, 46*(3), 69–74.

Tilson, D., & Rockwell, R. (2004). Latin America. In J. Merrill & A. de Beer (Eds.), *Global journalism.* Boston: Allyn & Bacon.

Wernick, A. (1991). *Promotional culture: Advertising, ideology and symbolic expression.* London: Sage.

2

The Other "New" Mexico

Public Relations Accelerates the Move to a Legitimate Democracy

Richard K. Long

Key Points

- Mexico is a "young" democracy.
- Mexico's economic future is closely tied to U.S. economic recovery; NAFTA is only one part of the equation.
- The real impact of the Vicente Fox presidency will be determined by the outcome of future elections, especially the 2006 presidential race.
- True freedom of the press will enhance Mexico's emergence as a stable democracy.

Convergence of the North American Free Trade Agreement (NAFTA), mass media reforms, and a sea change in the country's political landscape have created extraordinary public relations opportunities for organizations in Mexico, now the world's eighth-largest economy. The emergence of a truly independent mass media system, coupled with the first engagement of the public in issues of the day, signals progress in Mexico's development as an economic, social, and political force in the Western Hemisphere.

Mexico as an Emerging Democracy

To fully appreciate the "emerging" Mexico, it is important first to understand its unique history, where democracy has not always been the operative political system. Mexico's indigenous people first came under foreign domination in 1519, when Fernando Cortés claimed the territory for Spain. In 1821 the Spaniards were overthrown, and the young republic began to govern itself. Forty-one years later, the French made a short-lived attempt to bring Mexico into its colonial realm. The first Mexican victory over the French was a memorable one at the Battle of Puebla on May 5, 1862. It gave rise to the national holiday Cinco de Mayo. The Mexicans, led by Benito Juárez and aided by three thousand Union army veterans fresh from the U.S. Civil War, continued their fight against French rule. After three years of fighting, Emperor Maximilian surrendered and soon met his end before a firing squad.

After France's departure, Juárez assumed the presidency of the country. Then Mexico entered a period of more than thirty years under the authoritarian rule of Porfirio Díaz. When Díaz resigned under pressure in 1911, the country splintered, and various factions fought for control in a "revolution" that lasted three decades. In the words of an American diplomat, "Once Díaz was out of the way, the Mexican people set about slaughtering each other." Between 1913 and 1928, three Mexican presidents, one vice president, and the revolutionaries Emiliano Zapata and Pancho Villa were assassinated. All this turmoil was challenging enough for Mexico, but some of the upheaval spilled into the United States, which sent troops south of the border.

Mexicans were not amused by the U.S. expeditions, even if the intent was to restore order. For many, it was a reminder that its big and powerful neighbor was flexing its muscles again—with Mexico as the sure loser. After all, California, Nevada, Arizona, New Mexico, Utah, and Texas once *belonged* to Mexico. Texas won its independence in 1836 and became a republic. Then, in 1846, U.S. president James K. Polk sent troops south in what became known as the Mexican War. U.S. troops fought all the way to the streets of Mexico City before the two countries signed the Treaty of Guadalupe Hidalgo. *New York Times* reporter Tim Weiner observed, "The United States stole half of Mexico fair and square, taking everything from Texas to California and more. People here [in Mexico City] do not forget the invasions of the gringos, or their power and influence" (Weiner, 2001b, p. 3).

In the 1930s, one dominant political party emerged. Partido Revolucionario Institucional (PRI) took control of Mexico's political, social, and economic destiny and, as regular as clockwork, elected a new president every six years. The end of that seventy-one-year reign, with the election of Vicente Fox in 2000, is a key to Mexico's emergence as a legitimate democracy.

To the outside world—and to most Mexicans as well—Mexican elections were as predictable as the sunrise. In the presidential elections of 1958, 1964, 1970, and 1976, the PRI candidates won with margins of more than 85 percent. And virtually all of the winners since 1920 left office much richer for the effort, thanks to an ingrained system of graft and corruption.

Mexico is a land of contrasts. The country covers slightly more than 750,000 square miles, and is more than 2,100 miles wide at the U.S. border and as narrow as 135 miles in the south. The country has 97 million people (35 percent under the age of fifteen), but that figure is misleading. Mexico City, the capital, has an official population of 18.5 million. However, by some estimates, more than 20 million live in the huge bowl, surrounded on all sides by mountains. One of the country's challenges, typical of many developing nations, is the distribution of income. By one estimate, 43 percent of the population lives in "extreme" or "intermediate" poverty. Burson-Marsteller executive Roy Caple looks at it another way: "The upper classes account for 5% of the population. The middle class is another 20%. That means 75% of the people are living at or below the hunger level" (personal communication, July 3, 2001).

Despite the poverty, Mexico is a highly literate nation. According to 1999 government data, 93 percent of Mexican men over the age of fifteen are literate. For Mexican women the same age, literacy is 89 percent (Gower, Craddock, & Pruitt, 2001).

Mexico is catching up with the technology generation, though there are only 104 phone lines per thousand people (Mexico City has more cellular phones in use than telephone *lines*) and only 47 personal computers per thousand people. Newspaper circulation is only 115 per thousand people, compared to 227 radios and 261 televisions per thousand (Gower et al., 2001). For the population at large, radio and television are the dominant media and sources of entertainment. However, the country's decision makers rely heavily on newspapers and magazines for their information.

Oil and tourism have been the heart of Mexico's economy for many years. The world's fifth-largest oil producing country, Mexico is also rich in natural gas. "Black gold" provides about 35 percent of the government's total revenue base. Since 1994, when NAFTA took effect, Mexico has shown substantial growth in the manufacturing sector and a corresponding increase in exports.

The United States, Mexico, and Canada crafted NAFTA in the 1980s. The treaty called for eliminating tariffs on most manufactured goods over a fourteen-year period, opening all three markets for each country's products. U.S. environmental groups, labor unions, and some agricultural interests say NAFTA has cost U.S. jobs, as companies move production facilities south of the border to take advantage of lower labor costs. With a minimum wage of about seven dollars a day, Mexico does offer labor savings, though many jobs pay well above the minimum. (*Note:* All monetary figures in this chapter are stated in U.S. dollar equivalents.)

In its first five years of operation, NAFTA has had a positive impact on some sectors of Mexico, and the numbers fail to show any disadvantage for the U.S. economy. Trade between the United States and Mexico grew from $80 billion in 1993 to nearly $180 billion in 1998. Equally important is what *didn't* happen as a result of NAFTA. When the treaty was being debated in the U.S. Congress, one war cry was heard regularly: "Listen to that giant sucking sound as U.S. jobs move south." Though some U.S. production has moved to Mexico, the net negative effect on U.S. jobs has been minor. In actuality, according to the U.S.–Mexico Chamber of Commerce NAFTA Forum, from 1993 to 1998, 18 million new jobs were created in the United States, some 350,000 of them related to exports to Mexico (NAFTA Forum, 2001, www.usmcoc.org/-naftafor.html).

In 1997, Mexico surpassed Japan as the United States's second-largest trading partner, trailing only Canada. Many Mexican business and government leaders say it is only a matter of time before Mexico moves into the number one position.

The Mass Media of Mexico

It is axiomatic that for a true democracy to exist, certain freedoms must flourish. The history of modern nations would show how essential freedom of the press is in the maturing of a democratic society. In such a setting, the media keep people informed and help them make sensible decisions at the ballot box. The media also serve as watchdogs, to keep big government, big business, and other institutions accountable.

Mexico's mass media history is a mixed bag. At times, the media, as with the government and other institutions, have been a part of the entrenched corruption that afflicted Mexico for all of the twentieth century. Because the media received its marching orders—and frequently plain brown envelopes filled with pesos—from the dominant political party and other special interests, the media were seldom taken seriously.

Many Mexican opinion leaders, including journalists, openly refer to the years of the PRI as "authoritarian." People not following the dominant party line were subjected to reprisals, sanctions, threats, kidnappings, and, all too often, assassinations. And journalism as an institution heeled to the PRI dogma until well into the 1990s.

Consider the situation of newspapers, dependent as they are on newsprint and ink. For decades, a government entity, Productora e Importadora de Papel, S.A. (PIPSA), controlled the importation of newsprint, and newspapers that offended the government found their allocation reduced or temporarily suspended. Hardly subtle, this technique ensured certain obedience to government (i.e., PRI) expectations.

A second technique, now mercifully defunct, was the printing of *gacetillas,* which were government- or PRI-purchased advertising spaces designed to look like news stories. In some cases, entire pages of newspapers were covered with government propaganda. Pity the unsuspecting reader, if any were fooled by the technique, who may have thought he or she was really reading news.

The insidious nature of the *gacetillas* is not hard to divine. Newspapers became dependent on the insertions for their revenue flow, and there was a natural desire to make sure nobody harmed the cash cow. Reporters came to depend on them, too, because many papers gave a commission to those whose beats generated the income. Of course, the sources of the *gacetillas* had some expectations, too. When stories did not meet those expectations, the government often forced newspapers and radio stations to fire overly independent reporters.

A third way of swaying news coverage was with the plain brown envelope containing cash. In many cases, the cash changed hands before stories were written; on occasion, the envelope came in appreciation for a certain story or placement.

The fourth influence on media practices was pure terror. Numerous influential reporters and editors were killed in the 1980s and 1990s when their work angered or threatened drug lords, politicians, and others. For some journalists, death threats were enough to ensure moderation in their writing.

Changes began to appear in the late 1980s, during the presidency of Carlos Salinas. In an effort to give limited additional freedom to the press, the practice of *gacetillas* started to decline and PIPSA was privatized, meaning that newspapers were now free to go to the open market for their newsprint. The government, however, still controlled tariffs on imports, meaning that newspapers might not have a competitively priced alternative to PIPSA newsprint. Ironically, the decision to privatize PIPSA was actively opposed by many newspaper publishers who feared having to compete without subsidies and protection.

The Salinas government also suggested a solution to the chronic problem of unaudited newspaper circulation figures. Mexico City, with nearly two dozen daily newspapers, is a laboratory for trying to understand newspaper economics. How can a city of 18 million people sustain so many daily newspapers? Subsidies from unions and political parties are a good starting point.

One study in 1990 attempted to determine actual versus reported circulation for twenty-five newspapers. It found that most papers claiming daily circulation of more than 100,000 had actual sales of less than one-fourth that number. Some papers inflated their daily sales by factors of ten or fifteen times (Raymundo Riva, cited in Orme, 1997).

Salinas proposed an auditing system, such as the Audit Bureau of Circulation in the United States, but only three or four newspapers supported the concept. So as of 2001, the problem persisted as newspapers made circulation claims that could not be verified. As one reporter wrote, "Circulation figures are almost a state secret" (Lorenzo Meyer Cosio, personal communication, July 13, 2001).

Media authorities point to several breakthroughs in the emergence of a truly free press in Mexico. The magazine *Proceso* emerged during the 1980s and became a counter-voice to the government-controlled media. According to syndicated columnist Alberto Aguilar, "Everyone knew the government was allowing *Proceso* to publish for balance, but control of the rest of the media continued" (personal communication, July 24, 2001). Still, *Proceso* established a toehold that encouraged others.

Perhaps the first Mexican newspaper to establish its independence and withstand the fury of the PRI/government was *El Norte,* published in Monterrey since 1938. In the mid-1980s, the PRI withdrew its advertising from *El Norte* to punish it for overly aggressive reporting that was critical of the PRI, but the paper withstood the pressure and achieved considerable respect among Mexican journalists.

El Norte's success led its owner, Alejandro Junco de la Vega, to establish *Reforma* in 1994. The name was no mistake. It was intended to send a message that new journalism was coming to Mexico City to feed the new public opinion that was emerging. From its beginning, *Reforma* sent a clear message that it would not accept government advertising.

Reforma since has become the most influential newspaper in the capital—and perhaps in the country. Operating from a modernistic complex, *Reforma* employs seven hundred reporters and editors. The average age of the staff is slightly more than twenty-seven, and 80 percent of the news staff speak English. After three years of service, reporters are eligible for a one-year exchange with leading U.S. newspapers.

Reforma has seventy thousand regular subscribers and sells another eighty thousand copies daily on the street, this despite opting not to participate in the Unión de Voceadores de México, which controls newspaper and magazine distribution in thousands of kiosks and street-side stands throughout Mexico City and other population centers. To further express its independence, *Reforma* buys newsprint from U.S. sources, rather than from PIPSA.

Just as media organizations helped move Mexico into the new millennium, many journalists have also broken the historic mold of corruption and subservience to the government. One such person is Lorenzo Meyer, a political columnist who writes for *Reforma* and fifteen other Mexican papers. He also does a weekly radio commentary show and a historical issues program on Channel 11 in Mexico City.

Meyer's original calling was as a professor of political history at El Colegio de México in Mexico City. He continues to teach there, but his journalism endeavors have brought him considerable visibility and acclaim—and a few death threats. "I started doing short political commentaries for a local radio station about 1983. Two years later, I began writing a weekly column in *Excélsior,*" Meyer recalls. His academic experience had been in an authoritarian setting, that is, a closed atmosphere where there was little opportunity to say or do anything meaningful. "Writing for the media was an outlet for my expression," Meyer says (personal communication, July 13, 2001).

Meyer's political positions and, hence, his writings are left-of-center, which puts him in a position of critiquing government policies, including those of Vicente Fox, whose election he says benefited Mexico by "helping diminish the authoritarian elements of the central government" (personal communication, July 13, 2001). Though he downplays reports of death threats against him, Meyer knows journalism can be a dangerous profession in Mexico. "Reporters in Mexico City are relatively safe, but those covering drug cartels or other criminal activity are certainly at risk, especially in such states as Baja California, Oaxaca, Guerrero, Chiapas, and Tamaulipas. In some states, it doesn't pay to cross the governor or the PRI party machine," he says (personal communication, July 13, 2001).

In addition to an active Mexican media community, there is a large and growing cadre of foreign correspondents. The list changes regularly, but in the summer of 2001 these organizations were represented by at least one reporter: ABC, *Arizona Republic, Boston Globe,* CBS, Cable News Network, *Dallas Morning News, Financial Times of London, Houston Chronicle, Los Angeles Times,* NBC, *New York Times, The Economist, Wall Street Journal,* and *Washington Post.*

As the twenty-first century unfolds, so do many new journalistic practices and operating philosophies in Mexico. The changes should improve public understanding of complex issues and promote the cause of democracy. And as the media change in Mexico so, inevitably, will public relations practices.

Public Relations in Mexico

Given the country's political history, it is no surprise that public relations has been through many iterations. During the presidency of Lázaro Cárdenas in the 1930s, the function was called "press and political propaganda," and the primary task was "information management." Thirty years later, many organizations, especially in the government, used the term "news management." This, of course, suggested that the news was really being managed—and by most accounts, it was.

More professionally speaking, public relations got its start in 1960, when Mexico City's Universidad Iberoamericana offered its first degree program in "technical and information sciences." Incorporating journalism, advertising, corporate communications, and a smattering of organizational behavior, the program soon became "public communications" and finally "social communications." The latter term originated from a papal encyclical in the 1960s that challenged Catholic education to put greater emphasis on its social obligations. Implicit in the use of this term, however, is a long-standing disdain for "public relations." Thus, Mexico is engaged in a unique transition today. Domestic clients, especially large companies, tend to use the "social communications" designation. Agencies and foreign clients, most of them steeped in the U.S. and European practice of "public relations," are working to establish a better understanding of what the profession can be.

José Carreño, director of the Department of Communications at Universidad Iberoamericana, explains that historically public relations (PR) has had little or no strategic role in organizations. "As a concept, PR has been degraded. PR is the task of sending birthday gifts, scheduling special events, working one-on-one to keep friends," Carreño says. He adds that it is difficult to teach public relations at the university level because of the perception that it deals with "frivolous things" (personal communication, August 1, 2001). That change is afoot is demonstrated by the fact that Carreño directs a program that today includes 1,100 communications majors—10 percent of the total enrollment at the university. Their graduates work in advertising, public relations, broadcasting, film, and print journalism.

In the early days of public relations, companies turned to freelancers, many of whom were former journalists, for help. Large agencies were nonexistent in Mexico. This changed dramatically in 1994, when NAFTA went into effect. Most of the U.S.-based firms opened Mexico City offices in 1994 and 1995, primarily to service U.S. companies that were coming to Mexico, as well as to assist Mexican companies that began to see value in extending their reputation management beyond their customers.

Five Mexico City firms offer perspectives on the development of public relations in the country.

Zimat Golin/Harris

Bruno Newman is one of the recognized public relations pioneers of Mexico. A 1966 graduate of Universidad Iberoamericana, he began working in public relations five years later. In 1980, he founded Zimat Consultores. Four years after the firm's founding, Newman was joined by Marta Mejía, widely acknowledged as one of the outstanding women in Mexico's public relations community.

Newman recalls the early days of public relations in Mexico. "PR meant almost anything to different groups. If there was a complaint in a hotel, it was a 'PR matter.' People selling encyclopedias were considered to be in PR," he says (personal communication, July 27, 2001). A local joke at the time was that a PR practitioner was "The man with the cold hand," because much of public relations somehow involved holding a cocktail.

Zimat enjoyed 40 percent growth per year during the period from 1996 to 2000, and Newman suspects that the rest of the major firms in Mexico had similar success. Overall, he says, NAFTA has brought good times and opportunities for the profession in Mexico.

Mexico has had its share of economic downturns and boom years, and Newman believes the two extremes have been good for Zimat. In very bad years, he says, the firm has helped clients function in a crisis mode. In good years, clients have seen how much value public relations offers. "In some years, the cost of one 60-second TV spot would fund a year's consulting program," he remembers (personal communication, July 27, 2001).

Long an acquisition prospect for larger international firms, Zimat was purchased by Interpublic in 2000 and is now affiliated with Golin/Harris Communications, headquartered in Chicago. The firm has more than fifty consultants, 95 percent of whom speak English fluently. Their average age is about thirty-five, more than half are women, and their resumes reflect degrees from Georgetown University, Yale University, and the Sorbonne. Zimat clients usually begin by asking for help with strategic media relations, government affairs, and financial communications. Zimat does some product publicity work as well, but this service is harder to sell in Mexico than in the United States. The firm has a very broad client base that includes thirty-seven domestic and twenty-four foreign companies, ten public sector accounts, and a dozen nonprofit organizations. Some of its well-known clients are Pepsico, Gillette, Frito-Lay, Bayer, Hitachi, Mack Trucks, and Lucent Technologies.

Newman applauds the changes that have occurred in the Mexican media. "Media bribes have been almost eradicated," he says, adding, "Today those who take payments are an endangered species. Nobody controls the media in this country any more." Mexican reporters also are getting more aggressive. "Historically, there were three subjects the media couldn't touch—the president, the army and the Virgin of Guadalupe," he says. Now the first two are fair game. "For years, the media feared the government would lift its radio–TV concessions or its lucrative print advertising. No longer," he emphasizes (personal communication, July 27, 2001).

Hill & Knowlton

Hill & Knowlton (H&K) opened its Mexico City office in 1995 without a single account, but NAFTA optimism was in the air and the risk seemed worth taking.

Antonio Tamayo, president and general manager of the H&K operation, studied business administration and spent several years in the hotel industry. From there he went to Los Angeles and worked for a Hispanic advertising agency. When he returned to Mexico City, it was as marketing vice president for the Westin hotel chain. He joined Hill & Knowlton in 1995 and helped open the office. Because of his background as a user of public relations services, he brought a strong client perspective.

H&K has twenty-five professionals on its staff in Mexico City, and 90 percent of them are bilingual. Their client base includes Motorola, McDonald's, Warner-Lambert, Delphi Automotive Systems (the largest private employer in Mexico), and LALA Mexico (the country's largest milk producer). Much of H&K's client work is in the field of "reputation management," a reflection that in Mexico today competitiveness includes a company's reputation in the public and private sectors. For many Mexican companies, this requires a new mind-set. In the past, these companies only had to compete locally, and key people knew who they were and what they could do. Today, the picture is decidedly multinational, and a strong corporate reputation is a value-added proposition.

Tamayo recruits almost exclusively among college graduates but not always from communications or public relations programs. His team includes an engineer from Spain, a communications graduate from France, and a Harvard political science graduate.

Fleishman-Hillard Mexico

Now the largest public relations consulting firm in the world, with global billings of $343 million in 2000, Fleishman-Hillard is deeply committed to Mexico. Its Mexico City office opened in 1995, initially to assist Wal-Mart and Anheuser Busch.

Flavio Díaz, senior vice president and general manager of the Mexico City office, began his career in corporate public relations, spending eighteen years with IBM and two with Motorola in Latin American and the United States before joining Fleishman-Hillard in 1996.

The firm's early focus was on investor relations, then, increasingly, on media relations as many companies came to Mexico and needed help getting started there. Today the firm has about forty clients, including Yahoo! Mexico, Dell Computer, MTV, Sony Corporation, Merck, and the Mexican Association of Pharmaceutical Research Companies.

Díaz has a team of twenty-four bilingual professionals, and eight of them each speak three languages. All of the office's support staff speaks English fluently. Since 1997,

Fleishman-Hillard has had no turnover among its professional staff, and Díaz is proud of the office's record of having not lost a client because of service issues in that time frame.

Díaz hires solid writers with broad cultural backgrounds in areas including the arts, music, and politics. Candidates must be bilingual and also very adaptable because of the range of clients being served. Recruits do not come from any particular university or academic major. Experience in Mexico is a plus but not an absolute requirement.

NAFTA clearly changed Mexico and its public relations industry, says Díaz. "Mexican companies are looking for investors abroad, and they are much more aware today that their corporate reputation will impact their ability to attract capital. Good numbers and a bad reputation won't help them," he says (personal communication, June 28, 2001).

Díaz is enthusiastic about the dramatic changes in the Mexican media that began about 1985, when press credibility was at its lowest point. Older generations of Mexicans were brought up to ignore the media, and the industry made no effort to educate the public about itself. Today, younger Mexicans are becoming more trusting of the media, and reporters and editors are learning how to use the freedoms they acquired with the end of authoritarian rule. It is a given, says Díaz, that the public will gain from a better-informed media. "The only censorship that exists in Mexico today comes from within organizations," he states (personal communication, June 28, 2001).

Most of the true investigative reporting in Mexico is being done by two newspapers, *Reforma* and *Milenia,* says Díaz. He hopes the media will increase its commitment to debating public issues. In Díaz's view, there are still too many one-sided analyses in the media, and not enough give-and-take so people can decide for themselves.

Díaz believes public relations in Mexico is still in an immature state, but there are signs of growing sophistication. U.S. and European companies have very advanced programs, but many Mexican firms believe public relations is an expense, not an investment. Many Mexican companies still ask how much the media will be paid for publicity gained. "*Gacetillas* are almost dead, but many people do not realize it," says Díaz (personal communication, June 28, 2001).

Edelman Public Relations Worldwide

Edelman opened its Mexico City office in 1994, also essentially from scratch. Magdalena Carral, president and general manager, came to Edelman in 1996 after a six-year career as a government economist.

Carral became head of the Mexico City office in 1998. In that short time, she has seen the public relations field change significantly. "All the big global agencies are in Mexico today, and there is great competition for U.S. and Mexican accounts. Having the U.S. agencies here has helped improve the professionalism of PR in Mexico," she says (personal communication, June 27, 2001). Carral says Mexico's news media are becoming more professional. "We see many new, young and serious-minded professionals pursuing journalism, especially covering business and technology," she says. Still, despite growing professionalism, it is common in a client presentation to be asked, "How much of the budget goes to the journalists?" Today, the answer is "zero" in the business arena, though Carral recognizes that the practice of paying bribes to reporters may die more slowly in the political sector (personal communication, June 27, 2001).

Edelman's client base is about 70 percent American and the rest Mexican. Clients include Compaq Computer, General Electric International, Mars Inc., Mattel, Microsoft, New York Life, Televisa S.A., and United Parcel Service.

One of Carral's priorities is to raise understanding of public relations in Mexico. "American clients know what PR can do for them, and they have high expectations. Some day, it will be the same in Mexico," she believes. Carral and other agency heads recognize one characteristic of the Mexican public relations market—large local companies tend to have big internal staffs and are cautious about out-sourcing (one example is Petróleos Mexicanos—Pemex—which has a two-hundred-member Social Communications Department). U.S. companies are leaner and more decentralized, with decisions made locally even if budgets have to be approved at headquarters. One likely result of this practice is that Mexican companies will see the need to become leaner, eventually leading to more out-sourcing.

One dilemma faced by Edelman and other firms is that some U.S. companies are closing domestic plants and moving some production to Mexico because of NAFTA. With pressure from U.S. labor unions and others, the companies often want to keep a low profile in Mexico. At the same time, Mexico's trade ministry wants to publicize the new investment and include the company's name in lists circulating to other potential foreign investors.

Edelman has fifty consultants, about thirty of whom are bilingual, and two-thirds are women. The firm hires only local talent with expertise in journalism, international affairs, economics, and political science.

Burson-Marsteller

Roy Caple, managing director of Burson-Marsteller, picked another route to the top of a Mexico City firm. After graduating with a law degree from a Mexican university, Caple earned a master's degree in international affairs from Columbia University. In 1994 he joined Burson-Marsteller and worked in the firm's Venezuela, Colombia, and Chile operations before moving to Mexico City in 2001.

Burson-Marsteller (B-M), probably the first U.S. consultancy to succeed in Mexico in the early 1990s, has thirty-five professionals, 90 percent of them bilingual. B-M recruits graduates in journalism, law, international affairs, and social communications. "My biggest requirement is that they have common sense," says Caple, who acknowledges that Mexico City is a tight labor market for the specialists he seeks (personal communication, July 3, 2001).

Caple's client list includes Unilever, Grupo Modelo (a large Mexican brewing company), Grupo Cuervo (a leading liquor producer), Quaker Oats, Levi Strauss, Nestlé, Merrill Lynch, duPont, and Nextel.

Public Relations Services

Each firm offers similar services in Mexico. Media training, technology communications, crisis management, health care, investor relations, and reputation management are some of the consistent offerings.

The firms share many characteristics—young staffs, new undertakings and services that are quickly gaining currency, and the combination of public relations-savvy U.S. clients competing for agency time with Mexican firms that are quickly embracing sophisticated public relations approaches common in the United States, Canada, and Europe.

Two areas seem to lag in development and sophistication. One is issue management and the other is employee communication. Issue management is a complex process that has matured in the United States only during the past two decades. A sophisticated issue management process includes

- A system for environmental scanning to help anticipate issues and deal with them early;
- Substantial use of opinion research to help organizations distinguish between public *perceptions* and public *opinion;*
- A determination to create two-way (or even three-way) dialogue between affected stakeholders;
- A conscious effort to engage "the other side," that is, critics and adversaries, in meaningful discussion to seek middle-ground solutions; and
- Inclusion of government interests, especially from the legislative and regulatory sectors.

Issue management is emerging as a specialty in Mexico, but there is too little emphasis on dialogue between stakeholders. The tendency is to send a client's messages and consider the task completed. By its very name, issue management means a long-term process to affect public opinion and values. It is seldom a one-shot, one-way effort.

Employee communication is a second area for development in Mexico. For generations, the tendency in Mexico (and all of Latin America) has been to focus on the most-senior executive in the organization—interviews with the chief, photos of the boss, reprints of the CEO's speeches. Photos in many employee publications are unusually predictable, for example, a group of executives (mostly men) sitting at a conference table in a formal pose. Candid photography is not used extensively, nor is "lighter" fare, such as a humorous moment in a meeting.

The discipline needs to be less formal and to emphasize two-way communication— vertically and horizontally—within organizations. More focus on the rank-and-file would also create more empowerment.

Professional Development

Two organizations are working to improve the professionalism of public relations in Mexico. The Mexico Public Relations Association is a small academy focusing on individual members' skill development. The second, and most recent, addition is Asociación Mexicana de Agencias Profesionales de Relaciones Públicas (PRO-RP).

PRO-RP is a group of eight firms (including Zimat Golin/Harris, Hill & Knowlton, and Edelman Worldwide) that has established professional standards and a code of ethics, and is making an effort to extend the value of public relations to the Mexican market. The group has three primary concerns:

- The ethics statement includes an agreement not to hire people away from member firms without the knowledge of both parties. This "no-raid" policy is difficult to follow, because the Mexico market is short on skilled public relations people.

- The member firms also agree not to solicit business from a client who already has a working arrangement with another member. If a client notifies the incumbent agency that a new search is underway, all wraps are off.
- Any member firm paying reporters to place stories will be expelled.

Vicente Fox and Public Relations

The Fox administration made considerable and effective use of public relations in its first few months. Accredited reporters accompanied Fox wherever he went, and he made himself highly visible and accessible to the media.

Transition planning began immediately following Fox's election victory in 2000, and several veteran public relations practitioners offered advice on the structure of the communications organization. Ultimately, it was decided to split the job into two parts. Martha Sahagún, Fox's press spokesperson when he was governor of Guanajuato, assumed the press spokesperson role. The second position, coordinator of image management and public opinion, went to Francisco Ortíz, a former Procter & Gamble marketing official and Televisa S.A. executive.

This plan worked well for six months but then hit some snags. Sahagún had two significant challenges. One was her tendency to speak for the entire administration, including the cabinet, even when key ministers were saying other things publicly. This led to a number of embarrassing retractions and clarifications that made observers wonder who was making the policy calls.

The second challenge was a series of news stories that openly discussed Sahagún's "special relationship" with Fox. Rumors had circulated for some time, but the lid came off in a June 1, 2001, *New York Times* story by Ginger Thompson. She quoted Sahagún as confirming the romance, further raising questions of Sahagún's ability to separate her personal and professional agendas. The Fox administration was not amused and told Thompson so, but it was clear the story had gotten to the heart of the relationship. Fox and Sahagún resolved the matter on July 2, when they were married in a civil ceremony. Their wedding date was the first anniversary of Fox's election victory and also his fifty-ninth birthday.

With Sahagún now the First Lady of Mexico, Ortíz moved to Los Pinos, Mexico's presidential compound, and took over as press spokesperson. Few political observers expect Sahagún to shrink into the background.

Consider some of Fox's initiatives in the first six months of his presidency:

1. In their first face-to-face meeting as presidents, George W. Bush and Fox had serious discussions about a "guest worker" program that would allow Mexican nationals to work legally in the United States for certain time periods. Advocates of such a program said it would improve labor conditions and eliminate some risks of illegal immigration. Opponents said the imported labor force would undermine U.S. wages rates. Fox described the proposal as safe, organized, and realistic, a much safer alternative to the "coyotes" who prey on migrants near the border. In a press conference following the February 16, 2001, summit meeting, Fox said he had received a commitment from Bush to work toward migration reform.

2. In his first international trip, Fox traveled to several central California cities. While in Sacramento, he addressed a joint session of the legislature and urged lawmakers

to allow Mexicans seeking legal residency to qualify for resident tuition at the many state colleges and universities. Fox said extending this benefit, especially to the children of migrant families, would demonstrate what could be accomplished with educational opportunities.

3. To emphasize his point about ending corruption at U.S. border crossings, Fox boarded a helicopter and, along with a group of reporters, toured three of the busiest customs stations just before Christmas 2000. The point was to drive home his commitment to "zero corruption, zero dirty dealings." This high-profile, lead-by-example style is unusual in Mexico and no doubt left an impression, if only temporarily, that Fox would no longer tolerate business as usual.

4. Even the selection of an official presidential portrait proved a unique symbolic opportunity for Fox (see Figure 2.1). Instead of the usual formal portrait, Fox chose to have his photo taken with forty Mexicans from all parts of the country and all levels of society. Included in the photo are two women in wheelchairs, a firefighter and a police officer, children, a musician, and a dancer. To Fox's right and left are a man

FIGURE 2.1 *For the first time in Mexican history, the president's official portrait includes members of the citizenry. It reflects Vicente Fox's efforts to engage more and varied people in the process of making Mexico a country of citizens, rather than a nation of elite politicians.*

and a woman in traditional Indian attire. In the background is a large Mexican flag, and beneath the assembled group are the words, *Todos Somos México* ("We are all Mexico").

5. Fox conducts a Saturday morning radio talk show and takes questions from all callers. Some discussions turn into debates, but the program is entirely spontaneous. The tactic is revolutionary in Mexico, where the populace has never had such ready access to a president.

Fox also has made some mistakes along the way. His PAN (Partido Acción) party always had been the bridesmaid in presidential elections and is learning what it means to be in power today. Most of the party's stumbles have been minor, but each has given opposition groups a chance to attack.

One embarrassing incident was "Towelgate" in the summer of 2001. Fox was taking every opportunity to demonstrate the openness of his presidency. In a Mexico City speech, he illustrated this point by mentioning that even the costs of refurbishing Los Pinos, the presidential complex, were available on a government Web site. This prompted reporters to check the site, and soon stories appeared about $440 towels and remote-control curtains. The total cost of the upgrades was in excess of $1 million, leading one senior public relations practitioner to say, "More than half the population lives at or below the hunger level, which explains some of the reaction to President Fox's redecorating of Los Pinos" (Roy Caple Hernandez, personal communication, July 3, 2001).

Mexico and the Certainty of Change

Fox's landmark victory in the three-way race for president was proof positive that Mexico was ready for a change—or at least for an alternative to the PRI. He won with only 46 percent of the popular vote and was inaugurated without his party having a majority in the Mexican Congress.

Fox's early agenda focused on tax reform and an overhaul of the nation's electricity system. The former requires a simple majority vote in Congress—one that will be hard to obtain because Fox's program calls for a 15 percent tax on food products and medicine—whereas the latter is a constitutional issue and requires a three-fourths plurality in Congress. Beyond these two issues, though, are others that will require the support of Congress *and* the population at large. Each has abundant public relations challenges and communications implications.

Immigration

For the past half century, the United States has been the land of opportunity, especially when viewed from the perspective of its relatively poor neighbor to the south. Regardless of U.S. unemployment rates, there always have been thousands of U.S. jobs waiting for anyone, including illegal immigrants, willing to take them. In many cases, these have been unskilled positions that U.S. citizens are not interested in doing, such as in agriculture, hotels, and restaurants. Several studies suggest that if the United States had to get along without illegal immigrant labor, some sectors of the economy might be forced to shut down.

One assessment of the 2000 U.S. Census shows that as many as 11 million Mexican-born men and women are living illegally in the United States, about one-half of them in California and Texas. Many Mexicans obtain visas and make legal visits to the United States, but many more find a way across the border and then obtain work wherever they can. For those who do, there are few benefits attached to the jobs—no health care, no Social Security, and no unemployment benefits.

Traditional U.S. policy has been to patrol the border and detain anyone found entering the country illegally. In 2000, the U.S. government spent more than $2 billion on immigration and border control measures, and, on any given day, the Immigration and Naturalization Service had 20,000 immigrants (not all of them Mexican) in detention, waiting to be deported (Schmitt, 2001).

Impoverished Mexicans see opportunity to the north and are willing to take their chances crossing the border. Unfortunately, some three hundred to four hundred people die each year trying to cross the desert in 115-degree heat.

Fox named a U.S.-born college professor to head the Presidential Office for Migrants Living Abroad. Juan Hernández, who was teaching Mexican literature at the University of Texas (Dallas) before taking the position, grew up in the state of Guanajuato, where Fox served as governor. The first Mexican American (he has dual citizenship) to serve in a Mexican Cabinet, Hernández is the immigrants' link back to their home government. As he told the *Los Angeles Times,* "Immigrants should not be treated as second-class citizens of Mexico. These individuals are heroes who provide wealth to Mexico, and although we would prefer to keep them at home, if they decide to leave, we will be watching out for them" (Muñoz, 2001, p. M3).

The fact that immigrants "provide wealth to Mexico" is a little-known story. Many migrant workers leave wives and children behind while they seek jobs. Some are gone for years without seeing their families. Still, immigrants regularly send money home, to the tune of $8 billion annually. This makes these remittances the third-largest source of income for the entire country, behind oil and tourism.

Given the amount of money involved, the Fox administration is looking for ways to make it easier and less expensive to transfer money from the United States to Mexico. U.S. companies have pledged financial support, including a $10 million grant from 7-Eleven Inc. American Airlines, Mary Kay Corporation, and Western Union have also pledged help to simplify and reduce the cost of sending money electronically to families of Mexicans working in the U.S. (Romney, 2001).

One political initiative being discussed is to give citizens living abroad the right to vote via absentee ballot in Mexican elections. Until now this has not been allowed under Mexican law, but Hernández argues that if a Mexican citizen is sending money back home and plans to return to Mexico at some time, he or she should be able to participate in the political process back home.

Finally, the Fox administration has begun to cast the immigration issue in slightly different—but strategically unique—terms. Fox talks about the "migration" issue. Semanticists may argue the distinction, but from a public consumption standpoint, "immigration" seems a one-way journey. "Migration," however, is viewed by Fox as a phenomenon in which many Mexicans who journey north choose to return to their home country if and when economic conditions allow. In a similar change of perspective, Fox has urged Americans to "view the border more as a joining line than as a dividing line" (Barone, 2001, p. 27).

Fox has made many commitments to the Mexican people. If he is unable to maintain U.S. employment by Mexican nationals, his credibility will suffer and his revolution may be short-lived. Significant lobbying and communicating in the United States is a key part of the Fox strategy. Several U.S. industries are simply more dependent on immigrant labor than U.S. voters may realize.

Narcotics

It is no secret that the United States has a massive problem with illegal drug consumption. Because most of the drugs are not produced or processed in the United States, it follows that trafficking and importation are an equal (and connected) problem. Most recent estimates suggest that about 15 million Americans spend between $60 billion and $70 billion annually on illegal drugs. And in the past two decades, the U.S. government has spent more than $30 billion to stop the flow of drugs from "source countries" (Flunk the "report card," 2001, p. B8). For years, Mexico has been viewed with scorn by U.S. law enforcement agencies who developed a long list of Mexican officials, some highly placed in the government, who profited personally from the illegal drug activity. With the arrival of Fox came a commitment to stop the drug trafficking. It will not be easy because the illegal drug businesses are huge, profitable, and, at least until now, well insulated by protection from bribed officials in Mexico.

At their first meeting, Presidents Fox and Bush issued a joint statement that was remarkable for its candor. Fox acknowledged that Mexico has a drug trafficking problem, and Bush said that without U.S. consumption of illegal drugs, there wouldn't be a trafficking issue. Bush's comment, sensible in its simplicity, is a step that few U.S. politicians have been willing to admit: Drug *users* create the demand.

Fox's challenge is fourfold: Find the drug lords; arrest them before they can be tipped off by corrupt police officials; try them in legitimate courts of law; and then incarcerate them. U.S. and Mexican officials have added another consideration. With a favorable ruling from the Mexican Supreme Court in January 2001, Mexico has begun extraditing Mexican nationals and others to the United States to face trial on felony charges. Even though the two countries have had an extradition treaty in place for two decades, the actual return of indicted criminals did not begin until early 2001.

Since that time, several high-profile arrests have sent a clear message to organized crime in Mexico:

- The first major drug arrests of the Fox administration occurred on April 6, 2001, when an army general and two aides were charged with providing protection to cocaine and marijuana traffickers. Brigadier General Ricardo Martínez was the sixth general jailed on drug-related corruption charges since 1997.
- On May 7, 2001, Everardo Arturo Páez was arraigned in a federal courtroom in San Diego, to face charges involving shipments of cocaine into the United States, along with money laundering. Páez was arrested in Tijuana in 1997 and had been in a Mexican prison fighting the extradition request. At the time of his arrest, police estimated that Páez's cartel was spending $1 million per week on bribes to police and government officials.
- On May 25, 2001, Mario Villanueva was arrested in the resort town of Cancun. Villanueva, a former governor of the state of Quintana Roo in the Yucatán Peninsula,

disappeared in 1999, just two weeks before he was to leave office. Since that time, he had been one of Mexico's most wanted fugitives. The day after his arrest, prosecutors in New York City unsealed an indictment charging Villanueva with conspiracy to import two hundred tons of cocaine into the United States. According to the indictment, Villanueva received $500,000 for each cocaine shipment that went through Quintana Roo between 1994 and 1998. Villanueva faces twenty-eight criminal charges in Mexico, but Fox has said that if Villanueva can be extradited to New York right away, he will make that happen.

Fox's war declaration on narcotics means tremendous social and economic change for Mexico. He faces the difficult task of taking jobs—illegal though they are—from poor Mexicans to help rich Americans end their addictions. Fox's task of reminding Americans that they are creating the demand for drugs is a delicate one, and he cannot hope to accomplish it without substantial help from the U.S. government.

Corruption

Mexico is hardly the only country in the world with deeply entrenched corruption as an everyday fact of life. Nevertheless, the "system" was in place for at least a century and blossomed under seventy-one years of rule by one political party. The sins range from small bribes, called *mordida* ("the bite"), to fixing traffic tickets to widespread and megadollar graft at the highest levels of government.

Just how widespread is the corruption? Drug lords have escaped from prison with the help of bribed guards. Other criminals have escaped arrest because of tips from police officials "on the take." Mexicans returning home have found that they cannot bring goods into the country without paying customs officials unofficial taxes. At some border crossings, Mexican citizens must pass through two or three checkpoints before reaching their destination— each stop means more open palms expecting money in return for a hassle-free passage.

Soon after his inauguration, Fox fired eighteen of nineteen customs station directors along the border. Newly appointed directors have, in turn, fired customs agents found to be taking bribes. And the new rigor seems to be making a difference. In only three months, the station director at Ciudad Juárez, across from El Paso, seized 140 trucks carrying contraband. The taxes due on the seized merchandise were more than $2 million. He also presided over a unique bonfire fed by nearly two million contraband U.S. cigarettes that had been confiscated.

Largely because of illegal drug traffic, auto theft rings, and kidnappings, U.S. law enforcement agencies have extensive dealings with their Mexican counterparts. However, by Mexican policy, agents of the Drug Enforcement Agency and Federal Bureau of Investigation, for example, are not permitted to carry weapons on Mexican soil. This raises significant security concerns *if* they cannot trust their Mexican counterparts.

U.S. Attorney General John Ashcroft visited Mexico in May 2001 to discuss these trust issues. To his great satisfaction, he found his Mexican counterparts to be just as zealous as he was about cooperation between the law enforcement interests of the two countries. Adolfo Aguilar Zínser, special advisor to Fox on national security matters, went so far as to tell Ashcroft, "If I belonged to the F.B.I., I would not trust the Mexican police" (Ruiz, 2001, p. A19).

Fox proposed a solution in April 2001, when he offered U.S. law enforcement agencies the opportunity to conduct security checks on their Mexican counterparts. Although some would view this as an intrusion of Mexican sovereignty, Fox took the step in order to clean up his side of the law enforcement equation. As evidence of this commitment, twelve hundred federal district police were fired for corruption during the summer of 2001.

Why the passion about corruption? In part, because Fox says corrupt practices siphon off 5 to 7 percent of the nation's yearly gross domestic product (GDP), negatively influence the image of the nation, and send the wrong messages to potential investors, domestic or foreign. These are not trivial concerns for Fox, because 5 to 7 percent of Mexico's GDP equals $21 billion to $30 billion annually.

To attract the foreign investment Mexico needs, Fox must press his campaign for a reduction—if not an elimination—of corrupt practices. He is trying to end a way of life in which officials at all levels felt entitled to take bribes to supplement their paltry government paychecks.

Energy Policy

In 1938, President Lázaro Cárdenas nationalized domestic and foreign-controlled oilfields throughout Mexico. Since that time, the national oil company, Petróleos Mexicanos (Pemex), has enjoyed a monopoly on the exploration, refining, and sale of oil and natural gas. In Mexico, a driver has one choice for gasoline—a Pemex station.

Pemex and oil are important symbols of Mexican sovereignty. The company is also a major fiscal force because its profits are returned to the government. Despite this, Pemex and the Fox administration face some difficult decisions.

For all of its oil exploration, Mexico cannot keep pace with refining demand; hence, the country imports about $1 billion worth of gasoline from U.S. refineries each year. Some estimates say that Pemex needs to invest at least $20 billion to upgrade and expand its refining capacity simply to keep pace with domestic demand. And in order to meet demand for natural gas, the country needs to spend $500 billion in new drilling through 2010. Since these costs are beyond Mexican resources, one obvious (but politically sensitive) prospect is to invite foreign investors (and operators) into at least the natural gas sector.

An obvious challenge is to make Pemex more efficient. As with many monopolies, it is inefficient and often sluggish. With 140,000 employees, Pemex is the country's largest employer. And with 80 percent of that employment represented by strong unions, significant changes will be fought every step of the way.

One of Fox's early appointments was a new general director of Pemex. Raul Muñoz, head of duPont Mexico's operations, got the job, and he soon began talking about productivity and efficiency steps that would save Pemex $3 billion near-term. An obvious but politically sensitive starting point would be to reduce employment. Pemex produces about 3 million barrels of crude oil daily with 140,000 employees. Venezuela's state-owned oil company produces the same amount daily with one-third as many employees (Webb, 2001).

Muñoz also emphasized the need for Pemex to grow, especially in the refining arena, because Mexico's chemical product imports ate up almost 90 percent of the money generated by the country's oil exports in 1999. Critics insist that the $7.7 billion spent on chemical imports could have gone a long way toward improving Pemex's ability to make those products locally. But without the imports, other industries would have been without raw materials for their own production.

At the Fox–Bush summit in February 2001, the presidents discussed Bush's vision for a "hemispheric energy policy" that would include Canada, the United States, and Mexico. Bush's interest in the hemispheric approach is obvious. Electricity brownouts in California are a political nightmare, and Bush would like to reduce U.S. dependence on Middle East oil, but to do that he must find some way to overcome public resistance to more drilling in the United States. And Pemex needs to invest billions in exploration and transmission facilities in order to contribute.

The plan has its challenges. *New York Times* reporter Tim Weiner describes the hemispheric plan this way: "Only three obstacles stand in its way: the laws of physics, the laws of supply and demand, and the laws of Mexico. There may be a fourth: It would take many billions of dollars in American investment to make it happen" (Weiner, 2001a, p. A1).

Evelyn Iritani, a *Los Angeles Times* reporter, puts it another way: "As the world's biggest single consumer of energy, the U.S. has a point of view that to some outsiders—especially in the energy-producing countries such as Mexico and Canada—is purely one of self-interest. Critics liken the U.S.-led deregulation effort to economic imperialism disguised as free trade, where the U.S. forces other countries to open their energy markets to powerful American firms that then siphon off the energy for SUV-driving, electricity-gobbling Americans" (Iritani, 2001, p. C1).

Of all the steps Fox is taking, energy policy excites the most nationalistic fervor among his constituents. Making Pemex more efficient means eliminating jobs, and if this has to be done at the same time foreign investors are invited to enter the Mexican energy and petrochemicals markets, Fox will encounter huge resistance.

Conclusion

Although there is considerable optimism in Mexico, it is premature to close the books on the country's emergence as a world economic and political force. Mexico is much more of a democracy than it was before the 2000 election. Then again, it's impossible to tell exactly how the country will respond to the many changes being promoted by Fox. Lorenzo Meyer accurately describes Fox's near-term challenges:

> Fox has to be able to make good on all the demands and interests of the disenfranchised who have been waiting for almost two centuries for justice. The promises that the new government has made to the poor are vague. According to 1999 statistics by domestic and international agencies, impoverished people account for half of Mexico's population. Yet their needs have never been met because of a lack of public funds—80% of the budget is already allocated to internal costs and debt—and the fact that the free market economy has almost nothing to do with their interests. (Meyer, 2000, p. B7)

To be sure, there is much to celebrate. Political dialogue has increased in substance, and previously disenfranchised voters are clearly more immersed in public debate. The media are steadily improving, partly because of a desire to emulate some U.S. media practices. Public apathy is dwindling as the government takes increasingly bold steps to attack corruption and narcotics-related violence.

To fail in Fox's mission is to concede a return to Mexico's corrupt practices of almost the entire twentieth century. In the words of Flavio Díaz, general manager of Fleishman-Hillard Mexico, "The worst thing that could happen to Mexico would be for the people to become disappointed by change" (personal communication, June 28, 2001).

Discussion Questions

1. Why is a free and competitive mass media system an asset to a public relations effort?

2. If you were the public relations director of a U.S. company that is closing a facility and moving that production to Mexico, how would you explain the move to your U.S. employees? Your stockholders?

3. If you were the public relations director for a trade association that opposes Vicente Fox's "guest worker" program, what would be some of your arguments *against* it? Conversely, if you represent an organization that depends on migrant labor, what are some of your arguments *for* it? In either case, who are the key "publics" you will want to reach?

4. If you were a public relations consultant invited to assist a state-owned enterprise, such as Aeromexico or Pemex, how would you approach the assignment? The objective is to make the enterprise more efficient and competitive, but the process is fraught with political and labor sensitivities. Where do you start?

5. If you are advising Vicente Fox, how much importance do you put on U.S. media relations and how much on Mexican media relations? Why?

References

Barone, M. (2001, May 7). Why it's time for a new look at immigration-law reform. *U.S. News & World Report,* p. 27.

Flunk the "report card" on drugs. (2001, March 2). *The Los Angeles Times,* p. B8.

Gower, M., Craddock, C., & Pruitt, S. (2001). Mexico in transition. *Business Mexico, 11*(2), 24.

Iritani, E. (2001, February 16). Bush pushes energy plan in Mexico. *The Los Angeles Times,* p. C1.

Meyer, L. (2000, December 4). For Fox, now is the hard part. *The Los Angeles Times,* p. B7.

Muñoz, S. (2001, February 11). Mexican-American cabinet member looks after mexicans living abroad. *The Los Angeles Times,* p. M3.

NAFTA Forum of the United States–Mexico Chamber of Commerce (2001). Retrieved from www.usmcoc.org/-naftafor.html. [Accessed August 1, 2001].

Orme, W. (Ed.). (1997). *A culture of collusion: An inside look at the Mexican press.* Coral Gables: North–South Center Press, University of Miami.

Romney, L. (2001, March 5). Fox vows to trim cost of transferring U.S. fund. *The Los Angeles Times,* p. C1.

Ruiz, R. (2001, May 22). Building trust with Mexico. *The New York Times,* p. A19.

Schmitt, E. (2001, May 27). Ambivalence prevails in immigration policy. *The New York Times,* p. A14.

Webb, S. (2001). Pemex shake-up: Can Fox turn this lethargic giant into a lean moneymaker? *Business Mexico, 11*(4), 27.

Weiner, T. (2001a, February 13). Bush due to visit Mexico to discuss exporting energy. *The New York Times,* p. A1.

Weiner, T. (2001b, May 27). After a bailout, a wedding. *The New York Times,* p. 3.

3

Privatization and Government Campaigning in Ecuador

Caudillos, Corruption, and Chaos

Donn James Tilson

Key Points

- A societal culture of authoritarian rule, as evidenced by this study of past administrations in Ecuador, influences government public relations behavior more toward *one-way, asymmetrical* than *symmetrical* models of communication.

- A *caudillo*-style mind-set, rooted in a political tradition of corruption, ruled by physical force and manipulation, views communication as an end in itself and will employ deceptive public relations strategies, and violence if necessary, to advance its own interests rather than the common good.

- Governments that seek to influence public policy by command rather than by collaboration in societies that are increasingly mediated and politically conscious will encounter difficulty in managing conflict with key publics.

The 1980s in Latin America ushered in a wave of free-market reforms and the privatization of state industries from telecommunications to electricity. Given the initial success of such efforts in Chile, Argentina, and Brazil (Alman, 1995; Tilson, 1996b), other Latin American nation-states attempted to follow suit.

However, not all government campaigns to "sell" privatization have been well received. For example, the 1993–1996 campaign by the Durán-Ballén administration in Ecuador was opposed, often violently, by the full spectrum of publics from the military to

63

indigenous peoples. Some elements of the plan, called the Strategic Program of State Modernization, were defeated in Congress; voters rejected other measures in a November 1995 plebiscite.

A review of the Durán-Ballén campaign, as well as subsequent efforts by other administrations, suggests that (1) a societal culture of authoritarian rule influences government public relations behavior more toward *one-way, asymmetrical* than *symmetrical* models of communication; (2) a *caudillo*-style mind-set, rooted in a political tradition of corruption, ruled by physical force and manipulation, views communication as an end in itself and will employ deceptive public relations strategies, and violence if necessary, to advance its own interests rather than the common good; and (3) governments that seek to influence public policy by command rather than by collaboration in societies that are increasingly mediated and politically conscious will encounter difficulty in managing conflict with key publics.

Culture and Public Relations

It has been suggested that societal culture "form[s] the basis for individuals' communication styles" (Gudykunst et al., 1996, p. 510) and also has "a direct impact on the public relations practice of organizations because public relations is first and foremost a communication activity" (Sriramesh & White, 1992, p. 609), which may explain the "environmental impact [of organizations and their public relations departments]" (Verčič, Grunig, & Grunig, 1996, p. 47).

Culture, then, may affect the characteristics of excellent public relations practice (Grunig, 1993; Sriramesh, Grunig, & Buffington, 1992). For example, Sriramesh and White (1992) contend that public relations practitioners who operate in societies that display higher levels of authoritarianism and individualism "will tend to practice the one-way press agentry model of public relations . . . [while] holding the view that power should be concentrated in the hands of a few top managers" (p. 610). Further, practitioners who believe that "information flows out from the organization and not into it" and that "leaders of the organization know best" (Grunig & White, 1992, p. 43) "see public relations as a tool to be used in a war among opposing social groups" (p. 52). Conversely, public relations excellence is found "more often in societies whose cultures emphasize collaboration, participation, trust and mutual responsibility" (Grunig, 1992, p. 245). Those who practice excellent public relations view it as a "symmetrical process of compromise and negotiation and not a war for power" (Grunig & White, 1992, p. 39). Such cultures "display lower levels of power distance, authoritarianism and individualism" (Sriramesh & White, 1992, p. 611).

Public Policy and Issues Management

Political systems are considered an inherent part of societal culture and, as such, influence the practice of public relations (Sriramesh & White, 1992). Research shows that government agencies typically use the public information model of public relations (Grunig & Grunig, 1989, 1992), which views public relations only as the dissemination of information (Grunig, 1993). Moreover, in authoritarian, totalitarian, or communist political systems, government public relations is limited to the press agentry model, and lateral, symmetrical communication in society is difficult if nonexistent as is excellence in public relations (Verčič et al., 1996). The ruling elite in such societies seek to maintain their political and economic control through the use of propaganda "to dissolve communication between people in order to disable their ability to form publics" (Verčič et al., 1996, p. 42). In creating "constraints to [lateral] communication or one-sided information flow," such governments through propaganda demonstrate their "power to lie" inasmuch as the "lie . . . shows naked power behind itself" (Verčič et al., 1996, p. 43). Nevertheless, although power may maintain political control, "deception or manipulative communication can only be successful if its deceptive and manipulative characteristics are not recognized by receivers" (Deatherage & Hazelton, 1998, p. 69).

In societies that are in the early stages of development as mediated, emerging democracies, authoritarian managerial and asymmetrical communication styles by government may become more problematic. As awareness of better living conditions increases and standards begin to improve, a disadvantaged population may react with political strikes, demonstrations, and violence if it believes that the state is not offering sufficient symbolic reassurances that "a bad order will be changed" (Edelman, 1964, p. 169). Should a government fail through its public relations efforts to manage conflict with key publics, it will become increasingly difficult to establish the legitimacy essential for organizational survival. As Simões (1992) notes regarding the proper exercise of organizational authority and public relations management in a democracy:

> Its [the organization] actions must be geared toward the common good and never to its own interests . . . public relations will not have its existence justified as long as practitioners consider communication as an end in itself. . . . If there are no open communication channels, or if the organization lacks credibility, each party will be isolated from one another. . . . If it is not possible to organize a system of negotiation . . . the public may rebel with violence. (pp. 194–198)

Research in the emergence of social issues suggests that they are advanced in the arenas of public discourse by various social groups, institutions, and individuals who compete in promoting specific issues or their particular interpretation of an issue (Hilgartner & Bosk, 1988). However, although certain issues "by definition call for responses from government" (Solesbury, 1976, p. 381), government not only responds to issues but also presents them as well. Although governments must compete with other sources to establish primacy of both the issue and its interpretation (Hilgartner & Bosk, 1988), government sponsorship can give an issue a sense of legitimacy inasmuch as issues "only begin to become powerful once institutions within the political system become associated with them" (Solesbury, 1976, p. 383).

In promoting an issue, governments may take a proactive approach, employing a catalytic strategy that advances the issue through its natural life cycle (Crable & Vibbert, 1985). Such a process of issues management, as conceptualized by Chase and Jones (1980), is an elaboration of Marston's RACE (Research, Action, Communication, Evaluation) approach to public relations problem solving, which uses research to identify and analyze issues crucial to the organization's survival; formulates strategy options, policies, and action programs; implements programs using various communication channels; and evaluates the results. But it is in the formulation of objectives that support basic organizational goals where issues management approximates more strategic methods of planning, such as Management by Objective (MBO) and Research, Objectives, Program, and Evaluation (ROPE). In such methods, problems are identified; objectives are set that describe solutions and specify the audience and desired effect; programs are fashioned denoting themes, messages, and communication channels; and effects are evaluated given the objectives specified (Hendrix, 1989; Pearson, 1987; Tilson, 1996a).

In presenting issues, governments may enjoy structured habitual access to media channels based on their special status and institutional power (Molotch & Lester, 1974), but some studies suggest that such status does not always guarantee either access or credibility (Schlesinger, 1989; Sigal, 1986). Nonofficial, even alternative sources, can and do present their particular interpretations on an issue, both in the mass media and in other fora of public discourse, and may ultimately redefine the problem and seize ownership of it (Schlesinger, 1989).

Methodology

A combination of several qualitative methodologies was used in this study to obtain data on public relations strategies, the economy, the political environment, and public perceptions of and responses to government initiatives. In-depth, semistructured interviews were conducted with key government and corporate figures. During such interviews, various government documents, including a copy of the Durán-Ballén administration's *Strategic Program of State Modernization,* were provided. This plan fully outlines the government's public relations strategies, objectives, publics, and messages, and provides the essential direction for a textual identification of "themes and plots" (Turner, 1990, p. 148) and analyses of organizational media. Additionally, a textual analyses of press coverage of quality newspapers in Ecuador and in critical markets, such as the United States, provided an opportunity to compare such coverage with government efforts to communicate key messages to internal and external publics.

Ecuador: An Introduction

Ecuador is a microcosm of Latin America's societal culture, "with a highly unequitable distribution of income" where "historically, a small elite has dominated effective political participation" (Tenenbaum, 1996, pp. 451, 454–455). The country ranks among the worst in Latin America in terms of income distribution (35 percent of the population is poor, 15 percent live in extreme poverty; the figures for rural areas are 47 and 22 percent, respectively).[2] The defense of oligarchic privileges in the mass media "by the most competent professionals . . . is carried out under the pretext of being in the national interest" (Hurtado, 1980, p. 182). A political culture of "regionalism . . . [and] highly factionalized politics" (Tenenbaum, 1996, pp. 451–454) produced seventeen constitutions and twenty-two presidents, dictators, and juntas in one 23-year period (Gunther, 1967). Caudillo-style methods of governing have had a long tradition in Ecuador, where "force became the accepted method of transferring or retaining power. . . . Liberals, conservatives and opportunists relied on controlled elections, press censorship and extralegal coercion to limit the opposition" (Tenenbaum, 1996, p. 452).

Political corruption in Ecuador also has become institutionalized over the years. According to some estimates, only 40 percent of tax collections reach the treasury. The dictatorship of General Guillermo Rodriguez was overthrown in 1976 in part because of "the government's inability to administer public funds . . . honestly" (Hurtado, 1980, p. 295). During the administrations of the four presidents who governed Ecuador from 1979 to 1992, Congress often impeached government ministers and censored administrative officials for corruption. Past military governments built up a vast state bureaucracy—"one of the most corrupt and ineffective in Latin America"—and swelled the ranks of state industries that "ensured huge inefficiencies" while creating dozens of for-profit businesses owned by the army's holding company (General, 1995, p. 39). For example, the Social Security Office employed 22,000 workers, and the state telecommunications company had 6,000 employees.

Modernization Plans, Implementation Woes

The plan to privatize state industries in Ecuador, and to persuade key publics to support the reforms, targeted sectors developed under the two military juntas that ruled Ecuador from 1972 to 1979. Following a return to civilian rule in 1979, several administrations tried to implement economic reforms and develop key industries by attracting investment. Such efforts were thwarted by an opposition-controlled Congress and met with popular protest as austerity measures imposed to reduce high inflation and a growing public debt further aggravated the economy. After winning a bitterly contested race in 1992, Sixto Durán-Ballén and his vice president, Alberto Dahik, entered the political maelstrom, holding only seventeen of the seventy-seven seats in Congress.

The administration began its modernization program with a decree in January 1993 that allowed direct foreign investment in domestic companies without prior governmental approval. In December 1993, a modernization law was pushed through Congress allowing foreign concessions in public sectors. The law also created an agency, Consejo Nacional de Modernización del Estado, or CONAM, as an advisory council to the president to coordinate and implement the reform process. CONAM included representatives from the public and private sector. In March 1994, the administration appointed Marcel Laniado de Wind as CONAM executive director.

As Laniado took office, however, the administration already was in political trouble for its heavy-handed managerial style. The country's constitutional court declared illegal an executive decree raising gasoline prices by 71 percent. The administration claimed the hike was needed to offset a drop in oil prices (oil revenues represent about half the nation's income) and to lower the national deficit. The move also drew criticism from four former presidents who warned that "the democratic system was in danger" (Chorus of protests, 1994, p. 77).

As if to confirm their fears, the administration introduced legislation in Congress to abolish midterm congressional and local elections, claiming that campaigning was creating a "governability" crisis. When the bill failed, Vice President Dahik, the administration's privatization architect, called for a plebiscite to abolish the elections. The *Latin American*

Weekly Report noted, "the government . . . is determined to achieve by authoritarian means what it failed to bring about by democratic methods . . . by pushing through its unpopular programme by decree" (Dahik calls for plebiscite, 1994, p. 88).

On the eve of the May elections, nearly forty different organizations, including public service unions and indigenous peoples' groups, held a two-day strike demonstrating their opposition to privatization. An association of retired military officers publicly denounced the reforms, arguing that the state should retain a controlling interest in strategic industries. To calm the unrest, Durán-Ballén appointed someone who claimed direct descent from the Inca Atahualpa to a new cabinet post overseeing indigenous affairs; the minister, who wore a red poncho for his investiture, was a business graduate from Yale and a board director for Chiquita banana company. Indigenous groups were "not impressed" (Unions call strike, 1994, p. 190).

The elections became a referendum on the administration's privatization plans. Durán-Ballén lost six congressional seats to parties opposed to reform. He insisted, however, that "a couple of representatives less in parliament won't change the course of my government" (Government suffers vote setback, 1994, p. 592).

Over the next three months Durán-Ballén attempted to advance his privatization agenda before a stronger opposition took control of Congress. The administration gave the International Monetary Fund a letter of intent to accelerate reforms, and CONAM director Wind announced new privatization plans. The director of the Social Security Office, who opposed the agency's privatization, was replaced, prompting bloody street protests by employees. Durán-Ballén sent a bill to Congress to abolish the agrarian reform office and to sell land and water rights held communally by indigenous peoples to commercial interests. Indigenous peoples comprise 47 percent of Ecuador's population—the second highest in Latin America—and hold 58 percent of the nation's land. Such "modernization by brute force," as the Social Christian party leader described the ploy, brought violent demonstrations by indigenous peoples and a mobilization of the army (see Figure 3.1). A compromise finally protected indigenous peoples' water rights and limited land sales.

Concurrently, the administration announced plans to privatize the telephone company (EMETEL) within eight months, having just granted a concession for the first private mobile telephone service. Two bills were sent to Congress—one while most members were on vacation—and defeated. Undaunted, the administration declared it would privatize EMETEL "with or without a law"; CONAM president Patricio Peña added "the consensus of . . . congressmen is a relative matter" (Executive sneaks in new EMETEL bill, 1994, p. 353).

In yet another move, the government awarded foreign oil companies contracts to explore and develop several million acres of Amazon jungle and announced it would accept bids for the construction of a second Andean pipeline to carry the new oil to coastal ports. Arguing that deforestation was destroying the rain forest, indigenous peoples' organizations and ecological and human rights groups called for a fifteen-year moratorium on exploration in the Oriente.

Promotional Political Communication

Despite growing popular opposition, the administration forged ahead with efforts to develop a comprehensive plan of attack that would outline its agenda for the next several

FIGURE 3.1   *Miguel Pandám, leader of the Indigenous Federation of the Shuar Peoples, is escorted out of Ecuador's Government Palace after a discussion that led to a new agreement on land reform.*

Photo by Randy Olson, from *Discovering Ecuador and the Galapagos Islands,* 1994.

years. *The Strategic Program of State Modernization* developed by CONAM envisioned a proactive, probusiness campaign targeted at specific publics within a set schedule of prioritized activities and deadlines for 1994 to 1996. Indeed, "the original plan was the sale of 80% of state companies for an estimated $10 Bn (billion) by 1996" (Bequillard, 1995, p. 2). State industries, such as the airline Ecuatoriana "that will allow a fast and successful privatization, together with an effective publicity campaign," were slated for sale first in 1994 because they would "contribute to the gain of political consensus in favor of privatizations" and create "fast legitimacy so . . . modernizations will be in place before the resistance of rivals gains force" (CONAM, 1994, pp. 22, 26). Concessions were planned in 1994 for public works, the Civil Registration Office, seaports, and airports. Reform of the Telecommunications Law was planned by the end of 1994, with privatization in 1995, followed by Social Security, railroads, and electricity. Given the authoritarian nature of the administration's approach to the issue, the plan resolved "if legal reform of the Telecommunications Law . . . has not been passed . . . CONAM and EMETEL will focus their efforts on establishing . . . companies whose shares will be offered through an international call for bids and awarded" (CONAM, 1994, pp. 50, 52, 58).

Although the plan proposed an "informative and educational type public communication program," the campaign was essentially promotional in nature inasmuch as the reform process "implies a redefinition of the role of the State, which goes from being eminently managerial to that of being the promoter of private initiative" (CONAM, 1994, pp. 4, 10). As such, "it is CONAM's priority, to concentrate its efforts in . . . promotion of . . . widespread participation of citizens in private enterprise . . . [and] development of the capital market" (CONAM, 1994, pp. 6–8). In so doing, "it is important to 'sell' people a 'scenery' of a better quality of life . . . better telephone service, widespread availability of energy . . . better roads" and "to give the public the feeling that their interests have been taken into account" (CONAM, 1994, pp. 26–30).

Although the plan acknowledged the importance of *two-way asymmetrical communication*—"the public should be involved in the campaign of communications . . . reception points for claims and suggestions could be established" (CONAM, 1994, p. 28)—the campaign design was principally *one-way asymmetrical* and relied primarily on the mass media to convey key messages. Research was conducted to assist in "elaborating . . . a general list of the various publics and their key characteristics," and public opinion surveys were conducted "to discover the current position of the modernization process in the minds of the public" so that the communication campaign could be "oriented toward these indicators" (CONAM, 1994, p. 34). "Educational information" was to be provided to "potentially large investors, international organizations . . . journalists who specialize in economic themes . . . government officials, university teachers, members of parliament, workers representatives . . . [and] the young and receptive to change" through "pamphlets, lobbying, seminars, [and] events," but "messages should be . . . principally relayed by . . . massive radio and television campaigns" (CONAM, 1994, pp. 34–40).

Soon after the strategic program was presented to Congress and the media in September 1994, the administration ran into further trouble. Laniado argued with Finance Minister Cesar Robalino over plans to modernize the Customs Office and resigned as CONAM director. Durán-Ballén appointed the former industry minister, Mauricio Pinto, to head CONAM; his name appears on the final draft of the strategic plan. Robalino also clashed with Information Minister Carlos Vera, who resigned. By the end of the year, four cabinet members had resigned—the ministers of finance, health, foreign affairs, and energy—as congressional calls for impeachment and opposition to privatization grew.

A Campaign Unravels

Over the next year, the government continued to promote its privatization plans, but a series of events, including a border war with Peru, charges of widespread corruption by administration officials, and power shortages, effectively ended any hope for modernization. Moreover, as the administration gradually lost its political grip, its managerial style grew more authoritarian and its communication approach more one way and asymmetrical.

To "educate" key publics about privatization, the government organized a conference in Miami in early November 1994. With the support of its Federation of Exporters and several Ecuadorean-owned Miami banks, administration officials touted the advantages of doing business in Ecuador to two hundred South Florida executives. Federation President Juan Jose Pons told conferees Ecuador offered "social peace, absence of militant labor unions, [and] an open economy. . . . The media are constantly serving up news about bombings . . . in other countries, but not in Ecuador. . . . We are not in the news because nothing happens" (Bussey, 1994, p. C1).

A border war with Peru two months later not only marred Ecuador's "tranquil" image but also undermined investors' trust and the nation's economy. After three weeks of armed clashes and forty military deaths over a jungle area reportedly rich in gold and oil, the United States, Chile, Brazil, and Argentina—the guarantors of the Rio de Janiero Protocol that settled a war in 1941—arranged a cease-fire. To cover war-related expenses, Ecuador imposed a 10 percent tax on fuel, diverted resources from social programs to the military, rationed electricity, and initiated other austerity measures. When Durán-Ballén tried to increase the workweek to further pay for the war, unions clashed with police. The war cost Ecuador U.S.$383 million (of a U.S.$583 million 1995 deficit). Local and foreign investors withdrew millions of dollars from the country's banks, pushing up interest rates. Foreign investment in the nonoil sector fell 48.1 percent in 1995. Economic growth slowed from 4 percent (real GDP) in 1994 to 2.5 percent in 1995. In October 1995, the nation's currency was devalued by 6 percent.

The war and continued public protests, however, did not stop the administration from moving ahead with its privatization plans and using force on occasion. In April and May 1995, police used tear gas to break up union, student, and indigenous groups demonstrating against privatization even as the administration was accepting bids to sell a majority stake in Ecuatoriana. The airline, which ceased operations eighteen months earlier and consisted of only one DC-10 plane, was sold in August to a consortium of Ecuadorean investors and VASP, the Brazilian airline—much later than the administration originally had planned. As negotiators finalized the deal, oil and electric unions demonstrated against administration efforts in Congress to privatize their companies and to remove the right of public employees to join a union.

Corruption: The End Game

The final chapter of the administration's privatization efforts was written, however, not by angry crowds but by the administration itself. Media revelations of government corruption in June 1995 led to impeachment proceedings and resignations.

In drafting its privatization plan, the administration had boldly proclaimed its credibility. In a letter to investors, CONAM Director Pinto (who became finance minister in early 1995 and was impeached by Congress for misusing tax revenues and helping his father-in-law avoid paying taxes) declared "the bequeathal of culture, tradition, and hard work are emerging to encounter a modern era with decision and honesty" (CONAM, 1994, p. 1). Sensing, perhaps, the administration's vulnerability to investigations of its "honesty," the plan suggested creating a "semantic axle" to portray reform as "good . . . and innovative . . . [which] will determine the success or failure of our communication strategy" and warned that "we must avoid the turning of the axle against us . . . if our axle is corruption . . . someone . . . will say that modernization corruption will merely be 'moved' from the public . . . to the private sector" (CONAM, 1994, pp. 32, 34).

Corruption charges surfaced in September 1994, soon after the CONAM plan was finalized. Durán-Ballén was accused of securing a loan from the state credit agency for his granddaughter so her in-laws could expand a family-run business. The agency director resigned, and a judge issued a warrant for her arrest.

It was an off-the-cuff remark by Vice President Dahik, however, that opened the floodgates against the administration. In an off-the-record meeting with reporters in June 1995, Dahik said that the administration had given legislators U.S.$90 million in public works projects and posts in state oil and electricity companies in return for their support of privatization bills and had paid several Supreme Court Justices from a government account of "discretionary funds" to approve a reform law considered unconstitutional. Guayaquil's leading daily newspaper, *El Universo,* broke the story, explaining that, according to Dahik, such payoffs actually were "shakedowns" by justices and deputies.

Some media analysts suggest that *El Universo*'s boldness was prompted by a growing popular disgust with the administration and politics in general. Traditionally, most Ecuadorean media are "generally not aggressive and probing" and often practice "press release" journalism, accepting stories passed along by government officials (Vanden Heuvel & Dennis, 1995, pp. 88–89, 97). But in light of a growing list of impeachments, resignations, and scandals, public opinion had turned increasingly against the nation's political system and may have finally found a voice in the media.

The administration quickly went on the defensive and began relying increasingly on press conferences and news releases to communicate with its publics. Dahik responded in a television broadcast that the accusations were "electoral cannibalisms" (Vice presidente de Ecuador torea crisis de imagen, 1995, p. B3, author's translation) and sent a letter to the Supreme Court, explaining that he had referred to corruption "in general" and not to actual instances (Piden juicio contra el vice presidente ecuatoriano, 1995, p. B3, author's translation). In a radio and television press conference in late July, Durán-Ballén maintained that, since assuming office, he had tried to eliminate the "decades of corruption" in the justice system and Congress, and called for a referendum to implement anticorruption reforms in the judiciary (Gobierno ecuatoriano anuncia medidas contra la corrupción, 1995, p. B1, author's translation).

The Supreme Court conducted hearings into the allegations, and charged Dahik with embezzlement, bribery, misuse of public funds, and illicit enrichment. It ordered the arrest of former Foreign Minister Paredes and former government Press Secretary Enrique Proaño for using some of the "discretionary" funds for a down payment on the purchase of a radio station. Paredes went into hiding and protested his innocence through audiotapes sent to Quito radio stations. Congress initiated impeachment proceedings against Dahik, Finance Minister Pinto (who supposedly had transferred monies to the secret government account), Supreme Court President Miguel Macias Hurtado, and two other justices.

When Congress failed in a vote to impeach Dahik, the Supreme Court ordered his arrest. He quickly resigned and fled in a copiloted private plane to Costa Rica where he was granted political asylum. In April 1996, he campaigned on San José television stations and in the daily newspaper, *La Nación,* proclaiming his innocence and maintaining that "all expenses were reviewed by the Comptroller General" (Dahik insists on innocence, 1996, p. 14).

Lights Out, Election On

To make matters worse, a drought in southern Ecuador in August 1995 prompted electricity rationing nationally as water levels dropped at Paute, a hydroelectric station that produces 70 percent of the nation's power. Daily blackouts of eight to fifteen hours continued through January 1996, including during an international summit when the lights went out for Durán-Ballén and foreign heads of state at a dinner in the presidential palace. Obviously, the "embarrassing . . . cut . . . did nothing for the image of the state electricity company, which the government is trying to privatise" (Blackout brings back reality, 1995, p. 424).

Also during 1995, a respected television journalist, Freddy Ehlers, emerged as a popular spokesperson for political change. Ehlers, anchor for a Sunday night news program, *La Televisión,* on Teleamazonas, Ecuador's leading network, and well known for his investigative reporting of political corruption, proposed on-air that a constituent assembly be held to throw out the administration and change the electoral system. Viewers flooded the station with letters of support, and former President Rodrigo Borja and the labor unions endorsed the idea. Ehlers later ran in the 1996 presidential elections with the support of the unions, indigenous and women's organizations, and other left-of-center pressure groups, and placed third with 21 percent of the vote.

A public referendum on administration proposals to partially privatize social security and public health, ban strikes by public employees, and implement other political and economic reforms was defeated in November 1995. An average of 56 percent of voters rejected all eleven proposed constitutional reforms. A confederation of indigenous, union, and pressure groups vigorously campaigned for a "no" vote. The confederation arose during the Dahik investigations as did a mobilization of anticorruption human rights and citizen groups. Polls indicated Durán-Ballén's popularity fell to "the lowest of any president since democracy was restored in 1979" (Hayes, 1996, p. A14). By March 1996, 80 percent of Ecuadoreans opposed reform.

And yet the government continued to press forward with privatization. Just prior to the referendum, the administration was evaluating foreign bids to build a second trans-Andean oil pipeline. Striking workers, joined by electric company employees, finally forced the resignation of Energy Minister Galo Abril, the principal advocate of the venture. He later was prosecuted for complicity in a scam involving duty-free imports of fuel, a revelation that also led to the firing of all of PetroEcuador's senior management. Eventually, Petro-Ecuador bowed to public pressure, announcing that it would forego building a second line.

Still, the administration maintained a steady stream of promotional materials on privatization. A report for investors argued its "strategic program backed by the country as a whole is orienting the economy toward . . . confidence and freedom to invest" (*Ecuador: The Business Target,* 1996, p. 1). Another publication reported that "Ecuador is undertaking extensive public-sector reforms that include . . . reducing the size of the public sector and its interference in the economy" (Ecuador, 1996, p. 23).

By early 1996, the administration had decided on one method of "reducing" such interference as it pushed through yet another proposal in Congress to privatize the electricity company, INECEL. When workers occupied the main hydroelectric station and other stations in protest, the government sent troops to remove them and to guard the facilities from further demonstrations.

As the administration prepared to leave office as elections loomed in mid-1996, it was clear that privatization efforts had failed. Originally intending to privatize 160 state-owned industries, the Durán-Ballén administration managed to push through Congress the sale of only ten entities—39 percent of the state's electric company, the state airline, and several smaller enterprises (Oppenheimer & Ellison, 1996).

Back to the Future

Sadly, for Ecuador, political and economic conditions went from bad to worse with the election of Abdala Bucaram to the presidency in 1996. A millionaire rancher, lawyer, and former mayor of Guayaquil, Bucaram—who called himself "El Loco" (the crazy man)—shouted his way to power on a populist campaign that denounced free-market policies and promised to "exterminate the oligarchy" (Ex-governor appears to lead, 1996, p. A10) while improving conditions for the poor hurt by those reforms. His reputation, however, for an "authoritarian leadership style" (Ex-governor appears to lead, 1996, p. A10) and for corruption—"business people said he repeatedly shook them down for donations [as Mayor of Guayaquil]" (Johnson, 1996, p. A26)—soon became evident.

In his inauguration speech, he "promised to go ahead with free-market reforms" (Oppenheimer, 1996, p. A6) and named three millionaire businessmen and campaign donors to a newly created economic commission. He then kept the previous administration's Central Bank director, one of the key figures of reform, in his post and began "talking about cutting government subsidies for food and transportation, a proposal he attacked during his campaign" (Watson, 1996a, p. A14). Moreover, he also hired former Argentine Economic Minister Domingo Cavallo—the architect of that nation's privatization reforms—as an advisor to "transmit the Argentine economic experience" (Fired Argentine aide will advise Ecuador, 1996, p. A22). Further, Bucaram vowed to privatize the oil industry, ports, and highways and to sell 35 percent of the telephone company (Oppenheimer & Ellison, 1996). In December he unveiled an economic plan to reduce the national deficit that increased prices on basic commodities, and on gas and electricity, by as much as 300 percent, and eliminated government subsidies on transportation, propane gas, and other services (Watson, 1996b). The action echoed drastic price hikes taken by Durán-Ballén during the early months of his administration, which were bitterly opposed by Ecuadoreans. Bucaram also launched a controversial plan to peg the nation's currency to the U.S. dollar in order to control inflation. As expected, the measures angered most Ecuadoreans, and by January 1997 his popular support had fallen to 11 percent from a high of 67 percent at his inauguration only five months earlier (Johnson, 1997a).

But it was his "penchant for filling public offices with cronies and relatives" (Johnson, 1997b, p. A14) and his luxurious, bizarre lifestyle, coupled with the reforms that eventually led to calls for his ouster. Two days after his inauguration, observers already were noting that "nearly half of his Cabinet is made up of relatives and friends, many of whom have no credentials for their jobs" (Oppenheimer, 1996, p. A6). His advisors included his brother-in-law (finance minister), brother (social welfare minister), and campaign manager and childhood friend (energy minister). His son, "an informal 'customs broker' " (Johnson, 1997c, p. A20) at the port of Guayaquil, earned U.S.$1 million in only a few months in his post even as importers complained of new taxes and shakedowns for bribes from Bucaram's "friends and allies, including a handful who had criminal records" and who were "suspected of milking the state of tens of millions of dollars" (Escobar, 1997, p. A12). The president and his inner circle soon were being called "Ali Abdala and the Forty Thieves" by opponents (Johnson, 1997c, p. A20). Meanwhile, Bucaram, who chose to live in a plush suite at the Crown Plaza Hotel (owned by a friend) instead of in the presidential palace, organized and starred in a Christmas charity telethon and several rock concerts throughout

Ecuador to promote his for-charity CD, and entertained Lorena Bobitt in the palace (he and she became the godparents of the daughter of a local singer).

Some two million demonstrators filled the streets of Quito in February 1997 as a massive national strike shut down the country. An alliance of student groups, sports federations, business and agricultural associations, and indigenous confederations organized the protest calling for Bucaram's ouster. Congress responded the next day, voting Bucaram out of office for "mental incapacity" and installing its president, Fabian Alarcon, as a one-year interim chief until new elections could be called. The vote, however, only served to further complicate matters because Bucaram refused to leave office and challenged Alarcon to a public fistfight to determine the presidency. Simultaneously, Vice President Rosalia Arteaga declared herself to be the lawful president, arguing that Congress's vote was unconstitutional. When Alarcon and his supporters tried forcibly to enter the presidential palace, police repelled them, resulting in several injuries and one death. Meanwhile, the New York–based Council of the Americas canceled its "Investing in Ecuador" program that had been scheduled for the following week.

Ecuador had three presidents for almost a week—an oddity that had occurred three other times in the nation's history (1859, 1883, 1961). Congress and the military finally brokered a deal temporarily investing Arteaga until legislators could vote to designate a new interim president. Congress again chose Alarcon to lead the nation until elections in August 1998. Bucaram fled to Panama; half of his cabinet joined him in exile or escaped to Miami.

Reports soon revealed the extent of his administration's corruption. His private secretary and $4 million withdrawn from the Central Bank of Ecuador vanished. Aides stole paintings and furniture from the presidential palace. An investigation by a special corruption commission uncovered that the state telecommunications company president and other agency officials "signed dozens of 11th-hour bogus contracts with cronies and issued advances for work never done" totaling millions of dollars (Johnson, 1997d, p. A14). Bucaram's finance officer was arrested near the Peruvian border carrying $3.4 million in U.S. dollars. Congress dismissed thirteen legislators for "mishandling public funds," and the Supreme Court charged Bucaram and four of his presidential aides (including his spokesperson) with "squandering or stealing $88 million in government funds" (Ousted Ecuadorean president, 1997, p. A23), ordering him to stand trial. From exile, he conceded "that he may have withdrawn $4 million from the Central Bank . . . to take care of the country's internal security" and lamented that "it was a mistake not to have had better public relations with the media" (Oppenheimer, 1997, p. A10).

Alarcon immediately canceled the unpopular price hikes and promised that he would formulate economic policy by consensus rather than by decree. But before he could get his administration on track, he was accused of hiring more than 1,000 "phantom" legislative aides to pay salaries to his political supporters during his term as president of Congress. Cesar Verduga, his interior minister, moreover, was charged with misspending U.S.$5.3 million from a secret government fund and fled to Miami before he could be arrested. And according to Reyes and Johnson (1998), a presidential advisor was

> accused of pressuring U.S. and other companies holding state contracts to donate money to buy clothing for thousands of Ecuadoreans left homeless by El Niño flooding. The money

allegedly went to several firms in South Florida to pay for shipping containers of used clothing donated by local merchants. The clothing later was discovered being sold in stores in Guayaquil. (as cited in Tilson, 1999a, p. 71)

The advisor fled to Panama. Alarcon remained in office, however, until the August 1998 elections and finally was arrested in March 1999.

A New Beginning?

A centrist, Quito Mayor Jamil Mahwad, was elected president in 1998 with 53.6 percent of the vote and the support of the business community and the middle class; however, almost 37 percent of voters abstained, their absence blamed largely on "disillusionment with Ecuador's democracy" (Johnson, 1998, p. A6). Mahwad immediately faced a multiplicity of problems—falling prices (and revenue) for oil, Ecuador's main export; U.S.$1 billion in El Niño–related damages to main export crops; 40 percent inflation (up from 25 percent in 1996); 11 percent unemployment; U.S.$15 billion in foreign debt; a 25 percent drop in U.S. investment (Luxner, 1998); and a U.S.$1.2 billion budget deficit.

The wheels of the economy began falling off in March 1999 as nine private banks closed (three others fell in 1997 and 1998). The government allotted more than U.S.$1 billion to save them, and Mahwad shut down the banking system and partially froze most deposits. Angry depositors blamed bankers—some of whom fled the country—for losing their money in failed personal business ventures or for stealing it outright (Johnson, 1999a, p. E1). The government eventually took control of sixteen banks, representing 70 percent of the nation's U.S.$4.3 billion in banking assets, at a cost of U.S.$3 billion. By July 2001, Ecuador still owed U.S.$816 million of the frozen assets to depositors (Newport, 2001).

Mahwad aroused further public anger by announcing a series of economic austerity measures—higher taxes, fuel price increases of 165 percent (later rescinded), and a freeze on U.S. dollar bank accounts—which prompted street protests and strikes. By August 1999, the government announced it could not pay the interest on U.S.$6 billion in foreign "Brady bonds" debt as it also sought to restructure an additional U.S.$1 billion in commercial loans; the national debt of U.S.$13.3 billion almost equaled its GDP (Bussey, 1999). Inflation eventually would increase to 60 percent for the year, the highest in Latin America, and the economy would shrink by 7 percent (Hayes, 2000). Experts attributed the problems to "economic mismanagement and . . . political mismanagement" (Johnson, 1999b, p. E6).

To secure funding, Mahwad signed a letter of intent with the International Monetary Fund in September 1999 for a U.S.$400 million loan, but the deal required an increase in the national value-added tax, reduced deficit spending, and banking reforms, measures opposed by Congress (Johnson, 1999b). Mahwad also proposed replacing the nation's currency with the U.S. dollar to control inflation (an idea that Bucaram had launched earlier); privatizing state-run oil, electricity, and telecommunications companies; and freezing bank accounts for seven to ten years.

By January 2000, some fourteen banks had collapsed (and the government had spent hundreds of millions of dollars to save them), and inflation/devaluation had reduced monthly minimum wages to U.S.$45 to U.S.$50 and raised the cost of living for basic foodstuffs for a family to U.S.$200 a month. A "People's Parliament" of indigenous groups, students, and others announced its opposition to Mahwad's plan, declaring that it would "dollarize poverty, privatize wealth and repress the resistance" (Bussey, 2000a, p. A14). According to the World Bank, some 5.1 million Ecuadoreans (41 percent of the population) were living in poverty (Bussey, 2000b).

A military coup in January 2000 forced Mahwad from office as thousands of protestors seized Congress and the Supreme Court. The next day, however, the junta bowed to internal and external pressures to restore democracy and turned the government over to Vice President Gustavo Noboa, the nation's sixth president in only four years. Oddly, although he pledged to listen to protestors—to "launch a crusade against corruption"—he proceeded with "dollarization" (Johnson, 2000, p. A19). By March, Congress had passed "dollarization" legislation, which included various austerity measures and privatization plans. Noboa signed the bill into law, and the International Monetary Fund (IMF) and other international agencies announced U.S.$2 billion in loans (Bussey, 2000c). More than 80 percent of Ecuadoreans remained opposed to "dollarization," however. By August, though, monthly inflation had dropped from double digits, and in May 2001, slowed to its lowest rate in five years, standing at 39.6 percent annually, as "dollarization" seemed to have an effect on price hikes.

To unblock the IMF loan promised in March but still not delivered by January 2001, Noboa imposed 100 percent fuel price hikes and a 75 percent increase in transportation fares. The measures prompted immediate protests by indigenous peoples with some five thousand marching in Quito and seizing a university building. Noboa declared a state of emergency and sent the army to retake control. After ten days of civil disorder and three deaths, the administration agreed to a compromise—reduce cooking gas prices and only freeze gas prices until year's end. As one political observer noted, "The government thought they could solve the problem with a strong-arm approach, and they found out they couldn't" (Wyss, 2001, p. A23). In June the IMF made a partial loan payment—U.S.$190 million.

Privatization Déjà Vu

Even as protesters clashed with the army, Ecuador's finance minister and the Ecuadorian-American Chamber of Commerce of Greater Miami hosted a conference, "Ecuador 2001: Economic and Financial Projections," to attract investors to the country. As included in the "dollarization" legislation, privatization and new investment in state-run oil, electricity, and telecommunications companies were part of the "modernization" plan in order to develop the capacity necessary to meet increasing consumer demands and generate additional badly needed revenue for the government. During Alarcon's administration, Congress had voted to allow private capital in such "strategic" sectors of the economy, and the government began searching for investors inasmuch as "the state lacks the resources to make key investments in such sectors" (Ecuador: Groundwork for change, 1998, p. 1). The Central Bank later reported that foreign investment rose 51 percent in the first quarter of 2001, compared with the last quarter of 2000.

In April 2001, the government announced that it would open up the telecommunications market to private investment by selling ten wireless bands at an auction in August and hire a firm to administer the two state telecommunications companies; Ecuador, with a density of ten phone lines per one hundred people, has one of the lowest levels in the region (Dex, 2001a). The administration also said that it would put its electricity companies up for sale at an auction in September to secure the investment necessary "to ensure that we have sufficient power to meet the demands as the economy grows"; estimates are that only 54.3 percent of people in rural areas and 79 percent nationally have electricity (Dex, 2001b, p. C2).

To further develop its energy resources, the government awarded a contract in August 2001 to a U.S. firm to build a natural gas pipeline from a field in the Pacific Ocean to a new electric power plant. In August work began on building a second trans-Andean oil pipeline—a project that had to be scrapped in late 1995 during the Durán-Ballén administration as striking oil workers and indigenous and ecological groups protesting deforestation forced the resignation of Energy Minister Galo Abril, the plan's architect (Tilson, 1999b). The U.S.$1.1 billion pipeline, planned for 2003, will carry oil from the Amazon across the Andes to a Pacific port and is designed to double Ecuador's oil output. In June a rain-induced landslide ruptured the one existing pipeline and interrupted oil exports for four days. Opposition to the new pipeline immediately resurfaced as "environmentalists have vowed to tie themselves to trees . . . to block construction" (Oil conduit draws protest, 2001, p. C2).

By the end of 2001 the IMF released the final portion of its loan to Ecuador, noting that the country had stabilized its economy and would meet its inflation and growth targets but also warning that measures had to be taken to "reduce the . . . dependence on oil revenues and . . . maintain a sustainable fiscal balance" (IMF loans 95 million to Ecuador with warning, 2001, p. C2). Inflation indeed had fallen dramatically from 91 percent in 2000 to only 22.4 percent in 2001 (Inflation falls in dollar shift, 2002), but Ecuador also reverted from a U.S.$1.4 billion trade surplus in 2000 to a U.S.$360 million trade deficit (for the first eleven months) in 2001 (Trade deficit $360 million, 2002) as international oil prices fell. The administration immediately asked the IMF for a new standby loan agreement to help finance $400 million in debt payments due in 2002 (Dex, 2002). As suggested earlier by the IMF, the terms for the new loan would require Ecuador to speed up privatization and deregulation in telecommunications and electricity among other industries. After years of public opposition to such efforts—and an endless parade of presidents who unsuccessfully tried to force such reforms on the country—it seemed that nothing had changed in Ecuador. Ten years later, the nation was heading back to where it started under the Durán-Ballén administration.

Conclusion: Toward a New Ecuador

The failure of various administrations, and that of Durán-Ballén in particular, to promote privatization is a testament to the consequences of the absence of organizational credibility and the incongruence of authoritarian managerial styles and *asymmetrical* communication in societies that are emerging democracies. *Asymmetrical* worldviews, and the authoritarian cultures that historically have nurtured them, will lead public relations professionals "toward actions that are . . . ineffective" (Grunig & White, 1992, p. 40) as citizens in such nation-states begin to voice their expectations for a more participative culture.

Although large segments of Ecuador's population continue to be excluded from playing participatory roles in government decision-making, nevertheless, disenfranchised interests are becoming increasingly politicized and mediated, which does not bode well for administrations with elitist tendencies either in Ecuador or elsewhere in Latin America (Tilson & Rockwell, 2004). In the 1996 national elections, for example, indigenous peoples put forward their own presidential candidate, Freddy Ehlers, for the first time in history, as well as several congressional candidates. The election was the first in which an individual such as Ehlers could run without being nominated by a recognized party. In a country where network telecasts reach 86 percent of the population (and 94 percent of the nation's households have televisions) and some 759 radio stations blanket 97 percent of households, a politically aroused (and mediated) citizenry will find *caudillo*-style communication, official corruption, and *personalismo* government intolerable.

Further, the very notion of developing public relations strategies to manipulate the opinion of key publics toward an acceptance of privatization seems to be morally questionable in itself however laudable such modernization plans may be. Moreover, when the manipulation generates a response that is clearly disruptive to the social order, the promoters, particularly being democratically elected administrations, should pause to reconsider their actions not only for the good of their administrations but also for the good of society. Such governments, however deeply rooted in a political culture of corruption, deceptive public relations practices, and rule by force, must recognize that even caudillo-style behavior has its consequences as well as its limits.

An editorial in *El Comercio,* a Quito-based centrist newspaper, considered one of the most venerable in Latin America, perhaps best summarizes popular sentiment on government and public expectations:

> Society needs to feel. . . it is participating . . . [but] continues to be an abstraction for the political class . . . no one in their organizations is in touch with the people . . . as a result [government programs] are not viable . . . government needs to negotiate with the social sector . . . to institutionalize the exercise of societal authority . . . to harmonize contradictions is better than having to send in the police. (Un país pensante, 1996, p. A7, author's translation)

In the final analysis, future administrations will need to serve less as promoters of special interests, including their own, and more as the mediators of the full range of public groups. That will require both excellence in management and public relations—initiating dialogue not diatribes, fashioning programs out of compromise instead of conflict, and governing in a manner that, rather than being suspect, earns the trust and respect of all citizens.

Notes

1. Excerpts reprinted from Donn J. Tilson (1999), "Public relations in emerging democracies: The government campaign in Ecuador to sell privatization in key publics."

2. Following are useful Web sites for information about Ecuador's politics, economy, culture, and history:
   - www.ecuador.org (the official site of Ecuador's U.S. embassy)

- www.ecuanet.com (a news portal with links to tourism and business chambers; click on the Directorio tab to find links)
- Sites for information on Ecuador's financial markets:
  1. www.bce.fin.ec (Central Bank)
  2. www.bvg.fin.ec/default_eng.htm (Guayaquil Exchange)

3. www.ccbvq.com/bolsa/html/index.html (Quito Exchange)
4. www.superban.gov.ec/ (Superintendency of Banks)
5. www.supercias.gov.ec/ (Superintendency of Companies)

- U.S.-government and other sites:
    1. www.stat-usa.gov (U.S. State Department "Country Background Notes" for a subscription fee)
    2. www.odci.gov (Central Intelligence Agency with links to *The World Factbook*)
    3. www.worldskip.com (links to Web sites of information on countries)

Discussion Questions

1. In what way has culture shaped government communication and management styles in Latin America? How did the Durán-Ballén Administration's approach to promoting privatization reflect Ecuador's cultural and historical heritage?

2. What role did the mass media ultimately play during the course of the Durán-Ballén government's campaign to promote privatization?

3. Why have indigenous groups, students, labor unions, and other publics opposed government plans to privatize industry? To "dollarize" the economy? Do you think these plans are a good idea? Why or why not?

4. If your public relations firm were invited to counsel Ecuador's government in promoting its privatization and "dollarization" plans, what would you recommend? Would you conduct the campaign differently? If so, how?

References

Alman, K. (1995). Telecommunications privatization in Latin America: An overview of the process, issues, and implications. *World Communication, 24,* 32–38.

Bequillard, N. (1995). *Ecuador business plan.* Unpublished report. Quito, Ecuador.

Blackout brings back reality. (1995, September 28). *Latin American Weekly Report,* p. 424.

Bussey, J. (1994, November 4). Ecuador polishes its business image. *The Miami Herald,* p. C1.

Bussey, J. (1999, August 27). Ecuador defaults on bonds. *The Miami Herald,* p. C1.

Bussey, J. (2000a, January 14). Ecuador's "People's Parliament" plans economic counterplan. *The Miami Herald,* p. A14.

Bussey, J. (2000b, January 22). Revolt in Ecuador is from bottom up. *The Miami Herald,* p. A2.

Bussey, J. (2000c, March 10). Ecuador embraces U.S. dollar as its national currency. *The Miami Herald,* p. A12.

Chase, H., & Jones, B. (1980). Issues management to strategic management: Policy and action. Part 2. *Public Relations Quarterly, 25,* 5–7.

Chorus of protests continues to swell. (1994, February 24). *Latin American Weekly Report,* p. 77.

CONAM Informe de Actividades del Consejo Nacional de Modernización del Estado Correspondiente al año 1994. (1994). Quito, Ecuador.

Crable, R., & Vibbert, S. (1985). Managing issues and influencing public policy. *Public Relations Review, 11,* 3–16.

Dahik calls for plebiscite on polls. (1994, March 3). *Latin American Weekly Report,* p. 88.

Dahik insists on innocence. (1996, April 12). *The Tico Times,* p. 14.

Deatherage, C., & Hazelton, V. (1998). Effects of organizational worldviews on the practice of public relations: A test of the theory of public relations excellence. *Journal of Public Relations Research, 10,* 57–71.

Dex, R. (2001a, April 13). Ecuador ends state telecom monopoly. *The Miami Herald,* p. C2.

Dex, R. (2001b, July 6). Ecuador restructures electricity sale. *The Miami Herald,* p. C2.

Dex, R. (2002, January 9). Ecuador, IMF discuss standby loan accord. *The Miami Herald,* p. C2.

Ecuador. (1996, March), *World Guide,* pp. 23–26.

Ecuador: The Business Target. (1996). Miami: Ecuador Trade Center.

Ecuador: Groundwork for change. (1998, March 20). *Global View,* p. 1.

Edelman, M. (1964). *The symbolic uses of politics.* Urbana: University of Illinois Press.

Escobar, G. (1997, February 18). Allegations of corruption at Ecuador port. *The Miami Herald,* p. A12.

Executive sneaks in new EMETEL bill. (1994, August 11). *Latin American Weekly Report,* p. 353.

Ex-governor appears to lead first round in Ecuador voting. (1996, May 20). *The Miami Herald,* p. A10.

Fired Argentine aide will advise Ecuador. (1996, August 16). *The Miami Herald,* p. A22.

General, president, managing director. (1995, April 1). *The Economist,* p. 39.

Gobierno ecuatoriano anuncia medidas contra la corrupción. (1995, July 25). *El Nuevo Herald,* p. B1.

Government suffers vote setback. (1994, August 18). *Facts On File,* p. 592.

Grunig, J. E. (1992). What is excellence in management? In J. E. Grunig (Ed.), *Excellence in public relations and communication management* (pp. 219–250). Hillsdale, NJ: Lawrence Erlbaum Associates.

Grunig, J. E. (1993). Implications of public relations for other domains of communication. *Journal of Communication, 43,* 164–173.

Grunig, J. E., & Grunig, L. A. (1989). Toward a theory of the public relations behavior of organizations: Review of a program of research. *Public Relations Research Annual, 1,* 27–66.

Grunig, J. E., & Grunig, L. A. (1992). Models of public relations and communication. In J. E. Grunig (Ed.), *Excellence in public relations and communication management* (pp. 285–326). Hillsdale, NJ: Lawrence Erlbaum Associates.

Grunig, J. E., & White, J. (1992). The effects of worldviews on public relations theory and practice. In J. E. Grunig (Ed.), *Excellence in public relations and communication management* (pp. 31–64). Hillsdale, NJ: Lawrence Erlbaum Associates.

Gudykunst, W., Matsumoto, Y., Ting-Toomey, S., Nishida, T., Kim, K., & Heyman, S. (1996). The influence of cultural individualism–collectivism, self-construals, and individual values on communication styles across cultures. *Human Research Communication, 22,* 510–543.

Gunther, J. (1967). *Inside South America.* New York: Harper & Row.

Hayes, M. (1996, May 19). Ecuadorean elections framed by pessimism and poverty. *The Miami Herald,* p. A14.

Hayes, M. (2000, January 11). Ecuador to swap sucre for dollar. *The Miami Herald,* p. C2.

Hendrix, J. (1989). *Public relations cases.* Belmont, CA: Wadsworth.

Hilgartner, S., & Bosk, C. (1988). The rise and fall of social problems: A public arenas model. *American Journal of Sociology, 94,* 53–78.

Hurtado, O. (1980). *Political power in Ecuador.* Albuquerque: University of New Mexico Press.

IMF loans 95 million to Ecuador with warning. (2001, December 12). *The Miami Herald,* p. C2.

Inflation falls in dollar shift. (2002, January 3). *The Miami Herald,* p. C2.

Johnson, T. (1996, July 4). "El Loco" shakes up Ecuadorean election. *The Miami Herald,* p. A26.

Johnson, T. (1997a, February 6). "Crazy" leader must go, Ecuador crowds shout. *The Miami Herald,* p. A28.

Johnson, T. (1997b, February 7). Ecuador's president ousted by Congress on mental grounds. *The Miami Herald,* pp. A1, A14.

Johnson, T. (1997c, February 8). Patience ran low with leader's antics, excesses. *The Miami Herald,* p. A20.

Johnson, T. (1997d, February 27). Ecuador's ousted leader plundered the palace. *The Miami Herald,* p. A14.

Johnson, T. (1998, July 13). Ecuador exit poll: Harvard grad wins. *The Miami Herald,* p. A6.

Johnson, T. (1999a, March 28). On Ecuador streets, the crisis hits hard: "We are in ruins." *The Miami Herald,* pp. E1.

Johnson, T. (1999b, October 17). Ecuador on the brink of economic disaster. *The Miami Herald,* pp. E1, E6.

Johnson, T. (2000, January 23). Ecuadorean army backs down; new civilian president sworn in. *The Miami Herald,* pp. A1, A19.

Luxner, L. (1998, August 10). New leaders face a tough sell. *The Miami Herald Business Monday,* p. 11.

Molotch, H., & Lester, M. (1974). News as purposive behaviour: On the strategic use of routine events, accidents and scandals. *American Sociological Review, 39,* 101–112.

Newport, S. (2001, July 19). Ecuador delays bank auction. *The Miami Herald,* p. C2.

Oil conduit draws protest. (2001, June 21). *The Miami Herald,* p. C2.

Oppenheimer, A. (1996, August 12). "El Loco" puts family first as he fills jobs. *The Miami Herald,* p. A6.

Oppenheimer, A. (1997, March 24). Ecuador's Bucaram not giving up. *The Miami Herald,* pp. A1, A10.

Oppenheimer, A., & Ellison, K. (1996, August 17). Awaiting broader shift to private enterprise, Latin America frets over pitfalls of the past. *The Miami Herald,* p. A1.

Ousted Ecuadorean president, four aides charged with corruption. (1997, March 9). *The Miami Herald,* p. A23.

Pearson, R. (1987). Public relations writing methods by objectives. *Public Relations Review, 13,* 14–26.

Piden juicio contra el vice presidente ecuatoriano. (1995, July 20). *El Nuevo Herald,* p. B3.

Schlesinger, P. (1989). From production to propaganda. *Media, Culture and Society, 11,* 283–306.

Sigal, L. V. (1986). Who? "Sources make the news." In R. Manoff & M. Schudson (Eds.), *Reading the news* (pp. 22–37). New York: Pantheon Books.

Simões, R. (1982). Public relations as a political function: A Latin American view. *Public Relations Review, 18,* 189–200.

Solesbury, W. (1976). The environmental agenda: An illustration of how situations may become political issues or issues may demand responses from government; or how they may not. *Public Administration, 54,* 379–397.

Sriramesh, K., Grunig, J. E., & Buffington, J. (1992). Corporate culture and public relations. In J. E. Grunig (Ed.), *Excellence in public relations and communication management* (pp. 577–595). Hillsdale, NJ: Lawrence Erlbaum Associates.

Sriramesh, K., & White, J. (1992). Societal culture and public relations. In J. E. Grunig (Ed.), *Excellence in public relations and communication management* (pp. 597–614). Hillsdale, NJ: Lawrence Erlbaum Associates.

Tenenbaum, B. (1996). *Latin American history and culture.* New York: Charles Scribner's Sons.

Tilson, D. (1996a). Promoting a "greener" image of nuclear power in the U.S. and Britain. *Public Relations Review, 22,* 63–79.

Tilson, D. (1996b). The commodification of Latin America: A confluence of telecommunications, the media and promotion. *World Communication, 25,* 133–141.

Tilson, D. (1999a). Against the common good: The commodification of Latin America. *Media Development, 46,* 69–74.

Tilson, D. (1999b). Public relations in emerging democracies: The government campaign in Ecuador to sell privatization in key publics. *Equid Novi, 20,* 80–94.

Tilson, D., & Rockwell, R. (2004). Latin America. In J. Merrill & A. de Beer (Eds.), *Global journalism.* Boston: Allyn & Bacon.

Trade deficit $360 million. (2002, January 16). *The Miami Herald,* p. C2.

Turner, R. (1990). A comparative content analysis of biographies. In E. Oyen (Ed.), *Comparative methodology: Theory and practice in international social research* (pp. 134–150). London: Sage.

Unions call strike against sell-off. (1994, May 5). *Latin American Weekly Report,* p. 190.

Un país pensante. (1996, April 21). *El Comercio,* p. A7.

Vanden Heuvel, J., & Dennis, E. (1995). *Changing patterns: Latin America's vital media.* New York: The Freedom Forum Media Studies Center.

Verčič, D., Grunig, L. A., & Grunig, J. E. (1996). Global and specific principles of public relations: Evidence from Slovenia. In H. Culbertson & N. Chen (Eds.), *International public relations: A comparative analysis* (pp. 31–65). Mahwah, NJ: Lawrence Erlbaum Associates.

Vice presidente de Ecuador torea crisis de imagen. (1995, July 9). *El Nuevo Herald,* p. B3.

Watson, J. (1996a, August 9). Ecuadoreans puzzle over president-elect's new image. *The Miami Herald,* p. A14.

Watson, J. (1996b, October 28). Ecuador's man of the people—today. *The Miami Herald,* p. A8.

Wyss, J. (2001, February 8). Fuel price concessions end deadly protests in Ecuador. *The Miami Herald,* p. A23.

4

Peru's Fujimori

The Campaign to Sell the Administration's Neoliberal Policies

Alan Freitag

Key Points

- Public relations, as a profession that depends on the exercise of effective communication, is inextricably linked to the concept of culture, a term that scholars have said is synonymous with communication.

- The four traditional models of public relations practice can be linked on an international plane to concepts of cultural diplomacy (press agentry and public information models) and cultural relations (two-way asymmetric and two-way symmetric models).

- Through a detailed analysis of a case study, such as this one concerning a communication campaign conducted by the government of Peru, we can examine the influence of culture (including its social, political, economic, historical, and other dimensions) on the character and content of communication.

- By noting changes in communication patterns, particularly within a carefully planned, well-orchestrated communication campaign, analysts may be able to discern commensurate emerging changes and trends within a national culture, particularly in terms of political textures. In this case study, the subtle move from cultural diplomacy to cultural relations, as reflected in the campaign described, may portend a cultural shift in international relations. Of course, considerably more representative research would be necessary to confirm such a conclusion.

Since Grunig and Hunt (1984) first proposed a four-stage evolutionary model of public relations development based on each stage's goals, environment, and organizational behavior, scholars have made extensive use of the approach, with its *one-way* and *two-way*, *symmetric* and *asymmetric* profiles, to add to our understanding of public relations prac-tice. As a result, the multistage theory has undergone a variety of modifications as it has been applied in various settings, especially in public relations practice outside the United States. Van Leuven (1996), for example, examined the development of public relations practice in Singapore and Malaysia and presented an alternative pattern. He found in these two Southeast Asian nations a three-stage process that progressed from nation building, to market development, and, finally, to regional interdependence. Still discernible, how-ever, in Van Leuven's three-stage process is a gradual move from one-way to two-way communication.

Alternatively, Signitzer and Coombs (1992) have linked the four models, when applied to an international setting, with models of public diplomacy. The *press agent/publicity* model, they argue, is essentially a propaganda model, employing an aggressive language policy. The *public information* model equates to a self-portrayal approach in which the concern is for comprehension. The *two-way asymmetric* model mirrors the information model of pub-lic diplomacy wherein no change in one's own behavior is expected. The *two-way sym-metric* model equates to a dialogue view of public diplomacy, with change being a possibility on both sides. The first two models the authors categorize as *cultural diplomacy,* whereas the latter two they consider *cultural relations.* This link between culture and pub-lic relations is further supported by the common association of communication with each. Samovar and Porter (1988) note:

> Culture and communication are inseparable because culture not only dictates who talks with whom, about what, and how the communication proceeds, it also helps to determine how people encode messages, the meanings they have for messages, and the conditions and cir-cumstances under which various messages may or may not be sent, noticed, or interpreted. In fact, our entire repertory of communicative behaviors is dependent largely on the culture in which we have been raised. (p. 20)

And, though public relations has been defined in many ways, each definition invari-ably stresses the centrality of communication. Additionally, public relations research has addressed the importance of cultural components to the profession. Culbertson (1994), for example, has keyed on cultural beliefs as they impact public relations and posited that those beliefs contour group members' information-seeking and interpretation patterns. Sri-ramesh, Kim, and Takasake (1999) strongly agree, conducting metaresearch to conclude that culture, organizations, and the practice of public relations on behalf of those organi-zations are intrinsically linked. Moss and DeSanto (2002) concur as well, stating that "pub-lic relations needs to be understood in the context of the cultural climate in which practitioners operate" (p. 8); these authors call for further case studies to help discern and explain that link between culture and public relations practice.

This chapter on Peru is such a case study. As Culbertson, Jeffers, Stone, and Terrell (1993) have sought to place public relations practice within a context of its social, politi-cal, and economic (SPE) environment, this chapter continues to build the case that culture needs to be added to the "SPE" milieu that Culbertson and his colleagues describe. Of course, the first challenge is to come to an agreement regarding what is meant by culture. A plethora of texts have made an attempt to codify this slippery term, and it is not the pur-pose of this chapter to add to the confusion. However, most seem to agree that culture includes elements, such as shared beliefs and values, and that culture is learned or symbolically transmitted. Further, there is general recognition that this learned culture permeates individual and organizational behavior. It stands to reason, therefore, that public relations practice would reflect the culture from which it emerges. A collateral question is whether, as we move slowly toward universal standards of public relations excellence as prescribed, for example, by Verčič, Grunig, and Grunig (1993), we will see a strengthening of two-way models of practice. If so, there would be reason to hope that ethical practice could lead to positive changes within cultures. This case study examines just such a scenario. It begins with the description of a government agency striving to excoriate past public distrust toward the institution it represents, and ends with that organization, or at least elements of it, returning apparently to the same practices that begat earlier distrust. Will the public relations agency weather the new crisis? Will continued public relations excellence by the agency help restore confidence in the parent institution? As the announcer says, "Stay tuned."

The Case

In the center of one of the world's most prestigious English-language news magazines, a twenty-two-page advertising supplement touts a product through the use of splashy graphics, high-quality photographs, tables demonstrating the quantitative attributes of the product, "exclusive" interviews with the "CEO" and other top "executives," a litany of the product's successes, testimonies of "satisfied customers," and page after page of high-impact prose aimed at capturing the reader's attention and imagination, motivating him or her, it is obviously hoped, to "invest" in this exciting product. The expensive and extraordinary ad is a case study in marketing and public relations. It is image-making writ large. Even on a much smaller scale it is a technique reserved for only the most exceptional of products or services—the major redesign of an automobile, the launching of a new airline, the birth of a new media conglomerate.

This product, though, is very different from all those things. It is a country—Peru. The advertising supplement is an essay with photos, charts, and tables redefining a nation that had been associated for twelve years (preceding the advertising supplement) with violence, fear, death squads, an economy irretrievably lost, four-digit inflation, a place nobody visited and from which everyone who could, left. The ad supplement epitomizes a new message disseminating from Peru since 1990. It is a message of welcome to foreign investment, tourists, and professionals. It is also a statement of stability, promise, and potential putting the world on notice that Peru intends to become an economic force to be reckoned with, a player in the post–cold war global dynamics transforming Latin America into a major producing and consuming engine.

The purpose of this chapter, though, is not to address Peru's hope for economic renaissance but rather only one easily overlooked aspect of the promotional program's design—a relatively small government agency called PromPeru. It was PromPeru that contributed to the design and placement of the twenty-two-page supplement in *Far Eastern Economic Review*. Further, it was PromPeru that was behind an aggressive, comprehensive corporate-style communication strategy channeling the message of Peru's flamboyant president Alberto Fujimori (1990–2000) through a host of conduits in an effort to recast

Peru's image as part of a larger plan to restructure completely the nation's economy and politics.

In order to examine PromPeru with any degree of thoroughness, some underpinning is necessary. First, an analysis of the message itself is needed. What are the tenets of neoliberalism that define the new Peru? Second, simply, what is PromPeru? Third, and most importantly, how did PromPeru, its products, and programs reflect and project, in text and subtext, the policies of the Fujimori administration? The first task requires some contextual scene setting in order to appreciate the scope of Fujimori's reforms. As suggested in the preceding paragraphs, the social, political, economic, and cultural contexts are vital to fully understanding the nature of public relations practice in an international setting.

Off-the-Shelf Neoliberalism and Fujimori's Modified Design

The "neo" in neoliberalism is probably at risk of losing its credibility because an argument can be made that the political and economic philosophy bearing this sobriquet first emerged with Chile's authoritarian dictator, Augusto Pinochet, and his "Chicago Boys" in the years following the U.S.-backed coup that brought Pinochet to power in 1973 (Cockcroft, 1996). Pinochet's "shock" programs were along the lines of the International Monetary Fund's (IMF) recommendations aimed at restoring economic solvency, regardless of the social costs. They included wage freezes, consumer product price rises, currency devaluations, lower tariffs on imports, privatization of government-owned enterprises, and reduced government spending, all aimed at getting control of the economy, reducing inflation, and harnessing free-market forces. Despite Pinochet's fall from power in 1989,[1] the appeal of neoliberalism spread quickly throughout Central and South America as it was adopted by a host of nations smitten by the lure of an expanding free market in a post–cold war world, and by the hope that infusions of wealth from foreign investments would permeate their populations, raising living standards across the board.

The reality, at least in the near term, has been mixed. Some pointed to Chile, Argentina, Bolivia (Conaghan & Malloy, 1994), and even Mexico as evidence that neoliberal economic measures were working during the 1990s. Others cited the social costs that accompanied neoliberal austerity measures wherever they have been employed (Cockcroft, 1996). Those social costs include escalating unemployment; reduced social spending by government with a resulting spiral of poverty for the most disenfranchised of the population; and a widening chasm between the few, powerful elite who benefit from infusions of foreign investment and the vast majority who are too far down the economic chain to receive those benefits. Of course, Argentina's president Carlos Menem was forced from office in 1999 in the midst of the country's economic meltdown, and neoliberalism's promised benefits are increasingly questioned throughout Latin America (Gwynne & Kay, 2000).

But it has been almost thirty years since Pinochet first imposed neoliberalism, and the concept has undergone some changes in the interim, at the very least around the margins. Too, the tenets of neoliberalism have perhaps been found guilty by virtue of their association with coincidental phenomena such as corruption and feckless leadership, as in Brazil, and with cosmetic democracies, as in Argentina and Chile (Mainwaring, 1995).

Peru, however, redefined neoliberalism to suit its own peculiar historical, political, and economic situation—a situation that resulted in internal policy changes related to neoliberalism as the environment developed and unfolded in the 1990s. An in-depth review of Peru's history is not necessary, but a brief overview will help set the stage for Fujimori's dramatic entrance in 1990. This condensed history also helps in understanding the culture that helped shape public relations practice and continues to affect its development. However, the foundations of Peru's culture are far deeper.

Background

Roughly the size of Alaska, Peru includes three basic regions—rain forest in the east (about 60 percent of the nation's land area, but home to only 11 percent of the population, mostly indigenous peoples), some of the world's driest desert along the Pacific coastline from Ecuador to Chile, and the "sierra" region comprised of Andean peaks and fertile valleys. About half the population is indigenous (most of whom are monolingual in languages and dialects other than Spanish), and the remainder are a combination of European, mestizo, Asian, black, and mulatto. The result is "an immense geographical, linguistic, and cultural gap" that "divides Peru in half" (Cockcroft, 1996, p. 456).

The colonial experience in Peru was dramatically different from that of the United States. Early in the sixteenth century, Spain's Francisco Pizarro stormed brutally into what is now Peru, slaughtering or enslaving the indigenous Incas. The social structure was paternalistic and ruthlessly oppressive. By the nineteenth century, Europe had extracted Peru's resources, primarily silver, and established a dual society of elite whites and oppressed indigenous peasants (Cockcroft, 1996). The dominant feudal system resulted in conditions under which a disproportionate share of the wealth and power was concentrated at the top of the hierarchy, whereas the vast majority were relegated to poverty and dependency (Sharpe & Simões, 1996, p. 279).

Independence from Spain arrived violently in 1824, with the aid of the armies of Argentina's José de San Martín and Venezuela's Simón Bolívar. There followed forty years of a relatively chaotic Republic marked by thirty-four presidents. The economy shifted from silver to fertilizer and the focus from Spain to Great Britain, but societal dualism remained a hallmark.

In the final quarter of the nineteenth century, U.S. investment (and influence) surpassed that of Great Britain. The "aristocratic republic" from 1895 to 1919 included elections limited to a "small male electorate based on literacy and property qualifications" (Cockcroft, 1996, p. 161). By then the pattern was well established of a dependent economy, lacking production capability for internal consumption—a society in which only the elites could afford the high cost of imported manufactured goods, and one characterized by company stores, child labor, and foreign ownership. The societal pattern also included concentration of company ownership—including media—to a limited number of powerful families who, as a result, wielded increasing political influence.

It's not surprising, then, that labor unrest began to emerge in the early twentieth century, exacerbated by the Great Depression in the 1930s. Bloody confrontations between the army and labor movements ensued. The dictatorship of General Manuel Odría (1948–1956) saw increasing U.S. influence, severe repression of labor movements, and the continued dominance of an export-oriented oligarchy.

Elections beginning in 1956 brought some modest reforms, but social unrest continued to grow, occasionally turning violent. Lesser government appointments were routinely handed out to family members and friends in an environment that accepted patronage as a privilege of office (Sharpe & Simões, 1996). A brief ruling military junta in 1963 returned authoritarian measures, but the election of President Belaúnde (1963–1968, first term) saw the reinstatement of some reforms.

The cycle of military rule continued with a coup in 1968, but this time the thrust was nationalistic, even to some extent reformist and populist. Breaking with the past, the military government, under General Juan Velasco Alvarado, reflected more middle-class values and saw themselves as reformers who could lead Peru to its full potential. For the first time, military leaders recognized the need to influence public support through the media, though autocratic approaches continued to shape these efforts. For example, the government expropriated opposition newspapers and broadcast outlets, and invoked sanctions against any media criticism of the government. Clearly, the government recognized the impact the media could exert on public opinion, but their approach to media relations fell somewhat short of standards of public relations excellence (Alisky, 1981).

In 1975, a deepening economic crisis led to strikes, violence, and repression as conservative elements of the ruling junta came to the fore. Velasco was forced aside and replaced by General Francisco Morales Bermúdez, who reversed earlier reforms and came down hard on labor. Some industries were privatized, but most remained under government ownership. Morales adhered to the IMF's economic austerity measures with commensurate rises in consumer costs and escalating inflation that led only to more social unrest (Cockcroft, 1996).

When Belaúnde recaptured the presidency in the 1980 elections, he attempted to implement economic policies similar to those of Pinochet's "Chicago Boys"—fundamentally neoliberal. Three basic problems precluded the realization of any success, however. First, corruption became the stock and trade of the Belaúnde regime—a recurring element in the political culture. Second, the 1982 global recession drove down Peru's export income. Third, drug trafficking became a very serious drain on Peru's budget through the loss of legitimate revenue. Further, the emergence of the *Sendero Luminoso* terrorist organization, a group of Maoist zealots, began to exact enormous costs on the Peruvian economy: agricultural production diminished dramatically in a countryside gripped by fear, and government costs to fight the insurgency soared (Cockcroft, 1996). In addition, Belaúnde failed to recognize that neoliberalism required more than merely establishing programs—such programs needed to be supported with proactive ideological campaigns if they were to be embraced by political parties, business interests, and the general public (Conaghan & Malloy, 1994).

President Alan García Pérez (1985–1990) stepped back from neoliberalism with relatively arbitrary policies including the nationalization of banking. He enjoyed initial success, manifested by a 20 percent growth rate during his first two years, but the economy quickly faltered, and rampant inflation, coupled with his own corruption and the continuing battle with *Sendero Luminoso,* saw his party fall into deep disfavor by the 1990 elections (Cockcroft, 1996; Conaghan & Malloy, 1994).

Such history distinguishes the Peruvian experience from that of the United States, especially as it relates to the development of public relations. Molding of public opinion—

mobilization of public support—through the use of even the most rudimentary of sound, cohesive communication strategies simply does not have consistent precedent in Peru. Culturally and historically, persuasion in the region has been characterized and defined by personal interaction in contrast to the employment of U.S.-style, mass communication techniques (Culbertson, 1996).

But, in 1990, the stage was set for enormous change. Inflation stood at an unbelievable 7,650 percent. Prolonged depression and high foreign debt were conspiring to exacerbate the lingering poverty that permeated the economically dualistic society. Tax revenues had dropped from 15 percent of gross domestic product to 3 percent under President García. Public disorder was dangerously explosive. From 1980 to 1988, 12,870 Peruvians died in political violence, and the number would eventually climb to 26,000 by 1993 (Cockcroft, 1996, Conaghan & Malloy, 1994; Graham, 1994; Sheahan, 1994).

Fujimori—The Candidate of Change

The electorate in 1990 was faced with a difficult dilemma. To remain fused to traditional forms of government and policies would have meant a continuation of the worsening economic spiral and the attendant risks of corruption and civil unrest. However, radical changes aimed at improving long-term economic conditions required a considerable leap of faith along with the likelihood of considerable personal sacrifice, including personal freedoms (Bishop, 1973).

A relative unknown, Alberto Keinya Fujimori, fifty-two, and the U.S.-educated son of Japanese immigrants, seized on the economic crisis facing Peru and on the feckless leadership of the established policies. Moreover, his newly created *Cambio* (change) party ran in opposition to the neoliberal programs that President García had attempted, with little success, to implement. Fujimori's populist appeals captured voters' imaginations, and he was swept into the presidential palace (Roberts, 1995).

Within weeks of his inauguration, though, Fujimori imposed a sweeping economic stabilization program incorporating the very neoliberal tenets he decried during his campaign. First, price subsidies and social spending were drastically cut along with public sector employment. He increased interest rates and taxes on government services. He deregulated financial and labor markets, reduced tariffs, and began privatizing publicly owned enterprises. He took steps to reduce tax evasion and to tap international financial assistance (Roberts, 1995, Sheahan, 1994).

Although the economy improved under Fujimori's neoliberal policies—evidenced especially by the drop in inflation from 40 percent per month to 1 to 2 percent per month—social costs included sharp increases in unemployment and poverty. Nevertheless, his peculiar mix of populism and neoliberalism propelled his administration to unprecedented popular support, permitting him to launch an *autogolpe* (self-coup) in April 1992, which suspended the Constitution, dissolved Congress and all regional governments, and purged most of the judiciary. Although the coup enjoyed enormous popular support, Fujimori also had cultivated favorable relations with key components of the military that had backed the coup as well (Roberts, 1995).

The coup and the new Constitution, which voters narrowly approved in 1993 (Cockcroft, 1996), permitted Fujimori to be reelected to the presidency in 1995. In the interim, however, he fell back on more traditional populist techniques, such as ensuring he was present (with attendant media coverage) for the dedication of new schools and other community improvement projects, especially those in poorer sectors of the country. Those projects, and other substantial increases in social spending, would not have been possible without the successes of his neoliberal programs, primarily privatization, and the crackdown on tax evaders (Roberts, 1995).

President Fujimori broke new ground with his unique blend of neoliberalism and populism, made all the more effective by his skillful use of classic public relations techniques. As a result, he enjoyed continued popularity at home and admiration abroad. A looming question at the time, however, pertained to the sustainability of the programs that supported his popularity—in particular, those social programs implemented in the early 1990s, such as vast housing construction programs, school construction, health care and sanitation initiatives, transportation efforts, and even the promotion of small businesses. The cash that funded these programs was obviously finite and based heavily on privatization efforts. Clearly, the task was to build a sustainable agricultural, manufacturing, service, and small business infrastructure that would carry the burden through generated revenues once privatization income was drained.

Although some degree of that infrastructure capital could come from internal investment, most needed to come from foreign sources. The challenge was to attract that outside investment. Fujimori had demonstrated his ability to build public consensus through skillful communication techniques that stressed the benefits of his policies while enlisting public patience with the associated downsides. What remained to be seen was his degree of success in conveying a global image of economic stability and confidence for a nation whose extant image was characterized more by association with hyperinflation, periodic military dictatorships (with attendant "expropriation" of businesses), and violent guerrilla movements.

The remainder of this chapter examines the central agency tasked with overturning Peru's tarnished reputation and building confidence for global investment. Of course, the truth that festered beneath the surface, certainly during Fujimori's final years, was that the patterns of corruption, exploitation, and despotic control continued to infect Peru's political fabric. The legacy of the nation's troubled past was not so easily discarded. Fujimori's disgraceful departure in 2000 belied the optimism of the communication campaign that the world witnessed and betrayed the sinister duplicity of the nation's top leadership. Still, no suspicion has stained the government agency that this chapter addresses, and it may eventually stand as an example of ethical public relations practice having endured in spite of the turmoil surrounding it. The agency, in fact, continues at this writing to function in much the same manner as is described. It would appear that the integrity of its members and the excellence of its work, though having suffered a setback by the Fujimori political crisis, continue to serve the nation well.

A Communication Campaign Framework

Although there had been some past efforts at mobilizing public support through mass communication, such as during the military dictatorship of the late 1960s and early 1970s, there was no precedent for the scale of the campaign that was necessary to achieve Fujimori's lofty goals. Perhaps one could look for an example to the populism of Juan and Eva Perón in Argentina during the late 1940s and early 1950s when they made especially effective use of radio. Even Argentina's former president Carlos Saúl Menem had become something of a "media hound" during his administration (Sarlo, 1994). But, in both those cases, the audience was internal and the aims cosmetic. Fujimori faced a far more challenging task—a global audience and a substantive, enduring message.

Assuming the president understood the mechanics of what was needed in terms of a comprehensive communication campaign, the simplest route would have been to retain the services of a multinational public relations firm accustomed to designing and implementing projects of this scale. The problem then would have been one of subtext. Why would potential foreign investors accept a message of confidence in the Peruvian economy when the president himself did not exhibit confidence enough to entrust his own people with the task of conveying that message? To his credit, Fujimori opted instead to "invent" a government agency to carry that message—PromPeru.

Other nations have agencies that project and shape their own national image. The United Kingdom's BBC World Service brings British culture and character throughout the globe. The Voice of America puts a U.S. interpretation on events for a world audience. Most countries operate national tourist or information bureaus. Still, PromPeru was different then and it remains so today. It incorporates the latest technologies and proven public relations techniques to project a positive image of Peru in an effort to instill confidence in potential investors, tourists, and business interests. It is proactive, serious but lively, polished, and vibrant. Here's what the agency told the world in 1996:

> Welcome to the Worldwide Web of the commission for the promotion of Peru (PromPeru). It is a pleasure for us at PromPeru, to open this window of instant communications and be part of the Internet virtual community. PromPeru is the government agency in charge of fostering the image of Peru abroad. We provide information about investment opportunities, potential exports, tourist attractions, and our ancestral culture. Through a variety of publications, videos, CD ROM, missions abroad and special events, PromPeru disseminates the wealth of a centuries-old country reborn as a modern nation open to the world. Today, Peru shows rapid growth combined with solid business foundations. We hope that you enjoy your virtual visit to Peru.
>
> PromPeru . . . is the state entity that, in coordination with the private sector, fulfills the task of making Peru's new image known abroad. Through its publications, PromPeru provides the international community and foreign investors with valuable information about Peru, the vast opportunities it offers, and the regulations applicable to the different economic activities.
>
> We invite you to discover Peru's new image through our publications and videos.

This excerpt comes from its 1996 Web site; the rhetoric has been toned down considerably on the current site. The somewhat traditional style permeated dozens of well-designed and information-filled Web pages that PromPeru maintained beginning in the early 1990s. At that time, the Welcome page featured a photo of the PromPeru staff—a group of only twenty people, mostly young, looking very much like the eager, competent executives of any thriving, forward-looking corporation. Their leader then was Dr. Beatriz Boza, an energetic woman constantly alert for additional opportunities to convey her nation's message.[2] Essentially a public relations firm with one client, PromPeru's task from the beginning was to recraft Peru's image, conveying a climate of peace, safety, and stability, and making it attractive to foreign investors and tourists. In subtext, the mission was to tout the successes of President Fujimori's brand of neoliberalism.

The PromPeru Collection

PromPeru's campaign products included printed materials, videos, and a very sophisticated battery of World Wide Web pages even in the Web's earliest days. Because of their immediate availability to potential users around the world, the Web pages offered perhaps the most valuable insight into the agency's potential impact. While these 1996 pages are no longer available on-line, a review of their variety and content is useful.[3]

Following the style of many Web "home" pages, the initial screen contained merely a simple "welcome" design and a menu of optional topics to pursue, depending on the Web user's preferences and interests. This home page also offered the user the option of viewing pages in English or Spanish. Menu path options led to pages related to the following topics: business, figures, legal, current issues, women, and tourism. Other options led users to "El Dorado Magazine," "Perunet al dia," a "Catalogue," and "The Peace Offering Ritual." Because one of the major thrusts of the Fujimori administration was to attract investment, the "business" pages were of obvious importance to the campaign.

Here again, the first business page offered additional menu choices: investing in success, investing opportunities in manufacturing, forestry industry, investment opportunities in mining, and investing in Peru. Space does not permit an in-depth analysis of every Web page; rather an examination of key pages will illustrate main points.

"Investing in success" provided an overall view of the investment climate in Peru, addressing economic conditions; legal framework; privatization; and a cursory assessment of particular industries, such as mining, agriculture, manufacturing, fishing, and tourism. The page ostensibly was aimed at planting the seeds of consideration in the minds of potential investors without overburdening them at this early stage with ponderous facts and figures. The page was replete with references to traditional neoliberal hallmarks, stressing Peru's attractiveness to "foreign and domestic investors," "freely determined prices," "elimination of all barriers on international trade," and "freedom of remittance of capital and royalties to their country of origin." The page touted Peru's "impressive turnaround," "stable legal framework," and referred to a "consolidated democracy"—an oblique allusion to Fujimori's *autogolpe.*

Regarding the stable economy, the page highlighted the dramatic drop in inflation to 15.4 percent in 1994 and an anticipated rate of 10 percent for 1995. Also cited were an annual GDP growth rate of 12.9 percent for 1994 and a "significant increase in tax revenues"—a result, at least in part, from Fujimori's policy of cracking down on tax delinquency as part of his neoliberal program.

The brief description of the new legal framework clearly reflected the administration's neoliberal philosophy. Peru, the page noted, treated foreign and domestic investors equally in terms of rights and obligations, and promised stable tax laws. It boasted that there were no longer any taxes on exports and just a 15 percent tax on 97 percent of all imports. The deregulation of banking and insurance also was stressed.

Perhaps the most prominent element of the administration's neoliberal economic plan was the privatization of industry. Though other pages provided greater depth, this "investing in success" page offered an excellent summary. It argued that most privatization still lay ahead but that now was the time to become involved, citing anticipated privatization of government-owned companies in oil and mining, energy generation, agribusiness, and fishing.

For example, by 1996, when this page was viewed, firms already privatized included major enterprises engaged in mining, petroleum distribution, salt, cement, banking, telecommunications, and power generation. Even the national airline, Aeroperú, had been sold. The government had realized U.S.$2.8 billion in privatization proceeds in 1994. In the spring of 1996 the government announced an accelerated three-year "divestment blitz" expected to generate an additional U.S.$15 billion. In the following years, success has been less than anticipated, especially in mining and agriculture. Efforts continue, however, and, in 2002, control of Lima airport operations was sold to a German, U.S., and Peruvian consortium.

However, although Fujimori enjoyed public relations success abroad as a result of the privatization effort, his public at home was less enthusiastic. In 1996, for example, the oil workers' union mounted protests against the sale of a major refinery—obviously fearing that private (stockholder) ownership would lead to streamlining and the resultant loss of jobs. Fujimori conceded eventually that a 40 percent stake in the refinery would remain in government hands (Region begins new privatization drive, 1996).

A major sale in 1996 was that of Telefónica del Perú. Here, too, Fujimori encountered public relations challenges. Although the sale of stock on the New York Stock Exchange generated a greater international (especially U.S.) response than anticipated, raising U.S.$1.1 billion, oversubscription by foreign investors compelled the government to halve the number of shares available to domestic investors. However, Fujimori once again demonstrated his public relations savvy by appointing a *defensor del pueblo*—literally, a "defender of the people," but essentially an ombudsman representing the public's interest before the administration. This ombudsman seized on the Telefónica issue and demanded more transparency in any future privatization-related stock offers. Fujimori sensibly conducted some damage repair by announcing the domestic sale of a portion of the Telefónica stock still held by the government (Peruvians disappointed, 1996).

The PromPeru Web pages further touted specific neoliberal economic measures in its business page options. For example, the page (actually eighteen pages when printed) concerning "investment opportunities in manufacturing" provided extensive information on legislative and institutional frameworks for investors. It described, for instance, the National Commission of Foreign Investment and Technology (CONITE), the agency empowered to contract with foreign investors, granting assurances of guaranteed income tax rates, currency conversion procedures, and capital and profit repatriation. The page stressed that exchange rates were driven strictly by "free supply and demand"—a pillar of neoliberalism. The page also alluded to the "deregulation of labor"—a cause for concern among miners and other workers who feared they would be disarticulated by Fujimori's probusiness policies.

Again and again, Web pages, similar to the one on manufacturing and others covering forestry, agriculture, mining and industry, were peppered with references to "opening up of trade," "deregulation," "simplified and lower tariffs," "open and free trade," and "competitiveness." The pages expressed support for the Uruguay Round of the General Agreement on Tariffs and Trade (GATT) and embraced other global economic initiatives aimed at the free-market paradigm, such as the European Union's Generalized Preferences

System as well as those of Japan and the United States. The business pages of PromPeru conveyed key messages to project the Fujimori-designed image of Peru as a nation reborn in the neoliberal image.

Associated with the page group concerning investment opportunities was a page entitled "Perú al dia" ("Peru up-to-date"). The page was kept current and included brief business news items in wire service style, such as stories about a Peruvian mining company's accord with the Korean automotive manufacturer Hyundai, the investment of U.S.$16 million in a petroleum processing plant, the establishment of a branch office of Morgan Guaranty Trust in Peru, and even the decision of a Greek tourism firm to construct a U.S.$3.5 million casino. The intent of the news-style pages was to lend third-party credibility to PromPeru's messages of stability and confidence, and to project excitement and immediacy so as to suggest to the potential investor that the train is leaving the station and it would be unwise to be left standing on the platform.

Still another Web page group within the PromPeru stable was a series called "Peru in figures." Here the browser was able to access more than 150 separate tables and charts in categories reflecting those in the business page group—agriculture, fishing, mining, natural resources, manufacturing, tourism, and so on. A host of additional statistical graphics was available, including traditional subjects such as gross domestic product, farm production, mining products, crude oil reserves, manufacturing capacity, tourism revenues, export and import products, interest rates, employment, and air cargo traffic.

Tables and charts provided statistical information a potential investor might have found useful in assessing Peru's economic condition—for example, a profile of the educational system including enrollment, number of teachers, and size of libraries, which universities offer which degrees, and how many children under one year of age receive vaccinations. Although the figures and trends portrayed through these 150-plus graphics were significant, more important was the secondary message that all of Peru was open to inspection to the potential investor. It would appear that President Fujimori, through PromPeru, went to great lengths to convey an image of transparency in an effort to overcome many years of concealment bordering on the sinister.

Yet another block of PromPeru pages provided a detailed agenda of major political, cultural, educational, and other events involving Peru. These pages, too, were updated regularly and seemed to have had the purpose of elevating the nation's status through descriptions, in straightforward, diary-style entries, of key events. Sample entries for September and October 1996 included the following:

- Participation in an agribusiness tour in Los Angeles, California
- Observation of "Peru Week" at the Organization of American States in Washington, DC
- A presidential summit for the Rio Group in Bolivia
- Participation in a forum on social development in Chile
- Operation of a display on commercial Lima for the Taipei International Fair
- Operation of a display on Peru for the Korean World Travel Fair
- Participation in the International Market for Crafts and Light-to-Medium Industry in Italy
- Participation in the meeting of the American Society of Travel Agencies in Bangkok
- Participation in the meeting of ministers of defense of the Americas in Argentina

- Conduct of a seminar on Latin American economic opportunities held in Jakarta, Indonesia
- President Fujimori's visit to Bonn, Germany
- Participation in a meeting on rural agricultural financing held in Brazil

Again, the message here was more one of subtext. The point is clearly that Peru was taking a proactive approach to integration with the global economy and culture. The events reflected a broad scope of activities and a geographical spectrum encompassing the rest of Latin America, Europe, Asia, and North America.

Another category of PromPeru's pages was the group that included lengthier, and often more scholarly, articles concerning Peru's recrafted image. This group featured research-length essays on a variety of subjects directly related to those addressed in the previously discussed business and investment pages. Categories included trade and investment, banking and finance, market regulation, labor law, taxation, intellectual property, and others.

Beyond the Web

Although PromPeru's Web site articles, photos, features, statistics, and other elements offered a refreshing glimpse into a culture, a country, and its emerging image (there was even an audio page that permitted the browser to listen to an excerpt of authentic, Peruvian flute music), and were representative of the messages the agency projected on behalf of Fujimori, the effort certainly was not limited to this medium. As previously noted, magazine inserts and promotional activities around the globe were elements in the administration's communication campaign, but PromPeru had a more extensive media mix as well.

Dozens of glossy brochures, pamphlets, and information kits heralded everything from the tenets of neoliberalism to *Pisco,* the traditional grape brandy—"a miracle born from the fertile Peruvian desert and the mixture of Indians and Spaniards."

One of the brochures revealed another side of the agency—a sixty-page, high-quality, full-color magazine of more than a hundred photos of pre-Hispanic Peruvian art. The publication included a foreword and dedication by President Fujimori and was prepared for a PromPeru-coordinated display of artifacts in Miami's main library downtown in 1994 and 1995. Although the brochure and the event promoted understanding and appreciation for Peruvian culture and history, Fujimori, again in a classic application of public relations techniques, linked the event to his neoliberal program:

> By presenting this exhibition in Miami we also wish to give the visitor the opportunity to take a closer look at the values that nurture Peruvian identity in the hemispheric context. As Peru becomes a global player it does so as a bearer of modernity in change that is deeply rooted in Peruvian history and culture.

Other publications were less subtle in their message packaging, with titles such as

- Freedom to invest in a country of opportunities
- Peru: new horizons
- Investing in Peru: guide to business law

- Opportunities to invest in export industries
- Opportunities for investment in industrial timber
- Opportunities for investment in manufacturing (others cover mining, tourism, etc.)

Other publications, and parts of many, also engaged in a sound public relations tactic—being up front about negative information. The border dispute with Ecuador is a good example.[4] A separate publication entitled simply "The Peruvian Position Regarding Recent Events on the Border with Ecuador" included an essay obviously slanted toward the Peruvian view, but nevertheless offered considerable historical background on the issue and articulated clearly Peru's position. This public airing was not likely a tack that would have been taken during the nation's previous decades of isolation.

One final PromPeru product worth noting was a video, one of several the agency produced and distributed. Entitled "Peru: A Country Moving to the Future," it neatly encapsulated in roughly ten minutes virtually all the elements of the neoliberal message in visuals and narration. The images included the bustle of a modern city, the vibrant stock exchange, native craftspeople weaving, the muscles and sweat of hard-working factory laborers, drilling operations, scenes of modern agriculture, medical laboratory research, even high fashion. The rapid sequences and up-tempo music conveyed a subtext of a nation on the move. The deep baritone narrator stressed the size of the Latin American market to which Peru is the gateway and lauded its "solid democracy with a government strongly supported by the people, with international credibility . . . successfully controlling the problems which affected the country in the last years," such as "the economic crisis, terrorist violence, and the isolation from the international trust." The reassuring words accompanied a visual, first of people marching in amiable solidarity, then of a *Wall Street Journal* headline boasting, "Peru's progress: Fujimori has tamed terrorism and inflation." As the camera tilted down the headline, the image quickly faded before the reader could read the rest: "but means still rankle." Quick flashes of colorful shots showed the viewer how major companies were already investing; large neon signs for Goodyear, Sony, Toyota, Hyundai, Samsung, Pizza Hut, and others bore witness to an apparent flood of major investors. The narrator reminded the viewer that there were no more restrictions on profits or foreign investment. Skilled and semiskilled laborers appeared as the voice entoned "competition and private initiative."

One of the criticisms of neoliberalism, and generally of Latin America's approach to agriculture for the past 150 years, has been the emphasis on export crops at the expense of staple food crops, resulting in increased revenue for wealthy landowners, but insufficient basic food for the poor majority (Booth & Walker, 1993). Unfortunately, the video did little to contradict the charge. Scenes of abundant farm products include primarily cotton, grapes, and tobacco and stress the "strong demand in the world market" for such products.

Other elements of the video leave the administration open to additional common criticisms of neoliberal economics. The narrator boasted that "the majority of the coast is still to be *exploited*" (emphasis added). Using such a word is a hot button for those who accuse neoliberalism of neglecting ecological concerns. Similarly, images of mining operations depicted a scarred landscape in the otherwise stunningly picturesque Andes as the narrator added that there are opportunities for conversion of rain forest to production of resins, dyes, spices, rubber, and medicine, though he stressed they are "maintaining the ecological balance of the Amazon." Even public infrastructure projects were tied to commerce and investment, emphasizing road construction and seaport/airport facility expansion.

Overall, the positive, fresh and flashy video acknowledged briefly a troubled past, but brushed it aside as it sought to instill confidence and exuberance for a nation on its way to a bright, shining future. It was quintessential PromPeru, and quintessential Fujimori.

The Role of the "CEO"

All this discussion of PromPeru's efforts is not to say that President Fujimori delegated to the agency complete responsibility for a national public relations campaign, eschewing a personal role. Far from it. The president was a highly visible participant and took an extremely active role in projecting and shaping the national image while cultivating his own.

Fujimori's persona was that of the consummate, high-profile chief executive officer—the Lee Iacocca of Latin America. His public appearances and meetings, especially with foreign dignitaries, were no-nonsense, all-business affairs. He came across as someone who did not suffer fools gladly. Telling were his comments regarding his dissolution of the Congress: "The democracy of political parties is over. We have a democracy that brings benefits to people, in contrast to the other democracy, which was partyocracy" (Serrill, 1996, p. 30).

Peruvians called him *El Chino,*[5] and his foreign visits with attendant media coverage garnered considerable achievements. During his 1994 visit to China, for example, Fujimori obtained more than U.S.$100 million in soft loans with which to purchase Chinese products, such as tractors, construction equipment, and civilian aircraft (Kaye, 1994). He visited New York and hosted a lunch for three hundred institutional investors in May 1996, successfully promoting the sale of Telefónica shares as described earlier (Fujimori, 1996).

The president was surprisingly, and effectively, open regarding his negotiations with foreign investors. By releasing weeks in advance a letter of intent concerning his endorsement of IMF-prescribed economic targets, Fujimori secured a U.S.$2.7 billion natural gas contract with the Shell-Mobil consortium—Peru's biggest foreign contract to date. As a result of this and other successes, the important Swiss Bank Corporation generated a glowing report on Peru's economic prospects (Fujimori, 1996). The contribution of adroit public relations techniques to Peru's and Fujimori's string of economic successes cannot be overstated. Those techniques included openness, coordinated communication efforts, responsiveness to feedback, and program evaluation.

All these activities by President Fujimori, made highly visible through extensive media coverage, contributed to the high popularity ratings he enjoyed before his administration unraveled in its final months. However, as Gamboa (2001) points out, Fujimori enjoyed highly favorable media coverage, but it was coverage that did not match opinions and issues cited by the public in polls. It is not surprising, then, that, in 2002, an investigation of corruption in the Fujimori administration was extended to include possible manipulation of public opinion through considerable financial incentives extended to media that supported the government (Chauvin, 2001). The administration, in fact, outspent Procter & Gamble in 1999, becoming the nation's largest advertiser. By early 2000, four of the top spending advertisers in Peru were government agencies, lavishing tens of millions of dollars on sympathetic media. It is ironic that the final blow to the Fujimori administration was the repeated broadcast on Peruvian television of a hidden-camera video showing the president's sinister aide, Vladimiro Montesinos, handing a wad of cash to an opposition congressman in exchange for his switching parties. Others present on the video included a top advertising agency executive and the then-vice president of Peru's largest television network. In separate audio recordings Montesinos told the network vice president how to slant news coverage in favor of the administration. A panel of judges later viewed hundreds of related videotapes, while Montesinos waited in a Lima prison, charged with more than eighty crimes, including money laundering, organizing death squads, protecting drug lords, and illegal arms trafficking. In fact, more than seventy top military and intelligence officials tied to the scandal were arrested (Kopel & Krause, 2002). There is no indication that PromPeru was involved in any of these activities.

Even before the corruption scandal, there were common charges leveled against Latin American neoliberalism that economic reforms came at tremendous social costs, including growing unemployment, a widening gap between the few elite and the poor majority, drastic reductions in government-supported social programs, and environmental sacrifice (Walker, 1996). Fujimori seemed to be aware of the charges and appears to have tried to dispel them, though performance often fell short of promise. In April 2001, Fujimori began a legally questionable third term following a rigged election. By November of that year, following the revelations of corruption and fearing investigation and charges, Fujimori used the cover of a summit in Brunei to seek refuge in Japan. A decade of increasingly authoritarian policies and strongman politics culminated in his disgraceful resignation via fax from a hotel in Japan where today he remains in exile—his parents had immigrated to Peru from Japan, and Fujimori had retained his Japanese citizenship. Congress refused his resignation, instead ousting him and declaring him "permanently morally unfit" for office. Peruvian officials demanded his extradition so he could face charges of embezzlement and "abandonment of office," but Japan refused. The former president may also be linked, accusers say, to paramilitary death squads and disappearances (The future without Fujimori, 2000; Takayama, 2001).

Conclusion

Somehow, though, PromPeru, the small agency with an enormous task, seems to have weathered the scandal, continuing to inject an element of public relations excellence and a degree of hope for a nascent democracy into a culture struggling to overcome its past. Enormous economic challenges remain: Unemployment is at 8 percent and underemployment (having less than full-time, regular, or adequate employment) adds another 53 percent of the population to that figure; 90 percent of Peruvians spend 80 percent of their income on food; economic growth stands at 3 percent (5 percent was predicted); and external debt equals 60 percent of the nation's gross domestic product. Nevertheless, inflation has been trimmed from 7,500 percent in 1990 to 3 percent, terrorism is subdued, and the border dispute with Ecuador has been settled. There is a network of new roads and thousands of new schools and clinics. Privatization is moving ahead (Chauvin & Epstein, 2001).

The *cultural diplomacy* model that Signitzer and Coombs (1992) described appears to define the PromPeru approach, though this is less likely a conscious effort than it is, as Moss and DeSanto (2002) explain, a reflection of the culture out of which the agency emerges. This is a model characterized by publicity, self-portrayal, and one-way communication. Still, the agency can point to significant accomplishments. Further, the agency appears to reflect Van Leuven's (1996) market development stage, with its use of modern media channels, sophisticated management, coherent planning, and well-crafted messages promoting trade expansion. That is remarkable in light of the apparent corruption within the very administration that launched it.

Barbero (1993) has described the risks that accompany the promise of communication technology advances. Writing of the impact of the mass media on Latin American culture, he argues, on the one hand, that new communication capabilities offer the promise of industrial modernization, government and infrastructure efficiency, academic advancements, and even the deepening of democratic structures. On the other hand, he observes that there is peril for "manipulation and distortion" (p. 25) by those who would impose imperialistic, autocratic rule. For, at least since the appearance of the caudillos several hundred years ago, leaders in Peru have seemed to have fostered a legacy that views communication within a one-way paradigm—manipulative and controlled—and President Fujimori proved unable to escape the pattern. The apparent disregard for fact and impression accuracy bolsters that assessment.

Nevertheless, it would appear PromPeru may represent a hope for public relations in Latin America that places fundamental values, such as honesty, on a higher plane. Perhaps as it moves increasingly toward the *cultural relations* model, with its attendant emphasis on two-way communication, PromPeru may yet prove to be a positive change agent in Peruvian society despite the historic cultural dynamics there that argue against excellent public relations practice. At best, PromPeru represents the possibility that global standards of professional public relations excellence truly have the potential to rise above and make the world a better place.

Notes

1. Although Pinochet's candidate lost the election to Patricio Aylwin Azócar, Pinochet retained his position as head of the Chilean military along with the authority to appoint individuals to key government positions.

2. For example, in 1995, while awaiting a flight at the Miami airport enroute to a promotional visit to Europe, Boza seized the opportunity to address a group of U.S. scholars passing through the airport on their way to a Fulbright-sponsored tour of several Latin American nations (T. W. Walker, personal communication, July 15, 1996).

3. World Wide Web Sites (these sites were viewed in 1996 and are no longer on-line). As of this writing, the gateway to the PromPeru Web site can be found at www. peru.org.pe.

4. Ecuador and Peru waged a war over an unmarked Amazon border region from January 26 to February 28, 1995 (FBIS, 1995).

5. *El Chino* does not mean, as some have said, "The Chinese." Rather, the term appears to mean the equivalent of *Nissei* or *Sansei* (the first generation of Japanese who were born in Japan are known as the *Issei*. The second generation are *Nissei,* and are born in the U.S. of *Issei* parents. The third generation are the *Sansei*). Similarly, in Spanish, *Turco* refers to anyone of Arab extraction. According to F. LaSor, the then-director of the U.S. Information Service Office in Lima, Peru (personal communication, November 25, 1996), he would not be called *El Japoneso* since that would refer to persons born in Japan.

Discussion Questions

1. What recommendations would you make to the president and administration of Peru to increase the effectiveness of the campaign to foster trade, investment, and tourism? How would you recommend the campaign develop in order to foster continued progress from *cultural diplomacy* to *cultural relations*? What cultural characteristics might constitute barriers to that progress?

2. The most difficult culture to study and understand is your own. Using the characteristics described by Hall (high-context versus low-context communication), Hofstede (power distance, uncertainty avoidance, individualism-collectivism, and masculinity-femininity), or others, predict how your culture would "rate"? Consult your library to determine your accuracy. See Chapter 5 for a discussion of Hofstede's cultural dimensions.

3. The general description of a national culture certainly does not mean that every member of that culture reflects perfectly those characteristics. Do you perfectly reflect your national culture? How do you differ? What might account for those differences?

4. How do you think your national and individual cultural characteristics affect the way you understand and approach the practice of public relations? Give specific examples.

5. Select a national culture other than your own—Peru, for example—where you might someday conduct public relations activities. Do some library research on the cultural taxonomies listed in question 2, characterize that culture, and suggest how that culture might have a different understanding of and approach to public relations practice. In what areas might you have to make adjustments to accommodate those differences?

References

Alisky, M. (1981). *Latin American media: Guidance and censorship.* Ames: Iowa University Press.

Barbero, J-M. (1993). Latin America: Cultures in the communication media. *Journal of Communication, 43*(2), 18–30.

Bishop, M. (1973). Media use and democratic political orientation in Lima, Peru. *Journalism Quarterly, 50*(1), 60–67, 101.

Booth, J., & Walker, T. (1993). *Understanding Central America.* Boulder, CO: Westview Press.

Chauvin, L. (2001, February 26). Peru probe touches media, shops. *Advertising Age,* p. 24.

Chauvin, L., & Epstein, J. (2001, March). Construction ahead. *Latin Trade, 9*(3), 26–27.

Cockcroft, J. (1996). *Latin America: History, politics, and U.S. policy* (2nd ed.). Chicago: Nelson-Hall.

Conaghan, C., & Malloy, J. (1994). *Unsettling statecraft: Democracy and neoliberalism in the Central Andes.* Pittsburgh: University of Pittsburgh Press.

Culbertson, H. (1994, August 10). *Cultural beliefs: A focus study in cross-cultural public relations.* Paper presented at the convention of the Association for Education in Journalism and Mass Communication, Atlanta, GA.

Culbertson, H. (1996). Introduction. In H. Culbertson & N. Chen (Eds.), *International public relations: A comparative analysis* (pp. 1–13). Mahwah, NJ: Lawrence Erlbaum Associates.

Culbertson, H., Jeffers, D., Stone, D., & Terrell, M. (1993). *Social, political, and economic contexts in public relations.* Hillsdale, NJ: Lawrence Erlbaum Associates.

Foreign Broadcast Information Service (FBIS)—Latin America (1995, October 3), p. 53.

Fujimori takes hard sell to U.S.: President seizes back policy initiative after bad month (1996, June 27). *Latin American Regional Reports—Andean Group,* 2–3.

The future without Fujimori: Peru without Fujimori: The squalid exit of Peru's president leaves a caretaker with much cleaning up to do (2000, November 25). *The Economist,* pp. 38–39.

Gamboa, J. (2001). The politics of hope. *Hemisphere: A Magazine of the Americas, 10,* 10–13.

Graham, C. (1994). *Safety nets, politics, and the poor: Transitions to market economics.* Washington, DC: Brookings Institution.

Grunig, J. E., & Hunt, T. (1984). *Managing public relations.* New York: Holt, Rinehart & Winston.

Gwynne, R., & Kay, C. (2000). Views from the periphery: Futures of neoliberalism in Latin America. *Third World Quarterly, 21*(1), 141–156.

Kaye, L. (1994, June). Peru's "El Chino": Fujimori charms China. *Far Eastern Economic Review, 21.*

Kopel, D., & Krause, M. (2002, March 22). Losing the war on terrorism in Peru. *National Review Online.*

Mainwaring, S. (1995). Democracy in Brazil and the Southern Cone: Achievements and problems. *Journal of Interamerican Studies, 37,* 113–177.

Moss, D., & DeSanto, B. (2002). *Public relations cases: International perspectives.* London: Routledge.

Peruvians disappointed by their limited stake in Telefónica shares. (1996, August 1). *Latin American Regional Reports—Andean Group.*

Region begins new privatization drive: Peru leads the field with plans to treble receipts. (1996, May 23). *Latin American Regional Reports—Andean Group.*

Roberts, K. (1995). Neoliberalism and the transformation of populism in Latin America: The Peruvian case. *World Politics, 48,* 82–116.

Samovar, L., & Porter, R. (1988). *Intercultural communication: A reader* (5th ed.). Belmont, CA: Wadsworth.

Sarlo, B. (1994). Argentina under Menem: The aesthetics of domination. *Report on the Americas, 28,* 33–37.

Serrill, M. (1996, May 8). Back to the caudillos? Democracies under strain are seeing their elected civilian presidents turn to authoritarian measures. *Time,* p. 30.

Sharp, M., & Simões, R. (1996). Public relations performance in South and Central America. In H. Culbertson & N. Chen (Eds.), *International public relations: A comparative analysis* (pp. 273–297). Mahwah, NJ: Lawrence Erlbaum Associates.

Sheahan, J. (1994). Peru's return toward and open economy: Macroeconomic complications and structural questions. *World Development, 22,* 911–923.

Signitzer, B., & Coombs, T. (1992). Public relations and public diplomacy: Conceptual convergences. *Public Relations Review, 18(2),* 137–147.

Sriramesh, K., Kim, Y., & Takasake, M. (1999). Public relations in three Asian cultures: An analysis. *Journal of Public Relations Research, 11,* 271–292.

Takayama, H. (2001, April 16). Whatever happened to . . . Alberto Fujimori? *Newsweek,* p. 42.

Van Leuven, J. (1996). Public relations in South East Asia from nation-building campaigns to regional interdependence. In H. Culberson & N. Chen (Eds.), *International public relations* (pp. 207–222). Mahwah, NJ: Lawrence Erlbaum Associates.

Verčič, D., Grunig, L. A., & Grunig, J. E. (1993). *Global and specific principles of public relations: Evidence from Slovenia.* Paper presented to the Association for the Advancement of Policy, Research, and Development in the Third World, Cairo, Egypt. Also in H. Culbertson & N. Chen (Eds.), (1996). *International public relations* (pp. 17–30). Mahwah, NJ: Lawrence Erlbaum Associates.

Walker, T. (1996, September 10). *Neoliberalism in Latin America.* Lecture presented at Ohio University, Athens.

5

Public Relations in Latin America

A Survey of Professional Practice of Multinational Firms

Sandra L. Montenegro

Key Points

- Public relations is defined differently in Latin America than elsewhere.
- Historical and cultural factors have had an important impact on the practice of public relations in Latin America.
- Multinational public relations firms must adapt their practices to work in the region.
- The type of management style necessary for a multinational firm to successfully operate in Latin America is different from that in other regions of the world.

The greatest development for public relations worldwide in recent years has been increased cross-border activity challenging well-established public relations firms to explore other markets, often by following their clients. Today, the largest public relations firms, such as Fleishman-Hillard, Weber Shandwick Worldwide, Hill & Knowlton, and Burson-Marsteller, earn about half of their fees abroad according to *PR Week*'s global rankings for 2001.

During the late 1980s, when many multinationals expanded their businesses worldwide, Latin America became one of their target markets, particularly because several countries' repressive military regimes were democratized and their economies started to open during that time. In addition, the historical ties and proximity to the United States has made the region evolve as a key market for international public relations. Latin America represents a market of about 516 million people with two of the world's largest economies, Brazil and Mexico, with a combined population that accounts for half of Latin America's total population (eMarketer, 2000).[1]

The practice of public relations in Latin America challenges international public relations firms because it involves understanding the culture, the market capabilities of each country, and the particularities of each nation. This chapter presents the nature of public relations in Latin America and the influence of historical and cultural factors on the practice of public relations. A survey of the way multinational public relations firms work in the region provides a closer look at the actual practice of the profession and provides answers to three major questions. What is public relations in Latin America? What is the management style needed to operate in the region? And what is the Latin American market capability?

Public Relations: Definitions and History

Research conducted by the Communication School at the University of São Paulo identified eight thousand public relations professionals in Brazil, registered in the Professional Council of Public Relations (Salles Ferreira, 1993). Yet because many professionals identify themselves with titles in social communication, political marketing, and social marketing, the actual number of public relations practitioners in Brazil is much higher (Sharpe & Simões, 1996). It is the same for public relations professionals worldwide. The *1996 Reeds Directory of Public Relations Organizations* lists 155 national and regional public relations associations with an aggregated membership of 137,000 people. Such memberships, however, usually are only a partial indication because large numbers of public relations practitioners do not belong to professional organizations (Wilcox, Ault, & Agee, 1997).

The public relations field is commonly characterized by what it does rather than what it is; thus, there is not one definition of the profession on which academics agree. Bruning and Ledingham (2000) argue that, "ask a practitioner to define the field and the likely response is a listing of the activities that are included under the rubric of public relations: publicity, press agentry, advertising, events management, media relations and so on" (p. xi). They observe, "public relations is a field that continues to seek a theoretical framework to guide its practical application" (p. xi). In recent years public relations academics have agreed on the relational perspective that defines public relations as relationship management. The *Excellence in Public Relations and Communication Management* study (Grunig, 1992)[2] defines public relations as "the management of communication between an organization and its publics. The key element is the notion of managed communication—whether it is called, public relations, communication management or organizational communication" (p. 459). For Wilcox and colleagues (1997), the best definition of public relations is that of Long and Hazelton who describe public relations as "a communication function of management through which organizations adapt to, alter, or maintain their environment for the purpose of achieving organizational goals" (p. 4). For Cutlip, Center, and Broom (1994) public relations is "the management function that establishes and maintains mutually beneficial relationships between an organization and the publics on whom its success or failure depends" (p. 2). Likewise, Hutton (1999) proposes a paradigm that defines public relations as "managing strategic relationships" (p. 199). He considers that this definition "encourages the recognition and development of strategic relations as the dominant paradigm that the public relations field so desperately needs if it hopes to advance in either theory or practice" (p. 211).

In Latin America, the first two countries that regulated the public relations profession, Brazil and Panama, established specific laws that delineated the activities considered to constitute public relations, but none of these laws defined public relations. Brazil's 1967 legislation requires a degree in public relations and a license in order to practice. Panama's public relations legislation of 1980 recognized the exercise of public relations as a paid profession with the objective of continuously planning, establishing, and maintaining the mutual understanding between an institution, a public, or a private enterprise and the groups or persons who are directly or indirectly related.

Simões (1992) argues that there are six different professional approaches of public relations in South America: (1) *Communication* approach: In Brazil, the country with the most practitioners, the practice of public relations is viewed as a specialty within journalism. "Performance is viewed as informing the media about the organization, searching for space in the mass media, and also generating instruments to inform the internal public" (p. 190). (2) *Promotional* approach: For those with a marketing orientation, public relations is the activity that supports selling the product through the promotion of both the product and the organization. (3) *Ethical* approach: Public relations serves as disseminator of the organization's best performance. (4) *Motivational* approach: Public relations acts together with human resources to build and maintain organizational morale. (5) *Contact* approach: The public relations professional is the *contact* reference in the social, political, and technical relationships. (6) *Event planning* approach: Public relations is the organization and implementation of social and cultural events as ends in themselves (p. 190).

Simões (1992) proposes a new paradigm, a challenge to create a common professional code for the global public relations community, and a conceptual definition: "Public relations is the administration of the political function of organizations" (p. 191). According to Simões (1992), this activity is performed (operational definition) by analyzing tendencies, predicting consequences, advising the decision-making power, and implementing planned programs of information. Public relations is useful in that it helps to solve conflict imminent in the organization–public social system through the use of information. Therefore, Simões concludes, public relations ultimately facilitates the transactions of the organization with various key publics to legitimize and give credibility to organizational decisions. Consequently, society benefits inasmuch as public relations searches to establish harmony in behavior (p. 191).

The profession of public relations developed in Latin America by the middle of the twentieth century as foreign companies started business in the region. Hill & Knowlton was among the first public relations firms to follow clients by opening offices in the countries where the clients began operations. The firm's "involvement in the field of international public relations began in the mid-1950s when it became apparent that the expansion of industrial operations across national borders would bring a growing need for sound public relations counsel and action" (Hill & Knowlton, 1968, p. v). Hill & Knowlton established an office in Bogota, Colombia, for Avco Manufacturing Co. and, in 1949, a contract to promote Colombian tourism and trade in the United States followed (Miller, 1999).

Likewise, the Tropical Oil Company established a public relations department in 1948 in Colombia. In Chile, the public relations profession began in 1950 with the creation of a public relations department at the Branden Copper Company (Delano, 1990).

Brazil has been the leader in the development of public relations in the region. According to Sharpe and Simões (1996), the first corporate public relations department opened in 1914 at the São Paulo Tramway Light and Power Company Ltd. Also, the teaching of public relations in Brazil started in 1949 at the University of São Paulo Institute of Administration resulting in the creation of the School of Communication and Arts in 1967. By 1954, the Brazilian Association of Public Relations (ABRP) was founded in São Paulo with twenty-seven professionals. In 1967, Brazil became the first country in the world to regulate the profession of public relations. Then, the government issued guidelines for the performance of public relations within all communication units of government (Serra e Gurgel, 1985).

According to Salles Ferreira (1993), the profession in Latin America began to be shaped into an organizational framework after the first Inter-American Conference on Public Relations, held in Mexico City in 1960, where the Inter-American Federation of Public Relations Association (FIARP) was founded with headquarters in Caracas, Venezuela. FIARP was founded with the purpose of promoting and assisting public relations associations in its member countries.[3] In 1985, FIARP was recognized as the Inter-American Confederation of Public Relations (CONFIARP), with the same member countries (except for Canada). It is still an association of associations rather than of individuals, and its goal is to promote unity and reciprocal collaboration among public relations professional organizations (Sharpe & Simões, 1996). CONFIARP as a major regional grouping shares roles with other organizations to promote public relations seminars and conferences.

During the 1980s, public relations in South American countries truly began to develop with the fall of military governments in Brazil, Argentina, Paraguay, Chile, Uruguay, Peru, and Panama. Abolition of military control resulted in new freedom for the media (Sharpe & Simões, 1996). Since 1990, opportunities in Latin America for business and public relations executives have further increased with the development of free-market economies, the privatization of key industries, the proliferation of mass media outlets, and an increase of promotional activities—advertising, marketing, and public relations (Tilson, 1999b).

The development of public relations in the region has been directly linked to its economic growth. As various countries have established democratic governments with long-term economic policies, foreign investment, along with privatization, have progressively ameliorated the region as a whole. Stanley Fisher (2000), first deputy managing director of the International Monetary Fund, observes that the region has been able to move forward even after economic storms hit Mexico in 1994 and Brazil in 1999. He noted that Latin American economies improved sharply in 2000 and were doing better than expected a year later. At that time, economic growth had been running at a 4 percent annual rate; inflation was stable, fiscal positions had strengthened, and current account balances had improved.

International public relations firms in Latin America have established a network of offices in the region in recent years in order to better serve their clients, who have extended their business in the region given the improving economic climate. The expansion in the region has been led by such U.S. firms as Burson-Marsteller, Hill & Knowlton, Ketchum, and Fleishman-Hillard, among others. Yet growing the business is not the only reason for their expansion; there is also a strategic reason according to Ruben Aguilar, director of Ketchum Latin America—"the key is to be here because otherwise we could not retain many of our clients back home" (Dillenberger, 2000, p. 48). Public relations firms from Spain in recent years have also established themselves in the region. Sanchis & Asociados (S&A) created a Latin American division, Hispacom, which has strategically allied or partnered with the most prominent local public relations agencies. S&A's expansion was primarily a result of the importance of the Spanish-speaking market that represents 550 million people, as well as Spain's large investments in the region. Spain's largest multinational telephone company, Telefónica, invested $6 billion in Latin America between 1999 and 2001 (Navarro-Conley, 2000).

In Central America, in contrast, the development of public relations has been much more limited. Civil wars, poverty, and natural disasters in Honduras, Nicaragua, and El Salvador have stymied economic growth. Yet the Central American market in some countries, such as Costa Rica (the strongest economy), Panama, and Guatemala is growing. The first public relations firms to venture into the region have been Ketchum Public Relations Worldwide and Porter Novelli, yet local companies are the leaders into the region. Currently, "forecasters predict that as Central American countries continue to increase trade with their neighbors, with Mexico and with the U.S., the region will become a greater magnet for [public relations]" (Dillenberger, 2000, p. 51).

Nature of the Profession

Hector Cardona, country manager of Burson-Marsteller Colombia, provides an example of the way media relations is handled in his country. He considers the company's worldwide media relations methodology of formal relations with the press inapplicable because the methodology needs to be "colombianized." He argues, "it is necessary to create a closer relationship with the press; just sending press releases does not guarantee the publication of articles about clients." He considers it necessary to get to know journalists on a personal level by inviting them for lunch or participating in social gatherings. Once the friendship is established, it creates an "invisible" compromise between the journalist and the public relations practitioner. Cardona stresses that this close relationship is not a form of bribery; it is simply the way the media operates in Colombia (Montenegro, 2001). Understanding the culture, and particularly the way personal relationships evolve, are key to appreciating the way public relations operates in Latin America. A close look at the media landscape, the history, and culture are helpful in understanding the practice of public relations in Latin America.

Media Landscape

The media as a reflection of a society's form of expression is useful in understanding the practice of public relations. The media landscape in Latin America is both interesting and dynamic. The region has a long tradition of print media; by the mid-nineteenth century Argentina had a well-established newspaper system (Tilson, 1999b). Many newspapers provide excellent professional coverage (*Reforma,* for example, in Mexico), often modeling themselves after the *New York Times* and other high-quality newspapers such as *El País* in Spain. Traditionally, Latin American newspapers have been more literary and more political than their U.S. counterparts (Cole, 1996). Grupo de Diarios America, an association of eleven major Latin American dailies, headquartered in South Florida, represent more than two million subscribers and a vast network of internewspaper intelligence-sharing. Additionally, U.S. media conglomerates such as *Time, Newsweek, Fortune,* and the *Wall Street Journal,* among others, now have Latin American editions (Tilson, 1999b).

Television and radio, however, are the most dominant media in Latin America and continue to grow in influence. Virtually everyone has access to radio; it is the most pervasive and free communication medium (Cole, 1996). Throughout Latin America, radio and television, with their great proportion of entertainment content, such as *telenovelas* (soap operas), draw immense audiences, whereas newspapers are read more by the highly educated and those interested in politics (Cole, 1996). According to Tilson (1999a), "From 1970 to 1988 the number of television stations multiplied from 205 to 1,459 as countries and media conglomerates set up satellite and cable networks" (p. 70). For instance, Brazil has more "TV sets than the rest of Latin America combined. Its multinational, multimedia TV conglomerate, Rede Globo, is by most measures, the world's fourth or fifth largest network. Its regular primetime audiences of 60 million to 80 million are the largest of any network in the world" (Stevenson, 1994, p. 215). Cable television now reaches more than 15 million households in the region, and some thirty networks have established their operations in South Florida within the past five years. Among them are CNN en Español, ESPN, Sony TV, Discovery Communications Latin America, and HBO Latin America (Tilson, 1999b).

According to Tilson (1999a) and Tilson and Rockwell (2004), the commercialization of Latin American society has furthered the development of the mass media and the promotional sector, accelerating the region's consumer culture. Martin-Barbero (1993) agrees and contends that the penetration of multinational corporations, such as McDonald's, and DVDs in Latin America is creating a new problem of identity in its societies. Modern society stands in sharp contrast with traditional Latin American cultures (see Figures 5.1 and 5.2).

Despite the development of media outlets in Latin America, freedom of the press is a serious concern in several Latin American countries. In Mexico, historically, ties between newspapers, broadcasting, and the government have been particularly strong. As a result, most Mexican newspapers have been uncritical supporters of the government (Stevenson, 1994). Thus, some journalists consider, "Changing the media-state relationship in Mexico is far more complex than granting more interviews and allowing reporters more opportunity to question the president about his policies" (Hughes, 2000, p. 1L). In Venezuela, a provincial law passed by the state of Apure on April 24, 2000, allows local police to detain journalists who publish negative information about the regional authorities and politicians. According to Gregorio Salazar, secretary general of the Press Workers Union, "for some sectors of the government the freedom of speech today does not represent anymore that sacrosanct right that President Hugo Chavez, once proclaimed while being a presidential candidate" (Sindicato de Trabajadores de Prensa y Colegio de Periodistas, 2000). In Colombia, *The Economist* reported, "the enduring sense of insecurity, plus a deep economic recession, has driven Colombians to seek refuge abroad in record numbers" (The assault on democratic society, 2000, p. 34). For example, Francisco Santos, a popular activist against kidnapping and violence and the news editor of *El Tiempo,* Colombia's main newspaper, was forced to flee into exile. He is "only one among

FIGURE 5.1   *Caracas, a modern urban environment in Latin America*

FIGURE 5.2 *Traditional landscape in the* **Altiplanos** *or Highlands of Peru and its Andean Neighbors, Chile, Bolivia, and Ecuador*

many Colombian journalists, intellectuals and political activists who have been forced to flee after speaking out against the violence and intimidation meted out by Colombia's illegal armies of the left and right" (The assault on democratic society, 2000, p. 34). According to the Inter-American Press Association (IAPA), seventeen journalists were killed in Latin America for work-related reasons in 2000 (Inter-American Press Association, 2001, cited in Tilson & Rockwell, 2004).

Historical and Cultural Factors

The paradox between the proliferation of media outlets and the negative influence of some governments on the press reflects some characteristics of Latin America's political culture. Sharpe and Simões (1996) explain that major historical developments have influenced public relations and communication generally in Latin America.

Under Spanish rule, a viceroy or a representative of the crown was named to oversee each new territory and accumulate the wealth of the area for the crown. Under this feudal system, viceroys and lower-level officials were compensated poorly despite the riches they collected and returned to Spain. "A government culture evolved in which each level of government hierarchy attempted to compensate for low salaries by profiting from government service" (Sharpe & Simöes, 1996, p. 279). Over time, government graft and corruption became ingrained in the culture, "causing officials to see compensation as a privilege of government service rather than as unethical behavior" (Sharpe & Simöes, 1996, p. 280). In addition, many of the New World appointees wanted to build the status of their family name in Spain or Portugal and appointed family members to positions through nepotism. As a result, Sharpe and Simöes conclude, "families, as social groups, became dependent on government bureaucracies for jobs and economic security" (p. 280). Moreover, Spanish colonies often protected their own interests when new laws from Spain were not in the best interest of the colonists. Crow (1985) states that such views helped establish the local sentiment that the law "shall be respected but not enforced" (p. 175). He points out "the psychological significance of [this behavior] struck roots that ran deep into the character of Latin American political practice" (Crow, 1985, p. 175).

As a consequence, the overemphasis on familyownership and self-interest in social, political, and economic issues "failed to create the recognition of serving the community as a facet of public relations performance that public shareholder generates" (Sharpe & Simöes, 1996, p. 281). Family needs take priority over community needs, limiting the role of nonprofit social service organizations in society. Sharpe and Simöes (1996) point out that the concept of fund-raising from the public to serve community needs is absent. "Meeting the needs of the poor is viewed primarily as a responsibility of the church and the government rather than of private corporations and businesses or individual citizens" (Sharpe & Simöes, 1996, p. 284). This lack of concern also extends inwardly into organizations. The lack of communication between managers and employees has long been a historical tradition. Improved communication with employees and external audiences has evolved only very slowly (Sharpe & Simöes, 1996). Austin (1990) notes that the society generally is characterized by a hierarchical structure, "paternalistic manager–employee relations, and autocratic decision-making" (p. 354).

Family interests also are reflected in the region's business practices. For example, whereas in the United States "large media organizations tend to be publicly held and have an ethos of serving the public, Latin American media conglomerates are family businesses and are motivated by a desire to advance family's interests" (Vanden Heuvel & Dennis, 1995, p. 15).

Another historical influence on culture has been the Catholic Church's values related to usury. The biblical prohibition against allowing investors to make a profit from loans was encouraged by the Church, discouraging Spanish investments. Thus Spain and Portugal failed to provide investment that would have prevented much of the legacy of public dependency on government and much of the poverty that led to the revolutions within the colonies (Sharpe & Simöes, 1996).

Corruption and self-motivated family interests inherited and maintained in certain Latin American governments since colonial times are reflected in the long and controversial history of U.S. public relations firms that have served as counselors for some of the most violent regimes in Latin America (Tilson, 1999a). For example, Hill & Knowlton represented the repressive government of Duvalier in Haiti. Norman Wolfson of Norman, Lawrence, Patterson & Farrell served as public relations counsel for the late Nicaraguan dictator General

Anastasio Somoza. Ruder, Finn & Rotman represented the government of El Salvador during its bloodiest civil war years (Tilson, 1999a). According to the "Torturers' Lobby"[4] report, Patton, Boggs & Blow represented the government of Guatemala in Washington during 1991 and 1992 while hundreds of Guatemalans were executed for political reasons. Stauber and Rampton (1995) consider that repressive governments' "public relations efforts are targeted primarily at an international audience—in particular, to corporations, policymakers and news media responsible for shaping trade and foreign policy" (p. 148).

Vanden Heuvel and Dennis (1995) point out that Latin America shares a common history, achievements, and problems. Its countries won independence from Spanish and Portuguese colonial powers; new forms of governments were established that alternated between dictatorships and democracies. As mentioned earlier, the 1970s was the decade of suppressive dictatorships that were later replaced with democratic governments during the 1980s. The 1990s saw a movement toward privatization and the move of Latin America toward globalization. Yet according to Vanden Heuvel and Dennis (1995), problems common to Latin American countries are the unequal distribution of wealth (which produced a vast lower class), soaring crime rates, endemic corruption in the judiciary, and weak educational systems that are struggling to prepare a young generation for an increasingly competitive global economy. The chasm between city and country in parts of Latin America mitigates against national cohesion.

For example, as shown in Figure 5.3, less than 5 percent of the population had access to the Internet in 2000. Minority access to information technology serves to illustrate one way in which wealth is unequally distributed.

Despite these similarities, Latin American countries have important national peculiarities. The most obvious of these is Brazil's Portuguese colonial heritage, which sets it apart from the rest of Latin America (Vanden Heuvel & Dennis, 1995). For instance, StarMedia Network, the American Internet company that targets Spanish- and Portuguese-speaking Internet users, had to rethink its strategy when targeting the Brazilian market—"when Brazilians entered the StarMedia.com Spanish Web site and were asked to select what country they

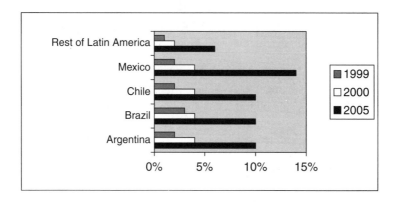

FIGURE 5.3 *Percentage of Latin American Households with Internet Access, 1999–2005*

Source: eMarketer, 2000.

were from off of a list, they would say what are we doing among all those other countries" (Elliot & Sokin, 2000, p. C1). The company created a Web site in Portuguese specifically for Brazilians—StarMedia.com.br. Likewise, Belize and Guyana, former British colonies, Suriname, a former Dutch colony, and French Guiana, an overseas department of France, inherited the languages of their colonizers, placing them as distinctive entities in the vast Latin American region.

Ethnicity varies from country to country, and often within a particular country, and is a variable that influences social class structure. With the conquest by Spain the process of *mestizaje* in Latin American began: First, whites and Indians gave birth to *mestizos,* then, with the arrival of black slaves from Africa, whites and blacks gave birth to *mulatos* and Indians and blacks to *zambos.* Martin-Barbero (1993) considers that *mestizaje* does not only represent something that happened in the past but it also represents what Latin America is today. He explains, "*mestizaje* is not simply a racial fact but the explanation of our existence" (p. 188). Venezuela, Brazil, and Colombia have a very mixed population, whereas Bolivia, Mexico, Peru, Guatemala, and Ecuador have large indigenous populations. Argentine and Chilean societies are predominantly of European descent. Southern Brazil is shaped by the large numbers of German and Italian immigrants who settled in the area; whereas the north is shaped by the Portuguese sugar cane plantation owners and their slave descendants (Sharpe & Simões, 1996). Social class distinctions based on race is a legacy of the Spanish and Portuguese colonial classifications of people. Fitch (1998) explains that the more closely descended to Spain, Portugal, or other European countries a person is, the higher he or she is in the social order; conversely, "The more pronounced indigenous heritage, the lower one's station is likely to be" (p. 19). Moreover, descendants of African slaves brought by the colonists generally occupy the lower social level. Fitch argues that there is a clear "correlation between race and social class, and social class status is a pervasive index of identity, relationships, and expectations for life" (p. 19).

Considering such historical and cultural factors, communication as an expression of culture can be viewed, therefore, as an expression of personal relationships. All professional activities in Latin America are built on personal relationships. It is very important to get to know someone at a personal level. Fitch (1998) points out that in Latin America "there is an involvement in people's lives that makes a richly woven fabric of social life. That involvement sustains families and friendships with a firmness that is enviable by U.S. standards" (p. 17). Foreigners operating in Latin America have encountered cultural obstacles. Austin (1990) gives an example of a U.S. sales executive who failed to close a deal in Mexico because he focused only on the business aspects rather than the personal relationship of the transaction. The Mexican buyer found that he and the American could not be friends; therefore, they could not do business together. He says,

> If we could be friends, he would feel obligated to me and this obligation would give me some control. Without control, how do I know he will deliver what he says he will at the price he quotes? (p. 352)

Latin Americans, in general, need to have face-to-face contact with the person with whom they are dealing. Ray Kotcher (1998), president and chief operations officer of Ketchum Public Relations Worldwide, agrees; he considers that successful public relations in Latin America requires a physical presence in the area because the culture of the region puts great emphasis on personal relationships. Therefore, foreign public relations firms have offices, partnership, or affiliations with local firms in several countries. Kotcher considers this association essential because "they provide us with a greater understanding of the cultural differences and political and economic climates in our client markets" (p. 26).

The hierarchical structure of Latin American society, with the predominance of family interests over community interests, affects the target audience of public relations practitioners. Some Latin American countries are more hierarchical than others and, to a great extent, that also translates to their economic development. Countries such as Chile, Argentina, and Costa Rica are more structurally developed, with open-market economies where the government fulfills a basic administrative function and the press is more open and diverse. In these countries public relations are more attuned to U.S. public relations practice; Argentina has the most sophisticated public relations market where local companies understand the importance of communicating their messages effectively to the public.

The hierarchical social structure linked to the economic and political context of a country also dictates which target audiences have decision-making power; for example, most leading mass media outlets are family-owned. Thus, these media are likely to be influenced to some extent by the interests of the family in question. As mentioned earlier, there are still violations of the freedom of the press, and the context of each country impacts that freedom. In countries that are undergoing economic problems, such as Venezuela and Colombia, civil discord and political uncertainty are factors that constantly limit the freedom of the press. In this type of context, public relations practice is also affected because the general public may no longer be the target audience; the government, the elite, and even guerrillas become the most important target audience because they have the decision-making power.

Such historical and cultural factors explain the particularities of the practice of public relations in Latin America. Culture, as is later examined, is the leading factor that public relations practitioners need to be sensitive to. Kotcher (1998) considers that U.S. companies, in particular, need to employ public affairs strategies to nurture public support. For example, Kotcher relates that when a company was constructing a large pipeline project in Peru, "the operation had to address the concerns of the indigenous peoples of the area and some two dozen international special interest groups who carefully monitored every movement" (p. 26). Kotcher concludes that "a coordinated presence and cultural sensitivity are fundamentals for successful public relations in Latin America" (p. 26).

Methodology

In order to analyze the nature and extent of public relations in Latin America as practiced by the leading public relations firms in the region, a survey was conducted among the chief executive officers of the leading public relations firms in Latin America (Montenegro, 2001). The survey examined the definition of public relations; the development of the public relations industry in terms of the type of clients; reasons for the firm's expansion to Latin America; and the management style needed to successfully operate in the region based on three variables: service, training, and geographical presence. The survey also examined the role of headquarters in supervising the implementation of public relations campaigns. Most importantly, the survey explored whether an international public relations firm's *know-how* is transferable to Latin America. The selection of the participating firms for the survey was based on their global public relations ranking (Table 5.1) as well as their geographical extension (Table 5.2). The participating firms were Burson-Marsteller, Hill & Knowlton, Fleishman-Hillard, Edelman Public Relations Worldwide, Grupo Link (a Weber-Shandwick company), Porter-Novelli, GCI Group, the Jeffrey Group, and the Spanish firm Sanchis & Asociados. The survey was conducted via e-mail, and personal and telephone interviews.

Impact of Culture on Public Relations Practice

In Latin America, as in other parts of the world, public relations is influenced by the cultures and political systems within and among which it works (Sriramesh & White, 1992). Verčič, Grunig, and Grunig (1996) examine the elements of culture that most influence the interaction between organizations and their publics. They argue that culture matters in the way that organizations and their public relations departments interact.

Hofstede (1980) considers that culture is to society as personality is to the individual. In a study of fifty countries, he identified four key cultural dimensions—individualism and collectivism, power distance, uncertainty avoidance, and masculinity/femininity (1980). *Individualism and collectivism* relates to intergroup processes; it consistently differentiates Eastern from Western cultures (Jaividi & Jaividi, 1991, as cited in Klopf, 1998); the former are typically homogeneous and collectivist; the latter, heterogeneous and individualistic. Klopf (1998) considers that, broadly speaking, Western cultures are individualistic, and Asian and Latin American collectivistic. The main distinction between these two cultural orientations rests in the concept of self. Klopf (1998) explains, "the self-concept is an integral part of the U.S. culture" in that Americans "assume that each person is not only a separate biological entity, but also a unique psychological being and a singular member of society" (p. 41). Anderson (1994, as cited in Klopf, 1998) argues that the extreme individualism of U.S. society as a whole makes it difficult for Americans to interact

TABLE 5.1   *Latin America Public Relations Agency Rankings, 2000*

Ranking			Latin America Income ($)		
'99	'98	*Agency Name*	*1999*	*1998*	*% Change*
1	1	Burson-Marsteller	9,348,000	10,326,000	–9
2	3	Shandwick'	6,974,000	3,260,000	114
3	2	Edelman	5,924,137	6,283,885	–6
4	5	Porter Novelli	3,487,000	1,592,000	119
5	4	GCI Group/APCO	2,039,824	1,714,748	19
6	6	Fleishman-Hillard	1,371,000	1,112,000	23
7	7	Brodeur Worldwide	200,000	100,000	100
		Totals	29,343,961	24,388,633	20

Source: PRWeek Agency Rankings, September 25, 2000.

TABLE 5.2   Country Presence in Latin America

Country	Burson-Marsteller	Hill & Knowlton	Grupo Link	Porter Novelli	Fleishman-Hillard	Edelman	Ketchum	GCI Group	Jeffrey Group	Sanchis & Asociados (Spain)
Headquarters	Miami	New York	Miami	Buenos Aires	Miami	Mexico City/Miami	Atlanta	Atlanta	Miami	Madrid
Start of operations	1977	1988	1999	1996	1993	1994	1995	1994	1993	1997 Hispacom
Argentina	Office	Office	Office	Office	Affiliate	Office	Affiliate	Office	Office	Affiliate
Bolivia										Affiliate
Brazil	Office	Office	Affiliate	Office	Affiliate	Office	Affiliate	Office	Office	Affiliate
Chile	Office	Office	Affiliate	Affiliate	Affiliate	Affiliate	Affiliate	Office	Affiliate	Affiliate
Colombia	Office	Associate	Office	Affiliate	Affiliate	Affiliate	Affiliate	Affiliate	Affiliate	Affiliate
Costa Rica				Affiliate	Affiliate	Affiliate	Affiliate			
Dominican Republic				Affiliate	Affiliate	Affiliate				
Ecuador					Affiliate			Office		
El Salvador			Affiliate	Affiliate						
Guatemala	Affiliate	Office	Affiliate	Affiliate	Affiliate		Affiliate			Affiliate
Mexico	Office	Office	Affiliate	Office	Office	Office	Office	Office	Office	Affiliate
Nicaragua				Affiliate						
Panama	Affiliate	Associate	Affiliate	Affiliate			Affiliate			
Paraguay		Associate								
Peru		Associate	Affiliate	Affiliate	Affiliate		Affiliate	Office	Affiliate	Affiliate
Puerto Rico	Office	Office	Affiliate	Affiliate	Affiliate	Affiliate	Affiliate	Office		
Uruguay		Associate		Affiliate						
Venezuela	Office		Affiliate	Affiliate	Affiliate	Affiliate	Affiliate	Affiliate	Affiliate	Affiliate

Note: Office refers to a firm's ownership of an office in Latin America. Associate refers to a firm's association with a local firm in which the foreign firm has some equity ownership. Affiliate refers to a firm's affiliate.

Source: 1999 O'Dwyers Directory of Public Relations Firms; URL of each company (O'Dwyer, 1999).

115

with and understand people from other cultures, especially cultures where interdependence rather than independence may determine a person's sense of self (Cordon & Yousef, 1983, as cited in Klopf, 1998).

Klopf (1998) explains that, in contrast, in collectivist cultures, the self is not in the foreground; people may not consider their own selves as much different from other selves because collectivist cultures perceive themselves as part of a group, whether it be a family, a clan, or an organization. Verčič and colleagues (1996) consider that collective cultures "value group goals above individual goals. They are characterized by interdependence and reciprocal obligations" (p. 48).

Power distance "reflects the extent to which power, prestige, and wealth are distributed disproportionately among people of different cultural strata or classes" (Verčič et al., 1996, p. 48). Hofstede conceptualized a power distance index (PDI) to measure the degree of distance. Thus, the greater the concentration of power in the elite members of society, the greater the score of PDI.

Uncertainty avoidance refers to the extent to which a society can tolerate ambiguity. Verčič and colleagues (1996) explain that lack of tolerance for uncertainty produces anxiety and often leads to formal codes of conduct in an effort to ensure uniformity among members of a particular culture and avoid deviant views within that culture. Hofstede (1980) found U.S. society to be low on his uncertainty avoidance index (46/100).

Masculinity/femininity refers to the value that society attaches to social roles based on gender. Hofstede (1980) measured the extent to which people of both sexes in a culture endorse masculine or feminine traits. Members of masculine cultures internalize their emotions; they value money and work to be successful and to be independent. Feminine cultures are characterized by free expression of emotions and caring for others. In contrast to the masculine group, they work to live rather than live to work (Klopf, 1998). Hofstede (1980) found Japan, Austria, and Venezuela to be the most masculine countries and Sweden, Norway, and the Netherlands to be most feminine.

Having looked at the concept of culture, Sriramesh and White (1992) argue that "the linkages between culture and communication and culture and public relations are parallel because public relations is primarily a communication activity" (p. 609). They contend that, inasmuch as society's culture affects the pattern of communication among its members, "it also should have a direct impact on the public relations practice of organizations because public relations is first and foremost a communication activity" (p. 609).

Considering that culture plays a key role in determining public relations practice of a particular country, and considering Hofstede's (1980) cultural determinants, Latin American societies are collectivistic, with individuals belonging to a group, to a family, as well as to a social class. As a result, family interests have priority over community interests. Thus, status differences are accepted, and paternalism is the prevailing hierarchical arrangement. In contrast, individualistic cultures reject status differences preferring an equalitarian approach (Klopf, 1998).

Organizations in collectivistic cultures have been shown to have tall, hierarchical structures and restricted upward communication (Sriramesh & White, 1992). Thus, Latin America's power distance is significantly high. It is not surprising, then, that the gap between the rich and poor is enormous. Poverty is one of the worst structural problems in Latin America, with about 240 million people living below the poverty line; almost one-half the population of Latin America earns less than one dollar a day (Rohleder, 1998).

This class antagonism has created an enormous mistrust between the poor and the rich, resulting in kidnappings and robberies of members of higher social levels.

Latin Americans, in general, are highly tolerant of uncertainty, particularly because law is respected yet not necessarily enforced, and time is viewed as infinite and abundant (Austin, 1990). Thus, Latin American societies tend to be more present-oriented or past-oriented than future-oriented. As a result, government decrees may not take place today, but perhaps tomorrow. Business meetings may not start on time, but will take place later on. This is in contrast with cultures such as that of the United States where time is a finite and scarce resource, and punctuality and time efficiency are a premium (Austin, 1990).

Hofstede (1980) found that some Latin American cultures are more masculine than others; Venezuela and Mexico ranked as the third and sixth most masculine countries. However, countries such as Chile and Peru ranked sixth and ninth as the most feminine countries. The masculinity/femininity determinant varies from country to country.

Management Styles and Public Relations

Having looked at the relationship between culture and public relations, and communication generally in Latin America, it is important to consider how international public relations firms in Latin America manage their international operations. Wakefield (1996) proposes four perspectives for understanding public relations management internationally and in Latin America: *comparative management* theory, *contingency* theory, *culture-free* versus *culture-specific* managerial behavior theory, and *generic* versus *specific* theory.

Comparative management theory explores organizational and cultural theories in international management studies. According to Adler (1983) cross-cultural management has identified management issues to be considered when dealing in an international arena—"the focus of cross-cultural management studies is the behavior of people of different cultures working together within organizational settings" (p. 7). Cross-cultural management concentrates primarily on the microlevel (the study of people within organizations). It comprises both international and domestic studies, the impact of cultural diversity across and within national borders. It examines the behavior of people from different cultures working within a single organization and compares people's behavior in organizations located in several cultures (Adler, 1983).

Wakefield (1996) considers that *contingency* theory is especially useful internationally because it takes into account the effects of the environment on an organization. Negandhi (1983) claims that open-systems management is best for multinational organizations. He considers cross-cultural management theory limited to the internal study of structures without considering environmental influences. Therefore, a midrange theory—*contingency theory*—recognizes the complexity involved in managing modern organizations but uses patterns of relationships or configurations of subsystems in order to facilitate improved practice (Kast & Rosenzweig, 1972).

Wakefield (1996) observes the debate in comparative management about whether managerial behavior is *culture-free* or *culture-specific*. Some argue that enterprises can operate *culture-free*, meaning an organization can operate the same way in any nation and be successful (Heller, 1988). Others contend that culture of origin strongly influences organizational behavior (Hofstede, 1980; Smith & Tayeb 1988).

The *culture-free* approach to management involves *ethnocentric* companies that believe what works at home will work abroad (Maddox, 1993). Thus, corporate strategy is made from a home–country perspective; as a result, environmental cultural factors are ignored. However, *polycentric* firms with a *culture-specific* approach, "believe that each foreign operation's environment is unique and difficult to understand and deal with from a home base; therefore, each foreign operation is given a great deal of autonomy to run its own affairs" (Maddox, 1993, p. 54). Yet, as *polycentric* firms expand, they become overwhelmed by the increasing differences in their operating environments (Thorelli, 1966). Consequently, the benefits of unified operations are lost if the subsidiaries move too far in different directions, and *polycentric* firms may lose their competitive edge in a global arena.

Brinkerhoff and Ingle (1989) argue that neither the *culture-specific* nor *culture-free* approach alone can be effective. They consider that effective organizations combine *culture-specific* and *culture-free* values and have developed *generic and specific management variables* through a "structured flexibility approach to management that integrates the blueprint model's planned structuring of action with the process model's flexibility and iterative learning orientation" (p. 487).

Brinkerhoff and Ingle (1989) designed the *blueprint model* as specific and unique to one culture. It "consists of following a set of prescribed steps beginning with problem specification and concluding with post-project evaluation" (p. 488). *Blueprint* project management is oriented toward structure and control to enable managers to make minor adjustments during implementation, in order for a project to be maintained on target. In contrast, the *process model,* is generic; it is adaptable to the needs of a particular culture. It has the notion that not enough is known in the preimplementation stage about what will be successful to specify all details in advance. Therefore, design and implementation are merged so that the project is modified and adapted as knowledge is acquired about the specific environment.

Considering the four perspectives of international public relations management, it is important to take into account the principles of each in order to understand how international public relations companies can be successful in an international arena. First, companies must consider the cross-cultural management differences among the headquarters and the subsidiaries. Organizational behavior varies across cultures. Adler (1986) points out that "researchers have found culturally based differences in people's values, attitudes and behaviors" (p. 30). Adler (1986) observes that to manage effectively in a multinational or domestic multicultural environment, it is necessary to recognize the cultural differences and learn to use them as an advantage rather than ignoring them or allowing them to cause problems.

Once an international firm considers cultural differences, it also needs to reflect on how the environment affects management effectiveness. Maddox (1993) considers that, as the global environment in which a multinational firm operates changes, the organizational structure must undergo a transformation. Austin (1990) contends that, "a distinguishing feature of more successful companies in developing countries is their superior ability to understand and interact with their business environment" (p. 3). Yet the environmental changes or contingency factors to which the company needs to adapt are not only structural but also cultural knowledge is needed to facilitate the cultural integration of the multinational.

Companies, in addition to considering cultural and environmental differences, must also determine whether their management style is *culture-free* or *culture-specific* and identify the *generic* and *specific* management variables that integrate the corporate planned structure of action with the actual process model implementation. First, according to Maddox (1993), companies could actually benefit from global integration and local differentiation and become culturally integrated. Yet Maddox (1993) considers that this cultural integration is only possible if the firm is multicentered, with each center being a major contributor to the overall company's global strategies. Second, there must be a strong corporate culture/management ethos throughout the organization that supports the multicentered approach and sustains the organization's values. Third, there must be the capacity in each part of the organization to ensure that local culture is adequately considered. "This consideration must be relative to the decisions that emanate from that part of the organization and that are being implemented by that part of the subsidiary" (p. 61).

Austin (1990) agrees that achieving cultural congruency in an international working environment is a strategic issue because of its importance and scope. He says, "Many business opportunities have been lost . . . because of failures in understanding or in managing cultural diversity; getting the economies right may be futile if you've got the culture wrong" (p. 345). In managing in developing countries, Austin (1990) advises, "managers need to identify, understand and managerially interpret cultural forces. This can be done by relating certain sets of cultural values, attitudes, and behavior to the organizational areas they most affect" (p. 358).

Multinational Public Relations Firms' Practice

All survey participants agreed that there is a misconception of public relations in Latin America. Most agreed that the general public understands it as media relations, event planning, and promotions. The types of clients are predominately multinational companies; for most firms, these represent more than 50 percent of their business in the region. For the Jeffrey Group, Fleishman-Hillard, and Ketchum, multinational clients represent 100 percent of their business, whereas Burson-Marsteller and GCI Group have the greatest percentage of local clients—50 percent. However, for all the firms surveyed, multinational clients represent the highest percentage of revenue.

Most participants agreed that the main reasons for targeting Latin America are its potential, their clients' business requiring their presence in the region, and the presence of their competitors in the region. For most firms, Latin America is an important market, and this is reflected in their revenues in the region. Overall, the percentage of the participant firms' worldwide revenues represented by Latin America ranges between 5 and 10 percent, with the exception of the Jeffrey Group, which derives 100 percent of its revenue from serving Latin America.

Four firms direct their operations from Miami: Burson-Marsteller, Fleishman-Hillard, the Jeffrey Group, and Grupo Link (a Weber-Shandwick company). They explain the leading reasons for choosing Miami are its proximity to Latin America, the availability of bilingual employees, and proximity to the firm's global headquarters. For Jeffrey Sharlach of the Jeffrey Group, Miami is the business capital of Latin America, and most multinational companies headquarter their Latin American operations in Miami. For Etienne Hernandez of Grupo Link, a Weber-Shandwick company, Miami is the Spanish-language media capital of the United States, thus, it is easier to communicate with both the U.S. Spanish-language and Latin American media because they have a presence in Miami.

However, two firms direct their Latin American operations from Atlanta—Ketchum and GCI Group—because their clients' Latin American operations are based in Atlanta.

For Juan C. Cappello, president of Hill & Knowlton Latin America, its clients require a presence in New York City, as the leading financial market of the Americas, and so Hill & Knowlton has located its office there. For Sanchis & Asociados, its Latin American operations are headquartered in Madrid, the firm's worldwide headquarters. Porter Novelli and Edelman choose to have their headquarters in the region. Porter Novelli headquarters are in Argentina because it is the most sophisticated office to manage the Latin American operation. Edelman's headquarters are based both in Mexico City and in Miami, given the offices' proximity to Latin America and the United States.

Management Style and Services

All firms surveyed offer the same portfolio of services in Latin America that they offer in the United States. Yet most of them agreed that the three leading services their clients demand are media relations, corporate relations, and technology; public affairs and government relations ranked fourth. Other services provided are crisis management, health care, and marketing.

All firms train their employees. For those that have a strong corporate culture, such as Burson-Marsteller, Hill & Knowlton, Fleishman-Hillard, and Ketchum, employees are trained in-house as often as possible, at least every six months. Firms that belong to communication conglomerates also take advantage of the resources offered by their parent organizations. For example, Ketchum employees attend Ketchum College as well as Diversified Agency Services University.

In terms of presence, there are two public relations tier markets, a first-tier market represented by Mexico, Argentina, and Brazil, and a second-tier market represented by Chile, Colombia, and Venezuela (Table 5.2). For smaller markets, firms tend to operate through affiliates. Guatemala serves as the hub for Central America. All firms surveyed have offices or affiliates in the first-tier market. Mexico leads the market in terms of geographical presence, inasmuch as 80 percent of the firms have proprietary offices in Mexico, and 20 percent of the firms operate through affiliates. Argentina is next with 70 percent of the firms having proprietary offices in the region, and 30 percent having affiliates. Brazil is third with 60 percent of the firms having proprietary offices in the country and 40 percent operating through affiliates. The second-tier market is also determined by the firms' geographical presence. In Chile, 30 percent of companies own offices, and 70 percent operate through affiliates. In Colombia, 20 percent have their own offices, 70 percent work through affiliates, and 10 percent operate through an associate. In Venezuela, only one firm owns offices (Burson-Marsteller), representing 10 percent of the firms surveyed, whereas 80 percent operate through affiliates, and 10 percent do not have a presence.

The geographical presence of the firms is reflected in the size of the staff each has in the region. The total number of employees regionwide ranges from fifty to three hundred. The geographical presence and size of staff confirm each firm's ranking—Burson-Marsteller has the largest proprietary network of offices and has the largest number of employees. Edelman, Ketchum, and Porter Novelli follow in extent of presence and staff size, coinciding with *PR Week* 2000 Latin America rankings.

Most firms are organized geographically, in that each Latin American country reports to a regional headquarters. Burson-Marsteller, Fleishman-Hillard and Porter Novelli also have a practice structure. Ketchum has a unique structure called "best teams"; according to a client's needs, a team is formed with employees specialized to fulfill those needs. The Jeffrey Group has one regional account team. For Burson-Marsteller, Edelman, and GCI Group, affiliates work independently and report only when necessary. Ketchum works closely with its affiliates because its only proprietary office is in Mexico; the firm oversees the affiliates, which report to the firm and also work independently. Firms that have their own network of proprietary offices rely on their affiliates for only 2 to 5 percent of their operations.

When conducting panregional campaigns for clients, most firms coordinate the work of their regional offices and affiliates from their Latin American headquarters. Generally, an account supervisor is designated to oversee the work of the regional team. At Edelman, affiliate offices work independently on a panregional campaign; the affiliate is responsible for the local side, and Edelman headquarters in Mexico oversees the affiliates. Hill & Knowlton and Sanchis & Asociados agree that the key to a successful panregional campaign is establishing objectives, or a structure of goals, to be implemented by the regional office or affiliates and then supervised by headquarters. Porter Novelli adapts to the client's needs; the Porter Novelli office that obtains the account forms the team. The client also may want to work with its own network of subsidiary offices that report to Porter Novelli affiliates, which, in turn, report to the account leader, who has been chosen according to the client's requests. Likewise, Burson-Marsteller operates according to the client's needs; if the client requires a regional strategy, one office in the region controls the strategy centrally, and then the campaign is coordinated in each market. If the client wants to work on a market-by-market basis, then the client works individually with the Burson-Marsteller office of a particular country.

Obstacles with Latin American Offices

Several participants agreed that, when dealing with Latin American employees, the major obstacles are cultural barriers. A closer relationship with employees is required. Jaime Marsal of Sanchis & Asociados explains that, even though he speaks the same language as the Latin American offices, the working culture is different, and he finds a lack of initiative from auxiliary employees. Ken Willis of GCI agrees; he finds that Latin American employee expectations and working culture are very different from those in the United States. They also have varying views of what public relations is; most focus on media relations and not much on strategy. Juan Carlos Lynch of Porter Novelli considers that the major obstacle is the different service standard provided. What makes the work difficult sometimes is the different understanding each market has of public relations. The challenge is obtaining a homogeneous quality of work. Juan Carlos Cappello of Hill & Knowlton considers that there is a lack of appropriately trained personnel, particularly in business communication and information technology. "Even in markets where there are communication-trained people they do not understand how business works" (Cappello, personal communication, October 19, 2000). Other obstacles are political barriers, such as elections, strikes, and religious holidays and technical barriers, such as a failure of the Internet server, which delays the circulation of e-mail messages.

All participants agreed that most clients have high expectations when initially extending their operations into Latin America. According to Juan Carlos Cappello, clients associate the region with low costs and high returns; however, doing business in São Paulo can be as expensive as doing business in Manhattan. Thus, they do not have a true understanding of business costs in the region. He also considers that there is a great myth of Latin America as a homogeneous region. Gabriel Guerra of Edelman agrees, saying clients see the region as a uniform block. All respondents agree that the major obstacle they face as clients begin operations in the region is cultural ignorance. There is a lack of understanding of the public relations and business particularities of each country. Rissig Licha of Fleishman-Hillard suggests that there is a lack of cultural sensitivity and understanding of suggests nuances.

Clients also expect to have the same standard of service in Latin America that they receive in the United States. All participants agree that clients expect consistent service and consistent public relations. Santiago Hinojosa of Burson-Marsteller says:

> When a client starts to work with Burson-Marsteller Latin America, they expect the same level of professionalism in the region. To the client that is Burson-Marsteller standard, and it is often disappointing. An employee from Latin America may not have the same years of experience and the skill set is not comparable to an employee in New York. (personal communication, September 5, 2000)

Juan Carlos Lynch of Porter Novelli agrees that in Latin America clients expect service comparable to that in Europe or the United States—"The fundamental obstacle derives from work methodologies of each country's agency. The problem is not Latin America, but working with somebody who does not understand the region" (Lynch, personal communication, September 28, 2000). Gabriel Guerra of Edelman considers one obstacle to be that public relations processes vary according to each country's culture and customs, thus the client's launch of a product can vary from country to country. Likewise, Ruben Ortega of Edelman explains that foreign companies that extend their business to Latin America must learn several lessons; they have to orient themselves locally in order to avoid mistakes.

Jaime Marsal of Sanchis & Asociados finds cultural particularities to be the major obstacle. His company deals largely with public affairs and government relations in the region. He considers the major obstacles are bureaucratic peculiarities, uncertainty in the political decision-making process, and political *clientelismo* (patronage from powerful politicians to those who follow them).

Most participants agreed that their firm's *know-how* is transferable and possible only through training. However, although the *know-how* is transferable, it must account for the cultural differences of each country in which a firm operates. Thus, all firms that seek to provide seamless service worldwide must recognize that it is only possible by taking into consideration local nuances even as they seek to offer employees professional development to constantly challenge and motivate them to perform their best and remain with the firm.

All survey participants expect continuous growth in revenue and in geographical presence. They believe that the potential in Latin America is real. Ketchum expects to establish equity relations with its affiliates; some of its affiliates have expanded operations to other countries, and Ruben Aguilar considers that, as Ketchum's affiliates grow, so will Ketchum. GCI Group expects to continue the centralization of its Latin American operations. Sanchis & Asociados expects to have a presence in all Latin American countries. Edelman wants to extend its roster of health care clients. The Jeffrey Group expects to continue growing; the company doubled in size from 1999 to 2000. Grupo Link, a Weber-Shandwick company, will continue growing as the company finishes acquiring equity in Brazil and Mexico and was projected to acquire equity in second-tier markets in 2001.

Conclusion

The public relations profession in Latin America faces several challenges—first, its definition. The survey generally confirmed Simöes' (1992) description that public relations in Latin America is generally understood by the public to be media relations and event planning, although in the first-tier markets, the public relations concept coincides with Hutton's (1999) definition of the management of relations with key publics. Despite the fact that public relations is a field that continues to grow—and in recent years has become a preferred field of study among students of communication—it is a profession that needs to be further developed and understood by the public, particularly corporations that could improve their image if they made public relations a key component of their managerial strategy.

Second, international public relations firms need to be sensitive to local culture and the way business operates in Latin America. They also need to educate the client to be sensitive to the different ways public relations is practiced in various countries. In Latin America, international public relations firms need a physical presence if they are to build strong relationships with employees of their own offices, affiliates, and associates, as well as their clients, inasmuch as one of a public relations firm's most valuable resources is its people. Operating successfully in Latin America, moreover, depends to a great extent on the strength of the relationships built among members of an organization, as well as with clients and key publics given the culturally based need of Latin Americans to build friendships with the people with whom they work.

Survey respondents agreed that Latin America is a strategic market for international public relations firms; in order to be fully global, multinational firms must be present in the region. However, it is important to keep in mind, according to the respondents, that Latin America cannot be considered as a uniform block. Although it has similarities, it also has unique local nuances. Thus, the practice of public relations as a communication activity is to a great extent determined by a country's culture.

International public relations firms can benefit from practicing across borders because public relations can be used as a lens to better understand how organizations in other cultures use communication to adapt their relationships with key publics (Botan, 1992). Also, public relations firms can benefit by learning from the knowledge and experience of other cultures' public relations practices. Botan (1992) considers that understanding the role of both clients and practitioners in an international environment is the key for ethical international public relations. Thus, Botan (1992) agrees with Maddox (1993) and Austin (1990) in the importance of identifying and integrating the cultural aspects for successful management process and public relations practice of a multinational company in a global scenario. As a result, a firm's *know-how* is transferable once local cultural differences and environmental factors are taken into consideration.

Lastly, the survey indicates that the Latin American public relations market is a sophisticated one. This is illustrated by the size of the markets, the types of services provided, and type of clients the firms have, which are primarily multinational. Argentina is the most developed market for public relations because local companies understand public relations as the management of relations with key publics. This is particularly important as Argentina faces economic problems and companies deal with critical issues, including the downsizing of employee staffs. In second-tier markets this relational concept of public relations is evolving.

Latin America is an important market for international public relations. To be fully global, international firms must operate in the region. The presence of international public relations firms has fostered the development of the profession, including the growth of academic programs offered by local universities. Yet public relations professionals also have the challenge of educating the public to understand that the true role of public relations is the management of relationships. Latin American public relations professional organizations can play a key role in this education effort. International public relations firms also should play a role in these associations, exchanging knowledge with local organizations and promoting the profession throughout Latin America. Further research will be needed to track the continuing evolution of the public relations profession in Latin America in light of recent economic developments in Argentina and changing geopolitical realities following the September 2001 terrorist attacks in the United States.

Notes

1. Brazil is the fifth-largest country in the world and the largest in Latin America; it occupies one-half of the South American continent, and it is slightly smaller than the United States. It ranks sixth in the world's population with 171.8 million people (July 1999 estimate), equivalent to one-half the population of South America. Brazil's economy is the tenth-largest in the world (Central Intelligence Agency, 2000).

2. This project conducted by six researchers studied "the characteristics that enhance the ability of public relations departments to contribute to organizational effectiveness" (Verčič and colleagues, 1996, p. 36).

3. Member countries include Canada, Mexico, Dutch Antilles, Costa Rica, Venezuela, Colombia, Ecuador, Peru, Bolivia, Paraguay, Chile, Argentina, Uruguay, and Brazil.

4. In 1992, The Center for Public Integrity, based in Washington, DC, published a study entitled "The Torturers' Lobby," revealing that Washington lawyers and lobbyists, who served as top political advisors to Presidents Reagan, Bush, and Clinton, were raking in more than $30 million a year by helping repressive governments improve their images (Stauber & Rampton, 1995).

Discussion Questions

1. You are the owner of a public relations firm in the United States that wants to expand into Latin America. You do not speak Spanish, and you need to expand in order to attract new business. What would your strategy be to expand to Latin America? If you were to open offices, where would they be located?

2. What do you consider to be the most important aspects that you need to be aware of when dealing with someone from Latin America? Based on your answer (and your answer to question 1), how would you establish relationships with the media when you are new in town?

3. You are the president of a U.S.-based firm that just won the public relations contract for an Argentinean beef export company. This client wants to penetrate the U.S. market and requests a very experienced person to lead the account. Linda is the ideal candidate to lead the account; she speaks Spanish and lived in Argentina for a few years. Yet your client demands that a male lead the account. How would you handle the situation? How do you ex-

plain to the client that Linda is the ideal candidate? What obstacles do you consider she would face when making a presentation to the client in Argentina?

4. Inka-Cola is the biggest competitor of Coca-Cola in Peru. It has been the beverage of tradition and illustrates the degree of loyalty Peruvians have to one brand, to the point that McDonald's menus include Inka-Cola instead of Coke. The public relations firm you work for just won the Crystal-Cola account, a clear beverage that tastes just like Coca-Cola. Your mission is to introduce the new beverage to Latin America, including Peru. Of what would your public relations campaign consist? What markets would you target first? Why? What would be the principal challenges, and how would you overcome them?

References

Adler, N. (1983). Cross cultural management issues to be faced. *International Studies of Management & Organizations, 13,* 7–45.

Adler, N. (1986). From the Pacific century: Cross cultural management reviewed. *1986 Yearly Review of Management of the Journal of Management, 12,* 295–318.

The assault on democratic society in Colombia. (2000, March 18–24). *The Economist,* p. 34.

Austin, J. (1990). *Managing in developing countries: Strategic analysis and operating techniques.* New York: Free Press.

Botan, C. (1992). International public relations: Critique and reformulation. *Public Relations Review, 18*(2), 149–159

Brinkerhoff, D., & Ingle, M. (1989). Integrating blueprint and process: A structured flexibility approach to development management. *Public Administration and Development, 9,* 487–503.

Brunig, S., & Ledingham, J. (2000). *Public relations as relationship management.* Mahwah, NJ: Lawrence Erlbaum Associates.

Burson-Marsteller. (2001). Retrieved January 24, 2000, from www.bm.com

Central Intelligence Agency. (2000). *The world fact book.* Retrieved October 13, 2000, from www.cia.gov/publications/factbook.

Cole, R. (1996). *Communication in Latin America: Journalism, mass media, and society.* Wilmington: Scholarly Resources Inc.

Crow, J. (1985). *Spain, the root and the flower: An interpretation of Spain and the Spanish people.* Berkeley: University of California Press.

Cutlip, S., Center, A., & Broom, G. (1994). *Effective public relations.* Englewood Cliffs, NJ: Prentice Hall.

Delano, B. (1990). *Las relaciones publicas en Chile* [Public Relations in Chile]. Santiago: Editorial Universitaria.

Dillenberger, D. (2000, September 25). Global rankings: Latin America. *PR Week,* pp. 48–54.

Edelman Public Relations Worldwide. (2001). Retrieved July 11, 2000, from www.edelman.com.

Elliot, S., & Sokin, A. (2000, May 28). Young and Rubican agrees to $5.7 million takeover by WPP. *The New York Times,* p. C1

e-Marketer. (2000). *eLatin America Report.* New York: e-Marketer.

Fisher, S. (2000, October 12). *Latin America 2000.* Speech at the LACEA 2000 Conference, Rio de Janeiro, Brazil, International Monetary Fund. Retrieved October 12, 2000, from www.imf.org.

Fitch, K. (1998). *Speaking relationally: Culture, communication and interpersonal connection.* New York: Guilford Press.

Fleishman-Hillard International Communications. Retrieved May 2, 2000, from www.fleishman.com.

The Freedom Forum. (2001). Retrieved August 25, 2000, from www.freedomforum.org.

GCI Group. (2001). Retrieved July 11, 2000, from www.gci.com.

Grunig, J. E. (Ed.). (1992). *Excellence in public relations and communications management.* Hillsdale, NJ: Lawrence Erlbaum Associates.

Heller, F. (1988). Cost benefits of multinational research on organizations. *International Studies of Management and Organizations* 18 (pp. 5–18).

Hill & Knowlton. (1968). *Handbook on international public relations.* New York: Praeger.

Hill & Knowlton Public Relations. (2001). Retrieved May 2, 2000, from www.hillandknowlton.com.

Hofstede, G. (1980). *Culture's consequences: International differences in work related values.* Beverly Hills: Sage.

Hughes, S. (2000, July 16). A not-so-modest proposal to free Mexican media. *The Miami Herald,* p. 1L.

Hutton, J. (1999). The definition, dimensions, and domain of public relations. *Public Relations Review, 25*(2), 199–214.

The Jeffrey Group. (2001). Retrieved May 2, 2000, from www.thejeffreygroup.com.

Kast, F., & Rosenzweig, J. (1972). General systems theory: Applications for organizations and management. *Academy of Management Journal, 447–477.*

Ketchum. (2001). Retrieved July 11, 2000, from www. ketchum.com.

Klopf, D. (1998). *Intercultural encounters: The fundamentals of intercultural communication.* Englewood, NJ: Morton.

Kotcher, R. (1998). The changing role of PR in Latin America. *Public Relations Tactics, 5,* 26.

Maddox, R. (1993). *Cross-cultural problems in international business.* Westport, CT: Quarom Books.

Martin-Barbero, J. (1993). *Communication, culture and hegemony* (E. Fox and R. White, Trans.). Newbury Park, CA: Sage.

Miller, K. (1999). *The voice of business: Hill & Knowlton and postwar public relations.* Chapel Hill: University of North Carolina Press.

Montenegro, S. (2001, December). *Public relations in Latin America: A comparative analysis of multinational public relations firms.* Unpublished thesis, University of Miami, Coral Gables, FL.

Navarro-Conley, E. (2000, October 27). Inversiones españolas seguirán apuntando a América Latina [Spanish investments will continue to target Latin America]. Mundo IT.com. Retrieved October 31, 2000, from www.mundoit.com/noticias.

Negandhi, A. (1983, Fall). Cross-cultural management research: Trend and future directions. *Journal of International Business Studies, 14*(2), 17–29.

O'Dwyer, J. (Ed.). (1999). *O'Dwyer's directory of public relations firms 1999.* New York: J. R. O'Dwyer Co. Inc.

Porter Novelli International (2001). Retrieved July 11, 2000, from www.porternovelli.com.

Rohleder, J. (1998). Dimension of neostructuralism: Poverty in Latin America. Neoliberalism and Neostructuralism, Internet Seminar. April–July 1998. Eberhard-Karls Universität, Institute of Political Science. Retrieved November 6, 2000, from http://tiss.zdv.uni-tuebingen.de/webroot/sp/barrios/themeB3a.htr.

Salles Ferreira, M. (1993). Public relations in Latin America. *International Public Relations Review, 16,* 4–5.

Sanchis & Asociados. (2001). Retrieved July 11, 2000, from www.sanchisyasoc.com.

Serra e Gurgel, J. B. (1985). *Cronologia da Evoluçao Histórica das Relacoes Publicas* [A chronology of the historical evolution of public relations]. Brasilia: Linhu Grafica.

Shandwick International. (2001). Retrieved May 2, 2000, from www.shandwick.com.

Sharpe, M., & Simöes, R. (1996). Public relations performance in South and Central America. In H. Culbertson & N. Chen (Eds.), *International public*

relations (pp. 273–297). Mahwah, NJ: Lawrence Erlbaum Associates.

Simöes, R. (1992). Public relations as a political function. *Public Relations Review, 18,* 189–200.

Sindicato de Trabajadores de Prensa y Colegio de Periodistas. (2000). "Gremios Periodísticos rechazan decreto de Apure" [Journalists reject Apure's decree]. *El Universal.* Retrieved April 24, 2000, from http://archivo.eud.com/2000/04/24/24112DD.shtml.

Smith, P., & Tayeb, M. (1988). Organizational structure and processes. In M. Bond (Ed.), *Cross cultural challenge to social psychology* (pp. 153–164). Newbury Park, CA: Sage.

Sriramesh, K., & White, J. (1992). Societal culture and public relations. In J. E. Grunig (Ed.), *Excellence in public relations and communications management* (pp. 597–614). Hillsdale, NJ: Lawrence Erlbaum Associates.

Stauber, J., & Rampton, S. (1995). *Toxic sludge is good for you: Lies, damn lies and the public relations industry.* Monroe, ME: Common Courage Press.

Stevenson, R. (1994). *Global communication in the twenty-first century.* New York: Longman.

Thorelli, H. (1966, July). The multi-national corporation as a change agent. *The Southern Journal of Business, 1,* 1–9.

Tilson, D. (1999a). Against the common good: The commodification of Latin America. *Media Development, 46,* 69–74.

Tilson, D. (1999b, April 28). *The media landscape in Latin America and crisis management.* Speech to the International Association of Tank Owners, INTERTANKO, Houston, TX.

Tilson, D., & Rockwell, R. (2004). Latin America. In J. Merrill & A. de Beer (Eds.), *Global Journalism.* Boston: Allyn & Bacon.

Vanden Heuvel, J., & Dennis, E. (1995). *Changing patterns, Latin America's vital media.* New York: The Freedom Forum Media Studies Center, Columbia University.

Verčič, D., Grunig, L. A., & Grunig, J. E. (1996). Global and specific principles of public relations: Evidence from Slovenia. In H. Culbertson & N. Chen (Eds.), *International public relations* (pp. 31–65). Mahwah, NJ: Lawrence Erlbaum Associates.

Wakefield, R. (1996). Interdisciplinary theoretical foundations for international public relations. In H. Culbertson & N. Chen (Eds.), *International public relations* (pp. 17–30). Mahwah: NJ: Lawrence Erlbaum Associates.

Weber Public Relations Worldwide. (2001). Retrieved July 11, 2000, from www.weberpr-worldwide.com.

Wilcox, D., Ault, P., & Agee, W. (1997). *Public relations strategies and tactics.* New York: Longman.

Part III

Around Europe

An Introduction

Hugh M. Culbertson

Many countries around the world appear to have sought advice from U.S. practitioners and educators in establishing public relations as an occupation and academic focus. Predictably, the Yankee version usually did not fit very well given the varied social, political, cultural, and economic contexts.

All is not culturally relative, however. James E. Grunig, Larissa A. Grunig, and Dejan Verčič (Chapter 6) have proposed several principles of public relations that appear to apply universally. And Chapters 6 through 9 report on valiant—if somewhat halting and uneven—attempts to apply these principles in three former areas in the communist sphere—Slovenia, Romania, and Russia.

Two scholarly formulations seem useful in examining the goals, progress, and barriers facing European public relations.

First, the four-stage evolutionary model of public relations (Grunig & Hunt, 1984) remains a lively focus of debate. As modified and applied recently, the model suggests two basic conclusions:

1. *Two-way communication pays.* A successful public relations shop needs to listen carefully and respectfully to various well-defined publics on behalf of the client organization, as well as to speak to these publics.
2. *Persuasion, along with building and maintaining ongoing relationships, are important.* Any organization needs inputs—money, supplies, labor, and so on—from its environment. The organization usually needs to count on these inputs' consistent availability. That requires the loyalty of key publics. And loyalty hinges on solid relationships built on mutual understanding that develops over time (Verčič, Grunig, & Grunig, 1996).

POLAND

CZECH REPUBLIC

SLOVAKIA

SLOVENIA
Ljubljana

HUNGARY

ROMANIA

Bucharest

SERBIA   BULGARIA

CROATIA

BOSNIA AND HERZEGOVINA

MACEDONIA

ALBANIA

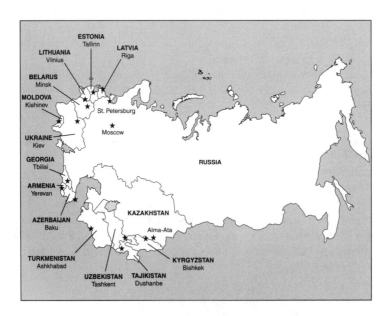

ESTONIA
Tallinn

LITHUANIA
Vilnius

LATVIA
Riga

BELARUS
Minsk

MOLDOVA
Kishinev

St. Petersburg

UKRAINE
Kiev

Moscow

GEORGIA
Tbilisi

RUSSIA

ARMENIA
Yerevan

AZERBAIJAN
Baku

KAZAKHSTAN

Alma-Ata

TURKMENISTAN
Ashkhabad

KYRGYZSTAN
Bishkek

UZBEKISTAN
Tashkent

TAJIKISTAN
Dushanbe

In a second formulation, Van Leuven (1996) notes that, in the developing world, public relations generally goes through three stages—sometimes, but not necessarily, in the sequence listed below.

1. *Nation building.* The goal here is to develop a sense of sharedness. Citizens of a nation must feel they have something in common. They must have a sense of commitment to the state that motivates them to pay taxes, honor a common flag, and even die in battle to protect that flag.
2. *Marketing support.* A nation needs a viable economy. And that requires marketing and public relations expertise to help stimulate sales and economic growth.
3. *Regional interdependence.* This requires a feeling that countries can profit from trade and foreign-policy alliances. At the very least, they need to avoid blowing one another up—a real danger with modern weapons of mass destruction.

In Europe, the collapse of the Soviet Union contributed to three trends, each requiring careful attention to one of the stages or activities just listed. Two of these trends—"breaking up" and "coming together"—seem to conflict with each other. Yet both have been going on at the same time. And both pose challenges and opportunities for public relations.

First, the *breaking up of nations requires nation building.* When the USSR imploded, several parts of it became independent nations, sometimes with disastrous civil strife. Armenia and Azerbaijan fought bitterly in the former Soviet Union. Also, Serbs, Moslems, Bosnians, and Albanians did the same in the former Yugoslavia.

Second, *joining together in alliances requires clarification of regional interdependence among nations.* In particular, the North Atlantic Treaty Organization (NATO) expanded. And the European Union developed a common currency as well as governmental structure (Morgan, 1999). Peoples with long histories of rivalry and hard-won independence from each other joined hands at long last.

The European Union (EU) is an organization of fifteen nations, with several others preparing for possible future membership. EU member states have resolved to create a single market in which goods, people, and capital move freely from country to country. Recently, these states established a common currency, the euro. Such moves involve discomfort—and public relations problems—partly because leaders of a given nation often believed they were surrendering their sovereignty to a degree (eurunion.org/profile/brief/htm, 2002).

Third, *privatization following the collapse of communism put a spotlight on marketing support.* Often privatization seemed unduly hasty, reckless, and corrupt. Acceptance of the process—and of the institutions taking part in it—has become problematic.

How well has public relations progressed in these realms? The literature in general, and the four chapters in this section, support both optimism and pessimism.

On the down side, several barriers stand in the way of public relations maturation and growth.

First, *power distance is high in many societies.* This appears to hamper public relations people as they seek representation in the leadership councils of organizations they serve (Sriramesh, 1996; Verčič, et al., 1996).

Power distance is the extent to which people in a society see substantial disparities in power and influence as inevitable—as part of the natural order of things (Hofstede,

2001). High power distance tends to go along with respect for the elderly. Thus, public relations practitioners—often the "new kids on the block" who are staff workers outside formal lines of authority—face uphill battles in gaining status within high-power-distance societies. And, as discussed in Chapter 6 of this volume, Grunig and colleagues regard such status as important in public relations management.

Second, *uncertainty avoidance also is high in some of these same countries in Europe.* People tend to feel threatened by unknown and uncertain situations (Hofstede, 2001). That leads them to strive hard for closure—perhaps before all relevant information has become available.

Taylor (2000b) suggests that high uncertainty avoidance and power distance can pose real problems for public relations. This became apparent a few years ago when Belgian schoolchildren became ill after drinking Coca-Cola. Belgian authorities immediately called a halt to the sale of Coke, and both France and Spain also reacted strongly.

All three nations have rated high on uncertainty avoidance and power distance. This apparently led people to expect strong, quick action by Coca-Cola executives, to blame them for the problem, and to demand firm conclusions before available evidence supported them. All of this has a downside. One axiom of public relations is that, when you do not know the answer to a question, you admit it. Then, of course, you work hard to find an answer. But you do not make one up to please an audience!

Three other countries—Denmark, Sweden, and Norway—reacted much more patiently and calmly to the episode. These nations rank quite low on both power distance and uncertainty avoidance.

Third, *openness has been resisted in societies with long histories of totalitarianism.* Leaders who suddenly feel insecure in a fast-changing environment understandably find it difficult to change their approach overnight. This holds in Russia (Chapter 9), Romania (Chapter 7), and Bulgaria (Karadjov, Kim, & Karavasilev, 2000).

Fourth, *educational institutions have been more or less purely practical or purely academic.* This leaves little chance for the twain to meet so students and scholars can link communication management with communication–technician activity (Dozier, 1992). Partly as a result of this, public relations practitioners often labor mostly as technicians.

Fifth, in Britain, a leader in European public relations, selection of practitioners for entry in the field has focused on "*experience and subjectively assessed, ill-defined personal qualities*" (L'Etang, 1999, p. 283). This view has hampered efforts by the British Institute for Public Relations to define and gain acceptance of a set of skills and body of knowledge as hallmarks for practice. That, in turn, has impeded efforts to gain professional status. (L'Etang, 1999).

Despite these barriers, progress has been made. Turning to the half-full part of the bottle, the literature suggests several pluses:

1. Growth of public relations theory in the Russian Federation (Chapter 8).
2. Successful marketing programs in Romania on behalf of material products (Turk, 1996) and tourism (Chapter 7).
3. Innovative steps to market hotels, restaurants, educational programs, and tourism services in Russia so as to build lasting relationships with actual and potential customers, tourism-related firms, and other important clients (Chapter 9).

4. Gradual acceptance on the continent of the European Parliament's role in Europe despite apathy and opposition in many countries, low visibility, and inherent difficulties in building press coverage of a deliberative assembly. Such problems stem in part from the fact that this body makes decisions slowly and follows complex procedures. Also, the Parliament has to contend with at least eleven official languages. And it often is upstaged by the EU Commission, a body that oversees operation of the European Union, as well as by national governments (Morgan, 1999).

5. Gradual embracing of two-way, relationship-oriented approaches in former communist states such as Russia (Chapter 9), Slovenia (Verčič et al., 1996), and Romania (Chapter 7).

6. Growth of management alongside technician-oriented public relations in Russian academic programs (Chapter 8).

7. An important role for nongovernmental organizations (NGOs)—using communication skills—in building civil society with widespread public participation and deliberation in Bosnia since the tragic conflict there during the 1990s (Taylor, 2000a).

All in all, public relations is alive and well in Europe—even in countries with totalitarian heritages that have impeded its growth (Bentele & Peter, 1996).

Slovenia

Government type	Parliamentary democratic republic
Capital	Ljubljana
Language	Slovene, Serbo-Croat
Ethnic groups	Slovene, Croat, Serb, Bosniak, Yugoslav, Hungarian
Religion	Roman Catholic
Major industries	Ferrous metallurgy and rolling mill products, aluminum reduction and rolled products, lead and zinc smelting, electronics (including military electronics), trucks, electric power equipment, wood products, textiles, chemicals, machine tools

Sources: National Geographic Atlas of the World Seventh Edition, CIA The World Factbook 2002

Romania

Government type	Republic
Capital	Bucharest
Language	Romanian, Hungarian, German
Ethnic groups	Romanian, Hungarian, Roma, German, Ukrainian
Religion	Romanian Orthodox, Roman Catholic, Protestant
Major industries	Textiles, footwear, light machinery, auto assembly, mining, timber, construction materials, metallurgy, chemicals, food processing, petroleum, refining

Sources: National Geographic Atlas of the World Seventh Edition, CIA The World Factbook 2002

Russia

Government type	Federation
Capital	Moscow
Language	Russian
Ethnic groups	Russian, Tatar, Ukrainian, Chuvash, Bashkir, Belarusian, Moldavian
Religion	Russian Orthodox
Major industries	Complete range of mining and extractive industries producing coal, oil, gas, chemicals, and metals; all forms of machine building from rolling mills to high-performance aircraft and space vehicles; shipbuilding; road and rail transportation equipment; communications equipment; agricultural machinery, tractors, and construction equipment; electric power generating and transmitting equipment; medical and scientific instruments; consumer durables, textiles, foodstuffs, handicrafts

Sources: National Geographic Atlas of the World Seventh Edition, CIA The World Factbook 2002

References

Bentele, G., & Peter, G. M. (1996). Public relations in the German Democratic Republic and the New Federal German States. In H. Culbertson & N. Chen (Eds.), *International public relations: A comparative analysis* (pp. 349–365). Mahwah, NJ: Lawrence Erlbaum Associates.

Dozier, D. (1992). The organizational roles of communications and public relations practitioners. In J. E. Grunig (Ed.), *Excellence in public relations and communication management* (pp. 327–355). Hillsdale, NJ: Lawrence Erlbaum Associates.

Eurunion.org/profile/brief.htm (2002). [Accessed August 19, 2002].

Grunig, J. E., & Hunt, T. (1984). *Managing public relations* (Chapter 2). New York: Holt, Rinehart, & Winston.

Hofstede, G. (2001). *Culture's consequences: Comparing values, behaviors, institutions, and organizations across nations.* Thousand Oaks, CA: Sage.

Karadjov, C., Kim, Y., & Karavasilev, L. (2000). Models of public relations in Bulgaria and job satisfactions among its practitioner. *Public Relations Review, 26*(2), 209–218.

L'Etang, J. (1999). Public relations education in Britain: An historical review in the context of professionalization. *Public Relations Review, 25*(3), 261–289.

Morgan, D. (1999). *The European Parliament, mass media, and the search for power and influence.* Aldershot, England: Ashgate.

Sriramesh, K. (1996). Power distance and public relations: An ethnographic study of southern Indian organizations. In H. Culbertson & N. Chen (Eds.), *International public relations: A comparative analysis* (pp. 171–190). Mahwah, NJ: Lawrence Erlbaum Associates.

Taylor, M. (2000a). Media relations in Bosnia: A role for public relations in building civil society. *Public Relations Review, 26*(1), 1–14.

Taylor, M. (2000b). Cultural variance as a challenge to global public relations: A case study of the Coca-Cola scare in Europe. *Public Relations Review, 26*(3), 277–293.

Turk, J. (1996). Romania: From publicitate past to public relations future. In H. Culbertson & N. Chen (Eds.), *International public relations: A comparative analysis* (pp. 341–347). Mahwah, NJ: Lawrence Erlbaum Associates.

Van Leuven, J. (1996). Public relations in South East Asia from nation-building campaigns to regional interdependence. In H. Culbertson & N. Chen (Eds.), *International public relations: A comparative analysis* (pp. 207–222). Mahwah, NJ: Lawrence Erlbaum Associates.

Verčič, D., Grunig, L., & Grunig, J. E. (1996). Global and specific principles of public relations: Evidence from Slovenia. In H. Culbertson & N. Chen (Eds.), *International public relations: A comparative analysis* (pp. 31–65). Mahwah, NJ: Lawrence Erlbaum Associates.

6

Public Relations in Slovenia

Transition, Change, and Excellence[1]

James E. Grunig

Larissa A. Grunig

Dejan Verčič

Key Points

- Slovenia, which was part of Yugoslavia until 1991, provides an example of transitional public relations in Eastern Europe—using public relations to help solve problems typical of countries changing from socialist planned economies and single-party communist rule to market economies and democratic government.

- Before its independence, Slovenia was a part of the Holy Roman Empire, the Habsburg (Austro-Hungarian) Empire, the Kingdom of Yugoslavia, and communist Yugoslavia.

- Throughout its history, Slovenia has been one of the most prosperous regions of Central and Eastern Europe. This prosperity has provided a fertile setting for the development of public relations.

- Although public relations did not develop formally until about 1990, a number of public relations-like activities can be found throughout the history of Slovenia. These included the initial development of the practice during socialist times and the use of public relations tools to break from Yugoslavia.

- Slovenian public relations practitioners developed the infrastructure for a profession beginning in the early 1990s, including a professional society, courses for practitioners, university education, and both scholarly and applied research.

- A small group of Slovenian public relations scholars and practitioners have searched throughout the world to learn advanced public relations principles and practices and have made important contributions to the advancement of public relations themselves.

- Pristop Communications, the largest public relations firm in Slovenia, has demonstrated that advanced generic principles of excellent public relations can be applied in the Slovenian context.

- In spite of the advanced state of some public relations practice in Slovenia, public relations has disseminated slowly to organizations in the country, and much Slovenian practice still is characterized by limited and confused concepts and a lack of qualified professionals.

On June 25, 1991, Slovenia declared its independence from Yugoslavia. Two days later, Yugoslavia sent a small army force into Slovenia, which Slovenia defeated in a well-planned ten-day war. As part of its preparation for the war, Slovenia "provided invitations and facilities for the Western media to base themselves in Ljubljana [the capital of Slovenia] rather than Belgrade [the capital of Yugoslavia]" (Lampe, 2000, p. 370). During the war, these media reported that Yugoslavian air strikes at the border "killed several foreign truck drivers, thus inflicting the first in the long series of black eyes shown immediately to the wider world on television" (p. 370). This negative media coverage of the war played a role in the decision of the Yugoslav leadership to abandon Slovenia and formally acknowledge its independence on July 18, 1991.

Public relations, therefore, played a role in helping Slovenia become a sovereign nation for the first time. Slovenians, like their former Yugoslav partners the Croats and Serbs, are South Slavs (the name "Yugoslavia" means South Slavia), descended from Slavs who migrated southwest into the region beginning in the sixth century (Lampe, 2000, p. 14). Their language is similar to, but distinct from, the Serbo-Croatian language. Although Croatia and Serbia were independent political entities in medieval times, Slovenians were dominated by German feudal lords from the eighth century on and then by the Austrian Habsburg empire until the end of World War I. Slovenia became a part of the Kingdom of Yugoslavia after World War I (the first Yugoslavia) and then became a constituent republic of communist Yugoslavia after World War II (the second Yugoslavia).

Slovenia has a population of nearly 2 million people (about the same population as the Seattle metropolitan area). It is slightly larger in size than New Jersey (20.296 square kilometers). The contribution of transportation services alone to the U.S. gross domestic product (GDP) equals Slovenia's total GDP of U.S.$21 billion. It is located in the middle of Europe between Austria, Croatia, Hungary, and Italy. From its capital, Ljubljana, it takes two and one-half hours to drive by car to Venice, Italy, or five to Vienna, Austria. When Slovenia gained its independence from Yugoslavia, it also began a transformation from a closed to an open society.

Slovenia is part of what was until recently called "Eastern Europe"—a term that developed after the Yalta Conference that ended World War II (Csaba, 1993). To most Americans, it means the world east of what Winston Churchill in his address March 5, 1946, at Westminster College named the "iron curtain." The World Bank Development Report for 1996 classified Eastern Europe as composed of the Central and Eastern European (CEE) countries of Albania, Bosnia and Herzegovina, Bulgaria, Croatia, the Czech Republic, Hungary, the Federal Republic of Yugoslavia, the former Yugoslav Republic of (FYR)

Macedonia, Poland, Romania, the Slovak Republic, and Slovenia. This classification also included the newly independent states (NIS) that formerly were part of the Soviet Union: Armenia, Azerbaijan, Belarus, Estonia, Georgia, Kazakstan, the Kyrgyz Republic, Latvia, Lithuania, Moldova, Russia, Tajikistan, Turkmenistan, Ukraine, and Uzbekistan (World Bank, 1996).

The European Union (EU) at its meeting December 12–13, 1997, in Luxembourg produced a further distinction between those countries that were politically and economically capable of starting negotiations to enter the EU in a first circle (the Czech Republic, Hungary, Estonia, Poland, and Slovenia); in a second circle (Bulgaria, Latvia, Lithuania, Romania, and the Slovak Republic); and the rest, which are for political or economic reasons (or both) considered still unacceptable for EU membership.

Major (1993) said that, despite their differences, Eastern European countries have one feature in common: "[T]he focus of power struggles and of economic transformation is the reallocation of property rights, including, first of all, privatization of the state-owned property" (pp. 1–2). This feature results in many small changes that have profound consequences. Since starting his public relations career in the early 1990s, for example, one of the authors of this chapter, Dejan Verčič, has been involved in the transition of his home territory from one country to another (the Yugoslav Federal Republic of Slovenia became the independent Republic of Slovenia), the change of currency (from Yugoslav Dinar to Slovenian Tolar), political system (from a one-party "people's democracy" to a multiparty parliamentary democracy), economic system (from socialist self-government to market economy), social system (from a closed to an open society), privatization of formerly "social-owned" capital, denationalization of the property that was nationalized under socialism, and internationalization of the economy into a broader European and global market.

Polish public relations scholar Ryszard Ławniczak (2001) described public relations in Central and Eastern European countries as "transition public relations"—public relations that helps organizations adapt to the change from a planned economy to capitalism and from socialism to democracy. Transition public relations, in particular, helps state-owned companies manage the process of privatization, privately owned businesses gain support for private ownership, government agencies introduce new instruments such as the value added tax (VAT) or pension reform, and foreign companies deal with prejudices against foreign capital or foreign ownership.

Ławniczak (2001) described three main tasks for transition public relations for the countries in the former Eastern Europe:

- "Firstly, to reverse the fears of and prejudices toward 'ruthless capitalism' instilled during the socialist era" and to build "capitalism with a human face" (pp. 14–15). The average Polish citizen, he said, associates capitalism with unemployment; the lack of a welfare safety net; social inequalities; monopolistic practices; and foreign capital, which is part of a plan to take over the country.
- "Secondly, to create public awareness of the wide range of possible alternative market economy models and of the fact that both in Poland and in other formerly socialist countries a struggle is currently under way to determine the final shape of the market economy by promoting value systems and lifestyles along with products and services" (p. 15).

- "Thirdly, to facilitate effective functioning of the market economy" by promoting entrepreneurship and the process of privatization, attracting foreign capital, and enabling domestic businesses "to participate in the process of creating a market economy" (p. 15).

Zavrl and Verčič (1995) emphasized the importance of change for transition public relations in Central and Eastern Europe. They quoted Edward L. Bernays who they said described public relations in the "very first book about public relations" written in the 1920s "as an applied social science with a capacity to bring order out of the chaos of accelerating social changes people have had a problem dealing with" (p. 21). They added:

> If that were so in the 1920s in the USA, it is even more so in the 1990s in Central and Eastern Europe. For individuals, groups, organisations, and even governments, events and processes in the region resemble chaos more than anything else: small interventions cause big results, without anybody being able to predict the final outcome. . . .
>   Who needs public relations today in Central and Eastern Europe? A very practical answer is: everybody—all kinds of organisations, both domestic and foreign, including governmental and paragovernmental agencies. (p. 21)

In the transitional societies of the former Eastern Europe, many of these types of organizations are tempted to use public relations to try to asymmetrically impose their idea of change on the publics who are affected by the change. Public relations has important power effects. It is easy to see the outcomes in a win–lose matrix. However, by playing a zero-sum power game the personal and public relationships needed as a background condition for present and future relations may easily be destroyed. Organizations create publics when their actions have consequences for other organizations or groupings of people (J. Grunig, 1997; J. Grunig & Hunt, 1984). Often, the consequences of organizational decisions fall on people who were not part of the decision-making process but who suffer the effects economists term "externalities" (Verčič, 1994; Verčič & J. Grunig, 2000).

Privatization and other changes that occur in societies in transition have many such externalities, and public relations professionals must help organizational decision makers manage their impact (Kaur, 1997). In Western countries, publics tend to develop into activist groups that limit the effectiveness of organizations (L. Grunig, 1992a; L. Grunig, 1992b). Publics in Eastern European countries have tended to suffer the effects of externalities without organizing into activist groups, but that is changing rapidly. Even if publics do not organize into activist groups, however, organizations have the social responsibility of reducing the impact of their decisions on publics and of including publics in the decision-making process.

Barlik (2001) studied government public information campaigns in Poland and Slovenia and concluded that two-way symmetrical communication (public relations based on dialogue and concern for the interests of the other party as well as self-interest) was crucial in these countries:

> Public relations programs relying on a two-way, symmetric flow of information contribute to the systemic transformation in Poland and other Central and Eastern European countries. The main difference lies in the use of active communication with target audiences, the fact that their views are accounted for, and that mutual understanding is sought. The most im-

portant goal of information programs that public relations firms conduct for state authorities should be to build two-way communication with target audiences and to ask their opinions not only on how effectively to realize programs forced upon them, but also to discuss such programs before making decisions. Programs aimed at promoting certain interests or "selling" certain opinions belong to the field of advertising and marketing rather than public relations. (p. 141)

Slovenia provides an excellent example of how public relations should be practiced in a transitional Central and Eastern European country. First, Slovenia provided a context in which public relations could thrive. Several years ago, Thurow (1993) predicted that Slovenia would be the most successful of the countries that used to make up Yugoslavia. The *Economist* (1997a) confirmed his prediction and noted that "Slovenia has remained the most prosperous country in ex-communist Europe" (p. 45; see also *Economist,* 1997b).

Second, and perhaps most important, Slovenian public relations professionals have demonstrated that they could import the most excellent public relations practices from developed countries and apply them in the context of a developing country. In addition, they have shown that educated professionals in a developing country could improve on the imported practices and, therefore, play a leading role in the development of enhanced public relations principles worldwide. The key to this success has been access to and development of a sophisticated body of theoretical knowledge—a body of knowledge missing from public relations practice in most countries.

We begin the discussion of how Slovenia became a laboratory for excellent public relations by looking at the historical context of this innovative little country. Understanding the history of Slovenia will provide perspective for understanding its contemporary public relations problems and opportunities. In addition, Slovenia's history reveals forms of public relations that existed in the country long before the term "public relations" was first used. In the United States, public relations historians and other scholars have debated when the practice of the function actually began. Some trace its origins to ancient times—to, for example, early Greek and Roman philosophers, Moses, and Jesus. Although communication activities were not called "public relations," they played a major role in the U.S. Revolutionary War. Others argue that the history of public relations did not begin until specialists began to call themselves public relations practitioners or similar names such as press agents or publicists. That history did not begin until the late nineteenth century.

In Slovenia, similarly, communication practices that J. Grunig and Hunt (1984) called "public relations-like activities in history" (p. 14) can be traced to the Early Middle Ages, probably before the year 1000 (Gruban, Verčič, & Zavrl, 1994). However, public relations in Slovenia, called by that name, did not begin until 1990 when practitioners started to call themselves so, organized into a professional society, and developed public relations education. There was no "public relations" in Eastern Europe before 1989 because the concept was not acceptable for socialism (see Gruban et al., 1994; Ivanov, 1993).

Historical Context of Public Relations in Slovenia

Since the breakup of the former Yugoslavia began in 1991, the world has heard a great deal about ethnic hatred and wars among Serbs, Croats, Bosnian Muslims, and Kosovar

Albanians in seven of the eight former federal units of Yugoslavia (Bennett, 1995, p. 233). Slovenia, however, has been notably absent from these conflicts since its ten-day war in 1991. Bennett explained:

> Slovenia has emerged virtually unscathed from the carnage and can look to the future with confidence. Indeed, given the devastation and despair in so much of the former Yugoslavia, it is almost as though Slovenia never belonged to the same country. However, the contrast should not come as too great a surprise since Slovenia has always been a special case. With Slovenes making up more than 90 per cent of the republic's population, the danger of ethnic strife was minimal. Moreover, in the absence of a Serb minority, Slovenia could not be a target for Serb nationalists and never formed part of the Greater Serbian vision of Yugoslavia. (p. 233)

Slovenians have long been the most prosperous of the South Slavs that made up Yugoslavia. In the middle of the nineteenth century, when Slovenians were under the control of the Habsburg (Austro-Hungarian) Empire, the Slovenian peasants, "once known for their poverty and backwardness," became "the most prosperous and literate among the South Slavs" (Benson, 2001, p. 16). In 1973, according to Bennett (1995), Slovenia's *"per capita* income was roughly double the Yugoslav average" (p. 102); and its unemployment was zero. In the 1980s, Slovenia had "the highest standard of living" and "by far the lowest unemployment" of the Yugoslav republics (Lampe, 2000, p. 349). Slovenia was paying for "one-quarter of the federal [Yugoslav] budget with only 8 percent of the population" (p. 350). Nevertheless, high inflation and increasing unemployment throughout Yugoslavia caused Slovenia's rate of economic growth to fall sharply by the mid-1980s (p. 349). Lampe added, "Improving connections with neighboring Austria, Italy, and Hungary seemed a better way to revive that growth than to respond to Belgrade's call for closer economic integration with the rest of Yugoslavia" (pp. 349–350).

In addition to their prosperity, Slovenians managed to retain their language, culture, and identity through centuries of domination by other ethnic groups or membership in different kingdoms or empires. Lampe (2000) explained that during the period between 800 and 1800:

> The medieval model for political integration in Southeastern Europe was a loosely structured, ethnically indistinct kingdom or empire, rather than a centralized state based on national identity. Such nation states were not conceivable before early modern England and France finished what Henry V and Joan of Arc set out to do in the fifteenth century. (p. 14)

Slovenia in Imperial Times

In medieval times, there were independent states of Croatia, Serbia, and Bosnia, but the Slovenians were dominated by the Frankish Germans and never established a state (Lampe, 2000, p. 14). Lampe added that "the populations of such medieval polities surely attached more importance . . . to their religious identity in newly accepted Christian churches than to brief native states" (p. 14). Slovenians and Croats were part of the Holy Roman (Catholic) Empire and the Serbs part of the Byzantine (Orthodox) Empire. Fewer than one hundred years after they converted to Christianity in the eighth century, the Slovenians fell under the domination of the Frankish feudal lords who ruled the Holy Roman Empire (p. 29).

During this time, the earliest public relations-like activities took place in Slovenia—in the form of persuasive writings. The first persuasive writings in the Slovenian language were the Freising Records, written before the year 1000 when Slovenia was part of the Holy Roman Empire. The Diocese of Freising included the Slovenian provinces of Carniola and Carinthia. According to Gruban and colleagues (1994), the Records (written by Ambraham, the bishop of Freising who died in 994) were a "traveling bishop's manual" that represents "the oldest known record of persuasive speech in the Slovene language" (p. 10).

The religious empires were succeeded by the Austrian Habsburg and Turkish Ottoman empires. The Habsburg family succeeded the Franks as emperors of the Holy Roman Empire, ruled that empire from 1438 to 1806, and then continued to rule after the Roman Empire fell. The Habsburg and Ottoman empires ruled the northern and southern parts, respectively, of what became Yugoslavia until these empires were destroyed at the time of World War I. As Benson (2001) explained:

> It took the destruction of two great empires to make room for the formation of the Kingdom of the Serbs, Croats, and Slovenes in 1918, a new state created out of the marcher [border] lands straddling the Ottoman and Habsburg dominions. The histories of the Slav tribes settled south of the Danube have diverged since earliest times, when the power of the Byzantium won the Serbs for the Orthodox rite, while the Croats and Slovenes adhered to Rome. (p. 1)

In the early sixteenth century in Slovenia, a sizable Protestant movement developed that was suppressed by the Habsburg rulers in Vienna. According to Lampe (2000): "Luther's tenets attracted Slovene and German adherents, first in the towns and then in the countryside. They openly opposed the authority of the established Catholic hierarchy. Jesuit zeal and military force soon suppressed them" (p. 29). This Protestant movement was led by Primož Trubar, who used public relations principles to lead the movement.

According to Gruban and colleagues (1994), Trubar (who lived from 1508 to 1586) was "not only the first renowned Slovenian great communicator but also the first author to have written on the importance of communications" (p. 10). Trubar, they explained, was "equally significant for Slovenians as Demosthenes was for the ancient Greeks, Caesar for the Romans, and Abraham Lincoln for Americans" (p. 10). He founded Protestantism in Slovenia and "was so successful in propagating the Protestant ideas that he was first persecuted and then banished from Slovenia to Germany" (p. 10).

According to Lampe (2000), political disarray and economic backwardness characterized the South Slavic region in the period from 800 to 1800. Its small population was spread across a difficult landscape: "Yet where they were intermingled, they coexisted constructively. There is scant evidence of the long-standing ethnic hostility that some journalists and politicians, but few scholars, have used to explain the recent warfare on the ruins of the second Yugoslav state" (p. 9).

Although Slovenians were under the control of the Habsburg Empire, their population was "scattered among six Austrian provinces or territories, most with German or Italian ethnic minorities" (Lampe, 2000, p. 69). Slovenians had a majority of the population in only two of these provinces, Carniola and Carinthia (Benson, 2001, p. 16). The largest Slovenian population was in Carniola, where today's capital of Slovenia, Ljubljana, is located. Nevertheless, according to Lampe (2000), "Not until the eighteenth century, however, did one Slovene scholar, Tomas Linhart, reject the lingering view that the Slovenes were ethnically German themselves and had no separate Slovene identity" (p. 29).

In 1867, the Ausgleich (compromise) between Vienna and Budapest created a dual monarchy within the Austro-Hungarian Empire. This compromise placed the Slovenians under the control of Austria rather than Hungary and protected Slovenians from the "aggressive language policy of Budapest" (Benson, 2001, p. 16) that had attempted, for example, to force Croats to speak Hungarian. In 1882, Slovenians won "an electoral majority in the Diet of Carniola and in Ljubljana itself" (p. 16). Mostly, however, Slovenians wanted to protect their language and culture:

> This limited political advance, coupled with some well-timed cultural concessions, mollified Slovene opinion, and Slovenian nationalism remained at heart a social movement aimed at greater acceptance of the use of the Slovene language in education and administration. It is not clear that the principle of nationality—the idea that nationals ought to occupy a defined territorial space with their own state—was something that the Slovenes seriously applied to themselves. (p. 16)

Between 1868 and 1871, however, Slovenians began to flirt with the idea of a South Slav province that would include Slovenians, Croats, and Serbs. According to Lampe (2000), a small group of Slovenians drafted a proposal, the Maribor Program, for "a single Slovene entity within the Habsburg monarchy" (p. 69). The proposal "had no practical prospects," Lampe added, "but the idea of a larger, South Slav province began to attract large crowds to a series [of] mass political meetings called *tabori,* or town meetings" (p. 70).

The *tabori,* according to Gruban and colleagues (1994), were held as part of a political program called "United Slovenia." The program demanded that all Slovenians in the Austro-Hungarian Empire be joined into one administrative unit, that the Slovenian language be given equal status with other languages, that there would be a Slovenian university, and that solutions should be found for local educational and economic problems. The largest *tabor,* held in 1971 near Ljubljana, attracted thirty thousand demonstrators. Gruban and colleagues (1994) explained: "All of these events have the same significance for Slovenia's history of persuasive communication as does the American Revolution to the American history of persuasive communication. The slogan United Slovenia can be compared to the slogan, 'no taxation without representation' and *tabori* to the famous Boston Tea Party" (p. 10). This was the largest campaign in Slovenian history, and *tabori,* according to Gruban and colleagues were the first pseudoevents in Slovenia—events that take place only for publicity purposes.

The First Yugoslavia

At the beginning of the twentieth century, Lampe (2000) added, "the uneven pace of accelerating economic modernization made the lack of Slovenian political leverage within the Austrian half of the Dual Monarchy more painful" (p. 70). At that time, the idea of a Yugoslavia became more attractive to Slovenians; and they played a major role as mediators between the Serbs and Croats in order to bring it about. As Lampe put it, "Yugoslavia began and ended with Slovenia" (p. 3).

Serbia had gained its independence from the Ottoman Empire during the nineteenth century, according to Lampe (2000), and developed a modern army, civilian government bureaucracy, and "a political culture that was based on more independent experience than any of the other South Slav peoples" (p. 47). Serbia won two Balkan wars with Turkey and Bulgaria in 1912 and 1913, which "fanned Croatian and Slovenian enthusiasm anew for some Yugoslav state" (p. 91). It took World War I to destroy the Austro-Hungarian Empire, however, and make the creation of Yugoslavia possible.

On June 28, 1914, a Bosnian Serb assassinated the heir to the Habsburg throne, Archduke Franz Ferdinand, in the Bosnian capital of Sarajevo. "Austria-Hungary declared war on Serbia a month later (28 July)," according to Benson (2001), "triggering the general European conflict, which was to obliterate the second imperial obstacle to South Slav unification" (p. 20). In 1915, Serbia and a committee of Croatian and Slovenian exiles, the Yugoslav Committee, declared that their goal for the war was to create "some sort of South Slav state" (Lampe, 2000, p. 102). In 1917, they signed an agreement, the Corfu Declaration, to create a kingdom of Serbs, Croats, and Slovenes ruled by the Serbian monarchy (p. 105). The new kingdom was recognized by the Allied powers (including the United States), the winners of World War I, at the Paris Peace Conference in 1919. A constitution was ratified in 1921, officially bringing the new country into being (p. 127). The first king, Aleksandar, "redesignated the Kingdom of Serbs, Croats, and Slovenes as the Kingdom of Yugoslavia" in 1929 (p. 163).

As described in Lampe's (2000) history of Yugoslavia, the new kingdom shared power between an elected parliament and the king from 1921 to 1929, when King Aleksandar assumed all power and created a dictatorial, authoritarian kingdom. Aleksandar was assassinated by the chauffeur of the leader of a Macedonian terrorist, separatist organization in 1934 and replaced by his cousin Prince Paul and two other senior regents. They were supposed to hold power until Aleksandar's son Petar reached his eighteenth birthday in September 1941. In March 1941, however, the Yugoslav government joined the Tripartite Agreement among Germany, Japan, and Italy—after resisting German pressure to join. Two days later, a military coup overthrew the government. Lampe explained the consequences: "The March 27 coup and Hitler's immediate decision to 'destroy the Yugoslav state as it currently exists' signaled the end of the first Yugoslavia even though German forces did not invade until April 6" (p. 200).

According to Lampe (2000), the first Yugoslavia faced a number of problems. It had to integrate the economies and legal systems of the former Habsburg provinces with those of Serbia. It also had to unify "Orthodox, Catholic, and Muslim religious communities from previously separate jurisdictions" (p. 129). It was successful, however, in "celebrating the cultural affinities" (p. 129) of the Serbs, Croats, and Slovenes. Most importantly, especially for Slovenia, the first Yugoslavia created a large, integrated economy.

Toward the end of the first Yugoslavia, specialized media and company publications appeared in Slovenia—early forms of what J. Grunig and Hunt (1984) called the public information model of public relations. Beginning in 1943, according to Gruban and colleagues (1994), the first specialized publications were published. These included *Agricultural and Handicraft News* (a popular science paper) and *Young Learner* (for children). In 1937, industrial journalism began, including such publications as *Our Metal*

Worker, Factory Gazette of the Industrial Society of Kranj, and *Gazette of the Laško Brewery Ltd.*

The Second Yugoslavia

During World War II, the Nazis destroyed virtually "all existing institutions" in Yugoslavia (Lampe, 2000, p. 201). The Germans invaded Serbia and installed the fascist Ustaša government in Croatia. Slovenia was divided between Italy and Germany. About 1 million Yugoslavs out of a population of 16 million people died in the war (Benson, 2001, p. 73). This destruction of Yugoslavia allowed the communist Partisans, led by Josip Broz Tito, to champion resistance to Germany and Italy; win a civil war against the Chetniks, who supported restoration of the Kingdom of Yugoslavia; and take power in 1945 (p. 75). Tito's government, according to Lampe (2000), originally followed the Stalinist model of the Soviet Union of centralized, hierarchical communist party control. After Tito broke away from Stalin and the Soviet bloc in 1948, however, the second Yugoslavia developed "a new theory of decentralized socialism" (p. 233). Tito was a Croat, born near the border of Croatia and Slovenia. He led Yugoslavia as the head of the League of Yugoslav Communists and then as president until his death in 1980.

The second Yugoslavia lasted almost twice as long as the first. Compared with other East European countries, Lampe (2000) said, Yugoslavia "became a more open and better place to live than anywhere in the nearby bloc" (p. 265). Government was more decentralized than in other communist countries, and Worker Enterprise Councils provided workers a system of self-management. The economy had more features of a market economy than in other socialist countries. And, according to Lampe:

> the regime granted some real breathing space to intellectual freedom by the 1960s. Educational standards rose, a more open if still monitored media began to have an impact, and the free expression of opinion and the practice of religion benefited from significant concessions. Urban culture prospered, its audience swollen by rural migration to the main cities. Ethnic mixing, exposure to Western training, and easier access for women buoyed most professions. (p. 266)

The partial introduction of a market economy and the Yugoslav variant of socialism, worker self-management, resulted in a form of business communication called "contacts with the public," which was another kind of public relations-like activity in Slovenian history. A textbook on the subject defined contacts with the public in this way, according to Gruban and colleagues (1994): " 'In self-management, contacts with the public differs from capitalist or communist public relations in ideology above all; however, it includes all the general elements of the activity necessary in a market economy.' The same textbook defined 'the number and positions of communists' in the organization as one of the major factors to be considered when preparing a business plan" (p. 12). Contacts with the public also was a function to be carried out by trade unions rather than by management. At the beginning of the 1970s, the largest Slovenian organizations reorganized their information and propaganda departments into departments of contacts with the public. In the period before Slovenian independence, however, the Yugoslav government removed many of the technocratic managers of Slovenian companies and removed departments of contacts with the public at the same time.

Yugoslavia had its greatest economic successes in the 1960s; and, in the words of Verčič (2000b), those years also were "a 'liberal' period in communist Yugoslavia" (p. 26). During this liberal decade, public relations was introduced as "a possible area of interest for social scientists and academic educators" (p. 26). According to Verčič, communication science was first institutionalized in Yugoslavia at universities in Ljubljana in 1966, Belgrade (the capital of Serbia and Yugoslavia) in 1969, and Zagreb (the capital of Croatia) in 1969. The founder of communication science at the University of Ljubljana, France Vreg, developed an interest in public relations: "On one of his visits to the U.S. universities, [Vreg] met Scott Cutlip and even started translating the second edition of his textbook *Effective Public Relations* (Cutlip & Center, 1960)" (p. 26).

The flirtation with public relations education ended, however, when the liberal period of Yugoslav communism ended. Verčič (2000b) described the rise and fall of public relations education in socialist Slovenia:

> Prof. Dr. Vreg was not alone in his interest in public relations at the UL [University of Ljubljana]. In the early 1970s, Mr. Pavle Zrimšek, MSc, who was a lecturer at the same department of communication, translated into Slovenian a German text on public relations by Hundhausen (1969). . . .
>
> In the early 1970s, everything was prepared for the introduction of public relations as a separate academic subject to be taught at the Faculty of Sociology, Political Science and Journalism (now Faculty of Social Sciences, FSS) at the UL. A teaching curriculum was prepared to be submitted to the academic authorities. Then came a political reaction that followed a broader conservative wave in Yugoslavia removing pro-liberal politicians (and university professors) from their offices. Prof. Dr. Vreg was criticized for his pro-Western "leanings," and one of the results of that criticism was the abolishment of the idea to introduce public relations at the UL. Public relations was explicitly ascribed the status of politically incorrect and unacceptable in the context of Yugoslav socialism (in contrast to advertising and marketing that were not politically stigmatized and had been developing at the UL since the mid-1970s). This was the end of that chapter in the history of public relations research and education in Slovenia. (pp. 26–27)

By the time public relations became established as a profession in Slovenia, just before and after its independence in 1991, both Vreg and Zrimšek had retired. However, in the foreword to a special issue of *Pristop* magazine on public relations in Slovenia published in 1994, Vreg (1994) described his 1960s theories of public relations in terms that public relations theorists in the twenty-first century call symmetrical public relations (e.g., J. Grunig, 2001).

In 1994, Vreg said: "This new discipline [public relations] is establishing itself during a time of emerging democratization. Along with political pluralism, parliamentary democracy, and [a] market economy, new structures of publics and public opinion are becoming relevant. These are the ground on which Public Relations can grow" (p. 4). Vreg explained that at the beginning of the 1960s, he had met several U.S. communication and public relations theorists and had tried to introduce their ideas in Slovenia. "I learned," he said, "that the ground at home was not ready for this kind of thinking. In those ideologically poisoned times it was heretical to write even that 'public activity of many public persons stops behind closed doors of conferences and other meetings' " (p. 4), which he had written in the Slovenian social science journal *Teorija in praksa* (Theory and practice).

In the article in *Teorija in praksa,* Vreg (1994) said, "I introduced into communication science in Slovenia at that time a model of 'horizontal communication and reciprocal vertical communications,' what public relations theory today terms as a symmetrical model of two-way communication" (p. 4). Vreg described public relations in terms that, first, reflected the German philosopher Jurgen Habermas' concept of an ideal communication situation: "The substance of the discipline is communicative interaction of participants in a situation which presupposes communicative competence of all participants" (p. 4). Second, he described public relations in symmetrical language:

> And here is the place for institutions of public relations. They must assure understanding between partners, build mutual trust, truthfulness and reliability (credibility) of messages, put away misunderstanding on an intersubjective level (different interpretations of messages), establish empathic dialogue (role taking and mutual development of expectations), solve interactual and interest conflicts (what some pragmatically call management of conflicts) and develop human relations.
>
> Such two-way reciprocal processes can be developed only by mediators, who are professionally educated, who open communication channels, explain, identify, persuade and negotiate. They must develop abilities for empathy, sensibility, flexibility, tolerance, high motivation and interactive experience. (p. 4)

Just as a conservative communist reaction killed public relations theories of the 1960s in Slovenia that were similar to contemporary theories, so Yugoslavia's economic successes in the 1960s gave way to an economic decline that began just before Tito's death in 1980, became severe in the 1980s, and eventually led to the end of Yugoslavia. According to Lampe (2000), unemployment increased, real earnings declined, and the annual rate of inflation "passed 100 percent" (p. 299). Hyperinflation reached 2,500 percent in 1989 (p. 355). Benson (2001) added: "Economic ruin, and the absence of a democratic framework within which the federation could evolve, killed off the second Yugoslavia" (p. 132).

Independence for Slovenia

After Tito's death, the Yugoslav government was headed by the chair of a Federal Executive Council, who was elected by the National Assembly to a four-year term and acted as prime minister, and a collective presidency with members from each republic and autonomous province (Lampe, 2000, p. 326). Members of the federal league of Communists dominated these bodies. By 1990, however, a single federal league had ceased to exist and only separate Leagues of Communists in each of the republics remained. By 1990, according to Bennett (1995):

> The existing state apparatus remained intact by default since nothing had emerged to replace it, yet clearly it had become anachronistic given the demise of the LCY [League of Communists of Yugoslavia]. The country was in a sort of limbo-land and Yugoslavs were conscious this state of affairs could not be permanent. The form a third Yugoslavia might take was the subject of debate and speculation in every republic. (p. 114)

During 1990, Bennett (1995) said, "three blueprints for Yugoslavia's future were on the table" (p. 115). The federal prime minister, Croatian Ante Marković, whom Lampe

(2000) described as "a more constructive leader" (p. 352), thought he could maintain Yugoslavia by improving the economy. However, according to Lampe, "he could not forge the political consensus needed to maintain support" (p. 352). Lampe added: "The post-Tito power vacuum at the federal level had already opened the way for leaders of the republic parties to assert themselves. In 1986, two younger men seized this chance—Milan Kučan of Slovenia and Slobodan Milošević of Serbia" (p. 332). Kučan and Slovenia wanted to make Yugoslavia a loose confederation of republics. The now-infamous Milošević and Serbia wanted to recentralize it under Serb control.

Milošević had four of the eight votes in support of his plan (Serbia, the autonomous Serbian provinces of Vojvodina and Kosovo, and Montenegro). Kučan, Lampe (2000) said, "could not bring the other four votes—Bosnia-Hercegovina, Croatia, and Macedonia, plus Slovenia—to agree on a common alternative" (p. 332). At the same time, according to Bennett (1995), Serbian media were stirring up ethnic hatred by claiming that Serbs had been "mercilessly exploited and persecuted in Tito's Yugoslavia" (p. 115). Milošević also "renewed efforts to destabilize the four federal units outside his control by stirring up the Serb communities there" (p. 115). In this context, Slovenians decided that their economic and political interests would be served better by independence than continued association with Yugoslavia. As Lampe (2000) pointed out, Yugoslavia was able to begin because it supported Slovenian interests; and it ended when it no longer served those interests. Without Slovenia, Yugoslavia could no longer hold together.

Several features of Slovenia's break from Yugoslavia are important for understanding the subsequent development of the public relations profession. First was the emergence of what Lampe (2000) called "a youth culture which emerged as a social movement" (p. 350). Student leaders at the University of Ljubljana and editors of the youth magazine *Mladina* were instrumental in challenging the Yugoslav federal order. Among these young people were Dejan Verčič and Franci Zavrl, two of the three founders of the first public relations firm in Slovenia, the PR Center, which eventually became a part of Pristop Communications. Zavrl, along with Janez Janša (who became defense minister at the time of Slovenia's ten-day war), were among a group of journalists and an army officer sentenced to prison (Gruban et al., 1994) for publishing a list of prominent Slovenians whom Lampe said supposedly would be arrested in case of a military emergency (p. 351).

According to Gruban and colleagues (1994), as a result of these arrests thirty-five thousand people demonstrated "against the encroachment of the army upon civilian life and over 100,000 people joined the Committee for the Protection of Janez Janša's rights" (p. 12). These protests, and other events leading to Slovenian independence, included many elements of activism and symmetrical communication—key components of the public relations activities of activist groups in the United States (see, e.g., J. Grunig & L. Grunig, 1997; J. Grunig, 2000). In Gruban and colleague's (1994) words: "Self-organization of people, lateral communications, independence of media, political pluralism, and a market economy brought about awareness of the significance of communication" (p. 12).

Zavrl's experience with the newly independent media during this time prepared him for his eventual role as Pristop's specialist in media relations. Verčič also headed the Slovenian press center, which played a key role in the battle for support from Western media during the events leading up to the war and independence (see Bennett, 1995, p. 162). In general, the youth culture in Slovenia presented an opportunity for young, innovative public relations practitioners to have unusual influence on the profession.

The other key features of Slovenia's break from Yugoslavia that affected the development of public relations were economic in nature. Although the other republics were concerned about divorcing themselves from the Yugoslav economy, Slovenia's economy was relatively detached from the rest of Yugoslavia—accounting for 15 percent of purchases and 21 percent of sales in 1989 (Bennett, 1995, p. 143). In 1990, Serbia had even imposed taxes on what it considered to be Slovenian "exports" to that republic (p. 143). Although Slovenia originally suffered from the loss of Yugoslav markets, it also had improving ties with Austria, Italy, and Hungary. Elements of a market economy had been introduced in Slovenia as early as the 1960s, but according to Bennett, the economy still was planned and it would be necessary to introduce a free-market economy:

> In the wake of economic restructuring a prolonged period of labour unrest and strikes appeared on the cards, with potentially destabilizing political consequences. However, as a result of the war, Slovenes were much better prepared psychologically to deal with the pain of restructuring and, in contrast to the rest of eastern Europe, labour unrest never materialized. War instilled a sense of discipline and national pride in the Slovene labour force which have helped facilitate a remarkably smooth economic transformation. (p. 233)

Slovenia joined the World Bank and the International Monetary Fund in 1993 and is now in the final stages of joining the European Union. Slovenia passed legislation to privatize the economy, which Bennett (1995) said "was supposedly designed to reflect the ownership structure which existed in Yugoslavia under Worker Self-Management but it has also proved fertile ground for a number of business scandals" (p. 234). Thus, Slovenia has had to cope with a number of the changes and the externalities brought about by those changes that are typical in what Ławniczak (2001) called "transition" public relations. As we will see, Slovenian public relations practitioners rose to the challenge admirably.

The Formal Development of Slovenian Public Relations

Throughout the history of Slovenia, we have identified communication activities that resemble contemporary public relations practices. However, public relations began to develop as a profession in Slovenia between 1989 and 1992. In 1989, Dejan Verčič and Franci Zavrl established The PR Center, a company that was later merged into today's largest public relations consultancy, Pristop Communications. On November 12, 1990, seven months before independence, ten people met at the founding meeting of the Public Relations Society of Slovenia (PRSS) (Gruban et al., 1994). Verčič, was among these founding members along with his business partners, Zavrl and Brane Gruban. The first two authors of this chapter, James and Larissa Grunig, soon became friends and collaborators with the Pristop founders and were named honorary members of the Public Relations Society of Slovenia in 1993.

As a result of our participation in the development of Slovenia public relations, we acknowledge that we perceive that development largely through the lens provided by our collaboration. Others might see the development of public relations differently. For example, we said that marketing and its component, marketing communication, were acceptable in socialist times in Slovenia whereas public relations was not. In 1993, two years after Slovenian independence, the PR Institute (the research arm of Pristop) conducted a survey of the largest Slovenian business firms (Gruban et al., 1994, p. 16). Of 255 companies that participated, only sixteen (6.3 percent) had organized public relations functions and only eleven (4.3 percent) had in-house public relations departments. However, 41.5 percent of these companies had marketing departments—including five (2 percent) that had organized public relations as part of marketing departments. The survey also showed that the marketing staff was responsible for communicating with external publics in 22.2 percent of the companies that had no public relations function. (CEOs and their deputies were responsible in 36 percent of these companies.)

Marketing communication has been taught in the Department of Communication at the University of Ljubljana since socialist times, whereas public relations education has struggled to gain acceptance in the university. Until recently, public relations had been taught mostly as a subject within the marketing communication curriculum. Advocates of the integrated marketing approach, which views public relations as part of the marketing function (e.g., Duncan & Caywood, 1996), probably would interpret these facts as showing that public relations developed during the socialist period, and continues to develop, as a component of integrated marketing communication.

This, indeed, was the position taken by Jančič (1994), a former practitioner in the firm Studio Marketing in Ljubljana and a faculty member in the Department of Communication Sciences at the University of Ljubljana. He said that Slovenian companies adopted marketing communication practices in the late 1960s "when in a period of liberalization many companies accepted marketing know-how from multinational partners" (p. 1). He also said that he believes the marketing function subsumes public relations and that Slovenian practitioners in the early 1990s understood public relations in that way. They became confused, he added, when Larissa and James Grunig lectured in Ljubljana in 1992 and argued that public relations was a distinct function from marketing.

In contrast, we believe public relations developed in Slovenia when it was established as a management function separate from marketing. We interpret the development of public relations in this way not to diminish the importance of marketing communication but to establish the idea that marketing communication is one of only many specialized areas of public relations and not synonymous with or the parent of public relations.

The Search for Knowledge and the Development of Professionalism

Many articles have been written about public relations in developing countries in professional publications such as the *Public Relations Journal, International Public Relations Review, Public Relations Quarterly,* and *Communication World.* An example is Black (1990–1991). These articles generally show that public relations practice, at least initially, is hindered by limited and confused concepts and a lack of qualified professionals. It is limited to media relations and marketing communication and confused with advertising and marketing.

Although these problems also occurred in Slovenia, Slovenians quickly reached out to other countries to adopt the most advanced public relations practices and to use the results of public relations research and theory. In addition, Slovenians quickly recognized the need for public relations education and conducted research of their own. This is in contrast to many other countries that adopted public relations practices from developed nations but in doing so adopted the most antiquated and ineffective practices (press agentry, publicity, and "image making")—thinking that is what public relations is about (see, e.g., Ali, 1995; Kaur, 1997; and Scholz, 1998).

Slovenia provides an example of how a country newly practicing public relations can leap to the forefront of practice by searching for and developing knowledge. The search for knowledge began in 1990 when Dejan Verčič and Franc Zavrl visited the Institute of Public Relations in London and several public relations agencies in the United Kingdom. In February 1991, Verčič traveled to the United States on a study tour sponsored by the U.S. Information Agency. During that tour, he met with James and Larissa Grunig in Washington, DC, and began the collaboration and sharing of knowledge that affected both the practice of public relations in Slovenia and the development of public relations knowledge and theory in both countries. The Grunigs visited Slovenia for the first time in January 1992 and gave a public lecture to practitioners.

In 1991, the first booklet on public relations was published in the Slovenian language (Gruban, Maksimovič, Verčič, & Zavrl, 1990); and the Slovenian chapter of the International Public Relations Association (IPRA) was formed. In 1992, Pristop Communications developed a magazine, *Pristop,* the first publication to publish public relations articles in Slovenia. The magazine organized the first roundtable on education in public relations with the participation of the minister of education and sport and the dean of the Faculty of Social Sciences at the University of Ljubljana. By the end of 1992, public relations was well established as a field of practice; and the first seeds for research and education were planted.

The next two years, 1993 and 1994, can be characterized as the search for recognition of the public relations profession. In the summer of 1993, the Grunigs visited Slovenia again for nearly a month and gave the first seminar on public relations at the University of Ljubljana and lectures to a number of organizations throughout Slovenia. The Public Relations Society of Slovenia became a member of the European Confederation of Public Relations (CERP). In 1994, Pristop Communications formed the PR Institute as its research arm and the Ministry of Science and Technology registered it as a research institution. This was the first time that public relations had received recognition by a Slovenian public body regulating scientific work. In that year, Slovenians who were members of the International Association of Business Communicators (IABC) received a charter and formed their own chapter—IABC Slovenia.

Also in 1994, public relations was introduced into the curriculum of marketing communications at the undergraduate level in the Department of Communication at the Faculty of Social Sciences, University of Ljubljana. In that same year students interested in public relations from both the University of Ljubljana and the University of Maribor (the only two universities in Slovenia) organized a student section of the PRSS and became members of CERP Students (the European organization of public relations students). By 1994, therefore, public relations had received full recognition in Slovenia not only as a well-developed practice but also as a subject of scientific and educational interest.

The period since 1995 can be characterized as the time in which public relations became institutionalized in Slovenia in books, journals, and educational institutions. Several examples illustrate that institutionalization. Verčič (1995) successfully defended the first master's thesis in public relations at the Department of Communication. (He has since earned a Ph.D. in social psychology from the London School of Economics and Political Science, completing a dissertation on the effect of media coverage on trust in organizations [Verčič, 2000c]). Hunt and J. Grunig's (1995) *Public Relations Techniques* was translated into Slovenian. In 1997, the first book on public relations written by Slovenian practitioners was published (Gruban, Verčič, & Zavrl). A special issue of *Teorija in praksa,* the major social science journal in Slovenia, was published on organizational communication. In 1998, Gruban, Verčič, & Zavrl edited the first book of readings on public relations in the Slovenian language. Also in 1998, public relations was introduced at the graduate level as an elective subject in the marketing communication program at the University of Ljubljana. In 1999, a second special issue of *Teorija in praksa* on organizational communication was published.

Thus, Slovenian public relations had made major strides toward excellence at the beginning of the twenty-first century. The engine of that excellence has been research and education.

The Development of Slovenian Research on Public Relations

Public relations research in Slovenia began with the collaboration between the largest Slovenian public relations consultancy, Pristop Communications, and James and Larissa Grunig from the University of Maryland in the United States. When Verčič, who is responsible for research and development at Pristop, met the Grunigs during his visit to the United States in 1991, they and four colleagues were beginning a major research project on excellence in public relations and communication management for the IABC Research Foundation (Dozier, 1995; J. Grunig, 1992; L. Grunig, J. Grunig, & Dozier, 2002). Pristop decided to use that study as a benchmark tool, translated the questionnaires developed by the Excellence team, and executed a comparative study—adding Slovenia to the original countries of the Excellence project (the United States, Canada, and the United Kingdom).

In addition to this research, Verčič, in his role as research director at Pristop, began to use a number of U.S. theories in its practice. In doing so, he made important contributions to the development of those theories—helping to truly globalize public relations theory. For example, Pristop began to use J. Grunig's (1997) situational theory of publics as part of its practice. Verčič & Žnuderl (1993) published a conceptual and empirical test of the theory in Slovenia. Verčič (1997) also used the theory in a case study of the Slovenian electrical company, which was faced with several publics with conflicting interests—a study that had original implications for the development and use of the situational theory.

Verčič also made important theoretical contributions when, writing with J. Grunig (Verčič & J. Grunig, 2000), he linked public relations theory to economic and strategic management theories. In particular, he suggested that public relations should be reconceptualized as the management of organizational externalities. In 1998, L. Grunig & Verčič (1998) applied some insights from research on public relations in Slovenia to small countries in general (countries with populations of less than 1 million). They pointed out that in Slovenia, smallness makes public relations personal: "It is very important who you are and whom you know. . . . Everybody personally knows everybody else (there is a joke in Slovenia that sooner or later everybody will get into the parliament). . . . That mixture of private and public relationships personalizes any social question and arranges the social fabric in cliques" (p. 2).

Also in 1998, Verčič began to head a team of researchers to initiate the European Public Relations Body of Knowledge project (for CERP Education and Research, the European Association for Public Relations Research and Education). The goal of the project is to develop a database of public relations literature in as many European languages and from as many European countries as possible.

Pristop did not keep its research and the research it used from other countries to itself, however. It has made a major effort to introduce research to other Slovenian practitioners and to bring the best international public relations researchers to the country. This dissemination began with the first two visits of the Grunigs to Slovenia, when they made presentations to the PRSS, the University of Ljubljana, and Pristop's clients. In 1994, Pristop took another step that not only brought the best public relations research to Slovenian professionals but also established Slovenia as the center of public relations research in Europe. Verčič and collaborators from universities in the United Kingdom organized an International Public Relations Research Symposium at Bled, a picturesque town on a lake in the Slovenian Alps. That conference has been held each year since and has become the premier annual research conference on public relations in Europe.

Academics and practitioners from more than twenty countries on every continent have participated, including a large audience of Slovenian practitioners each year. Conference presentations have been published in two books (Moss, MacManus, & Verčič, 1997; Moss, Verčič, & Warnaby, 2000); in special issues of the *Journal of Communication Management,* which is published in the United Kingdom; and in annual proceedings.

The Development of Public Relations Education

When public relations practice appeared in Slovenia in the early 1990s, education was being developed first by the professionals themselves. At that time, Verčič (1993) estimated that at least four business training centers had organized twenty-four public relations seminars per year. Pristop, itself, was among the organizations offering public relations seminars.

Public relations was introduced to the academic curriculum of students of marketing communication in the Department of Communication Science in 1994. The first lecturer in this subject was Dr. Andrej Škerlep, who still teaches it today. In 1998, public relations was introduced as an elective to graduate students of marketing communication in the same department—also taught by Škerlep. In 1999, business communication (in the sense of corporate communication) was added as a new subject in that same department. In 2001, the title of that subject was changed to communication management, a term that is becoming the most popular name for public relations in Europe.

After completing his doctorate in London in 2000, Verčič also became a part-time faculty member at the University of Ljubljana with the title of assistant professor for public relations and communication management. The educational system in Slovenia allows him to be on a track toward a full professorship even though he is not employed by the university. He is employed by Pristop, and the University of Ljubljana pays Pristop for the time he spends teaching. In 2003, Verčič taught an elective course in communication management to third- and fourth-year undergraduate students within the area of marketing communication. He also taught public relations and communication management to graduate students in American studies in the Faculty of Social Sciences; and, with Škerlep, Verčič teaches public relations to graduate students of marketing communication.

In 1999, the dean of the Faculty of Social Sciences invited professors at the Department of Communication Science to a meeting to explore possibilities of introducing public relations as a separate area of study at the University of Ljubljana. They agreed to start with a postgraduate program, and that program was still awaiting approval in 2003. An undergraduate program would take more time because undergraduate education is fully publicly funded in Slovenia; whereas graduate education is partly or fully funded by the students themselves. For that reason it is much easier to start with a new graduate than with a new undergraduate program. Within the past decade there also were several attempts to introduce public relations to the second Slovenian University, the University of Maribor. They failed primarily because qualified faculty members were not available to teach the subject.

In little more than a decade, therefore, Slovenia not only established a twenty-first century public relations practice but it also assumed a leadership role in the discipline. Slovenians have won many awards from IPRA and IABC. Their research is at the cutting edge in Europe and the world. In the next two sections, we look closer at that practice.

Normative and Positive Practice of Public Relations in Slovenia

Because Slovenia has made such a rapid leap into the forefront of public relations research and practice, we have found it to be a useful laboratory for developing a global theory of excellent public relations practice. Scholars and practitioners of public relations as well as of disciplines such as general management, marketing, and advertising have asked whether their discipline should be practiced in the same way in different countries or whether the discipline must be practiced differently in each country.

Public relations would have to be practiced differently in each country if the differences in such characteristics as history, culture, religion, language, or the political and social system were so great that the same theories and forms of practice could not be used. If that were the case, scholars and practitioners around the world could not share theories of public relations; and professionals could work only in their home countries or in countries they knew as well as their own. However, it is possible that theories and practices of public relations are universal so that a knowledgeable professional could work equally effectively in any country.

In Verčič, L. Grunig, and J. Grunig (1996), we developed a global theory of public relations that falls between these two extreme views of international practice and, in a sense, acknowledges merit in both approaches. We believe that if public relations is to be a global profession, scholars and professionals throughout the world must be able to share theories and practices, learn from each other, and collaboratively build the public relations profession. At the same time, we believe that communication professionals must take differences in countries and their cultures into account when they practice in different parts of the world. In developing this theory, we adopted Brinkerhoff and Ingle's (1989) idea that a global theory should consist of generic principles and specific applications.

Such a theory means that the principles of public relations, at an abstract level, are the same, or generic, in all countries. However, at a practical level, those principles must be applied differently in different settings. To apply generic principles in a country, a public relations professional must have extensive knowledge of the generic public relations theory as well as extensive knowledge of the country where he or she is working. Public relations scholars and practitioners from throughout the world, therefore, could develop generic principles together; but they would be able to apply them only in countries they know well or with the assistance of other professionals who understand a country.

To grasp this approach, it is important to distinguish between a normative and positive theory. Our global theory is a *normative* theory. It includes concepts that explain how public relations *should* be practiced throughout the world to be most effective. Public relations may be practiced in other ways, however, and many writers have *positively* described and explained how and why public relations is practiced differently throughout the world. The fact that the global theory is a normative theory does not mean no one actually practices it. In fact, we have found many instances of its practice throughout the world—including in Slovenia. As a normative theory, we say simply that the public relations practices it describes will be more effective than other ways of practicing public relations that may, in fact, be practiced more often.

For the case of Slovenia, then, we consider whether a set of normative principles can be applied in that country and, if they can, how knowledgeable practitioners have applied them. Then, we consider positive research and cases for examples of both excellent and less-excellent practice to show how transitional public relations is actually practiced in Slovenia.

Generic Principles

The generic principles of our global theory were developed from the fifteen-year research project on excellence in public relations and communication (Dozier, 1995; J. Grunig, 1992; L. Grunig, J. Grunig, & Dozier, 2002). In general, the generic principles require knowledge and professionalism by the public relations unit. They also require understanding of and support for public relations by senior management. The characteristics of an excellent public relations function can be placed into four categories, each containing several characteristics.

1. *Empowerment of the public relations function.* For public relations to contribute to organizational effectiveness, the organization must empower communication management as a critical management function.

* *The senior public relations executive is involved with the strategic management processes of the organization, and communication programs are developed for strategic publics identified as a part of this strategic management process.* Public relations contributes to strategic management by scanning the environment to identify publics affected by the consequences of decisions or who might affect the outcome of decisions. It communicates with these publics to allow them to participate in organizational decisions that affect them.
* *Programs to communicate with strategic publics also are managed strategically.* Communication programs are based on formative research, have concrete and measurable objectives, and are evaluated either formally or informally or both.

- *The senior public relations executive is a member of the dominant coalition of the organization or has a direct reporting relationship to senior managers who are part of the dominant coalition.* The senior public relations executive is part of or has access to the group of senior managers with the greatest power in the organization.

The fourth characteristic of empowerment defines the extent to which practitioners who are not white males are represented and promoted in the public relations function:

- *Diversity is embodied in all public relations roles.* Excellent public relations departments empower both men and women in all roles as well as practitioners of diverse racial, ethnic, and cultural backgrounds.

2. *Communicator roles.* Communication technicians are essential to carry out most of the day-to-day activities of public relations departments, and many practitioners are both technicians and managers. In less-excellent departments, however, all of the communication practitioners—including the senior practitioner—are technicians or simply administrative managers who coordinate the work of technicians. If the senior communicator is not a strategic manager, it is not possible for public relations to be empowered as a management function.

- *The public relations unit is headed by a strategic manager rather than a technician or an administrative manager.* Excellent public relations units must have at least one senior communication manager who conceptualizes and directs public relations programs.
- *The senior public relations executive or others in the public relations unit have the knowledge needed for the managerial role.* Excellent public relations programs are staffed by professionals—practitioners who have gained the knowledge needed to carry out the managerial role through university education, continuing education, or self-study.
- *Men and women have equal opportunity to occupy the managerial role.* The majority of public relations professionals are women. If women are excluded from the managerial role, the communication function may be diminished because many of the most knowledgeable practitioners will be excluded from that role.

3. *Organization of the communication function and its relationship to other management functions.* Many organizations have a single department devoted to all communication functions. Others have separate departments for programs aimed at different publics such as journalists, employees, the local community, or the financial community. Still others place communication under another managerial function, such as marketing, human resources, legal, or finance. Many organizations also contract with or consult with outside firms for all or some of their communication programs or for such communication techniques as annual reports or newsletters.

- *Public relations is an integrated communication function.* An excellent public relations function integrates all public relations programs into a single department or provides a mechanism for coordinating programs managed by different departments.
- *Public relations is a management function separate from other functions.* Even though the public relations function is integrated in an excellent organization, the function should not be placed in another department whose primary responsibility is a management function other than communication, such as marketing or human resources.

4. *Models of public relations.* An excellent department designs its communication program on a two-way symmetrical model of collaboration and public participation rather than on the press agentry (emphasizing only favorable publicity), public information (disseminating accurate information but engaging in no research or other form of two-way communication), or two-way asymmetrical (emphasizing only the interests of the organization and not the interests of publics) model.

- *The public relations department and the dominant coalition share the worldview that the communication department should base its goals and its communication activities on the two-way symmetrical model of public relations.*
- *Communication programs developed for specific publics are based on two-way symmetrical strategies for building and maintaining relationships.*
- *The senior public relations executive or others in the public relations unit have the professional knowledge needed to practice the two-way symmetrical model.*
- *The organization has a symmetrical system of internal communication.* A symmetrical system of internal communication is based on the principles of employee empowerment and participation in decision making. Symmetrical communication within an organization fosters a participative rather than an authoritarian culture as well as improved relationships with employees.

Specific Applications

After identifying these generic principles of global public relations practice, we identified six contextual conditions that differ across countries that public relations practitioners must understand and consider when they practice public relations in different countries. These include:

- Culture, including language
- The political system
- The economic system
- The media system
- The level of economic development
- The presence of activist groups (also known as pressure groups or nongovernmental organizations [NGOs]) and the nature of their activities

Slovenian Public Relations as a Test of the Global Theory

We believe that the generic principles of how excellent public relations should be practiced globally will be supported by research in different countries. In doing research, it is important to remain open to the need for revision of these principles and to the addition of new ones so that the generic principles are truly global and not ethnocentric. In that regard, as reported in Verčič and colleagues (1996), L. and J. Grunig conducted qualitative interviews in 1993 with Verčič, Zavrl, and Gruban,[2] who were then the three principal owners of the public relations firm Pristop, to determine if they agreed that the Excellence principles are generic, to ask them how they adapted the principles in their country, and to suggest additional principles.

The interviews confirmed that the generic principles we identified from research in the United States, Canada, and the United Kingdom also applied in Slovenia. The Pristop participants in our research said that four of these principles had been most important in their practice:

1. *Empowerment of the public relations function.* Because so few organizations had specialists in public relations after independence and even fewer had knowledgeable specialists, public relations consultants had to have direct communication with CEOs to be successful.
2. *Knowledge of the managerial role and symmetrical model.* The knowledge of the Pristop managers allowed them to develop public relations as a profession and set them apart from other practitioners who claimed to be practicing public relations but in reality knew little about it.
3. *Separation from other functions.* It was important to help clients understand that public relations is different from marketing and should not be integrated into marketing.
4. *Symmetrical employee communication.* Under the socialist system of Worker Self-Management, management was required by law to keep employees informed so that they could make decisions. When Worker Self-Management was replaced by private ownership, the system of employee communication collapsed. As a result, Pristop found symmetrical communication to be essential—achieved by making employee newsletters more responsive to employees and through upward communication processes such as focus groups and small-group meetings.

The Slovenian professionals also suggested one new generic principle: ethics as a necessary component of excellent public relations. They pointed out that in the post-socialist context of Slovenia, corruption was common and the suspicion of corruption even more common. Therefore, they suggested that ethical practice was a crucial element of excellent public relations in order to avoid damage both to their individual reputations as professionals and to the reputation of the public relations profession. As a result, we have added ethical practice to our list of generic principles.

The interviews also revealed specific applications of the generic principles in the Slovenia context:

1. In working with clients, public relations consultants needed to make the heads of the public relations function more visible to top management and help to empower them. Most Slovenian organizations were authoritarian and did not respect public relations heads, who generally were technicians. As a result, the consultants included communication heads in meetings with CEOs and helped them to develop strategic plans.
2. Because of the lack of knowledge of public relations among practitioners, Pristop developed its own training programs and worked to develop public relations education in the country.
3. The problems of visibility and respect for public relations were even greater when the practitioner was a young woman. Sometimes it was necessary to put a man's name on a proposal or have a man make a presentation. More important, however, was working with women to help them gain experience and demonstrate success.

4. Clients generally were unwilling to pay for the formative and evaluative research necessary for strategic public relations. To compensate, Pristop initially provided research at no cost to demonstrate its value.

5. Few organizations had experienced activist pressure, so Pristop sometimes had to organize activists so the client had someone with whom to talk.

6. Clients typically were preoccupied with negative media coverage and requested consultations with Pristop to counteract this. Adverse publicity, however, typically occurred because of poor relationships with the community, employees, and the government. Therefore, Pristop used media relations problems as a way to gradually alert clients to the need for programs to cultivate better relationships.

7. Most clients in Slovenia had little idea of the nature of public relations. Therefore, Pristop had to help clients develop a worldview of what its function is and what it can accomplish before developing specific communication programs.

8. The remnants of the socialist political and economic system were more conducive to asymmetrical than symmetrical communication. As a result, symmetrical public relations had to be introduced incrementally and its effects sometimes described in asymmetrical language.

In addition to this qualitative research, we also replicated the quantitative part of the Excellence study in Slovenia. As we have already discussed, Verčič translated the three questionnaires used in the study into the Slovenian language in 1991 and administered them in 1992 to CEOs, heads of public relations, and employees in the thirty Slovenian organizations that had public relations departments. We analyzed the data in exactly the same way as we did the Excellence data from the three original countries and reported the results in L. Grunig, J. Grunig, and Verčič (1998). We found that the principles of excellence clustered into the same index of excellence in Slovenia as they did in the United States, Canada, and the United Kingdom in spite of a different cultural, political, and economic context—thus providing strong support that the general principles are the same in the four countries.

Although the principles were the same, our research showed differences in the extent to which Slovenian organizations practiced excellent public relations. Slovenian practitioners were less involved in strategic management and were less valued by senior management than practitioners in the English-speaking countries. In addition, the employee data showed that the old Yugoslav cultural, political, and economic context in Slovenia had left its remnants inside Slovenian organizations, which still had more authoritarian cultures, asymmetrical communication systems, and low levels of job satisfaction than organizations in the Anglo countries.

We also found that privatization and political change in Slovenia had encouraged activism to the extent that our research participants estimated its prevalence at levels similar to participants in the other countries. As reported in J. Grunig and L. Grunig, (1997), we found that Slovenian organizations experienced about the same level of activist pressure as organizations in Canada, the United States, and the United Kingdom. Slovenian organizations, however, had not developed the same effective means of dealing with activism as had organizations in the Anglo countries. Activism was relatively new in Slovenia in the post-socialist period, so even excellent public relations departments had not learned how to cope with it.

These differences again explained why the public relations professionals we interviewed in Slovenia said they needed to counsel CEOs to support and empower public relations managers, develop education in public relations to deal with the lack of public relations knowledge, emphasize employee relations because of the negative context (structure, culture, and communication system) inside Slovenian organizations, and work both with clients and activists so that they could learn to communicate with each other.

Examples of Slovenian Practice

Ašanin Gole and Verčič (2000) edited a volume of case studies of Slovenian public relations programs and techniques from the period 1990 to 2000 that provides a picture of what public relations professionals actually do there. Most of the cases were compiled for professional awards programs and, therefore, describe some of the most excellent public relations examples from the country. A sampling of these case studies also illustrates the nature of transitional public relations in a postcommunist country.

- *SKB Banka (Bank)* (Gruban & Verčič, 2000). After Slovenia developed its independence, SKB Banka was transformed from a socially-owned company into a joint-stock company. Because of negative economic growth at the time of independence, citizens lost their trust in domestic banks. SKB Banka hired Pristop Communications in 1991 to formulate and implement an integrated communication program to gain trust—including public relations, advertising, and direct mail for employees, present and potential clients, journalists, and foreign clients.
- *Krka Chemical Company* (Požar, 2000). Until 1996, Krka was a socially owned company typical of the former Yugoslav economic system. After privatization, the public relations department became an integral part of the transition to a shareholder-owned company—in particular by developing a communication program to attract and keep shareholders.
- *The Slovenian Chamber of Commerce* (Verčič, 2000a). In 1994, the Chamber of Commerce learned that the Slovenian government was preparing a bill that would abolish the chamber as a public legal body and replace it with several smaller, private, legal bodies. The chamber hired Pristop to help transform the organization into a reputable trade association and increase the likelihood that it would survive.
- *The Environmental Development Fund* (Verčič & Pek Drapal, 2000). Socialist countries in transition typically experience high levels of air pollution from the use of fossil fuels such as coal, wood, and heavy oil by formerly government-owned electric companies. In 1996, Pristop was hired by the Environmental Development Fund, founded by the Slovenian government, to conduct a communication campaign to encourage households to convert to more environmentally-friendly heating systems.
- *Healthcare Union of Slovenia* (Grdadolnik, Šetinc, Nacevski, & Kapun, 2000). The Healthcare Union, a union of nurses and health care technicians, wanted to negotiate a labor agreement with the government health care system but could not because the union was disorganized and unknown. The SPEM Communication Group of Maribor, the second-largest Slovenian city, worked with the union from 1996 to 1999 to develop communication among members, increase the union presence in the media, and develop relationships with governmental bodies and other medical associations.

• *Economic relationships with Japan* (Serajnik Sraka, 2000). Slovenia and Japan had been economic partners for many years, but most Japanese either did not know of Slovenia or thought of it as still part of Yugoslavia. Likewise, most Slovenians thought of Japan as a distant and uncertain market. The PR and Media Office of the Slovenian government worked with a number of associations and government agencies to develop a program of communication and exchanges with Japan called "Slovenia: Your Landing Point to Europe."

The Diffusion of Public Relations Excellence

We have looked at the experience of public relations practitioners in Slovenia from a normative standpoint and found evidence that a small, developing country without a history of democracy or experience with public relations can quickly establish mature and excellent public relations practices if it can develop or acquire the knowledge that is necessary for excellence. The actual practice of public relations by most practitioners, however, may lag considerably behind the normative ideal of a few members of the field.

For approximately fifty years, communication researchers have studied the diffusion of new ideas and practices to potential users of the practices—including farmers, medical doctors, and consumers (see, e.g., Rogers, 1983). Consistently, they have found that only a small number of potential users adopt ideas quickly. It takes many years before the majority of a population adopts the ideas and even longer before the ideas are used by nearly everyone. Although excellent public relations practices have been adopted by a group of innovators in Slovenia, showing that our generic principles can be applied in a transitional society, we would not expect that they would be used by most, or even a majority, of Slovenian practitioners. Indeed, the Excellence study showed that most public relations practitioners do not use or even understand these principles, even in the United States, Canada, and the United Kingdom where public relations has been practiced for at least a hundred years.

L. Grunig and Verčič (1998) reported that a survey conducted in 1993 of Slovenian businesses by Pristop showed that 56 percent of the largest companies had no kind of organized public relations function, including those operated through marketing. That number dropped to 46 percent in a 1996 survey. Only 4 percent had an independent public relations department in 1993 and 14 percent in 1996. A third survey, conducted in 2001 and reported in Verčič and Van Ruler (2002), showed that 37 percent of medium and large companies had no specialist in public relations or communication management. On the average, most of the companies had two employees specializing in public relations and most had no budget for the function.

In addition, in 31 percent of the companies the marketing department was responsible for external communication compared to 6 percent for the public relations department. In 19 percent of companies, marketing also managed internal communication, compared to 4 percent for public relations and 6 percent for human resources, which would be a more logically related function to employee communication than marketing. More to be expected, 50 percent of the companies made marketing responsible for marketing communication, compared to 2 percent for public relations. According to Verčič and Van Ruler (2002), "many respondents had a problem understanding what they were really being asked about and how could that be different from a 'normal' marketing and/or sales operation" (p. 9).

When the survey participants were asked questions about the roles played by communication specialists, operational (technical) roles were most common. CEOs who took responsibility for public relations activities were more likely to perform strategic and managerial communication tasks than were public relations people. Verčič and Van Ruler (2002) concluded: "It can be said for Slovenian practitioners in general that they write, read, and advise. This does not mean that there are not many exceptional high-quality professionals, but they are exceptional by being exceptions" (p. 10).

These studies suggest that public relations is diffusing to Slovenian organizations but that it is diffusing slowly. It also shows that, as in other countries where public relations is developing, public relations still suffers from limited and confused concepts—limited to technical activities and confused with marketing and advertising—and a shortage of qualified professionals. In the words of Verčič and Van Ruler (2002), "public relations in Slovenia is relatively young and only beginning to specialize," and "public relations and communication management in Slovenia is a qualitatively less-developed profession" (p. 17).

Conclusion

The development of public relations in Slovenia provides a good example of how the former socialist countries of Eastern and Central Europe can begin to practice public relations when they change from a planned economy and single-party communist government to a market economy and democratic government. Slovenia has long been among the most prosperous and outwardly oriented republics in the region, however, which has increased the opportunities for public relations.

Beginning just before Slovenia's independence, a leading group of Slovenian public relations professionals began to search for a body of knowledge to use in their practice and quickly became innovators in further developing that body of knowledge. As a result, their experience demonstrates that generic principles of excellent public relations can be applied within the context of a country with a history of authoritarian governments and less-developed economies—both of which were typical in the two Yugoslavias and the European empires, of which Slovenia was a part, that preceded today's independent Slovenia.

Nevertheless, new ideas and practices, such as those embodied in the Excellence principles, diffuse slowly throughout a social system. As a result, most Slovenian organizations still do not have public relations functions and most of those that do practice public relations limit it to technical activities and confuse it with marketing.

Notes

1. Portions of this chapter have been adapted from L. Grunig & Verčič (1998) and Verčič (2000b).

2. Gruban left Pristop and founded the management consulting firm Dialogos in 1999.

Discussion Questions

1. What does Slovenia tell you about the history of public relations? Does it begin when practitioners begin to call themselves public relations experts, or can public relations activities be found throughout history? Compare your answer with the history of public relations in the United States. When did the practice begin in the United States? Did the United States really invent public relations and disseminate it to other countries, or have other countries participated equally in the development of the field?

2. Can public relations be practiced in a socialist country ruled by a single party or are capitalism and democracy necessary for public relations to exist?

3. If you lived in another transitional country in Eastern Europe, such as Romania, Bulgaria, Croatia, or Macedonia, what institutions do you think you would have to develop to begin to introduce and diffuse public relations in that country?

4. Select another country with which you are familiar and discuss how you would apply the global theory of generic principles of public relations and specific applications in that country. Describe the culture, political system, economic system, media system, level of development, and extent and nature of activism in that country. How would you apply the normative, generic principles of public relations in that context?

5. How does the confusion of public relations with marketing affect the establishment of public relations in developing countries? What could you do to resolve this problem?

6. Where does the body of knowledge in public relations come from, based on the Slovenian experience? Do practitioners learn it from experience? Is it developed from research and formal education? Does the body of knowledge come mostly from the United States and other developed countries or can scholars and practitioners from newly developing countries contribute equally to it?

References

Ali, D. J. (1995). *Societal culture and public relations: A comparative analysis of Trinidad and Antigua, West Indies.* Unpublished master's thesis, University of Maryland, College Park.

Ašanin Gole, P., & Verčič, D. (2000). *Slovenian public relations theory and practice 1990–2000.* Ljubljana: Public Relations Society of Slovenia.

Barlik, J. (2001). Public awareness campaigns in Poland and Slovenia: Lessons learned by government agencies and PR practitioners. In R. Ławniczak (Ed.), *Public relations contribution to transition in Central and Eastern Europe: Research and practice* (pp. 123–142). Posnań, Poland: Biuro Usługowo-Handlowe, Printer.

Bennett, C. (1995). *Yugoslavia's bloody collapse.* New York: New York University Press.

Benson, L. (2001). *Yugoslavia: A concise history.* Houndmills, Basingstoke, Hampshire, England: Palgrave.

Black, S. (1990–1991). Public relations in China today. *Public Relations Quarterly, 35*(4), 29–30.

Brinkerhoff, D. W., & Ingle, M. D. (1989). Integrating blueprint and process: A structured flexibility approach to development management. *Public Administration and Development, 9,* 487–503.

Csaba, L. (1993). After the shock: Some lessons from transition policies in Eastern Europe. In L. Somo-

gyi (Ed.), *The political economy of the transition process in Eastern Europe* (pp. 88–107). Aldershot, England: Edward Elgar.

Cutlip, S. M., & Center, A. H. (1960). *Effective public relations* (2nd ed.). Englewood Cliffs, NJ: Prentice Hall.

Dozier, D. M. (with Grunig, L. A., & Grunig, J. E.). (1995). *Manager's guide to excellence in public relations and communication management.* Mahwah, NJ: Lawrence Erlbaum Associates.

Duncan, T., & Caywood, C. (1996). The concept, process, and evolution of integrated marketing communication. In E. Thorson & J. Moore (Eds.), *Integrated communication: Synergy of persuasive voices* (pp. 13–34). Mahwah, NJ: Lawrence Erlbaum Associates.

Economist. (1997a, November 22). Slovenia: Canny survivor. *Economist, 40,* 45.

Economist. (1997b, November 22). A survey of business in Eastern Europe: Eastern Europe recast itself. *Economist,* Supplement.

Grdadolnik, V. O., Šetinc, B., Nacevski, D., & Kapun, N. (2000). Negotiations for collective agreement campaign for the Healthcare Union of Slovenia. In P. Ašanin Gole & D. Verčič (Eds.), *Slovenian public relations theory and practice 1990–2000* (pp. 103–109). Ljubljana: Public Relations Society of Slovenia.

Gruban, B., Maksimovič, M., Verčič, D., & Zavrl, F. (1990). *ABC PR: Odnosi z javnostmi na prvi pogled (ABCs of PR: Public relations at first sight).* Ljubljana: Tiskovno središče Ljubljana.

Gruban, B., & Verčič, D. (2000). SKB Banka: "Proving what we can do." In P. Ašanin Gole & D. Verčič (Eds.), *Slovenian public relations theory and practice 1990–2000* (pp. 43–44). Ljubljana: Public Relations Society of Slovenia.

Gruban, B., Verčič, D., Zavrl, F. (Eds.). (1994). Public relations in Slovenia: Research report. *Pristop* (special issue).

Gruban, B., Verčič, D., & Zavrl, F. (1997). *Pristop k odnosom z javnostmi (An approach to public relations).* Ljubljana: Pristop.

Gruban, B., Verčič, D., & Zavrl, F. (Eds.). (1998). *Preskok v odnose z javnostmi: Zbornik o slovenski praksi v odnosih z javnostmi (A step into public relations: A reader on Slovenian practice in public relations).* Ljubljana: Pristop.

Grunig, J. E. (Ed.). (1992). *Excellence in public relations and communication management.* Hillsdale, NJ: Lawrence Erlbaum Associates.

Grunig, J. E. (1997). A situational theory of publics: Conceptual history, recent challenges and new research. In D. Moss, T. MacManus, & D. Verčič (Eds.), *Public relations research: An international perspective* (pp. 3–48). London: International Thomson Business Press.

Grunig, J. E. (2000). Collectivism, collaboration, and societal corporatism as core professional values in public relations. *Journal of Public Relations Research, 12,* 23–48.

Grunig, J. E., & Grunig, L. A. (1997, July). *Review of a program of research on activism: Incidence in four countries, activist publics, strategies of activist groups, and organizational responses to activism.* Paper presented to the Fourth Public Relations Research Symposium, Bled, Slovenia.

Grunig, J. E., & Hunt, T. (1984). *Managing public relations.* Orlando: Holt, Rinehart & Winston.

Grunig, L. A. (1992a). Activism: How it limits the effectiveness of organizations and how excellent public relations departments respond. In J. E. Grunig (Ed.), *Excellence in public relations and communication management* (pp. 503–530). Hillsdale, NJ: Lawrence Erlbaum Associates.

Grunig, L. A. (1992b). Power in the public relations department. In J. E. Grunig (Ed.), *Excellence in public relations and communication management* (pp. 483–501). Hillsdale, NJ: Lawrence Erlbaum Associates.

Grunig, L. A., Grunig, J. E., & Dozier, D. M. (2002). *Excellent public relations and effective organiza-tions: A study of communication management in three countries.* Mahwah, NJ: Lawrence Erlbaum Associates.

Grunig, L. A., Grunig, J. E., & Verčič, D. (1998). Are the IABC's excellence principles generic? Comparing Slovenia and the United States, the United Kingdom and Canada. *Journal of Communication Management, 2,* 335–356.

Grunig, L. A., & Verčič, D. (1998). PR in Slovenia: Doing public relations in a small country in transition in Eastern Europe. In J. Felton (Ed.), *Crises in a wired world: How does PR handle the instant transmission of problems globally? Proceedings of International Symposium 2.* Gainesville: The Institute for Public Relations, University of Florida.

Hundhausen, C. (1969). *Public relations: Theorie und systematic (Public relations: Theory and method).* Berlin: de Gruyter.

Hunt, T., & Grunig, J. E. (1995). *Tehnike odnosov z javnostmi (Public relations techniques)* (Branko Gradišnik, Trans.). Ljubljana: DZS.

Ivanov, V. (1993). From propaganda to public relations. *Newsletter of the European Association of Public Relations Education and Research, 3*(1), 8–10.

Jančič, Z. (1994, July). *Relationship marketing and public relations.* Paper presented to the First International Public Relations Research Symposium, Bled, Slovenia.

Kaur, K. (1997). *The impact of privatization on public relations and the role of public relations and management in the privatization process: A qualitative analysis of the Malaysian case.* Unpublished doctoral dissertation, University of Maryland, College Park.

Lampe, J. R. (2000). *Yugoslavia as history: Twice there was a country* (2nd ed.). Cambridge, England: Cambridge University Press.

Ławniczak, R. (2001). Transition public relations—An instrument for systemic transformation in Central and Eastern Europe. In R. Ławniczak (Ed.), *Public relations contribution to transition in Central and Eastern Europe: Research and practice* (pp. 7–18). Posnań, Poland: Biuro Usługowo-Handlowe, Printer.

Major, I. (1993). *Privatization in Eastern Europe: A critical approach.* Aldershot, England: Edward Elgar.

Moss, D., MacManus, T., & Verčič, D. (Eds.). (1997). *Public relations research: An international perspective.* London: International Thomson Business Press.

Moss, D., Verčič, D., & Warnaby, G. (Eds.). (2000). *Perspectives on public relations research.* London: Routledge.

Požar, J. (2000). Communication of Krka during the privatization process and communication with the shareholders (1993–1997). In P. Ašanin Gole & D.

Verčič (Eds.), *Slovenian public relations theory and practice 1990–2000* (pp. 53–60). Ljubljana: Public Relations Society of Slovenia.

Rogers, E. M. (1983). *The diffusion of innovations* (3rd ed.). New York: Free Press.

Scholz, J. (1998). *A normative approach to the practice of public relations in the Eastern part of Germany.* Unpublished master's thesis, University of Maryland, College Park.

Serajnik Sraka, N. (2000). Presentation of Slovenia and its economy in Japan: Slovenia: Your Landing Point in Europe. In P. Ašanin Gole & D. Verčič (Eds.), *Slovenian public relations theory and practice 1990–2000* (pp. 117–121). Ljubljana: Public Relations Society of Slovenia.

Thurow, L. (1993). *Head to head: The coming economic battle among Japan, Europe, and America.* London: Nicholas Brealey.

Verčič, D. (1993). Privatisation fuels PR growth. In R. Sarginson (Ed.), *Hollis Europe: The directory of European public relations & PR networks* (4th ed., pp. 389–390). London: Hollis Directories Ltd.

Verčič, D. (1994, November). *Cultural biases in U.S. public relations: Constraints and advantages.* Paper presented to the Research Center in Public Communication and the College of Journalism Graduate Student Association: University of Maryland, College Park.

Verčič, D. (1995). *Odnosi z javnostmi: Nastanek, zgodovina in teorije (Public relations: Emergence, history, and theories).* Ljubljana: FDV— magistrska naloga.

Verčič, D. (1997). Towards fourth wave public relations: A case study. In D. Moss, T. MacManus, & D. Verčič (Eds.), *Public relations research: An international perspective* (pp. 264–279). London: International Thomson Business Press.

Verčič, D. (2000a). Prevention of governmental intrusion into the organization of the Slovenian Chamber of Commerce and its pre-emptive transformation. In P. Ašanin Gole & D. Verčič (Eds.), *Slovenian public relations theory and practice 1990–2000* (pp. 64–66). Ljubljana: Public Relations Society of Slovenia.

Verčič, D. (2000b). Public relations research and education in Slovenia. In P. Ašanin Gole & D. Verčič (Eds.), *Slovenian public relations theory and practice 1990–2000* (pp. 25–38). Ljubljana: Public Relations Society of Slovenia.

Verčič, D. (2000c). *Trust in organizations: A study of the relations between media coverage, public perceptions and profitability.* Unpublished doctoral dissertation, The London School of Economics and Political Science, the University of London, London.

Verčič, D., & Grunig, J. E. (2000). The origins of public relations theory in economics and strategic management. In D. Moss, D. Verčič, & G. Warnaby (Eds.), *Perspectives on public relations research* (pp. 7–58). London: Routledge.

Verčič, D., Grunig, L. A., & Grunig, J. E. (1996). Global and specific principles of public relations: Evidence from Slovenia. In H. M. Culbertson & N. Chen (Eds.), *International public relations: A comparative analysis* (pp. 31–65). Mahwah NJ: Lawrence Erlbaum Associates.

Verčič, D., & Pek Drapal, D. (2000). Public communication campaign for the Environmental Development Fund in Slovenia. In P. Ašanin Gole & D. Verčič (Eds.), *Slovenian public relations theory and practice 1990–2000* (pp. 81–89). Ljubljana: Public Relations Society of Slovenia.

Verčič, D., & Van Ruler, B. (2002, July). *Public relations and communication management in the Netherlands and Slovenia: A comparative analysis.* Paper presented to the International Communication Association, Seoul, Korea.

Verčič, D., & Žnuderl, B. (1993). Kdo ali kaj so javnosti: Prvi slovenski test (Who or what are publics: The first Slovenian test). *Pristop, 1*(2), 18–21.

Vreg, F. (1994). Foreword. In B. Gruban & D. Verčič (Eds.), Public relations in Slovenia: Research report (pp. 4–7). *Pristop* (special issue).

The World Bank. (1996). *World development report 1996: From plan to market.* Oxford, England: Oxford University Press.

Zavrl, F., & Verčič, D. (1995). Performing public relations in Central and Eastern Europe. *International Public Relations Review, 18*(2), 21–23.

7

Public Relations and Romania

Tourism and Dracula's Homeland

Rachael E. Doksoz

Key Points

- Propaganda is a *one-way* approach of sending information to the public in attempt to get rid of a problem rather than communicating a way through the problem.
- During communism, propaganda was used to promote a positive image of Romania externally while internal publicity promoted its dogma; the media were used to promote all of the regime's successes but none of its failures.
- Currently, public relations practitioners desire proper training and wish to develop their use of the *two-way symmetric* approach, but that is still in the early stages of development.
- Efforts are being made to communicate with internal and external publics in order to regain and strengthen tourism as a dependable source of income for Romania.
- Based on the worldwide popularity of Dracula and because of Romania's failing tourism industry, Romania wants to open a Dracula theme-based park in 2004.

Romania, ruled by communism for nearly three decades, gained its freedom in 1989. Now that democracy is emerging, Romanians are using not only their natural resources but also their cultural resources, such as legends and superstitions, in order to develop the national economy. Romania is home to the well-known region called Transylvania, which inspired the mysterious tale of Dracula. Dracula, the fictional character in Bram Stoker's novel published in 1897, is based on the historical Prince Vlad Tepes Dracula, who ruled over Wallachia and was infamous for impaling criminals and prisoners of war. This fusion of

Vlad Tepes and the mythical Dracula is now being used promotionally to attract tourists to Transylvania and to stimulate the Romanian economy.

Public relations is beginning to play an integral role in the promotional campaign to transform Dracula into an international tourist attraction. For decades, the Dracula legend interested tourists traveling to Transylvania; however, Romania was under the rule of Nicolae Ceausescu who stunted tourism, (Heibert, 1992). Without the income of tourism, along with various other economic catastrophes, Romania's economy continued to be depressed. After the revolution, many tourists feared Eastern Europe's fragile condition, further limiting Romania's potential for income from the tourist industry (Baker, 1995). Nevertheless, the government slowly started to reestablish tourism in many areas of the country, including resorts in the Black Sea area, the Danube Delta, the capital, Bucharest, and Transylvania. Even so, many travelers have been reluctant to come. Now, however, independent travel agencies in Romania are using marketing strategies to attract more tourists, and the government is working with outside investors to develop a "Dracula Land" theme park.

Romania's Political History

Romania, along with other Eastern European countries, fell under the control of the Soviet Union at the end of World War II. The Romanian Communist Party (RCP) dramatically changed the social, political, and cultural realities that existed (Papacostea, 1996). In 1964, the RCP announced its independence from the Soviet regime and headed in the direction of national communism. From 1970 to 1980, Nicolae Ceausescu's power increased, and he launched the "cultural revolution." The propaganda combined national exaltation with his cult of personality. He enjoyed popular support but only for a short period. The RCP quickly put a stop to those who opposed the party and those with Western ideologies (Papacostea, 1996).

The RCP's main goal was to isolate Romania from the rest of the world. This led to the reconstruction of a totalitarian, national communism approach (Papacostea, 1996). Certain measures were taken to adjust history according to RCP ideologies and to manipulate public opinion through the RCP's Department of Propaganda and the Institute of History.

In December 1989, the party fell, and Ceausescu and his wife were executed. Romania, having suffered one of the most repressive communist regimes, paid a fearsome toll in bloodshed as the regime collapsed (Papacostea, 1996). The move to democracy, however, was not an easy transition and difficulties continue. Ion Iliescu led the new government as president after the fall. A former leading communist (Ramet, 1992), Iliescu's leadership did not prove to be successful in aiding the growth of democracy in Romania.

In November of 1991, a new constitution was created. It affirms political pluralism as a right, along with cultural and religious freedoms, and also states that Romanian citizens have the same rights as declared in the Universal Declaration of Human Rights (Ramet, 1992)—the rights to privacy; confidentiality of correspondence; and freedom of conscience, expression, assembly, and association. Also, there are rights of private property, judicial independence, and freedom of the press. With all of these freedoms, though, many Romanians still feel ill at ease without political stability (Ramet, 1992). There are democratic institutions and a free press, but corruption is also present (Lauer, 1999). Iliescu returned to office in December 2000, under the political banner of the Social Democracy Party of Romania (PDSR), replacing Emil Constantinescu as president after the most recent election. Iliescu's earlier administration had been criticized for its unenthusiastic reform policies that strengthened Mafialike conduct and aroused anti-Western feelings in the country (Lauer, 1999). Following his election, Iliescu made promises to reform Romania's economy. Emerging from forty-five years of communism, Romanians still are skeptical of political parties, trade unions, and parliament (Rose, 1999).

Marketing and Public Relations in Romania

After World War II, Romania emerged as industrial nation with a centralized economy. Moreover, the move to industrialize was marketed to outside nations (Lascu, Manrai, & Manrai, 1993) with public relations, as it was understood in Romania, playing an important role in the marketing campaign. Propaganda was used to promote a positive image of the nation externally even as publicity internally promoted the dogma of communism; the media, in particular, were used to promote all of the regime's successes and none of its failures (Lascu et al., 1993).

After the fall of communism, the economy suffered severely. High inflation rates, recession, and stagflation were some of the consequences of such rapid political change (Lascu et al., 1993). The business sector tried to survive as managers surveyed Romanian consumers to find out what products they most wanted, and marketing organizations relied heavily on advertising, especially television, to promote products. Such promotion pushed prices to the point where Romanians could not afford many of the items being advertised (Lascu et al., 1993).

Romania's newspapers, radio stations, and television stations, are now controlled by desire for income rather than communism. Cable television is growing in popularity; nearly 40 percent of Romanians have cable. More television programming means more advertising venues. Private stations also are increasing in number, but they do not overstep their independence. They have good relations with the government and do not want to risk going beyond their boundaries because this relationship allows them to stay lucrative. If they were to go beyond the boundaries that the government established for them, they could be forced to forfeit their businesses (Carothers, 1996). Therefore, stories in the media focus more on sensationalism and fiction rather than economic, political, and social concerns (Turk, 1996).

Public relations, mainly practiced by government agencies and independent firms, is largely nonstrategic and *one-way asymmetric* in nature. *Press agentry* or *publicity, one-way asymmetric* models of public relations, are most commonly used. Indeed, Romanians use the word *publicate* to describe both propaganda and publicity and consider both concepts interchangeable. Propaganda is a primal stage of public relations that aims to rid itself of a problem rather than trying to communicate a way through the problem or issue at hand with the public. Propaganda is basically a *one-way* approach of information sending. Because of this, propaganda does not really fit into public relations at all because it does not adhere to the sender–receiver *two-way* function of the communication process. Public relations practitioners in Romania view the external public as a mass audience that is reached through the media (Turk, 1996). Practitioners do not adhere to the nine generic principles that characterize excellence in public relations (Verčič, Grunig, & Grunig, 1996):

- Involvement of public relations in strategic management
- Empowerment of public relations in the dominant coalition or a direct reporting relationship to senior management
- Integrated public relations function
- Public relations as a management function separate from other functions
- The role of the public relations practitioner
- Adherence to the *two-way symmetrical* model of public relations
- Following a *symmetrical* system of internal communication
- Knowledge potential for managerial role and *symmetrical* public relations
- Diversity embodied in all roles

For instance, strategic management and the separation of public relations from other functions, such as marketing, does not take place; public relations and marketing functions, in fact, tend to go hand in hand in Romania (Turk, 1996).

According to J. E. Grunig and L. A. Grunig (1992, cited in Verčič et al., 1996), "practitioners of professional public relations rely on a body of knowledge as well as technique and see public relations as having a strategic purpose for an organization, which is to manage conflict and build relationships with strategic publics that limit the autonomy of the organization" (p. 41). For Romania, as well as other former communist countries, public relations is not about building communication between an organization and its publics but about deteriorating communication among people, which breaks down their ability to form publics, which in turn hinders them from following their causes. Some argue that the current public relations mind-set is a remnant of Romania's communist past (Turk, 1996). Others suggest that it stems from the lack of professional education. It was not until 1993, for example, that the first college-level public relations course was taught at the University of Bucharest. Moreover, faculty members had no real training or experience in public relations (Turk, 1996). Most public relations practitioners lack formal training and have degrees in engineering, economics, or philosophy.

Public relations practitioners desire proper training and wish to develop their use of the *two-way symmetric* approach, which would represent a step toward professionalism. That is still in the developing stages, though, because of Romania's current authoritarian approach to public relations. However, Romania is beginning to develop social responsibility in public relations (Turk, 1996). This can be seen through some private organizations, such as IDEE. IDEE is a Romanian-based public relations and marketing firm that represents USAID (United States Agency for International Development) and various worldwide private and government-run industries in Eastern Europe, such as one of Romania's public television stations and the Department of Public Information (see www.idee.ro). The firm has more than fifteen years of experience in handling government relations' communication campaigns (IDEE, 2001).

The government is working with independently owned firms in a concerted attempt to stimulate the economy. In addition, efforts are being made to communicate with internal and external publics in order to regain and strengthen tourism as a dependable source of income for the country (Heibert, 1992). One major source of tourism is Transylvania, not only the place but also the mystery that lies therein.

Vlad Tepes—The "Real" Dracula

Prince Vlad Tepes Dracula (see Figure 7.1) was born in 1431 in the Transylvanian city of Sighisoara. The name "Dracula" comes from the word *dracul,* which means "devil" in Romanian. When "ya" is added, the words mean "one of the dragon or devil." Stories have been told that Vlad Tepes would sign his name as "Draculya." Other stories suggest that the King of Luxembourg initiated his father, Vlad II Dracul, into the secret Society (or Order) of the Dragon and that is the origin of his name (Johnson & Clifford, 1994). Created by the Roman Catholic Church in the thirteenth century, the Order of the Dragon was originally intended to help keep the Turks out of Europe.

Vlad Tepes's father, who was of royal lineage, was living in exile in Transylvania. He planned to seize the throne of Wallachia, an independent province contested by Romania, Hungary, and Turkey. In 1436, Vlad II Dracul seized the throne of Wallachia but lost it shortly thereafter to Turkey; he then pledged his loyalty to Turkey. A few years later, the Hungarians reportedly assassinated him as well as his oldest son. The Turks kept Vlad Tepes and his younger brother, Radu, captive until Vlad was seventeen. Vlad was released but Radu remained with the Turks. In 1451, Vlad offered his allegiance to Hungary against the Turks and invaded Wallachia in 1456, seizing the throne (Baum, 2000).

FIGURE 7.1 *Vlad Dracul Tepes.*
16th century portrait, German artist unknown.

Courtesy of the Kunsthistorisches Museum, Vienna, Austria.

Constant battles with Turkish forces followed. The Turks, in an attempt to halt Vlad, sent a note to his wife saying that he had been killed in battle. Distraught by the news, she threw herself out of a window and drowned in a river. This portion of the river is still known as the River of the Princess. In revenge, Tepes impaled one-fourth of a Turkish army at the battle of Giurgiu in 1460, at which point Tepes (pronounced *tepish*), which means "impaler," was added to his name. Impaling is a method of torturous death in which a body is placed on a spike with weights tied to the feet driving the spike up through the body until it reaches the victim's heart. A sultan of the Turkish Empire is reported to have wandered through a valley of twenty thousand impaled victims, including Turkish prisoners of war and political opponents of Vlad Tepes (Kessler, 1997; Johnson & Clifford, 1994). The Hungarians captured Tepes in 1462 and held him prisoner for four years. He finally was accepted into the Hungarian royal family and married one of the king's daughters (Baum, 2000). During this time, his younger brother, Radu, ruled Wallachia under control of the Turks. In 1475, Tepes invaded and took control of Wallachia again.

Tepes fiercely ruled Wallachia, harshly punishing anyone for the smallest of crimes. He impaled robbers, gypsies, enemies, tax evaders, and even small children (Kessler, 1997). He was known to have boiled heads in kettles, roasted people alive, and cut bodies into pieces to drink their blood. He is reported to have killed more than one hundred thousand people (Montgomery, 1997).

Vlad Tepes Dracula eventually was killed in battle, and the Turks were said to have preserved his head in honey and placed it on a spike in Constantinople. His body was buried in an island monastery in Snagov near Bucharest. In 1931, however, an excavation of the burial site revealed only animal bones; there was no sign of his coffin or remains, thus adding to the legends of Dracula as one of the undead (Baum, 2000).

The Popularization of Dracula

Bram Stoker created the popular view of Dracula in the nineteenth century. Stoker sought out the history and legends of Vlad Tepes, whose thirst for blood inspired Stoker to use him for the main character in his horror novel (Kessler, 1997). Stoker placed the story in a contemporary setting. Because horror stories were exceedingly popular at the time, he knew his tale would capture the public's imagination (Kessler, 1997). Dracula is based on legend, reality, fiction, superstition, and fearful fantasy. Stoker studied religion, ethnography, medicine, the occult, and accounts of Jack the Ripper. He incorporated all of these elements, as well as the superstitions that still exist in Transylvania, to create a horror story that soon became a cult classic.

Transylvania is a land filled with local superstitions of the undead, ghosts, and vampires. For example, a ribbon is placed around the head of the newly dead to prevent evil spirits from possessing the body, and many precautions are taken—including the use of garlic—to ward off vampires. Modern medicine offers an explanation for some of the superstitions. Vampires and vampire-like behavior/appearance may be explained scientifically. Christian Honigsmann, a Viennese dermatologist, has suggested that porphyria, once a widespread genetic illness in Transylvania, may explain vampirism (Kessler, 1997). Porphyria is a disease that destroys the skin, especially when in contact with sunlight; people with this disease can suffer extreme pain—described as a burning sensation—after only a few minutes of exposure of sunlight. The disease also can cause teeth to glow a red/orange color and gums to recede making the teeth appear larger. In addition, those afflicted with porphyria are said to sometimes commit violent acts, which can be mistaken as vampirism. The treatment for porphyria is bloodletting or blood transfusions. Some with the disease have said that drinking animal blood offers relief. Porphria is inherited but only if both parents are carriers. In the Middle Ages, inbreeding was common among royalty and those living in remote villages, such as Transylvania, thus sparking episodes of the disease (Bleasel & Varigos, 2000; Kessler, 1997).

The legend of Dracula has inspired musicals, ballets, television shows and miniseries, films (the most recent being Francis Ford Coppola's 1997 version), fan clubs, and Web sites, and has transformed Transylvania into one of the country's top tourist attractions (French, 1995). It was not until 1991, however, that the novel was translated into Romanian. Many Romanians, over the past several years, have only now been learning about Stoker's novel for the first time because Ceausescu banned many Western books during his dictatorship (Voss, Nettleton, Dhue, & Oswald, 1998). They previously only knew of Vlad Tepes (French, 1995). Romanian history characterizes Tepes as a totalitarian ruler who used his strength to build an army and help establish trade routes with neighboring countries (Fernz, 2000). Many Romanians consider him a national hero for having defeated the Turkish army. (Kessler, 1997; Waterfall, 1997).

Tourism and Dracula's Legend

Romania is one of Europe's poorest countries; the average salary is less than $100 a month (Chiriac, 2001; Waterfall, 1997). The government is trying to improve the economy, in part, by boosting tourism. The number of visitors to Romania declined from 6.5 million tourists in 1990 to 5.9 million in 1994 (Marsh, 1995). In 1996, the number of tourists increased but declined once again in 1997 to 2.8 million foreign tourists, which represented 2 percent of Romania's gross domestic product (Reuter, 1997). The majority of tourists come from Germany, Bulgaria, the Ukraine, and Turkey. The National Authority for Tourism in Romania tried to attract tourists through its "Eclipse 99" and "Millennium" programs, which attempted to lure tourists who wanted to witness the last solar eclipse of the millennium, which Romanian promoters said could best be seen in their country. Other promotions were established to promote rural, ecological, and cultural tourism but have not generated the level of tourist activity desired (Foreign tourists look for adventure, 2000). Government and private travel agencies also have been promoting tourism in Bucharest, the Black Sea region, the Danube Delta, and Transylvania. Bucharest is a city of art and history with more museums per capita than any other capital in the world (Museums in Bucharest, 2001). The tourism industry is planning to build a new resort, called Europa, near the Black Sea, at an estimated cost of $800 million. Many large hotel corporations have expressed interest in the project. If this project is a success, it could double tourism revenues from 2000, which was about $500 million (Chiriac, 2001). The Danube Delta, covering more than 5,500 square kilometers, is the confluence of the rivers of Central and Eastern Europe. It has the world's largest area of reed beds and is filled with a myriad of flora and fauna and wildlife. Pollution, however, discourages visitors from vacationing at this once-popular destination as factories dump phosphates, nitrates, oil residues, mercury, and pesticides into the rivers, threatening the entire ecosystem (Cazacu, 1994).

Transylvania is perhaps the most promising of the tourist regions in Romania because of the legend of Dracula. The "Dracula industry" has been growing over the past few years and shows continued promise (Voss et al., 1998). For example, there are many on-line sites promoting the Dracula phenomenon in Romania. The on-line sites are mostly privately run by those interested in the legend and travel agencies using the legend of Dracula to promote business in Romania. Some sites are Romanian, but many are from all over the world (see the note at the end of this chapter for a list of Web sites).[1] The First World Dracula Congress in 1995—a mixture of academics, historians, and Dracula followers from Canada, the United States, Great Britain, France, and Italy—stimulated early interest. The conference was held in Bucharest and the conferees discussed both the historical and fictional Dracula (Rodina, 1995; Stephen, 1995), one of its intended purposes (Dascalu, 1995). The May 2000 Second World Dracula Congress debated the myths and reality of Dracula (Brasov, 2000). Future congresses are planned. Nicolae Paduraru launched the first conference "forced" on him by fans and tourists interested in the mythical Dracula. Nicolae Paduraru founded the Transylvanian Society of Dracula in order to promote Dracula and tourism, which, as noted by Minister of Tourism Matei Dan, boosts the economy (Devotees whip up Dracula frenzy, 1995). The Transylvanian Society, a not-for-profit organization with more than five hundred members globally, organizes tours in Transylvania that explore both the facts and the legends of Dracula and Tepes (Fangs are what they used to be, 1998). The society offers members a line of wine, travel discounts, and honorary titles (Marks, 1995). Membership in the society includes an annual fee of U.S.$50 and a one-time U.S.$27 fee. Once a year the organization has a symposium for those interested in the myth and legend of Dracula where academic papers are presented. In addition to a newsletter, members can keep up with events through Web sites that the organization has created. The Canadian Web site (www.ucs. mun.ca) is hosted by Elizabeth Miller, current president of the Canadian division of the society. It includes lists of Web sites with Dracula-related themes, including publishers, discussion groups, research, scholarship, arts, books, authors, merchandise, and more. The society also works closely with other organizations with similar themes.

A typical week-long vacation package, including tours and hotel stays, costs about $1,200. The trip starts in Bucharest and continues to Sighisoara, Tepes's birthplace. The tour includes a stop at Bran Castle, which was captured by the Saxons in the thirteenth century in order to protect Brasov, an important trade center at that time. Although Tepes spent some time at Bran, he never resided there but lived instead at Poenari Castle in Wallachia (Fernz, 2000); his brief stay at Bran, however, is a good enough "hook" for Dracula enthusiasts (Montgomery, 1997). The last stop on the tour is the monastery in Snagov that supposedly houses Tepes's remains (Voss et al., 1998). Along the way, depending on the tour, there are side-trips to medieval castles and small villages, filled with the landscapes that Stoker's novel depicts—misty mountains, bats, howling wolves, and gothic architecture. A lavish meal in a good restaurant costs only twenty-five dollars per person (Shapiro, 1996). The "Dracula-ified" hotels sell drinks such as "Dracullina," also known as "women vampires' delight," and "Dracula's Spirit," a blood-red vodka. These "spirits" sell for five times the price in Dracula country than they do elsewhere in Romania (Dascalu, 1995). There are, in fact, many businesses in Romania, especially in Transylvania, associated with the Dracula tours. Businesses, especially entrepreneurs, typically use the *press agentry* public relations model to attract Dracula tourists and purposely restrict information to positive messages, particularly since there has been so much negative media coverage concerning the problems of pollution and the economy.

Romanians are not particularly fond of the Dracula myth but are willing to endure the count for the sake of the tourism income that it generates (Scott, 1995). Similarly, the Ministry of Tourism is not happy with the Dracula industry but realizes that tourism in the Black Sea resorts and the Danube Delta is not enough. The entrepreneurial class views Dracula tourism as an excellent way to make money (Gilbert, 1995) and argues that it only makes sense to exploit the legend for the benefit of the country. Indeed, the tourist industry has benefited from being the place in Stoker's book where Dracula was born (Wilkinson, 1997). Tourism, for example, provides jobs for many unskilled laborers, who maintain tourist sites and their grounds (Harrop, 1994). Moreover, international tourism can provide many other jobs for and help project a positive image of Romania to the outside world (Vospitannik, Littlejohn, & Arnot, 1997).

Dracula Land Theme Park

Under communism, Romanians were not allowed to mention Dracula, but now the head of the Romanian Ministry of Tourism, Matei Dan, hopes that this once-forbidden legend will attract tourists (McAleer, 2001). The Romanian government and German investors have been working together to build a Dracula theme park. Westernstadt Pullman City, a German company that operates a Wild West theme park in the United States, will likely design and build the park. The Romanian government originally tried to interest Walt Disney Co. as an investor. According to Dan, Romania has an earning potential of U.S.$1 billion, double what it currently earns from tourism. Neighboring Bulgaria already earns more than U.S.$1 billion annually from tourism (Romania: a lot at stake, 2001; Romania plans to bleed tourists, 2001).

Sighisoara, Tepes's birthplace, has been discussed as the location for the theme park, which would be jointly funded by the government and investors at a cost of U.S.$15.62 million with an additional U.S.$19 million for infrastructure improvements. Plans are to complete the 148-acre park by the fall of 2004, a project expected to create nearly three thousand jobs. Hotels and golf courses also are planned as part of the park complex (Germans to build Dracula theme park, 2001). Romania estimates that 1 million tourists will visit the theme park annually (Bucharest okays Dracula theme park, 2001).

Some are skeptical of the park, though. The president of the Transylvanian Society of Dracula and head of the Romanian Division, Nicolae Paduraru, says that any theme park should be "culturally correct," and Canadian historian Elizabeth Miller fears that the park will focus more on the myth than on historical accuracy. Some suggestions of a divided park have been made, but sponsors have not yet revealed details of the design layout (McAleer, 2001). From a marketing perspective, using Dracula as a theme park character caters to the needs of both those interested in the fictional character and in the historical Tepes. Although those interested in the latter fear that the park will accentuate the myth over the historical reality, with some four thousand Dracula clubs worldwide, the income from visitor-devotees to that myth may soothe some of the complaints (Heibert, 1992; McAleer, 2001). In answer to the skeptics, Raul Mihai, the director of Bran Castle, has argued that the park will boost Romania's economy and that many other museums, such as the Sherlock Holmes museum in London and Romeo and Juliet attractions in Verona, Italy, bank on fiction to generate tourism (Thurston, 2001).

Conclusion

In the final analysis, Dracula alone cannot generate a sufficient number of tourists to sustain the tourism industry in Romania. The Romanian National Tourist Office does its best to promote the nation as a whole but has limited resources (Dracula revives tourism, 2000). The Romanian Tourist Agency did promote Dracula in cooperation with state-approved Transylvanian Tours at one point, but the state tours have since stopped. Entrepreneurs now have picked up where the state left off.

Romania is still struggling as a nation with economic and political problems, but with the right public relations and marketing mix, tourism may be one way to stimulate the economy (Baker, 1995; Velea, 1996). The country's natural beauty is underdeveloped and has great potential as a promotional attraction. Although many tourists simply have not yet discovered this particular area of the world, it does offer a new travel experience (Harrop, 1994). Tourism authorities are trying to attract investors but with some difficulty. Some of the problems are based on the socioeconomic status of the country (Harrop, 1994). Hotels and other facilities associated with tourism do not have the funds to cater to the expectations of most Western guests. Westerners find the standards of service unacceptable (Woodard, 1995). Other problems with tourism have to do with the government itself. Those in the tourist industry must pay their taxes all at once at the beginning of the year. If they cannot, they must either take out loans or liquidate their assets. In order to pay both their debts and operational costs, they must raise prices, which results in a further loss of real income (Velea, 1996).

Miscommunication further inhibits tourism. Tour operators, hotel and restaurant managers, and transportation providers have yet to coordinate their efforts, which is critical to developing the industry. Further, they must grow, develop, and maintain services required to satisfy travelers (Vospitannik et al., 1997).

Romania does have a long way to go in many aspects, but considering the present state of the economy, the legend of Dracula has really been a blessing in disguise for Romania. Tourism means money for impoverished Romanians (Bridge, 1995; Mutler, 1995; Stephen, 1995); this income would otherwise never enter the country. Travelers to Transylvania are learning about a historical figure who exhibited some of the same characteristics as the legendary Dracula they have come to know through literature and film. And tourists who visit Romania also are discovering resorts, lodges, and places of retreat set in geographically beautiful areas.

Little public relations research exists on this topic, fascinating though it is. Romania has suffered so much devastation and social turmoil, it was refreshing for this author to identify something leading the society in a positive direction. Public relations is in its beginning stages in Romania, but with proper training and education the profession will mature. If Romania can develop its tourism industry through effective public relations and marketing, then the economy will grow and the country will have an opportunity to actively participate in the global economy.

Dracula Park Update

Since the summer of 2001 there has been much concern over the location of the Dracula theme park. Proponents of locating the park in Sighisoara have argued that the project would provide badly needed jobs in the surrounding area, which currently suffers serious unemployment. Opponents have countered that the park would destroy not only the city's thirteenth century medieval atmosphere rich in culture and history but also a nearby forest of ancient oaks (Dracula theme park would suck life, 2002; Marinas, 2002; Thorpe, 2002).

To decide what was best for the city, the Romanian government contracted PricewaterhouseCoopers in June 2002 as the consultant firm for the park (Chelminski, 2003). The firm conducted an assessment of the park's location and financial projections and reported that it would be more profitable for the park to be closer to Bucharest (Dracula theme park could be switched, 2002; Dracula theme park would suck life, 2002). Consequently, in November 2002, the Romanian government announced it would move the location of the park to Snagov, just north of the Bucharest airport (Chelminski, 2003). The decision also followed objections by UNESCO, the United Nations cultural organization, that the park would inflict significant damage on Sighisoara (Dracula theme park would suck life, 2002; Marinas, 2002; Thorpe, 2002). Moreover, Prince Charles backed opponents to the Sighisoara location and led protests against the park's originally proposed location (Dracula theme park could be switched, 2002).

As of November 5, 2001, the investment cost for the park was estimated at U.S.$31.5 million and is expected to reach U.S.$100 million (Marinas, 2002). The park is expected to attract more income from international markets, including the Coca-Cola Company, which is negotiating to be the sole beverage provider of the Dracula park. Groundbreaking was scheduled for May 2003 (Chelminski, 2003).

Note

1. Following are a few of the more interesting Web sites with information about Dracula and Romania.

Dracula Tourist Information
www.draculand.com/
http://draculea.homestead.com/
www.draculatour.com
www.draculascastle.com
www.dracastle.bigstep.com
www.activelifestyle.com/romania/draculanew.htm
www.transylvaniainc.com/Transylvania/Dracula.htm
www.transylvania.com
http://members.aol.com/atamas/transylvania.htm
www.undiscoveredlands.com/Transylvania/Dracula.htm

Romanian Travel Sites
http://hometown.aol.com/patraulius/index.html
www.ilovetotravel.com
http://goeaster
http://goeasteurope.com/
http://www.toursandevents.com/
www.romtour.com—Romania National Tourist Office
http://www.top100.ro/

Transylvanian Society of Dracula Sites
www/afn.org/~vampires/tsd.html
www.afn.org/tsd.html
www.chebucto.ns.ca

Discussion Questions

1. As a public relations professional for the Dracula theme park, what would you do if certain organizations began publicizing accusations that the park was "culturally incorrect" and that only those interested in the myth of Dracula would find it entertaining?

2. During the first few days of the grand opening of the Dracula theme park, an elderly person has a heart attack because of one of the "scary" attractions in the park. There were no

signs posted warning those with heart conditions. What crisis management techniques might a public relations professional use?

3. After some bad weather, a ride at the Dracula theme park becomes inoperable while passengers are still on board. They eventually all get out safely. What would a public relations professional do to ensure the rides are safe?

4. In a non-Dracula theme park sponsored tour, a couple gets severe food poisoning and has to be hospitalized. The incident generates international news coverage except some information gets crossed, and the theme park is blamed. How would a public relations professional handle this situation?

5. The Romanian National Tourist Office's latest report shows that there have been far fewer tourists than expected. Your team of public relations practitioners is asked to come up with a media-related way to get international attention. What, as a public relations professional, would you do?

References

Baker, G. (1995, August 26). Draculaian measures: Impaler's birthplace haunting. *The Gazette,* p. H8.

Baum, T. (2000). Timeline: The life of Vlad Tepes III Dracula. [On-line]. Available: www.usanetwork.com/movies/darkprince/history.html.

Bleasel, N., & Varigos, G. (2000). Porphyria cutanea tarda. *Australas J Dermatol, 41,* 197–206.

Brasov, P. (2000, May 26). Romania host Dracula gathering. *The Vancouver Sun,* p. A11.

Bucharest okays Dracula theme park in Romania. (2001, July 8). *Deutsche Press–Agentur,* International News. [On-line.] Available: www.lexisnexis.com (Retrieved November 18, 2002).

Carothers, T. (1996). Romania: Projecting the positive. *Current History,* 118–123.

Cazacu, M. (1994). The Danube Delta. *Unesco Courier, 47,* 34–38.

Chelminski, R. (2003, April). The curse of Count Dracula. *Smithsonian,* pp. 110–115.

Chiriac, M. (2001, May 18). Tourism-Romania: Renewed efforts to attract tourists. [Transcript]. Inter Press Service. [On-line.] Available: www.lexisnexis.com (Retrieved November 18, 2002).

Dascalu, R. (1995, May 26). Dracula's followers gather for Vladfest. *The Calgary Herald,* p. A2.

Devotees whip up Dracula frenzy in Transylvania. (1995, May 29). *The Associated Press,* International News Section. [On-line.] Available: www.lexisnexis.com (Retrieved November 18, 2002).

Dracula revives tourism. (2000, March 6). *Travel Trade Gazette UK & Ireland,* p. 46.

Dracula theme park could be switched to Bucharest. (2002, October 8). [On-line]. Available: www.ananova.com. (Retrieved on November 18, 2002).

Dracula theme park would suck life out of medieval town: UNESCO. (2002, October 2). ABC News On-line. [On-line]. Available: www.abc.net.au/news/newsitems/s691168.htm (Retrieved on November 18, 2002).

Fangs are what they used to be in Romania: Kevin Pilley follows in the flight path of the legendary Count Dracula. (1998, October 31). *The Financial Times–London,* p. 19.

Fernz, H. (2000, November 24). Visiting Dracula's castle is not as scary as you think. *New Straights Times Press Malaysia Berhad,* p. 13.

Foreign tourists look for adventure and originality in Romania. (2000, July 25). *Romanian Business Journal.* Financial Times Information. Global News Wire. [On-line.] Available: www.lexisnexis.com (Retrieved November 18, 2002).

French, S. (1995, April 18). Where tourism needs a little bite. *The Northern Echo.* Available: www.lexisnexis.com (Retrieved November 18, 2002).

Germans to build Dracula theme park in Transylvania. (2001, July 18). *The Associated Press,* Business Section, International News. [On-line]. Available: www.lexisnexis.com (Retrieved November 18, 2002).

Gilbert, R. (1995, August 27). The First World Dracula Congress in Transylvania in pursuit of a myth that refuses to die. *The Independent–London,* p. 47.

Harrop, J. (1994). The role of tourism in the EC and prospects for Eastern Europe. *European Business Review, 94*(2), 20–25.

Heibert, R. (1992). Global public relations in a post-communist world: A new model. *Public Relations Review, 18,* 117–126.

IDEE. IDEE Communications Strategies. (2001, July). (Address: Iancu de Hunedoara 37, sc.D,#1, apt. 1, Bucharest, Romania). [On-line]. Available: www.idee.ro. Available e-mail for general information: idee@idee.ro.

Johnson, M., & Clifford, G. (1994). Dracula is dead and well and attracting tourists to Transylvania. *Life, 17*(11), pp. 66–72.

Kessler, M. (Director). (1997). *Dracula: The true story*. [Videotape]. (Available from Janson Video, Inc. www.janson.com/videos/history/dracula.html)

Lascu, D., Manrai, L., & Manrai, A. (1993). Marketing in Romania: The challenges of the transition from a centrally-planed economy to a consumer-oriented economy. *European Journal of Marketing, 24*(11/12), 102–120.

Lauer, K. (1999, December 14). Ceausescu casts a shadow in Romania: A decade after his death. *Deutsche Presse-Agentur.* [On-line]. Available: www.lexisnexis.com. (Retrieved on November 18, 2002).

Marinas, R. (2002, July 2). Romanian Dracula park plan "undead." Reuters. [On-line.] Available: www.draculaland.com/news2002.html#2jul02. (Retrieved on November 18, 2002).

Marks, J. (1995). Dracula's new lease on life. *U.S. News & World Report, 118*(21), pp. 45–46.

Marsh, V. (1995, May 25). Romania prepares for Dracula without tears: First World Dracula Congress heralds start of Transylvania tourism drive. *Financial Times–London,* p. 3.

McAleer, P. (2001, July 14). Dracula emerges from his tomb: Forbidden recognition by Romanian's Nicolae Ceausescu, the vampire has been unearthed to entice the tourists with terror, says Phelim McAleer. *The Financial Times,* p. 20.

Montgomery, L. (1997, December 28). Following Dracula's trail through Romania. *The Herald.* [On-line.] Available: www.lexisnexis.com (Retrieved November 18, 2002).

Museums in Bucharest. (2001, January 11). *Romanian Business Journal.* Financial Times Information. Global News Wire. [On-line.] Available: www.lexisnexis.com (Retrieved November 18, 2002).

Papacostea, S. (1996). Captive Clio: Romanian histiography under communist rule. *European History Quarterly, 26,* 181–208.

Ramet, S. (1992). Balkan pluralism and its enemies. *Orbis, 36*(4), 547–564.

Rodina, V. (1995, May 23). Romania hosts First Dracula Congress. *United Press International.* [On-line.] Available: www.lexisnexis.com (Retrieved November 18, 2002).

Romania: A lot at stake; Dracula land hopes to lure blood money. (2001, July 20). *The Toronto Sun,* p. 50.

Romania plans to bleed tourists. (2001, March 22). *The Houston Chronicle,* Business Section, p. 1.

Rose, R. (1999). Another great transformation. *Journal of Democracy, 10*(1), 51–56.

Reuter UPI AP News. (1997, March 31). Hungarian American List. [On-line]. Available: www.hungary-request@majordomo.umd.edu. Newsgroup: www.soc.culture.magyar.com.

Scott, K. (1995, June 3). A legend they can count on. *The Hearld,* p. 25.

Shapiro, H. (1996, July 26). Travels in the land of Dracula. *The Jerusalem Post,* p. 13.

Stephen, C. (1995, May 29). Romanians stake all on the myth of Dracula. *The Daily Telegraph,* p. 10.

Thorpe, N. (2002, June 27–28). Romania scraps Dracula Land. BBC News. [On-line]. Available: http://newsbbc.co.uk/l/hi/world/Europe/2071513.stm. (Retrieved on November 18, 2002).

Thurston, M. (2001, May 5). Romania sinks teeth into Dracula dollars. *Agence France Presse,* International News.

Turk, J. (1996). Romania: From publicate past to public relations future. In H. Culbertson & N. Chen (Eds.), *International public relations: A comparative analysis* (pp. 341–347). Mahwah, NJ: Lawrence Erlbaum Associates.

Velea, G. (1996, April 4). Romania–economy: A tourism boom, on shaky foundations. International Press Service. [On-line.] Available: www.lexisnexis.com (Retrieved November 18, 2002).

Verčič, D., Grunig, L. A., & Grunig, J. E. (1996). Global and specific principles of public relations: Evidence from Slovenia. In H. Culbertson & N. Chen (Eds.), *International public relations: A comparative analysis* (pp. 31–65). Mahwah, NJ: Lawrence Erlbaum Associates.

Vospitannik, N., Littlejohn, D., & Arnot, R. (1997). Environments, tourism and tour operators: 1985–1995 in Central and Eastern Europe. *International Journal of Contemporary Hospitality Management, 9*(5–6), 204–214.

Voss, V., Nettleton, S., Dhue, L., & Oswald, S. (1998, October 31). Exploring the Real Transylvania. [Transcript]. CNN Travel Guide.

Waterfall, C. (1997). Reality bites. *Geographical Magazine, 69*(2), 34–36.

Wilkinson, P. (1997, June 14). Whitby takes fright at the spectre of a Dracula invasion. *The Times.*

Woodard, C. (1995, May 10). A mimic of Miami misses the boat in ex-red Romania. *Christian Science Monitor,* p. 7.

8

Theoretical Development of Public Relations in Russia

Katerina Tsetsura

Dean Kruckeberg

Key Points _____

- Russian public relations theory has been developed under the influence of the U.S. theoretical body of public relations.

- There is a historical association between public relations and propaganda.

- An absence of a communication tradition in Russia has led to the evolution of two separate approaches to public relations education—a business and a journalism perspective.

- Female public relations practitioners have a unique place in Russia and work in every area of public relations as the profession has broadened in function.

- Public relations ethics offers an international challenge.

- "Black" versus "white" public relations is currently associated with a discussion of ethics in modern Russia.

Perhaps nowhere has contemporary public relations evolved more quickly than in Russia, where today a high level of professional practice exists after a mere fifteen years of development. Russian public relations is well on its way to achieving acknowledgment and respect, both within the country itself and globally: Public relations firms throughout Russia are representing a range of clients, and internal public relations departments have been formed within many Russian companies; government departments are employing specialists in public affairs; and nonprofit organizations have hired public relations specialists. Moreover, Russian public relations scholars have been actively examining the theories and practice of public relations, both in Russia and in Western developed countries—especially the theories and practice of public relations in the United States.

Global Market Offers Opportunities

To determine the significance of Russian public relations research and scholarship, one must first understand the worldwide importance of contemporary public relations practice. The trend of global market expansion offers public relations a unique opportunity to create an effective worldwide communication infrastructure for its global practice. Russian scholar Alyoshina (1997) emphasizes that globalization is an important factor of public relations development. She reports

> Global companies, modern leaders of world markets, bring to Russia high-concurrent management methods and business culture. Theory and practice of public relations have already been formed in Western countries. That is why today the high, world-standard level of business management cannot exist in Russia without public relations management. (pp. 4–5)

Thus, public relations becomes an extremely important, indeed essential, professional practice in the modern world. Public relations literature reveals that its contemporary practice is heavily guided by theory (Kruckeberg & Starck, 1988). That is why public relations theoretical foundations should be examined in detail, and the findings of such examination should be applied in practice. U.S. experience in public relations clearly has shown that a theoretical framework continues to lead public relations practice into the new century and helps to form and to perfect modern practice.

U.S. Theory Influences Russian Public Relations

Russian public relations theory has been developed under the influence of the U.S. theoretical body of public relations. To Russian scholars this seems logical and rather obvious: Public relations began to develop in Russia not longer than fifteen years ago, whereas U.S. public relations theory is at least a century old.

Alyakrinskaya (2000) confirms that public relations in Russia is borrowed from U.S. practice and that the U.S. perspective on public relations practice is being internalized in Russia. However, any national character of public relations practice in Russia is not yet clear, and no formula for the evaluation and examination of Russian public relations practice has yet been defined. Rather, Russian public relations theory is developing impetuously. Nevertheless, the U.S. scientific tradition in public relations, coming from a country where public relations evolved as a separate professional area, has had a tremendous impact on the developmental process of Russian public relations practice. Russian research and educational materials on public relations theory and practice, including essays and textbooks, clearly reflect Russians' tendency to adopt U.S. theoretical perspectives (Borisov, 2000; Tsetsura, 2000a).

Of course, Western Europe also has made its contributions to Russian public relations. Russian public relations theory has many similarities with modern European theory and practice because of a range of geopolitical factors (Lebedeva, 1999). However, one must remember that European theory, in turn, was also formed to a great extent through the influence of the U.S. body of knowledge in public relations. Verčič (1994) argues

> Public relations came to Europe only after the Second World War together with American "scientific management" as a part of the Marshall Plan. I am not saying that there were no individuals in Europe practicing public relations on a limited scale before the 1950's. But isolated individuals do not make a profession. Public relations started to develop late in Europe compared to the U.S. (p. 10)

Nessmann (1995) points out that the development of the field in the United States and Europe might be characterized by ideas moving in both directions, "with Americans influencing Europeans much more than vice versa in the past and present" (p. 153). Nessmann continues

> In other words, theoretical and practical elements were devised by Americans (especially by Bernays), taken up by European authors . . . and further developed in their own right in a European context. . . . It should not be forgotten that European public relations is strongly oriented towards the American scene. (p. 153)

Thus, we can only conclude that Russian public relations is heavily based on U.S. research, scholarship, and knowledge. No formal research described any connections between theories in the United States and in Russia or the impact that United States's theory has had in forming Russian public relations theory before Tsetsura (2000a) made the first attempt to identify and characterize the extent to which U.S. public relations theory has affected Russian theory. After examining major theoretical frameworks covered in the most popular U.S. and Russian textbooks, she concluded that Russian public relations theory depended heavily on U.S. theory. However, her research showed that many Russian textbooks lacked discussion about the latest developments in U.S. public relations theory, which demonstrated that Russian public relations theory is still underdeveloped.

To understand the reasons behind the theoretical development of public relations in Russia, we must closely examine the circumstances under which public relations has emerged in Russia and how it continues to develop in that country. The next section of this chapter analyzes historical and cultural particularities of the development of public relations in Russia.

Development of Russian Public Relations Theory

Twenty years ago, Russians were not familiar with the concept of public relations; a definition could only be found in reference to "marketing" in *Marketing: Collected Essays,* by Kostukhina (1974), a book about "modern problems of capitalistic markets":

> Public relations—1. Establishment of relations with publics. 2. Department for establishing such relations (its goal is to develop positive attitudes toward a company among needed publics, including a number of actions and sometimes advertising). (p. 86)

Of course, marketing was a part of capitalistic economic theories, and for many years in Russia public relations was considered a marketing function that was used in countries with capitalistic economic systems; thus, public relations was only considered in a marketing context in Russian business studies of that time.

With political and economic changes in Russia, public relations came to life, and the old literature, as well as the old comprehension of public relations, was first brought into use. Scholars having business backgrounds began talking about public relations as an effective tool of marketing. At the same time, publishing houses began translating and releasing U.S. literature on popular economic subjects, which included some discussion about the concept of public relations. Russian professional translators, who did not have any "real-life" experience with public relations, translated public relations terms into Russian, creating several controversial definitions: "Indirect advertising (from English—public relations)—any contacts with public and media"; "propaganda (from English—publicity)—method of indirect advertising, which includes the usage of editorial, non-paid space in the media" (Ozhegov, 1984, p. 156).

Even *Sovremennyj Slovar Insotrannyx Slov*, a Russian modern dictionary of foreign words (1993), explained publicity as "advertising and popularity." Today, these translations seem inappropriate and illogical, but at the time in which they had appeared, nobody in Russia had yet comprehensively studied public relations, its history, and its ultimate goals, and so the definitions were accepted.

Modern public relations theory in Russia uses many English words to decide concepts, thereby preventing precise translations into Russian. Such practice began in the mid-1980s when public relations began to evolve as an independent area of study. Literal, word-for-word translations did not reflect the essence of the concepts. Moreover, because of a lack of historic context in Russia, the Russian language often did not have synonyms for some words, such as *publicity*. Thus, traditional scholars began to accept "loaned" translations.

Public Relations Established in Russia

Public relations has quickly become established in Russia, and several public relations concepts, as well as many marketing terms, have become a part of the Russian lexicon as public relations and marketing have become parts of the Russian social/economic infrastructure. Active development of public relations professional practice has led to an active examination of public relations by scholars.

Researchers who had switched from studying economics to studying public relations had broadly supported an already existing understanding of public relations simply as a part of marketing. Such scholars advocated the practice of public relations only as a means of marketing support. Golubkov (1994), in his marketing dictionary, emphasized public relations as an effective and inexpensive way to communicate with publics. Publicity as a major component of public relations was being defined as a business tool that was being used in Western countries. So economists Feoktistova and Krasnuk (1993) developed this definition:

> Publicity—any positive commerce messages, presentations or materials about goods or services, releasing through the media and non-paid by parties concerned. (p. 125)

At the same time, another approach to public relations was also evolving. Scholars who were examining U.S. and European perspectives on public relations were developing a competing philosophy. Utkin and Zaitsev (1993), in one of the first Russian works on the subject, argued that public relations was an ideology of creating reputation, responsibility, and trust, rather than simply a method of gaining immediate profits. Moreover, translated and original works in public relations from other countries were accentuating these ideas by providing well-supported explanations of the nature of public relations.

Some of the scholars who were especially interested in public relations began a diligent investigation of its practice. They developed theories that created the substance of modern Russian public relations. Others, as Tsetsura (2000b) pointed out, were persistent in their attempts to prove that public relations was unnecessary and that attention to public relations was undeserved:

> The latter scholars argued that public relations methods were unfair and manipulative and that the only goal of this "pseudo-study" was to create a positive image without spending much money, i.e., by using any direct or indirect means, including free advertising in the media. Some journalism educators and editors actively supported this idea. They felt cheated by the new public relations practitioners who were trying to get publicity. Such opinions were very popular, and it was easy to find an explanation for these contentions: anyone who wanted to learn more about public relations and publicity used definitions from earlier published works and dictionaries. This "double nature" of public relations could only be erased through the process of exercising true public relations practice and constantly explaining public relations' true philosophy to the various Russian publics. (p. 5)

Therefore, public relations—as is the case in any new scholarly and professional area—was not recognized for some time in Russia. It took several years of active practice and many scholarly and practitioner discussions about the true nature of public relations before positive perceptions of public relations began replacing negative perceptions. Although the problems of understanding and accepting the nature of public relations seem to be irrelevant for modern Russian public relations, some questions still exist about defining public relations. In many cases, Russian scholars use definitions of Western scholars, for example,

> Public relations is a management function, which evaluates relations among publics, identifies politics and actions of individuals or organizations with publics' interests and realizes a program of actions to gain publics' understanding and acceptance. (Mencher, 1993, p. 347)

The following definition of public relations, offered by British author Black (1993), is also popular among Russian educators:

> Public relations is an art and study of reaching a harmony through mutual understanding based upon truth and full information. (p. 17).

At the same time, some scholars provided their own definitions of Russian public relations. According to Pocheptsov (1998), public relations, in general, is a study of public opinion management.

Because public relations can be used, and is used in many areas, it is sometimes difficult to identify what literature is employed in each particular case. To understand Russian public relations, we have to examine its origins.

Public Relations—Historically Associated with Propaganda

Historically, public relations is associated with propaganda, although some U.S. public relations theorists vigorously resist this legacy, arguing that the term *propaganda* should not be used in discussions about public relations (Tsetsura, 2000a).

In the mid-1980s, the negative connotations of "Soviet propaganda" were broadly cited in discussions about Russian public relations. Such associations with propaganda were very common among Russians during that time because they had just been given freedom of speech and they were reevaluating their beliefs and values related to the societal role of communication.

However, during this same time, Russian scholars were beginning to explore a "neutral" theory of propaganda, a concept that was shocking to most Russians. Western authors Pratkanis and Aronson (1991) were among the first educators who presented such an approach, which was actively extended by Russian scholars. In their book, *Age of Propaganda* (1991), Pratkanis and Aronson supported the idea of the synonymous meanings of "propaganda" and "persuasion." They used those words together, distinguishing them by definitions of "mindless propaganda" and "thoughtful persuasion," thus giving the term "propaganda" a neutral meaning: it might be positive (open and honest explanation) or negative (lying, manipulative, based on total inspiration, but not on argued evidence).

This concept seemed acceptable but created problems outside of the scholarly community. Some Russian publics, overwhelmed by negative perceptions of propaganda and remembering the old definitions of publicity and public relations, made inaccurate connections between the two concepts, thereby relegating the term "public relations" a mere double-speak of "propaganda." The differentiation between public relations and propaganda that Western public relations scholars had distinguished for years became immediately an urgent issue to resolve to the Russian scholarly world.

The discussion went beyond theoretical and geographical borders. A European scholar, Nessmann (1995), pointed out that many practitioners still believed that public relations sought to manipulate public opinion and that these communicators practiced unethical and asymmetrical communication. This position might be explained easily by the lack of theoretical knowledge of public relations. Borisov (2000), president of the Russian Public Relations Association, warned practitioners that modern "public relations is risked to become the synonym of manipulating of public consciousness, the tool to initiate the information wars, the tool that is able to make black white, and the new issue of old agitation" (p. 1).

Of course, U.S. practitioners and educators had faced similar problems not that long ago. Even today in the United States, questions of the manipulative nature of public relations are debated. Stevens (1985) said that public relations' success does not happen because of manipulation. Although the myth about public manipulators was popular once, it has started to disappear. Yet, there are always some supporters of this myth. Stevens observed

> This myth of the super-manipulative PR man harms the professional in a number of ways. Clients sometime confuse expertise with omnipotence. They think the PR professional can gain unlimited access to any given page in the newspaper, any magazine, any TV show, simply by using a combination of flattery and expense account lunches. (p. 105)

Thus, the relationship between propaganda and public relations might not be so easy to define, and the examination of their mutual influences and coexistence creates fascinating discussions. It is especially important now to continue examining these issues because of the recent tendency to reevaluate communication phenomena in the context of public relations.

Absence of Russian Communication Tradition

Perhaps the primary difference in the evolution of public relations theory in the United States and its origins in Russia is the absence of a communication tradition in the latter country. Areas that U.S. communication schools customarily have studied were split in Russia among several schools, which becomes the key to understanding the major differences between Russian and U.S. public relations and remains the best explanation for the journalism foundation and the consequential journalistic impact on Russian public relations.

In Russia, scholars of journalism and business education programs began to define and to discuss conceptual frameworks and global points of view concerning public relations, and professionals in the two areas have argued about the principles of public relations as well as the methods of teaching in this professional area. Business schools concentrated on the management–marketing functions of public relations (we could call it "business-type public relations"), whereas journalism programs focused on the management–communication function ("journalism-type public relations").

After ten years of active development of public relations in programs of higher education in Russia, the significant impact that those first courses and their creators had on public relations education in Russia have become obvious. This impact can be identified not only through the existence of these two schools of thought and the scholarly debates about the business or communication nature of public relations but also through the contemporary curricula for public relations education programs in Russia.

Popularity and growth of public relations motivated many school administrators and faculty to create their own programs in which students could have emphases, minors, or majors in public relations. Faculty members who became interested in public relations started to prepare syllabi and to promote public relations courses within their departments. Again, depending on the backgrounds and views of those scholars, public relations education followed a business or a journalism core.

Today, Russian higher education has equally strong public relations schools from both backgrounds. Existing public relations education programs at Moscow, St. Petersburg, and Voronezh State Universities, founded in the beginning of the 1990s (Tsetsura, 2000a), are examples of journalism-oriented public relations education programs. Meanwhile, schools such as Moscow State Academy of Management, St. Petersburg Electro-Technical University, and Voronezh Politechnical University offer business-oriented public relations education programs. As of April 2000, fifty-six Russian universities (about half of them situated in schools of journalism) offered majors in public relations (Konovalova, 2000).

There is no need to further discuss the advantages and disadvantages of both given that the purpose of this chapter is to examine the journalism-oriented approach. However, it is important to note that the public relations scholarly establishment has come from a journalism background, which dictates Russian public relations theory and practice because of the relatively greater success of public relations education programs that are offered by journalism schools.

The early 1990s became the foundation years of public relations education in Russia, as well as in other countries in the Commonwealth of Independent States (CIS). Names of the scholars who entered the public relations education field (e.g., Blazhnov, Vikentiev, Krylov, Alyoshina, Pocheptsov, and Zverintsev) have appeared in professional journals and monographs (Tsetsura, 2000a). Quickly, those people became known as the pioneers of Russian public relations. Nowadays, these scholars continue to form a theoretical core of Russian public relations. Different issues on the practical side of the field, such as publicity, crisis management, consumer and community relations, as well as public affairs (particularly political campaigns), are the most popular areas of study.

Writing about developing public relations in different countries, Kogan (1970) explained the typical idiosyncrasies in Europe. Great economic progress came when many of the old economic and social structures were being changed. Business was receptive to new ideas and new techniques, and the influence of a younger generation of professional managers was making itself felt. This statement reflects the scheme of building public relations in postcommunist Russia. Goreigin and Nikolaev (1996) remarked that public relations in Russia as a new study has already seen an interesting, albeit very short, history. This history deserves a review not only because it provides a look at the evolution of a profession but also because it represents a new dimension in communication. Goreigin and Nikolaev established three stages in the history of Russian public relations: (1) 1989 to 1992—the journalism stage, which focused on openness and politics; (2) 1992 to 1993—the bureaucratic stage, which focused on controlling the message; and (3) 1993 to the present, which is focusing on measuring the effect of communication. However, today the situation in Russia has already changed, so it will be useful to add some other stages to this conception.

An alternative explanation for the development of public relations in Russia also deserves to be mentioned. Tsetsura (1999) proposed that women played a significant role in the growth of Russian public relations in its earliest stage of development. A discussion of women's roles in the process of public relations development is not only a tribute to feminism but also a necessity that must be included in any accurate historical account. Of course, women had had an impact on public relations history in the United States as well. In the 1920s Edward L. Bernays and his wife, Doris E. Fleischman, founded one of the first public relations firms. Their firm worked well thanks not only to Bernays but also to his wife. However, the predominance of men in the field was a key factor at that time. Many historians have pointed out that Bernays tried to avoid associating his wife's name with public relations. Even later, when feminism in the United States had become popular, and after Bernays had encouraged his wife to pursue her career, he nevertheless set some parameters for her. We can see the result of those efforts today. Edward L. Bernays "is viewed as the founder of the profession they pioneered together" (L. Tye, 1998, p. 127).

The same fate awaited Russian women who began working in public relations in the 1980s. Although equal rights for men and women had been recognized in Russia, it was difficult for females to present themselves as leaders in this new professional occupation. The problem of male–female leadership in public relations remains a vital issue today in both Russia and the United States. Nevertheless, Russian women, as well as their U.S. counterparts, occupy a variety of leading positions, and they work in a wide range of areas in public relations. For example, most of the Russian public relations practitioners who currently work in nonprofit organizations are women (Tsetsura, 1999). A female practitioner, Veronika Moiseeva, is an executive director of the Moscow agency, Imageland PR Worldwide. She also was one of the first presidents of the Russian Association of Consulting Companies in Public Relations (AKOC) (Tsetsura, 1999).

As mentioned earlier, public relations in Russia has had several antecedents, including journalism and advertising. Professionals who worked in those areas watched the Western experience in using public relations and understood the extent of influence public relations might have on Russian publics. They began using public relations methods to achieve specific goals to establish good long-term relationships between their organizations and these organizations' publics. Moreover, the need for public relations was accelerated because of Russia's emerging democracy and free-market economy.

Public Relations and Media Relations

As in most countries, public relations in Russia started with media relations. Female journalists found public relations to be a fresh opportunity to realize their career ambitions. It is considered general knowledge that, in Russian journalism, men predominate, and they leave to women only the opportunity to cover relatively unimportant or entertainment-type stories. That is why public relations, which was regarded as work in the second-tier of newsworthiness, provided the best opportunity for careers for Russian women.

However, in the middle of the 1980s, public relations began to grow and to develop so quickly that it soon became a highly desirable career in which to work. In addition, journalists and behavioral scientists began to appreciate the power of public relations to influence publics and to form global images. Thus, Russian men began turning to public relations as well, and they soon began to replace women in the highest positions. "The best journalists are leaving journalism for richer pastures in public relations (including serving as political spokespersons)," noted Johnson (1995, p. 181) in his essay for *Global Journalism: Survey of International Communication,* describing that moment in time of Russian journalism history. Nevertheless, many women already had valuable experience in Russian public relations, so they were able to keep their high-level professional positions.

Thus, female public relations practitioners were drawn early on to this new professional career and thereby received credit for their part in its development. For instance, the first public relations agency in Voronezh (the Black-Soil Region of Russia), a city with a population of more than one million, was founded by a female journalist (Tsetsura, 1999).

Today, Russian female practitioners work in every area of public relations, including public affairs, media, and customer relations, as well as in financial relations. Women chair four of the sixteen Moscow public relations agencies that specialize in political consulting (National News Service Agency, 2000). Many other women work for public relations and advertising agencies, as well as in public relations departments of commercial companies in the entertainment and fashion industries. Russian women also practice public relations for nonprofit and government organizations, banks, media, and trade nets. They conduct public relations research, and they teach public relations at Russian universities.

Russian public relations theory continues to develop dramatically. Indeed, the Russian educational system has developed and codified requirements for a public relations curriculum; the Federal Russian Committee of Higher Education has certified an official public relations major that recognizes public relations as a separate area of study (Department of Higher Education of Russian Federation, 2000).

The practitioner side of public relations, however, concentrates its efforts on specialized areas of public relations, such as corporate and governmental public relations, and, in many cases, ignores other areas of public relations. Novikov (1999) indicates that political consulting and corporate public relations are two main areas of current Russian practice. It is not surprising that the majority of research and articles in professional journals are focused on these areas. Nevertheless, the public relations field has defended its right for professional autonomy and today has become a vital part of Russian life, which helps promote modern social-economic changes at the national level. In 1996, U.S.$100 million were spent for public relations services in the Russian market (Novikov, 1999). Primarily in Moscow, public relations firms and whole alliances of firms are forming and engaging in campaigns that are designed to attract attention and to generate interest in these firms among professional publics and society at large. For example, some agencies conduct seminars, whereas others sponsor competitions. They also invite foreign colleagues to speak to Russian practitioners and create other types of linkages and relationships (Eremin & Borisov, 2000). Russian scholars Goreigin and Nikolaev (1995) note that the creation of public relations professional associations, the most prominent of which are the Russian Association of Public Relations (PACO) and the Russian Association of Consulting Companies in Public Relations (AKOC), have helped to legitimize public relations as a profession in Russia; these associations also have helped to create professional standards for public relations practitioners as well as to facilitate professional communication.

Russian public relations has gone down a twisted path of development, in many ways similar to the historical evolution of U.S. public relations. As is discussed later in this chapter, contemporary issues in public relations theory of both Russia and the United States are similar to one another. At the same time, many researchers emphasize the challenges that educators and practitioners might face working in international public relations as well as in public relations at the global level. International ethics is one of such challenges.

Ethics as an International Challenge

At a national level, public relations is both complex and difficult. This complexity grows when members of diverse communities with different cultures, nationalities, histories, and geopolitics start practicing public relations among one another. Because public relations practice is based on experience and on repeated use of public relations methods, many cultural assumptions and unique characteristics nevertheless can be applied universally in public relations practice (Botan, 1993).

Wakefield (1997) identified various general principles of public relations that can be applied universally, pointing out that professional ethics is one of them. The results of a recent study of Russian public relations practice have confirmed Wakefield's results, confirming the principle of professional ethics as the most important general principle (Egorova, 2000).

Although many strategic principles can be applied worldwide, tactics must be adapted to each country. Previous studies (Ferguson, 1998; Sriramesh, 1996; Wakefield, 1997) suggest that the level of a nation's development as well as its cultural, economic, and political environment affect the way public relations is practiced within each country as well as internationally. Tulupov (1996) supports this statement, providing evidence that U.S. methods of resolving public relations problems did not bring positive results in Russian public relations practice. He warns public relations professionals of the danger in using campaign actions specifically created for U.S. publics in Russian public relations practices. Cultural and psychographical particularities of Russia must be considered, according to Pheophanov (2001). He claims that advertising as well as public relations practice in Russia copies Western examples and brings values alien to Russian publics. However, Pheophanov fails to provide substantive evidence of such claims. Describing examples of German, Spanish, and U.S. products advertised in Russia, he makes contradictory observations. He criticizes, for example, Russian adaptations of names for German-produced vodkas, such as Tzar, Kazak, Rasputin, and at the same time complains that Russian professionals and Western producers "very infrequently use . . . national specifics" (Pheophanov, 2001, p. 54).

Undoubtedly, the practice of public relations depends on the national idiosyncrasies of each country. Earlier, Durbin (1968) described European differences in the practice of public relations where many companies encountered problems in using common public relations methods that they had imported from the United States. He noted that organizations and firms had to remember national differences every time they tried to conduct U.S. public relations campaigns in Europe. Years later, Culbertson and Chen (1996) stated that "a nation's political system and culture do help shape its practice of public relations" (p. ix). Tsetsura (1997) demonstrated how some public relations practices, such as the distribution of press releases through the mail, did not work during a campaign to promote an annual festival of Children's Computer Creation "KidSoft," but such difficulties seem to be more of a technical rather than a conceptual nature.

Scholars have advocated the theme of global public relations in the consideration of public relations ethics and professionalism. Starck and Kruckeberg (2001) define globalization as "the economic and cultural ways in which nations' activities have become increasingly interlinked" (p. 56). Kruckeberg (1998) earlier proposed, "As the level of public relations professionalism increases, multicultural perspectives will tend to become subsumed by a global professionalism that will tend to result in a solidarity of ethical assumptions based on increasingly common professional beliefs and ideologies" (p. 46). Kruckeberg referred to Creedon's work on "strategic ethics" in international public relations, which means building relationships from a mutually accepted sense of values. With an increasing level of professionalism, ethics becomes more universal, and therefore, similar values become recognized by practitioners from different countries. Kruckeberg concludes, "As professionalism increases, as the value of public relations is increasingly recognized and as practitioners increasingly become part of an organization's dominant coalition, the range of multicultural perspectives in public relations will correspondingly decrease" (p. 48). Mortensen (1996) concurs and calls for "the development of new international perspectives, more sophisticated, research-based operational models, and intensified drives toward universally accepted professionalism" (p. 338). Thus, universal practice and professional ethical norms will dominate over multicultural perspectives in public relations.

Russian scholars agree on the universality of public relations practice. Pocheptsov (1998) contends that Russian public relations practice today in many ways depends on the Western experience; however, he fairly notes that such tendency characterizes any new discipline. He argues that Russian professionals should learn more about public relations experiences in other countries, so they can develop better practices in their own country.

Theoretical foundations of public relations also stay the same throughout the world, although, in some cases, they attract more theories outside of the field as well as new directions for theories within public relations. For instance, Wakefield (1997) organized research in international public relations into several groups that unite major theories in the fields of global society, culture, management, and communication and that interact with separate public relations theories, providing the context for public relations in international areas.

Several leading theories form and expand the international public relations body of knowledge. Among these is the concept of the "global village" as conceptualized in the past several decades and examined by Kruckeberg (1996, 2000) in the context of international public relations and modern globalization; cultural dimensions and the practice of "excellent" public relations described by Sriramesh and White (1992); media help in integrating publics and issues worldwide based on coverage of activist agendas (Hiebert, 1992); and implications of other communication theories (structural functionalism, evolutionary perspective, social conflict, and symbolic interactionism) for public relations research (Newsom, Turk, & Kruckeberg, 2000). These theoretical concepts have to be considered when developing international public relations theories and, therefore, when formulating applications for international public relations practice. More importantly, international scholars who are seeking to develop the theoretical foundation of public relations in their own countries should examine these concepts. In the search for ethical public relations, public relations scholars must turn to modern theories that emphasize the importance of community and activism in modern public relations.

Another popular modern theory in public relations is a "reconstructed theory," which is linked with the phenomenon of an organization's social responsibility. Kruckeberg and Starck (1988) define public relations as cooperative, interactive, and complex communication and argue that public relations is best practiced when used as an active attempt to restore and maintain a sense of community that could be practiced as a process of communication among publics. Thus, community relations is not a specialization within public relations, but the main element of community-building theory. Kruckeberg and Starck argue that a public relations professional should not concentrate on being a "news person." "Such attitude today is anathema to those schooled in contemporary public relations," the authors observe (p. 70). Likewise, media relations should be revised and focused on communication with publics. Because a sense of community has become less strong in modern mass society, Kruckeberg and Starck propose that the public relations practitioner can help satisfy the need to restore this sense of community that was lost through modern means of communication and transportation.

> Our argument is that an appropriate approach to community relations should be an active and direct attempt to restore and maintain a sense of community. Only through such a conceptual approach does the practice of community relations deal directly with the problems shared by the organization and its geographical public. (p. 83)

This argument generated ideas of activism, which later helped to create a theory of activism in public relations in connection with the theory of excellence. L. Grunig (1992) argues that the behavior of activist groups is the crucial element of the environment in which public relations programs are practiced. Activists can play a critical role in limiting the organization's ability to achieve its goals. Grunig's research shows that organizations that practice successful public relations view activist groups as strategic publics and respond to activists' actions using the two-way symmetrical model. In a continuation of this theory development, Holtzhausen (2000) points out, "The fact that public relations as activism receives so little attention supports the theory that public relations has become part and parcel of the maintenance of metanarratives and domination in society" (p. 100). She suggests emphasizing the role of activism in modern public relations. L. Grunig views activism as one of the necessary components of democracy and, therefore, of public relations practice. A study by Egorova (2000) confirms the idea that public relations practice is more effective if activism is present. She shows that, compared to the United States, activism in Russia has not gained sufficient power to influence government and organizations to change their politics. This is an important phenomenon for Russian public relations practice, whose influence and significance, unfortunately, remain to be discovered by Russian public relations theorists.

So far, discussions about media relations and mass communication in Russian public relations practice dominate Russian contemporary public relations research (Tulchinsky, 1994; Vikentiev, 1998). Research efforts concentrate on mastering techniques of image creation and reputation (Chumikov, 1999). Public affairs is also a well-represented topic in Russian literature (Miroshnichenko, 1998) as well as media relations (Alyoshina, 1997; Tsetsura, 1997).

Currently, the most popular discussion associated with ethics in modern Russian public relations (PR) theory is built around the problem of "black PR" versus "white PR." The terms were introduced in the beginning of the theoretical development of public relations in Russia and soon became popular among scholars and professionals. "Black PR" is associated with manipulative techniques that can be used mostly in election campaigns and advertising. "White PR" represents the Western-type public relations practice that is based on the philosophy of "excellent" public relations (Maksimov, 1999).

Some scholars dislike the idea of dividing public relations into "black" and "white." Instead, they explain that "black" public relations is actually not public relations at all, but rather "propaganda" (Tulupov, 1996). Many public relations specialists point out that "white versus black PR" discussions exist mainly because there is a lack of a commonly adopted definition of the profession as well as a lack of understanding of the philosophy and ethics of public relations (Novinskij, 2000). U.S. scholars agree with the opinion of the nonexistence of public relations' "black nature," stating that "any misuse or abuse of public relations is a question, not of 'bad' public relations of which only an individual practitioner can be held responsible, but rather such misuse or abuse becomes a question of unethical professional practice which is of collective concern and which must be the collective responsibility of all practitioners" (Kruckeberg, 1992, p. 34).

Meanwhile, ethics remains the weakest point in Russian public relations. Although Russian professionals cite Western codes of ethics and even create their own, including the codes of ethics of the Russian Public Relations Association and other professional associations, ethics are frequently not applied or considered in modern Russian public relations practice (Pocheptsov, 1998). In contrast, modern U.S. public relations is overwhelmed with propositions on modern ethics including the collective work of such authors as J. Grunig and Hunt (1984), Heath (1992), and Kruckeberg (2000). A philosophy of ethical public relations has formulated modern values of public relations, one of which is "its ability to contribute to the collective shared reality that brings harmony, a shared perspective that leads people to similar, compatible conclusions" (Heath, 1992, p. 318). Heath concludes, "To achieve its full potential in this regard requires constant and aggressive critical re-examination of the rhetorical substance, form, practices, ethics, and strategies that are employed in public relations" (p. 318). Russian scholars will need to follow this path to be able to develop the public relations body of knowledge further.

Conclusion

Public relations has an impact on our work, our points of view, and on our world understanding. That is why this field can be considered as the art of dealing with publics to achieve mutual understanding and constructive activity in the world (Black, 1993). The profession of public relations and its views have changed tremendously within the past ten years not only in Russia but also in other countries (Clarke, 2000; Sparks & Conwell, 1998). Professionalism in public relations is expressed in a wide diapason of values and beliefs that parallel the wishes of organizations and their publics. Public relations plays a vital role in today's philosophy of relationships. Socially responsible behavior of any organization becomes one of the most important goals of modern public relations. Currently, public relations practice in Russia struggles for continuous exercise of social responsibility. Many unethical practices in the field have generated discussions about "black PR" among professionals and members of society. However, public relations educators and scholars believe that, as the level of professionalism rises, more ethical practices will appear and more severe unethical practices will be punished. One of the ways to ensure the professional development of the field in Russia is to continue the development of theoretical foundations of Russian public relations. Not only scholars but also practitioners can play a vital role in such development by using Russian public relations in ways that challenge negative perceptions of the actively growing field. Since the beginning of its development in Russia, public relations has matured considerably both in theory and practice. Learning from the experience of the Western world, Russian public relations now uses conceptual foundations and shares fundamental views of the field. At the same time, Russia has its own cultural and historical particularities that are reflected in the Russian public relations practices at the technical level.

Today, the profession is more than simply a "seeking" process for strategies and tactics to ensure successful communication between organizations and publics; rather, public relations is viewed as an "establishing and maintaining" process of creating mutual responsibility for a better society not only within one particular country but also throughout the world. That is why it is extremely important to continue to develop, study, and apply new theoretical concepts in public relations practice. It is hoped that this shared meaning of the significance of public relations theory will soon be recognized by U.S. and Russian scholars of the twenty-first century.

Discussion Questions

1. In what ways can public relations help ameliorate twenty-first-century social problems? Describe specific examples in the United States and elsewhere throughout the world in which public relations addressed not only clients' public relations problems but also social problems.

2. Why does Russia look predominantly to the United States for its public relations theory as opposed to Western Europe or elsewhere, such as the Pacific Rim countries?

3. Can the concept "propaganda" be truly "neutral"? Explain the differences between "mindless propaganda" and "thoughtful persuasion."

4. What are some differences you might expect between journalism-oriented public relations and business-oriented public relations in Russia, as described in this chapter?

5. What unique problems might women public relations practitioners in Russia have that their counterparts in the United States have not had to overcome or have already overcome?

6. As a society that is redefining and rebuilding itself, what opportunities exist in Russia for community building as recommended by Kruckeberg and Starck?

7. In what ways can public relations scholars in Russia ensure that public relations is both practiced ethically and perceived as practiced ethically?

References

Alyakrinskaya, M. (2000, Spring). In search of the national formula. *Dialog* [On-line serial]. Available: http://www.pr-dialog.newmail.ru/Alyakrinskaya.html.

Alyoshina, I. (1997). *Public relations dlja menedgerov I marketerov* [Public relations for managers and marketers]. Moscow: Gnom-press.

Black, S. (1993). *The essentials of public relations.* London: Kogan Page Ltd.

Borisov, A. (2000). PR ne brannoe slovo [PR is not a bad word]. RUPR [On-line]. Available: www.rupr.ru/news/165206.html?section=articles.

Botan C. (1993). A human nature approach to image and ethics in international public relations. *Journal of Public Relations Research, 5,* 71–81.

Chumikov, A. (1999). Kreativnye tekhnologii public relations. [Creative technologies of public relations]. Yekateringurg, Russia: Basko.

Clarke, T. (2000). An inside look at Russian public relations. *Public Relations Quarterly, 45,* 18–22.

Culbertson, H., & Chen, N. (Eds.). (1996). *International public relations: A comparative analysis.* Mahwah, NJ: Lawrence Erlbaum Associates.

Department of Higher Education of Russian Federation. (2000). *Novyj gosudarstvennyj obrazovatel'nyj standart po spetsial'nosti "Svjazi s obschestvennostiju" (350400)* [New governmental standard in the major "Public Relations." Official document]. [On-line]. Available: www.pr-news.spb.ru/.

Durbin, W. (1968). International public relations. In M. Johnson (Ed.), *Current thoughts on public relations* (pp. 118–128). New York: M. W. Lads.

Egorova, A. (2000). International public relations: Order out of chaos. A Delphi study focusing on Russia. Unpublished master's thesis, University of Louisiana, Lafayette.

Eremin, B., & Borisov, A. (2000, April). PR epohi uporjadochennoj demokratii [PR in the era of organized democracy]. Electronic version of magazine *Sovetnik* [On-line series]. Available: www.sovetnik.ru/archive/2000/4/article.asp?id=100.

Feoktistova, E., & Krasnuk, I. (1993). *Marketing: Teorija i practica*. Moskva, Russia.

Ferguson, S. (1998). Constructing a theoretical framework for evaluating public relations programs and activities. *Communication Yearbook, 21,* 191.

Golubkov, E. (1994). *Marketing: Slovar'*. Moskva, Russia.

Goreigin, A., & Nikolaev, A. (1995). The value of PR association to Russians. *Communication World, 12,* 7–10.

Goreigin, A., & Nikolaev, A. (1996). Evolution of modern Russian communication. *Communication World, 13,* 68–70.

Grunig, J. E., & Hunt, T. (1984). *Managing public relations.* New York: Holt, Rinehart and Winston.

Grunig, L. A. (1992). Activism: How it limits the effectiveness of organizations and how excellent public relations departments respond. In J. E. Grunig (Ed.), *Excellence in public relations and communication management.* Hillsdale, NJ: Lawrence Erlbaum Associates.

Heath, R. (1992). Epilogue: Visions of critical studies of PR. In E. Toth & R. Heath (Eds.), *Rhetorical and critical approaches to public relations* (pp. 315–319). Hillsdale, NJ: Lawrence Erlbaum Associates.

Holtzhausen, D. (2000). Postmodern values in public relations. *Journal of Public Relations Research, 12,* 93–114.

Johnson, O. (1995). East Central and Southeastern Europe, Russia, and the newly independent states. In J. Merrill (Ed.), *Global journalism: Survey of international communication* (pp. 177–185). White Plains, NY: Longman.

Kogan, I. (1970). *Public relations.* New York: Alexander Hamilton Institute.

Konovalova, E. (2000, April). A za PR otvetish' pered . . . sovest'ju [And for PR you are responsible . . . yourself]. Electronic version of magazine *Sovetnik* [On-line serial]. Available: www.sovetnik.ru/archive/2000/4/article.asp?id=2.

Kostukhina, D. (Ed.). (1974). *Marketing: Collected Essays.* Moskva, Russia.

Kruckeberg, D. (1992). Ethical decision-making in public relations. *International Public Relations Review, 15,* 32–37.

Kruckeberg, D. (1996). Answering the mandate for a global presence. *International Public Relations Review, 19,* 19–23.

Kruckeberg, D. (1998). Future reconciliation of multicultural perspectives in public relations ethics. *Public Relations Quarterly, 43,* 45–48.

Kruckeberg, D. (2000). Public relations: Toward a global professionalism. In J. Ledingham & S. Bruning (Eds.), *Public relations as a relationship management: A relational approach to the study and practice of public relations* (pp. 145–157). Mahwah, NJ: Lawrence Erlbaum Associates.

Kruckeberg, D., & Starck, K. (1988). *Public relations and community: A reconstructed theory.* New York: Praeger.

Lebedeva, T. (1999). *Public relations. Korporativnaja i politicheskaya rezhissura* [Corporate and political directing]. Moskva: MGU.

Maksimov, A. (1999). *"Chistye" i "gryaznye" teknologii vyborov: Rossijskij opyt* ["Clean" and "dirty" technologies of elections: Russian experience]. Moskva: Delo.

Mencher, M. (1993). *Basic media writing.* Madison, WI: Wm C. Brown.

Mortensen, M. (1996). Public relations: An alternative to reality? In H. Culbertson & N. Chen (Eds.), *International public relations: A comparative analysis* (pp. 317–338). Mahwah, NJ: Lawrence Erlbaum Associates.

National News Service Agency of Russia, the official website (2000). [On-line]. Available: www.nns.ru/.

Nessmann, K. (1995). Public relations in Europe: A comparison with the United States. *Public Relations Review, 21,* 151–160.

Newsom, D., Turk, J., & Kruckeberg, D. (2000). *This is PR: The realities of public relations* (7th ed.). Belmont, CA: Wadsworth.

Novikov, A. (1999, July). Khronologija rossijskih public relations [Chronology of Russian public relations]. Electronic version of magazine *Sovetnik* [On-line series]. Available: www.sovetnik.ru/archive/1999/7/article.asp?id=4.

Novinskij, B. (2000). PR: nauka ili remeslo? [PR: science or skill?]. RUPR [On-line]. Available: www.rupr.ru/news/173192.html?section=articles.

Ozhegov, S. (1984). *Slovar' Russkogo yazyka.* (Dictionary of Russian language). Moskva: Russkij Yazyk.

Pheophanov, O. (2001). *Reklama: novye tekhnologii v Rossii* [Advertising: New technologies in Russia]. St. Petersburg: Piter.

Pocheptsov, G. (1998). Public relations, ili kak uspeshno upravljat' obschestvennym mneniem [Public relations, or how to successfully manage public opinion]. Moskva: Tsentr.

Pratkanis, A., & Aronson, E. (1991). *Age of propaganda.* New York: W. H. Freeman.

Sovremennyj Slovar Inostrannyx Slov (Modern dictionary of foreign words). (1993). Moskva: Russkiy Yazyk.

Sparks, S., & Conwell, P. (1998). Teaching public relations—Does practice or theory prepare practitioners? *Public Relations Quarterly, 43,* 41–44.

Sriramesh, K. (1996). Power distance in public relations: An ethnographic study of Southern Indian organizations. In H. Culbertson & N. Chen (Eds.), *International public relations: A comparative analysis* (pp. 171–190). Mahwah, NJ: Lawrence Erlbaum Associates.

Sriramesh, K., & White, J. (1992). Societal culture and public relations. In J. E. Grunig (Ed.), *Excellence in public relations and communication management* (pp. 597–614). Hillsdale, NJ: Lawrence Erlbaum Associates.

Starck, K., & Kruckeberg, D. (2001). Public relations and community: A reconstructed theory revised. In R. Heath (Ed.), *Handbook of public relations* (pp. 51–59). Thousand Oaks, CA: Sage.

Stevens, A. (1985). *The persuasion explosion: Your guide to the power and influence of contemporary public relations.* Washington, DC: Acropolis Books Ltd.

Tsetsura, K. (1997). Public relations kak socialnyj institut v Rossii [Public relations as a social institute in Russia]. Unpublished master's thesis, Voronezh State University, Voronezh, Russia.

Tsetsura, K. (1999, April). Women and the development of public relations in Russia. Paper presented at the sixty-seventh annual convention of Central States Communication Association, St. Louis.

Tsetsura, K. (2000a). Conceptual frameworks in the field of public relations: A comparative study of Russian and United States perspectives. Unpublished master's thesis, Fort Hays State University, Hays, KS.

Tsetsura, K. (2000b). Understanding the "Evil" nature of public relations as perceived by some Russian publics. Paper presented at the International Interdisciplinary PRSA Educators Academy Conference, Miami.

Tulchinsky, G. (1994). *Public relations: Reputatsija, vlijanie, cvjazi s pressoj i obschestvennostiju, sponsorstvo* [Public relations: Reputation, influence, media relations and community relations, sponsorship]. St. Petersburg: St. Petersburg State University.

Tulupov, V. (1996). Public relations in Russia as a new social institution. Speeches at the conference "Public relations in Russia today and tomorrow" (pp. 17–21). Voronezh, Russia: Voronezh State University.

Tye, L. (1998). *The father of spin: Edward L. Bernays and the birth of public relations.* New York: Crown.

Utkin, E., & Zaitsev, V. (1993). Public relations, ili dobroe imja firmy [Public relations, or a good name of a company]. *Torgovlja, 4–6,* 36–39.

Verčič, D. (1994). Public relations—research perspectives. *International Public Relations Review, 17,* 9–11.

Vikentiev, I. (1998). Priemy reklamy i public relations [Techniques of advertising and public relations]. St. Petersburg: St. Petersburg State University.

Wakefield, R. (1997). International public relations: A theoretical approach to excellence based on a worldwide Delphi study. Unpublished doctoral dissertation, University of Maryland, College Park.

9

The White Nights

A Public Relations Case Study of a Russian Company

David Ritchey

Key Points

- Cultural differences can make it difficult for a public relations practitioner and a client to work together creatively and successfully. In this case study dramatic cultural differences made teamwork almost impossible.

- A public relations practitioner often treats a company's different holdings as one company. The White Nights Company owns several distinct businesses. Sometimes a public relations practitioner should treat each holding as a distinct business, not associated with the holding company.

- The Citizens for Democracy Corps (CDC) and the White Nights Company provided little background information for the public relations practitioner before his arrival in Russia. One of the public relations problems was that the White Nights Company listed on the Internet is not the same White Nights Company represented by the CDC and the public relations practitioner.

- Russian citizens have only recently discovered public relations, and few have any formal training in public relations. Of course, most private entrepreneurs in Russia want successful public relations. Unfortunately, many Russians still have a view of the media that is a holdover from the Communist Party era.

The CDC provides opportunities for U.S. executives to volunteer their business expertise in Russia, Azerbaijan, Georgia, Thailand, and the Ukraine. The CDC was started by President George H. W. Bush in an effort to help the growing democratic movement in Russia. Georgia and the Ukraine since have left the former Soviet Union and formed separate countries.

The CDC also services those countries. In working with the CDC the U.S. government's goal is to help companies in those countries become more westernized and, therefore, more democratic. Russia's economic well-being, for example, is important to the world's financial communities. For this reason, in the summer of 1998, the International Monetary Fund announced it would lend about U.S.$11 billion to Russia to help the country stabilize its shaky financial markets.

Many of the owners and managers of companies in CDC countries have not been exposed to the principles of marketing, advertising, or public relations. Consequently, company presidents or managers lack the skills to deal with available channels of communication. Moreover, many are skeptical of the newspapers, magazines, and electronic media, believing they are still controlled by the government. Those tendencies provide CDC volunteers with ample opportunities to hone their skills in these countries. The CDC recruits volunteers in the United States and pays roundtrip airfare from the closest airport to the destination. The client provides the accommodations. Volunteers are responsible for their food and personal expenses.

The White Nights Company

The CDC recruited the author in 1998 as a volunteer to assist the White Nights Company in St. Petersburg, Russia, in developing a public relations plan. Julia Pashkova, twenty-nine, president of the White Nights Company, inherited the business on the death of her father. The White Nights Company consisted of five units: the White Nights Hotel (see Figure 9.1), with about 320 rooms; the White Nights Restaurant and Bar (in the White Nights Hotel); the Education Center where foreign languages (French, Spanish, English, and Finnish) are taught to Russians; a second White Nights Restaurant in another section of town; and the White Nights Tourism Office, an end-user tourism office for people planning to travel to St. Petersburg.

The name, White Nights, comes from the location of St. Petersburg, a city so far north that in June and July the sun sets for only a few hours each night. In May, dusk falls at midnight, and sunrise is about 4 A.M. The "white night," of course, is the first day of summer when the sun does not dip below the horizon.

St. Petersburg, the fourth-largest city in Europe, is located across the Gulf of Finland from Finland. Founded in the early 1700s, St. Petersburg was named for Peter the Great, the Russian Czar. The city is dotted with statues of political leaders and castles from the time of Peter and Catherine. When the communists came to power here early in the twentieth century, the name of the city was changed to Leningrad. During World War II, the Germans surrounded Leningrad (the Siege of Leningrad) and held it captive for 900 days. More than a half-million people starved to death in Leningrad during the siege. After the fall of communism, citizens voted to change the name of their city back to St. Petersburg. The city is now known, in part, for the Hermitage, one of the greatest art museums in the world, located in the castle of Catherine the Great.

Those of us who are not Russian may have to change our concept of that country and its people. No matter how ancient we might think Russia is, we are wrong. Think of Russia as existing only since perestroika, 1988. With that time line as a framework, divide the pop-

FIGURE 9.1 *The White Nights Hotel (and author),*
St. Petersburg, Russia. Note the new neon sign on top
of the building and the heavy fence around the building.
Courtesy of David Ritchey.

ulation into two groups. First, senior citizens who lived most of their lives under communism and now find their world turned upside down with talk of elections, free-market economies, and public relations. They find the change unsettling.

Russians under the age of fifty, however, told me, "Life is better. Not everything is perfect. Things are better than they have been." They are optimistic that the political changes will improve the quality of their lives.

Getting Started

When I arrived in St. Petersburg, CDC officers instructed me to develop a frugal public relations plan that could be executed without my presence. Typically, CDC volunteers work with a client for only two or three weeks, and the client must be able to continue to execute the project without the volunteer. In addition, the public relations plan could not suggest that the client spend a great deal of money.

Spending too much money was not an option for my client. Frugality was a key word in her vocabulary. When I suggested that she and the heads of her different companies have business cards, she said, "Impossible. Too expensive." To me, that seemed too frugal.

The client's frugality, however, seemed more reasonable as I got to know her. She was fearful that the communists might come to power again. She is Jewish, and, with many other Jews, suffered during the communist reign. She saves every ruble she can in order to leave Russia should the communists win an election.

Because the CDC client provides the accommodations for the CDC volunteer, the White Nights Hotel, of course, was where I lived. The large block-style building is made of beige/yellow brick and resembles the apartment buildings constructed during the Stalin era. It has not been refurbished since its construction during that era. Those who stay there walk the last two blocks from the bus stop to the hotel, first on a sidewalk and then on a gravel road. In the mud-based parking lot, automobile tires are half buried in the ground to provide a stopping place for each car. A very young, armed guard sits in the lobby and watches television. The halls are wide, with little lighting. However, the floors of the halls and the rooms of the hotel are scrubbed each day by several cleaning women. My room had a small narrow bed, a small refrigerator, a television, and a private bath. The floor of the bathroom sloped toward a small drain in the middle of the floor. When guests take a shower, they stand in the middle of the floor and use a hand-held sprayer. Television programming featured news, game shows, and comedy shows. U.S. television programs are often shown on Russian television, including *90210* in its European version, with nude scenes.

The hotel caters to truck drivers and school groups on education tours to St. Petersburg. The truck drivers check in by midafternoon and drink beer until the hotel's restaurant/bar closes at 6 A.M. They resume drinking when the bar opens at 9 A.M. Large groups of children between the ages of ten and fifteen stay in the hotel while on school trips to St. Petersburg.

A second CDC volunteer, Ed Michalski, a food/restaurant expert, also worked with the same client. We ate one meal a day in the hotel's restaurant in order to help the hotel's economy. After a tour of the kitchen and the area where the food was stored, however, he announced, "No more." He told the staff to get the cat and the kitty-litter box out of the kitchen. He told other food stories that sent me to the local market to buy bottled water and candy bars.

To get to the CDC office in the central section of St. Petersburg, I had to walk three blocks from the hotel to the bus stop and ride the bus for four stops. Then, I rode on the subway for three stops to reach Nevsky Prospekt, one of the world's most beautiful streets. Russians like to compare Nevsky Prospekt with New York City's Fifth Avenue. Nevsky Prospekt is lined with fashionable stores and resembles U.S. streets with its two Pizza Huts, a Kentucky Fried Chicken outlet, Baskin-Robbins, and several McDonald's restaurants. The street features the Stroganoff Palace, the home of the Duke and Duchess Stroganoff, who invented the beef dish that carries their name.

One Sunday night, at about 10:30 P.M., with the sun still high above the horizon, I stood on a street corner while a Dixieland jazz band played familiar music. When the band played "Hello, Dolly!" a woman stepped out of the crowd and started dancing by herself. The people in the crowd at first grew very quiet and then started applauding and cheering the solo dancer. This was a special moment for me in Russia. Why? When the communists were in power they said that "if you listen to jazz today, you'll kill your grandmother tomorrow" and "if you listen to or play jazz today, you'll commit treason tomorrow." The implication, of course, was that U.S. jazz is a corrupting influence on the Russian people and should be avoided.

Change comes slowly here. It might begin with a woman dancing to "Hello, Dolly!" played by a jazz band on a street corner. Or, with a U.S. public relations practitioner attempting to persuade a Russian business executive to buy business cards for those who head the departments in her company. Each represents a hard-won change. Each is a slow, tentative change, one small step at a time. The band starts playing "Hello, Dolly!" and slowly and deliberately a woman steps out in front of a crowd. She's scared. But, it is safe. The tempo increases, and she dances with abandon. Maybe tomorrow, executives will be secure enough to buy business cards.

Setting Goals

Julia Pashkova established the following goals for each of the units in her White Nights Company:

- The White Nights Hotel sells at a 20 to 50 percent capacity. However, during holiday periods, occupancy may reach 100 percent. Pashkova's goal is to increase total occupancy by 20 to 25 percent. However, she said she does not have the money for needed renovations.
- The Education Center is a major drain on her resources. It loses about U.S.$3,000 each month. She wanted to close the center, but government officials have asked her to keep it open because it is the only language school in the district. The center attracts university graduates, who have launched their careers, and who find that they need to learn a new language or to perfect conversational language. The quality of the education seems to be high. The problem is that the general public is not aware of the center. Pashkova could have a graduation ceremony for students when they finish the two-year program, but the center's director says the building is in such bad shape she is ashamed to have a graduation program there. Could the ceremony be moved to the White Nights Restaurant nearby? Pashkova says that perhaps she will close the center and reopen it again once she knows the amount of governmental support.
- The second restaurant is doing well. Well managed, the restaurant provides quality food to customers. The restaurant is physically connected to a school, so the manager sells more than one hundred meals to students daily. Pashkova says the second restaurant is not near a metro station or the bus line, which is inconvenient for the general population. However, that inconvenience could be overcome. If people knew the location of the restaurant, the quality of the food, how reasonable the prices are, and how comfortable the facility is, they likely would go to that restaurant. The restaurant is surrounded by apartment buildings. Enough people live in the area to make the restaurant a success. However, many people do not eat in restaurants, a holdover from the days of communism. I suggest that management post signs outside the building to identify it as a restaurant. Perhaps, flyers could be posted in the apartment buildings to make neighbors aware of the restaurant.

- The Tourism Center is successful. It has a good reputation, attracts a large number of repeat clients, and is profitable. I suggest hiring some recent college graduates who have degrees in tourism finance. Pashkova says that she usually hires women whom she has known for a long time and trusts. Once she hires them, she trains them to do the work her way. Several of the workers in the Tourism Center complain about being overworked. They have a fierce loyalty to Pashkova, and she has been able to bank on that loyalty, but she needs to hire at least one more employee in order to relieve current employees. She also needs to expand operations. I suggest that she write letters to groups that use her service, place newspaper stories about the service, and, perhaps, buy ad space in newspapers and magazines. This unit of the White Nights Company is profitable enough to carry some of her less profitable areas.
- One large problem that Pashkova does not want to address is that there is a second company named the White Nights Company in St. Petersburg. This other White Nights Company has a hotel, a language school, and a tourism office; is on the Internet; and works to be visible. Pashkova insists her company is better known and has a good reputation. I do not doubt her but anyone who accesses the Internet will discover a White Nights Company and can make reservations through that company. This is a problem and will become a greater problem for her business.

Recommendations

After reviewing her situation, I made the following recommendations:

1. First, the White Nights Hotel and the White Nights Tourism Department need an awareness campaign to remind some of their publics that these services exist. Second, the awareness campaign could introduce the White Nights Company to other important publics. A public is a group of people who have an interest in a company—the public could be customers, employees, or any others who have an interest in the White Nights Company. The general population is not aware of the White Nights Company. Although the company has been in existence for about ten years, many of its potential customers do not know it exists. This lack of awareness is complicated by the fact that St. Petersburg has a second White Nights Company. It is imperative that the White Nights Company has a good reputation with its clients. The purpose of this public relations plan is to make the company more visible, and therefore, attract more customers.

2. Raise rates at the hotel by 10 to 25 percent. Then, offer discounts that will bring the price down to the current level. It is admirable to have kept the prices low. However, customers think they are getting a real bargain when you offer a discount. A discount of up to 25 percent will provide the company with more opportunities to work with clients. This is typical of U.S.-style hotels. If a tour brings fifty people, give them a 10 or 15 percent discount for bringing a large group. You do not lose money, and the customers think they are getting a bargain. Most of the other hotels in St. Petersburg offer discounts to groups. Members of the Tourism Department staff can check on the discounts other hotels in St. Petersburg offer.

3. Business cards are a marketing tool and a necessity for all managers and directors. Those who receive the business card will use it to contact the White Nights Company. Employees who have business cards should make an effort to give them to all possible business contacts.

4. Write and send thank you letters to the schools and organizations that use your services. When schoolchildren return to their schools, they should find a thank you letter waiting at the school. In the letter, write, "I look forward to serving you and your school again in the near future." Also, mention in the letter the leaders who accompanied the students. Use the names of people as often as possible. Also write thank you letters to other organizations that use the services of the White Nights Company. For example, write letters to the trucking companies or other companies that have truckers who use your services. If drivers from a trucking company stay in the White Nights Hotel, make sure they get a thank you letter. Can you establish a working relationship with trucking companies? Offer a discount (perhaps 10 percent) to the drivers from a certain company if they use White Nights's services in St. Petersburg.

5. Write to the officers in the travel agencies that send business to you and let them know that you appreciate their business. Offer to help them again. Suggest other tours the White Nights Company can plan for them. If they liked the first tour, they will love the second tour.

6. Write to schools that do not do business with White Nights. Tell school officials about the success other schools have had with the programs offered by the White Nights. Invite the school officials to ask for more information about your programs.

7. Target marketing is defined as marketing to a specific group of people. White Nights officials have decided to which groups to market the hotel and tourism programs. Target market according to geography. The White Nights has served people from all areas of Russia. However, the White Nights does not have to target the entire country. Target areas from which you get the most customers—those cities between St. Petersburg and Moscow. This is a manageable geographic area that is large enough to make a financial impact on the White Nights.

- Contact schools in the target area. Send school officials a description of what you have done for other schools in the area. Invite their business.
- Contact business and industry in the target area. Let those companies know that you are available to help if they want to send groups to St. Petersburg.
- Contact newspapers in the area. Send news stories about the White Nights Hotel and the other White Nights companies. Ask for information about the cost of advertising.
- What companies in this area have truck drivers? Write letters encouraging the truck drivers from those companies to stay in the White Nights Hotel.

8. Target people who are important to White Nights tourism.

- Contact school officials.
- Contact officials in companies that employee truck drivers. Offer their drivers discounts at the hotel.
- Contact truck drivers who know your hotel. Offer them discounts (10 percent) in cash if they can bring a new customer to the hotel.

- Contact important people. Read newspapers to find out who is important in each city and village. Invite these people to consider contacting the White Nights Tourism Office the next time they are planning a trip to St. Petersburg.
- Ask your customers to give you the names and addresses of other people who could use the White Nights's services.

9. Participate in tourism shows or exhibits. You and members of your staff should attend, meet people, and distribute business cards and other information about your company. Set a goal of getting to know at least ten new people and companies at each trade show. Distribute brochures or other printed materials about the services White Nights Tourism offers. Do you have photographs of people enjoying your tours? A brochure is expensive. However, it will give the people something to take with them by which to remember your company, as well as the information they need to contact you and use your services. A brochure that is well written, well designed, and persuasive is a good investment and will almost guarantee a profit on the investment.

10. Consider hiring part-time employees who have studied tourism finance at one of the local universities. Such students have contacts and knowledge that can be important to the White Nights Tourism Office.

11. Consider sending some of the current employees to a university training program in tourism. Tourism in Russia is changing every day. It is important for everyone on your staff to be up-to-date on changes in tourism.

12. Prepare to invest a little money in the tourism business.

- Print flyers—one-page documents that describe the hotel and the tours.
- Print brochures, larger documents that will easily fit into envelopes and can be mailed to people around the country. The purpose of a brochure is to sell a product, in this case, the tourism industry.

13. Consider hiring a secretary (at least a part-time secretary). The secretary's job would be to write the many letters that need to come from the president of the White Nights Company and the director of the Tourism Office. In addition, this person should keep accurate records of the people, companies, and organizations that use its services. This information will help you know who to contact, what organizations have successfully used your services, and who might spend more money with your company. If the customer has a successful experience with White Nights Tourism, that customer is likely to return for more and more vacations offered by White Nights Tourism as well as to recommend White Nights to friends and colleagues.

14. Record keeping is important. Create files of names, addresses, and telephone numbers of organizations, businesses, and people who use the White Nights Tourism service. Without adequate records, the company will lose contacts with important clients. Much of this can be maintained and updated on the computer in your Tourism Office. If you don't know where you've been, you won't know where you're going.

15. Personally call on both Russian-language and the English-language newspapers. I talked to an editor at the *St. Petersburg Times* who said a business reporter would be happy to interview you. News stories will generate awareness or visibility for the White Nights

Company. You must call on the newspapers repeatedly. They will not use every story you submit to them. However, call on each newspaper once a week. At first, stop at the office in person. Later, after you've established a relationship with the reporter, you might simply telephone. Suggest news stories. What is special about your company, your employees, and yourself?

16. Don't be a victim of the word *impossible*. When people use the word *impossible,* they shut off possible discussion and solutions to a company's problems. Keep everything open and honest and visible to the world. Not every suggestion can be used. However, every suggestion provides a starting place for a discussion that may lead to a solution.

17. The White Nights Company has accomplished much. The company must continue in that tradition. By contacting the CDC and by working with its consultants, you have taken a major step forward in modernizing the company and making it financially stronger.

Conclusion

When my three weeks as a CDC volunteer ended, I had to leave St. Petersburg. The CDC does not provide an opportunity to extend the visit. The client executed part of the public relations plan. However, her insecurities about the stability of the government and its economy make her timid about making important, frugal changes in the way she manages the White Night Company. The client has to make tough choices in a difficult setting.

Discussion Questions _____

1. One of the problems between the public relations professional and the client was a difference in cultural backgrounds. Cite five differences in this case. How could the public relations professional have helped to bridge some of these differences?

2. The culture in Russia was changing during the time that the public relations professional was consulting with the client. How can a public relations professional help a client whose culture suddenly no longer exists or is in the process of changing?

3. The public relations professional was asked to represent five different entities with the same company name, the White Nights. Having several different companies under the umbrella of one name is not unusual in many parts of the world, but it does present several public relations problems. How does a public relations professional create an awareness campaign for each company to make it separate and distinct? What are some other problems that a public relations professional might encounter in attempting to define and promote each company?

4. *Frugality* was the key word in the client's vocabulary. A public relations professional needs to know the budget allocated to a project in order to effectively represent a client. Yet in this case the client was sabotaging the public relations effort by not providing a budget. One suggestion was that the client be expected to spend as much money on the program as the U.S. government had invested in the program when it sent the public relations professional to help the White Nights Company. Is that a fair request of the client? What are other ways a public relations professional could help a client who has a severely limited budget?

5. The client established several goals for the White Nights Company. Were the goals realistic? Should the public relations professional be involved in the goal-setting process? What should the public relations professional's role be in the goal-setting process?

6. In truth, all of the White Night companies needed a public relations awareness program. Now, several years after this case study, Russia has changed. What would you recommend to a public relations professional working on the White Nights account today?

Part IV

Around Africa

The Quest for Public Relations in Africa

An Introduction

John Fobanjong

Public relations is largely about the perception that an organization or nation-state establishes in the minds of others about itself. If such a perception is good, it increases the chances that others will want to interact positively with the organization. If the perception is bad, however, it reduces the desirability of others to want to interact with that organization.

Prior to coming into contact with the outside world, Africa had a largely positive image in the minds of those who read or heard the accounts of explorers who visited the continent. The history of many of the early explorers who discovered Africa is replete with lavish accounts of tales that would be perceived today as public relations. The tales created a strong desire in the minds of the rest of the world to visit or even invest in Africa. But as Africa became increasingly familiar to the outside world, the positive tales soon turned into negative depictions of Africa, which, in turn, quickly translated into increased negative public relations for the region. As time passed, the history of Africa's golden age was gradually replaced by a history of Africa's dark ages. Today, Africa is known more for its debilitating tales than for its proud accomplishments. For Africa, nothing has done more to stave off foreign capital than such negative public relations.

From attracting foreign investors to economic growth and political stability, public relations affects everything. Africa's inability to attract and retain foreign investment has much to do with the negative public relations that surrounds its social institutions. In this introductory chapter, we attempt to explain how and why Africa has come to find itself in the economic doldrums. We will see that not only has history failed Africa but contemporary Africa has failed itself as well. Endowed with a rich variety of natural resources,

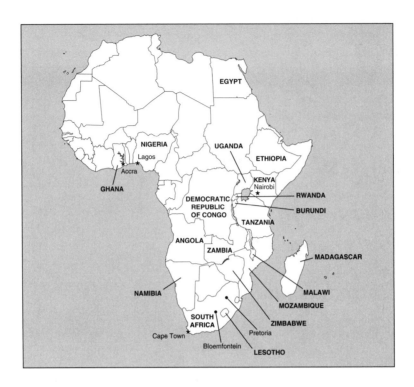

Africans, both past and present, have failed to invest these resources in the development of its public relations industry. As a result, Africa is unable to market many of the goods and services that it produces both at home and abroad. Indeed, Africa is the only continent that produces much of what it does not consume (in the form of raw materials) and consumes much of what it does not produce (in the form of manufactured goods). With the international economy now global, it is those nations that invested substantially in developing their public relations industry that are in a position to attract much of the external capital that has become the engine of global competitiveness.

Glory Found and Lost

The end of the cold war and the dawning of the New World order raised expectations for the demise of the Old World order in Africa. As the winds of change blew across the continent, they augured in a breath of optimism for Africa, and expectations were high that, at long last, Africa would finally find itself on the path to political stability and economic prosperity. The African intelligentsia was euphoric. So, too, were Africa's civil society and other advocates for change within and outside the continent. The sense of optimism that created this euphoria was second only to that which was witnessed in the early years of Africa's independence from colonial rule.

Among the realities that contributed to this more recent sense of optimism was the collapse of the last vestiges of colonial rule in Africa and the release of Nelson Mandela from prison. The collapse of the Soviet Empire and the reverberation of the winds of democracy that sailed across the continent in the early 1990s also gave the civil society, which was until now suppressed in Africa, a sense of confidence. This confidence was particularly high among the African intelligentsia, who thought that it was now going to be in a position to influence the political destiny of their respective societies. African scholars at home and abroad rushed to analyze and interpret this new and sudden reality that had unexpectedly dawned on the continent. At various intellectual discourses that ensued, terminology developed to explain the changes went from "Afro-optimism" to "African renaissance" (Shraeder, 2000). Unfortunately, the euphoria was unusually ephemeral. Some long-term African rulers quickly capitulated and gracefully bowed out to popular demands for the democratic reforms that were ushered in by the New World order. Others remained stubbornly resistant to any attempts that were directed at changing the status quo. Like a cat, the old order appeared to have more than one life. It was soon realized that rulers who were initially receptive to the winds of change only did so to placate the demands civil society and threats of sanctions from foreign donors. Before long, the sense of optimism that accompanied the dawning of the New World order soon flickered into pessimism, with domestic political order in most African states returning to the status quo ante. Hope among the intelligentsia for an African renaissance soon turned into despair (Shraeder, 2000).

Traditionally, among the most optimistic of African intellectuals, there has always been a hopeful sense of expectation—albeit wishful—that someday, in some distant future, Africa was going to somehow regain its historic greatness. Many of these scholars are inspired by the history of Africa's golden past. From their readings of African history, they are informed that great kings and queens once ruled Africa, milk and honey were aplenty, and gold and diamonds floated on riverbanks (July, 1980). Lavish spending by African leaders traveling through the Middle East brought inflation that destabilized the economies of Arab and Southern European nations along the Mediterranean Sea. Timbuktu was the global center of learning, and Ethiopia, Egypt, Ghana, and Zimbabwe were producers of great minds who developed architectural wonders. Western scholars traveled from Greece to study in Africa. For these scholars, Africa, not Greece, was the true birthplace of modern civilization (July, 1980), and some, influenced by religious readings, believe that Garden of Eden was located in Africa.

Over time, however, Africa lost its greatness, and the center of civilization shifted north to Greece and later to the Roman Empire, the Ottoman Empire, and the British Empire. By the middle of the twentieth century, global hegemony shifted from Europe to North America. Dispossessed of its power and dominance in global affairs it was not in the least pleasing to Europe. States on the eastern half of the continent soon organized to challenge the U.S. dominance in global affairs. This ignited an ideological rivalry that soon turned into an arms race. The race went nuclear, with arsenals of weapons pointing at each other. There was enough nuclear weapons buildup on both sides that East and West were guaranteed mutual assured destruction in the event of nuclear war. Africa opted for neutrality. Along with other regions in the Third World, it signed a nonalignment pact. It was a pact that was expected to keep African out of harm's way in the event of the outbreak of nuclear war between the East and the West. Given its declared neutrality and its geographic location in the Southern Hemisphere, Africa would be likely to avoid such a war and possibly regain its historic place as the center of global influence.

Before the end of the twentieth century, the Soviet Empire unexpectedly called for a truce. The East collapsed, and the United States consolidated its place both as a global power and as the center of global influence. In the absence of the much-dreaded nuclear apocalypse, Africa's utopian aspirations of regaining its historic place as the center of global influence were dashed. At the same time, the winds of democracy that blew across the African continent in the aftermath of the collapse of the Soviet Empire rekindled hopes of a different kind in Africa, hopes that superpower intervention in the internal affairs of African states would cease, and that the continent would eventually be allowed to exercise self-determination and political autonomy. But before the end of the 1990s, that euphoria was transformed into pessimism. For the first time in modern history, new terminology and phraseologies were developed to describe events that were occurring in Africa. In place of the "African renaissance," it was now common to hear political pundits allude to the epidemic of civil conflicts that had become endemic in the post–cold war era as "Africa's First World War." The phenomenon of *warlordism,* which had fallen into disuse in more than a hundred years, resurfaced in Africa in the form of fratricidal civil strife. Determined to acquire power by any means necessary, leaders from West to Central Africa transformed themselves into warlords, and with the backing of foreign and domestic supporters, sought a reordering of Africa on their terms. Among other post–cold war pathologies that continued to afflict Africa were debt crises, genocide, child-soldiers, AIDS, crime, and drug and diamond trafficking.

Unless Africa's debt crisis is resolved, as many as 20 million African children are expected to die every two years (Power, 1998). Financial resources that ought to be invested in health care, education, and food production are now directed at servicing foreign debt. As a result of their heavy debt burden, many African nations were not able to share in the historic economic growth that was realized by much of the world at the dawning of the new global economy that began in the 1990s. As much as 15 to 41 percent of the gross domestic product (GDP) of most African nations went into servicing foreign debt. Nowhere is this more telling than in Cote d'Ivoire, a country that is frequently cited as one of Africa's most stable economies. As shown in Table IV.1, between 1981 and 1992, interest payment on Cote d'Ivoire's U.S.$18 billion foreign debt was 41 percent. During that same period, Cote d'Ivoire had an annual inflation rate of 26 percent. Thus, each year inflation—and in-

TABLE IV.1 *Economic Indicators in Selected African States, 1981–1992*

	Cote d'Ivoire	*Guinea*	*Mali*	*Niger*	*Senegal*
Population	14.9m	6.7m	9.7m	9.4m	8.7m
GDP*	$8.0bn	3.2bn	$2.7bn	$2.2bn	$5.8 bn
GDP/per capita	$650	$500	$270	$270	$750
Debt Service	41%	15%	19%	33%	29%
Inflation	26%	5%	23%	8%	32%
Average Growth Rate	–0.8%	3.4%	4.6%	0.2%	3.6%

*Gross Domestic Product

Source: Calculated from 1996 *World Bank's Annual Report,* Washington, DC.

flation alone—drain away 67 percent of the GDP from the economy. Only 33 percent of Cote d'Ivoire's GDP is left for domestic consumption and reinvestment. No doubt that the economy of Cote d'Ivoire, as well as that of most other African states, have, since the dawning of the New World order, been characterized more by negative growth rates than by positive growth rates.

Almost every African country, including those not depicted in Table IV.1, has to contend with the dilemma of directing a substantial portion of its annual GDP away from alleviating hunger, poverty, sickness, and illiteracy, to paying interest on the debt it owes to foreign financial institutions. Between 1998 and 2000, for example, as much as U.S.$1 billion of Ethiopia's national income went into interest payments on such debt. Research by Power (1998) has shown that the number of those who die as a result of social spending cutbacks that are made as a result of payments on foreign debt is at least fifteen times the number of slaves who died during the transatlantic slave trade. Today, it is estimated that in Mozambique before every baby leaves its mother's womb, it has already incurred a foreign debt of U.S.$350.

As devastating as Africa's debt crisis is, it pales when compared to the epidemic of AIDS that is currently spreading across the continent. Described as the greatest tragedy to strike Africa since slavery, as many as 24 million lives have been claimed by the disease. Presently, as many as six thousand Africans die daily from AIDS—provoking a new humanitarian crisis that has led the international community to describe Africa as the "orphaned continent" (Lustig, 2002). Of the 13.2 million AIDS orphans who were reported worldwide in 1997, 95 percent of them lived in Africa. Wehrwein (1999) estimates that more than one-quarter of working-age adults are infected with HIV in some communities in sub-Saharan Africa, a statistic that brings profound economic repercussions for families and communities. Wehrwein has found that when AIDS claims the lives of people in their most productive years, grieving orphans and the elderly must contend with the sudden loss of financial support. Eventually, communities must bear the burden of caring for those that are left behind, and countries must draw on an increasingly diminishing pool of trained and talented workers.

Today, in much of postcolonial Africa, genocidal war has become a ready-made response to groups that demand political self-determination, including groups that are seeking to reorder Africa along lines that are different from the political arrangement that was left behind by former colonial powers. A myopic culture of greed, self-interest, and a relentless quest for self-aggrandizement have all but transformed Africa from a continent that is replete with vast amounts of natural resources to one that is caught up in political and economic stagnation. In a rather dismal and incomprehensible paradox, the very blessings that endow Africa's subsoil have been turned into a destructive curse on the continent. Proceeds from the sale of its gold, diamonds, oil, wood, and various other resources are used for the arming of child-soldiers rather than for the development of the human capital needed to pull Africa out of economic underdevelopment. Much of Africa today is reminiscent of the slogan "political power grows out of the barrel of the gun," which was used by Mao Tsetung to mobilize his supporters during the Chinese cultural revolution (Kesselman & Joseph, 2002, p. 519).

Among the many challenges that Africa faces is this challenge of governance. It is a challenge that requires the transformation of Africa's political systems from military and civilian dictatorships to competitive free-market democracies. Although the concept of democracy is not new to Africa, the authoritarian legacy inherited from colonial rule makes such transformation arduous. In their study of Africa, Joseph, Lewis, Kew, and Taylor (2002) found out that several precolonial societies, including the Igbos and the Yorubas of Nigeria, had elements of democracy in their traditional governance structures that promoted political accountability and representation. These were values that "ensured that the ruler and the ruled adhered to culturally mandated principles and obligations" (pp. 551–553). Crime against society was punished more severely than crime against individuals. Unfortunately, these democratic values were systematically destroyed during years of colonial occupation. In its place, a culture of authoritarianism and self-aggrandizement was instituted. In almost every part of Africa, indigenous popular participation was restricted, and the ruler's accountability to the governed weakened (Joseph et al., 2002).

Media, Democracy, and Society

The media is one of many of the modern institutions that play an indispensable role in facilitating the democratic process. They provide an enabling forum for active policy debates, political participation, and democratic competition. Unfortunately, most African governments find open political competition threatening. As a result, on gaining independence from colonial rule, most African governments immediately placed the major media outlets in their societies under state control. Those that could not be immediately brought under state control were closely monitored and censored to prevent the publication of any material that appeared to challenge the ruling party's hold on paper. The strategy worked very well during the cold war. However, with the growing globalization of the international system, governments in Africa are no longer in a position to keep an effective lid on the increasingly sophisticated web of communications outlets that have suddenly transformed the world into one global village. Forced by the growing globalization of the international community, government-controlled media outlets in Africa now have to compete with new communications technologies that cannot be effectively brought under state control. Citizens in Africa now have access to alternative sources of information that range from the Internet to cable and satellite communications. With the proliferation of new technologies in Africa, the viewership on most state-controlled television stations is rapidly dwindling. The television station of choice in much of Africa today is CNN.

The viewers of these cable and satellite television stations come largely from the middle class. In Africa, as in much of the Third World, the middle class mostly consists of government officials. Oddly, the very government officials who have chosen to keep a close lid on communications media in their societies are the same people who are loyal viewers of foreign satellite and cable television programming. On a daily basis, public officials in Africa are as interested in finding out what policies are coming out of Washington as they are about what is happening in their national capitals. As a result, Washington has become the capital by default of the new global economy.

For the rest of society, the implication of viewing television programming that is foreign is a lot more complex. Television programming in the market economies of advanced industrial societies is intended largely for the promotion and sale of goods and services. Broadcasting such programs by cable or satellite to Africa helps develop new tastes and new markets in Africa for Western producers. Frequently, however, many of the social implications of foreign television programming on the domestic economy remain largely hidden.

We know that television advertising whets consumers' appetites and helps create demand. What we do not know is what happens when the development of such appetites fails to come with the purchasing power necessary for the viewers to legally afford the products seen on television everyday. In other words, what happens when Africans who watch Western television programming cannot afford to buy the products or live the lifestyles that are promoted on their satellite and cable television screens? The annual per capita income in most African countries is less than U.S.$500. It is barely enough to buy three pairs of the brand name sneakers that are worn by many of the American and European youth whom they see on cable and satellite programming. To live the lifestyles that they see on television, Africans need money. If they cannot earn it honestly, they will undoubtedly try to earn it unscrupulously. This may include robbery, bribery, prostitution, or drug trafficking.

Thus, the unanticipated outcome of the globalization of cable, satellite, and other media outlets is its indirect contribution to the growth of the crime in Africa. It is now a common sight to see child-soldiers in Nike T-shirts playing Rambo with AK-47 automatic machine guns on the streets of Liberia and Sierra Leone. There is no doubt that the rapid growth in crime is related to the images seen on foreign cable and satellite television programming. Frequently, these images come uncensored. Despite the ability of African governments to control domestic communications programming through monopolistic control and censorship, they are helpless when it comes to controlling or censoring cable and satellite television programming. In the United States for example, explicit sexual scenes in programs such as the *Jerry Springer Show* are often blurred or blanked out when featured on network television. In much of Africa, *Jerry Springer* is shown unedited on prime-time television. Television violence and sexually explicit scenes, including X-rated movies, have become a daily staple for viewers in much of Africa. Many of these viewers are children and young adults. Even in societies where public officials are interested in keeping such images off the air, they do not have the technological ability to do so.

Other hidden social implications abound. What will happen to a child who is raised in the African interior, watching nothing but foreign television programming? Given the powerful influence that television has on society, and particularly on the minds of young people, it is very likely that in the not too distant future, much of Africa is going to become culturally westernized in its tastes and lifestyles. Children may very well grow up in Africa but refuse to speak or dress African, preferring instead to speak and dress like the stars they see on foreign television. Already, most African youths are more likely to buy U.S.-brand-name T-shirts than a new suit produced in Africa. There is no question that the United States has outdone Africa in its public relations, advertising, and marketing campaigns. But what Africa will do to catch up is unknown.

With the current trends, the televised commercialization of Western products to Africa will ultimately succeed in accomplishing what imperialism failed to accomplish—that is, to acculturate Africa and turn its peoples into dependent consumers of Western products. As imperialism sought to extend Western rule over Africa, it went beyond simple political domination, to actively working to replace the language, the tastes, and the cultural values of Africans with Western ones. The quest was unexpectedly interrupted when African states overwhelmingly clamored for their independence seventy-five years after having been colonized. Today, the exclusive ownership and control of modern communications outlets by the West makes it possible for imperialism to achieve its objectives without being physically present in Africa.

Public Relations and Revenue Potential for African Economies

The primary medium for creating demand in market economies is public relations. A market, or laissez-faire, economy is an economic system driven mainly by supply and demand. As large numbers of producers compete to produce and sell, it is the producer who has a mastery of the art of public relations who will gain increased market share. The same is true of nation-states. As countries compete for market share in the new international economic system, it is those countries with highly developed public relations infrastructures that are going to gain increased market share. Unfortunately, in the case of Africa, where governments have gained monopolistic control of national public relations resources—newspapers and radio and television stations—their ability to compete in the new global economy remains bleak. Particularly so as these resources are frequently directed more at self-promotion, self-preservation, and self-aggrandizement than at national development. It is this quest for self-aggrandizement that has blinded many African governments to the potential benefits of public relations for their citizens. Whereas countries in other parts of the world, particularly in the Western world, are generating hundreds of billions of dollars from the public relations industry, African countries are running out of revenue sources.

Paradoxically, as African rulers rush to hire the services of public relations firms in the West, they are working to inhibit the development of industry in their societies. This was the case with the governments of Nigeria, Angola, and even apartheid South Africa, which, in the 1980s, hired public relations firms in U.S. and European capitals to promote the image of their regimes to Western policy makers. At the same time, they refused to implement the domestic reforms necessary to open up their regimes to political participation and economic competition—conditions under which the public relations industry best flourishes. A specific example of a public relations move that provoked public outcry was a U.S.$5 million award by Nigeria's president General Abacha in 1995 to New York University for research on malaria. Many of his critics immediately saw the award as a public relations ploy aimed at promoting his image and cultivating goodwill with the U.S. public. While Abacha was giving away the U.S.$5 million to a university in the United States, he presided over the shutting down of those universities in his country that were critical of his rule. Malaria is a tropical disease, and, therefore, much of the data needed to conduct research on it is more readily found in Nigeria than in the United States. But because the quest for self-promotion and self-preservation was far greater than the quest for national development, Abacha found it more expedient to conduct a public relations campaign in the United States than to support institutions developing the resources necessary for the growth of public relations in Nigeria. Yet given the revenue potential of Nigeria's public relations industry, Abacha could have achieved his goal of self-preservation and self-promotion and promoted national development at the same time. In Nigeria, as elsewhere in Africa, policy makers do not appear to understand the revenue-generating potential of public relations. As evidenced in Table IV.2, the public relations industry remains a largely untapped industry in Africa; not a single firm among the top twenty-five public relations firms in the world is located in Africa.

Each of the top twenty-five public relations firms shown in the table generates annual revenues that run into the billions of dollars—revenues far greater than the annual

TABLE IV.2 *Worldwide Revenues of Top Twenty-Five Public Relations Firms, December 2000*

Firm Name	Pro Forma			Organic		
	Rank	Revenues	% Growth	Rank	Revenues	% Growth
Fleishman-Hillard	1	$342,841,000	60.8%	4	$272,377,000	27.7%
Weber Shandwick Worldwide	2	334,961,000	26.7	1	317,494,000	20.1
Hill & Knowlton	3	306,264,000	25.9	3	298,757,000	22.8
Burson-Marsteller	4	303,860,000	11.6	2	303,860,000	11.6
Citigate/Incepta	5	243,938,000	96.9	7	169,731,000	37.1
Edelman PR Worldwide	6	238,045,000	28.0	5	229,439,000	23.3
Porter Novelli International	7	208,157,000	22.6	6	195,529,000	15.2
BSMG Worldwide	8	192,195,000	32.3	9	168,500,000	16.0
Ogilvy PR Worldwide	9	169,454,000	36.4	8	169,454,000	36.4
Ketchum	10	168,247,000	17.3	10	168,247,000	17.3
GCI Group/APCO Associates	11	150,662,000	33.6	11	150,662,000	33.6
Golin/Harris International	12	136,933,000	35.1	12	122,929,000	21.2
Manning, Selvage & Lee	13	118,844,000	24.7	13	118,844,000	24.7
Euro RSCG	14	107,959,000	53.9	—	N/A	—
Brodeur Worldwide	15	84,200,000	20.1	14	84,200,000	20.1
Ruder Finn	16	84,125,000	41.9	15	84,125,000	41.9
Cordiant Communications Group	17	79,810,000	26.3	—	N/A	—
Cohn & Wolfe	18	64,409,000	36.4	16	63,220,000	33.9
Waggener Edstrom	19	57,905,000	14.5	17	57,905,000	14.5
Rowland Communications Worldwide	20	45,391,000	<8.7>	18	45,391,000	<8.7>
The MWW Group	21	37,723,000	38.5	19	37,723,000	38.5
Text 100	22	33,682,000	65.5	20	33,682,000	65.5
Schwartz Communications	23	33,186,000	57.8	21	33,186,000	57.8
Publicis Dialog	24	32,646,000	38.9	22	29,394,000	25.0
Magnet Communications	25	26,652,000	173.7	23	13,934,000	43.1

Source: Council of Public Relations Firms. Available: www.prfirms.org.

budgets of most African economies. Public relations revenue-generating potential for the continent is, therefore, substantial. But because policy makers in Africa are blinded by the frantic quest for self-aggrandizement, their economies are deprived of these benefits. Even as their economies stagnate, African governments prefer to turn to international financial institutions for advice and loans than to work themselves on implementing the reforms needed to open their economies for market competition. The World Bank and the International Monetary Fund seldom include advice on the potential benefits of public relations to emerging societies—that is, public relations strategies that can be implemented to help attract foreign investment, create demand, and gain market share. In looking at the figures it is evident that revenue potential from a healthy public relations industry is much greater than the revenue potential derived from a World Bank loan. Instead of turning to international financial institutions for loans and other financial solutions to Africa's stagnant economies, African rulers should be implementing reforms to enable the development of a domestic public relations industry.

Conclusion

At independence, the primary task of most African countries was to preserve and to consolidate the power handed over to them by departing colonial rulers. Everything else, including national economic development, was of secondary importance. Consequently, a disproportionately high percentage of national resources were directed at political self-preservation rather than at national development. In placing individual self-interest over national interest, African rulers indirectly contributed to the underdevelopment of the very continent they pledged to develop when they inherited power. Today, with various national economies around the world poised to go global, Africa remains caught up in a debilitating state of political and economic stagnation.

In failing to develop the skills and technologies to allow for gainful participation in the New World order, Africa has, through a dismal process of self-elimination, excluded itself as a relevant player in the new international system. Among the key national assets that would enhance Africa's competitive position are the interplay of domestic political stability, economic growth, and public relations. Political stability establishes the necessary conditions conducive to economic growth; and economic growth, in turn, contributes to the consolidation of political stability. With globalization, the stimuli for domestic economic growth are increasingly external rather than internal. To succeed, Africa must master the art of public relations. It is by mastering this art that Africa will be able to attract the external resources needed to enhance its productivity and global competitiveness.

If Africa, and, particularly, Africans who describe themselves as "Afroptimists" (Kaplan, 1994) expect someday to realize their dream of a return to the continent's golden age, they will have to begin first by investing in the development of a public relations industry

Kenya

Government type	Republic
Capital	Nairobi
Language	English, Swahili (both official), indigenous languages
Ethnic groups	Kikuyu, Luhya, Luo, Kalenjin, Kamba, Kisii, Meru, other African, non-African (Asian, European, and Arab)
Religion	Protestant (including Anglican), Roman Catholic, indigenous beliefs, Muslim
Major industries	Small-scale consumer goods (plastic, furniture, batteries, textiles, soap, cigarettes, flour), agricultural products processing, oil refining, cement, tourism

Sources: National Geographic Atlas of the World Seventh Edition, CIA The World Factbook 2002

Nigeria

Government type	Republic transitioning from military to civilian rule
Capital	Abuja
Language	English, Hausa, Yoruba, Igbo
Ethnic groups	Composed of more than 250 ethnic groups; the following are the most populous and politically influential: Hausa and Fulani, Yoruba, Igbo (Ibo), Ijaw, Kanuri, Ibibio, Tiv
Religion	Muslim, Christian, indigenous beliefs
Major industries	Crude oil, coal, tin, columbite, palm oil, peanuts, cotton, rubber, wood, hides and skins, textiles, cement and other construction materials, food products, footwear, chemicals, fertilizer, printing, ceramics, steel

Sources: National Geographic Atlas of the World Seventh Edition, CIA The World Factbook 2002

Ghana

Government type	Constitutional monarchy
Capital	Accra
Language	English, African languages (including Akan, Moshi-Dagomba, Ewe, and Ga)
Ethnic groups	Black African (major tribes—Akan, Moshi-Dagomba, Ewe, Ga, Gurma, Yoruba), European
Religion	Indigenous beliefs, Muslim, Christian
Major industries	Mining, lumbering, light manufacturing, aluminum smelting, food processing

Sources: National Geographic Atlas of the World Seventh Edition, CIA The World Factbook 2002

South Africa

Government type	Republic
Capital	Pretoria (administrative); Cape Town (legislative); Bloemfontein (judicial)
Language	Afrikaans, English, Ndebele, Pedi, Sotho, Swazi, Tsonga, Tswana, Venda, Xhosa, Zulu (all official)
Ethnic groups	Black, white, Indian
Religion	Christian, traditional and animistic, Muslim, Hindu
Major industries	Mining (platinum, gold, chromium), automobile assembly, metalworking, machinery, textile, iron and steel, chemicals, fertilizer, foodstuffs

Sources: National Geographic Atlas of the World Seventh Edition, CIA The World Factbook 2002

in their various societies. It is through an active public relations program that Africa will be able to change the negative perception that the outside world currently has of the continent. It is only by marketing Africa positively that the continent eventually will be in a position to attract and retain foreign capital, and possibly reverse the epidemic of "brain drain" that the region suffers today. Inevitable, such marketing will require sustained investment in the development of this sector on which so many political and economic development efforts are hinged.

References

Joseph, R., Lewis, P., Kew, D., & Taylor, S. (2002). In M. Kesselman & D. Joseph (Eds.), *Introduction to comparative politics* (pp. 551–552). Boston: Charles Scribner's Sons.

July, R. (1980). *A history of the African people.* New York: Charles Scribner's Sons.

Kaplan, R. (1994). The coming anarchy. *The Atlantic Monthly, 273*(2), pp. 44–76.

Kesselman, M., & Joseph, D. (2002). (Eds.). *Introduction to comparative politics.* Boston: Houghton Mifflin.

Lustig, R. (2002). AIDS in Africa: Breaking the silence. [On-line]. Available: http://news.bbc.co.uk/hi/english/ static/indepth/africa/2000/aidsinafrica/overview. stm.

Power, J. (1998). The millstone of African debt must be lifted at the annual World Bank/IMF meeting about to begin in Washington. [On-line]. Available: www.algonet.se/~d58155/forum/power/1998/ pow30-09.html.

Shraeder, P. (2000). *African politics and society: A mosaic of transformations.* New York: Bedford/St. Martin's Press.

Wehrwein, P. (2000). Harvard AIDS review fall 1999/winter 2000. [On-line]. Available: www.hsph.harvard.edu.

10

Public Relations, Decolonization, and Democracy

The Case of Kenya

Jacquie L'Etang

George Muruli

Key Points

- The emergence of public relations in Kenya took a different path from that of the United States or the United Kingdom, which raises considerable questions over the legitimacy of the dominant model of public relations practice based on the historical experience of one (the United States) culture.
- The colonial government depended on harmonious interracial communication despite intrinsic racism and injustice.
- The Mau Mau emergency provides some evidence that the British government tried to distinguish between their "public relations" and "propaganda" activities.
- The Kenyan case illustrates the point that in some cultural contexts it is difficult to separate government political propaganda from public relations practice.

One of the major themes of the twentieth century was the dissolution of European empires in Africa and Asia (Ochieng' & Atieno-Odhiambo, 1995) and the establishment of new forms of government in Africa, some of which posed considerable challenges to democracy. The role of public relations during such monumental changes has been little explored, and this chapter seeks to redress some of that gap in the literature by presenting a brief history of some key developments in one of Britain's former colonies—Kenya.

The chapter sketches some of the key political developments and identifies the role that public relations played. Furthermore, it proceeds to outline the way in which the occupation became established in Kenya. The chapter demonstrates that significant influences were British government propaganda, nationalism (including the activities of Mau Mau), decolonization and development, race relations, and religion. The colonial heredity is shown to have shaped Kenya both in terms of the role of public relations as a democratic practice, if only a limited one, as well as in terms of reinforcing colonial structures in the postcolonial world via private and state-sector economic relationships. Decolonization led to economic dependency and enhanced the emergence of an African elite. This structural feature necessitated the establishment of a public relations occupation that emerged distinct from the propaganda activities of both the British government and the nationalist movement Mau Mau.

The research is based on oral history interviews, archives, and documentary research in Kenya and the United Kingdom and may be categorized as sociological history. Because the dominant approach taken is historical, it has been judged inappropriate to impose conceptual frameworks from later periods of history or from other cultures.

Likewise, the chapter is sociologically rigorous in that it does not use the term *profession* in relation to public relations. The sociological literature on professions can be roughly divided into a typology encompassing research on the necessary and sufficient traits for an occupation to be recognized by society as a profession; research that tries to capture the generic stages of the process; ethnographic research; research drawing on Marx and Weber that emphasizes the profession's effectiveness in monopolizing a field of work and negotiating high status, known as the "power approach"; research that focuses on the "professional project" and the transformation of specialist knowledge and skills into social and economic rewards; and finally, research that takes a systemic approach in looking at occupations as a linked system in which changes in one occupation will have an impact on other occupations. Of particular importance are questions of jurisdiction or the degree of control an occupation has over a range of tasks. To sum up, the literature on the sociology of the professions has established as the key features of a profession:

> A specialised skill and service, an intellectual and practical training, a high degree of professional autonomy, a fiduciary relationship with a client, a sense of collective responsibility to the profession as a whole, an embargo on some methods of attracting business and an occupational organisation testing competence, regulating standards and maintaining discipline. (Elliott, 1972, p. 152, cited in Pieczka & L'Etang, 2001, p. 224)

and the processes through which an occupation must pass to achieve that status:

> (1) the emergence of the full-time occupation; (2) the establishment of the training school; (3) the founding of professional associations; (4) political agitation directed towards the protection of the association by law; (5) the adoption of a formal code. (Johnson, 1972, p. 28, cited in Pieczka & L'Etang, 2001, p. 244)

Thus, because public relations does not meet these criteria it is referred to more appropriately as an "occupation" rather than a "profession," even though it is acknowledged that this is an important aspiration for most practitioners and most academics.

British Colonial Rule in Kenya

Kenya was established as a colony as part of the "scramble for Africa" in the 1880s when the European powers partitioned Africa among themselves as they sought to establish spheres of geographical influence and to obtain raw materials for domestic production. As Ochieng' and Atieno-Odhiambo (1995) point out:

> In the ten years between 1885 and 1905 . . . Kenya . . . was transformed from a footpath 600 miles long into a harshly politicised colonial state. . . . The transformation of Kenya from a polyglot of strangers [adventurers and refugees] into a coherent state was the work of force. (p. xiv)

Some of the best land was given to Europeans thus limiting the African access to fresh land. This forced many Africans to work as laborers and servants for the incoming Europeans. Although some African colonies were ruled as protectorates under the jurisdiction of the Colonial Office from the outset, others, including Kenya, were initially under the control of chartered companies. Thus, a pattern of involvement with international capital was established at an early stage (Ochieng', 1995).

The relationship between Britain and its colonies was very different from that of the French (the French controlled one-third of Africa), which focused on the assimilationist notion of *La France d'outre-mer*—"France overseas" (Chamberlain, 1999, pp. 70–71). By contrast, the British were generally less inclined to intervene in local cultures and instead relied on various versions of "indirect rule" in which traditional rulers operated within an overall British framework. This model, therefore, depended heavily on good interpersonal relations between the British administrator and the African chief. Thus, the maintenance of relationships and the importance of communication were essential parts of colonial rule to achieve continued acceptance of the colonial condition. Nevertheless, however benign and regardless of the degree of local acceptance, the imperial relationship was characterized by the very obvious benefits that accrued to Britain in terms of international status, natural resources, a labor market, and, for those who settled in Kenya's pleasant climate, a good lifestyle. These benefits contrasted sharply with a pattern of underinvestment in the host country by imperialist capitalists and government (Chamberlain, 1999). It was only after World War II (which, in Britain, lasted from 1939 to 1945), when nationalist aspirations became much stronger, that a real effort was made to contribute to the development of the country and that it was recognized that there was "an obligation to finance the development of social services such as health and education in the British colonies, as well as trying to lay economic foundations" (Chamberlain, 1999, p. 35).

There were British settlers in Kenya prior to and after both World Wars and, because in the early part of the twentieth century Kenya was seen as a "new Australia," white settlers had high expectations for the acquisition of wealth, power, ownership, and political autonomy (Chamberlain, 1999, p. 49). Such hopes were dashed by a government White Paper in 1923 that made it quite clear that self-government was not being considered and that furthermore:

> Kenya is an African territory, and His Majesty's Government think it necessary definitely to record their considered opinion that the interests of the African natives must be paramount,

and that if and when those interests and the interests of the immigrant races should conflict the former should prevail. (Chamberlain, 1999, p. 50)

Despite these sentiments, the exercise of colonial power by a few in the ostensible interests of the many required careful management of relationships supported by appropriate rhetorical strategies and tactics.

A legislative council was established in 1906, and this was reconstructed in 1927, comprised of twenty official members, eleven of whom were elected Europeans, five elected Indians, one elected Arab, and one nominated member to represent Africans. The first African association was the Kikuyu Association formed in 1920, which consisted of a conservative collection of older tribesmen and chiefs. In 1921 the more radical Young Kikuyu Association (later the Kikuyu Central Association) was formed, which fell foul of the authorities during World War II for allegedly seditious (basically nationalist) activities.

From the early 1920s British civil servants at both local and national levels had been aware of the importance of public relations. They detected the necessity for government to manage public opinion in an emerging democracy partly because of the extensive social and political legislation passed in Britain from the 1830s onward. This legislation forced a profound change in the relationship between government and people both at national and local levels. Improved social welfare and progressively greater educational opportunities increased citizens' aspirations but also raised fears among the ruling classes. These fears were articulated as problems of management and communication within the bureaucratic elite of the country, and, hence, it was Britain's politically neutral civil servants who first gave proper attention to the subject of public relations. The Institute of Public Administration was formed in 1922 as "the leading independent British organization with expertise in public sector management" (Royal Institute of Public Administration RIPA, 1998, p. 10). Its journal, *Public Administration,* included many articles on public relations, propaganda, and "general relations with the public" (Grant, 1994, p. 48). "Public relations," in contrast to "intelligence," was seen literally as relations with the general public; it provided rather than collected information. It was argued that an essential aspect of the role of the public servant was "his obligation to stand as the representative of the vast, unrepresented, anonymous public" (Finer, 1931, p. 30). The evidence in *Public Administration* suggests that by the 1930s there was an understanding of the importance of good public relations to facilitate smooth administration. Achieving better understanding between the public and local government began to become of intrinsic importance to the job of administration and to the improvement of democracy because:

> a more vivid realisation of the state of public opinion on administrative matters . . . will show how [the administration of government policy] can be better adjusted to the environment in which it must work. . . . Publicity . . . should ensure that the public will be able to contribute informed but constructive criticism. (Cowell, 1935, p. 292)

Thus, in the British context, government peacetime public relations presented itself as a beneficent, socially responsible activity acting on behalf of the public interest. It is easy to see how readily such values could be transported to the colonial context in order to maintain the status quo. The British case illustrates very clearly the links between democratic practice and the growth of public relations activities. Whereas on the one hand these can be seen as a way of enhancing communication and understanding within society, on the other hand they can be interpreted as a rearguard action to preserve the class system of privileged access to power.

It is worth noting that civil servants responsible for communication at local and national levels during this period in the United Kingdom were integrated into specialist areas or ministries, for example, the Ministry of Health, and not under one ministry. Interest in public relations in central government was the result of a number of different historical developments: the rise of totalitarian regimes in Italy, Germany, the Soviet Union, and elsewhere; increasing tensions in international politics; reactions to the increased democratization of society; methodological developments in understanding public opinion; and, ultimately, modern warfare and the development of communications technology. The British government needed to control and censor unfavorable information that might harm morale; to penetrate enemy communication networks in order to confuse or to demoralize; and to win and maintain alliances from which political, economic, or military support might be forthcoming. The distinctions between propaganda, public relations, information, intelligence, persuasion, and psychological warfare became harder to draw. Although a proper conceptual discussion of these terms is beyond the scope of this chapter, the historical data presented does go some way to demonstrate the difficulty in distinguishing aspects of these different activities in a way that is rarely acknowledged in public relations literature.

The size and geographical scope of the British Empire and its dominions presented a challenge but also offered opportunities. The growth of an international network of news agencies connected by electric telegraph in the late nineteenth century ended governments' ability entirely to control news and also offered new opportunities for debate and comment. The British government offered subsidies to cable companies in order to encourage them to route cables through British territories, thus giving the British security services the chance to monitor and censor news as well as to gather intelligence (Pronay, 1982). Control over technology facilitated British control of news flow.

British propaganda in World War I was placed under the control of the specially created Department of Information. However, the British also set up a secret information and intelligence unit under the auspices of the Foreign Office from 1914 to 1917, and for three years this was the source of information targeted at the then-neutral Americans aimed to encourage them to enter the war on Britain's side. When the Americans eventually did enter the war in 1917, this unit became less important, and the Department of Information was upgraded to ministerial status and made responsible for propaganda in allied and neutral territories under the leadership of the press baron, Lord Beaverbrook. Another press baron, Lord Northcliffe, was given responsibility for the newly created Department of Enemy Propaganda. At the end of World War I the Ministry of Information was dissolved, largely because it was believed that its activities were inappropriate for a democratic country. It reopened for business in 1939 at the outset of World War II and closed again in 1945.

Colonial Kenya fell under the responsibility of the Colonial Office and the Foreign Office. The country comprised the imperial expatriate class; Asians (Indians, Pakistanis, and Goans), who made use of the railways to foster the development of business; Arabs, who were largely involved in small-scale agriculture and industrial production; and the indigenous Africans (Ochieng' & Atieno-Odhiambo, 1995, p. xv). Relations between Africans and Asians tended to be poor because Asians were the more prosperous group. There were many religions also—Hindus, Muslims (Sunni and Shia), Sikhs, and Christians. The assumption of racial superiority was a feature of the expatriate community in Kenya at the same time that it acquired the deservedly debauched and degenerate reputation of the "Happy Valley" crowd (Chamberlain, 1999). They were from the British upper classes and their motivation for living in Kenya was its lifestyle, big-game shooting, and easily available servants. Their self-indulgence and wild parties were well captured in James Fox's novel *White Mischief,* published in 1982 and subsequently made into a film (Chamberlain, 1999, p. 49). Racist assumptions were endemic, for example, in the early twentieth century some even preferred that Africans did not speak English because if they conversed with Europeans in English, they might be tempted to suppose that they could become the equals of Europeans (Watkins, 1939, p. 17).

Nevertheless, colonial government was dependent on harmonious interracial communication despite the intrinsic racism and injustices and, as Muruli argues, "in a multicultural/racial setting such as colonial Kenya, it is the strained social/human relationships that call for public relations action—hence giving public relations a unique role in society" (Muruli, 2001, p. 17). Interpersonal relations were paramount because there were no mass media and, until 1927, there was no broadcasting system in existence (Abuoga & Mutere, 1988). The colonial government contracted Cable and Wireless to relay news in English on its transmitting station at Kabete after monitoring the BBC for European consumption (Abuoga & Mutere, 1988). Radio was important because literacy was low but it was also a source of colonial domination because the English language dominated. Television was not introduced in Kenya and East Africa until 1960. As late as 1988 Abouga and Mutere argued that

> radio broadcasting is . . . the only medium of mass communication in Kenya. It has largely overcome the communication barriers of illiteracy and geographical isolation. (1988, p. 100)

It can be argued that British government public relations existed in Kenya from the inception of the colony in terms of building and maintaining relationships with key publics (the various racial groups and many different rural communities) but used interpersonal and social relations as the main technique to achieve harmony and acceptance of its goals.

A major British development in terms of its international public relations and public diplomacy was the creation of the British Council in 1934, founded to achieve goodwill for Britain through promotional work and exchange of persons. In broad terms its function was cultural propaganda and its mission was defined as follows:

> To make the life and thought of the British peoples more widely known abroad; and to promote a mutual interchange of knowledge and ideas with other peoples. To encourage the study and use of the English language . . . to bring other peoples in closer touch with British ideals and practice in education, industry and government; to make available to them the benefits of current British contributions to the sciences and technology; and to afford them opportunities of appreciating contemporary British work in literature, fine arts, drama and music. To co-operate with the self-governing Dominions in strengthening the common cultural tradition of the British Commonwealth. (White, 1965, p. 7)

However, at least one commentator saw a more substantial political agenda underlying the apparently benign cultural front:

[the Council] was created partly to perpetuate the appearance of power in the minds of foreigners at a time when hostile propaganda was beginning to expose the harsh realities of Britain's decline. Although the Council itself would not have considered itself to be in the business of myth-making, the very fact that there was felt to be a need to project British achievements abroad was in itself symptomatic of Britain's declining influence in international affairs. (Taylor, 1981, pp. 129–130)

In short, the British Council was an essential tool in communicating British national identity. This identity incorporated those of the colonies, and the British Council's work can be seen not only as the simple promotion of Britain abroad but also as a way of encouraging colonial peoples to identify with Britain. This became increasingly important as *uhuru*—independence—moved onto the agenda.

According to articles written by British practitioners in the 1920s and 1930s, British peacetime propaganda emphasized the breaking down of barriers among social groups through information, education, and persuasion, often using personal relationships as the means to achieve this (L'Etang, 1998). The council's success relied heavily on the benefits accruing to individuals who benefited from international visits and exchanges, conferences, exhibitions, cultural events, knowledge transfer, and networking. Within government circles such activities were seen as governmental tools, ostensibly to ensure the smooth working of democracy but in reality to help maintain the status quo.

The British Council began work in Kenya in 1947, following communications in 1946 between the governor of Kenya and the director general of the British Council in London (Muruli, 2001, p. 20). They expressed the need for the British Council to start work in the colony and the urgency of establishing an institute to provide cultural facilities and promote interracial understanding (Muruli, 2001, p. 20). The British Council's representative had specific instructions from the secretary of state, on his arrival in Kenya in May 1947, to establish a cultural center and a National Theatre where "educated members" of the different races could meet (Frost, 1978, p. 72). This demonstrates the council's interest in the emerging middle class not least because the British government was beginning to develop an awareness that this group, whose status depended on wealth and education, not lineage, were likely to be politically conscious and to regard the traditional rulers as "unenlightened, incompetent and British-inspired" (Hodgkin, 1956, p. 46). Longer term, the British Council's aims can be broadly encompassed as targeting the "successor generation" to facilitate relationships beneficial to Britain in the future, though the complexities and tensions of African politics made this sometimes difficult to achieve.

Nevertheless, the establishment of the British Council in Kenya signaled the beginning of a new era of interracial cooperation, specifically on the cultural front, and in 1947 hosted the first interracial concerts at which Europeans and Africans appeared on the same program (*East African Standard*, 1947).

Emergence of Media and Public Relations

A key development in the story of public relations in Kenya was the founding of the British Broadcasting Company (BBC) in 1922. The BBC developed broadcasting in the British dependencies, and the creation of a mass medium necessitated a system of journalists and sources to feed the medium. In a sense too it created the opportunity for a different and mediatized notion of public opinion to develop and supplied an important structure in terms of the replication of Western democratic practice. As has been noted

> Kenya, in 1928, was the first dependency to set up a wireless broadcasting station . . . a more effective instrument for promoting both local and imperial interests. (Central Office of Information, No: R 2644 of 1953)

The broadcast service began when Cable and Wireless was granted a license to broadcast by the colonial government. Broadcasting continued in English only until the beginning of the World War II in 1939, when programs for Asian and African listeners were introduced (Roberts, 1953, p. 12). The services to Africans and Asians were started to spread information and to create attitudes likely to assist the war effort (Muruli, 2001, p. 21). Unsurprisingly, this increased the government's interest in publishing for African publics. British officials were concerned that Africans would misinterpret and distort the information they received by radio and insisted on follow-up articles in news sheets to be distributed in areas that received radio (Muruli, 2001, p. 21). In 1939 the colonial government began publishing *Baraza* ("Forum"), a weekly bulletin that served to supplement the Department of Information's weekly bulletin *Habari Za Vita* ("War News") (Muruli, 2001, p. 22). It also served as a medium for disseminating news and information to the parents and relatives of African soldiers on the battlefront (Muruli, 2001, p. 22). Along with *Baraza,* a number of district news sheets appeared as well as a weekly news sheet in Kiswahili, *Pamoja* ("Together") (Muruli, 2001, p. 22).

The U.K. Ministry of Information gradually recruited a number of communication specialists during World War II, including posts responsible for press liaison, film, publications, broadcasting, and photography. Many of those initially appointed were Europeans, and it was not until the late 1950s that Africans began to reach more senior positions (Abuoga & Mutere, 1988). In 1940, the government inaugurated the Mobile Information Unit as another technique for its public relations activities in Kenya. Official records noted that

> an interesting experiment was made in Nairobi by sending round loud speaker vans to give information and propaganda to the African population. They were used regularly throughout the emergency Training Exercises, during the ARP Exercises, and at the end of October when there was a considerable danger of widespread strikes. (*Kenya Information Office Annual Report,* 1941)

The Government Information Services expanded, adding sections for European, Indian, and African publics, as well as French and Italian sections and a photographic section. The main function of the European section was the reception and distribution of written material (especially on the war effort) and broadcasting summaries of war news to schools (Muruli, 2001, p. 22). The target listenership of the European section was free citizens, Europeans in the occupied enemy territory, and prisoner of war camps (*Kenya Information Office Annual Report,* 1941). A range of written material was used to support the broadcasts, such as newspapers, magazines, pamphlets, posters, and handbills (*Kenya Information Office Annual Report,* 1941). The Indian and African sections were responsible for distributing government information about the war in order to create and direct public opinion appropriately. Programs included news, background briefs, and contextual information as well as health, agricultural, and labor propaganda. Chiefs and local native council elders contributed talks on the war and urged continual support and increased commitment toward the overall war effort.

There was no specialized member of staff for press, public relations, or information work until 1940. Prior to that date, press handouts (the term for press releases in that era in Britain) and bulletins were issued directly from Government House by an administrator (Abuoga & Mutere, 1988). The first journalist to be hired was Mervyn Hill, who was contracted as information officer for two years after which he returned to journalism (Abuoga & Mutere, 1988). Others who became involved in information work tended both to be technical specialists, for example, photographers or film specialists, and British.

The creation of the post of principal information officer (PIO), the representative of the Ministry of Information on the East African Command in 1942, led to a shift in responsibilities. The PIO took over information and press duties from the Kenyan Information Office (KIO). From then on, the PIO was responsible for military communiques and information about occupied territories as well as for the home front and news for African troops away from home. The PIO passed material directly to the Kenya Information Office for distribution to Kenyan media (*Kenya Information Office Annual Report,* 1942). Having been relieved of much of its duties, the KIO then focused on mass communication

> [i]n an endeavour to improve the activities of the information office as a public relations office by keeping the public informed of the activities and intentions of the government. (*Kenya Information Office Annual Report,* 1942, p. 3)

At this time there were no educational or training facilities available and, as late as 1992, a leading light of Kenya public relations, Shabanji Opukah, lamented the fact that "training facilities are either badly inadequate or totally lacking" (Opukah, 1992, p. 16).

In 1944 a specialized post of public relations officer was created within the KIO with a greater strategic responsibility for fostering favorable public opinion toward the war effort. Subsequently, the KIO became more of a technical service department charged with the responsibility of producing and supplying publicity materials.

From the late 1940s business became increasingly aware of publicity's virtues (Muruli, 2001, p. 36). Simultaneously, dramatic shifts occurred in public attitudes toward business and in the roles played by several institutions (Muruli, 2001, p. 36). In what appeared to be an increasingly diverse society, consensus was breaking down with a rise in the incidence of conflict and confrontation (Muruli, 2001, p. 36). As early as 1940, workers had begun to organize themselves into unions, largely organized along racial lines (Muruli, 2001, p. 36). Between 1939 and 1963 there were major strikes in most state corporations. Examples include twenty-three thousand African ports and railways worker strikers in 1959, a dockers' strike in 1960, and a major strike called by the East African Posts and Telecommunications African worker's union (Muruli, 2001). Such strikes could be partly attributed to the lack of internal communications within most organizations at that time, thus demonstrating the need for public relations. Growth of private sector public relations was a postwar, and largely postindependence, phenomenon that took place first in organizations such as Kenya Power and Lighting, Kenya Shell, and the East African Harbours Corporation (Muruli, 2001). This followed the pattern of the colonial power, Britain, where private sector public relations was fairly limited until after World War II. There, consultancies developed from advertising agencies, but this was not a significant feature of the public relations scene until the British economy had recovered in the 1960s (L'Etang, 2001). However, corporate public relations did develop earlier and faster in the postwar era, partly in response to the perceived threat of nationalization that emerged from the Labour Party's policy on state ownership (L'Etang, 2001). There were public relations departments prior to 1930 in London Transport, the Port of London Authority, Gas Light and Coke Company, ICI, British Overseas Airways Corporation (BOAC), Shell, J. Lyons & Company, and Rootes Motors and Brooklands Racing Track (Gillman, 1978). There were also some public affairs and political lobbyists and specialists in financial communications.

A British practitioner with African experience was based in Kenya on behalf of the British Army's East African Command prior to the Mau Mau emergency. He described the role of public relations as one that smoothed over social relationships between different classes and races:

> My main work there was with the *East African Standard*. . . . The English colonial papers were like the English provincial papers and they could cause a great deal of trouble—there was a lot of work to be done between settlers and the armed forces who were not always on the most friendly terms because here were these chaps coming out to our favourite land—the Happy Valley crowd. So one spent a lot of time getting people together. The proprietor of the *East African Standard* and a number of Swahili papers was a chap called Eric Anderson who was a very very nice man so of course I got to know him and then one would have him to dinner with the General and that sort of thing, and gradually begin to build relationships which is what it's all about. . . . If you're a good PRO . . . you should be on Christian name terms not only with the editor but also the proprietor and although it's always said the editor's independent of the proprietor that's not, as you know, wholly true. (personal communication, August 14, 1996, in L'Etang, 2001, p. 81)

The colonial experience was defined in an article in the Institute of Public Relations journal in 1951 that laid out the special qualities required for a PRO "in the Colonies." In addition to language skills, diplomacy, and the ability to create media for communication, it was deemed necessary to have

> the sort of intellectual and social background that will enable him to work in a very small community of well educated and overworked officials. . . . The sort of man who can discuss high policy with the Governor over dinner and the next day get down to the composing room of a newspaper in his shirt sleeves and talk to the printer as one old hand to another. (Johnson, 1951, p. 9)

Decolonization did not solely affect the British government but also relations between British private companies and the African populace as the following passage from an interview with a practitioner who worked for Unilever in Africa makes clear:

> The Board realized that in post-war black Africa there was going to be a big resurgence of political agitation working for independence from the British Commonwealth . . . [it was therefore] proposed that we should practice public relations . . . anticipating where African desires were going to lead and what sort of attitudes they were going to formulate. . . . It was a question of impressing people with the idea that we were a good thing

for them and their country. Public relations was very restricted because the press was very underdeveloped—radio was in its infancy and television didn't exist. . . . A lot had to be done by word of mouth—our managers mixing with the local community. We ran the first strip cartoon . . . in an African paper, and through it the African reader would learn what capital was, what profit was, what employment was, what training was and all those basic things. (personal communication, March 26, 1997, in L'Etang, 2001, pp. 80–81)

So Unilever reacted to decolonization by introducing public relations, which began by developing personal relationships in the community to win friends and influence people. The campaign aimed to counteract any latent alienation and preserve company interests in the postcolonial context. The function of public relations can be seen in this context to have engaged in helping to shore-up colonial economic structures.

More generally these examples highlight the interpersonal nature of public relations in the colonial period as indicated by Muruli (2001).

Decolonization, Nationalism, and Mau Mau

Britain ended World War II as the world's largest debtor nation, short of labor and food, with reduced productivity, and visible exports down to less than one-half of the prewar level. Although Britain in 1947 was described as "an impoverished, second-rate power, morally magnificent, but economically bankrupt" (Sissons & French, 1963, p. 247), the country's rulers attempted to maintain imperial rule. In the 1940s and 1950s, the United Kingdom was paying up to 8 percent of its gross national product on defense as the cold war escalated. Recovery was slow, and Britain's growth was much slower than its major competitors, Germany, Japan, the United States, and other Western European countries. Although British capital investment, output, and exports gradually expanded, revenue was insufficient to cover domestic commitments to welfare and employment, let alone support its overseas empire (Porter & Stockwell, 1989). Although the logical solution might have been to reduce overseas commitments, some, such as conservative politician (later Prime Minister) Harold Macmillan, advocated imperial regeneration as a solution to a perceived national crisis of confidence after the long years of war:

> a policy which will reinspire the masses and restore their pride and confidence. This is the choice—the slide into a shoddy and slushy socialism, or the march to the third British Empire. (Cabinet Memo, 1952)

The sheer cost of nuclear weapons and other instruments of mass destruction forced a change in military deployments within the empire as it was argued:

> Everything possible should be done to build up local Colonial forces in order to reduce the demands on our own Army. . . . [Colonial forces are] the front line of defence against subversion. (Defence Policy Review, 1954)

Thus, notions of dependency can be seen not only in terms of that of the former colonies on the United Kingdom but also of the United Kingdom on its territories. Postwar concepts of empire remained important to British identity as well as in terms of economic, political, and military contributions. At this point in history, however, African aspirations were developing, partly as a consequence of the wider world that Africans had glimpsed in their own wartime experiences. The growth of nationalism (first articulated through protests and the formation of the Kikuyu Central Association [KCA] in the 1920s, and by the Kenyan African Union [KAU] from 1944) was a logical consequence of this development, and, in Kenya, the emergence of the terrorist group Mau Mau forced all those who lived there to reconsider the colonial relationship and alternative futures. Such reflection was the necessary preamble to the process of change and the emergence of Kenyan identity to which public relations also made its contribution.

After World War II, African discontent in Kenya grew steadily. Little constitutional progress had been made, although by 1948 there was an unofficial majority in the Legislative Assembly, the four African members were still nominated rather than elected. Only in 1952 were Africans elected to the legislative council and then by a complicated indirect system (Chamberlain, 1999). Very few educated Africans achieved any kind of influence in government or the economy. British propaganda of World War II had attacked racism and stressed equality, but little of this idealism was evident in Kenya. Segregation and the color bar were entrenched in virtually all aspects of life, and the European settlers were particularly contemptuous of educated Africans. There was a mass exodus of Africans from the rural areas seeking employment in the cities, especially Nairobi (Abuoga & Mutere, 1988). The problem of land shortage and control of land by British landowners became severe in the face of the rising African population. Strong resistance developed against government attempts to enforce land use and soil conservation rules. Back in Nairobi, wages and living conditions were extremely poor for most Africans. The rising crime rates were symptomatic of deep social and economic problems that were not being tackled effectively. In both the urban and rural areas, an important radical vanguard was made up of army veterans who had served abroad and had their horizons expanded only to find little economic or political opportunity at home.

Increased militancy was accompanied by a rise in violent acts largely against fellow Africans. These were largely spontaneous expressions of frustration rather than tactics planned by a central coordinating body and, least of all, by the president of the KAU, Jomo Kenyatta. Kenyatta's association with Mau Mau has never been clearly identified, but Kenyatta was arrested and banished to a remote part of the colony on suspicion of the British government that he was involved. The Mau Mau name was an acronym for the Swahili phrase, *Mzungu Aende Ulaya, Mwafrika Apate Uhuru,* which translates as "the European should go back to Europe, so that the African can achieve self-government." Mau Mau was a nationalist, anticolonial, peasant-based guerrilla movement that used terror to challenge the status quo. According to Maloba (1998), the Mau Mau phenomenon was a consequence of state violence that had, through colonial policies, destroyed the traditional political economy and, by introducing international capital, had displaced peasants, squatters, and tenant farmers from the land. Assassinations and murders were committed at the same time that Mau Mau extended its network of supporters through secret oathing ceremonies and bestial rituals (some conducted on dead bodies). Mau Mau sought to mobilize landless peasants but did not attempt to educate them politically and subsequently failed to develop into a revolutionary party as had comparable movements in China, Cuba, Algeria, Vietnam, Guinea-Bissau, Mozambique, and Angola (Maloba, 1998).

Traditionally, folk communication in Africa employed oral (speech), aural (drums), and visual (smoke) techniques that were accessible to all (Magaga, 1982, p. 11). Technologized communication introduced problems of access, a degree of alienation, and the formation of a communication elite (Magaga, 1982, p. 13). Magic and witchcraft had always played a major role in Kikuyu society. Imported religions also played a major unifying role and, as Magaga (1982) points out:

> There is not a single aspect of communication that has been so perfected and has thrived so well in Kenya as religious communication. . . . Communication about God and religion . . . occupies a special, central and privileged position in Kenyan society. (pp. 84, 86)

Christianity and Islam have both played a dominant role in Kenyan society, and Christianity has been attributed with a major role in the rehabilitation of society following the Mau Mau Emergency. Mau Mau was seen by some parts of the Christian church as a specifically demonic threat, and the crisis stimulated and renewed evangelical fervour within Kenyan Christianity so that Roman Catholics and Protestants cooperated to an unprecedented degree to defeat the "anti-Christ" (Maloba, 1998, p. 14). For Mau Mau, Christianity was seen as a colonial religion, but Christianity's hold on the colony was very strong and thus those belief patterns generally prevailed. It seems that in Kenya a variety of mystical belief systems have long been a crucial part of society and a focus for communication. Although it is beyond the scope of this chapter to engage in a detailed conceptual discussion, it is nevertheless worth noting the association between some definitions of propaganda that depend on notions of irrational belief patterns, and religious communication, which is necessarily based on faith, rather than reason and sound empirical evidence.

Mau Mau was a temporary and fractured phenomenon lacking a clear ideology but with the ability to terrorize the population. Mau Mau was able tap in to strong cultural mores that gave considerable credence to belief in magic. Mau Mau relied organizationally on forest organizations based on traditional Kikuyu military organizations in which magic and witchcraft played a crucial role and thus reinforced the notion that nationalist sentiments were rooted in traditional culture (Maloba, 1998). However, it was clearly in the interests of the colonial power that such claims were delegitimized and that Mau Mau and anyone who could be associated with them be discredited as irrational, violent criminals.

The colonial power responded to the crisis with propaganda (news bulletins, press releases) that has had some considerable influence on the historiography of the literature about Mau Mau as has been identified by Maloba (1998). Demonization and a strategy to shape the population's view of Mau Mau by focusing on violence characterized much of the British effort. In the absence of any competing interpretation, the British view dominated. Thus, African nationalism was discredited as a criminal endeavor, and considerable efforts were made to attribute direct linkage between Jomo Kenyatta and others and the Mau Mau. Subsequently, it was important for Kenyan political parties, even though they partly owed their position to Mau Mau, to discredit it; as a consequence, political propaganda against Mau Mau has continued to the present day. Mau Mau propaganda efforts were considerably disadvantaged by their nomadic structures and lack of access to mass media. Mau Mau is an interesting example of a liberation movement engaging in terrorism that was not motivated to do so by news values. As Maloba (1998) points out, "The movement did not have a propaganda organisation that could rival the colonial state's bulletins and analyses" (p. 10).

At the outset of the colonial emergency in 1952 the colonial power defined Mau Mau and other nationalist tendencies seeking *uhuru*—independence—as illegitimate ungratefulness in return for the education, Christianity, commerce, rational government, and other features of Western civilization that colonialism had apparently delivered (Maloba, 1998). As 1952 wore on and violent acts continued in the Central Province, the Rift Valley, and Nairobi, European settlers became more and more uneasy. Calls were heard for strong action. In addition, government policy seemed to drift, as Governor Sir Philip Mitchell retired early in the year and his successor, Sir Evelyn Baring, did not arrive until September. Shortly after Baring's arrival, one of the most prominent Kikuyu chiefs and a firm supporter of the colonial regime, Chief Waruhiu, was assassinated in the Central Province. This act led Baring to declare a state of emergency on the almost hysterical advice of his subordinate, and, on October 20, 1952, he ordered the arrest of Jomo Kenyatta, Fred Kubai, Bildad Kaggia, and other KAU leaders. Governor Baring was forced to call in a substantial number of British troops to deal with the emergency and many more Africans (especially Kikuyu) were arrested and screened.

In the middle of the crisis the Lyttleton Constitution was introduced (named after the British colonial secretary). This was a complicated system intended to give Africans more opportunity to gain ministerial experience and was strongly opposed by the most conservative white settlers. But the zeitgeist of the times was independence, and gradual progress was made toward accomplishing that mission.

The Mau Mau emergency provides some evidence that the British government did in fact distinguish between public relations and propaganda activities and catered for these separately in terms of its organizational structures and personnel. For example, they did not use existing public relations channels, and within the first year of the emergency actually scaled down the information offices and cut the number of community development officer posts. The colonial state ran their campaign in coordination with their antiterrorist policies. In January 1954, however, the Department of Information in Kenya was officially constituted with a brief to ensure that the people of Kenya of all races were kept fully informed of the government's plans, policies, and achievements so as to gain their support and cooperation, and to build up public opinion in other countries so as to present the government's plans, policies, and achievements in such a way as to gain support for them and for British colonial policy more generally (Reiss, 1955, cited in Muruli, 2001, pp. 28–29). British government public relations was designed to create public opinion on the issue of Kenyan nationalism both in Britain and more widely in the international community. Thus, public relations functioned as a tool of Britain's diplomatic effort. The conceptual and practical overlap between public relations and diplomacy has been noted in the public relations literature (L'Etang, 1996; Signitzer & Coombs, 1992) and demonstrates the intrinsic connections between public relations and power; for this reason alone it cannot be assumed that government public relations will necessarily operate on behalf of democratic interests. Britain was a democratic state and ruled Kenya paternalistically and idealistically but, nevertheless, as a colony. Yet British government communications cannot be solely defined as propaganda, although they certainly included such activities because British government policy from the 1920s clearly intended the increasing involvement of Kenyans in government, even though progress was painfully slow.

In supporting political and diplomatic aims, public relations work was acknowledged as an important ingredient in the organizational decision-making process and hence efforts were made to ensure that it was part of the management mainstream. According to Abraham Ikobwa, a retired senior civil servant in the Kenyan Ministry of Information and Broadcasting, the director of the ministry was responsible for

> policy direction and co-ordination within the department following the lines laid down by the Minister, and the general planning and administration of the work of the department . . . the assistant Director . . . carried the particular responsibility of directing and co-ordinating the work of the field staff and planning the execution in the field of specific information projects. (personal communication, June 14, 2001, in Muruli, 2001, p. 30)

Included in this division was the post of public relations officer, who dealt with more than merely press matters and worked with filmmakers and broadcasters as well as "acting as an advisor to government in their dealings with all such professionals and publicists" (Reiss, 1955, p. 8, cited in Muruli, 2001, p. 30). Significantly, public relations was conceived as a strategic problem-solving function and was not limited to technical communications. In addition, public relations was clearly conceived as networking, and effective public relations was defined as dependent on

> personal relationships between the staff of the department and visiting journalists, broadcasters etc . . . [People] who usually themselves have large and elastic expense accounts and who expect the Government of Kenya to entertain them while they are in the colony. (Reiss, 1955, p. 11, cited in Muruli, 2001, p. 31)

The KIO press office focused on the reporting of emergency operations; preparation of press releases dealing with all aspects of government policy and activities; reporting activities of ministers and the deputy governor; writing feature articles that explained government policy and activities for use in the Kenyan and overseas press, especially the United Kingdom; acting as liaison with the United Kingdom Central Office of Information, the Colonial Office Press Organisation, and other British Information Posts outside the United Kingdom; and media relations, such as tours for newspaper correspondents, press conferences, news digests, information, booklets, tourist information, and material for film (Matheson, 1962). According to Mohammed Amin Sayid, formerly of the Department of Information, there were specialist units for publications and district news sheets that not only provided local news but also national and international news as interpreted by the Department of Information (personal communication, June 16, 2001). There were separate African and Asian sections responsible for information to those communities. During World War II the Asian public had been supplied with information from the Indian section of the Kenyan Broadcasting Services (set up in 1940), but this was abolished in 1946 in order to redirect resources to the African Information Services. It was reestablished in 1955 to provide both information for Asians in Kenya as well as information for India and Pakistan.

Independence

As already indicated, facing the challenge of nationalism (partly inspired by early Japanese victories in World War II) required considerable adaptation on behalf of the British administration, particularly in relation to the emergent Kenyan middle class. By the end of World War II, power could no longer be taken for granted, and British thinking became increasingly dominated by concepts of tutelage, development, and trusteeship (Boyce, 1999, p. 195).

Politically, a British move from colonial empire to commonwealth evaded severing the ties implied by "independence." It also helped to reinforce the historical relationship during the cold war. In his famous "Wind of Change" speech in 1960, then-British Prime Minister Harold Macmillan raised the issue of political spheres of influence explicitly when he asked:

> [Will] the uncommitted peoples of Asia and Africa . . . swing to the East or to the West. Will they be drawn into the Communist camp?

Despite local conditions, U.K. Colonial Office *intentions* were apparently based on "a profound commitment to the goal of multi-racial politics" (Porter & Stockwell, 1989, p. 57). Labour members of Parliament (MPs), such as Barbara Castle and A. Wedgwood Benn, argued the case for equality in Kenya particularly strongly. Wedgwood Benn, in particular, suggested that the struggle in Africa was akin to that of working-class people in Britain for political, economic, and social rights in the nineteenth century and went on to suggest that, in any case, Britain was partly responsible for the aspirations of Africans:

> We cannot stop this advance of the African people . . . for one reason, because here in this Chamber is the greatest revolutionary inspiration of the lot. If we can do it, why cannot they do it? We bring Africans here on Government grants to study at our universities. They are trained to be 'the white man's burden' and, when they return home, they discover, when they advocate the same sort of course themselves, that they are liable to be locked up as extremists. Extremism begins in the institutions, particularly the educational institutions of this country. (Hansard 1959–1960)

Three main principles were established as conditions of independence by the Kenya Constitutional Conference in 1960—that Africans should take a share in government; that the franchise should be widened to allow different views to be expressed; that individuals of every community should have full opportunity to participate in the administration of the country "in a spirit of mutual tolerance" (*Command Paper 960*). These principles of democracy emanated from the dominant political will and diplomacy of the time and did not arise specifically from the practice of public relations as such. Public relations is a consequence of political and economic change rather than as the proactive idealistic force for democratic enlightenment suggested in much of the public relations literature.

By the early 1960s there were two main political parties, the Kenyan African National Union (KANU), which stood for centralized government, and the Kenyan African Democratic Union (KADU), which stood for a federal form of government. KANU, led by Kenyatta, won in 1963, just prior to independence on December 12, 1963. Subsequently, Kenya became a one-party state and, although a multiparty system was introduced in 1992, KANU continued to dominate elections.

At the beginning of 1963, the Information Services in Kenya were a subordinate department of the Ministry of Constitutional Affairs and Administration. With the implementation of self-government, its status was raised to that of a full ministry and included the extra responsibilities of broadcasting and tourism, and the Ministry of Information became more preoccupied with publicity for government development projects and other related activities suitable for mass education. To this end, *Kenya Yetu,* a local newspaper, was preferred as a key medium of communication because it reached the remotest part of the country (Abuor, 1969).

A second major preoccupation of the postcolonial government public relations effort was that in support of Kenya's foreign policy. After independence in 1963 many citizens of Asian origin were uncertain about their security under an African government because they controlled a high percentage of the Kenyan economy. There was a mass exodus to Britain which, according to the Kenyan government of the time, "reflected [a picture of Kenya] . . . in the world press that does not do justice to Kenya" (Wangalwa, 1968, p. 1). This resulted in a major propaganda effort encompassing tourist boards, embassies, and public relations firms in countries where there were no diplomatic missions (Wangalwa, 1968).

After independence in 1963, the need for planned public relations was also recognized both by business owners and unions. Speaking to the Central Organisation of Trade Unions (COTU), the Ministry of Labour chief industrial relations officer argued:

> the most efficient communications techniques can be useless and even dangerous without a deep feeling for public relations. (*Daily Nation,* 1968)

Organizations that espoused and developed their communications included the Kenya Power and Lighting Company, whose activities included internal communications, sponsorships and exhibitions, and philanthropic fund-raising for famine relief. Likewise, Kenya Shell Ltd. developed a wide program of corporate social responsibility, including environmental conservation, sponsoring a secondary school for orphaned and underprivileged children and various charities for the disabled and disadvantaged, according to Toni Sitoni, former Public Relations Officer (personal communication, June 20, 2001, in Muruli, 2001, p. 41). The East African Harbours Corporation also practiced a wide range of public relations techniques including financial public relations. One can only speculate as to whether the motivation to act as good citizens was directed by philanthropy or the need to guard interests in the postcolonial context.

The first public relations consultancy in Kenya was Dunford Hall & Partners, which was established in 1955 (Abuoga & Mutere, 1988). However, it was not until after independence that consultancies became established as a feature of public relations practice in Kenya. Key consultancies in the early era included James Smart Ltd., Church Orr & Associates, Koor Public Relations, Kibao Publicity, Bob Dewar Publicity, Sealpoint Publicity, and Crawford & Ellis Ltd. According to Muthiaga Muthoni, most firms were foreign owned, employing Africans at the technician level (personal communication, February 8, 2001). These firms were more interested in global public relations than in developing local consultancy businesses. Nairobi was seen as a convenient gateway to the rest of the continent. Most multinational corporations preferred foreign-based firms to Kenyan consultancies. According to Abuoga and Mutere (1988), Africans were only employed if they had been recommended by a non-African friend or "godfather" (p. 90). African-owned consultancies generally were forced to rely on technical-level contracts for the production of house magazines and translations. These features of the Kenyan public relations political economy illustrates the endemic racism intrinsic to the colonial mentality.

Postcolonial Developments:
Social Welfare and Education

Postcolonial Kenya faced major political, economic, and social challenges. Politically, a priority was increased access and status for Africans and the provision of social welfare and education. This required the provision of a basic infrastructure. The economy needed rebalancing because it was largely dependent on foreign capital and was underdeveloped. Furthermore, economic power had to be transferred to the indigenous population.

Independent Kenya opted for a mixed economy, which still relied heavily on Western capital, especially from Britain, thus providing the necessary background framework for the growth of public relations. The colonial ties were facilitated by the fact that key leaders (including Kenyatta, who studied anthropology at the London School of Economics) had received some education in Britain. Thus, the long-term policy of the British Council to target "successor generations" was justified. Much remained unchanged, however, in the civil service, police, social services, economics, education, and provincial administration (Ochieng', 1995). The main shift was the emergence of the African middle class who benefited most from policies of "Africanization." The creation of Kenyan citizenship meant that the vast majority of Europeans and many Asians left Kenya. The African middle class took advantage of the many opportunities offered to consolidate and enhance their class position, so that society now became stratified by class and wealth rather than by race.

Nevertheless, opportunities for all Africans improved, and the mission of *harambee* ("let's pull together") created many opportunities, particularly in the secondary school movement, which had a broad educational commitment to involve as many people in formal and informal teaching and learning as possible. *Harambee* can be seen as a crucial plank in the democratization of Kenyan society.

An important aspect of independence was that of nation building, and public relations strategies were required to construct and promote the new Kenyan identity. The Ministry of Information was the government's main arm to pursue the goals of modernization and integration. This effort included a range of activities, such as attempts to make Swahili the national language rather than English, the construction of key symbolic monuments, and the Africanization of street names. However, a major difficulty in the promotion of national identity involved the absence of Kenyan media. At independence Kenyans relied on British and American TV imports, and both the main newspaper groups were foreign owned though some radio was locally produced in Swahili.

The establishment of the Institute of Development Studies in 1965 was a major public relations exercise to disseminate knowledge about Kenyan culture and Kenyan values. Its cultural division eventually became the Institute for African Studies in 1970 and was responsible for carrying out research in African archaeology, history, social anthropology, musicology, linguistics, oral literature, arts, and crafts (Ogot & Ochieng, 1995). An important part of its scope was its political priority to liberate Kenya from cultural imperialism. It aimed, therefore, to promote Kenyan culture throughout Kenya via the dissemination of research, lectures, exhibitions, and national cultural programs that included curriculum development in schools (especially in relation to language and literature). Thus, it would seem that nation building required considerable promotional efforts, and these led, in turn, to an opening up of debate among Kenyans as to their identity and Kenya's relationship to the shared colonial past, not solely in the immediate postindependence era, but, subsequently, when independence did not deliver all the hoped-for dreams.

Emergence of an Occupation: Toward Professionalization

Although it has been indicated that persuasive communication in Kenyan society was sponsored by the colonial power and by both indigenous and imported religious institutions, it was not until the postwar era that public relations became fully recognized as a distinct occupation. To this extent Kenya shared the heritage of its colonial power in that public relations was largely practiced by a government simultaneously engaging in political propaganda, and it was not taken up by the private sector to a significant extent until after World War II. As elsewhere, the public relations occupation encountered difficulties in establishing itself as a legitimate practice, and, by 1971, some serious concerns were being expressed about public relations status and viability as an occupation in Kenya. For example, Yohanna (Our roles, 1971) argued:

> A host of the problems of public relations units in many of our local organisations is the general lack of understanding and appreciation of the value of public relations machinery— failure among the management to grasp the values into which public relations organs could be converted. . . . In order to have viable meaning, a public relations organisation must be granted constant and direct contact with the chief executive of the organisation concerned. Being the mouthpiece of its group, it needs to be responsible to the policy makers (the board) in its external communication deliberations through the chief executive. It must therefore, invariably be attached to the office of the chief executive from which channel it can best help in the creation of an identity for the organisation. (p. 10)

J. A. Opembe, a founding member of Kenya's professional institute, the Public Relations Society of Kenya, alerted colleagues to the dangers of poor quality entrants to the occupation:

> some organisations and companies in this country when they decide to employ a public relations officer, because of lack of knowledge of the basic principles of public relations, recruit someone on a clerical salary that is used as a messenger to provide one way traffic message. He is not well informed about the functions of the company and its policies nor is he consulted in any formation of a policy he is expected to explain to its public. (*East African Management Journal,* 1971, cited in Muruli, 2001, p. 48)

Opembe has been seen as the "father" of public relations in Kenya. Originally a teacher, he moved to the Maize Control Board in 1947 as a clerk and a shop steward before being appointed to a post as public relations assistant in 1960. The following year he was awarded a British Council scholarship to study management and public relations, even though at that time formal educational opportunities in the United Kingdom were subdegree level and limited to the intermediate and final examinations set up by the Institute of Public Relations (IPR) in the late 1950s. In view of the lack of formal education it is likely that

Opembe's scholarship included visits to major consultancies and large organizations that maintained established departments of public relations. In 1969, Opembe joined the Institute of Public Relations, thus exemplifying the maintenance of links between Britain and its former colonies. He played a key role in the formation of the Federation of African Public Relations Association (FAPRA) and was the first African to be awarded the IPR President's Golden Award for exemplary services to the public relations profession. Opembe became a top-level manager whose career included the establishment of the Kenya Sugar Authority, managing director of Kenya Cashews Ltd., and jute controller of Kenya (Opukah, 1993). In the latter part of his career, he entered politics and became assistant minister for planning and national development, thus illustrating the overlap between the worlds of politics and public relations. Other Kenyan practitioners who have made their mark on the international scene include Colin Church, president of IPRA in 1996; David Keli-Killu and Yolanda Tavares, who both served on IPRA's executive council; and Shabanji Opukah, public affairs manager of British American Tobacco (BAT) Kenya Ltd. and a past chair of FAPRA.

It is noticeable that the early appointments into government and corporate public relations work were British. This was consistent with other patterns of employment in the colonial era, and public relations became subject to "Africanization" in due course. One can only speculate as to whether entry to public relations was easier for Africans than other managerial positions simply because it was seen as a nonmanagerial function. According to Muruli, most of the early public relations practitioners were men because women were still restricted to the home (personal communication, August 2001, to L'Etang). Those women who went to university tended to go into the teaching profession at the primary level and by the early 1970s they formed the majority of those taking the B.A. in education (personal communication, August 2001, to L'Etang). It was not until women started enrolling for courses in journalism at the University of Nairobi and the Kenya Institute of Mass Communications (KIMC) that they began to move into public relations (personal communication, August 2001, to L'Etang).

Another prominent practitioner who reviewed the early period, Shabanji Opukah, commented:

> public relations in Africa had no focus, seemed to have no future, and prospects were generally relegated to the lowest realms of management in most organisations. The situation was so pathetic that the most common joke about PR in much of the continent was that it was the job assigned to anybody in the organisation who did not have something productive to do. PR was perceived as the off man's job. . . . It was, at best, the climax of the "gin and tonic" PR on the continent. (Opukah, 1992, p. 14)

As a consequence of the poor status granted to public relations, the term *public relations* began to be replaced by such terms as *public affairs, corporate communication,* and *public information* just as in other countries. A key turning point was the International Public Relations Association's (IPRA) professional development seminar held in Nairobi in 1992. Held in the context of rapid international change, such as the end of the cold war, the rapid weakening of apartheid in South Africa, and the freeing of Nelson Mandela, the seminar encapsulated the zeitgeist of the times and looked toward increased democratization and transparency, values that facilitate the growth of public relations (Opukah, 1992).

Among others, L'Etang and Pieczka (1996) and Pieczka and L'Etang (2001) argue that education is crucial for the professionalization process. In Kenya it was not until after the Ministry of Information and Broadcasting had lost many senior officers to fill press attaché posts overseas that the government considered the establishment of an Institute of Mass Communication. Before then, training for information officers was conducted primarily through in-service and refresher courses, training at the Kenya Institute of Administration, and training overseas (*Annual Reports,* 1963, 1965, 1969).

According to Mrs. Grace Lomada, head of department of the Kenya Institute of Mass Communication, the postindependence Africanization program and the demands of the new information order forced the Kenyan government to recognize urgent training needs, and the KIMC was founded in 1965 to train media personnel and communicators (personal communication to Muruli, June 28, 2001). Graduates have worked as public servants, public relations officers, news agency reporters, information officers, broadcast journalists, radio and TV producers, broadcasters, photojournalists, audiovisual producers, and film producers, according to lecturer Geoffrey Adambo (personal communication, June 28, 2001). According to Absalom Mutere, former director of KIMC, now director of the School of Journalism at the United States International University, Nairobi, the School of Journalism, University of Narobi was established in 1970 to train journalists in the East and Central African region. The introduction of a one-year postgraduate diploma course in mass communication gave students a choice between media management and public relations in the final term (personal communication to Muruli, July 2, 2001). By the end of the twentieth century public relations had become established as a distinct occupation with its own educational structures.

Conclusion

The emergence of public relations activities in Kenya was largely the consequence of the desire of powerful interest groups to create and manage public opinion. The role of the colonial power was important but, significantly, it only engaged in more formal public relations at a time of international conflict and threat. The challenge of Mau Mau facilitated the growth of a genuine Kenyan public opinion regarding propaganda activities, though these were carefully managed by the British government during the emergency at international, national, and local levels. Following the emergency, a Kenyan consensus began to emerge within the new middle class about the nature of the state, the economy, and political structures; and on independence, considerable promotional activities took place to forge a new postcolonial Kenyan identity. Private-sector public relations emerged partly as a consequence of industrial labor conflict but, more significantly, as a consequence of the important role that international capital came to play in the Kenyan postindependence economy.

The development of public relations has often been linked to the growth of mass media and industrial strife, particularly in the United States. However, the pattern of evolution in Kenya took a rather different path. If we understand the role of public relations as the management of relationships, then public relations preexisted mass media in the Kenyan context. Partly because of the multiracial context, interpersonal relations remained an important part of public relations postwar as seen in the efforts of the British government agency, the British Council. Furthermore, as the Kenyan example illustrates, in some cultural contexts it is difficult to separate government political propaganda from public relations practice. This is partly a result of the colonial heritage because the historical relationship between government propaganda and public relations in Britain is equally unclear. The important role of religion in Kenyan culture introduces another connection with propagandistic activities. A discussion of conceptual definitional problems is rather beyond the scope of this chapter. It is suggested that analyses that argue that public relations, rather than propaganda, is a distinguishing feature of democracy may be overdrawn. As Kenya moved from colonialism to independence and the development of its economic requirements forced a renewed dependence on international capital and, to some degree, the ideological underpinnings. Internally, grassroots promotional activities were important to support government nation-building initiatives in social welfare, education, and national identity.

Ultimately, the Kenyan case provides a good example of how public relations is an outgrowth of deeper political and economic structural features of a society in the international context, which typically emerges from powerful elites who need to manage public opinion. It also appears that the growth of public relations is not so much associated with one particular political arrangement but a consequence of change in the aforementioned deep structures.

Discussion Questions _____

1. What *alternative* frameworks or typologies of public relations practice emerge from the aforegoing review of British and Kenyan public relations history? What do these reveal about the *limitations* of the dominant paradigm?

2. Why might it be inappropriate to apply notions of "Excellence" or "symmetry" to the British and Kenyan cases?

3. Discuss the role of interpersonal relations in situations where there is an asymmetry of power between an organization and its publics.

4. Consider the links between public relations and diplomacy. Where does one practice begin and the other end?

5. The British government appeared to distinguish between its propaganda and public relations activities. Is this distinction clear, and how may one judge the difference in (a) the historical cases presented and (b) any other case?

6. Were the Mau Mau engaged in propaganda or public relations? Give reasons for your view.

7. Discuss the links between religious communication and definitions of propaganda.

References _____

Abuoga, J., & Mutere, A. (1988). *The history of the press in Kenya.* Nairobi: ACCE.

Boyce, D. (1999). *Decolonization and the British Empire 1775–1997.* London: Macmillan.

Chamberlain, M. (1999). *Decolonization.* Oxford: Blackwell.

Cowell, F. (1935). The uses and dangers of publicity in the work of government. *Public Administration 13,* pp. 290–3.

D. T. (1997). *Which Way Africa?* Nairobi: Government Press.

Elliott, P. (1972). *The sociology of the professions.* New York: Herder & Herder.

Finer, H. (1931). Officials and the public. *Public Administration, 9,* 30.

Fox, J. (1982). *White mischief.* Jonathan Cape.

Frost, R. (1978). *Race against time: Human relations and politics in Kenya before independence.* Nairobi: Transafrica Press.

Gillman, F. (1978, April). Public relations in the UK prior to 1948. *International Public Relations Association Review,* 43–50.

Grant, M. (1994). *Propaganda and the role of the state in inter-war Britain.* Oxford: Clarendon Press.

Hodgkin, T. (1956). *Nationalism in colonial Africa.* London: Frederick Muller, Ltd.

Johnson, Brigadier. (1951). You cannot get such men. *Public Relations 4,* p. 9.

Johnson, T. (1972). *Professions and power.* London: Macmillan.

L'Etang, J. (1996). Public relations as diplomacy. In J. L'Etang & M. Pieczka (Eds.), *Critical perspectives in public relations* (pp. 14–34). London: Thompson.

L'Etang, J. (1998). State propaganda and bureaucratic intelligence: The creation of public relations in twentieth century Britain. *Public Relations Review, 24*(2), 413–441.

L'Etang, J. (2001). *The professionalisation of British public relations in the twentieth century: A history.* Unpublished doctoral thesis, University of Stirling, Stirling, Scotland.

L'Etang, J. (in press). *Public relations in Britain: A history of professional practice in the twentieth century.* Mahwah, NJ: Lawrence Erlbaum Associates.

L'Etang, J., & Pieczka, M. (Eds.). (1996). *Critical perspectives in public relations.* London: Thompson.

L'Etang, J., & Pieczka, M. (Eds.). (in press). *Public relations: Critical debates and contemporary practice.* Mahwah, NJ: Lawrence Erlbaum Associates.

Magaga, A. (1982). *People and communication in Kenya.* Nairobi: KLB.

Maloba, W. (1998). *Mau Mau and Kenya: An analysis of a peasant revolt.* Oxford: James Currey.

Mitchell, S. (1954). *African afterthoughts.* London: Hutchinson & Co.

Muruli, G. (2001). *Public relations in Kenya: The missing link 1939–71.* Unpublished master's thesis, University of Stirling, Stirling, Scotland.

Ochieng', W., & Atieno-Odhiambo, E. (1995). On decolonization. In B. Ogot & W. Ochieng (Eds.), *Decolonization and independence in Kenya 1940–93* (pp. xi–xviii). London: James Currey.

Ochieng', W. (1995). Structural & political changes. In B. Ogot & W. Ochieng (Eds.), *Decolonization and independence in Kenya 1940–93* (pp. 83–109).

Ogot, B., & Ochieng, W. (Eds.). (1995). *Decolonization and independence in Kenya 1940–93.* London: James Currey.

Opukah, S. (1992). Challenges for public relations in Africa. *International Public Relations Review, 15*(2), 14–17.

Opukah, S. (1993). The First J. E. Opembe Memorial Lecture. Nairobi: BAT.

Pieczka, M., & L'Etang, J. (2001). Public relations and the question of professionalism. In R. Heath (Ed.), *Handbook of public relations* (pp. 223–236). London: Sage.

Porter, A., & Stockwell, A. (1989). *British imperial policy and decolonization 1938–64 Volume 2 (1951–64).* Cambridge Commonwealth Series: The Macmillan Press.

Pratt, C. (1985). Public relations in the Third World: The African context. *Public Relations Journal, 41*(2), 11–12, 15–16.

Pronay, N. (1982). *Propaganda, politics and film 1918–45.* London: Macmillan.

Signitzer, B., & Coombs, T. (1992). Public relations and public diplomacy: Conceptual convergences. *Public Relations Review, 18*(2), 137–47.

Sissons, M., & French, P. (1963). *Age of austerity.* London: Greenwood.

Taylor, P. (1981). *The projection of Britain 1919–39.* Cambridge, England: Cambridge University Press.

White, A. (1965). *The British Council: The first 25 years: 1934–59.* London: The British Council.

Archival Documents

Abuor, C. (1969). Features from provinces: A government circular to all provincial information offices. Nairobi: Ministry of Information and Broadcasting.

Annual report. (1941). Kenya Information Office (KIO).

Annual report. (1942). Kenya Information Office (KIO).

Annual report. (1949). Kenya Information Office (KIO).

Benn, A. (1959, November 2). Colonial policy. Speech to House of Commons. *Hansard Parliamentary Debates* (1959–60), vol. 612, cols. 770–778.

Cabinet memo. June 17, 1952.

Cabinet papers. (1954). CAB 129/71, C(54) 329. Defence policy review by secretary of state for commonwealth relations, 3/11.

Daily Nation October 22, 1968.

Davies, A. (1941). Circular to District Commissioners. Ref A/A/16/2, File No. PUB 7/1/2.

The development of broadcasting stations in the British dependencies. (1953). Central Office of Information, No. 2644 of 31/7.

East African Management Journal. (1971). 5(4).

East African Standard. (1947, December 25).

East African Standard. (1956, March 16).

East African Standard. (1966, September).

Economic policy: Cabinet memorandum by the minister of housing and local government. (1952, June 17).

Gould, J. (1952). Secretarial establishment, Circulars Nos. 5 & 6, File No. PUB 7/1/2.

Handbook on broadcasting services in the colonies. (1954). Colonial information office (COI) (6th ed.).

Heed Public Criticism. (1968, October 22). *Daily Nation.*

Hola Camp, Kenya. *Hansard Parliamentary Debates.* (1958–59), vol. 610, cols. 219–237.

Hutchinson, G. (1941). Letter to news agents in the reserves.

Huxley, E. (1946). A personal letter to the acting information officer, Hutchinson. File No. S/H I&P 9/3/4.

Kenya Information Services Annual Report. (1949).

Macmillan, H. (1960, February 3). The wind of change. Speech to both houses of the Parliament of the Union of South Africa, Cape Town.

Mombasa Times. (1959, 1960).

Opukah, S. (1992). Challenges for public relations in Africa. *International Public Relations Review 15*(2), 14–17.

Our roles in public relations context. (1971, November/December). *Gateways of Eastern Africa,* no. 4, 10.

Report of the Kenya Constitutional Conference. Command Paper 960, February 1960 PP (1959–60) X, 891.

Riding a hobby horse. (1954). *Public Relations, 6*(4), 36.

Roberts, W. (1953). *History of the technical development of broadcasting in the colonial territories: A report.*

Royal Institute of Public Administration, 1998.

Royal Institute of Public Administration. (1998). 10.

Staff Magazine. (1962, June). The East African Power and Lighting Company, No. 2.

Turner, R. (1940). Circular to all district commissioners in Nyanza Province. File No. PUB 7/1/2 MIL 18/2.

Udoji, J. (1962). Report of the Africanisation of public services of the East African Common Services Organisation, Nairobi.

Wainwright, R. (1952). A letter to Mr. Hill, 21 November. Blundell 12/7.

Wangalwa, J. (1968, June 28). Proposed government propaganda: A paper submitted to the permanent secretary, Ministry of Information and Broadcasting. Quarterly Publication.

Watkins, C. (1939, November 19). Letter to the information officer, J. Silvester. Ref.: ML. 18/2, File No. PUB 7/1/2.

11

Public Relations Exigencies in a Developing Democracy

A Case Study of Nigeria's Fourth Republic

Emmanuel C. Alozie

Key Points

- Nigeria was amalgamated by Britain in 1914 and became independent in 1960.
- With a population estimated to be more than 100 million people, Nigeria is the largest democracy in Africa. The country has experienced about thirteen years of democratic rule in its forty-two years of independence.
- The main source of Nigerian revenue is oil. Prior to the discovery of oil in the 1960s, agriculture was the mainstay of the nation's economy, but has more recently been neglected.
- The Nigerian press and mass media sector is free and vibrant. Nigerian media strive to promote nation building.
- The various tiers of Nigerian government have not adequately employed public relations as a tool for national development.

Nigerians elected Olusegun Obasanjo president in February 1999. In May, when he took the oath of office, he told his citizenry that they were entering a new era of governance—an era of political freedom, economic stability, international recognition, and government accountability and transparency. Obasanjo ruled Nigerian from 1976 to 1979 as a military head of state.

Soon after taking over the reins of power in Nigeria for a second time, the president and members of his cabinet embarked on their first public relations effort. They undertook a goodwill and familiarization tour of the nation. The purpose of the tour was to listen to and to learn about the concerns of the various constituencies and to promote the administration's policies and programs (Agwu, 1999). After fifteen years of military rule, the president and several members of his cabinet visited many foreign countries in an attempt to repair Nigeria's battered image (Obasanjo lists gains, 1999). These tours affirmed the importance that past and current Nigerian administrations attached to public relations as a vehicle for nation building and development. Pratt (1985) stated that the economic and social realities of any society determined the role public relations played in a society. It could also be added that the political needs of the administration in power influences both the role public relations plays and the strategies the administration adopts (Boafo, 1985). If these assumptions are correct, it could be argued that the Obasanjo administration's first public relations effort proved their validity.

Obasanjo assumed office at a time when Nigeria was on the brink of economic collapse and national disintegration as a result of economic mismanagement, political turmoil, and military dictatorship. The country also suffered from an unfavorable foreign image, thus discouraging foreign investment. Nigerians lost faith in their government. To fulfill his campaign promises to promote Nigerian unity and to raise the social welfare of the people, the Obasanjo administration needed the understanding and cooperation of many constituencies. These constituencies include Nigeria's diverse population (made up of more than 300 ethnic groups), Nigerians in the diaspora, foreign governments, multinational corporations, international government, and nongovernment organizations (see Figure 11.1).

This study explores the role public relations has played during the first year of the Obasanjo administration (May 29, 1999, to May 29, 2000). It attempts to determine whether the administration used public relations to promote its programs. The study also explores the strategies and tactics the administration used by relating and comparing them

FIGURE 11.1   *Vice President Atiku Abubakar (center) commissioning a developmental project during his tour of Rivers State.*

Courtesy of *Conscience International 2001.*

with those of previous administrations. To accomplish this task, the following subjects are examined:

- The history and political development of Nigeria
- The prevailing economic and social conditions of Nigeria
- History of public relations in Nigeria
- The theory of communication and functions of public relations in nation building and development
- The major policies adopted by the administration as well as events that occurred in Nigeria from May 29, 1999, to May 29, 2000
- The public relations strategies used by current and past administrations

History and Political Development of Nigeria

Nigerian politics and elections could serve as guides to understanding the psyche of Nigeria's distinct peoples and the nation's political development. There are more than 350 recognized tribal groups with almost the same number of languages and dialects in Nigeria. Estimates of the Nigerian population range from 100 million to 120 million, but the country is dominated by three groups—the Hausa-Fulani tribes in the North, the Yorubas in the Southwest, and the Igbos in the Southeast. These three groups combined make up about 60 percent of the population. The largest minority groups in Nigeria include the Angas, Baribas, Chambas, Edos, Ekois, Efiks, Gwaris, Ibiobios, Idoma-Igas, Ijaws, Itesekiris, Jarawas, Jukuns, Kambaris, Kataos, Marghis, Nupes, Ogonis, Tivs, and Urohobos (Metz, 1991; *World Factbook,* 1997).

British enterprises arrived in West Africa in the 1600s. By 1861, formal British administration spread from the Lagos coast to the interior of Nigeria. British colonial administration was resisted in the South but was more successful in the North. That success in the North prompted British colonial rule to favor the northerners in most political decisions about Nigeria (Agbagha, 1999). In the 1800s, the British began the gradual consolidation of Nigeria for its commercial benefits and material exploitation at the expense of the political, cultural, and economic welfare of the people. Britain completed its creation of Nigeria with its amalgamation in 1914. The amalgamation, according to Madiebo (1980), created the Federation of Nigeria as it exists today, a nation that "has never really been one homogenous country, for its widely differing peoples and tribes are yet to find any basis for true unity" (p. 3). Rupert (1998b) described Nigeria and other countries the European colonial masters left behind in Africa as "business-colonies meant to profit the European governments and traders who controlled them" (p. A18). The distinct nature of these tribes and peoples contributed to the various social and political upheavals Nigeria has suffered since independence.

Nigeria held parliamentary elections in 1959, a year before it became independent in 1960. The elections ushered in the first independent and indigenous administration under Tafawa Balewa, a northerner, as prime minister. The first postindependence national elections were held in 1964, one year after Nigeria became a Republic. Tribal division, irregularities, and political instability marred both of these elections. The 1964 elections were particularly divisive, filled with political infighting and violence, overwhelmed by rigging and other forms of election irregularities (Sklar, 1997).

Under both Balewa administrations, northerners dominated Nigerian politics. During his administration, it was alleged that unqualified northerners rose to prominent positions as a result of nepotism. Southerners who held prominent positions were largely displaced. Hence, it was alleged, the Balewa administrations were riddled with corruption, nepotism, tribalistic tendencies, and religious conflict (Anosa, 1998). These problems have existed in every northern-led administration, prompting other ethnic groups, including the Igbos and Yorubas, to contend that they were marginalized (Abasilim, 1998; Ugbomah, 1998).

These intractable problems that plagued both Balewa administrations continued for six years after independence. The persistence of these problems prompted some junior officers to stage a coup, who overthrew the Balewa administration in January 1966. General Aguiyi Ironsi, an Igbo, became Nigeria's first military head of state. Although Igbo officers from the Southeast dominated the January coup that brought General Ironsi to power, he did not participate in its planning and execution. Most of the prominent politicians and army officers killed in the coup were from the North and the Southwest.

Objective Nigerian commentators agree that the intentions of the coup plotters were honorable. The coup was staged to save the country from disintegrating. However, the killings of prominent northerners and southwesterners led to a backlash (Ugbomah, 1998). Six months later, a second coup staged by northern officers, resulted in the death of the head of the first military head of state, General Ironsi. General Yakubu Gowon, a Tiv from the northern region, became head of state. During the upheaval that followed, a pogrom ensued in Northern Nigeria, in which thousands of Igbos and ethnic groups from the Southeast were killed. In 1967, the deaths forced the Igbos to declare the creation of the Republic of Biafra under the three-year long civil war. More than one million people, mostly Igbos, were killed during the war (Copson, 1997).

According to Sklar (1997), when the war ended in 1970, General Gowon promised to integrate Nigerians. He also promised to hand over power to a civilian administration by 1976 after a period of reconstruction and reconciliation. In 1972, he lifted the ban on political activities. Shortly after lifting the ban, he hinted that he would postpone the transition to civil administration. Gowon's decision attracted public outcry and was overwhelmingly condemned by opposition leaders. His administration had become corrupt, nepotistic, and incompetent. In 1975, Gowon was overthrown. The new administration, led by General Murtala Muhammed, a northerner, cited corruption and ineptitude as the reasons for staging the coup. Muhammed implemented policies that won his administration popular support. In 1976, General Muhammed was killed in another unsuccessful coup attempt.

General Olusegun Obasanjo, a Yoruba from the Southwest, succeeded him. Obasanjo became the first military head to organize general elections and to deliver power to the civilian administration in 1979. Like the two previous postindependence elections, the 1979 elections that ushered in the Second Republic were plagued with tribal divisions and rigging. A northerner from the Fulani ethnic group, Shehu Shagari, became the president. He was reelected in 1983 and his administrations were marked by incompetence, corruption, and cronyism. General Muhammadu Buhari, a Hausa from the North, overthrew the Shagari administration in December 1983. The Buhari administration implemented strict disciplinary policies, which some considered repressive. But a majority of Nigerians liked his disciplinary policies (Nigeria: A history of coups, 1998; Sklar, 1997).

In 1985, General Ibrahim B. Babangida dethroned the Buhari administration. Babangida, a northerner from the Gwari ethnic group, became head of state. Sklar (1997) noted that two unsuccessful coup attempts (1985 and 1990) were conducted to overthrow the Babangida administration. Babangida engaged in a protracted transition from a military to a civilian administration. Corruption and political maneuvering flourished under his administration, and it was beset with numerous economic problems (Dellios, 1998).

In 1993, general elections were held in which Moshood Abiola, a Yoruba from the Southwest, won. Many international observers regarded the elections as the fairest in the nation's history. However, intense pressure from the northern oligarchy and top military officers forced the Babangida administration to annul the elections. This resulted in the installation of a caretaker government. Six months later, Sani Abacha, the defense minister, another northern general, sacked the caretaker administration of Ernest Shonekan, a southwestern Yoruba, in a palace coup. He was installed as the head of state (Adejare, 1998). Abacha imprisoned Abiola, the apparent winner of the 1993 elections, when he declared himself president during the anniversary of Abiola's election. He died in prison about five years later (Writer brands Abiola's death, 1998).

Under the five-year regime of Abacha, Nigeria experienced the most iron-fisted government in its thirty-nine-year history. All kinds of freedoms were curtailed, and many citizens were imprisoned without trial (World: Analysis of Nigeria, 1998). Corruption reigned. Abacha implemented programs that would have made possible his election as civilian president in 1998, but he died suddenly as a result of a heart attack in 2000 (Rupert, 1998a). After Abacha's death, General Abdulsalami Abubakar handed over power to a civilian administration headed by Olusegun Obasanjo in May 1999. In April 2003, President Obasanjo was reelected for a second term under the banner of the ruling Peoples Democratic Party. The president's party dominated the gubernatorial and national assembly elections. Opposition parties accused the ruling party of rigging the elections. Although some national and international observers claimed the elections were free and fair, others agreed with the opposition parties the elections were marred with irregularities (Abuh, 2003). Despite the controversies that ensued, the 2003 elections marked one of the few times Nigeria conducted a successful and peaceful transition of a civilian administration.

Nigerian Economic and Social Conditions

Regarded as one of the most economically viable states in Africa in terms of natural resources, human talents, and industrial base, Nigeria has earned about U.S.$250 billion from windfalls in oil revenue from the time of her independence in 1960 through 1997 (Enyinnaya, 1998). Under military rule for more than thirty of its forty-one-year-history, Nigeria has been plagued by ethnic, regional, religious considerations, ruthless exploitation of impoverished people, wars, economic stagnation, instability, corruption, and maniacal leaderships (Ihonvbere, 1997). According to Stanbic Merchant Bank Nigeria Limited, a subsidiary of Standard Bank of South Africa Group, Nigeria's share of Africa's foreign debt is estimated to be between U.S.$30 billion and U.S.$35 billion (MBendi, 1998).

Abdullahi Aliyu, Nigeria's director general and chief executive officer of the Family Economic Advancement Program, explained that after the oil boom of the 1970s the real income per capita dropped sharply. As a result, the quality of life of Nigerians continued to decline. He added that by 1986, the inflation rate averaged about 3.5 percent and increased to 57 percent by 1993 and 77 percent by 1994. Data from Nigeria's Office of Statistics demonstrated poverty incidence between 1972 and 1980 averaged 45 percent, 43 percent by 1985, 34 percent by 1992, and about 50 percent by 1996. The real per capita income of Nigeria in 1972 was 1,300 naira (Nigerian currency). It increased to 3,000 in the 1990s with the poverty rate remaining at 45 percent (Enyinnaya, 1998).

Aliyu explained that despite Nigeria's vast resources, the per capita income of Nigerians from the 1970s to date has remained lower than that of the 1960s. He blamed the federal government for the poor performance of the economy. He pointed out that Nigeria's economic malaise and stagnation were caused by poor management of government agencies and poor monetary and fiscal policies. These failures hindered the development of infrastructures that were intended to provide the foundation for the nation's industrialization. Aliyu explained that the "Nigerian economy has not been moving forward due mainly to kleptomania, corruption and political instability" (Enyinnaya, 1998, p. 1 of on-line printout). He added that Nigeria's monetary policies have not been targeting the issue of inflation.

History of Communication in Nigeria

Nwosu (1990) has credited the British with introducing public relations to Nigeria. He stated that organized public relations in Nigeria began within government agencies on January 1, 1944, when British colonial administrators set up the first Public Relations Office in Lagos, the nation's former administrative capital. By 1948, the colonial administration established public relations outlets in the regional capitals of Ibadan, Enugu, and Kaduna. At independence, the government established a full-fledged Federal Ministry of Information and an in-house public relations department at each ministry. At present, Nigeria has thirty-six states. Each has its own ministry of information, headquartered in the state capital. The headquarters of the federal ministry is located in Abuja, the administrative capital, and maintain offices in each state. Every federal and state ministry, as well as most government departments and parastatals, maintains an in-house public relations component. The state governments have information officers posted outside their capitals. The officers of the federal and state ministries of information and departments are responsible for informing the public of government activities and policies. They also analyze feedback in order to refine their messages to further promote government policies and to attract favorable responses from the public.

Although formal public relations was first organized as a government activity, it has grown tremendously among nongovernment organizations, such as commercial banks and corporations. Pratt (1985) states that various Nigerian administrations tend to delegate and view public relations activities as social responsibilities of the nation's leading corporation—activities they are encouraged to conduct as their contributions to promoting nation building and development. Consequently, these nongovernment organizations tend to sponsor and apply sophisticated public relations strategies and campaigns, whereas various administrations depend on publicity-related tactics and programs as their primary public relations strategies.

Nwosu (1990) credits the growth of public relations among commercial organizations on the importance that organizations attach to the process and their willingness to use public relations practices and strategies extensively. Of the sixty-six full-fledged advertising agencies in Nigeria, some offer public relations services (Amuzuo, 2000; Okigbo, 1989). The number of independent public relations firms and practitioners have been growing (Amuzuo, 2000). It should be noted that ethnic groups in Nigeria have conducted traditional forms of public relations for centuries. For example, Africans hold consultations, dialogues, and conflict resolutions with each other as a way of promoting mutual understanding and resolving issues. Other forms of African public relations include visits, gift giving, festivals, sports events, intermarriage, and the use of town criers and dispatchers to relay messages.

Literature Review of Theory and Function of Public Relations

The thrust of public relations functions are aimed at building, maintaining, and changing relationships in order to promote mutual understanding between organizations and their audiences (Seitel, 1995). For decades, scholarship on public relations processes relied on the symmetrical communication function of public relations—the exchange of information between organizations and the public. Scholars argue that symmetrical communication allows organizations to dominate the exchange, thus inhibiting the contributions of the public in the public relations process. However, a change of approach occurred when scholars developed a public relations typology that elaborated on the evolution of the role of public relations (Cutlip, Center, & Broom, 1985; Dozier, 1992). The typology offered four roles of public relations: *expert prescriber* (one who defines and researches a problem, and implements a campaign), *communication facilitator* (one who serves as mediator between an organization and the public), *problem-solving facilitator* (one who helps managers determine how to solve problems), and *communication technician* (one who produces campaign materials). Cutlip and colleagues and Dozier's typology tended to focus on one-way communication from organizations to their public. However, Grunig and Hunt's (1984) model established the fact that the public relations process involved both *one-way* and *two-way* forms of communication consisting of *publicity/press agentry* (campaigns to gain awareness at the expense of accuracy), *public information* (campaigns that depend on accurate information to gain understanding), *two-way asymmetrical* (involving sharing and exchanging information with the public aimed at promoting mutual understanding and benefit), and a *two-way symmetrical* model.

As Pratt (1985) notes, the Nigerian government and others in the developing world have used public relations as a vehicle for nation building and public-issue-oriented communication (Taylor, 2000). Their public relations campaigns are aimed at creating awareness, generating acceptance of government programs and policies, and mobilizing public support for development programs (Alanazi, 1996). To realize these goals, Third World governments have adopted the concept of development communication. Oliveira (1993) defined development communication as instilling awareness among a target group. As currently practiced, development communication involves systematic utilization of interpersonal and mass communication channels to motivate, stimulate, and promote social development programs and developmental habits among Third World masses.

Nation-building campaigns (development communication) then serve as strategic efforts to achieve specific effects on a large group of people in a predetermined time period.

However, studies have found that development communication has often failed because campaigns are plagued with many problems. Studies have found that nation-building campaigns are value laden and disregard traditional values. They are often used for the political benefits of the leaders, instead of solving society's social problems (Boafo, 1985; Taylor, 2000). A single campaign is often used to reach diverse groups and to achieve multiple purposes. This might account for the difficulty most Nigerian government-sponsored communication and public relations efforts aimed at promoting social development programs have encountered. In a country as diverse as Nigeria, where ethnic tensions exist and national unity dangles on the throes of ethnic division, economic malaise, corruption, and political instability, it may be difficult to reach Nigerian masses and achieve the goals of any single campaign within a brief specific period. Nation-building campaigns in a country as diverse as Nigeria require well-planned and long-term strategic campaigns, such as those the Malaysian government adopted (Taylor, 2000). Malaysia is a diverse nation.

To understand this difficulty, it is important to understand two communication models that dominate nation-building literature. One of these is Geertz's (1973) *primodalist* concept, which argues that communication brings to the fore deeply held ethnic prejudice, thus generating competing loyalties that inhibit nation building. This might be the case in Nigeria, where several ethnic clashes have broken out since the return to civilian rule. Some have alleged these ethnic and communal clashes are a result of accusations being traded by leaders of different ethic groups on the front pages of Nigerian newspapers and magazines. However, Deustch's (1963) *integrationist* approach posits that concerted organized communication conducted over a long period of time tends to breakdown barriers, thus promoting nation building.

Nigerian Government Public Relations Strategies

George and Ogbondah (1999) identified specific public relations strategies used by past Nigerian administrations (Nwosu, 1990). Nwosu states that the federal and state ministries of information and in-house public relations components of various departments and parastatals are staffed by information officers. The main duties of these officers include providing information to the public, assessing public reaction, and then refining government public campaign messages in order to generate support for any administration's policies and programs (see Figure 11.2). This practice is in keeping with Grunig and Hunt's (1984) public information model. Although Nigerian information officers are required to obtain feedback from the public, few, if any, systematic studies have been conducted to determine if this function is performed effectively.

Nwosu (1990) notes that poor implementation of public relations strategies by Nigerian governments could be attributed to policy and structural factors, including neglect, lack of cooperation, and misunderstanding of the importance of public relations. Structural factors that contribute to the ineffective use of public relations strategies include budgetary constraints, lack of facilities, inadequate training of government public relations officials, and failure to contract to independent agencies. As stated earlier, studies have found that the extent to which public relations strategies are employed by the government depends on the intentions, needs, and interests of the government (Boafo, 1985; Pratt, 1985). That view was supported by the activities of two military regimes: Ibrahim Babangida and Sani

FIGURE 11.2   *President Olusegun Obasanjo (center) and Governor Peter Odili take the floor with Justice Mary Odili (far right) and Dr. Christie Toby at the state banquet in honor of the President.*

Courtesy of *Conscience International 2001.*

Abacha. These regimes were known for their mismanagement and corrupt and harsh dictatorial tendencies. For example, after annulling the 1992 elections won by M. K. O. Abiola, a southerner, Babangida engaged in a publicity and lobbying campaign to explain his decisions. Sani Abacha used public relations strategies in his efforts to succeed himself. He organized a million-man march to garner support among Nigerians for his self-succession bid. When his administration tried and executed Ken Saro-wiwa, an environmentalist, on what most believed to be false charges, he attracted international condemnation. To repair his image and promote his administration, the Abacha administration engaged in an extensive public relations effort. The administration used lobbying, publicity, press conferences, and special advertising inserts to explain its action (George & Ogbondah, 1999).

The Babangida and Abacha administrations spent a great deal of money on public relations campaigns to save their administrations, instead of using the money to initiate and promote social programs on agriculture, business, housing, illiteracy, and education that would advance nation building and national development. These past abuses accounted for Obasanjo's pronouncement that his government would usher in a new era for Nigeria.

On assuming office in May 1999, Obasanjo banned government ministries and departments from using government funds to buy space or time in Nigerian media to congratulate him or to send members of his cabinet congratulatory messages. It had been common practice among government agencies and commercial corporations to buy space or time in Nigerian media to send congratulatory messages and announcements to an incoming administration. They also offer similar messages to any administration in power during annual celebrations such as Independence and Christmas.

Obasanjo's Major Policies and Events in Nigeria

To assess the extent to which the Obasanjo administration has used public relations strategies to promote its policies and to deal with other issues confronted in its first year, an outline of the administration's major policies and key events in Nigeria between May 29, 1999, and May 29, 2000 is necessary:

- Obasanjo appoints a cabinet. Supporters praise him for appointing a cabinet that reflects the federal character, whereas critics accuse him of marginalization (Obafemi, 1999).
- Obasanjo purges the Nigerian army of politicized officers—described as officers who held political positions during the military administrations or having political tendencies. About thirty military officers were affected (Timeline: a year of democracy, 2000).
- Ethnic and religious riots break out in most regions of Nigeria. The estimate of those killed in these riots is set at about two thousand with thousands more displaced. Estimates of property damaged are in the millions of naira. Calls for devolution increased (Corruption: Obasanjo toughest challenge, 2000).
- After assuming office, Obasanjo straddles on the withdrawal of Nigerian troops from Sierra Leone. He withdraws a large number, while retaining some as part of a Western African contingent (ECOMOG) (Phillips, 2000). In May/June of 2000, Obasanjo agrees to return Nigerian troops as part of a Western African contingent in Sierra Leone after UN troops are captured by rebels (Nigeria on the agenda, 2000).
- The federal government recovers money (about 100 billion Nigerian naira and U.S. $2 billion frozen) looted by officials in the Abacha administration from foreign and domestic banks. The administration confiscates properties acquired illegally by former government officials (Corruption: Obasanjo toughest challenge, 2000; Nigeria on the agenda, 2000).
- The administration introduces social programs including Poverty Alleviation and Universal Basic Education (Nigeria on the agenda, 2000).
- Obasanjo's economic policies are credited with stabilizing the economy and currency (Ibagere, 2000, May 28). Nigerians claim their economic conditions have not improved. The administration introduces new paper currency bearing the portraits of outstanding Nigerian leaders (Phillips, 1999).
- The federal government launches an anticorruption campaign (Nigeria on the agenda, 2000).
- The federal government institutes panels to investigate corruption and human rights abuses under previous administrations. Critics accuse Obansanjo of not making the scope, time, and those being investigated wide enough to include people in every military administration (Timeline: a year of democracy, 2000).

- Clinton promises to visit Nigeria (State refuses senator's claim, 2000). In an interview, he names Obasanjo as one of ten world leaders he admires.
- The federal government introduces a bill establishing a parastatal (Niger-Delta Development Commission) to deal with development programs in the region.
- Obasanjo declares May 29 a holiday (Democracy Day) to observe Nigeria's return to democracy. He offers full pardon to soldiers who fought on the side of Biafra during the civil war. He also pardons S. Buhari, speaker of the House of Representatives, who was impeached earlier for falsifying documents relevant to his age and education.

Obasanjo maintains that the cornerstone of his administration's policies is to strengthen the bonds that unite Nigerians and promote their economic well-being. An examination of the administration's policies and events that occurred in the country between May 29, 1999, to May 29, 2000, demonstrates that the administration had ample opportunities to employ public relations strategies to promote its social and economic programs, engender national stability, and encourage mutual understanding.

The current study, based on a field study and reports from three leading Nigerian newspapers (*Guardian, Vanguard,* and *Post Express*) available on the Internet, attempts to explain how the administration met that challenge.

On assuming office in May 1999, Obasanjo selected a cabinet that reflected the federal character. His appointments demonstrated that the president was committed to giving every region a fair share of the "nation cake," as most Nigerians would say. During past military regimes, northerners dominated the administrations. When critics from various ethnic groups—especially the North—accused Obasanjo of marginalization, Nigerian media and masses rallied in support and praised his appointments. Following their appointments, members of his cabinet were dispatched to their home regions to promote the policies and programs of the administration. The visits enabled the masses to hold meetings, dialogues, and consultations with top government officials from their regions. During these tours, welcome celebrations, concerts, folk dances, and prayer meetings were held and gifts were exchanged. These activities represented a well-founded traditional African public relations strategy. Van Leuven (1996) reports that similar strategies are viewed as appropriate public relations in some Asian countries. These visits embarked on by his ministers fostered a sense of belonging among ethnic groups that had earlier felt disenfranchised.

In June 1999, Obasanjo purged the military of soldiers who held political positions or had political leanings. The purpose of the purge was to rid the military of those officers who had tasted political power and might be tempted to stage a return. Having dominated past military administrations, most of the officers affected were northerners. That prompted northern leaders to accuse the president of marginalization. Regarding the use of public relations to explain the need for the purge, Obasanjo failed woefully. The administration did not promptly hold a press conference or issue a press release to explain his rationale for taking such a drastic action. Most Nigerians learned of the purge through media reports and rumors. As tensions rose over the purge, Obasanjo delegated his defense minister, T. Danjuma, a northerner, and chiefs-of-staff, mostly northerners, to explain his action. If the president had held a press conference or had issued press releases prior to the purge, the administration would have been able to promote understanding, instead of the country suffering the rancor that occurred. However, it should be noted that making such a decision public before dismissing the officers might have jeopardized his administration. Based on editorial comments and letters to the editor in Nigerian newspapers, most Nigerians welcomed his action.

In 1999 and 2000, several events occurred that threatened the unity of Nigeria. These events included the introduction of *sharia* law (a legal system in Islamic society based on the Koran) in the North, which caused religious and ethnic riots. Thousands of people were killed or displaced. Properties were damaged. Border disputes in communities in the East, West, and Middle Belt frequently occurred. Communal clashes claimed many lives and caused the destruction of properties estimated to be in the millions of naira. The Niger Delta region remained volatile as Ijaw youths and others in oil-producing areas continued to stage violent protests against oil companies operating in the area. The protests were aimed at disrupting the operations of the oil companies for polluting their environment, failing to build social infrastructures, and not investing in economic development in the areas. The protests were also used to call attention to the suffering of the indigenous people and neglect of the areas by previous administrations. Nigeria relies on oil produced from these areas for more than 90 percent of its revenue.

During one of these protests in the city of Odi, Bayelsa State, in the Delta region, Obasanjo sent federal troops to quell the protest. Many residents of Odi were killed and their homes and properties destroyed. Following ethnic and religious clashes in the North, which resulted in the deaths of many easterners, Igbo groups began clamoring for secession and a return to Biafra—a separate nation easterners fought for in the late 1960s following a similar pogrom. With the renewed violence against the Igbos and other easterners in the North, five Igbo governors called for confederation. These upheavals called for nation-building campaigns to drive home to Nigerians the need to avoid violence and to work together. Such a campaign would also explain the administration's plans to resolve the problems that caused the clashes. However, the administration did not adequately employ public relations strategies.

The president reacted differently to each event. For example, the administration was accused of keeping silent when some northern states introduced *sharia* law, which led to riots and loss of lives and properties. However, critics accused the administration of being heavy-handed when federal troops were sent to Odi to quell the uprising. Obasanjo was also criticized for using the military in the Delta, while being reluctant to do so in the West and North. Critics condemned his harsh criticism of Igbo leaders who called for confederation. The president described the Igbo leaders as traitors. He was criticized for making such a statement in the face of the killings and property loss Igbos and other easterners suffered in the North. The failure to promptly organize a press conference as rumors swelled remained a public relations shortcoming of the administration. The administration could have launched nation-building campaigns to send the message that these events were a result of the freedom Nigerians were enjoying in a democratic state. Opinion leaders writing for Nigerian newspapers that tended to share a similar view would have supported these campaigns.

Tensions regarding the introduction of *sharia* in the country calmed down when the administration held consultations with members of the council of state. The council includes past presidents, traditional leaders, and current federal and state executive officers. The northern governors who introduced the code agreed to abrogate it. The president also held meetings with Igbo leaders and those from the Delta region to assure them he was aware of their plight. At the end of these consultations, which could be regarded as two-way symmetrical communication, the participants held press conferences and issued statements that offered Nigerians hope that the administration remained committed to fairness and to ensuring the security of their lives and properties. The introduction and the passage of the Niger-Delta Development Commission served an important step toward redressing the neglect of Nigeria's oil-producing regions.

Beginning in late 1999 and early 2000, the Obasanjo administration launched a number of social welfare programs. These included the introduction of poverty alleviation programs, universal basic education, and public service campaigns to curb the spread of HIV-AIDS. The administration also launched programs to curb corruption and to recover funds from former officials. It also set up several panels including those to investigate past human rights abuses and corruption. The implementation of these programs afforded the administration ample opportunity to use public relations strategies to educate Nigerians about the values and success of these programs. Broadcast (especially radio) campaigns, if well tailored and conducted in ethnic languages, would educate millions of Nigerians in rural areas who cannot read. The campaigns launched by the administration could be described best as "feeble attempts." They were not conducted in a consistent manner. However, some leading corporations attempted to fill the vacuum by incorporating developmental messages in their advertising campaigns. Alozie (1999) noted this practice but found these advertisements reached only a few elites. To promote its efforts, the Nigerian government must launch nationwide campaigns aimed at reaching the masses. The campaigns must be consistent and must be designed to last long enough to determine their effectiveness.

One year after Obasanjo assumed office in 1999, the economic policies of his administration seemed to be bearing fruit. The nation's currency had stabilized. The economy had grown, inflation had been reduced, capital flight had been curtailed, and foreign investments had been trickling in. To help stabilize Nigerian currency, the administration introduced higher denomination (100 naira) bills using the portraits of Nigerian heroes. The portraits of these heroes serve as important symbols, a sound economic policy, and a great public relations strategy. Honoring these heroes demonstrates and teaches Nigerians that sacrificing for the unity and welfare of the nation remains a most rewarding virtue. Nigerians learned that possessing enormous wealth by cheating and depriving other citizens would not earn an individual a place in history. Service and virtue have been etched positively in the annals of Nigerian history. This is a major lesson for citizens to learn in a society where corruption and lack of patriotism have been described as the nation's economic ruin and on impediment to national unity.

After winning the 1999 election, Obasanjo embarked on a worldwide tour to enhance the image of Nigeria. The newly elected president realized that for his administration to succeed and to attract foreign investment he needed to repair the image of Nigeria abroad. In addition to his domestic policies of running an open government, setting up panels to investigate human rights abuses and corruption, and working to recover funds looted by past leaders, Obasanjo took decisive action to make Nigeria a leading actor on the stage of international affairs. His ardent work to resolve the crises in the Horn of Africa, Central Africa, and West Africa won him praise. When former U.S. President Bill Clinton was asked to name the top ten world leaders whom he admired, he identified Olusegun Obasanjo as one based on Obasanjo's domestic and international policies.

However, the administration has not exploited these achievements and the changing image of Nigeria to attract foreign investment. For example, it should be recalled that at a critical juncture when he faced condemnation, Abacha embarked on an aggressive public relations campaign abroad to justify his actions and policies. He hired lobbyists in foreign capitals, advertised his policies in foreign media, and dispatched his spokespeople to explain his actions and policies. Abacha was moderately successful (George & Ogbondah, 1999). The Obasanjo administration should have followed Abacha's lead by retaining lobbyists, and using insert advertisements and publications to sell Nigeria's new position in foreign countries in order to attract investments.

Conclusion

Based on this analysis, it could be argued that the Obasanjo administration has used public relations strategies to promote its policies. However, the administration has not employed public relations strategies consistently and adequately. The administration's attempts could be described best as "haphazard." The administration tends to rely on press conferences to relay and promote its policies. These conferences have frequently been poorly organized. For an administration that has the daunting task of relaying its policies to a disparate group at home and abroad, the efforts shown so far remain feeble. It should be noted that the administration recognized its failures. This was demonstrated by the earliest cabinet changes in the administration. Believing that his messages were not getting out, Obasanjo moved Dapo Sarumi, his first minister of information, from the Ministry of Information to the Ministry of Integration and Cooperation in Africa. He replaced him with Professor Jerry Gana, who headed the Africa ministry. A former university professor, Gana served as minister of information during the Babangida and Abacha administrations (Jerry Gana is new information minister, 2000). He is viewed as a public relations and communications genius. He may have been responsible for the earlier administrations' aggressive public relations campaigns. He left the Abacha administration when the former head of state embarked on a campaign to succeed himself. He joined a group of Nigerian statesmen calling for Abacha's resignation. After assuming office as minister of information, Gana promised to address the nation and hold weekly press conferences (every Thursday) to clarify and promote the policies of the administration (Jerry Gana addresses nation, 2000).

The current and future administrations should be advised to launch public relations campaigns to complement and promote their policies of his administration. For example, nation-building campaigns should be complemented with public relations strategies. In 2000 as he entered his second year, Obansanjo began emulating the late President Franklin D. Roosevelt by hosting a weekly radio show called "Presidential Saturday Talk" (Obasanjo to start weekly radio talk, 2000). This represents a step in the right direction for Nigerian leaders. Through such an interactive forum, the president and other administrators would be able to measure the pulse of the masses while they sense the direction in which they plan to take the nation. Present and future leaders should appoint spokespersons who would do a better job of articulating their policies to the various constituencies at home and abroad. Obasanjo and other Nigerian leaders should make themselves available to the press in order to interact and to take and answer questions. They should hire foreign lobbyists to expertly articulate their policies to their governments and corporations. Nigerian leaders should also press their policies abroad through lobbying, publications, and special advertisements in the media.

These efforts might require huge expenses in terms of money, energy, and time, but the strategies provide a vehicle for changing the fortunes of Nigeria. Administrators should view the expenses as investments that will attract foreign investment, and promote the economic and social welfare of Nigerians, thus fulfilling their goals of strengthening the bonds that unite Nigeria and making the nation a leading country in Africa and the world.

Discussion Questions

1. What are the dominant public relations tactics used by the government administration?

2. To what extent did the government use public relations strategies?

3. In a society as diverse as Nigeria, do you think public relations could serve as an important vehicle for national development and integration?

4. If hired as a consultant by the government, what forms of public relations tactics and strategies would you suggest that the government use?

References

Abasilim, M. (1998, August 21). The Igbo marginalization. *Post Express Wired*. [On-line]. Available: www.postexpresswired.com/post.

Abubakar, Gen. A. (1998, October 2). We have learned from our post errors. *Post Express Wired*. [Online]. Available: www.postexpresswired.com/post.

Abuh, A. (2003, April 23). Buhari urges calm, Fawehinmi sad, Ojukwu, others want polls voiced. *The Guardian* [Online]. Available at www.guardianewsgr.com/news/ Retrieved April 23, 2003.

Adejare, O. (1998, August 8). Beyond IBB's crocodile tears. *Post Express Wired*. [On-line]. Available: www.postexpresswired.com/post.

Agbagha, M. (1999, November 11). Perhaps, a new scramble. *Post Express Wired*. [On-line]. Available: www.postexpresswired.com/post.

Agwu, A. (1999, June 20). Obsanjo's statesmanship. [Online]. Available: www.postexpresswired.com/post.

Alanazi, A. (1996). Public relations in the Middle East. The case of Saudi Arabia. In H. Culberston & N. Chen (Eds.), *International public relations: A comparative analysis* (pp. 239–256). Mahwah, NJ: Lawrence Erlbaum Associates.

Alozie, E. (1999). *Communication and social modernization: An analysis of cultural reflections and the role of advertising in the economic and national development of Nigeria.* Unpublished doctoral dissertation, University of Southern Mississippi, Hattiesburg.

Amuzuo, C. (2000, April 17). Modern advertising business thrives on diversification—Onyia. *The Vanguard.* [On-line]. Available: www.vanguardngr.com.

Anosa, V. (1998, August 21). Nigeria: Whose nation? *Post Express Wired*. [On-line]. Available: www.post-expresswired.com/post.

Boafo, S. (1985). Utilizing development communication strategies in African societies: A critical perspective (development communication in Africa). *Gazette, 35,* 83–92.

Copson, R. (1997, December 3). Nigeria fact sheet. Foreign and National Defense Division, Congressional Research Service. [On-line]. Available: www.3.senate/seracg/s97.

Corruption: Obasanjo toughest challenge. (2000, May 28). *BBC News*. [On-line]. Available: news.bbc.co.uk.

Cutlip, S., Center, A., & Broom, G. (1985). *Effective public relations*. Englewood Cliffs, NJ: Prentice Hall.

Dellios, H. (1998, July 15). Nigeria transitional leader feels familial tug of a schemer. *Chicago Tribune.* [On-line]. Available: www.chicago.tribune.com.

Deustch, K. (1963). Nation building and national development: Some basic issues for political research. In K. Deustch & J. Foltz (Eds.), *Nation-building* (pp. 1–16). New York: Atherton.

Dozier, D. (1992). The organizational role of communications and public relations practitioners. In J. E. Grunig (Ed.), *Excellence in public relations and communication management.* (pp. 327–355). Hillsdale, NJ: Lawrence Erlbaum Associates.

Enyinnaya, B. (1998, August 19). Government earns $250b from oil. *Post Express Wired*. [On-line]. Available: www.postexpresswired.com/post.

Geertz, C. (1973). *The interpretation of culture.* New York: Basic Books.

George, A., & Ogbondah, C. (1999). The Ogoni crisis: A critical analysis of Nigeria's military Junta's international image-laundering campaign. *Southwestern Mass Communication Journal, 15*(1), 73–89.

Grunig J., & Hunt, T. (1984). *Managing public relations.* New York: CBS Public Publishing.

Ibagere, E. (2000, May 28). Nigeria: So what changed? *BBC News.* [On-line]. Available: news.bbc.co.uk.

Ihonvbere, E. (1997). Democratization in Africa: Challenges and prospects. In G. Agbang (Ed.), *Society and politics in Africa—Issues and trends in contemporary African politics: Stability, development and democratization* (pp. 337–366). New York: Peter Lang.

Jerry Gana addresses nation Thursdays. (2000, May 3). *Vanguard.* [On-line]. Available: www.vanguardngr.com.

Jerry Gana is new information minister, Sarumi moved. (2000, April 4). *Vanguard.* [On-line]. Available: www.vanguardngr.com.

Madiebo, A. (1980). *The Nigerian Revolution and the Biafran War.* Enugu, Nigeria: Fourth Dimension Press.

MBendi. (1998, October 10). Stanbic Merchant Bank Nigeria Limited. Nigeria. Economic Indicators. [On-line]. Available: www.mbendi.co.za/stanbic.

Metz, H. (Ed.). (1991). *Nigeria: A country study.* Washington, DC: Federal Research Division, Library of Congress.

Nigeria: A history of coups and countercoups. (1998, July 7). *BBC Online Network.* [On-line]. Available: news.bbc.co.uk.

Nigeria on the agenda. (2000, May 31). *Post Express Wired.* [On-line]. Available: www.postexpresswired.com/post.

Nigerian leader promises democracy. (1998, September 23). *Associated Press.*

Nwosu, I. (1990). Public relations and advertising in the process of governance and economic recovery in Nigeria. In I. Nwosu (Ed.), *Mass communication and national development—Perspectives on the communication of environments of development in Nigeria* (pp. 231–242). Aba, Nigeria: Frontiers Publishers Limited.

Obafemi, O. (1999, June 29). Marginalization of wolf-cry too soon. *Post Express Wired.* [On-line]. Available: www.postexpresswired.com/post.

Obasanjo lists gains of world tour. (1999, April 9). *Post Express Wired.* [On-line]. Available: www.postexpresswired.com/post.

Obasanjo to start weekly radio talk. (2000, March 30). *Vanguard.* [On-line]. Available: www.vanguardngr.com.

Okigbo, C. (1989). Communications ethics and social change: A Nigerian perspective. In T. Cooper, C. Christians, F. Plude, & R. White (Eds.), *Communication ethics and global change* (pp. 124–135). New York: Longman.

Okongwu, A. (1998, September 9). Roadblocks to the nation's democratic highway. *Post Express Wired.* [On-line]. Available: www.postexpresswired.com/post.

Oliveira, M. (1993). Communication strategies for agricultural development in the Third World. *Media Asia, 20*(2), 102–108.

Phillips, B. (1999, December 29). Big banknote too much for Nigeria. *BBC News.* [On-line]. Available: news.bbc.co.uk.

Phillips, B. (2000, May 5). The view from Nigeria. *BBC News.* [On-line]. Available: news.bbc.co.uk.

Pratt, C. (1985). Public relations in the Third World: The African context. *Public Relations Journal, 41*(2), 11–16.

Rupert, J. (1998a, June 9). Corruption flourished in Abacha's regime: Leader linked to broader plunder. *Washington Post: Washington Post Foreign Service,* p. A1.

Rupert, J. (1998b, November 9). Denied wealth, Nigeria's poor take dire steps. *Washington Post: Washington Post Foreign Service,* p. A18.

Seiter, F. (1995). *The practice of public relations.* Englewood Cliffs, NJ: Prentice Hall.

Sklar, R. (1997). Crises and transitions in the political history of independent Nigeria. In P. Beckett & C. Young (Eds.), *Dilemmas of democracy in Nigeria.* (pp. 15–44). Rochester, NY: University of Rochester Press.

State refutes senator's claim over Clinton's trip. (2000, March 29). *Africa News Online.* [On-line]. Available: www.africanews.org.

Taylor, M. (2000). Toward a public relations approach to nation building. *Journal of Public Relations, 12*(2), 179–210.

Timeline: A year of democracy. (2000, May 28). *BBC News.* [On-line]. Available: news.bbc.co.uk.

Ugbomah, E. (1998, August 20). Who is marginalized? *Post Express Wired.* [On-line]. Available: www.postexpresswired.com/postexpress.

Van Leuven, J. (1996). Public relations in South East Asia from nation-building campaigns to regional interdependence. In H. Culberston & N. Chen (Eds.), *International public relations: A comparative analysis* (pp. 207–222). Mahwah, NJ: Lawrence Erlbaum Associates.

World: Analysis of Nigeria: General Abacha's era of dictatorship. (1998, April 25). *BBC News Online Network.* [On-line]. Available: news.bbc.co.uk.

World Factbook (1997). Nigeria. Central Intelligence Agency (pp. 346–348). Pittsburg: Superintendent of Documents.

Writer brands Abiola's death "heinous crime." (1998, July 10). *BBC News Online Network World News Watch.* [On-line]. Available: news.bbc.co.uk.

12

Fire at Nigeria's Treasure Base

An Analysis of Shell Petroleum's Public Relations Strategies in the Wake of the Niger Delta Crisis

Chris W. Ogbondah

Amiso George

Key Points _____

- Shell Petroleum Development Company (SPDC) has drilled oil in the Niger Delta region of Nigeria where it has made billions of dollars in profits since 1958.

- Inhabitants of the Niger Delta allege that SPDC's oil drilling activities have not only polluted their communities but also that the multinational oil giant has not behaved like a good community neighbor.

- Consequently, Niger Delta communities have embarked on demonstrations, arson, ransom taking, hostage taking, abduction, and the killing of oil workers (including expatriate staff), vandalism, destruction of drilling equipment, and disruption of SPDC's full ability to drill oil.

- Shell's initial response to the ensuing Niger Delta crisis consisted of denials and the use of instruments of violence and coercion as well as brute force that only increased the conflict.

- Shell's public relations policy in the Niger Delta should consist of two-way communication with its community neighbors. In particular, listening, dialogue, collaboration, honesty, openness, ethical considerations, and respect for cultural values and human rights should be at the center of SPDC's public relations policy in the future.

- This will enable the company and its host communities to build mutual trust and understanding, thus reducing the likelihood of crises in the future.

> *The Delta is on the boil. Youths are taking over oil rigs, flow stations and installations everyday.*[1]

The preceding statement epitomizes the dilemma and crises in which Shell Petroleum Development Company (SPDC) has been embroiled over the past twelve years in the Niger Delta region of Nigeria where it drills crude oil. As Onyenwenwa (2000) has observed, "These ubiquitous crises . . . in the oil-producing communities though had been for a long time subterranean and suppressed by the military, have now surfaced and assumed frightening dimensions" (p. 122). Iyayi (2000) made a similar observation, "Today, no week passes without some report on the situation in the Niger Delta: gas flares, spillage and environmental degradation, hostage taking, explosion of pipelines . . . violence, the murder of demonstrators, the squalor and deprivation of whole communities etc." (p. 151). Shell also acknowledges that the Niger Delta crises are precipitated by an intense feeling of neglect and anger on the part of the inhabitants of the region (Corzine, 1996).

Two major issues underpin the intense feelings of neglect and anger and are therefore central to the ongoing crises that Shell faces in the region. One is environmental pollution resulting from SPDC's operation, which has decimated the ecology of the Niger Delta, Nigeria's breadbasket. The second issue is the mostly justifiable allegation that Shell has failed to be a good neighbor in the Niger Delta where it has drilled oil for nearly half a century. In other words, Niger Delta communities allege that Shell's oil drilling activities have left the region environmentally polluted, and the company has woefully failed to maintain a sense of social responsibility and concern for its host communities. Residents of the region say that Shell has failed to embark on socioeconomic development projects that would enable them to overcome the deleterious effects of oil drilling. This is why Taiwo (2000) has described the Niger Delta crisis as the problem of "killing the goose that lays the golden egg" (p. 207).

Consequently, the communities have embarked on demonstrations, arson, ransom taking, hostage taking, abduction and the killing of oil workers (including expatriate staff), vandalism, and destruction of Shell's drilling equipment. In many communities the crises have disrupted SPDC's ability to drill oil. In Ogoni, local residents sacked Shell for more than six years. The result has been huge monetary losses for Shell and its Nigerian government partners. Demonstrations against Shell are yet to abate in the oil-producing communities. College students of the Isoko community in Delta State have protested against Shell for what they described as SPDC's marginalization in the award of scholarships and industrial training programs.

This chapter presents a critical analysis of Shell's public relations response in the wake of the Niger Delta crises. It begins with a brief description of the Niger Delta region in order to highlight the environmental peculiarities that are central to the ongoing crises. Next, it provides a historical overview of the region's neglect in order to place today's intense feeling of neglect and anger by Niger Delta communities in perspective. The chapter then describes the courses and causes of the crises, and Shell's public relations strategies. A critical analysis of the effectiveness of Shell's public relations is made. The chapter concludes with recommendations that should have implications for policy implementation in resolving the crises.

Historical and Global Operations of Shell

SPDC of Nigeria is a subsidiary of two Anglo-Dutch groups of companies—the Royal Dutch and Shell. The Royal Dutch Company for the Exploitation of Petroleum Wells in the Netherlands East Indies was registered in the Hague in 1890. Its name was abbreviated in 1949 to Royal Dutch Petroleum Company. The other company in the group, Shell, was first registered in London in 1897 by the brothers Marcus and Sam Samuel as the Shell Transport and Trading Company, Ltd. (now Plc: public limited company). Royal Dutch Petroleum Company (Koninklijke Nederland) and Shell Transport and Trading Company, Plc own 60 percent and 40 percent respectively of Shell Petroleum NV (Netherlands), Shell Petroleum Company Ltd. (UK), and Shell Petroleum Inc. (USA).

The three companies and their operating subsidiaries (including SPDC of Nigeria) are managed worldwide by Shell International. Operating subsidiaries are divided into the following divisions: (1) exploration and production; (2) oil products; (3) chemicals; and (4) gas and power. Other small divisions include coal, hydrogen, forestry, and renewables (mainly in forestry and solar energy).

In 1999, oil and gas accounted for 88 percent of net proceeds, whereas chemicals accounted for 12 percent. The company's interests in power generation and renewable resources are considerably smaller. Its various activities are conducted in more than 135 countries, including Nigeria, where SPDC is the leader in the petroleum and gas business. It is the pioneer and the largest hydrocarbon exploration and production company in the country. Originally known as Shell D'Arcy, and later as Shell-BP, it was jointly financed by the Royal Dutch/Shell Group of Companies and the British Petroleum (BP) Group on an equal basis. The company was granted an oil exploration license on November 4, 1939, although geological reconnaissance work started in 1937.

The company discovered the first commercial oil field at Oloibiri in Rivers State in 1956. From a modest production of six thousand barrels of crude oil per day in 1958, when the first cargo of oil was exported, the rate of SPDC's daily production has steadily increased to the current production potential of more than one million barrels. The production quota of 950,000 barrels per day represents just under half of Nigeria's oil production exported mainly from two oil terminals—Bonny in Rivers State and Forcados in Delta State.

The Niger Delta Environment

The Niger Delta region of Nigeria, where the bulk of the country's oil is produced, spans more than seventy thousand square kilometers and four ecological zones. Situated in the southeast and parts of southwestern sections of the country, the region is made up of six states of the Nigerian federation: Akwa Ibom, Bayelsa, Cross River, Delta, Edo, and Rivers states. As a specific geographical phenomenon, however, the Niger Delta is within Rivers, Bayelsa, and Delta states. This is an area covering about 3.5 million hectares of land, approximately the area of Belgium. It is among the biggest expanses of wetland, and includes the ninth most vast drainage area in the world and the third largest mangrove forest (Oyerinde, 1998; World Bank, 1995).

The region consists of a vast network of rivers and creeks with a coastal zone of beachfront and barrier islands. The area is a triangular-shaped landmass through which one of Nigeria's distinguishable features, the River Niger, empties into the Atlantic coasts that define the southernmost part of the country.

A particular feature of the Niger Delta is the exploitation of oil in densely inhabited areas. The processes involved in petroleum exploitation—exploration and production (E and P)—create significant adverse externalities for the environment and people of the Niger Delta. A vast expanse of the limited land area in the region is lost to oil wells and an extensive network of pipelines. This undermines the agricultural space. Of the effects of oil production in the Niger Delta, Taiwo (2000) said, "First, we have environmental pollution which encompasses the terrestrial, atmosphere and marine environments. The most common sources of the pollution are oil spillage and gas flaring, while the effects include extensive damage to surface vegetation, agriculture, human health and aquatic life" (p. 208).

Continuous gas flaring contributes to acid rain in the region. This, in turn, reduces soil fertility and pollutes drinking water sources. Petroleum pollutants destroy the food sources of higher species by the incorporation of carcinogens into food chains, fishery resources, and human food resources. This poses significant health risks in addition to other less tangible psychological and cultural consequences of oil production, including breakup of families and the desecration of ancestral shrines. Women, in particular, have had to contend with multiple difficulties arising from the operations of the oil industry (Hutchful, 1985a).

Beyond any doubt, therefore, activities associated with oil exploration and oil production in the Niger Delta have significant deleterious effects on the environment. Seventy-five percent of the gas brought up with oil in Nigeria is burned off. This compares with less than 1 percent in the United States and about 20 percent in Iran, Libya, and Saudi Arabia. Table 12.1 presents the levels of gas flaring in Nigeria compared with gas-producing countries in other parts of the world.

The gas flared up in Nigeria, according to World Wide Fund for Nature, emits more than 34 million tons of carbon dioxide annually (*World Press Review,* 1996). The Nigerian Environmental Study/Action Team (NEST) notes that, "gas flaring has major adverse

TABLE 12.1   *Flaring Levels in Gas-Producing Countries*

Nigeria	76.0%
Saudi Arabia	20.0
Iran	19.0
Mexico	5.0
Britain	4.3
Algeria	4.0
Former USSR	1.0
United States	0.6
The Netherlands	0.0

Source: Ashton-Jones (1998)

socio-economic and environmental impacts which include atmospheric pollution by combustion contaminants; thermal pollution of air, land and water; destruction of vegetation and associated wildlife . . . damage to soil and crops by heat and the deposition of primary and secondary contaminants" (Nigerian Environmental Study/Action Team, 1991, p. 45).

In an eight-page pamphlet, *Challenges of Gas Flares-Out,* Shell pledges its commitment to ending gas flaring by 2008 (*The Shell Bulletin,* 2002). A $70 million contract that Shell has signed with the Nigerian Gas Company (NGC) aims to speed up the oil company's flare-out policy. Under the terms of the contract, SPDC is to refurbish twelve of the NGC stations, most of which have been in poor operating condition for ten years.

In addition to the environmental effects of gas flaring, oil spillage constitutes a major threat to the environment, human life, and livestock in the region. From 1970 to 1982, 1,581 oil spills involving almost 2 million barrels of crude oil were reported in Nigeria (Nigerian National Petroleum Corporation, 1995). Ogbondah (2001) provides accounts of some of those oil spills. Impacts of the spills include "loss of fish, crustaceans and other aquatic animals, eutrophication of water bodies, de-vegetation and other ecological bodies, loss of drinking and industrial water, destruction of agricultural and related activities and impairment of human health" (Ogbondah, 2001, p. 44).

Ashton-Jones (1998) reported the devastating effects of gas flaring and acid rain on the health of residents in the Niger Delta, which include cancer and stroke. Table 12.2, as reported by the Committee for the Defense of Human Rights, presents some of the health complaints during oil spillage from the *Sea Express* oil tanker off the Pembrokeshire coast between February 16 and March 16, 1996 (Ashton-Jones, 1998).

TABLE 12.2 *Pembrokeshire Oil Spillage Health Complaints*

Symptoms/Diagnosis	Prevalence in Controls	Prevalence in Exposed	Significance
1. Generally ill	7.3%	23.2%	Yes
2. Headache	12.0	32.5	Yes
3. Nausea	5.8	2.6	Yes
4. Vomiting	2.5	2.8	No
5. Diarrhea	4.5	7.6	Yes
6. Sore eyes	4.9	15.6	Yes
7. Running nose	11.3	18.5	Yes
8. Sore throat	10.5	26.5	Yes
9. Cough	9.6	19.1	Yes
10. Itchy skin	4.7	10.4	Yes
11. Skin rashes	2.9	6.7	Yes
12. Blisters	0.4	1.1	Yes
13. Shortness of breath	4.4	10.4	No
14. Weakness	12.7	21.7	Yes

Source: Ashton-Jones (1998)

Others who have highlighted the environmental effects of oil production in the Niger Delta include Oyerinde (1998), Ikporukpo (1985), Ikein (1990), Awobajo (1981), and Agbese (1995). Therefore, complaints of environmental devastation and ecological despoliation resulting from multinational oil companies' drilling activities in the Niger Delta are quite legitimate.

Oil, Niger Delta Communities, and Neglect

Today's complaints of neglect by communities in the oil-rich Niger Delta are not new. During the last days of British colonial rule in Nigeria these complaints were so intense that the colonial government set up the [Henry] Willink Commission to look into the issue. The 1957 commission recommended that attention be paid to the accelerated socioeconomic development of the region.[2] Under the arrangement establishing the commission, industries, roads, health facilities, educational institutions, and other socioeconomic infrastructures were supposed to be set up to enhance the economic development of the region. But as Horsfall (1999) has noted, the Niger Delta Development Board (NDDB) that was established to ensure accelerated development of the region failed in its charge.

When minority groups in the region felt that socioeconomic developments in their communities were not being addressed, their demands took a dramatic turn. For example, in 1967 Isaac Adaka Boro, Samuel Owonaru, Nottingham Dick, and a few young men of the Niger Delta organized a short-lived rebellion. Boro and a group of like-minded youths took up arms and declared that the Niger Delta had seceded from Nigeria and had become an independent Niger Delta Republic (Tebekaemi, 1982). The rebellion was put down within twelve days, but the issues of neglect, environmental pollution, socioeconomic marginalization, and deprivation that Boro and his compatriots raised did not die with the rebellion.

Today, crises precipitated by complaints of environmental pollution and neglect in the Delta communities have resulted in a public relations nightmare for Shell. Even though the shipment of oil from the coasts of Nigeria began as far back as 1958, it was not until about three decades later that indigenes of the oil-producing region drew very serious attention to the havoc wreaked on the environment by oil companies (Soremekun & Obadare, 1998). The complaints, however, have taken a new dimension since 1990.

Prior to 1990, complaints by oil communities were frequently channeled through petitions to the oil companies and the Nigerian government. Usually included in the petitions were demands for compensation for farmlands and fish ponds destroyed by oil spills and oil well blowouts (Lolomari, 1995). The petitions, although ostensibly written on behalf of entire villages or clans, were actually, in most cases, initiated by a handful of individuals without much communal input.

Ogoni Community

As Agbese and Ogbondah (1998) observed, the strategy of petition writing, considered largely ineffectual, changed dramatically in 1990 with the formation of the Movement for the Survival of Ogoni People (MOSOP), the sociocultural organization that Ogonis, one of the Niger Delta communities, used to articulate their demands from Shell. MOSOP eschewed the strategy of writing petitions and charging occasional lawsuits against oil companies. Instead, it demanded self-determination and the right to use revenues derived from oil extracted on Ogoni land for the benefit of the Ogonis. It mobilized the Ogonis, and has since waged an intense struggle against the Nigerian government and Shell.

MOSOP explained that it took these actions because oil exploration has polluted Ogoni lands, streams, and creeks with acid rain, oil spillage, and oil blowouts.

Through the Ogoni Bill of Rights, a document issued by traditional heads of various ethnic clans of Ogoni and leaders of the MOSOP, the organization enumerated the environmental effects of Shell's oil drilling activities in Ogoni since 1958. The document laments the suffering of the Ogoni people as a result of oil exploration and the decimation of agricultural and fishing farms. It also highlights the economic and political marginalization of the Ogoni people as well as the lack of social services and infrastructural amenities such as electricity, drinking water, health facilities, educational institutions, and so on in Ogoni land (Saro-Wiwa, 1992; Sha'aba, 1998). As Agbese and Ogbondah (1998) noted, MOSOP used mass protests to draw international attention to Shell's environmental pollution on Ogoni land. The Ogoni Study Group (1995) points out that the Ogonis "sacked all police stations [in Ogoni land] . . . , harassed law enforcement agents, chased out magistrates from court sessions, beat up oil workers, blew up oil installations, mounted over 150 road-blocks, and in fact, made the whole Ogoni land unsafe for human habitation and regular business activity" (p. 4). MOSOP drove Shell out of Ogoni land and, by the end of 2001, Shell had not quite resumed full operations in Ogoni.

The Ogoni uprising against Shell signaled the beginning of what has recently become a quest for ethnic rights and social and economic justice by communities in the Niger Delta. Other groups in the Niger Delta have similarly waged their own struggles against Shell because they allege that their oil-producing communities have borne the brunt of oil production and gained very little from it.

Itsekiri Community

The Itsekiris, who occupy the westernmost part of the Niger Delta, have also confronted Shell. They claim that, even though Shell produces approximately 275,000 barrels of oil (i.e., $5 million per day at the rate of $18 per barrel) or $1,802 billion per year from Itsekiri land (Fregene, 2000), the company has neglected its social responsibilities in the community. Oil-related crises in the Itsekiri communities has resulted in the kidnappings, killings, arsons, ransom taking, and piracy against Shell (Fregene, 2000).

Egbema Community

Another oil community is the Egbema in Rivers State where Shell has extracted crude oil from sixty-three wells since 1958. Its residents say they detest Shell's policy of aloofness in the community (Onyenwenwa, 2000). Prominent among the community's grievances are (1) Shell's failure to employ residents of the community; (2) Shell's inability to provide infrastructures, such as roads, health facilities, educational institutions, and scholarships for the community; (3) Shell's failure to provide an economic welfare package for the community; and (4) Shell's failure to clean up environmental wastes stemming from its operations in the community. Onyenwenwa (2000) also explains other important causes of the crises between Shell and Egbema as well as other communities in the Niger Delta.

> The multinational oil companies did not involve the oil-bearing communities, *ab initio.* Since there is no negotiated Memorandum of Understanding (MOU), the companies have no Insurable Interest. Therefore they have no bargain to keep. They became flagrant and indeed cavalier. This amounts to complete rape of the people and not merely a case of communication gap.
>
> In the Niger Delta, oil pipelines pass under people's houses; beneath their farmlands and under the waters. Sometimes the oil spills into the rivers/farms. The hitherto serene, beautiful natural environment is destroyed. Animals are driven away, the others which couldn't escape perish. The people's traditional occupations of farming and fishing are automatically disrupted.
>
> Developmental needs of the people are ignored. No basic infrastructure, no human capital development scheme, no economic empowerment. Where, in some cases, the communities extract some promises from the companies, they are never kept. (p. 126)

According to the Egbema community, the discovery of oil has amounted to pauperization, misery, and nightmares for its residents. The residents say that the Niger Delta crisis can be resolved if Shell addresses the grievances of their people, and implements a Marshall Plan for the community.

Etche Community

The grievances of the Etche people, the third-largest ethnic group in Rivers State, are similar to those of other Niger Delta communities. Nwauzi (2000) said, "The Etche ethnic nationality has little or nothing to show for over four decades of oil exploration and exploitation in the area, apart from wanton and reckless destruction of the ecosystem. Etche has got no compensation for the enormous amount of revenue it provides to the national economy" (p. 136).

Residents of the community particularly complain that there are no roads in the area. They say that if Shell were a good community neighbor the company would have provided hospitals, electricity, and good drinking water for the people. They also complain that, despite the huge oil and gas resources Shell has tapped from their community, SPDC has neglected to even build bridges across the three rivers that traverse the community. Their sentiments were well echoed by Nigeria's former Petroleum Minister, Jibril Aminu:

> I am extremely sympathetic with the people of Rivers and Delta States. I am very concerned about what I saw in Escravos, Focados, and even in Warri. And the same things in Rivers State, the moment you go there, or fly in helicopter. There are no roads. No power line, no telephone line.[3]

On October 30, 1990, the people of Etche held their first public demonstration to draw attention to the community's problems resulting from oil drilling. On that day, youths from the Umuechem village carried out a demonstration to press the community's demands from Shell: the provision of electricity, roads, water, and other essential social amenities, and compensation for oil pollution of their farmlands and rivers. However, security forces of the state, Shell's partners in petroleum activities, attacked the unarmed demonstrators with tear gas and gunfire (Akaruese, 1998; Nwauzi, 2000). Fifty residents of the community were killed. Livestock and houses were also destroyed during the confrontation with Shell (Nwauzi, 2000).

Other crises in the Niger Delta involving Shell included that of December 4, 1993, in Nembe Creek in Rivers State where armed youths sacked Shell employees, and vandalized and looted the company's property. On June 25, 1995, angry youths in Egbema vandalized Shell's property and assaulted its staff.

It is incontrovertible that communities in the Niger Delta do not have access to basic infrastructure and amenities such as paved roads, electricity, and portable water. There are few industries to absorb the large population displaced from agriculture and aquatic activities as a result of oil exploration in the area. Communities in the Niger Delta are particularly infuriated by observed patterns of employment in the oil industry. They have sensed patent discrimination in the seeming preference of the oil companies to hire Nigerians, other than the indigenes of the Niger Delta, even for menial jobs. Few indigenes of the region are involved in the lucrative practice of "lifting" oil.

There is little doubt that the immediate problem of the oil Delta is socioeconomic deprivation and environmental injustice. This is made more acute by the situation in which the region that produces the bulk of the nation's wealth is neglected in the distribution of infrastructure and basic amenities. A situation in which Nigeria's wealth is redistributed in a manner in which the region that produces the most wealth receives the least in socioeconomic development amounts to grave social injustice. As far as the Delta communities are concerned, the failure of multinational oil corporations to be involved in the socioeconomic development of the region constitutes part of this social injustice.

Although there are six multinational oil companies that operate in the Niger Delta, this study focuses only on Shell's public relations campaign in the region. The study examines the policy thrust of foreign oil companies' public relations in the Niger Delta with particular attention to Shell's public relations response to the crises inasmuch as Shell is the dominant player and the largest of the oil companies in the region. Table 12.3 lists the major oil companies in the Niger Delta and attests to Shell's dominance in the oil sector.

Table 12.3 shows that, although the Nigerian government through the Nigerian National Petroleum Corporation (NNPC) holds the controlling share in each of the six major oil companies, operational and, hence, real control is vested in the foreign companies. Shell was the first to arrive on the oil scene and accounts for almost half of the total oil production in the country. Human Rights Watch (1999) also notes that Shell is the biggest oil producer in Nigeria with the longest history from 1957, and has dominated the industry for as long as oil has been produced in Nigeria. It also notes that in the early days of its arrival in Nigeria, Shell enjoyed a monopoly and a privileged relationship with the government.

This case study of Shell's public relations response to the Delta crises is supported by a study of oil companies and the politics of community relations in Nigeria (Iyayi, 2000), which notes, "understanding the dynamics and essence of the relations between SPDC and the communities in the Niger Delta will be more than sufficient to account for

TABLE 12.3   *Major Oil Companies in the Niger Delta*

Oil Company	Shareholders		Operator	Share of National Production
Shell Petroleum Development Company	NNPC Shell Elf Agip	55% 30 10 5	Shell	42.0%
Mobil Producing Nigeria	NNPC Mobile	50 42	Mobile	21.0
Chevron Nigeria	NNPC Chevron	60 40	Chevron	19.0
Nigeria Agip Oil	NNPC Agip	60 40	Agip	7.5
Elf Petroleum Nigeria	NNPC Elf	60 40	Elf	2.6
Texaco Overseas (Nigeria) Petroleum	NNPC Texaco Chevron	60 20 20	Texaco	1.7
Total				93.0

Source: Iyayi (2000)

the totality of relations existing between the oil companies and the host communities of the Niger Delta" (p. 156).

Shell's Public Relations Strategies

Shell has employed a number of strategies in its relationship with the various communities in the Niger Delta. Although some of its actions in response to the Niger Delta crisis are commendable, others are not.

Detrimental Strategies

Among other things, the company has used violence as a way to end community protests against its perceived noninvolvement in the socioeconomic development of the Niger Delta. At other times, Shell has used silence and an "I-don't-care" attitude responding to the demands by Niger Delta communities. Other strategies have included defiance, denial, payment of money to selected community leaders, divide and rule, blaming victims, promotion of false consciousness, and cooptation.

Violence and Denial.   Violence is one of Shell's most frequently used strategies in responding to community protests against oil spillage, and compensation for the destruction of livestock, fishponds, and farmlands. Iyayi (2000) observes that, "Today, violence represents by far the most important community relations strategy that is adopted by the oil com-

panies in collaboration with the Nigerian state in the Niger Delta" (p. 164). Rather than engage in two-way dialogue with its communities, Shell acquiesces to the use of soldiers and
the state police to forcefully break up peaceful demonstrations and protests. The Nigerian
state feels obliged, as the major shareholder in the oil sector, to join forces with Shell and
other oil companies in using instruments of violence and coercion to disperse peaceful
demonstrations in the Niger Delta. Human Rights Watch (1999) notes that repression and
suppression of peaceful demonstrations are common daily occurrences in the Delta region:

> Virtually every oil producing community has experienced an incident along the following
> lines. Community members stage a protest demanding compensation for oil company ac-
> tivities. . . . In response to the protests, members of the Mobile police or other security
> forces come to the scene, the security forces carry out indiscriminate beatings, arrests and
> detentions; the protest is then abandoned. . . . In virtually every community there have been
> occasions on which the paramilitary mobile police, the regular police or the army have
> beaten, detained, or even killed those involved in protests, peaceful or otherwise, or indi-
> viduals who have called for compensation for oil damage, whether youths, women, chil-
> dren, or traditional leaders. (p. 11)

One of the numerous examples that illustrate Shell's use of violence in responding to
community protests was that of the Umuechem people in Etche. As noted earlier, on October 30, 1990, youths of the community staged a peaceful demonstration at Shell's facility to
press their demands for the provision of electricity, roads, water, and other social amenities,
and for compensation for oil pollution of their farmlands and rivers. In response, the Mobile
Police force attacked the unarmed demonstrators with tear gas and gunfire. Nwauzi (2000)
notes that fifty Umuechem people (including the paramount ruler of the Igbo-Agwuru-Asa
clan, Chief A. A. Ordu, and three of his family members) died in the violence. About 550
houses were destroyed, while members of the police force turned the episode into a festival
to feast on the people's domestic animals and food crops (p. 136). Of SPDC's use of violence
in responding to the Umuechem protest, Human Rights Watch (1999) reported that

> On October 29, 1990, the divisional manager of SPDC's eastern division had written to the
> Rivers State Commissioner of Police to request "security protection" with a preference for
> the paramilitary Mobile Police, in anticipation of "an impending attack" on SPDC facilities
> at Umuechem allegedly planned for the following morning. Following peaceful protests by
> village youths on SPDC's premises on October 30, SPDC again made a written report to the
> governor of Rivers State, a copy of which was sent to the commissioner of police. On Octo-
> ber 31, Mobile Police attacked peaceful demonstrators with tear gas and gunfire. (p. 123)

In 1994, Shell was also implicated in a joint use of violence with government forces
to suppress demonstrations in the Ogoni community. In response to Shell's request for the
state's assistance in protecting its facilities against demonstrations of Ogonis under the
aegis of MOSOP, Nigerian soldiers and members of the special mobile police attacked and
killed many of the demonstrators. Iyayi (2000) notes that

> Shell was implicated not only in the murders committed by the Rivers State Internal Secu-
> rity Task Force in Ogoniland but also in the murder of Ken Saro Wiwa and his eight other

Ogoni compatriots. Shell has been known to provide money for the purchase of sophisticated and up-to-date weapons for the security forces deployed by the Nigerian state to the communities in the Niger Delta. (p. 165)

Another example of Shell's use of violence in the oil communities was that which occurred at the Ahia Flow Station in Omodioga in Ikwerre Local Government Area. In January 1997, more than one hundred youths from Omodioga held a demonstration to protest Shell's failure to tar the village road, and to provide electricity and good drinking water in their community. In response, members of the paramilitary Internal Task Force of the Rivers State arrested twelve of the youths, and subsequently detained them at the Bori military camp for a month. Human Rights Watch (1999) noted that "for the first five days they were beaten every morning, and tear gas canisters were fired into their cells on a number of occasions" (p. 145). The youths were eventually released without charge, and warned to desist from future protestations against SPDC. Shell denied knowledge of the violent incident, and said its relationship with the Omodioga community had been cordial and harmonious.

Another act of violence occurred after an oil spill in 1998 at Shell's Opukoshi Flow Station around Obotobo in Delta State. Following the spill a delegation of the community was sent to meet with a Shell contractor at the site. The delegation requested that a water tank and generator provided earlier to the community by Shell be activated. In response to the community action, a team of security officers arrived in two speedboats and shot bullets into the bushes forcing members of the delegation to take cover for several hours. Although there were no fatalities, Shell denied knowledge of the incident.

Most recently, Shell also used violence—and the assistance of the new government under President Obasanjo—to respond to public protests at Odi in 1999. With Shell's acquiescence, Nigerian soldiers were drafted to disperse the protesters. The protest got out of hand when irate natives killed twelve security officers. The violent response to the protest led to mayhem, killings, destruction, and sacking of the entire Odi community by the soldiers.

Shell also uses denial as a strategy to defend itself and delegitimatize its opposition. At the onset of the Niger Delta crisis, Shell denied that environmental pollution in the Niger Delta was a result of its oil production in the region. It claimed that oil spillage, though of concern, was not caused by Shell but by saboteurs who sought financial compensation from the company.

Divide and Rule.   The divide-and-rule strategy is frequently used by Shell in collaboration with the Nigerian government to exploit the communities of the Niger Delta. The strategy involves preferential siting of development projects in certain communities; promotion of hatred for particular communities through, for example, the change of local government headquarters or an important facility of Shell; and the provision of support for some communities, including the supply of arms during inter- and intracommunal conflicts. During the Ogoni–Andoni conflicts in the 1990s, the Ogonis, for example, alleged that Shell provided moral and material support to the Andonis through third parties because of the Ogoni opposition of the company's oil policy.

Another example of this strategy can be seen in a protest letter sent to Shell in February 2002 by the people of the Okia community in Delta State. The letter accused Shell of masterminding the conflict between the Aggeh and Okia communities by awarding a contract for the surveillance of the Okia section of the Trans-Ramas Pipeline to a non-Okia indigene in order to incur the wrath of the people. The letter said that "there was no consultation with the people of Okia community as regards employment . . . and contract on the surveillance of the pipeline, the community did not present the contractor, the contractor is a non-indigene of Okia community."[4] In other words, the letter said, Shell was trying to set up a conflict between the Okia and Aggeh communities by awarding a contract for the surveillance of Okia community to a non-Okia indigene.

Iyayi (2000) notes that "this strategy has been so effective that several host communities in the Niger Delta are now up in arms against each other" (p. 162). Shell uses this strategy to divert the attention of the oil communities to internecine conflicts and away from protest.

Defiance.   Defiance, according to Iyayi (2000), consists of the activities of oil companies designed to show the host communities that there is nothing the latter can do to force the companies to take the particular course of action desired by the communities. In this respect, Shell issues statements strongly indicating that it will not change its position despite community protests. Defiance also involves threatening or taking court actions against the communities or simply continuing with a particular course of action even in the face of protests by members of the oil communities.

Since the mid 1990s, for example, the people of Rumuobiakani, where SPDC's headquarters is located, have pressed Shell to employ qualified indigenes of the community at the managerial level in the company. The community says its indigenes are professionals in several disciplines, including business management, law, accountancy, finance, economics, engineering, and so on. They have also persistently requested Shell to extend the award of its huge sums of contracts to experienced contractors from the Rumuobiakani community. In response, Shell defiantly says it cannot yield to community pressure.[5]

Cooptation.   Cooptation involves the payment of money, medical and vacation bills, and the award of lucrative contracts to selected community leaders so they will discourage protests and demonstrations against Shell's policies in their communities. It also involves making special or regular financial payments to members of the state's security forces. Those coopted become spokespersons and defenders of Shell's policies in the communities. Shell's use of such persons who are not trained in communication skills as spokespersons is certainly an unethical public relations strategy.

In several instances, this approach has worsened Shell's relationship with its host communities. For example, in Ogoni, the strategy led to the assassination of four prominent community leaders in May 1994 by irate members of the MOSOP. Members of MOSOP alleged that, by accepting financial favors from Shell, the four chiefs were willing to allow SPDC's policy to supersede the Ogoni communal interests. In response to that incident, as alluded to earlier, a special military tribunal under the then-military dictatorship of General Sani Abacha arrested and prosecuted MOSOP's leader Ken Saro-Wiwa and eight other Ogoni members of the peasant organization; they were found guilty and hanged in November 1995. The incident sparked international condemnation of Shell and the Nigerian military government (Ogbondah, 1999). With the Ogoni experience, Shell and other oil companies have realized the limitations of this strategy in their relationships with the Niger Delta communities.

Commendable Strategies

Although SPDC has engaged in certain reprehensible actions, nevertheless, it has adopted some commendable strategies in its relationship with the Niger Delta communities. These include the building of community clinics, schools, and youth and skills training centers; awards of scholarships; and the creation of jobs for indigenes of the oil-producing areas. Its social responsibility program in the communities has included the tarring of some roads, provision of good drinking water, rural electrification, building of health and recreational centers, supply of educational equipment, and so on.

Educational and Skills Training Programs.   Starting in the 1950s, Shell began to provide scholarships and training programs for some residents of the Niger Delta. Shell's public relations officer Omuku (2000) observed that "SPDC social investments programme dates back to the 1950s when we launched an agricultural initiative. . . . We have trained agricultural graduates as extension advisers and they live in the communities, helping farmers with improved varieties and farming techniques, and helping to get them organized in co-operatives" (p. 203). In 1970, Shell awarded scholarships to three Baptist High School students in Rivers State to study at the Imperial College, United Kingdom. "In 1998 alone, the company built over 71 classroom blocks for communities in the Niger Delta, providing in the process, decent learning environment for about 11,000 children" (p. 204).

According to a February 6, 1997, SPDC press release (Shell in Ogoni youth training initiative), that year the company launched a six-month training program at Bori Polytechnic for 350 Ogoni youths. The program was administered by Community Development Partners (CODEP), a nongovernmental organization specializing in rural development. The press release also said that Shell took over the maintenance and the supply of drugs for the Gokana General Hospital at Terabor, Ogoni. It said SPDC started supplementing the wages of the hospital's staff from 1997.

The press release further said Shell donated drugs to health centers at Bodo, Nchia, and Taaba in Ogoni. It said Shell "is planning to renovate and re-equip three other government health centers at Kpite, K-Dere and Kwawa as part of its 1997 health care programme, which involves building or refurbishing 13 hospitals or health centers throughout its area of operations in the Niger Delta." The press release enumerated other things that SPDC planned to do for the Ogoni community; for example, it said that "a science teacher sponsorship scheme will be extended to two Ogoni schools at Bori and Eleme."

Infrastructural Projects.   Omuku (2000) noted that Shell began to provide good drinking water, school buildings, and roads in its host communities from the 1980s. The company began to provide health facilities (clinics and hospitals) in the Delta region between 1992 and 1994. By 1998, Shell's community projects supported twenty-two hospitals and health centers, nine of which were started from the scratch. Shell said that in 2000, its medical personnel treated more than eighty-five hundred patients at its mobile clinics, com-

TABLE 12.4   *SPDC Hospitals Built or Renovated in Niger Delta*

Hospitals Built by SPDC	*Hospitals Renovated/Taken Over by SPDC*
Aminigboko Cottage Hospital	Bonny General Hospital
Umuebule Cottage Hospital	Nembe General Hospital
Soku Cottage Hospital	Egbema General Hospital
Owaza Cottage Hospital	Terabor General Hospital
Okoroba Cottage Hospital	Obio Health Center
Erhoike Cottage Hospital	Kpite Health Center
Ogulagha Cottage Hospital	Kwawa Health Center
Egbemo-Angalabiri Cottage Hospital	K-Dere Health Center
Oben Cottage Hospital	Igbide Health Center
Okpare Health Center	Ekakpamre Health Center
Oti-Jeremi Health Center	Effurun-Otor Health Center
Otuasega Cottage Hospital	Okrika General Hospital
Ellu Cottage Hospital	Iko Health Center
Tomagbene Cottage Hospital	Peremabiri Cottage Hospital
Kalaibiama Cottage Hospital	Edagberi Cottage Hospital
	Anieze Health Center

Source: SPDC *2000 People and Environmental Annual Report*

pared to nearly six thousand in 1998. Additionally, the company said it built three new cottage hospitals in the host communities, bringing to thirty-one the number of hospitals built, renovated, or supported by SPDC in 2000. A breakdown of the health facilities is listed in Table 12.4.

According to Omuku (2000), the company provided about 950 projects in the Niger Delta between 1992 and 1997. These included classroom blocks, water projects, and flea markets. Shell said that by 2000 it awarded 3,587 scholarships for primary through university-level education to indigenes of the Niger Delta. A breakdown of the number of scholarships from 1996 to 2000 is shown in Table 12.5.

TABLE 12.5   *SPDC Scholarships in Niger Delta*

	1996	*1997*	*1998*	*1999*	*2000*
University scholarships (area of operation awards)	427	430	430	430	430
University scholarships (national awards)	130	130	153	150	153
Postprimary scholarships	2600	2600	2600	2600	2600
Science teachers	266	252	383	360	349
Schools with science teachers	14	57	63	64	55

Source: SPDC *2000 People and Environmental Annual Report*

Shell also argues that in 2000 it spent $60 million in executing different projects in its host communities in the Niger Delta. According to SPDC, this represents almost double the amount it spent for similar efforts in 1996 (*2000 Annual Report*). A breakdown of its spending (U.S. dollars) on community projects is shown in Table 12.6.

Environmental Safety.   As part of its social responsibility program in the oil-producing communities, SPDC is now embarking on environmental safety projects. For instance, in 1996 the company replaced or buried old flow lines in order to reduce crude oil spillage. It also embarked on massive restoration of the vegetation of the mangrove swamp that was destroyed when the company cleared the paths for seismic exploration. In 2000, SPDC completed seventeen environmental impact assessments and fourteen environmental evaluation reports that were approved by Nigeria's Federal Ministry of Environment (*2000 Annual Report*). The company also claims its rapid response capability to oil spillage increased to 75 percent in 2000. Further, SPDC said that, in 2000, it initiated environmental awareness training for more than sixteen thousand of its staff, contractors, host communities, and students.

Although some Shell public relations strategies in response to the Niger Delta crisis are indeed commendable, generally speaking, the overall effort can be characterized as "public information" (Grunig & Hunt, 1984). Such a strategy consists of one-way communication aimed at making SPDC look good through propaganda and dissemination of only favorable information. Shell has not only overrepresented its community development projects but, more important, has also consistently failed to admit or volunteer negative information, including the deleterious environmental effects of its flaring of gas and oil spillage.

TABLE 12.6   *SPDC Community Projects Spending—*
Niger Delta, 2000 (in millions of U.S. dollars)

	U.S. Dollars in millions
Health care	$5.9
Vocational training	1.2
Science teacher scheme	0.3
Agriculture	1.9
Water scheme	8.5
Classroom blocks	2.9
Science blocks	0.2
Roads/bridges	33.6
Market stalls	0.3
Science equipment	0.5
School furniture	0.7
Town halls	0.2
Electrification	1.0
Secondary scholarships	2.5
Grants and donations	0.5
Others	0.03
Total	60.23

Source: SPDC *2000 People and Environmental Annual Report*

As far as its community development efforts are concerned, although the company has readily publicized its agricultural and health projects in some Niger Delta communities through the media, it has not concomitantly admitted that the projects lack sustainability. For example, one of Shell's numerous public relations press releases said that, by 1996, SPDC's seed multiplication farm projects in the Delta had benefited some seventy-nine thousand farmers in the region. However, Shell did not say that, until mid-1997, it had neglected to maintain and restore the farm project it started in Bori, Ogoni, in the early 1960s. Omuku (2000), Shell's public relations officer, even observed that, by 1997, only 57 percent of the company's projects were fully functional, whereas another 28 percent were partially functional.

Furthermore, the projects that Shell showcases represent a mere fraction of its profits from Niger Delta operations. For example, Shell's *Annual Community Report* in 1998, detailing the policy thrust of its community relations and its achievements, promotes the company's involvement in development projects in the oil communities. The report (Iyayi, 2000) said

> We continue to play a role in improving living standards in host communities. Our community spending increased by some 37 percent to $43.0 million in 1998, a larger than normal rise which was due to a significant number of high value projects that were undertaken during the year. SPDC's new approach to community development, mentioned in last year's report increasingly focused on long term goals in partnership with the communities themselves. (p. 163)

Although Shell salutes its 37 percent increase in community spending, the report does not say what this percentage represents in relation to the total profits the company made that year from oil drilled and exported from the Niger Delta.

Similarly, a 1996 SPDC press release said that the company had taken over the maintenance and drug supply for the Gokana General Hospital at Terabor and started supplementing staff wages. However, the release did not specify the amount of money spent to supplement wages. Even if the company were to do so by a substantial amount, it would still only constitute an infinitesimal percentage of the millions of dollars SPDC makes daily in profits from oil drilling in the Niger Delta.

Additionally, increases in social spending may barely keep pace with inflation. According to *People and Environment,* a fifty-four-page annual report that publicizes the company's socioenvironmental activities in the Niger Delta, Shell increased its expenditure for community development from $52 million in 1999 to $60 million in 2002 (*The Shell Bulletin,* 2001). But the SPDC document did not say that the $8 million increase in community development expenditures amounted to little or nothing in view of the spiraling inflation in Nigeria's dependent economy.

Finally, it should be noted that, although the company had the capability to embark on community development projects, it did not begin to do so until the crisis in the Niger Delta erupted. It is also significant that SPDC began to inform the public of its involvement in the socioeconomic development of the communities only once the crisis had erupted. A truly sound corporate public relations philosophy instead would incorporate two-way communication between SPDC and its host communities in which the latter are given opportunities to voice their concerns, as well as being continually informed of Shell's socioeconomic development efforts.

Conclusion

Shell's response to the Niger Delta crisis has been a public relations disaster. By and large, Shell's initial denials of complicity in oil spillage, environmental degradation, and ecological despoliation, its use of violence and force, as well as its involvement in socioeconomic development projects in the Niger Delta that were not sustainable, have only deepened the crisis rather than resolving it. Shell has lost millions of dollars through the disruption of its operations, destruction of its equipment, and payment of ransom for those workers kidnapped by irate community neighbors. These losses, consequences of questionable public relations strategies, should serve as object lessons for indigenous and other multinational corporations operating in less developed countries. Most important, Shell has lost the confidence of its host communities.

Moreover, as Iyayi (2000) notes, Shell's actions have heightened community protests against the company and its partners:

> Although the purpose of violence is to demoralize the peoples of the Niger Delta and to force them to abandon their protests, it is significant that protest has, in fact, increased. The increase in protest has come not only from the activities of the oil companies but from a growing level of awareness in the communities about the implication of these activities and how, over the years, the ruling elite in Nigeria has looted the revenue from the oil for the benefit of members of the ruling elite. (p. 167)

Arguably, the Nigerian government must share the blame for the situation in the Niger Delta. As a key investor in Nigeria, Shell has had a sweetheart relationship with successive governments since the company discovered oil in 1956. A substantial portion of foreign exchange earnings supporting Nigeria's economy comes from oil, about half of which Shell produces. The government's share in taxes, royalties, and equity is $13.92 per barrel (with an oil price of $19 per barrel), representing about 90 percent of Shell's net revenues from operations. Given such a healthy ongoing deposit into the Nigerian Federation Account, it is not surprising that the government hardly criticizes Shell for its environmental pollution, ecological despoliation, and woeful community relations in the Niger Delta. The partnership also helps explain why federal and state governments respond rapidly to Shell's requests for the use of force to disperse and suppress demonstrations in the Delta region. Shell sees community demonstrations as disruptive to its operations and profits. It is ironic that Shell, which prides itself as a human-rights-minded multinational, has supported such autocratic Nigerian government abuses in the Niger Delta. Moreover, inasmuch as Nigeria has joined the family of democratic nations, the new government must eschew the arbitrary and extralegal actions that have led too often to human rights abuses during various military dictatorships. Indeed, it would behoove both Shell and the Nigerian government to pursue policies in the Niger Delta that are congruous with democratic values—respect for human rights, cultural values, morality, transparency, accountability, openness, dialogue, and collaboration.

Shell's Niger Delta public relations policy instead should incorporate two-way symmetrical communication to build understanding between SPDC and its key publics. Although the model has been criticized by some as impractical (Cancel, Cameron, Sallot, & Mitrook, 1997; Leichty & Springston, 1993; Miller, 1989; Pavlik, 1989; Rakaw, 1989; Van de Meiden, 1993), its propensity to help secure symbiotic changes in the behaviors of both an organization and its publics (Grunig, 1989; Grunig & Grunig, 1989, 1992; Grunig

& Hunt, 1984) could enable Shell and its host communities to resolve the conflict in a mutually satisfactory manner.

For example, a major attraction of the model is that it allows public relations practitioners to use research to learn how members of an organization's publics perceive the organization. This research can then be used to advise an organization's management on public relations policies and actions and how they can be changed to better serve the public interest (Grunig & Hunt, 1984). Additionally, research can be used to determine how well members of an organization's publics understand management and how well management understands its publics. This can help an organization in choosing specific communication objectives (Grunig & Hunt, 1984). Further, inasmuch as this approach sensitizes an organization to its publics, the process, ultimately, can make it more effective in achieving its goals and objectives.

The model, moreover, consists of dialogue rather than monologue (Grunig & Hunt, 1984) and allows the question of what is right to be settled through negotiation, communication, and compromise and not through force, manipulation, coercion, or violence (Grunig, 1989); this is particularly important because every contending party in a conflict believes its position on issues is right. Grunig (2000) has argued that symmetrical public relations professionals lift organizations above the wrangle in the marketplace to help them understand that they will further their self-interest more by tempering advocacy with collective collaboration. According to Grunig (2000), not only will organizations accomplish their goals more often when they engage in collaboration with their publics but they also will develop a reputation of being moral and socially responsible.

Finally, and most important, the fact that the model bases public relations on negotiation and compromise makes it more ethical than any other model (Grunig & Grunig, 1992). It enables an organization to treat members of its publics as equals and to respect them as fellow human beings (Grunig, 1989). This is why it can be argued that SPDC should use this model in its public relations campaign in dealing with the Niger Delta crisis. By so doing, for example, Shell would change its noninvolvement in sustainable development in its host communities and cease its use of violence as a strategy. Such an approach would encourage the Delta communities concomitantly to also change and eschew arson and destruction of Shell's equipment as well as kidnapping, demonstrations, and hostage taking of SPDC's staff.

Overall, Shell's public relations strategies should be guided by a policy of openness, honesty, and dialogue with its host communities. Only in this way can SPDC find an early end to the crisis. At the same time, such an approach can enable Shell to build, preserve, sustain, and maintain a positive, long-term relationship with the residents of the Niger Delta. According to Grunig and Huang (1999) the development and maintenance of relationships should be the goal of an organization's public relations strategies.

Further, Shell's public relations policy in the Niger Delta should consist of more than listening and dialogue inasmuch as Grunig (2000) admits that two-way symmetrical practice is not the only characteristic of excellent public relations. Rather, SPDC's public relations strategies should be guided by ethical considerations as articulated by Kruckeberg (2000) and Martinson (1995–1996). Such considerations—collaboration, honesty, openness, ethics, and respect for cultural values—should be at the center of SPDC's public relations policy thrust in the future. This will enable the company and its host communities to build mutual trust and understanding, thus reducing the likelihood of further crises in the future.

In addition, SPDC should develop a sound crisis communication plan. Crises seem almost inevitable in today's business dealings with increasingly diverse stakeholders. This is why Birch (1994), Gonzalez-Herrero and Pratt (1995), Dyer (1995), and Zoch and Duhe (1997) have articulated the need for corporations to develop crisis communication plans. Caponigro (2000), for example, points out that a crisis communication plan enables an organization to know what to say and do once a crisis erupts, a point underscored by Benoit (1995, 1997), Combs (1995), Combs and Holladay (1996), and Adams (2000).

Shell's actions during the crisis do not indicate that it had a sound crisis communication plan. The company did not open any lines of communication with members of its host communities. Rather, it became defensive, first through denial and then through violence. At the onset of the Niger Delta crisis, Shell denied that environmental pollution in the host communities was related to its crude oil drilling activities. It claimed that oil spillage, though of concern, was not caused by Shell but by saboteurs in the host communities who thought that spilling oil would gain them monetary compensation from the company or the government. Then, it used coercion, force, and violence against the communities. As Seitel (2001) observes, the "key communication principle in dealing with crisis is not to clam up when disaster strikes but to provide prompt, frank and full information" (p. 213), a point that Barton (1996) also confirms.

The absence of an effective communication plan exacerbated Shell's ability to contain the crisis when it erupted. In developing an effective crisis plan SPDC instead should examine the following model designed by Birch (1994, p. 32):

Precrisis
- Develop crisis plan
- Train, with simulated crisis situation
- Create relationships with potential allies and adversaries
- Build/enhance corporate reputation

Crisis
- Identify problem; set up target group feedback
- Control the process and message
- Work the plan
- Respond quickly, honestly, people-to-people
- Communicate continually; confirmed facts only

Postcrisis
- Continue maintaining relationships
- Continue proactive communications
- Continue reputation building

According to Adams (2000), during a crisis, everything an organization says or does should reflect concern. But when the Niger Delta crisis broke out, SPDC's behavior did not reflect any concern for its host communities. Instead, SPDC's concern and sympathy was not shown until much later when the crisis was out of control. Newsom, Turk, and

Kruckeberg (2000) have noted that responses from a company or organization that seem devoid of sympathy for victims are serious mistakes.

It can be argued that SPDC's lack of sympathy, responsibility, and concern for the inhabitants of its host communities was a strategic public relations error. As Sha'aba (1998) argues, Shell should have obeyed environmental laws, used globally accepted techniques, and returned, by way of community-oriented projects, a portion of the $3 per barrel that it earned from the millions of barrels it extracted (p. 78).

Today, SPDC says it has reversed its behavior toward the oil-producing communities in the Niger Delta region. In this regard, a spokesperson for the company, Omuku (2000), said inter alia:

> To maintain our relevance in the ever-changing developmental needs of the people, SPDC has changed its social investment approach to one which puts the communities in the driving seat. It is based on participatory planning of each community's development aspiration, implementation and monitoring of community projects. The approach, which is fashioned to deliver increased incomes and improve living standards, will also boost the confidence and self reliance of the communities, delivering thereby a high sense of ownership of the projects. (p. 204)

Admittedly, Shell has contributed in some tangible ways to the welfare of the local communities, but when compared with its profits from the oil-producing areas, these contributions are paltry. The crisis has highlighted some areas of neglect in Shell's community relations. One of those areas is a lack of sensitivity and sympathy for community concerns. A continuous monitoring of the communities to ascertain their perceptions and opinions of SPDC's performance will enable Shell to anticipate any future crisis and to take steps to stop or minimize its effects. Community monitoring can only be effective if opinion leaders and influential community groups are encouraged to participate in the planning of community development projects or events. Such partnerships should help reduce the possibility of crisis in the future.

Notes

1. Jiti Ogunye, Preface. In W. Raji, A. Ale, & E. Akinsola (Eds.), *Boiling point: A CDHR publication on the crises in the oil producing communities in Nigeria* (pp. i–vi). Lagos: Committee for Defense of Human Rights.

2. *Report of the commission appointed to enquire into the fears of minorities and the means of allaying them.* London: HMSO, 1958, p. 3.

3. For a detailed understanding of Jibril Aminu's observation about the plight of the Niger Delta region, see *The Vanguard,* November 4, 1994.

4. For a detailed understanding of the contents of the protest letter, see *The Guardian,* February 18, 2002.

5. Interview with Emeka Wopara, Secretary of Rumuobiakani Youth Club, July 18, 2001.

Discussion Questions

1. How would you describe the major problem facing SPDC in Nigeria?

2. How would you evaluate Shell's initial response to the crisis? Should the company have done anything differently? If so, what?

3. How much of SPDC's behavior in the wake of the Niger Delta crisis was a result of a lack of preparation? Of arrogance? Using this crisis as an example, compare and contrast the attitudes of multinational corporations in other host communities in less developed countries and in more advanced Western cultures.

4. What could Shell have done to avoid the crisis?

5. How would you describe Shell's postcrisis communication strategy? Develop a public relations/crisis communications strategy for Shell's managing director to use in the event of another crisis.

6. Do you think Shell can rebuild its credibility with its host communities? If so, how?

References

Adams, W. (2000). Responding to the media during a crisis: It's what you say and when you say it. *Public Relations Quarterly, 45*(1), 26–28.

Agbese, P. (1995). Nigeria's environment: Crises, consequences, and responses. In P. Dwivedi, & D. Vajpeyi (Eds.), *Environmental policies in the third world: A comparative analysis* (pp. 125–144). Westport, CT: Greenwood Press.

Agbese, P., & Ogbondah, C. (1988). Environmental justice in Nigeria: Beyond ethnic mobilization. *International Journal of African Studies, 1*(2), 73–90.

Akaruese, L. (1998). Crises in oil yielding communities: Causes and dimensions. In O. Olorode et al. (Eds.), *Ken Saro-Wiwa and the crises of the Nigerian state* (pp. 144–156). Lagos, Nigeria: Committee for the Defense of Human Rights.

Ashton-Jones. N. (1998). *The ecosystems of the Niger Delta: An ERA handbook.* Ibadan: Kraft Books.

Awobajo, S. (1981, November). *An analysis of oil spill incidents in Nigeria: 1976–1980.* Paper presented at the Seminar on the Petroleum Industry and the Nigerian Environment, Petroleum Training Institute, Warri, Nigeria.

Barton, L. (1996). *Community relations handbook.* J. Zukowski (Ed.). Boston: NYNEX Properties Company.

Benoit, W. (1995). *Accounts, excuses, and apologies: A theory of image restoration strategies.* Albany: State University of New York Press.

Benoit, W. (1997). Image repair discourse and crisis communication. *Public Relations Review, 23,* 177–180.

Birch, J. (1994). New factors in crisis planning and response. *Public Relations Quarterly, 39*(1), 31–34.

Cancel, A., Cameron, G., Sallot, L., & Mitrook, M. (1997). It depends: A contingency theory of accommodation in public relations. *Journal of Public Relations Research, 9,* 31–63.

Caponigro, J. R. (2000). *The crisis counselor: A step-by-step guide to managing a business crisis.* Lincolnwood, IL: NTC/Contemporary Books.

CDHR: Report of the committee for the defense of human rights. (1998). Lagos, Nigeria: Committee for the Defense of Human Rights.

Combs, W. (1995). Choosing the right words: The development of guidelines for the selection of the "appropriate" crisis response strategies. *Management Communication Quarterly, 8,* 447–476.

Combs, W., & Holladay, S. (1996). Communication and attributions in a crisis: An experimental study of crisis communication. *Journal of Public Relations Research, 8,* 279–295.

Corzine, R. (1996, July 6). Shell faces up to distrust in delta province. *Financial Times,* p. 18.

Dyer, S. (1995). Getting people into the crisis communication. *Public Relations Quarterly, 40*(3), 38–41.

Fregene, P. (2000). Oil producing communities; First hand testimonies: How Nigeria plundered and underdeveloped the Itsekiri people. In W. Raji, A. Ale, & E. Akinsola (Eds.), *Boiling point: A CDHR publication on the crisis in the oil producing communites in Nigeria* (pp. 111–121). Lagos, Nigeria: Committee for Defense of Human Rights.

Gonzalez-Herrero, A., & Pratt, C. (1995). How to manage a crisis before—or when it hits. *Public Relations Quarterly, 40*(1), 25–30.

Grunig, J. E. (1989). Symmetrical presuppositions as a framework for public relations theory. In C. Botan & V. Hazleton (Eds.), *Public relations theory* (pp. 17–44). Hillsdale, NJ: Lawrence Erlbaum Associates.

Grunig, J. E. (2000). Collectivism, collaboration, and societal corporatism as core professional values in public relations. *Journal of Public Relations Research, 12*(1), 23–48.

Grunig, J. E., & Grunig, L. A. (1989). Toward a theory of public relations behavior of organizations: Review of a program of research. In J. E. Grunig & L. A. Grunig (Eds.), *Public relations research annual* (Vol. 1, pp. 27–66). Hillsdale, NJ: Lawrence Erlbaum Associates.

Grunig, J. E., & Grunig, L. A. (1992). Models of public relations and communication. In J. E. Grunig (Ed.), *Excellence in public relations and communication management* (pp. 285–326). Hillsdale, NJ: Lawrence Erlbaum Associates.

Grunig, J., & Huang, Y. (1999). From organizational effectiveness to relationship indicators: Antecedents of relationships, public relations strategies, and relationship outcomes. In J. Ledingham & S. Bruning (Eds.), *Relationship management: A relational approach to public relations* (pp. 23–53). Mahwah, NJ: Lawrence Erlbaum Associates.

Grunig, J. E., & Hunt, T. (1984). *Managing public relations.* New York: CBS College Publishing.

Horsfall, A. (1999). *The OMPADEC dream.* London: Imprint Publications.

Human Rights Watch. (1999). *The price of oil: Corporate responsibility and human rights violations in Nigeria's oil producing communities.* New York: Human Rights Watch.

Hutchful, E. (1985a). Oil companies and environmental pollution in Nigeria. In C. Ake (Ed.), *Political economy of Nigeria.* London: Longman.

Hutchful, E. (1985b). Texaco's Funiwa-5 oil well blowout, Rivers State, Nigeria. *Journal of African Marxists, 7,* 51–62.

Ihonvbere, J. (2000). A recipe for perpetual crisis: The Nigerian state in the Niger Delta question. In W. Raji, A. Ale, & E. Akinsola (Eds.), *Boiling point: A CDHR publication on the crisis in the oil producing communities in Nigeria* (pp. 73–109). Lagos, Nigeria: Committee for Defense of Human Rights.

Ikein, A. (1990). *The impact of oil on a developing country.* Westport, CT: Praeger.

Ikporukpo, C. (1985). Management of oil pollution resources in Nigeria. *Journal of Environmental Management, 20*(1), 199–206.

Iyayi, F. (2000). Oil companies and community relations in Nigeria. In W. Raji, A. Ale, & E. Akinsola (Eds.), *Boiling point: A CDHR publication on the crisis in the oil producing communities in Nigeria* (pp. 151–178). Lagos, Nigeria: Committee for Defense of Human Rights.

Kruckeberg, D. (2000). The public relations practitioner's role in practicing strategic ethics. *Public Relations Quarterly, 45*(3), 35–39.

Leichty, G., & Springston, J. (1993). Reconsidering public relations models. *Public Relations Review, 19,* 327–340.

Lolomari, O. (1995). Oil companies and oil communities as partners in development. In K. Soremekun (Ed.), *Perspectives in the Nigerian oil industry* (pp. 38–45). Lagos: Amkara Books.

Martinson, D. (1995–1996). Client partiality and third parties: An ethical dilemma for public relations practitioners. *Public Relations Quarterly, 40*(4), 41–44.

Miller, G. (1989). Persuasion and public relations: "Two Ps" in a pod. In C. Botan & V. Hazleton, Jr. (Eds.), *Public relations theory* (pp. 45–66). Hillsdale, NJ: Lawrence Erlbaum Associates.

Newsom, D., Turk, J. V., & Kruckeberg, D. (2002). *This is PR: The realities of public relations* (7th ed.). Belmont, CA: Wadsworth Thompson.

Nigerian Environmental Study/Action Team. (1991). *Nigeria's threatened environment: A national profile.* Ibadan: NEST.

Nigerian National Petroleum Corporation. (1995). *Proceedings of the 1985 national oil seminar.* Lagos: NNPC.

Nwauzi, L. (2000). Etche and oil exploration in the Niger Delta. In W. Raji, A. Ale, & E. Akinsola (Eds.), *Boiling point: A CDHR publication on the crises in the oil producing communities in Nigeria* (pp. 133–143). Lagos, Nigeria: Committee for Defense of Human Rights.

Ogbondah, C. (1999). The Ogoni inferno and fire fighters: Has the government's public relations campaign extinguished the flame? In J. VanSlyke Turk & L. Scanlan (Eds.), *Fifteen case studies in international public relations* (pp. 153–168). Gainesville, FL: The Institute of Public Relations.

Ogbondah, C. (2001, May). *Nigerian media and ecological protection in the Niger Delta: A proposal for more socially responsible environmental reportage.* Paper presented at the Conference on Environmental Issues and Development in Africa, The Center for African Studies, Ohio State University, Columbus.

The Ogoni Study Group. (1995). *Response to Shell activities in Ogoniland.* Port Harcourt, Nigeria: The Ogoni Study Group.

Omuku, P. (2000). A representative perspective of oil corporations. In W. Raji, A. Ale, & E. Akinsola (Eds.), *Boiling point: A CDHR publication on the crises in the oil producing communities in Nigeria* (pp. 197–205). Lagos, Nigeria: Committee for Defense of Human Rights.

Onyenwenwa, I. (2000). Oil mineral and the Egbema paradox: Unmasking the crises. In W. Raji, A. Ale, & E. Akinsola (Eds.), *Boiling point: A CDHR publication on the crises in the oil producing communities in Nigeria* (pp. 122–132). Lagos, Nigeria: Committee for Defense of Human Rights.

Osaghae, E. (1995). The Ogoni uprising: Oil, politics, minority agitation and the future of the Nigerian state. *African Affairs, 94*(376).

Oyerinde, O. (1998). Oil disempowerment and resistance in the Niger Delta. In O. Olorode et al. (Eds.), *Ken Saro-Wiwa and the crises of the Nigerian state* (pp. 55–70). Lagos, Nigeria: Committee for the Defense of Human Rights.

Pavlik, J. (1989). *The concept of symmetry in the education of public relations practitioners.* Paper presented at the International Communication Association (ICA) conference, San Francisco.

Rakaw, L. (1989). From the feminization of public relations to the promise of feminism. In E. Toth & C. Gline (Eds.), *Beyond the velvet ghetto* (pp. 287–298). San Francisco: International Association of Business Communicators.

Saro-Wiwa, K. (1992). *Genocide in Nigeria: The Ogoni tragedy.* London: Saros International Publishers.

Seitel, F. (2001). *The practice of public relations.* Upper Saddle, NJ: Prentice Hall.

Sha'aba, R. (1998). MOSOP and the Ogoni struggle. In O. Olorode et al. (Eds.), *Ken Saro-Wiwa and the crises of the Nigerian state* (pp. 71–85). Lagos, Nigeria: Committee for the Defense of Human Rights.

Shell in Ogoni youth training initiative. (February 1997). SPDC Press Release.

Shell Petroleum Development Company of Nigeria Limited (SPDC). 2000 Annual Report.

Shell Petroleum Development Company of Nigeria Limited (SPDC). 2000 People and Environment Annual Report.

Shell Petroleum Development Company of Nigeria Limited (SPDC). 2001 Annual Report.

Soremekun, K., & Obadare, E. (1998). Politics of oil corporations in post-colonial Nigeria. In O. Olorode et al. (Eds.), *Ken Saro-Wiwa and the crises of the Nigerian state* (pp. 36–54). Lagos, Nigeria: Committee for the Defense of Human Rights.

Taiwo, F. (2000). Nigeria and other oil producing countries: A comparative analysis of oil revenue sharing formula. In W. Raji, A. Ale, & E. Akinsola (Eds.), *Boiling point: A Cdhr publication on the crises in the oil producing communities in Nigeria* (pp. 207–226). Lagos, Nigeria: Committee for Defense of Human Rights.

Tebekaemi, T. (1982). *The twelve-day revolution.* Benin City, Nigeria: Idodo Umeh Publishers.

Van de Meiden, A. (1993). Public relations and "other" modalities of professional communication: Asymmetrical presuppositions for a new theoretical discussion. *International Public Relations Review, 16,* 8–11.

World Bank. (1995). *Environmental economic study of the Niger Delta, Nigeria.* Document prepared for the World Bank by Carl Bro. International, Denmark.

World Press Review. February 1996, p. 28.

Zoch, L., & Duhe, S. (1997). Feeding the media during a crisis: A nationwide look. *Public Relations Quarterly, 42*(3), 15–19.

13

Applying Reconstructed and Social Responsibility Theories to Foreign Direct Investment and Public Relations for Social Change in Sub-Saharan Africa

Cornelius B. Pratt

Charles Okigbo

Key Points

- The reconstructed theory of public relations holds that organizations have challenges that arise from people's sense of anomie and disconnection, that is, a loss of organization–public engagement and minuscule relationships between them.
- Social responsibility refers to the expectations that publics have of an organization as a meaningful contributor to society's interests.
- The development of sub-Saharan Africa can benefit immensely from foreign direct investment (FDI) by individuals, by corporations, by other groups, and by rich countries, such as members of the group of eight—Britain, Canada, France, Germany, Italy, Japan, Russia, and the United States.
- FDI as a developmental tool can benefit from professional public relations practices, which are guided by reconstructed theory and by the principles of the social responsibility of organizations.
- Our communication reflects our worldviews and so does our public relations.

The purpose of this chapter is twofold. First, it responds to a call by Sriramesh, Kim, and Takasaki (1999) "for the need to expand our knowledge of public relations in other parts of the world" (p. 289). Second, it provides propositions on an emerging theory of public relations for developing countries in light of an earlier observation by Botan (1992), namely, that multinational corporations' use of transborder public relations can result in significant harm to their constituencies in the long run. Both purposes are accomplished within the context of developing a public relations theory of sustainable development in developing countries.

This chapter has six sections. The first outlines the chapter's theoretical framework, identifying the importance of applying Kruckeberg and Starck's (1988) and Starck and Kruckeberg's (2001) reconstructed theory and the social responsibility theory to public relations for social change in sub-Saharan Africa. The second outlines the region's potential for, and benefits of, attracting foreign investment, even as it notes that, of all the world's regions, none is in more dire straits than sub-Saharan Africa. Such a notion is premised on the far-reaching contributions of businesses to economies worldwide and to national development in developing regions in particular. Further, it recognizes foreign direct investment as a key player in promoting social change. The third section reviews social change issues and developmental models that have historically provided the framework for social change in developing countries in general. It supports the evolving notion iterated by Abrokwaa (1999) that African-oriented development strategies of the twenty-first century abandon "imported Western development strategies in favor of African-oriented ones if any meaningful strides are to be made to better the conditions of its suffering masses" (p. 664). The fourth section discusses the integrated practice of public relations in sub-Saharan Africa and argues that, given the worldviews of such practice, both the reconstructed and social responsibility theories be applied to the practice if communication practitioners are to contribute meaningfully to sustainable development. The fifth section discusses some of the characteristics of public relations in Africa as a preamble to the sixth section, which outlines worldviews and a number of theoretical implications for identifying a point of departure for building propositions for a general theory of public relations for development in developing countries. A list of useful public relations Web sites follows at the conclusion of this chapter.[1]

Theoretical Framework

This section presents two society-grounded theories that guide this chapter: Kruckeberg and Starck's (1988) and Starck and Kruckeberg's (2001) reconstructed theory of public relations and the theory of the social responsibility of organizations.

The Reconstructed Theory

The reconstructed theory argues that the root of a number of organizations' communication problems lies in humankind's growing sense of anomie, which can be reduced through modern communications that build and enhance a desirable sense of community. FDI-related activities in sub-Saharan Africa historically have challenged cultural and economic systems, necessitating social changes and threatening a sense of national communication, while paying lip service to formulating community ties. According to the Kruckeberg and Starck (1988) theory, then

> an appropriate approach to community relations should be an active and direct attempt to restore and maintain a sense of community. Only through such a conceptual approach does the practice of community relations deal directly with the problems shared by the organization and its geographic public. (pp. 82–83)

This theory is relevant to understanding development communication—the process of employing communication to bring about positive changes in a community. Development must engender a sense of community (not anomie) and promote mutual relationships between organizations and their key publics. This is not always the case, which explains the high incidence of nationalization of multinational enterprises by various African governments, such as Uganda, Nigeria, and Zimbabwe. Since 2000, there have been violent confrontations between white Zimbabwean farmers and black settlers. The latter erroneously perceived the former as "perpetual foreigners," whose continuing presence in Zimbabwe was associated with that country's colonial history. There was a glaringly missing sense of community between the white farming community and black settlers: White farmers, in the view of the majority black population, had failed to cultivate a true sense of community and to identify with the blacks. Whites had failed to challenge the status quo. Negative perceptions and a poor image contributed to diminishing productivity, to social conflicts, and to an overall decline in Zimbabwe's economy. Building a desirable sense of community, as stated in the reconstructed theory of public relations, can resolve many issues that multinational organizations experience in their business relations in sub-Saharan Africa. Building such relations is, in effect, an expectation that borders on both social desirability and responsibility.

The Social Responsibility Theory of Organizations

Social responsibility is a universal ethical principle for communicators, as well as a desirable strategy for organizations. Peterson, Schramm, and Siebert (1971) explain this in the context of media philosophies as one of four typologies of press systems. That typology refers to the notion that the press is obligated to fulfill certain essential functions, for example, the public's right to know. For corporations in Africa that translates into becoming involved in some development activities not directly related, at least in the short run, to the well-being of one's institution. In developing countries, that responsibility is usually interpreted as being responsive to a nation's developmental needs.

Carroll (1979) defines an organization's social responsibilities as "the expectations or responsibilities that society has for business" (p. 500). In his view, it has four parts—legal, economic, discretionary, and ethical. Organizations, in general, are constituted bodies governed by and subject to legal requirements. Like the public at large, they are obligated to demonstrate respect for the laws of the land, and, as large corporate entities, serve as models for upholding those laws.

Economic responsibilities are the most important of the four; they require that organizations contribute to the economic well-being of the constituencies they serve; they should provide jobs, services, and products; and they should play their part in fueling economies.

Discretionary (or volitional) responsibilities are those that do not have clear-cut expectations from society but are left to an organization's judgment and choice. Organizations engage in them because of the need to demonstrate their civic responsibilities.

Ethical responsibilities transcend legal boundaries, raising issues that are (a) deontological, which emphasizes adherence to moral duties without consideration for *only* the consequences or results of an act; (b) utilitarian, which emphasizes actions or consequences that lead to the greatest happiness for the greatest number; or (c) morally relativistic, which is based on the notion that all moral values are good ("I'll determine what's right for me, and you can decide what's right for you" [Day, 1997, p. 56]). L'Etang (1994) underscores the implications of all three for corporate social responsibility, arguing that corporations should find moral justifications for their activities and ensure that their practice of corporate social responsibility live up to claims made publicly by their public relations staff.

Social responsibility as a guiding principle for individual and corporate activities is well respected in African communities. This is as much the case in business organizations as in the media. Okigbo (1994) argued that whereas the single most important philosophical value in U.S. journalism is freedom, its African equivalent is responsibility. But it is the responsibility as defined by the community or group institutions that are supreme in African communities. The notion of the self, that is, autonomy, is counterproductive to the African penchant for communitarianism, which, again, explains the African deference to and reverence for group institutions. Triandis (1995) and Gudykunst (1997) describe the individual–collectivism phenomenon as the cultural variability in communication. Moemeka (1997, 1998) distinguishes among individualistic, collectivist, and communalistic cultures. Both individualistic and collectivist cultures, on the one hand, are common in industrialized societies, where emphasis is on the individual; even in situations where collective actions are taken in collectivist societies, the group temporarily convenes to achieve a specific goal. In communalistic societies, on the other hand, "the community is given pride of place as a supreme power over its individual members" (Moemeka, 1997, p. 174), unlike the situation in societies where the emphasis is on the individual.

Thus, communalistic African cultures lend themselves to group supremacy—a kind of *groupthink.* This is the "mode of thinking that people engage in when they are deeply involved in a cohesive in-group, when the members' strivings for unanimity override their motivation to realistically appraise alternative courses of action" (Janis, 1972, p. 9). For example, many Africans think and behave in ways consistent with group norms and thought patterns (Nwankwo & Nzelibe, 1990). Obeng-Quaidoo (1985) referred to the phenomenon as the nonindividuality of the African. Similarly, Moemeka (1997) contends that the African is guided by the cultural belief in "I am because we are" (p. 174). Communalistic values often express themselves in professional communication activities that illustrate a belief in utilitarianism—providing the greatest good to the greatest number of people in the community. Nigerian journalists showed preference for utilitarian ethics in editorials about development issues (Pratt, 1990; Pratt & McLaughlin, 1990). African communication professionals tend to embrace *groupthink,* social responsibility, and utilitarianism.

This is not peculiar to African communities. Societal culture is reported to influence public relations in India (Sriramesh, 1992), Greece (Lyra, 1991), and Taiwan (Huang, 1990). That influence brings to the fore an interplay between culture and communication, and between communication and business. These relationships have implications for public relations practice and the development of FDI in Africa. FDI is a requirement for sustainable development of Africa, as addressed in the next section. Promoting the investment potential of sub-Saharan Africa requires the application of public relations strategies that are grounded in principles and theories.

Investment Potential of Sub-Saharan Africa

A renaissance of sorts—a reformist tide propelled by corporate-sensitive investment policies and civil liberties—is occurring in Africa, particularly in the sub-Saharan region. The region is readying itself to reap the benefits of that development fervor. The World Bank calls for a "business plan" and an increase in governments' consultations with business as key elements in the region's four-pronged action plan to stimulate investment: (a) improve governance and conflict management; (b) increase equity and investment in its people; (c) increase competitiveness and diversification of its economies; and (d) attract better support for the international community, while reducing dependency on aid (The World Bank Group, 2000).

In an address at the Foreign Press Center, in Washington, DC, on February 23, 1999, U.S. Trade Representative Charlene Barshefsky (1999) said:

> In many African nations, governments have adopted economic reforms, from liberalizing exchange rates, to privatizing state enterprises, reducing subsidies and cutting barriers to trade and investment. These have been joined by free elections in many countries. And the early results are clear: since 1994, inflation has dropped, growth rates have doubled, and our own exports to Africa are up by nearly 50%. African exports to the U.S. have risen as well. (p. 2)

Several recent events underscore renewed corporate interest in the region's business potential and the U.S. government's resolve to contribute more directly to its economic revitalization.

First, in mid-March 1999, eighty-six ministers from forty-six sub-Saharan countries held a historic meeting with then-President Clinton and some of his top officials. It was an opportunity for the African ministers to discuss the U.S. government's commitment to trading with, and investing in, the region. In April 1999, the Corporate Council on Africa sponsored a conference in Houston, Texas, titled "Attracting Capital to Africa." It was attended by more than 750 U.S. executives, many of whom represented Fortune 500 companies, eight African heads of state, and officials from twenty-two African countries. At that conference, five African countries—Botswana, Egypt, Ghana, Mauritius, and Namibia—received the 1999 Global Marketplace Awards for "continued efforts to open their economies to the world market" (USA ready, 1999). The council's third biennial U.S.–Africa Business Summit held September 16 through 20, 2001, underscores the continent's improving economic and political stability that is attracting foreign investment and stimulating new domestic economic ventures.

Second, by passing the African Growth and Opportunity Bill on May 18, 2000, the U.S. government demonstrated its firm commitment to increasing economic growth in Africa and to accelerating integration of the region into global markets (that trade pact is now commonly referred to as Africa's equivalent of the North American Free Trade Agreement, which has expanded trading opportunities between the United States and Mexico). It is potentially a boon to foreign investment. It authorizes quota- and duty-free imports, particularly textiles and apparel, from forty-eight sub-Saharan African countries for ten years. In return, the region has pledged to lift controls on investment by U.S. corporations, to make free-market reforms of their economies, and to show progress toward institutionalizing civil liberties. The continent is expected to benefit through improved access to U.S. markets and increased U.S. investment that might be worth more than U.S.$650 million annually.

Third, in February 1999, the U.S. government signed a Trade and Investment Framework Agreement (TIFA) with Ghana and with South Africa. TIFA was inteded to establish the platform for broadening trade relations. A similar agreement was signed July 1999 with Egypt.

Fourth, even before congressional approval of the African Growth and Opportunity Bill, two thousand African Americans met in Accra, Ghana, in May 1999 at the Fifth African African-American summit. With the theme, "Business, trade and investment," the summit also attracted twelve African heads of state, five vice presidents, and more than five thousand government officials, business executives, and tourists. At the summit, Ghana's then-President Jerry Rawlings called on African Americans to invest in Africa.

Fifth, during the Organization of African Unity summit in June 1999 in Algiers, Algeria, its Presidential Patrons Group of the Alliance for African Industrialization pledged to offer incentives to domestic and foreign private investors by, among other things, removing all barriers to FDI.

Sixth, the Conference on Industrial Partnerships and Investments in Africa, held October 20 through 21, 1999, in Dakar, Senegal, publicized the fact that Africa had consistently provided the highest return on investment (ROI), yielding more than two and one-half times the world average (Dakar Summit, 1999).

Finally, a summit, "Partnership with the Private Sector for Financing Africa's Growth through NEPAD (The New Partnership for African Development)," held April 15 through 17, 2002, in Dakar, Senegal, provided participants with opportunities to review several public–private projects in information technology, energy and agriculture, trade and finance, and health, among many others. NEPAD is working to attract foreign investment by individuals, by corporations, by other groups, and by rich countries, such as members of the group of eight—Britain, Canada, France, Germany, Italy, Japan, Russia, and the United States.

Efforts to meet Africa's long-term economic goals require, at the minimum, that the region meet three conditions. First, it has to reexamine its domestic, economic, and social policies, and privatize its economies. Second, it must comply with World Trade Organization rules that include cutting tariffs and opening service sectors to foreign investment. Third, it must adopt currency and investment deregulations. To date, many African countries have instituted economic reforms, improved macroeconomic management, liberalized markets and trade, improved private-sector activities, and experienced increased interest from domestic and international business and higher investment.

How Can the Region Be of Benefit to Investors and What Challenges Are They Likely to Face There?

Aside from Africa's preferential policies for exports to the United States and to the European Union, it has vast untapped natural, mineral, and human resources that make it even more of an investment haven. U.S. transnational corporations (TNCs) have made particularly profitable investments there. In 1995, the ROI on their African operations was 35 percent; in 1996, 34 percent; and, in 1997, 25 percent; compared with their average of 12 percent elsewhere (*United Nations,* 1998). In 1995, Japanese firms report average returns of 6 percent on their FDI in Africa, compared with 2 percent for the rest of the world. The ROI for British direct investment increased by 60 percent between 1989 and 1995.

FDI also plays an important role in stimulating economic growth, which creates local jobs, increases demand for exports and services, and reduces abject poverty and civil unrest. Aside from bringing capital to a country, FDI also transfers technology as well as managerial and marketing expertise. Sustained recovery and rapid growth in Africa and its economies' competitiveness will require enormous productive private investment and foreign direct investment (The National Summit on Africa, 1998).

Since the 1980s, FDI has become an important new instrument for integrating countries into the global economy. It is also an increasingly important factor in the economic development of a number of developing countries. According to a UN study on direct investment trends and policies in Africa, many African countries have concluded bilateral treaties with capital exporting countries as part of a policy to improve their investment climate and to attract FDI. By January 1995, about 230 bilateral treaties had been signed by countries in the region (United Nations Conference, 1995).

The Multilateral Investment Guarantee Agency (MIGA), an affiliate of the World Bank, notes that until quite recently many African governments were suspicious of the private sector in general, including those in their own countries. Foreign investors, notably multinational corporations (MNCs), were particularly feared as neocolonialists who sought to exploit Africa's natural resources and peoples.

However, African countries are competing to attract MNCs because their general business climate is improving and the private sector is increasingly regarded as a trusted and an inseparable partner in national development. During the past three and one-half decades, for example, there has been rapid expansion in education, health services, and in physical infrastructure (Lancaster, 1999). There has been an increase in literacy rates; a decline in childhood mortality; and an increase in life expectancy, not to mention an expansion of ports, airports, roads, and communication facilities.

Africa, with low FDI flows relative to other regions, showed more than 600 percent increase in FDI between 1990 and 1997 (see Table 13.1). An estimated U.S.$4.7 billion worth of FDI flowed into Africa (excluding South Africa) in 1997, although that amount was 3 percent of the total worth of FDI flows (U.S.$149 billion) to developing countries and was U.S.$188 million less than that in 1996. South Africa alone received U.S.$1.7 billion in FDI flows, from U.S.$760 million in 1996. Other leading recipients included Nigeria, U.S.$1 billion; Egypt, U.S.$838 million; Morocco, U.S.$588 million; Tunisia, U.S.$368 million; Angola, U.S.$358 million; and Tanzania and Uganda, U.S.$258 million. They all accounted for two-thirds of the total flows into Africa. In all, North Africa accounted for 39 percent in 1997 (up from 29 percent in 1996) and continues to receive higher investment flows than sub-Saharan Africa. Matching the size of Africa's FDI stock against the region's domestic market yields, a 10 percent share, compared with 14 percent for Asia, 18 percent for Latin America and the Caribbean, and 13 percent for Europe, suggests that even small FDI flows (in absolute terms) into Africa can still be significant to its economies (Stocker, 2000).

TABLE 13.1   *FDI Flows to COMESA¹ and SADC² Countries by Year (in millions of U.S. $)*

	1990	1997
Angola	–335	350
Burundi	1	1
Democratic Republic of Congo	–12	1
Egypt	734	891
Ethiopia	12	5
Kenya	57	20
Lesotho	17	29
Madagascar	22	14
Malawi	0	2
Mozambique	9	35
Namibia	29	137
Rwanda	8	1
South Africa	NA	1,725
Sub-Saharan Africa	834	5,222
Tanzania	0	158
Uganda	0	180
Zambia	203	70
Zimbabwe	–12	70

[1]Twenty-one member states of the Common Market for Eastern and Southern Africa: Angola, Burundi, Comoros, Democratic Republic of Congo, Djibouti, Egypt, Eritrea, Ethiopia, Kenya, Madagascar, Malawi, Mauritius, Namibia, Rwanda, Seychelles, Sudan, Swaziland, Tanzania, Uganda, Zambia, and Zimbabwe.

[2]Twelve member states of the Southern African Development Community: Angola, Botswana, Lesotho, Malawi, Mauritius, Mozambique, Namibia, South Africa, Swaziland, Tanzania, Zambia, and Zimbabwe.

Note: Data are not available for six COMESA countries and for two SADC countries.

Source: The World Bank (2000)

To strengthen their economies, sub-Saharan African countries particularly need to attract more FDI. Recent political and economic reforms there have made them more attractive to such investments. Namibia, for example, has an export processing zone (EPZ) that attracts FDI. In only three years, seventy-five national and international enterprises were granted EPZ status. Similarly, Mauritius has an export-oriented economy, an EPZ, an efficient infrastructure, a strong entrepreneurial culture, a National Productivity and Competitiveness Council, and several fiscal and administrative initiatives to attract FDI. Regionally, Africa's investors should have an economic responsibility to the region. They should strive for complementarity between their programs and those of Africa's regional integration schemes, such as the Common Market for Eastern and Southern Africa (COMESA), the Southern Africa Development Community (SADC), and the Southern African Customs Union (Mwenda, 1999).

Unquestionably, to reduce poverty significantly and to attract FDI, the region must have sustained growth. Since 1965, diamond-rich Botswana has had the world's fastest-growing economy, with an average annual growth rate of 13 percent; its government has an average budget surplus of 7.2 percent.

Paradoxically, a number of firms in Africa are becoming transnational, that is, outward investors. Even though African TNCs remain relatively rare and small, their development shows that there are firms in Africa that can be competitive internationally, not only through trade but also through production in foreign markets. Some seek short-term, high-yield investments abroad rather than investing in productive activities in their home countries. South African-based firms lead that development, followed by those from Nigeria. Between 1993 and April 1999, South African companies pledged about U.S.$240 million in investments in Zambia alone. Mauritian investments in Madagascar have already created twenty-five thousand jobs, whereas some Mauritian companies also are investing heavily in Mozambique. Three Southern African Development Community (SADC) countries—Malawi, Mozambique, and Tanzania—are developing the Mtwara transport corridor, an interregional outlet for boosting investment and trade. Projected to be launched early in 2005, it will be a medium for shipping imports and exports from southern Africa to the Tanzanian port of Mtwara, which is being remodeled.

Admittedly, as the World Bank Group (2000) noted in its report released May 31, 2000, the region faces massive challenges that are undermining its progress toward sustainable development, yet the twenty-first century offers the promise of better momentum for development if more effective partnerships between Africa and its development partners can be established. Because the success of these partnerships is rooted in the participation of multinational corporations whose public relations practices tend to be homegrown, they tend to be "ethnocentric" (Botan, 1992, p. 152) and result in significant harm to their hosts in the long run. Public relations in the industrialized countries, on the one hand, tends to focus on outcomes—that is, on its effects on corporate profitability. In Africa, on the other hand, the professional emphasis is on process—that is, how decisions are reached socially and the methods of their implementation. It is, therefore, a premise of this chapter that such partnerships are a global reality; in the African context, their success depends on the strategic application of theories to their constituencies.

Issues in Social Change

Development and social change are two sides of the same coin. Social change, otherwise known as "behavior communication change," has the following hallmarks: directions of change (some ideas or products are good, some are bad), rate of change (some ideas are adopted faster than others are), originality or adoption of a trend that originates from outside a society or organization, enduring or ad hoc (some changes last, others are short-lived), and strategic planning.

Applying this to national development, the goal is to provide the living standards to which a people aspire. It is a situation that enables a society to attain living conditions that are consistent with values that can provide a greater control of its environment. Consequently, development agendas tend to vary from one society or nation to another. Such variation makes comparison of development levels troublesome to some developmental economists. Moreover, some indices of development are not subject to quantitative analyses; hence, comparative analysis tends to be fraught with cross-national inaccuracies. This means, for example, that the heritage and culture of a people cannot be compared with those of another group because such a group may have qualities, nurturing practices, and norms that are unique. Further, indices used by the World Bank to measure a country's economic development—for example, gross national development—ignore the often pervasive nonpecuniary, difficult-to-measure sectors of developing economies (e.g., informal partnerships and networks). Nonetheless, the bank categorizes countries as either developed or developing, based on indices such as gross national product, life expectancy, and the accessibility of educational opportunities to a country's citizens.

Even though our ideas of development may vary, we can explain development planning with recourse to accepted theories or paradigms. The common approaches to development programs have been influenced by a number of development theories and models, which Narula and Pearce (1986) categorized into four types: modernization, interdependency and dependency, basic needs, and communications. The modernization paradigm was proposed in generally similar forms by Lerner (1958), Rogers (1976, 1995), and Inkeles and Smith (1974). It is in two forms: the dominant paradigm of the earlier phase and its revised version, the new paradigm (Narula & Pearce, 1986). The dominant paradigm, on the one hand, equates underdevelopment with poverty and the lack of division of labor, specialization, differentiation, and material goods. Thus, because a number of industrialized nations have substantial evidence of the presence of these indices, the only way for developing nations to move into developed status is for them to acquire these Western attributes of development.

On the other hand, the dominant paradigm holds that, because developing countries' value systems are not conducive to development, modernization can only occur if changes are made in such value systems. Whereas the earlier dominant paradigm is essentially one dimensional in its approach, the new paradigm is relatively multidimensional, examining other factors such as labor-intensive technology and social systems that are also considered keys to development. Melkote (1991) notes that because developmental theories are rooted in Western civilization, their communication approaches have major limitations. For example, developmental approaches need not focus on economic growth and industrialization but on "meeting specific needs of particular poverty groups; fulfilling such basic needs of people as health care, nutrition, sanitation and shelter; . . . and self-determination, self-reliance and cultural autonomy" (p. 176).

In recognizing these failures of the earlier dominant paradigm, "the new paradigm has a less restrictive purview, encompassing labor-intensive technology, decentralization in planning, both domestic and international economic factors, and the characteristics of the local social structures" (Narula & Pearce, 1986, p. 33). The paradigm recognizes the importance of traditional (that is, endogenous) values but calls for their blending with non-local (or exogenous) values.

The second approach to development is the interdependency/dependency model (Narula & Pearce, 1986), a critique of the dominant paradigm's focus on the domestic environment as if it truly hampers development. The interdependency model holds that "the international sociopolitical system decisively determines the course of development within each nation" (Narula & Pearce, 1986, p. 45).

The third category, the basic-needs model, is a commitment to meeting the basic needs of the poor through decentralization and integration. Decentralization is crucial for local autonomy in planning development programs and for communicating with the poor. Integrated development planning requires the restructuring and provision of the infrastructure necessary for attaining community-determined development goals.

Finally, the communication perspective orients development strategists and practitioners to interactions with (or participation in) their environment and with other publics. Melkote (1991) describes the need for such interactions through the use of "another development" in which communication models "allow for knowledge-sharing on a co-equal basis rather than be a top-down transmission of information and persuasion" (p. 270). Of all the theories used in research published between 1987 and 1997 to assess mass media impact on developing nations, the most frequently used was participatory development (Fair & Shah, 1997).

All these perspectives on development provide useful strategies for public relations practitioners who increasingly are being called on to serve on management teams that play key roles in policy and economic decisions that affect the development of nation-states. To meet the challenges of their management positions, they need integrated knowledge of public relations, developmental communication, and management of information technologies. The modern practitioner is much more than a wordsmith; she or he is a strategic thinker, a planner, an executor, an evaluator, and an advocate for both the organization and its publics. Above all, she or he engages in conflict resolution through symmetrical dialogue. Public relations is a coordinated and an integrated practice, which requires that its practitioners be involved at once in several programs: advertising, event participation, sales promotion, direct marketing, and publicity. It is such integration, then, that will enable the practitioner to apply effectively meaningful theories to FDI-related activities and to the role of public relations in fostering economic growth in developing nations.

The Practice of Integrated Communication

In the task of attracting foreign investment to sub-Saharan Africa, integrated communication is desirable in ensuring that positive development develops from unfolding political and economic changes in the region. A coalescence of economic and political factors have created substantial fluctuations in FDI flows to Africa (United Nations Conference, 1995). Nonetheless, seven countries—Botswana, Equatorial Guinea, Ghana, Mozambique, Namibia, Tunisia, and Uganda—are marketing their natural resources and expanding national and regional markets and other conditions to attract foreign investors. Even so, some investors are reluctant to do so because of perceived, exaggerated investment risks. Although there is merit to that perception, Mutharika (1997) argues that it is "correct only to the extent that in some African countries obsolete laws and excessive bureaucratic practices still exist and create unfavorable investment climate" (p. 280).

Three factors determine the investment locations of MNCs (*United Nations,* 1998). The first is the host countries' core FDI policies, which include rules and regulations on the entry and operations of foreign investors and trade and privatization policies. The second factor is the proactive measures host countries adopt to facilitate and promote investment.

They include investment incentives and measures that reduce the costs of doing business. The third factor is economic characteristics, which include host countries' resource-seeking, market-seeking, and efficiency-seeking practices.

Integrated communication can enable host countries to maximize their benefits from those three factors. C. Mwitwa of the Zambia Investment Center notes a reason for Africa's modest record in attracting FDI—"Americans have the American Dream; Malaysians, 'Vision 2020.' What package is Africa using to market itself?" (personal communication, May 17, 1999).

Granted, generating investor interest in Africa is fiercely competitive. And, as noted, it has been difficult for sub-Saharan Africa to attract FDI not so much because of the stiff competition from other developing regions but because of its poor image as an investment destination. To what extent can and do Africa's various national and regional investment centers play a key role in liberalizing the region's investment policies? That is, how do centers such as the South African Trade Center, the Zambia Investment Center, the Zimbabwe Investment Center, and the Center de Promotion des Investissements en Côte d'Ivoire promote an environment conducive to FDI? How much lobbying is done to harmonize the interests of both foreign investors and national governments?

Minuscule efforts in this direction have begun with a mix of sustained communication programs: marketing, public relations, advertising (particularly advocacy), lobbying, publicity, and group meetings. Such programs present to potential investors the liberalizing investment climate of the region vis-à-vis its infrastructure improvements and its market growth and potentials for further growth. Under the auspices of the Zambia Investment Center, for example, the Dynamic Dimensions Training Academy in Ndola, Zambia, provides on-the-job training in marketing and sales, supervision, management, customer service, and hydraulics. Since its founding in 1963, Zambia's Evelyn Hone College of Applied Arts and Commerce has provided a skilled regional workforce in commerce, accounting, the arts and social sciences, allied sciences, and, more recently, in computing technologies. The Zimbabwe Investment Center has, since its establishment in 1992, used exhibits and targeted campaigns to attract major investors from the United Kingdom, South Africa, and Malaysia to the construction, mining, and service sectors of its economy.

Some of the foremost institutional arrangements undertaken to stimulate economic development in the region have been the formation of the Preferential Trade Area of Eastern and Southern Africa in 1981, transformed into the COMESA in 1994, and the Southern African Development Coordination Conference, transformed into the Southern African Development Conference (SADC) in 1992.

COMESA has a potential market of 385 million people in twenty-one member countries. It imports more than U.S.$17 billion worth of goods annually and exports U.S.$13 billion worth. Those range from industrial and consumer products, petroleum, and precious stones, to textiles and food products. COMESA was established to assist the private sector to operate efficiently within the framework of good governance. Its immediate goal was to establish a free trade area by 2000, whereas the ultimate goal is to create an Economic Community for Eastern and Southern Africa.

The twelve-member SADC focuses on gaining approval of economic development projects, programs, and regional strategies. SADC adopts projects under its overall plan, permitting member countries to seek donor funding and encouraging private sector involvement.

COMESA is more concerned with regional economic integration and SADC with political issues. But how much of their work is visible beyond Africa? To what extent are businesses in the United States, for example, familiar with their investment-related activities? Both COMESA and SADC would be powerhouses for attracting more investment if they engaged in sustained, strategic communication on a global scale—and smoothed the potential investors' paths toward investing in Africa. Currently, the organizations' communication programs are generally limited to three tools: trade exhibits, the Internet, and print media. But how familiar are Africans with these media, even in their own countries?

Both African organizations could learn a lesson from the African Trade Institute of the World Trade Center in Chicago. The latter holds special events and high-profile meetings in an effort to educate businesses about trade opportunities in Africa. And it is expanding its information base on trade with Africa.

As interest in available business opportunities in sub-Saharan Africa increases, it is to its advantage to pool its communication resources through activities directed by such regional organizations as COMESA and SADC, and national investment centers. Therefore, the theory-grounded communication challenge for Africa is not simply that of lobbying for institutionalizing conducive policy frameworks prospective investors will find attractive. More important, it is to communicate worldwide the availability of an enabling environment that has the potential and commitment to offer foreign investors opportunities comparable to those found in other developing countries that have had greater successes in attracting FDI.

To what extent do political pronouncements foster or reduce FDI flows to Africa? Do national and provincial governments send a consistent message to the investor community? Are government representatives open and forthright in communicating publicly about economic development issues—and risks? Foreign investors tend to gauge their risks based on their perceived answers to those questions and tend to associate business in some developing countries with unacceptably high long-term political risks. That risk assessment has reduced, stabilized, or increased FDI flows to Africa (The World Bank, 2000).

Understandably, few investors are prepared to risk their investments in a country where there is uncertainty unless the stakes are unusually high. Policy shifts or reversals, usually made by politicians, create unfavorable perceptions of investment environments.

Zambia, once characterized by mass nationalization, took steps in 1992 toward the creation of an environment conducive for investment. Its Mulungushi Reforms of 1968 led to the establishment of the Zambia Privatization Agency (ZPA) in 1992 through an act of parliament. ZPA is an autonomous agency whose function is to plan, implement, and manage the privatization of state enterprises in Zambia in cooperation with the government by selling them to those competent to raise the necessary capital and to operate them. It is an avenue for FDI.

Even though Zambia's privatization program improved both the country's investment policies and climate, it has not attracted the expected level of FDI flows, partly because of pronouncements in the news media by opposition-party politicians who threatened to repossess some privatized companies if voted into office in 2001.

Today, sub-Saharan Africa's privatization policies and International Monetary Fund-directed structural adjustment programs are transforming Africa's economies, building and expanding investor confidence in a host of countries: Angola, Botswana, Burkina Faso, Cape Verde, Côte d'Ivoire, Egypt, Eritrea, Ghana, Kenya, Morocco, Mozambique, Namibia,

Nigeria, Senegal, South Africa, Uganda, and Zimbabwe. But they require integrated promotional campaigns beyond the use of trade exhibits, the Internet, and the print media. They need to more forcefully engage in symmetrical communication and to communicate the status of their programs, their after-investment services, their contributions to the economy, and their potentials for further fueling the transnationalization of their economies. And they need to more forcefully use cause-related marketing strategies (e.g., by sponsoring special events or socially responsible programs of nongovernmental organizations that attract instant credibility to themselves), spokesmen and spokeswomen, and reprints of corporate testimonies on industrial experiences in Africa.

Finally, in a further attempt to encourage more FDI, the sub-Saharan region is also demonstrably embracing the 1960s mantra, "trade, not aid." Trade stimulates industrial ingenuity and economic growth; aid results in dependence and decadence. The region has improving business initiatives, enabling investment frameworks, and sustaining, if not increasing, FDI flows. Therefore, individual and corporate investors would do well to respond favorably to those overtures. After all, nothing ventured, nothing gained.

Characteristics of Public Relations in Africa

Modern public relations in Africa, like journalism practiced on the continent, is a European import that is being adapted to African societies. Nonetheless, there are marked differences between the practice in the developed economies and that in the developing nations.

There are no published studies on the classification of public relations in developing countries practiced by dominant role models. Perhaps the most significant effort to date was that undertaken by Botan (1992), who developed a matrix of public relations from a global perspective. That matrix suggests the delineation of global public relations by four discriminators: the level of national development, the type of primary clients, the level of legal protection and of the political role of the practice, and the uniqueness of the history of the practice. Botan's (1992) argument is that these factors determine, in large measure, the amount and kind of public-relations resources, which, in turn, influence both the worldviews and role of the practice.

Within this matrix, developing nations' public relations suggests a consistency with the press-agentry, publicity, and public-information models (Bhimani, 1986; Pratt, 1985; Pratt & Ugboajah, 1985; Sriramesh, 1992; Sriramesh et al., 1999), and less of an adherence to two-way communication and symmetrical models. In essence, practitioners in the developing nations are "less inclined to seek information from their publics because they do not intend to shape the organizational activities to the needs of their environment" (Sriramesh, 1992, p. 204). Beyond that, even if they demonstrate an interest in shaping an organization's culture, they usually cannot do so because they tend not to be a part of an organization's dominant coalition, which is the group most influential in charting an organization's response to its strategic publics and to the threats of its environment.

Since the turn of the twentieth century, it has been more than forty years since a number of developing nations became politically independent. But such independence is simply one of the hurdles that they have attempted to overcome. Other hurdles are even more challenging. Asia and Africa have the notoriety of having two of the world's most economically disadvantaged nations: Bangladesh and the Sudan, respectively. Therefore, establishing economic and social infrastructures and workable political systems is a major item on the development agendas of most developing nations. The very nature of public relations encourages the form of "alternative development" and "communication perspective" proposed by Melkote (1991) and by Narula and Pearce (1986) as crucial to national development.

Ideal public relations is inarguably a two-way symmetrical process, which means that the interests of the development agency are balanced in favor of both the agency and the receivers of the agency's messages. In such a process, message dissemination is not the driving force of such relationships. Rather, the agency and its receiver publics have mutually beneficial relationships that enhance information delivery, acceptance, and understanding. This notion is consistent with Hiebert's (1992) argument that a new public relations theory is needed to "depict levels of effectiveness—the extent of impact of a message on a receiver, and the impact of feedback on a sender. Only if both these impacts are powerful will the communication be truly effective" (p. 124).

Practitioners also can contribute to decision making vis-à-vis the sustainable developmental process, using communication strategies to promote government programs to the poor, the needy. With the obvious limitations of the dominant paradigms, and renewed interest in alternative paradigms of development, it behooves Africa's public relations practitioners, most of whom are government staffers, to contribute to the developmental process by applying public relations strategies that are sensitive to the public interest. In doing this, practitioners will necessarily be applying the social responsibility dimension to the public relations process. The point here is that the social responsibility aspects of sub-Saharan Africa's public relations underscore and invoke the alternative/communication paradigms of development.

In the final analysis, to whom *is* the public relations practice responsible in developing countries? And to whom *should* it be responsible?

Positivistically speaking, public relations in developing nations, as noted earlier, is largely a communications, information-generating function, not a management function (e.g., Mohamed, 1984; Pratt, 1985; Sriramesh, 1992). In China, for example, the two-way symmetric model of a municipal government coexists with the one-way symmetric or persuasive-marketing approach of the central government (Chen & Culbertson, 1992). Because public relations focuses on giving information, its role in developing countries is largely functionary. This focus on communication makes it more of a conduit for communicating "programmed" development news than for nurturing development-oriented norms among audiences. Its responsibility is largely to the limited interests of whichever government is in office, a point iterated by French philosopher Jean-François Revel (1991):

> The claim of Third World countries to their own "cultural identity" enables the ruling minorities in many of them to justify, among other things, the censorship of information and the exercise of dictatorship. Under the pretext of protecting their peoples' "cultural purity," these leaders do their utmost to keep them ignorant of what is going on in the world and what the rest of the world thinks of them. They let a trickle of news seep through, inventing, when necessary, scraps of information that permit them to mask their own failures and to perpetuate their impostures. (p. 12)

The situation is changing now because of new information technologies, such as cell phones, satellite receivers, and cable stations, all of which are minimally vulnerable to censorship and government controls. Nevertheless, it is still true that governments in developing countries are eager to establish information offices staffed with officers who are likely to provide the much-needed government publicity. Publicity, in its narrowest sense, not public relations, in its broadest sense, is the emphasis of such communication programs. And it has been the benchmark for evaluating the effectiveness of public relations in developing nations. Public relations' efforts geared toward communicating the wishes of the powers that be are consistent with the asymmetrical, two-way communication model of the function; that is, they are driven largely by the self-interest of government development agencies, which are usually subservient to the government, not necessarily to their strategic publics, and much less to the common good.

Because of these limitations on public relations efforts in developing countries, there has been a continuing search for ways to achieve national development and to demonstrate the social responsibility of the public relations practitioner. Oftentimes, the practitioner's responsibility is defined in terms suggestive of mandated, unified national development roles. This means that the sub-Saharan African practitioner is considered socially responsible only when she or he makes a direct contribution to national development. Governments usually assume responsibility for national development plans and expect loyalty and compliance from communication practitioners. However, as Hiebert (1992) observes, many practitioners in developing countries question the development policies by which leaders in the developing world legitimize their control. Similarly, activist, nongovernmental organizations, and other interest groups criticize such policies.

The few developing nations' development programs that are driven by a symmetrical, two-way public relations model strive to attain a symmetry of interests between those of the agency and its publics. Such a symmetry should encourage businesses and development agencies to innovate as a first step toward bringing about changes in their environments. Grunig and Grunig (1990) argue that organizational innovation in developing countries is predicated on changes in management and communication techniques, changes that are crucial to the overall development of developing countries. They are a first step toward attaining development. Further, public relations should be reflective of the sociopolitical environment in which it is practiced. Because practitioners develop programs that can influence their publics in a variety of ways, they are expected to act in ways that demonstrate an organization's responsibility to its publics. Practitioners in developing nations should be responsible primarily for fulfilling professional ideals, applying them to meeting the needs of their strategic publics, and fomenting national development, not merely meeting the interests of their organizations' management. The potential for such a national role was reaffirmed in the Kampala Declaration of November 1991, a twelve-point communiqué by the umbrella organization, the Federation of African Public Relations Associations (FAPRA). Signatories to that declaration were members of Africa's institutes of public relations such as the Nigerian Institute of Public Relations, the South African Institute of Public Relations, and the Zimbabwe Institute of Public Relations. The declaration states, in part, that FAPRA shall promote social, economic, and political development in Africa; shall be involved in conserving, improving, and protecting the African environment; and shall work toward enhancing democratic practices and the observance of human rights in Africa. Public relations inherently and universally promotes social expression and a marketplace of ideas, both of which augur well for economic and political development. Public relations promotes a worldview—in itself an expression of a world vision.

Worldviews, Propositions, Emerging Theories

The term *worldviews* means the often-subjective images or dominant views that people have about an object. As defined by Kearney (1984), it is a way of looking at reality. Kearney explains:

> It consists of basic assumptions and images that provide a more or less coherent, though not necessarily accurate way of thinking about the world. A world view comprises images of Self and of all that is recognized as not-Self, plus ideas about relationships between them. . . . Assumptions about reality vary considerably from one group to another, and at bottom they depend upon and affect the actual perception of it. (p. 41)

Whereas some philosophers (e.g., Bohm, 1977; Feyerabend, 1970; Kuhn, 1970) argue that people or groups do not develop their worldviews through reason or compromise, others (e.g., Kearney, 1984; Vroom, 1989) maintain that they are developed through quasi-rational methods. Since public relations became a full-fledged industry in the mid-twentieth century, it has developed its own worldviews—most of which suggest organizational misunderstanding about the role of the practice and public doubts about its credibility.

Mowlana (1986) reminds us that developing any reasonable international ethic requires more than formulating and disseminating a printed code. However, given the tottering economies of most developing nations, it is critical that their practitioners develop mechanisms for business conduct, mechanisms that also will heighten their professional obligations and their contributions to their clients' and nations' development agendas.

Reconstructing a theory of public relations to provide a community-relations framework for development is "among the most important and among the most typical in the application of public relations skills" (Kruckeberg & Starck, 1988, p. 23). In the context of developing nations, the theory suggests that the public relations practitioner communicate community-oriented development news, using both traditional and modern communication channels to provide information on the publics' civic responsibilities in making national development a continuing reality. Such a framework is premised on relating with the publics through the use of communication programs and research tools. The application of specific public relations techniques and principles in supporting development goals and objectives constitutes the use of public relations for development. Taylor's (2000) public relations approach to addressing ethnic relations in Malaysia, that is, building community, focuses on communication-centered nation building that creates and maintains relationships and participation at both the interpersonal and organization–public levels. In doing so, FDI agents, as communication practitioners, demonstrate social responsibility.

The public relations theory for developing countries that emerges from this discourse, therefore, underscores the importance of Kruckeberg and Starck's (1988) and Starck and Kruckeberg's (2001) reconstructed theory and the relevance of organizational social responsibility. This means that practitioners need to engage in a balancing act that is responsive to overall national interests and to the importance of professional do's and don'ts that perpetuate such interests. That theory is guided by the following propositions (P's):

- P1: If foreign direct investment is to be effective in improving the well-being of the constituencies in which it is made, then investors must demonstrably respond to the environmental and cultural sensitivities of their hosts.
- P2: If businesses are to be demonstrably and socially responsible, then they will exceed their common obligations to their global markets to the advantage of their clients to whose immediate needs they are responding.
- P3: Organizations whose activities are grounded in culture-sensitive ethics (e.g., utilitarianism) are more likely to contribute, in large measure, to both the discourse on the need for social change and to that change itself.
- P4: Foreign direct investment directly involved in community development activities will more likely follow the participatory model of development.
- P5: If communication programs of the foreign private investor are community focused and relational, they are more likely to be effective in contributing to sustainable community and national development.

Conclusion

This chapter avers that theory-driven partnerships between private foreign investors and developing countries can promote economic development, trade, and investment. It reviews the limitations of current development models in developing nations and discusses the potential for the contributory roles of foreign direct investment and of public relations to those nations' development. The traditional exclusion of public relations from an organization's dominant coalition and other limitations inherent in the practice are also noted. Practitioner-formulated program development and implementation need be undergirded by relevant ethical theories that suggest sensitivity to Kruckeberg and Starck's (1988) and Starck and Kruckeberg's (2001) reconstructed theory and the theory of the social responsibility of organizations. In doing this, development efforts become anchored on a framework that is particularly sensitive to the development status of the environment.

The current development scenarios in many developing countries, particularly those in sub-Saharan Africa, while cognizant of the failures of the dominant development paradigms of the 1960s and 1970s, need to demonstrate further community-based programs that apply public relations skills and strategies to establish, maintain, and enhance development benefits for both organizations and the community. These ingredients of the effective use of public relations for development suggest a viable starting point for an emerging general theory of public relations for development of developing countries, much like the theory of organizational innovation in the Third World developed by Grunig and Grunig (1990). Therefore, to develop such a general theory within the context of sub-Saharan Africa requires that researchers examine the region's practitioner perceptions of ethical theories and organizational pressures, the extent to which public relations programs indicate such perceptions and the Kruckeberg and Starck's (1988) and Starck and Kruckeberg's (2001) reconstructed theory, and the various encroachments on practitioners in their applications of such theories. It is possible that the results of such investigations will shed much-needed light on the professional and nonterritorial determinants of practitioner contributions to national developments and to their enabling influences on the enduring benefits of FDI.

Note

1. Each of the following Web sites provides valuable information, current news, and recent development in the public relations industry. Each also provides links to Web sites for various public relations agencies. And they are convenient gateways to a wide range of public relations services available in major international agencies.

www.odwyerpr.com
http://ogilvyworldwide.com

www.bsmg.com
www.ruderfinn.com
www.hillandknowlton.com
www.porternovelli.com
http://bursonmarsteller.com
http://shandwick.com
http://edelman.com
http://ketchum.com
http://fleishmanhillard.com

Discussion Questions

1. Explain the major thrust of the Kruckeberg and Starck (1988) and Starck and Kruckeberg (2001) reconstructed theory. How relevant is it to sub-Saharan Africa and to other developing regions?

2. What is the theory of the social responsibility of organizations? Suggest an application to your contemporary social environment.

3. An African renaissance built on FDI from multinational organizations can benefit exceedingly from planned public relations and communication interventions, or what the World Bank Group calls a "business plan." Identify elements of such a plan.

4. What roles can public relations play in the development and sustenance of FDI in Africa?

5. The developmental programs of the developing countries have been influenced by a number of developmental theories and models. Describe some of these, and for each show its relationship to responsible, professional, public relations practice.

6. Describe and explain each of the following concepts, showing how each applies or could apply to the public relations practice in Africa: (a) participatory development, (b) utilitarianism, (c) the two-way symmetrical process, and (d) organizational innovation in developing countries.

7. Review critically each of the five propositions presented in this chapter. Argue for and against the practical limitations of each.

References

Abrokwaa, C. (1999). Africa 2000: What development strategy? *Journal of Black Studies, 29,* 646–668.

Barshefsky, C. (1999, February 23). *American trade policy in Africa. Paper presented at the Foreign Press Center,* Washington, DC. [On-line]. Available: www.ustr.gov/speech-test/barshefsky/barshefsky_30.html.

Bhimani, R. (1986). Status of PR in India: The image of a peacock and the status of an ostrich. *International Public Relations Review, 10*(2), 19–23.

Bohm, D. (1977). Science as perception-communication. In F. Suppe (Ed.), *The structure of scientific theories* (pp. 374–391). Urbana: University of Illinois Press.

Botan, C. (1992). International public relations: Critique and reformulation. *Public Relations Review, 18*(2), 149–159.

Carroll, A. (1979). A three-dimensional conceptual model of corporate performance. *The Academy of Management Review, 4*(4), 497–505.

Chen, N., & Culbertson, H. (1992). Two contrasting approaches of government public relations in Mainland China. *Public Relations Quarterly, 37*(3), 36–41.

Dakar summit to trigger African industrial revolution. (1999, September). *African Business,* 34.

Day, L. A. (1997). *Ethics in media communications: Cases and controversies* (2nd ed.). Belmont, CA: Wadsworth Publishing Company.

Fair, J., & Shah, H. (1997). Continuities and discontinuities in communication and development research since 1958. *The Journal of International Communication 4*(2), 3–23.

Feyerabend, P. (1970). Consolations for the specialist. In I. Lakatos & A. Musgrave (Eds.), *Criticism and the growth of knowledge* (pp. 197–230). Cambridge, England: Cambridge University Press.

Grunig, L. A., & Grunig, J. E. (1990). Strategies for communicating on innovative management with receptive individuals in development organizations. In M. Mtewa (Ed.), *International science and technology: Philosophy, theory and policy* (pp. 118–131). New York: St. Martin's Press.

Grunig, L. A., Grunig, J. E., & Ehling, W. (1992). What is an effective organization? In J. E. Grunig (Ed.), *Excellence in public relations and communication management* (pp. 65–90). Hillsdale, NJ: Lawrence Erlbaum.

Gudykunst, W. (1997). Cultural variability in communication: An introduction. *Communication Research, 24,* 327–348.

Hiebert, R. E. (1992). Global public relations in a post-Communist world: A new model. *Public Relations Review, 18*(2), 117–126.

Huang, Y. (1990). *Risk communication, models of public relations and anti-nuclear activism: A case study of a nuclear power plant in Taiwan.* Unpublished master's thesis, University of Maryland, College Park.

Inkeles, A., & Smith, D. (1974). *Becoming modern: Individual change in six developing nations.* Cambridge, MA: Harvard University Press.

Janis, I. (1972). *Victims of groupthink.* Boston: Houghton Mifflin.

Kearney, M. (1984). *World view.* Novato, CA: Chandler & Sharp.

Kruckeberg, D., & Starck, K. (1988). *Public relations and community: A reconstructed theory.* New York: Praeger.

Kuhn, T. (1970). *The structure of scientific revolutions.* Chicago: University of Chicago Press.

Lancaster, C. (1999). *Aid to Africa: So much to do, so little done.* Chicago: The University of Chicago Press.

Lerner, D. (1958). *The passing of traditional society: Modernizing the Middle East.* New York: Free Press.

L'Etang, J. (1994). Public relations and corporate social responsibility: Some issues arising. *Journal of Business Ethics, 13,* 111–123.

Lyra, A. (1991). *Public relations in Greece: Models, roles and gender.* Unpublished master's thesis, University of Maryland, College Park.

McElreath, M. (1993). *Managing systematic and ethical public relations.* Dubuque, IA: Wm C. Brown.

Melkote, S. (1991). *Communication for development in the Third World: Theory and Practice.* New Delhi: Sage.

Moemeka, A. (1997). Communalistic societies: Community and self-respect as African values. In C. Christians & M. Traber (Eds.), *Communication ethics and universal values* (pp. 170–193). Thousand Oaks, CA: Sage.

Moemeka, A. (1998). Communalism as a fundamental dimension of culture. *Journal of Communication, 48*(4), 118–141.

Mohamed II, R. (1984, January). Public relations in Lebanon: No task for the timid. *Communication World,* 35–38.

Mowlana, H. (1986). *Global information and world communication.* New York: Longman.

Mutharika, P. (1997). Creating an attractive investment climate in the Common Market for Eastern and Southern Africa (COMESA) region. *ICSID [International Center for Settlement of Investment Disputes] Review, 12*(2), 237–286.

Mwenda, K. (1999). *Multiple listings and the setting up of a regional stock exchange as means to stimulating increased liquidity on stock markets in eastern and southern Africa.* Paper presented at the African Studies Center, Michigan State University, East Lansing.

Narula, U., & Pearce, W. (1986). *Development as communication: A perspective on India.* Carbondale: Southern Illinois University Press.

The National Summit on Africa. (1998, June). Economic development, trade and investment, and job creation. (Thematic Working Paper Series).Washington, DC: Author.

Nwankwo, R., & Nzelibe, C. (1990). Communication and conflict management in African development. *Journal of Black Studies, 20,* 253–266.

Obeng-Quaidoo, I. (1985). Culture and communication research methodologies in Africa: A proposal for change. *Gazette: International Journal for Mass Communication Studies, 36,* 109–120.

Okigbo, C. (1994). Toward a theory of indecency in news reporting. In F. Kasoma (Ed.), *Journalism ethics in Africa* (pp. 70–87). Nairobi, Kenya: African Council for Communication Education.

Peterson, T., Schramm, W., & Siebert, F. (1971). *Four theories of the press.* Urbana: University of Illinois Press.

Pratt, C. (1985). Public relations in the Third World: The African context. *Public Relations Journal, 41*(2), 11–12, 15–16.

Pratt, C. (1990). Ethics in newspaper editorials: Perceptions of sub-Saharan African journalists. *Gazette: The International Journal for Mass Communication Studies, 46,* 17–40.

Pratt, C., & McLaughlin, G. (1990). Ethical dimensions of Nigerian journalists and their newspapers. *Journal of Mass Media Ethics, 5,* 30–44.

Pratt, C., & Ugboajah, F. (1985). Social responsibility: A comparison of Nigerian public relations with Canadian and U.S. public relations. *International Public Relations Association Review, 9,* 22–29.

Revel, J-F. (1991). *The flight from truth: The reign of deceit in the age of information.* New York: Random House.

Rogers, E. (1976). *Communication and development: Critical perspectives.* Beverly Hills, CA: Sage.

Rogers, E. (1995). *Diffusion of innovations* (4th ed.). New York: Free Press.

Sriramesh, K. (1992). Societal culture and public relations: Ethnographic evidence from India. *Public Relations Review, 18*(2), 201–211.

Sriramesh, K., Kim, Y., & Takasaki, M. (1999). Public relations in three Asian cultures: An analysis. *Journal of Public Relations Research, 11,* 271–292.

Starck, K., & Kruckeberg, D. (2001). Public relations and community: A reconstructed theory revisited. In R. Heath (Ed.), *Handbook of public relations* (pp. 51–59). Thousand Oaks, CA: Sage.

Stocker, H. (2000). Growth effects of foreign direct investment—myth or reality? In J. Chen (Ed.), *Foreign direct investment* (pp. 115–137). New York: St. Martin's Press.

Taylor, M. (2000). Toward a public relations approach to nation building. *Journal of Public Relations Research, 12*(2), 179–210.

Triandis, H. (1995). *Individualism and collectivism.* Boulder, CO: Westview.

United Nations Conference on Trade and Development. (1995). Foreign direct investment in Africa. New York: Author/DTCI/19, Current Studies, Series A, No. 28.

United Nations world investment report 1998: Trends and determinants. (1998). New York: Author.

USA ready to launch investment invasion. (1999, June). *African Business,* 8–10.

Vroom, H. (1989). *Religions and the truth.* Grand Rapids, MI: Eerdmans.

The World Bank. (2000). *Entering the twenty-first century: World development report 1999/2000.* New York: Oxford University Press.

The World Bank Group. (2000, May). Can Africa claim the twenty-first century? Washington, DC: Author.

14

Public Relations in Emerging Democracies

The Case of Ghana

Isaac Abeku Blankson

Key Points

- Public relations in emerging democracies, such as Ghana, focuses primarily on government relations and development communication.

- The 1990s liberal and democratic reforms in Ghana have provided a stable political environment, economic growth, and created a plural media environment that is encouraging freedom of speech and public expression.

- Since the reforms, Ghanaian public relations is being transformed into a more professional and relationship-management practice that includes increased importance for corporate and media relations and increased attention to public opinion.

- The Institute of Public Relations, Ghana, is also playing a significant role in promoting professionalism in the practice and redefining the functions and role of public relations.

Public relations practices in sub-Saharan African countries have been described as "public communication and persuasion programs that focus on national development" (Al-Enad, 1990, p. 26; Pratt, 1985, p. 12; Van Leuven & Pratt, 1996, p. 44). Pratt and Ugboajah (1985) noted that "Third World practitioners are considered socially responsible only when they contribute directly to national development" (p. 12). This means that public relations in sub-Saharan Africa is far from the ideal Western standard in which organizations use two-way symmetrical communication strategies to build positive relationships with their active publics (Brunig & Ledingham, 2000; Grunig, 1992; Grunig & Hunt, 1984). While the characterizations may still hold for the majority of the sub-Saharan African countries, recent developments in countries such as Ghana are having a significant impact on public relations practice that cannot be ignored.

Public relations in Ghana has been evolving toward a more professional practice since the country launched its International Monetary Fund (IMF)-directed democratic and liberal reform policies in the late 1980s. The intensification of the reforms in the 1990s ushered in a period of privatization of state enterprises and private sector growth (Booth, 1999; World Bank, 1999). These reforms are positively transforming some sectors of the economy and institutions. The Ghanaian public relations community is also being transformed.

Using data from interviews with Ghanaian public relations practitioners, government officials, public and private broadcasters, and communication scholars obtained from August 1998 to July 2000, this chapter examines the evolution of public relations practices and functions in Ghana. Although the major focus is on the impact of the country's 1990s democratic and liberal reforms on public relations, the historical developments and factors responsible for the nature of public relations practice in Ghana also are discussed. In essence, the question, "What role does the development of democratic and civil society have in shaping public relations practice in Ghana?" is investigated. This is based on the assumption that the development of civil society based on the principles of democracy, competitive market structure, public participation, and media pluralism can positively influence public relations practice in Ghana.

Ghana's experiences offer a unique opportunity for examining the role of the development of a democratic and liberal economy on the practice of public relations in emerging African democracies. As one of the emerging democratic nations in sub-Saharan Africa, Ghana continues to implement democratic and liberal policies that have propelled the country toward political stability, economic growth (UN Development Program, 1997), plural and independent private media environments, press freedom, and public participation in civic discourse (Blankson, 2000). These developments, the first of their kind in the history of Ghana, have significant implications for public relations practice in the country. Hitherto, Ghanaian public relations had been described as having "no clearly defined functions and as a tool primarily for public campaigns and persuasion programs" (Osam, 1989, p. 25). Do the liberal and democratic reforms offer opportunities for changing the way public relations is practiced in Ghana? Are they moving the practice toward a more professional and relationship-building function? Before looking into these issues, the history of public relations in Ghana is examined.

Brief History of Public Relations in Ghana

Public relations practice in Ghana can be traced to the British colonial administration that ruled the nation until Ghana achieved its independence in 1957. During the colonial period, public relations activities were performed solely by British and European expatriate practitioners. The primary function of the expatriate practitioners was to serve as the communication and information ministry for the colonial administration. They also served the interests of the multinational corporations (MNCs) operating in the country at the time.

Ghana's independence in 1957 brought some changes to the practice. As a deliberate postindependence policy to localize the Ghanaian administration, the Ghana government and the British colonial administration sought to gradually transfer key executive and managerial positions from expatriate to Ghanaian hands. The Nkrumah government (Convention Peoples' Party) that took over from the colonial administration gradually replaced expatriate administrators in key sectors of the civil service and government ministries with local Ghanaians as principal secretaries. As time went on, the MNCs operating in Ghana, such as the United African Company (UAC), Barclays Bank, GB Olivant, and petroleum companies, such as Mobil, Texaco, Shell, and BP Oil, followed the civil service initiative and employed local Ghanaians as "liaisons" or as "go-betweens" to the local Ghanaian administrators in the ministries and other businesses. The MNCs felt a compelling need to localize part of their management positions in order to maintain effective communication between their corporations and the civil service, which was increasingly being filled with Ghanaian administrators. It was this quest for "effective communication and subsequent employment of replacement officers" that brought about the first changes in public relations in Ghana (Gyan, 1991, p. 11).

However, replacing expatriate practitioners with local Ghanaians was hindered by the lack of qualified Ghanaian public relations practitioners. Consequently, the MNCs employed Ghanaians with journalism backgrounds as public relations officers to replace the expatriate practitioners. The lack of trained Ghanaian practitioners led Harold Macmillan (former British prime minister) and Jimmy Moxon (the district commissioner and mayor of Accra, Ghana, and subsequently the director of information services of Ghana and public relations advisor to President Kwame Nkrumah of Ghana) to start the Ghana Institute of Journalism (GIJ) in the 1960s to help train the officers already employed. Since then, the GIJ has been and continues to be one of the major public institutions that trains public relations practitioners in the country.

During the 1960s and 1970s, many of the local businesses and organizations did not understand or recognize the importance of public relations and, consequently, failed to establish public relations departments. Instead, officers in departments such as administration, marketing or sales, and personnel carried out the public relations duties. The few organizations that recognized the importance of public relations employed people with diverse backgrounds, education, and training to serve as press and information officers to perform publicity and press agentry duties. According to Gyan (1991), the emphasis on press relations favored those who had previously worked in media houses, especially the print media. It also created the impression that journalism and public relations were the same, a misleading thought still held by many in Ghana today. This misconception and other problems the Ghanaian public relations managers were facing were enough to motivate some of them to form the Public Relations Association of Ghana (PRAG) in 1971. PRAG has since changed its name to the Institute of Public Relations, Ghana (IPR).[1]

The Institute of Public Relations, Ghana

The Institute of Public Relations, Ghana, the brainchild of Hermann Alah, one of the early practitioners in Ghana, began as a social group in the early 1960s. The founding members, a small group of retired and practicing Ghanaian journalists employed as public relations managers in some MNCs, met to discuss issues they were facing and to share their experiences. As their numbers increased over the years, the social gatherings turned into weekly club meetings.

By the late 1960s, some of the Ghanaian public relations practitioners had become members of the Institute of Public Relations, United Kingdom,[2] and the Public Relations Society of America.[3] Though they were recognized by membership in foreign public relations organizations, many of the Ghanaian practitioners also believed they needed their own public relations association in Ghana (Gyan, 1991). Their membership in these foreign associations and the quest for local recognition provided the impetus for starting a national association similar to the foreign ones. To aid in the formation of a professional public relations association in Ghana, expatriate practitioners such as Dennis Buckle (former head of public relations in Unilever) and Frank Jenkins (former public relations educator and practitioner in Britain) organized training courses and seminars on public relations for the Ghanaian public relations managers and those interested in public relations as a future career.

It was through the collaborative efforts of the Ghanaian public relations managers and a few expatriate practitioners that PRAG was created in 1971. Its membership grew from 200 in 1975 to 342 in 1982. As of November 2001, IPR had 400 registered members. Unfortunately, the association became dysfunctional between 1984 and 1989 until it was reorganized in 1992. Membership was composed of a mixture of older journalists, who became public relations managers, and younger, trained public relations practitioners from the Ghana Institute of Journalism and the Ghana School of Communication Studies.

The formation of PRAG proved significant for public relations in Ghana. The 1970s marked an increase in awareness of public relations activities in state and private organizations. Ansah (1976) recognized that the 1970s witnessed a substantial increase in public relations departments attached to business houses; financial enterprises; universities; voluntary organizations and other institutions, public or private; and profit making or charity-oriented organizations in the country.

Public relations in Ghana also received a boost when, in 1972, PRAG hosted the third All-Africa Public Relations Conference in Ghana. The conference was very well attended. Approximately one hundred delegates from six African countries, as well as foreign participants and observers from Europe and the United States, attended the conference. It was sponsored by the Federation of African Public Relations,[4] the Public Relations Association of Ghana, and the government of Ghana (Sattler, 1981). Chief Olu Adebanjo, then the special advisor for information to former Nigerian president Shehu Shagari, recognized the growing importance of public relations in Ghana during the 1970s when he remarked that:

> No organization can hope to maintain its position or make progress without sound public relations practice. Any progressive and democratic government that ignores public opinion and does not consider the public relations implications of its actions and utterances is risking detriment to its image. (Sattler, 1981, p. 29)

Similarly, when Yaw Opoku-Afriyie, former minister for information for Ghana, opened the conference, he set down the challenge for public relations practitioners:

> While I urge you to place your expertise at the disposal of your countries and their peoples, I do so in the belief that you would first have succeeded in convincing them of what they stand to gain from your profession. It is not easy selling ideas, whether to management or

governments. But it is your duty, certainly your lot, to succeed in the endeavor of creating understanding around you. Your governments and countries will be the better for it if they see the things your professional training and knowledge can accomplish for them. (Sattler, 1981, p. 39)

Contrary to events in the 1960s and 1970s, the 1980s was a challenging period in the history of PRAG. The association became dysfunctional from 1984 to 1989, largely because of membership and leadership problems that ensued between the senior and older public relations managers and the new, younger, trained practitioners. Most of the senior public relations managers became disgruntled, frustrated, and disinterested in the organization they had nurtured when the younger practitioners doubted their credibility and professional skills and questioned their legitimacy in leading the association. This led many of the senior practitioners to leave the association. Their departure created a power vacuum that led to constant power struggles among the younger public relations practitioners over who should lead the association (Gyan, 1991). The crisis eventually plunged the association into disintegration until 1989, when an interim management committee was appointed to reorganize it. In 1992, PRAG was restructured into what exists today as the Institute of Public Relations, Ghana (IPR).

Public Relations Prior to 1990s
Liberal and Democratic Reforms

The nature and function of public relations in Ghana prior to democratic and liberal reforms in the mid-1990s were as varied as the backgrounds of those who performed public relations duties. To understand the character of practitioners in Ghana until the mid-1990s, Boachie-Agyekum (1992), Gyan (1991), Turkson (1986), and Osam (1989) examined the profile of some public relations practitioners, their educational backgrounds and professional training, and their positions and roles in the organizations where they were employed.

Profile of Ghanaian Public Relations Practitioners

Public relations practice in Ghana has always been male dominated. Gyan's (1991) study of the profile of Ghanaian practitioners revealed a twenty-three to three ratio in favor of male practitioners. The majority (about 53 percent) of public relations practitioners had some university education. In fact, most of them had postgraduate qualifications. The rest held diplomas from the Ghana Institute of Journalism or other diploma-awarding institutions. Some of them started with their organizations in some other capacity before being employed as public relations managers. A majority of the managers started working with their organizations in the mid-1980s. Very few of the Ghanaian public relations managers worked or headed separate public relations departments. Many worked as public relations managers in departments such as marketing and personnel.

Position of Practitioners in Organizations

Studies have shown that an overwhelming majority of Ghanaian public relations practitioners did not occupy senior level positions in their organizations (Gyan 1991; Osam,

1989; Turkson, 1986). Most occupied midlevel positions in both private and government organizations. Although some of the practitioners reported to a chief executive officer or a director, the majority reported through a chain of other senior-level administrators and had generally not been part of the decision-making body in their organizations. Turkson's (1986) study of the position of the public relations manager at the University of Cape Coast in Ghana revealed that the person holding that position reported to the registrar for municipal and estate services, who, in turn, reported to the deputy registrar, who also reported to the registrar. Another study by Osam (1989) that focused on a private insurance company, the Great African Insurance, showed that the public relations manager reported to the head of the marketing department.

Because the majority of Ghanaian practitioners occupied midlevel positions within the organizational chart, they were marginalized when institutional policies were being formulated. The low recognition received by the public relations practitioners did not only reflect in their low positions but also was reflected in the sizes of their units or departments. The majority of the Ghanaian public relations managers worked in very small departments that employed not more than five people (Gyan, 1991).

Roles and Functions of Practitioners

Prior to the mid-1990s, public relations practitioners in Ghana performed a variety of duties (Boachie-Agyekum, 1992; Gyan, 1991). The vast array of daily duties they performed mirrored the lack of clearly defined job responsibilities in their organizations. Gyan's (1991) study found that more than 80 percent of Ghanaian public relations practitioners performed press agentry, publicity, and protocol roles. The most performed daily activities included mass media monitoring, public opinion evaluation, speech and report writing, arranging and attending meetings, counseling management, and responding to public complaints. Other duties included organizing parties, picking up the children of top management from school, renewing passports for senior personnel, and ensuring that traveling arrangements for institutional heads were carried out (Boachie-Agyekum, 1992). Very few practitioners in Ghana had management responsibilities, such as advising management on communication and publicity issues. They also planned and executed programs, managed relationships with other organizations, and organized staff development and social activities (Boachie-Agyekum, 1992; Gyan, 1991).

A prominent practitioner and member of Parliament observed during the launching of the year 2000 IPR week conference in Accra, Ghana, that public relations in Ghana has been limited to protocol duties. He drew on instances in government departments, sporting clubs, religious organizations, and even political parties where public relations is found relevant only when it comes to distributing prepared speeches or looking for someone who can speak well in public.

Historical Factors that Shaped Ghana Public Relations

The development of public relations in Ghana and the varied and nonprofessional roles most practitioners performed during the 1970s until the mid-1990s were the results of several historical factors (Gyan, 1991; Osam, 1989; Turkson, 1986). These included (1) the nature of recruitment of Ghanaian public relations managers, (2) the different and contrasting regime types and ideologies, (3) the government as the key target of public relations, (4) the media and press system, and (5) the inactivity of the Ghanaian public.

Practitioner Recruitment by Ghana
Information Services Department

Public relations in Ghana prior to the mid-1990s was influenced greatly by the way Ghanaian practitioners were recruited and hired by corporations and organizations. Shortly after Ghana's independence in 1957, the Ghana Information Services Department (ISD) was charged with the sole responsibility of providing information, press, and public relations services for all government ministries and departments in the country. Government ministries and departments initially issued their press releases through the ISD. However, because of the workload and the slow nature of the process, the ISD was forced to send officers known as press secretaries or information officers to select ministries to perform public relations functions. Eventually, the ISD, which became known as the Public Relations Department in the Second Republic, decided as a matter of policy to assign information officers to all ministries (Gyan, 1991), a practice that continues to this day.

The majority of practitioners were recruited from the GIJ and the Ghana School of Communication Studies, University of Ghana,[5] the only schools that trained journalists and public relations practitioners. Based on their performance in the civil service placement examinations, the practitioners were subsequently hired by corporations and organizations to replace retiring practitioners or fill vacancies. The recruitment of journalists into public relations fields created a situation whereby public relations became synonymous with journalism.

Given the journalism background of these managers and the fact that little or no further training was given them even after being employed, the Ghana Information Services Department contributed to creating the low regard and negative perception of the practitioners.

Authoritarian Regimes and Ideologies

Until 1992, Ghana's political stability was challenged by an interchange of civilian and military governments. Each regime had its own political ideology that either facilitated public relations practice in Ghana or thwarted all efforts of public relations practitioners. Since independence in 1957, the country has gone through ten changes of government, including five military coups. Three ideological tendencies, namely state socialist, populist, and liberal, have competed for power over a long history of civilian and military regimes supplanting one another by coups and returns to civilian rule. Although the civilian governments generally practiced some form of democratic and liberal policies, the military regimes carried out authoritarian and socialist/communist policies (Terkper, 1996).

Several of the Ghanaian practitioners interviewed contend that authoritarian military governments negatively influenced their roles and activities especially in the 1970s and 1980s. It was explained that during the times of authoritarian military regimes, public relations activities were either directly or indirectly mandated to promote the government's agenda and focus campaigns on crisis management, publicity, and building a positive image for the government in the interest of "state security and national development" (Pratt, 1985, p. 12). The activities of many Ghanaian public relations practitioners in both the public and private sectors were mainly determined by government policies. The practitioners explained that it was because these were times when "the nation was in crisis, socio-political institutions had broken down, public fear and intimidation was at its highest level, and the authoritarian governments sought to limit further the already powerless civil society while at the same time increased the power of government" (Taylor, 2000, p. 3). For instance, between 1972 and 1978, the Supreme Military Council (SMC) under the leadership of General I. K. Acheampong mandated that every institution and individual in the country promote its controversial, overambitious, and unsuccessful agricultural policy, "Operation Feed Yourself," that aimed at convincing Ghanaians that self-sufficiency in food production could be achieved if every institution and individual engaged in backyard gardening (Terkper, 1996).

Government as Target of Public Relations

Some studies reveal that the Ghanaian government has historically been the major target of public relations efforts in the country (Osam, 1989; Turkson, 1986). The majority of the Ghanaian practitioners interviewed indicated to this researcher that, prior to the mid-1990s, more than 65 percent of their daily activities were targeted at a government or public official. This finding supports the findings of Kent and Taylor (1999), Taylor (2000), Pratt (1985, 1986), Pratt and Ugboajah (1985), and other scholars that Third World governments have been the most important publics in public relations practices in these nations.

There are several reasons why most of the public relations activities prior to 1995 targeted the government. As the most powerful institution of state with monopoly control over many sectors of the economy, the government regulated business and organizational practices, allocated business permits, controlled the media, and employed the largest workforce in the country. In addition, key government officials were perceived to have substantial decision-making powers, social status, and access to resources and the media. Consequently, for a Ghanaian public relations practitioner to be effective, he or she had to cultivate a favorable relationship with a government institution or official.

The majority of the public relations practitioners interviewed agree that, because most of their activities during the 1980s and early 1990s focused on government relations, other significant functions of their practice, such as community relations, were ignored. This hindered the flexibility and creativity required to be an effective practitioner because most practitioners relied on government apparatuses and resources for their publicity and communication needs. It also contributed to the creation of corrupt and unethical practices among practitioners. Many practitioners pay financial or material incentives to government officials in order to gain access to state and national resources and publicity in the state-controlled print and electronic media. These practices have contributed to the negative image of Ghanaian practitioners.

State-Owned and Controlled Media Environment

Media access in public relations practice in developing countries is very important (Taylor, 2000). Al-Enad (1990) rightly argues that in an ideal situation "an independent and free press will promote public relations activities whereas a controlled press will hinder its efforts" (p. 24). Until 1995, when Ghana's media, particularly the broadcasting radio and television environment, was pluralized and private ownership allowed for the first time, the country's media system, Ghana Broadcasting Corporation (GBC),[6] was state owned and controlled. While authoritarian military regimes favored the authoritarian press mode with heavy government control and censorship, democratic civilian governments practiced a quasi-liberal and developmental press model that allowed for some press freedom and public participation (Pratt, 1985; Siebert, Peterson, & Schramm, 1963; Taylor, 2000). These have been the media conditions under which public relations in Ghana has evolved.

In my interviews conducted with public relations practitioners in Ghana between 1998 and 2000, it was found that until private radio and television stations arrived on the Ghanaian scene in 1995, the media relations function of Ghanaian public relations practitioners was underutilized. Media relations also was conducted in a controlled environment. Only 25 percent of the practitioners interviewed relied frequently on the state-controlled media for their publicity and communication activities. Whereas only 34 percent frequently wrote news releases or organized press conferences, the majority, 66 percent, rarely wrote press releases or organized press conferences for their organizations. Most of the practitioners held the perception that the Ghanaian public had a deep distrust in the state media. Other practitioners simply found it difficult to get direct access to the media, especially during military regimes. About 60 percent of the public relations practitioners did not have direct access to the state print and electronic media but relied on third party and interpersonal connections to gain access to the media for their publicity.

The controlled media environment made it difficult for organizations to develop flexible relationships with the media and allowed for only one-way asymmetric communication between organizations and their publics. It also made it difficult for private organizations, especially smaller ones, to get publicity for their activities.

Inactive Ghanaian Publics

Ghanaian public relations practice also has evolved within an environment of public apathy and inactivity. The importance of an active public who participates in an organization's activities and voices its concerns through public relations has been stressed (Grunig & Repper, 1992, p. 128; Hallahan, 2000, p. 499). Inactive publics have been defined as "groups with which an organization wishes to establish and maintain relationships but who, for a variety of reasons, demonstrate low knowledge, involvement, and concern about the activities of the organization" (Hallahan, 2000, p. 499). This study found that, prior to 1995 when former President Jerry Rawlings and his National Democratic Congress (NDC)[7] government, which ruled Ghana from 1982 to 2000, allowed the public to exercise its democratic rights to freedom of speech and public participation in the affairs of the state, the Ghanaian public with whom practitioners had to communicate was very inactive. The inactive public was recognized in 1999 when former President Jerry Rawlings criticized Ghanaians as having developed a "culture of silence."

The public inactivity was a consequence of multiple factors, including decades of manipulation, suppression, and control by powerful forces in society, such as the military governments. It was also a result of purposeful and deliberate attempts by authoritarian regimes to discourage and inhibit both lateral and upward communication, denial of public access to the media, lack of opportunities to participate in sociopolitical discussions, and, consequently, public disappointment in the state media and its inability to represent their views (Ansah, 1985). In addition, sociocultural factors, such as high illiteracy and poverty, negatively affected public attitudes and behaviors.

The inactivity of the Ghanaian publics affected public relations practices in the sense that practitioners paid little or no attention to public opinion. They believed that public opinion could have little or no significant impact on their organizations' activities. The practitioners believed that their publics possessed low levels of knowledge about their organizations and showed very little interest and involvement in their activities. The publics' inactivity made the efforts of practitioners to communicate with their organization's publics very difficult. It determined the strategies and channels used for communication with the publics. The Ghanaian practitioners had the difficult task of seeking out their organizations' publics because the publics did not engage in any deliberate information-seeking efforts, other than to satisfy routine personal needs.

However, public relations practice in Ghana has been undergoing some changes as a consequence of the liberal and democratic reforms begun in the mid-1990s by the government of former President Jerry Rawlings.

Toward Professionalism in Ghanaian Public Relations

Despite the factors and events that have hindered the growth of public relations practice in Ghana, practitioners have observed significant opportunities and changes in their practice since the country launched extensive democratic and liberal reforms in the 1990s.

The 1990s Liberal and Democratic Reforms

In the mid-1990s, Ghana's structural adjustment policies turned into a long-term goal of establishing a democratic, liberal, and free-market economy. Because of pressure from international donor agencies, such as the IMF and the World Bank, and internal pressure mainly from the Ghanaian academic community, Jerry Rawlings and his NDC government agreed to democratize and liberalize the economy. International donor agencies, particularly the IMF and World Bank, made democratic and liberal reform a condition for continued external grants to the Ghana government (Booth, 1999).

The internal pressure came in the form of organized conferences aimed at putting democracy and liberalization on the public agenda. For example, at the opening ceremony of the Unda/OCIC[8] Africa General Assembly of Catholic Media Organizations jointly held Conference in Accra on September 6, 1992, the academic community picked on a speech delivered by the information minister of Ghana when he declared a major policy change:

> The political changes taking place on the continent are likely to lead to the review of state monopoly in the electronic media. We in Ghana, have the framework of our national communication policy, proposed a degree of deregulation in the electronic media set within clearly defined guidelines. (Bonnah-Koomson, 1995, p. 1)

This official policy declaration signaled a change in the attitude of the ruling Rawlings' NDC government. According to Bonnah-Koomson (1995), it was a source of inspiration to the School of Communication Studies, University of Ghana, to initiate public discussion on the issue of democracy and liberalization, and, more specifically, on media independence and pluralism in Ghana and in other African countries (Karikari, 1994, 1995). With support from the West Africa Regional Office of the International Development Research Center (IDRC) in Dakar, the Friedrich Ebert Foundation, and the Panos Institute, the School of Communication Studies organized two conferences, first in March 1993 and a follow-up conference in November 1994, on media pluralism and privatization. One of the objectives of the conferences was to influence public opinion to promote legislation supportive of the democratization and pluralization of the media as guaranteed by the 1992 Constitution of Ghana (Blankson, 2000).

Following international and internal pressure, the NDC government launched its liberal and democratic policies that began to transform the Ghanaian economy. For the first time in decades, Ghana began to experience economic growth, as well as growth in local and foreign private investments (Booth, 1999; UN Development Program, 1997; World Bank, 1999). The government also privatized some of the state enterprises and the media to allow for private ownership and operation. Consequently, the Ghanaian public, which hitherto had been inactive and uninvolved, began to show interest and to participate in the activities of the government and organizations. Organizations, both public and private, saw the need for communicating with each other and with their publics.

These developments are having significant effects on public relations in Ghana. Serious initiatives are being taken by the IPR to promote professionalism among public relations practitioners in the country. Corporate relations are gaining importance and prominence within the practice as well. In addition, more effective media relations practice is being fostered, and organizations have begun to be more responsive to public opinion and community concerns because of the increase in public awareness and involvement.

IPR Initiatives to Promote Professionalism

Under the leadership of Nabanyin Pratt, IPR aimed at promoting professionalism in Ghanaian public relations and improving the image of practitioners in the country. It launched major initiatives that included educating management and the public on public relations roles, promoting a better understanding and appreciation of public relations in Ghana, establishing proper education standards and professional criteria for practicing public relations in Ghana, and seeking legal recognition as the professional body responsible for all public relations practitioners in Ghana. Other initiatives aimed at defining what constitutes the body of knowledge in public relations in Ghana, setting standards for public relations practice and conduct, and eliminating those practicing public relations without the necessary educational and professional training (Gyan, 1991). IPR obtained legal status as a professional organization in 1992. This empowered the IPR to fully regulate and monitor the activities of all public relations practitioners and to mandate every public relations practitioner to register with the institute.

In 2001, the IPR signed a memorandum of understanding with four international public relations organizations in the United Kingdom, South Africa, Ireland, and Canada. Under the agreement, the five professional organizations would mutually recognize IPR and provide equal recognition to Ghanaian practitioners who visited the participating countries. This memorandum was developed to promote mutual international cooperation among professional public relations associations (IPR, 2001).

Through the IPR's efforts, a National Communication Bill passed by the Ghana Parliament in late 2001 bars nonmembers of IPR from practicing as public relations practitioners in Ghana. It also allows the IPR to enforce Article 2 of its bylaws, as stated in its constitution, "No person shall practice in Ghana as a public relations practitioner unless he is registered to practice as such in accordance with the constitution and bylaws of the Association and any law being in force in Ghana" (Constitution of the Public Relations Association of Ghana quoted from Gyan, 1991, p. 43). This is a significant attempt to eliminate all nonqualified individuals who are practicing as public relations practitioners. Interestingly, many companies have even started using nonmembership of IPR as a prerequisite for disqualifying applicants for public relations positions. In addition, the IPR is represented on job interview panels in organizations seeking to employ public relations or communication officers. Gradually, the practice of public relations in Ghana is gaining a higher profile, respect, and recognition.

The IPR has been active in organizing workshops and seminars and sponsoring studies and research on public relations. The IPR adopted the International Public Relations Association's Code of Professional Conduct[9] in order to identify with and conform to international public relations standards. It also has instituted membership and accreditation examinations. Finally, the IPR has established an office (secretariat) to run the affairs of the institute and is also constructing a Web site where both members and nonmembers can seek information.

In part because of these positive initiatives, IPR's membership has been growing. Between 1999 and mid-2001, the institute added 78 new members, bringing the total membership to 354 in 2000. These include 8 fellows or honorary members, 164 accredited members, 127 associate members, and 55 affiliate members. Corporate membership stood at nine in 2000 and included organizations such as Social Security and National Insurance Trust,[10] State Insurance Company, Vodi Technik Motors Limited,[11] Standard Chartered Bank,[12] Ghana Airways Company,[13] and others (IPR, 2001). According to the IPR secretariat, its membership stood at 400 in November 2001.

Increased Importance of Corporate Relations

The 1990s liberal and democratic reforms have moved the Ghanaian economy toward political stability, a free-market economy, and economic growth. Consequently, the confidence of private investors, both local and foreign, has been boosted. Ghana's stable economy and signs of future economic growth have attracted private investors who were previously reluctant to invest in the country. For example, the post and telecommunication industry, which hitherto was state controlled, was privatized. In 1997, it became known as Ghana Telecom[14] after it was purchased by a consortium led by Malaysia Telekom, a private telecommunications company in Malaysia. The UNDP also reported modest economic growth in Ghana's economy (UN Development Program, 1997).

These developments in Ghana's economic and political landscape in the 1990s led to the influx of private investments, particularly in mineral exploration, telecommunications, service, and consumer industries. Several multinational corporations, including

American, Japanese, Korean, and European corporate giants, either entered or reentered the Ghanaian business landscape. A few examples include Malaysian TV3, Motorola Communications, and Sprint Communications. This new phase of business and economic realities in Ghana is causing the development and maintenance of local as well as international competitiveness among businesses and organizations. It is also forcing the businesses and organizations to develop and maintain positive interrelationships as well as to adopt more professional business practices, accountability, and effective communication management.

The current economic and business climate is having positive implications on the Ghanaian public relations profession. The importance of corporate public relations is gaining attention and prominence among organizations and Ghanaian public relations practitioners. Management consciousness of public relations practice has been awakened as a result of the growing competitiveness of industries. The former deputy minister of environment, science, and technology asserted during the 1998 IPR Week conference "Raising Environmental Awareness through Public Relations" held on October 26, in Accra, Ghana, that "the dynamics of business ushering us into the 21st century needs public relations to manage industrial, marketing, environmental, financial and communication problems" (IPR, 1999, p. 1). Similarly, another prominent practitioner remarked during the 2001 IPR conference on October 2 in Accra:

> The current business climate in Ghana demands that we [Ghanaian practitioners] attach greater importance to inter-corporate communications, both local and foreign. More importantly, we have to re-examine the way we have done business in the past and probably adopt the western-style, two-way communication and relationship building practices. (IPR, 2001, p. 12)

With these developments, public relations practitioners have felt a greater need than ever to set up a communication bridge between organizations. A prominent executive with the State Insurance Corporation (SIC) remarked:

> Chief executives are being judged on their ability to identify, cultivate and exploit core competence that make growth possible in their organizations. Companies are competing for key people, not corporate cash. With the economic scenario going on in the country, it had become obvious that until public relations initiatives are integrated in the overall business activities of organizations, public image would be at stake. (IPR, 2001, p. 7)

Another executive, the manager of the Ghana Commercial Bank, observed:

> Events in recent times had instilled in almost all organizations a sense of obligation to give public relations its rightful place. Success of any corporate body depends largely on the public's perception of it and also the kind of relationship that exists between the organization and its publics. (IPR, 2001, p. 8)

Ghanaian executives and management are beginning to realize that effective corporate public relations results in improved productivity, increased profitability, and growth. The implication of this recognition is that the primary mission of public relations in Ghana is being redefined to focus more on the management of relationships between organizations and between the organizations and their publics (Broom, Casey, & Ritchey, 1997; Brunig & Ledingham, 2000; Grunig & Hunt, 1984).

Independent Media and Increase in Media Relations

Since independence in 1957, Ghanaian public relations operated under a state-controlled and monopolized electronic media system, the GBC. The print media, especially national newspapers such as the *Daily Graphic*[15] and the *Ghanaian Times,* were no different. However, in 1995, as a result of internal and international pressure, the NDC government, for the first time in the country's history, allowed for private ownership and operation of media. This led to the growth in competitive and independent media operations in the country. By 2000, as many as eleven private FM radio stations and three television stations were operating alongside the state media in Ghana's capital city of Accra alone (Blankson, 2000). On the television scene, Accra has three free on-air stations: GTV[16] (the state television station), and the newer and privately owned TV3[17] and Metro TV.[18] Other cable television and pay-TV operations also exist, though they are not well established. Among the dozens of independent and commercial radio stations that began operating alongside the state radio network, GBC 1, GBC 2, and Radio GAR, are Radio Gold, Vibe FM,[19] Peace FM, and Joy FM.[20]

The independent and commercial media operations have provided Ghanaian public relations practitioners with alternative and multiple channels of communication, thereby changing public relations practice as it existed prior to 1995. According to private broadcasters interviewed, the new print and electronic media operations have started to serve as gatekeepers, controlling information flow between organizations and their publics. The broadcasters also acknowledge that, through the private media, several organizations have begun to report information to their publics, to mobilize public support for their activities, and to influence public policy. More importantly, through newly created phone-in talk programs, private radio and television stations are reporting timely information and offering public, social, and activist groups the avenues through which to voice their opinions and concerns. The private media operations also are providing opportunities to report abuses of government, public and private officials, and even individual citizens, and in the process have become significant change agents in the Ghanaian society.

Generally, Ghanaian practitioners report significant changes in their media relations activities. More than 85 percent of the practitioners interviewed agree that the task of sustaining media relations with the private stations has assumed a central role in their daily activities. Most have increased their communication efforts, especially via radio, because it has become easier and simpler. The private stations are also supporting the efforts of organizations that articulate public needs and opinions by allowing them to reach various publics with information, and to speak to and listen to their relevant publics.

The plurality of media channels has made it easier for practitioners to develop and maintain media contacts, arrange press conferences, place news releases, and determine what the media finds newsworthy about their organizations. This is because practitioners no longer have to rely on the state media alone for publicizing their organizations' activities and programs. Because of the competitive nature of the broadcasting environment, the state radio and television stations are becoming more responsive to their requests for publicity about their organizations' activities and programs.

Finally, the public relations practitioners also report an increase in their efforts to monitor public opinion expressed in the media. This has become a critical part of their daily activities because the independent media operations are serving as self-appointed watchdogs of the government and organizations by exposing organizational fraud, abuses, negligence of duty, and social irresponsibility. This is of concern to organizations because the private media is telling the Ghanaian public what the state-controlled media does not. However, the vigilance and timely reporting by the independent and commercial broadcasting stations have forced public relations practitioners to pay increasing attention to the media, and especially to public discussions in radio and television programs.

Increase in Public Interest and Participation in Society

Though public involvement in the development of issues in public relations is important, public relations in Ghana has not benefited from an active public. Decades of denial of the publics' freedom of speech and lack of avenues for public participation created a "culture of silence" among the Ghanaian publics. This inactivity began to change after 1995, when the Ghanaian public was awakened to an open, free, and independent media environment that began to expose problems and issues of societal concern and interest. Furthermore, they were awakened to a political system that allowed such developments. The public realized that their involvement and voice in government and organizational issues mattered in the newly created civil society. In addition, the growth in the private sector business and in mass media in Ghana created a critical discerning public and advocacy groups who demanded more information and accountability from organizations. These developments have begun to influence the way in which organizations relate to their publics and communities, and, for that matter, the way public relations is practiced.

The majority of the public relations practitioners interviewed acknowledge the increasing importance public opinion has assumed in their daily practices. More than 90 percent of them stated that they spend a significant amount of their time listening to and monitoring issues and questions discussed on the phone-in programs. One practitioner reported that the increase in public interest and involvement in society and affairs of organizations is forcing Ghanaian practitioners to pay more attention to the importance of public opinion in their practices. Another noted that organizations were moving from being the sole initiators of communication with their publics to an environment where the Ghanaian publics are exerting more effort to communicate and to engage in the activities of organizations via the independent media stations, particularly through radio talk programs.

The Ghanaian public has become what Hallahan called an "aroused public" (Hallahan, 2000, p. 505). They are beginning to recognize the power they have to influence the activities and policies of the government, and state and private organizations. They have also realized the need to voice their opinions through the many radio and television phone-in programs that have become part of the media environment and Ghanaian society. The phone-in programs allow both public and private officials and organizations to communicate with the publics. They also allow the public to voice their opinions and concerns on diverse issues and to ask officials and leaders difficult but important questions. Consequently, public awareness and participation in societal issues have increased dramatically.

In addition, there has been an increase in the formation of interest groups and social movements around issues of common interest, such as child abuse, community sanitation, family relationships, health issues, and women's issues. For example, several Ghanaian women have joined forces with a popular actress in television drama, Maame Dokono, to expose abuses of children and women and to seek help for the victims.

Problems and Limitations

Though these opportunities and positive developments seem to be moving public relations practice in Ghana toward a more professional practice, there are still many problems. According to Niagia (2001), although some public relations practitioners in Ghana are at the forefront of the execution of business plans, their importance and crucial roles are still seriously discounted. Public relations in several Ghanaian organizations continue to exist under departments such as marketing, personnel, and advertising. Consequently, they do not have a well-defined set of independent functions, responsibilities, and job descriptions. This is because of management's inability or refusal to see public relations as an integral part of the organization. It is also because of the inability of both management and public relations practitioners to properly define what public relations should do.

In many cases, the job descriptions of the Ghanaian public relations practitioners are carved out of existing departments. Boachie-Agyekum (1992) reported that public relations appears "fragmented, underdeveloped and occupies an appendage role in many organizations in Ghana" (pp. 43–46). In a speech by the head of the IPR, Nabanyin Pratt, during the year 2000 IPR week conference, complained that a number of organizations still insist on using their public relations practitioners for mainly protocol purposes, thus ignoring the key roles that practitioners should play.

Implementation of public relations campaigns continues to pose a major challenge for Ghanaian public relations practitioners. Because public relations is not accorded a management function in many organizations, many practitioners struggle with a small staff, an inadequate budget, and limited freedom and flexibility to plan and implement their programs. This, coupled with other problems, makes Ghanaian practitioners seem like "errand boys" (Niagia, 2001, p. 2).

The public also has limited knowledge of what public relations entails. Although no data exist to confirm this claim, practitioners interviewed genuinely believe that the majority of the Ghanaian public does not understand what public relations practitioners do. Speaking at the year 2000 IPR week celebration, the chair of the National Media Commission, Dr. Bonnah Koomson, blamed Ghanaian practitioners for not making any serious progress toward educating the public on what public relation is and what functions it plays in society.

Lack of adequate education and professional training opportunities also have hindered the growth of public relations practice in Ghana. The majority of public relations practitioners are not educated beyond the two-year diploma certificate issued by the GIJ, the public institution under the School of Communication Studies, University of Ghana. The school offers mainly general communication and journalism courses. Besides, the

GIJ is the only educational institution in the nation that offers a diploma degree in public relations. The GIJ and the University of Ghana do not have separate bachelor's- or master's-level education programs in public relations. To compound the situation, the majority of the instructors of public relations courses have master's-level educations. Very few of the public relations instructors have doctoral degrees in public relations. Most have specializations in communication studies granted by foreign universities. Consequently, the educational standards for practicing public relations professionals in Ghana has been very low and not well defined, a problem that the IPR is working diligently to improve (PRAG, 1991). Furthermore, other professional development opportunities, such as workshops, seminars, and refresher courses that focus on public relations, are rare.

Ghanaian practitioners generally have limited knowledge of and access to modern communication technologies useful for enhancing their public relations activities. New communication technologies, such as the Internet and the World Wide Web, are not readily available to the majority of the Ghanaian public, or to the majority of practitioners. However, the IPR recently received one year of free access to the Internet from a private Internet provider, National Communication Systems (NCS). Several organizations and public relations agencies in Ghana, including IPR, do not have Web sites. Though many public relations practitioners in Ghana believe that such technologies are vital communication tools for simplifying information handling and delivery, most rarely use them in their daily activities. As a result, the ability to plan and implement successful and diverse public relations programs is impaired.

Though the IPR has initiated several changes to alleviate some of the problems in Ghanaian public relations, its initiatives have been limited by lack of funds and resources (IPR, 2001). The majority of IPR's members do not pay their membership fees, which is the major source of revenue for the institute. For instance, in September 2000, only 167 (47 percent) of the total 348 members were in good standing. Of those in good standing, 84 were accredited members, 41 were associate members, and 42 were affiliate members (IPR, 2001, p. 4).

Conclusion

Public relations in Ghana has come a long way. From its early days, through the turbulent times in the 1980s, the practice is beginning to improve its image. As Ghana continues along its economic and political development path, and the march toward democracy and a liberal economy strengthens, opportunities will expand for public relations practice in Ghana. As the reforms continue to be successful, public relations will eventually be recognized as an important function in organizational settings. Organizations have started to increase their public relations staffs and budgets and have even begun to expand their scope of activities in areas such as media relations, corporate relations, and community relations. In addition, the continued growth in independent media will offer more opportunities for Ghanaian public relations practitioners. Consequently, it will force organizations to keep open relations with the media and to attend to public concerns. Organizations that fail to respond to public demands will probably find themselves and their problems exposed. Excellent public relations practice thrives on the good performance of the individual practitioner. Where a public relations practitioner fails to assert himself or herself, he or she will not be able to convince management to give him or her greater responsibilities. It also appears that success in the practice hinges largely on managerial support, adequate public relations budgets, and cooperation by all parties concerned. In this regard, the efforts of the IPR to promote professionalism and improve the poor image of Ghanaian public relations practitioners are well in order and must be encouraged. Certainly, public relations practice in Ghana faces an optimistic future.

Notes

1. The Institute of Public Relations, Ghana, was recently given free Internet access. As part of the reconstruction, the IPR is in the process of constructing a Web site.

2. Institute of Public Relations, United Kingdom (www.ipr.org.uk)

3. Public Relations Society of America (www.prsa.org)

4. The Federation of African Public Relations is headquartered in Nairobi, Kenya.

5. The Ghana Institute of Journalism is the only institution in the country that trains public relations practitioners. It is under the School of Communication Studies, University of Ghana (www.ug.edu.gh).

6. GBC is the national broadcast network that oversees the operation of both radio and television broadcasting in the entire country. Since 1995, GBC has undergone drastic changes in response to private competition (www.gbc.com.gh).

7. The NDC was born out of the Provincial National Defense Council (PNDC) military government led by former President Flight Lieutenant Jerry Rawlings. Rawlings came to power in 1979 as a result of a military coup. The PNDC was later transformed into a political party, NDC, to allow Rawlings to stand for presidential elections in 1989. For more of NDC's platform visit their Web site at www.ndc.org.gh.

8. Unda was founded in 1928 and is the International Catholic Association for Radio, Television, and related Media (www.unda.org/association.htm). OCIC is the International Catholic Organization for Cinema and Audio-visual (www.ocic.org). The two have since merged to form SIGNIS (www.signis.net).

9. For more information about IPRA's Code of Professional Conduct visit www.ipranet.org/codes.htm.

10. See www.ssnit.org.gh for more information about SSNIT.

11. Visit www.vodi.com.gh for more information about Vodi Technik Motors Limited.

12. Visit www.standardchartered.com/gh/index/html for more information.

13. Visit www.ghana.airways.com for more information on the state airline.

14. Visit www.ghanatel.net for more information on the operations of Ghana Telecom.

15. Both the *Daily Graphic* and *Ghanaian Times* are state newspapers. Visit www.graphic.com.gh for more on the *Daily Graphic*. The *Ghanaian Times* does not have an operational Web site.

16. GTV is the television branch of the state-owned GBC network. Visit www.gbc.com.gh for more on the network.

17. TV3 is owned by a private consortium led by Malaysia TV3.

18. MetroTV is privately owned. It is geared mainly toward entertainment and movies. For more information visit www.metrotv.com.gh

19. Visit www.vibefm.com.gh for more information on the private radio station Vibe FM.

20. Visit www.joy997.fm.com.gh for more information on the private radio station Joy FM.

Discussion Questions

1. Public relations practitioners in Ghana are considered socially responsible only when they contribute to national development. What do you think this statement means? How has this social responsibility role helped shape public relations functions and activities in developing countries such as Ghana?

2. In the light of recent democratic and liberal reforms, and the subsequent economic and political changes occurring in Ghana, what do you foresee the future of public relations in Ghana to be? Do you think there will be a significant transformation of the functions and activities of practitioners? Explain.

3. Politics, governments, and their ideologies are very important when discussing public relations in many developing countries. Several scholars argue that, in the interest of national development, unity, and security, it is necessary for governments in such countries to control important sectors of the economy, such as the media and organizational behavior. In your view, what are the pros and cons of governments' heavy involvement in such activities? What are the political influences that hinder the effectiveness of public relations practitioners in Ghana?

References

Al-Enad, A. (1990, Summer). Public relations roles in developing countries. *Public Relations Quarterly, 35*(2), 24–28.

Ansah, P. (1976, June 11). A two way mirror. *The Daily Graphic,* p. 12.

Ansah, P. (1985). *Broadcasting and national development.* Accra: Ghana Broadcasting Corporation.

Blankson, I. (2000). *Independent and pluralistic broadcasting development in Ghana: Perceptions of audiences in Accra.* Unpublished dissertation, Ohio University, Athens.

Boachie-Agyekum, F. (1992). *A comparative study of PR practices in selected state and private establishments. A case of Ghana Commercial Bank, Standard Chartered Bank, State Insurance Corporation, Great African Insurance Company, Ghamot, and Japan Motors.* Unpublished research project, University of Ghana, Legon.

Bonnah-Koomson, A. (1994). Independent broadcasting stations in rural areas. In K. Karikari (Ed.), *Independent broadcasting in Ghana. Implications and challenges* (pp. 83–96). Accra: Ghana University Press.

Bonnah-Koomson, A. (Ed.). (1995). *Prospects for private broadcasting in Ghana.* University of Ghana, Accra: Gold-Type Limited.

Brunig, S., & Ledingham, J. (2000). Perceptions of relationships and evaluations of satisfaction: An exploration of interaction. *Public Relations Review, 26*(1), 85–95.

Grunig, J. E. (1992). (Ed.). *Excellence in public relations and communication management.* Hillsdale, NJ: Lawrence Erlbaum Associates.

Grunig, J. E., & Hunt, T. (1984). *Managing public relations.* New York: Holt, Rinehart & Winston.

Grunig, J. E., & Repper, F. (1992). Strategic management, public and issues. In J. E. Grunig (Ed.), *Excellence in public relations and communication management* (pp. 117–158). Hillsdale, NJ: Lawrence Erlbaum Associates.

Gyan, M. (1991). *A profile of public relations practice in Ghana.* Unpublished thesis, University of Ghana, Legon.

Hallahan, K. (2000). Inactive publics: The forgotten publics in public relations. *Public Relations Review, 26*(4), 499–515.

Institute of Public Relations, Ghana. (1999, March). *IPR Newsletter, 3*(1), 1–3.

Institute of Public Relations, Ghana. (2001, June). *IPR Newsletter, 5*(1), 1–12, 16–17.

Karikari, K. (Ed.). (1994). *Independent broadcasting in Ghana. Implications and challenges.* Accra: Ghana University Press.

Karikari, K. (1995). Political and technological constraints on the development of independent broadcasting in Ghana. In A. Bonnah-Koomson (Ed.), *Prospects for private broadcasting in Ghana* (pp. 9–16). University of Ghana, Accra: Gold-Type Limited.

Niagia, S. (2001, April). Public relations: A taxing task. *Business Watch Online, 3*(10). [On-line]. Available: www.africaonline.com.gh/bwatch/page11.html.

Osam, V. (1989). *Public relations outfits in private and public institutions.* Unpublished thesis, University of Ghana, Legon.

Pratt, C. (1985, February). Public relations in the Third World: The African context. *Public Relations Journal, 41*(2), 11–12, 15–16.

Pratt, C. (1986). Professionalism in Nigerian public relations. *Public Relations Review, 12*(4), 27–40.

Pratt, C., & Ugboajah, F. (1985). Social responsibility: A comparison of Nigerian public relations with Canadian and U.S. public relations. *International Public Relations Review, 9,* 22–29.

Public Relations Association of Ghana. (May, 1991). *Policy paper on accreditation of public relations education and practice.* Accra: Public Relations Association of Ghana.

Sattler, J. (1981). PR in Africa: Impressive strides. *Public Relations Journal, 37*(6), 28–29, 39.

Siebert, F., Peterson, T., & Schramm, W. (1963). *Four theories of the press.* Urbana: University of Illinois Press.

Taylor, M. (2000). Media relations in Bosnia: A role for public relations in building civil society. *Public Relations Review, 26*(1), 1–14.

Taylor, M., & Kent, M. (1999). When public relations becomes government relations. *Public Relations Quarterly, 44*(3), 18–23.

Terkper, S. (1996). *VAT in Ghana: Why it failed.* Development Discussion Paper No. 556. Cambridge, MA: Harvard Institute for International Development.

Turkson, D. (1986). *PR section of the University of Cape Coast.* Unpublished thesis, University of Ghana, Legon.

UN Development Program. (1997). *Ghana: Human Development Report.* Accra: United Nations Development Program.

Van Leuven, J., & Pratt, C. (1996). Public relations' role: Realities in Asia and in Africa south of the Saharan. In H. Culbertson & N. Chen (Eds.), *International public relations: A comparative analysis* (pp. 93–106). Mahweh, NJ: Lawrence Erlbaum Associates.

World Bank. (1999). *African Development Indicators.* Washington, DC: World Bank.

15

Public Relations in South Africa

A Communication Tool for Change

Arnold S. de Beer

Gary Mersham

Key Points

- Public relations in a multiethnic society, such as South Africa, presents professionals with a variety of challenges, from the need for diversity on government, corporate, and higher education staffs to the important role played by nongovernmental organizations (NGOs) and nonprofit organizations (NPOs).

- South Africa became a democratic society in 1994, and, unlike the situation in most other countries where a minority oligarchy was replaced by a government elected by the majority of voters, the transition was relatively peaceful.

- Public relations and interpersonal communication are often dealt with as though they belong to different aspects of the social sciences. Note the interaction between these two fields of study and especially the role "mutual understanding" plays in this regard as it concerns South Africa.

- For many decades public relations was believed to be confined to financial and business organizations. Note in this chapter how public relations can be deployed in a developing country.

- Public relations also is often regarded as only the promotions side of an organization. Note how in the case of South Africa it also can be part of the management of change.

Background

Fossil evidence on the evolutionary history of the family of humankind had, according to recent research, its earliest origins in southern Africa. The Koi-San people inhabited the most southern point of the continent some 1,500 years ago. In 1652 the Dutch East Indian Company set up a station to supply passing ships to the East with provisions. This European settlement was the beginning of what was later to become South Africa. During the Napoleonic wars, the British seized the Cape Colony (as it was then known) as a desirable strategic base controlling the sea route to the East. Since 1803 the Cape Colony was integrated into the international trading empire of an industrializing Britain, and the closed and regulated system of the Dutch period was swept away.

In the process of finding themselves on a new continent the Dutch (and later French and German) immigrants moved into the hinterland where they met the Bantu tribes, such as the Zulu and Xhosa, who had emigrated from mid-Africa to the south. The settlers, later to become known as Afrikaners or Boers, tried to find a new independent country not under British rule and moved to the north during the 1830s in what was to become known as the Great Trek. The Boers then formed two republics, one across the Orange River (the Republic of the Orange Free State) and one across the Vaal River (the South African Republic). In the meantime, the British also colonized the area where most of the Zulus lived and founded the colony of Natal. Between 1899 and 1902, the Anglo–Boer War was fought when the British tried to extend their influence into the two Boer Republics in order to lay claim to rich diamond and gold fields. After a prolonged guerrilla campaign, the British responded with a scorched earth policy, establishing concentration camps in which 26,000 Boer women and children died. Africans from Boer farms and towns were similarly incarcerated.

In 1910, the Union of South Africa was founded, consisting of the four colonies Cape, Natal, Free State, and Transvaal. The long process of segregation and apartheid began when the first Union Government enacted the seminal Black Land Act in 1913. This was the beginning not only of the repression of black Africans but also of other people of color. In 1948 the National Party came to power and segregation was formally legalized into apartheid. The struggle against apartheid became well-known throughout the world and came to a head at Sharpeville in 1960 when sixty-nine antipass demonstrators were killed in a clash with police. After Sharpeville, the black nationalist liberation movements, the African National Congress (ANC) and the Pan African Congress (PAC), abandoned their nonviolent resistance against apartheid and turned to armed struggle. This led to the Rivonia trial in 1963, in which ANC leaders, such as Nelson Mandela, were sentenced to life imprisonment. In 1976 were the Soweto uprisings and the beginning of the end of apartheid, which lasted another two decades.

White minority rule, growing black nationalism, and increasing international public opinion against apartheid led to an extended negotiating process in the early 1990s, culminating in the first democratic elections in April 1994. Nelson Mandela was elected president and FW de Klerk, the former president and leader of the National Party, vice-president. Soon thereafter, South Africa adopted one of the world's most liberal–democratic constitutions with a guarantee for freedom of the press and speech. In 1999, the second democratic elections were held, and Thabo Mbeki was elected president.

The peaceful political transition in South Africa in 1994 could not have occurred without open communication, freedom of speech, and the crucial role that public relations played to help create a political climate susceptible to change. The idea that democracy cannot exist without freedom of speech is a well-established norm of open- or free-market societies. There are also some fundamental relationships between public relations, communication, and democracy (Mersham, Rensburg, & Skinner, 1995) that are important foundations of the public relations practice in a still-democratizing South Africa.

Democracy and Public Relations

Public relations requires freedoms, communication/media, a democratic society, and personal truths. First, public relations in its modern sense can only function in accord with the fundamental rights of freedom of speech and of information. Every individual in a democratic society has an equal right to be heard. This includes the right to communicate, in a professional capacity, on behalf of the government, a company, organization, or individual.

Currently, South Africa is, unlike the apartheid years (1948–1994), characterized by a healthy debate on these matters, particularly between the media and the government. This is particularly evident in media relations as part of the broader concept of public relations. In fact, a public relations war exists. Government, with a multitude of public relations sections in state and semistate departments, argues that it does not get a fair hearing from the media. Government failures are well reported but their successes are not. It has, it says, equally the right of access to the media to communicate its policies and actions to its citizens. For some in government, media attacks on President Thabo Mbeki are only one facet of a general antagonism toward government (De Beer, 2002).

The South African news media claim (De Beer, 2002) they are only doing what the media should do: exposing corruption and misadministration and exposing the famous and powerful. The news media are ever wary of state attempts to infringe on freedom of speech. They point to their role in the fall of the apartheid regime, and the fact that the interventions by the Apartheid State must never be reinvented and used to silence and manipulate journalists. Meetings between President Mbeki and top South African editors in April 2001 may eventually lead the way to a better understanding of each others' interests, but, because of the past, there is a healthy concern that the government must not be allowed to dominate or force the media to carry its messages.

Public relations thrives on these freedoms and could not exist without them. Each individual, pressure group, and institution has a right to use public relations counsel and, in most democracies, do so. South Africa is no exception to this rule. Second, public relations is indispensable in modern and modernizing democracies with mass societies and mass communications. As South Africa engages massive social, political, and economic change, the role of the media increases in order to take the various developmental messages to people. Historically throughout the world, the various techniques of public relations were formed organically within the processes of industrialization and mass communication, and today in South Africa the wide spectrum of interests and groups state their messages in a variety of media.

Third, public relations, as it is defined today on the basis of an open communication process, can only exist in democratic societies. The plethora of media conferences and media releases by previously banned and marginalized groups in South Africa prior to and since the democratic elections is testament to this thesis. Public relations cannot and does not exist in authoritarian, dictatorial, or totalitarian regimes—except perhaps in name. In governments in which one party, or one leader, determines public policy, there can be no true role for public relations. According to the Johannesburg *Sunday Times,* this was emphasized by the situation in South Africa's neighbor, Zimbabwe, in 2002, when almost all vestiges of open public relation activities disappeared in the run-up to the presidential election (Time for you to go, Africa tells Mugabe, 2002, p. 1). The party or leader might use communication techniques as a form of propaganda to keep the people "in line" (as was the case in Zimbabwe), but there would be no need for professionals to practice on behalf of those who wanted to challenge or criticize the status quo and propose different ideas, policies, and procedures. Clearly, such communication practices would be labeled subversive and unlawful in a nondemocratic environment.

Fourth, public relations is linked to democracy because everyone has a right to articulate their version of the truth. There is no one truth because absolute truth exists only in the one-party totalitarian state. At the risk of falling foul of philosophy, history seems to suggest that social truth is evolutionary and in a state of flux. In any case, even where a majority view predominates on a given issue, the right of the individual to his or her own version of the truth is inviolable in a democracy. Public relations can only exist in open societies where civil society, business, and government are amenable to freely expressed opinion and the right to criticize existing and proposed policies.

Democracy and Communication

In practice, professional organizational communications, such as public relations, must be given the scope to operate on either a reactive or proactive basis (Mersham et al., 1995). In South Africa public relations is characterized by the early facilitation and establishment of communication relationships and networks with a variety of stakeholders (such as local communities, union representatives, local government, etc.). South Africa has become a country with one of the largest number of diverse forums in the world (according to country size) on all manner of interests and issues.

This approach, which Grunig and Hunt (1984) call the two-way symmetrical model, stresses that communication is two way and exchange leads to change on both sides of the organization–publics relationship. In the two-way symmetrical model, the practitioner serves as a mediator between the organization and the stakeholders. It encourages dialogue, rather than simply disseminating information (Grunig & Hunt 1984; Grunig & Grunig, 1992; Grunig & White 1992). South African practitioners quickly acknowledged the relevance of the work of these scholars for South Africa. Mersham and colleagues (1995) and Holtzhausen and Verwey (1996) argue from a South African perspective that the two-way symmetrical model provides a normative model of how corporate communication should be practiced in order to be ethical and effective under South African circumstances.

Public relations practitioners in South Africa largely acknowledge that they have to set about repairing and constructing bridges of trust between the "haves" and the "have nots," between those with growing political power and those with existing economic power. Public relations practitioners, as communicators in a new democratic society, inevitably find themselves center stage of the convergence of competing interests in the process of social change. In a sense public relations practitioners have become involved in "selling" the concept of democratic process. As large organizations find themselves under pressure to change, it is the public relations practitioner who has to explain these changes to both the organizations' internal and external communication partners.

Public Relations and Social Change

The challenges of social change and intercultural communication, and the growing influence of globalism are of increasing importance to professional communicators in South Africa. Because communication plays a major role in social change and development in South Africa, it has become essential for public relations practitioners to grasp basic issues surrounding democratic development regardless of their own cultural baggage or worldview. South Africa is "both developing and developed" at once (Pahad, 2001, p. 19) and reflects the challenges of resolving Mbeki's "two nations in one."

Corporate and government social investment are two of the key driving forces in South African public relations (Mersham et al., 1995). The centrality of public relations practice to democratic and developmental concerns in South Africa requires the practitioner to be sensitive to the needs and practices of developmental pursuits by the private sector and government. As Nina Overton-De Klerk (1994) puts it, corporate social investment is not a "sideline speciality" of public relations in South Africa but has become "the only way in which the South African business sector can ensure its survival in a turbulent South Africa in transition" (p. 73). Mersham (1992, pp. 54–55; 1993, pp. 112–13) draws attention to corporate social responsibility as a national philosophy, namely that

> the concept of social responsibility includes an organization's relationship to the society in which it operates, and its involvement in problems of national significance that fade that society.

As might be expected, the impact of burgeoning global culture, driven by a revolution in communications, is forcing forms of structural adjustments. The public relations practitioner plays an important role in marrying internal to external policy action and broad social movements. The private sector and government are clear in their shared commitment to democratic development. Essop Pahad, minister in the presidency charged with the public relations functions of the presidential office, argues that the role of South African government "is to bridge the developmental divide" (Pahad, 2001, p. 19). Being "both developing and developed" at once, government's public relations pitch is that it "gives us a voice born out of varied experience, one worth listening to across the board in world politics. . . . We have deep empathy for, and understanding of, the developing world. We can speak with Cuba and Libya and, at the same time, with the US and Europe. We are a 'linchpin nation' " (Pahad, 2001, p. 19).

History and Structure of Public Relations in South Africa

A decade or three ago public relations was considered by some in South Africa not to be a very serious form of communication. Public relations practitioners were often portrayed as members of the wine-and-dine or backslapping club who would hang around the so-called nineteenth hole at golf clubs. Success was often measured in the amount of space in publications that public relations practitioners could wrangle from journalists.

But what was true for countries such as the United States (Pember, 1987) was also applicable to South Africa. As society grew more complex and communication techniques and research methods more sophisticated, the need arose for communication experts who could deal with intricate socioeconomic, political, and other forces as they related to the communication needs of modern-day organizations. This was even more the case after the first democratic elections held in 1994, and then followed up by the next in 1999.

With the turn of the twenty-first century public relations is more and more becoming an ingrained part of not only corporate management but also all spheres of South African society. As elsewhere in the free-market world (Agee, Ault, & Emery, 1991), it involves research and analysis, policy formation, communication, and feedback from publics involved. Of all applied fields of communication, public relations in South Africa is presently the one discipline more concerned about the education and training of its practitioners, and with the process of professionalization, than any of the other older or traditional mass media fields, such as journalism.

Even so, the field and even the term *public relations* are not clearly demarcated. On the one hand, it is still seen by a minority as some sort of bribery by unscrupulous lobbyists, whereas on the other hand, it is acknowledged as an important management function with a wide range of communication activities. Or, as the well-known authors on public relations in South Africa, Skinner and Von Essen (1991), put it almost a decade ago, "public relations has emerged in South Africa today as a sophisticated, multifaceted discipline able to help forge effective two-way communication between an organization and its various publics" (p. 1).

The first public relations officer in South Africa was appointed by South African Railways in 1943, and the first public relations consultancy was established in Johannesburg in 1948. The introduction of several public relations departments in the private sector followed soon after, especially in the mining industry.

Though public relations has since developed in South Africa as a sophisticated discipline, and is increasingly recognized as an essential component of organizational and business activities, there is still debate about its exact role in society. The debate deals, as in many other countries, with the question of professionalism and how a professional code of ethics might be effectively enforced. South Africa was one of the first countries to research and evolve a formal body of knowledge of public relations—an attempt by the Public Relations Institute for South Africa (PRISA) to define the theoretical and practical knowledge required by a professional practitioner. As Brian Cullingworth, a former president of PRISA, put it, one of the paradoxes of the discipline is the extent to which it is misunderstood despite being populated by people whose business is planning, communicating, and image building. Consequently, the value of professional public relations is not yet apparent to all in South Africa.

Over the years there have been a number of individuals who have made substantial contributions to the field of public relations practice, education, and organization in South Africa. Among the pioneers who were also involved in establishing public relations in the field of education and publishing are Jacques Malan and J. A. L'Estrange (1965), Bob Krause (1977), Chris Skinner and Llew Von Essen (1991), David Hilton-Barber (1991), and Gary Mersham (Mersham & Skinner, 1998). As South Africa moved toward a more democratic society, these authors—academics such as Mersham from the Department of Communication at the University of Zululand, and public relations administrators such as

Margaret Moscardi—have played a pivotal role in placing public relations not only within the scope of a newly democratic society but also in making it work as a forceful communication tool.

The Nature and Scope of Public Relations

In South Africa, public relations as a communication field operates no differently than the practice does elsewhere in the free world. It is based on two assumptions. First, that in a modern democracy every organization survives ultimately only by public consent; and second, that this consent cannot exist in a communication vacuum. South African public relations follows this very basic notion.

Fundamental to public relations in South Africa and elsewhere is the establishment of mutual understanding between the organization on one hand and the various publics and general community on the other. This needs to be based on open, two-way communication that allows the organization to explain its policies, products, procedures, and so on while simultaneously allowing it to monitor feedback. Implicitly, this also allows the organization to influence public opinion, judgment, and behavior of its various publics.

Practitioners in the South African profession operate as elsewhere on two distinct levels: externally as consultants or advisers to their clients or to a company's management, or internally as in-house corporate public relations officers performing a multiplicity of functions. One of the marked developments in postapartheid society has been the increased use made by government of not only in-house public relations but also of outside consultants.

Taking its cue from such public relations organizations as the World Assembly of Public Relations (Mexico City, 1978), the International Public Relations Association (IPRA), and the Public Relations Society of America (PRSA), PRISA defined public relations as "the deliberate, planned and sustained effort to establish and maintain mutual understanding between an organization and its publics, both internal and external" (Nel, 1994, p. 213). This definition emphasizes the fact that public relations is a deliberate and intentional part of an organization's policy, a conscious effort to provide information and create goodwill. Public relations is designed to influence, gain understanding, propagate information, and ensure feedback from those affected by an organization's activities. It means that messages are tailored to meet identified target groups according to a definite set of objectives.

It describes public relations as a planned effort in which public relations activities are not haphazardly undertaken but systematically organized. It also implies that it is an activity that plans ahead for difficulties and emergencies. Research is undertaken, problems are identified, strategies are adopted, and objectives decided on. The goals may be short, medium, or long term, and planning involves detailed steps according to carefully determined priorities and aims. It also subsumes the conscious evaluation of the organization's activities that have a bearing on its reputation. For clarity's sake and in line with modern-day trends, the term *communication* could be added to specify the nature of the planned effort.

It is a sustained activity, a never-ending effort that recognizes that the public is continually changing, that there are numerous causes clamoring for its attention, and that it must be kept continuously informed. The definition draws attention to the proactive quality of good public relations. Instead of responding to crises with knee-jerk type reactions, public relations practice anticipates and plans for community concerns and possible crises. Public relations, therefore, implies an ongoing analysis of all sides of the communication equation—sender, message, channel, destination, and feedback within a particular system.

The need to establish and maintain understanding follows from the preceding, but the words *mutual understanding* form perhaps the crux of the definition. The products, services, policies, and practices of an organization may be excellent, but unless the public understands that, and recognizes them for what they are, they will not be used or appreciated. At the same time, unless the organization understands the public's likes and dislikes, it cannot adjust its products, services, policies, and practices to the desires of the public it serves.

In the modern world, and even more so in South Africa, very little remains static and unaffected by social change. Planning must be flexible enough to cope with a changing environment. Thus, for there to be mutual understanding, there must be a two-way flow of ideas, a continuous interchange of thought. To ensure this, arrangements for feedback from the various publics and evaluation of that feedback must be made on an ongoing basis.

Effective public relations reflects actual policies and performances by organizations, companies, and individuals. Acceptable performances and policies cannot be manufactured by the practitioner, and no amount of public relations activities can hide, for example, a company's poor employment policies or unresponsiveness to its community or its direct public's concerns (see the two case studies cited at the end of this chapter).[1]

Public relations activities are to be found in every sphere of South Africa's commercial, social, and political life:

- Government—national, regional, local, and international
- Business and industry—small, medium, transnational
- Community and social affairs
- Educational institutions, universities, and colleges
- Hospitals and health care
- Charities and good causes
- International affairs

Each of these institutions has a certain identity it wishes to portray, while at the same time, individuals and groups have certain perceptions or images of the particular organization, including the following:

- Corporate identity
- Corporate image

In South Africa, as elsewhere in the world where public relations is an important corporate communication tool, the functions of the public relations practitioner include:

- Programming and counseling
- Media relations
- Organizing
- Writing
- Production (creation of various messages using appropriate media)
- Speaking (face-to-face communication and public speaking)

- Research and evaluation
- Training (training and advising executives and management to deal with the media, make presentations, and give public appearances)
- Management

Professionalization

Ideally, the head of public relations should be equal in status, rank, and remuneration with other department heads. This is not yet the case in all South African corporations. In many instances public relations is still viewed as a function to be dealt with (if at all) by personnel or marketing.

Educational requirements, education, and training in public relations, however, are no longer dealt with in an ad hoc way. On the contrary, of all communication occupations, public relations was the first in South Africa to organize itself and develop minimum educational and training structures.

Public relations has come to the fore as the most general aspect of communication or mass communication taught at the tertiary level in South Africa. Almost all universities with communication departments or schools teach public relations to some degree, with some offering it as a major leading to master's and doctoral degrees (e.g., Potchefstroom, Rand Afrikaans, Free State, Zululand). At *technikons,* or technical universities, public relations is offered within an own school (e.g., Pretoria, Natal, Port Elizabeth). There are a large number of private colleges (evening or correspondence) offering public relations programs (e.g., Damelin). Recently, public relations has started to lose its independent position as a separate field of study because the trend is to combine it with, or see it as part of, corporate communication (which includes internal and external public relations, advertising, and promotion). At some universities, public relations is seen as part of marketing communication (Pretoria).

The driving force behind education is PRISA. Founded in 1957, PRISA now has more than three thousand members. Its main objectives are:

- To bring together those engaged in public relations work for the interchange of views and experience and for mutual consultation and advantage.
- To establish and maintain the full professional status and dignity of public relations work among members, practitioners, employees, and the general public.
- To foster and encourage the close observance of the highest professional conduct by its members and to prescribe such conduct.
- To give a united voice to the practice of public relations and to enhance its influence.
- To undertake all such activities as are likely to be of benefit to the practice of public relations and in the interest of its members.

Through its Public Relations Institute, PRISA runs ongoing professional development courses, seminars, and workshops in major centers around the country with the assistance of its regional chapters; short and midterm courses, in particular, are offered for new practitioners, midcareer professionals, and managers. Through a process of accrediting university and other courses, as well as its own courses, PRISA has developed a system whereby its members can succeed in obtaining the highest public relations ranking, namely that of APR (accredited in public relations).

After many years of activity by successive chairs and office bearers of PRISA, the Public Relations Ethics and Accreditation Council of South Africa was formed in 1985 (now the Ethics and Accreditation Council of PRISA). As an independent and autonomous body, the council's role is to monitor the practice of public relations, operating in much the same way as the Medical Council, Law Council, and other professional councils. The council serves the interests of both the general public and public relations practitioners by seeking to prevent malpractice in public relations. The tasks of the council are:

- The voluntary professional accreditation of public relations practitioners holding the required minimum educational and empirical qualifications
- The maintenance of a code of professional conduct and recognized ethics.

The aims of the council are:

- To set standards for the professional registration of public relations practitioners, these being a combination of appropriate academic qualifications plus relevant practical public relations experience, which may include the teaching of public relations.
- To examine applicants who meet these requirements by way of written and oral examinations based on the Public Relations Council's own published standards.
- To maintain an enforceable code of professional conduct and apply this code.
- To maintain a register of accredited professional public relations practitioners.
- To award the right to use the title accredited in public relations (APR).
- To create an awareness and positive perception among public opinion leaders of the role and value of the accredited public relations practitioner.
- To initiate and publish research, and formulate bylaws necessary to achieve its objectives.

Public Relations and Issues in South Africa

Many of the following issues are interrelated. Some of these issues have a global significance, whereas others have particular significance for South African practitioners. Against the background of the urgent need to establish communication between all the peoples of South Africa in a new political dispensation, the public relations profession has a vital and growing role to play. By promoting better understanding and cooperation, public relations could make a major contribution to the future peace and prosperity of democratizing South Africa.

Professional Values

Practitioners must adopt professional orientations or approaches. How can practitioners demonstrate their collective professionalism? Three aspects may be identified.

First, every public relations practitioner should apply a body of knowledge and techniques, which is standardized, systematic, and scientific in approach to the activities of public relations. As in any other profession, this requires formal training. Second, practitioners must subscribe to a code of professional standards that provides principles and guidelines for the appropriate ethical standards of operation. Enforceable codes of ethics, conduct, and standards of practice are a prerequisite to professionalism. Members of a professional body must accept these requirements and must be disciplined for transgressions. Third, practitioners must consciously exemplify professionalism by their behaviors at all times.

Membership in a Professional Organization

The existence of a professional body to which entry is restricted by qualifications and experience is essential for a discipline striving for professional status. In South Africa PRISA is the representative body. Membership in a professional organization affords individuals a platform to discuss, debate, and make decisions on issues and matters of common concern. It also provides a basis for further training and development of skills. The workshops and seminars organized by the various regional chapters of PRISA are good examples of how this works successfully in practice.

Social Responsibility

Organizations do not exist in a social vacuum. In the present day, the creation and provision of goods and services cannot be treated only as a profit-making operation. Contemporary society expects an organization also to exercise social responsibility with regard to the impact of its operations on the communities in which it is established and on the nation as a whole. This includes dealing with such problems as those associated with the environment, black advancement, health, education, and equality of opportunity.

These days, pressures from customers, consumers, publics, stockholders, and other pressure and interest groups stimulate corporate responsiveness. Corporations, as public entities, seek social approval by being good corporate citizens. An organization's set of responsibilities may be thought of as its social contract. It is generally accepted that a large company or corporation demonstrates its responsibility by devoting a sum of money specifically to projects that are not part of its everyday business. Social responsibility calls for an acceptance that the survival of an organization depends on its being seen as socially accountable—that it can rise above immediate economic interest and anticipate the impact of its actions and operations on all individuals and groups.

Types of Financial Support

Three main categories of financial support may be defined as donations, sponsorships, and subsidies. Broadly, donations are made to support a wide range of national, regional, and local concerns and projects—for example, educational grants, upliftment projects for the underprivileged and the disadvantaged, community health and welfare projects, and antipollution and conservation drives. The support may or may not be widely acknowledged, and although the organization might receive some recognition, the benefit is aimed toward the community concerned. In the case of sponsorships, more emphasis is placed on gaining wide publicity, especially with respect to sporting and cultural events. Subsidies may take various forms—transport, housing, and educational subsidies are three important areas.

It is clear that the concept of social responsibility is not limited to support for people and areas outside of an organization's field of operations. It also includes the organization's internal relations with personnel, its employment practices. For example, adherence is expected to the government's policy of affirmative action and black empowerment, chambers of commerce guidelines, business ethics, and the general well-being of employees. Ultimately, undertaking social responsibility should result in an actual social benefit. Goodwill and favorable publicity that accrues, although welcome, is often not seen as the major objective. It is often argued that in view of the problems facing black South Africans, the greatest part of any social responsibility program or funds should be directed toward the benefit of black people because they are, as a majority, the most in need.

Employment

One of the main problems in the area of employment is the relative lack of skills among black people. Increased training of skilled black labor in all sectors, especially in the engineering and technological fields, is imperative. On-the-job-training programs can contribute to skills acquisition and upgrading in the formal employment sector, and support for educational programs offered by *technikons* and training centers can be offered in the form of apprenticeships, bursaries, and scholarships.

Support for basic skills programs open to the general public, such as bricklaying, plumbing and electrical wiring, welding, basic accountancy, small-business financing and advice centers, and so on, can contribute to the development of the small-business and the informal sector. The informal sector is said to account for nearly a third of the productivity profile of the country and forms an indispensable foundation for larger business operations.

Industrial Relations

Industrial relations is an important arena where much can be done in terms of corporate responsibility programs. Trade unionism and industrial relations are virtually in their infancy in this country, and only in the past decade has labor relations legislation been freed of discriminatory implications. Trade unions are growing in strength, and this trend will probably continue in the near future. Public relations can assist in keeping all communication channels open, developing skills to handle disputes, and helping to bridge the gulf that exists between management and workers.

Housing

As a result of the rapid urbanization that black people are experiencing, the need for housing is widespread. Increasingly, organizations are realizing that productivity is linked to the living conditions of workers and that a settled worker having acquired freehold property and house ownership is a most productive worker. Social responsibility programs embrace assistance with financing for home purchasing and, in the case of larger organizations, the introduction of company-developed housing schemes.

Community Involvement

The ethic of community involvement runs strongly through black culture and recognition of this by an organization can only benefit it in the long term. A firm commitment to improving the situation of people will ensure successful operation in the future. Educational resources programs, such as the funding of local schools and teachers, and the funding of facilities and services projects, such as the provision of sanitation, running water, and electrical reticulation, are key areas where the quality of life of employees can be improved.

Education

Some aspects of education such as social responsibility have been referred to previously. Two main areas can be identified. The first is organizational education, which has to do with on-the-job training and specialized training that is associated with the work the employee carries out for the organization. The second refers to a more informal kind of education—education for survival—with which employers can assist. It concerns the economic system and how it works. Employees need to be shown how the system works to their benefit; for example, educational programs can present information concerning the importance of contributing to pension funds, worker unemployment insurance, and so on. It also includes encouraging and advising people about the value of freehold land and home ownership, the payment of rates and taxes, the provision of services, and the workings of a democratic system.

Environmental Issues

The reduction of pollution and protection of the environment is a worldwide problem that will continue to be a major issue in the future. Concern about the finite limits of the planet's air, water, and natural resources has become deeply embedded in the public's consciousness, and an organization cannot afford to underestimate the strength of the movement. In South Africa, for many years, the release of dangerous chemicals into the air and pollution-laden discharges into waterways was seldom questioned.

The opposite is true today. Environmental activist groups challenge every indication of industrial pollution and destruction of natural habitats that they discover. As the U.S. experience has shown, environmental protestations sometimes become major issues and engender substantial public support. From a global point of view, the green wave has only just arrived on South African shores and will no doubt gather momentum in the coming years. There is great scope, therefore, for the promotion of successful environmental projects.

Sometimes the assumptions of corporate environmental wrongdoing are based on inadequate information or a slanted approach. The best course for corporations with an environmental problem is to seek common ground with their critics. Informal meetings between company executives and environmentalist leaders can break down barriers and lead to the establishment of common objectives, toward which the opposing sides agree to work. From the public relations point of view, the minimum effect is that the organization is perceived to recognize its problem and to desire to solve it. Emphasis should be placed on long-term relationships and programs that dispel the image of a quick fix and show a strong commitment to the future.

Consumer Relations

Rising inflation and economic pressures are forcing consumers to speak out on matters they consider important. Business is already feeling the effects of pressure groups on such matters as pollution, environmental control, detergents, pesticides, and other ills of a social nature. The consumer movement in South Africa is gaining momentum and will increasingly become a force with which to be reckoned.

Trading, Sporting, and Cultural Opportunities

The lifting of trade sanctions and cultural boycotts during the 1990s provided many opportunities to reestablish old trading links and establish new business contracts. The countries of the African continent offer a huge potential for South African products, services, and expertise. Similarly, South African participation in the world sporting arena and a wealth of cultural activities will open vast new opportunities for the practice of public relations.

Importance of the Black Public

There is hardly a product or service in South Africa that does not enjoy the benefits of a black market. Nearly 60 percent of all retail sales are made by black consumers, and this trend is likely to increase as black people become more urbanized. By the year 2002, the black population will be 80 percent of the total, and at least two-thirds of all urban dwellers will be black. Public relations activities in this mushrooming urban sector will grow enormously in future years.

Concomitant with the increasing pace of social change in South Africa is the questioning by black people of all aspects of their social, political, and economic environment. Social change requires the rapid dissemination of appropriate information that allows people to not only bring about much needed change but also to help people adapt to such change with a minimum of disruption to their lives. Because the workforce in South Africa is predominantly black and is currently embroiled in the many currents of change presently being manifested, it is important for organizations to spell out clearly where they stand on such issues as human rights, freedom of association, freedom of speech, and so on. At the same time they have a right to clearly articulate their position on workers' duties and obligations to the organization, productivity, company loyalty, and the effects of disruptive practices.

The aspirations of the disadvantaged majority will lead to increased demands on natural resources and an easily understood impatience with cautious, sustainable utilization philosophies and conservation policies. Radical adjustments will have to be made to our definitions of environmental conservation and pollution. The urgency of dealing with the state of environments in informal settlements in and around major urban centers will form part of the priority for funds in education, health, and housing. For the black majority, these are the real environmental issues. Unfortunately, it seems that few of the traditional conservation and environmental professionals in South Africa are adequately prepared to pursue policies that will ameliorate these problems.

Communication and the Management of Change

Communication, as the free exchange of views and opinions between people in South Africa, is vital to growth, progress, and development. The process of communication within the organization takes place in many ways—through training courses, meetings, reports, newsletters, social activities, and consultative committees, to name a few channels. Essentially, in the South African context, the process is complicated by the number of languages spoken and different educational standards. Face-to-face meetings between senior staff and employees can help to reaffirm and evaluate decisions made at consultative committee or union representative levels. All of these factors point to the necessity of establishing a sound communication strategy based on a comprehensive view of the employee's life work.

The nature and success of social change in South Africa will depend on the business community's social vision and basic conception of humanity. In the parable, the Good Samaritan lifted the unfortunate person on the side of the road, cared for him, and put him back on his feet. The alternative, in public relations terms, is the casting of coins to the needy but not in the way that achieves a lasting economic transformation. Many social responsibility programs amount to coin casting rather than encouraging participative development at grassroots levels. Public relations practitioners can play a role in convincing organizations to adopt the mutual development philosophy.

None of the above has influenced society and public relations in particular more than the affirmative action drive. The overwhelming majority of the South Africa business community believes progress depends on an essentially self-interested response to prevailing circumstances and that equality of opportunity is based on the philosophy of the survival of the fittest. Public relations practitioners can assist in bringing about the change from a winners and losers mind-set to one of the harmonizing of human interests.

Engineers, accountants, computer scientists, and other technicians—who often have no grounding in the humanities or social sciences—often become the key arbiters of industrial fate. They are influential because they speak in terms that management understands—the cold hard immutable realities of profitability and units of production. Mass unemployment is a looming specter in South Africa: Management is resorting to computerization and mechanization to concentrate skills in fewer hands and effectively exclude and deskill the vast majority of the labor market. A possible result could easily be the intensification of the widespread reaction against what is perceived as an uncaring and discriminatory capitalism.

Affirmative action programs specifically aimed at channeling the behavior of the business community in ways that are responsible to South African society should form a major brief of the public relations practitioner in South Africa. Some of the key areas are creating opportunities for people to accumulate capital through land ownership, assisting in achieving parity in educational resources, and offering programs aimed at redressing language disadvantages.

Other issues dealt with in tandem with affirmative actions and black empowerment include:

- Counseling management and workers in social practices acceptable in South Africa
- Conducting research into opinions, attitudes, and expectations of the workforce
- The adoption and promotion of the ethics of mutual respect and democratic process

Achieving organizational change in South African business has become an important brief of the practitioner. Efforts toward assisting workers and senior management to accept substantial changes in the workplace are commonplace in industry. The corporate public relations practitioner is often at the center of such programs because they require substantial communication efforts. Some of the significant areas for practitioners include:

- Labor laws
- Recognition of the rights of workers and of management
- Affirmative action
- Increased productivity requirements
- Skills training
- Lifelong education
- The impact of new technologies
- Support for entrepreneurial programs and small to medium enterprises
- Capacity building in local communities

In the past, both government and business have tended to adopt a prescriptive route to their dealings with stakeholders. Only recently have South Africans developed a culture that responds to consensus, so it is important for the practitioner to consolidate and continue with this new cultural initiative. A positive trend in South African communications culture has been the shift toward consensus seeking at a national level between the trade union movement, business, and government. Another element that is receiving more attention in organizational change is the recognition of the voice of local communities.

Globalism and Public Opinion

Globalization refers to the increasing importance of international markets and competition for national economies. It designates the progressive intrusion of the economic rationality of a profit-driven system into areas that had hitherto not been touched by it. In many cases these interventions impact on areas of traditional life and national cultural heritages in South Africa. The apartheid era had the effect of cutting off South Africans from the broad currents of global change, but the ending of South Africa's status as an international pariah has opened up a range of exciting opportunities and fresh contacts for this country and its people. It has both sharpened ordinary South African awareness of the force of international opinion and change, and has exposed many of its leaders from all sides of the political spectrum to international thought and emerging global universals. South African businesspeople, politicians, academics, diplomats, technocrats, and bureaucrats are increasingly becoming members of international organizations and groups, attending a string of international conferences and meetings across the globe. We are witnessing the rapid integration of South Africa into the many streams of global political, social, and economic discourse. The new South Africa finds that its influence is not limited to continental Africa; it is much broader, reaching issues such as the Middle East, Northern Ireland, reform of the UN Security Council, the World Bank, IMF, poverty, debt relief, and closing the digital divide (Pahad, 2001).

Government is now "competing" on the world stage of international relations. This means adapting South Africa's economic and political institutions to the emerging economic and political universals of the global village. As trade barriers between nations are reduced and removed, companies and institutions have to compete in world markets and arenas. Practitioners have to deliver these messages to their stakeholders internally as they increase activities in foreign markets. South Africa's transition to democracy not only coincides with these major international developments but also stands as a symbol of global integration and reconciliation, of black renewal and the demise of Afro-pessimism, and of economic realism on a continent that for decades had been marked by economic failure. One result of the introduction of a democratic government in South Africa and the nation's subsequent "return" to the society of nations has been recognition of the importance of the global connection to ordinary citizens. South Africa's reconnection to the world has introduced a wider set of global values, trends, and integrative movements than were possible during the apartheid years of isolation.

What are the implications of the development of internationalism and globalism for South African public relations practitioners? Today, in South Africa and throughout the African continent, many traditional institutions are crumbling or being subjected to new pressures. The extended family, kinship structures, and the traditional bases of authority and identity are a few of the areas that may be mentioned in this respect. The result is that there is a greater responsibility on practitioners in business and government to assist their stakeholders through the social change process.

In more sense than one, public relations in South Africa has become the face of the new democratic society. Many, if not most, major organizations started their affirmative action or black empowerment programs in their public relations departments. However, it did not have a very smooth beginning, as research into the positions of black people in public relations shows. A Media Tenor South Africa-Institute for Media Analysis study reported that 83 percent of 7,393 company representatives quoted from February 2000 to January 2001 in five major daily and five major weekly newspapers, as well as on five major TV news channels, were white, despite efforts to put black people in media relations positions.

In traditional international relations theory there were two kinds of opinion: *Domestic opinion*—what a country's own people thought about an issue—was always vital to governmental decision making; and *foreign opinion*—what other countries and peoples thought about an action or issue—grew greatly as communication technologies developed. A third type of opinion—*global public opinion*—is growing in importance as a result of greater global communications activity through media such as the Internet and global news agencies. The impact of CNN's (Cable Network News) coverage of the Gulf War is sometimes referred to as a landmark in highlighting this trend clearly for the first time. Today global debates are more commonplace—the AIDS pandemic; the recent events in Bosnia, Somalia, Rwanda, and Zaire and the associated questions surrounding United Nations intervention—have all become controversial, global issues.

Political leaders in South Africa now find it impossible to attend only to domestic and foreign opinion; they have to heed the opinion expressed by the world at large. The powerful global response to President Thabo Mbeki's controversial position on the nature of AIDS transmission (see the cover story of *Newsweek,* March 4, 2002, "Mbeki against the world"), the South African government's lack of action on mother-to-child HIV/AIDS transmission, and its "quiet diplomacy" approach to President Robert Mugabe of Zimbabwe illustrate this clearly (see earlier reference). In the recent past, political leaders in South Africa could exercise a great deal of control over domestic and foreign opinion through control of information and communication. Local news media infrequently quoted from editorials or opinion pieces that appeared abroad. But today, global electronic networks have changed all this—in many instances electronic communication media (for example, e-mail and the Internet) allow two-way interaction between people who fall outside of the traditional webs of "mainstream" broadcast and print media. These observations also apply to business leaders. In many cases there is a great deal of mistrust of Western-dominated multinationals in South Africa. Exploitation of natural resources and the repatriation of profits to foreign shareholders are not believed to be in the interests of citizens. Multinational companies have long been the target of activist groups who seek to force the large multinationals to be accountable to local communities.

An important shift has been in the economic sphere in South Africa. Rationalization and privatization of state assets and previously state-run industries has taken place through the government's national development and economic programs. The South African government has committed itself to programs that support private enterprise and foreign investment. The shift has been toward a capitalist-oriented, free-market and free-enterprise system. This has required that government justify its stance, in a number of public relations exercises, in the face of opposition from Cosatu (Congress of South African Trade Unions) and the Communist Party, its political partners in the so-called tripartite alliance. For practitioners, downsizing and job layoffs, mainly the result of globalization, have meant they have had to carry out similar exercises on behalf of their organizations.

Toward a New South Africa

There is little doubt that the international public relations opportunities around the concept of a "new" and "successful" South Africa represent a turning point for Africa. It marks the beginning of an opportunity for South Africa to be one of the driving forces in the creation of effective economic continental cooperation and integration. Perhaps the biggest pan-African public relations effort is that of President Mbeki's Millennium African Recovery Program (MAP). In essence MAP calls for disseminating the notion that Africans have truly committed to continental economic recovery, sustainable development, and democratic governance. Regardless of whether this plan will meet its lofty objectives in whole or part, there is no doubt that the idea and principles espoused have led to huge growth in the power of social, political, and professional networks to interact across borders.

The negative media portrayals of Africa need to be addressed by Africa's public relations professionals. Salim Ahmed Salim, previously the secretary general of the Organization of African Unity (OAU), emphasized that Africa had not been fairly treated by the international media, namely:

> the achievements of the continent are not fully understood and appreciated abroad. Here, the public relations practitioner can make a difference. While Africa's wrongs need to be exposed, its achievements and efforts need also to be recognized.

As each African crisis surges to the headlines of the world media, it is characterized by sensational and often simplistic reporting. Complex issues are reduced to "stories" that are designed to meet the constraints of time, finance, reader interest, and African government censorship (Hawke, 1992). As outlined earlier, professional public relations practitioners are "change agents" and have a social role to play in assisting to bring about positive change. What should public relations professionals focus on with regard to Africa's image?

For a country still finding its feet on the road to full democracy, a number of issues have to be addressed:

- *The "Dark Continent" image.* Africa continues to be stereotyped as backward and barbaric—"the world basket case"—in the world media. African public relations practitioners can help to promote a more balanced view.
- *Better communication.* African governments need to establish better communication with local, foreign, and international media representatives. Greater openness by government is required with respect to disclosing failures and, by the same token, foreign media need to report more fully and regularly on positive achievements.
- *The debt problem.* Servicing debt is crippling African governments' initiatives to stimulate development and ameliorate poverty. Public relations practitioners should join the call for debt forgiveness by the North, a call made by many African heads of state.
- *Hunger, poverty, and disease.* Practitioners can play a major role in mobilizing African people to address hunger, poverty, and disease. National awareness programs mounted by national public relations bodies need to be directed toward African heads of state.
- *Mistrust and suspicion.* A major problem inhibiting the development of Africa is that of mistrust and suspicion by the leaders of Africa. Practitioners have a responsibility to make it clear that Africa's salvation can only come through African cooperation.
- *Continental trade.* Practitioners have an obligation to support efforts aimed at the implementation of protocols that will make an African "common market" or "trading bloc" functional.
- *Political instability.* Practitioners have a role to play in disseminating messages that call for respect for human rights, political transparency, and guaranteed protection of the life and property of citizens. African governments need to be urged to promote peace, democracy, and stability through good governance.
- *Social problems.* Tribalism, ethnic differences, religious intolerance, and corruption impede development. Practitioners have a responsibility to highlight these impediments to development.
- *Public relations techniques.* Public relations technologies can be used to mobilize the people of the continent to be self-reliant, confident, and enterprising.

Conclusion

Africa has many strengths that are underplayed and need to be highlighted. A new concern for democracy, coupled with the resilience and self-reliance of the African people, and an emerging, revitalized communications media are the building blocks of future progress. Africa remains a land of opportunities with untapped human and natural resources. The philosophy of *Ubuntuism*—the idea of being one's brother's/sister's keeper—runs deeply throughout African thought and action.

Professional public relations has yet to realize its full responsibilities to the urban and rural classes of Africa. A tremendous gap separates the practice of public relations from the needs and aspirations of millions of people in Africa. Practitioners face problems of poverty, ignorance, and social disruption caused by the penetration of capitalism and democracy into indigenous communities. To meet these problems, new kinds of approaches to public relations practice need to be devised through communication and collaboration with the African social and political order. In the fields of education, consumerism, community self-help programs, and corporate social investment can be seen the beginnings of a new approach to public relations in Africa. Public relations practitioners need to enhance the ability of the dispossessed to determine their development needs and set about fulfilling them. Public relations educators can make a meaningful contribution to the future of Africa by playing their part in this movement.

Public relations in South Africa in the past ten years or so is a far cry from the often misinformed stereotypes some people have of this important branch of the mass communication tree. New fields are opening up to qualified and concerned public relations practitioners. Professional public relations can offer to South Africa's developing and democratizing society, which is still very much in turmoil in many spheres, a meaningful and necessary communication basis on which to build the future.

Note

1. Two South African public relation case studies of note (one positive, one negative) are

Nieman, I., & Grobler, A. (2001). The M-Net "Face of Africa" competition: A study on the evaluation of public relations success story from the African continent. *Communicare, 20*(1), 1–27.

De Beer, A., & Schreiner, W. (2002). Golden silence the reason for the demise of Saambou. *Media Tenor South Africa Quarterly, 3*(1), 1–2.

See also www.gcis.gov.za.

Discussion Questions

1. Is public relations a communication function that could only be successfully implemented in a democracy? If so, why did public relations develop as a strong field of communication during the apartheid years in South Africa?

2. Find the Web site for the Public Relations Institute of South Africa (PRISA) and compare its contents with that of the Web site of the Public Relations Society of America (PRSA). What are the main similarities and differences?

3. Is public relations an independent field of study, or should it rather be dealt with within the broader context of corporate communication as is happening in South Africa?

4. Public relations, as it is traditionally known, has not yet fully come to its own in all countries of Africa, whereas it is a very viable field in South Africa. Why is this?

References

Agee, W., Ault, P., & Emery, E. (1991). *Introduction to mass communications.* New York: HarperCollins.

De Beer, A. (2002). To criticize or support government: The media in the spotlight. *Media Tenor South Africa Quarterly, 2*(1), 1–2.

De Beer, A. (in press). The South African Press—No strangers to conflict. In E. Gilboa (Ed.), *The media and conflict—International perspectives* (pp. 263–280). New York: Transnational Publishers.

Grunig, J. E., & Grunig, L. A. (1992). Models of public relations and communication. In J. E. Grunig (Ed.), *Excellence in public relations and communication management* (pp. 285–325). Hillsdale, NJ: Lawrence Erlbaum Associates.

Grunig, J. E., & Hunt, T. (1984). *Managing public relations.* New York: Holt, Rinehart and Winston.

Grunig, J. E., & White, J. (1992). The effect of worldviews on public relations theory and practice. In J. Grunig (Ed.), *Excellence in public relations and communication management* (pp. 175–195). Hillsdale, NJ: Lawrence Erlbaum Associates.

Hawke, B. (1992). *Africa's media image.* New York: Praeger.

Hilton-Barber, D. (1991). Public relations: What it is and how to use it effectively. In M. Leahy & P. Voice (Eds.), *The media book—1991/1992* (pp. 20–32). Bryanston, South Africa: WTH Publications.

Holtzhausen, D., & Verwey, S. (1996). Towards a general theory of public relations. *Communicare, 15*(2), 25–56

Krause, R. C. (1997). *Understanding public relations.* Cape Town: David Philip.

Malan, J., & L'Estrange, J. (1965). *Public relations practice in South Africa.* Cape Town, South Africa: Juta.

Mersham, G. (1992). The challenges of teaching public relations practice in Africa in the 90's. *Communicatio, 18*(1), 54–59.

Mersham, G. (1993). Public relations, democracy and corporate social investment. *Ecquid Novi, 14*(2), 107–126.

Mersham G., Rensburg, R., & Skinner, C. (1995). *Public relations, development and social investment: A southern African perspective.* Pretoria, South Africa: Van Schaik.

Mersham, G., & Skinner, C. (1998). Public relations: A vital communication function of our times. In A. De Beer (Ed.), *Mass media—Towards the millennium* (pp. 347–374). Pretoria, South Africa: Van Schaik.

Nel, F. (1994). *Writing for the media.* Midrand, South Africa: Southern.

Okereke, M. (1993, May 5). *Challenges of public relations practitioners in Africa and recent development in the practice.* Paper presented by chairman of the Federation of African Public Relations Associations (FAPRA) at IPRA Professional Conference, Cape Town.

Overton-De Klerk, N. (1994). Corporate social responsibility. In B. Lubbe & C. Puth (Eds.), *Public relations in South Africa* (pp. 173–190). Isando, South Africa: Heinemann.

Pahad, E. (2001, June 24). SA is bridging the developmental divide. *Sunday Times,* p. 19.

Pember, D. (1987). *Mass media in America.* Chicago: SRA.

Public Relations Council of South Africa. (2000). Code of Professional Conduct and Standards for Accredited Public Relations Practitioners. Johannesburg: Public Relations Council of South Africa.

Skinner, J., & Von Essen, L. (1991). *The South African handbook of public relations.* Johannesburg, South Africa: Southern Books.

Time for you to go, Africa tells Mugabe. (2002, March 3). *Sunday Times,* p. 1.

Around Asia

Introduction to Asian Public Relations

Mazharul Haque

Asia consists of forty-nine countries that include some of the largest and smallest, most developed and least developed countries in the world. Asian countries also represent the most diverse administrative and political systems. Some countries grant individual rights, free press, and democratic political systems, whereas others are authoritarian, repressive, and dictatorial. The continent has some of the most populous but also the smallest, most literate and illiterate countries in the world. There are also many ethnic, religious, and linguistic groups that separate nations and peoples within nations. The diversity that exists in religious, ethnic, linguistic, social, and cultural terms present a great challenge to communication specialists or public relations practitioners in reaching their publics both within and beyond national boundaries.

The continent may be divided into several geographical regions, namely, South West Asia, South Asia, Southeast Asia, East Asia, and North Asia. These regions differ not only in density of population but also in religious beliefs, literacy rate, socioeconomic development, and quality of life. Public relations practitioners and scholars in countries within these regions have to deal with these differences and function within different models of public relations that could include press agentry, one-way public information, two-way asymmetrical, and two-way symmetrical models. In the *press agentry* model the public relations agent wishes to propagandize and gain favorable publicity for the client without much concern for the accuracy of the message. In the *public information* model the agent disseminates certain kinds of desirable information about the organization for which he or she works. Both of these modes of communication fall under the *one-way asymmetrical* model. Under the *two-way asymmetrical* model agents gather information

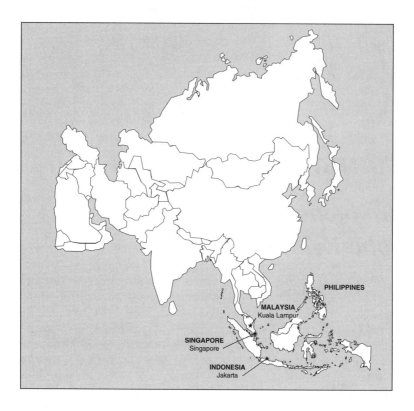

about the publics through modern scientific methods but the information is for propaganda purposes or engineering consent. Under the *two-way symmetrical* model, the public relations practitioner uses all the information not only for persuasion but also for promoting understanding and communication with the publics.

The level of literacy and socioeconomic development clearly affect and influence how public relations practitioners employ specific techniques of communication. In most Asian countries, communication practitioners have to engage in development communication that requires employing the available channels of media, including interpersonal, to mobilize public participation in the socioeconomic goals set by the national authorities. Many Asian countries try to achieve strategic developmental goals through short-term, medium, and long-term plans in the public health, educational, industrial, agricultural, and transportation sectors. The communication workers in the public sector have a crucial role to play in helping the country achieve these national objectives as part of a massive information and public relations campaign.

This part includes an overview of public relations in Asia and three chapters on specific Southeast Asian countries, namely, Singapore, Indonesia, and Malaysia. In her chapter, Newsom points out that Singapore is a high-tech society that has built a highly developed information infrastructure where the Internet is widely used by the residents of the city-state. This makes it possible for public relations practitioners to engage in two-way communication and build relationships with constituencies. In addition, they can present the viewpoints of their clients or organizations directly to key publics and stake-holders without a distorting press filter serving as an intermediary. Considering the still restrictive media environment existing in the country, the interactivity of the Internet and its wide diffusion in the society makes it a particularly effective medium for practitioners wishing to reach their desired publics. Despite having one of the highest standards of living in Asia and its emergence as a major trading center of the world, the major share of Singapore's public relations activities is still occupied by the government sector, but business-to-business public relations is gaining increasingly in importance. Newsom states that Singapore has one of the most sophisticated and established public relations professions in the world.

In his chapter on Indonesia, Thomas examines the historical developments that have occurred since the country's independence from Dutch colonial rule in 1949 and the recent *Reformasi* political reform process that began during the late 1990s. This process not only toppled the thirty-five-year politically repressive Soeherto regime but also brought about revolutionary changes in media policies and practices with deep implications for public relations in this vast multilingual and multicultural society of 240 million people.

In addition to government information agencies that operate in the public sector, there are several dozen private public relations agencies and a few joint-venture international consultancies in the country. In Indonesia, business public relations practitioners typically place less emphasis on corporate image building and more on advertising and sales promotion for their products and services. Because of the reformation process, however, Thomas suggests that there is far greater political awareness and activism in the general public. People currently have greater access to unrestricted media, including the Internet, than before. There is, therefore, greater scrutiny of both the governmental and corporate decisions and policies, and officials and executives alike are potentially subject to greater accountability as well. In this new environment, characterized by free press and public activism, public relations agents both in the public and private sectors need to engage in environmental scanning, monitoring of the media, opinion polling, and issues and crisis management. An element of complexity is added to the picture by the fact that corporations currently act in a globalized environment in which they have accountability to global publics that consist of internationally networked civil society groups, labor unions, environmentalists, and a host of other highly visible and vocal interest groups. Public relations practitioners have to proactively take action to not only project a positive image for their corporations or organizations but also to respond to a multiplicity of demands arising out of a greater availability of information through a diversity of media, public concern for economic justice, and a generally higher level of public awareness.

Venkateswaran, in her chapter on Malaysia, points out that the telecommunication sector in the country has experienced significant growth during the past decade. The government adopted a policy of creating a multimedia supercorridor (MSC), analogous to the information superhighway in the United States, and consequently, the country has invested in the creation of an extensive, state-of-the-art fiber optic network that facilitates services, providing e-commerce, distance learning, video-on-demand, and multimedia content.

Since independence in 1957, the government has promoted a policy of nation building trying to unify a country divided into different ethnic, religious, and linguistic groups. Subsequently, the country adopted the national ideology of *Rukunegara* that has promoted national integration, social equity, and progressive thought while maintaining distinctive cultural values. The public relations and communication workers were given the responsibility of providing the necessary information and ideological support to achieve these national goals. Venkateswaran states that in Malaysia the government remains the largest single communicator. Major media still carry news that is largely government oriented, and public relations in the country still may be understood as government relations. Malaysia seems to have transitioned from the initial phase of nation building into the market development and regional interdependence phases.

Because countries on the vast continent of Asia vary widely in terms of political and socioeconomic development as well as the level of literacy and quality of life, public relations issues, concerns, and problems also vary. In most countries on the continent, however, communication practitioners during the nation-building phase have to contribute to development communication by launching communication campaigns designed to motivate publics to participate in the huge task of achieving broad socioeconomic goals set by national authorities, including fostering a sense of community and nationhood. This is notable in view of the colonial or semicolonial history of many Asian nation-states. During the market development phase, with the emergence of an industrial and consumer society, practitioners resort to different techniques and strategies that may shift from one-way asymmetrical persuasive communication to organizing special events, grand openings, product launches, and so on. In the advanced stage of market development in Asia, corporations develop business interests that transcend national boundaries and make a transition into multinational and regional interdependence. Naturally, the role of a public relations agent changes with the broader social, economic, and political context in which he or she has to operate. In the context of a developed regional or international market the practitioner has to be prepared to deal with issues and communication management.

Singapore

Government type	Parliamentary republic
Capital	Singapore
Language	Chinese, Malay, Tamil, English
Ethnic groups	Chinese, Malay, Indian
Religion	Buddhist, Muslim, Christian, Hindu, Sikh, Taoist, Confucianist
Major industries	Electronics, chemicals, financial services, oil drilling equipment, petroleum refining, rubber processing and rubber products, processed food and beverages, ship repair, entrepôt trade, biotechnology

Sources: National Geographic Atlas of the World Seventh Edition, CIA The World Factbook 2002

Indonesia

Government type	Republic
Capital	Jakarta
Language	Bahasa Indonesia, English, Dutch, Javanese, and other local dialects
Ethnic groups	Javanese, Sundanese, Madurese, coastal Malays
Religion	Muslim, Protestant, Roman Catholic, Hindu, Buddhist
Major industries	Petroleum and natural gas, textiles, apparel and footwear, mining, cement, chemical fertilizers, plywood, rubber, food, tourism

Sources: National Geographic Atlas of the World Seventh Edition, CIA The World Factbook 2002

Malaysia

Government type	Constitutional monarchy
Capital	Kuala Lumpur
Language	Malay, English, Chinese
Ethnic groups	Malay and other indigenous, Chinese, Indian
Religion	Muslim, Buddhist, Hindu, Christian, Confucianist
Major industries	Peninsular Malaysia—rubber and oil palm processing and manufacturing, light manufacturing, electronics, tin mining and smelting, logging and processing timber; Sabah—logging, petroleum production; Sarawak—agriculture processing, logging, petroleum production and refining

Sources: National Geographic Atlas of the World Seventh Edition, CIA The World Factbook 2002

16

Overview o. Relations in Asia

Mazharul Haque

Key Points

- The geographic, demographic, and cultural conditions in which communication policy makers have to operate in Asia are varied and challenging.
- Public relations practitioners must be particularly mindful of the various cultural determinants on the culturally diverse Asian continent.
- As the public relations profession develops in Asia, it is essential for practitioners to identify their target publics from among various stakeholder groups and for public relations managers to become part of the dominant coalition in their organizations.
- In Asia, as elsewhere, there are specific characteristics of excellent public relations departments that contribute to superior management in organizations.
- There are various models of public relations activities and approaches used in public-sector and private-sector public relations in Asia.

Asia is the largest of the seven continents in both size and population, occupying almost one-third of the world's land area and 60 percent of the global population. The forty-nine countries of Asia represent a wide diversity of nations. They include some of the largest and smallest in terms of population, some of the richest and poorest in gross national product, literate and illiterate, and the most developed and underdeveloped nations of the world. The two most populated nations in the world are China and India, two Asian giants. One has 1.3 billion people, whereas the other has about a billion, but two-fifths of the Asian countries have populations of less than 5 million people. China and India are countries of continental proportions, but three Asian nations—Bahrain, Maldives, and Singapore—each covers less than three hundred square miles.

The countries of Asia have a great variety of administrative and political systems. China and Vietnam are ruled by communist governments; most Middle Eastern countries have monarchies with varying degrees of rights of expression and individual freedoms, but some countries, such as India and Japan, have democratic political systems with a free press and individual rights. Some countries, such as Pakistan, Indonesia, and Mayanmar, have had military rulers for much of their history as independent states. Asia is known to be the cradle of human civilization. Asians founded the first cities, started agriculture and trading, set up the first systems of law, invented writing, paper and moveable type, and created the earliest literatures. But it fell behind the West during the sixteenth century allowing West European nations to conquer large parts of Asia between the 1500s to 1800s. The economic gap between Asia and the West widened greatly during colonial rule.

Population in Asia is unevenly distributed. Some countries in Asia are among the most densely populated in the world. Bangladesh, India, eastern China, Hong Kong, Singapore, much of Japan, and the island of Java in Indonesia are among the most densely populated areas of the world. High density of population in the poorer countries has created a hugely complicated demographic situation causing problems of chronic underdevelopment leading to a high rate of illiteracy, hunger, poor health care, and ecological degradation. Communication and public relations policy makers in many Asian countries have to function within a resource-poor environment where the challenge is to motivate masses to participate in programs of social mobilization to improve the general quality of life.

The continent also has dozens of ethnic and communal groups. These groups dispersed within or across national boundaries often get into violent conflicts threatening international political order and national integration, a major concern for communication and public relations practitioners in developing countries.

It is notable that all the major religions in the world originated in Asia, namely Buddhism, Confucianism, Hinduism, Taoism, Shintoism, in addition to the three monotheistic faiths—Islam, Judaism, and Christianity. Unfortunately, the diversity of religions also has contributed to destructive rivalry for a greater share of political and economic power or geopolitical dominance leading to violent conflicts among groups. Interracial, interreligious, or interethnic conflicts have occurred between Arabs and Jews, Greeks and Turks, Hindus and Muslims, Malays and Chinese, Armenians and Azerbaijanis, to name a few.

Asians speak many languages and dialects within nations and across national boundaries. All the major language families, except for African, are widely used in the continent. This poses a tremendous barrier to communication. In a large country such as India, the national constitution recognizes more than a dozen and a half major languages but numerous dialects are spoken by large numbers of people. For example, in one of the twenty-three Indian states, Madhya Pradesh, more than 375 languages and dialects are spoken (*The World Book Encyclopedia,* 1999). This contributes not only to the great cultural diversity of the nation but also to linguistic conflicts and chauvinism. Public relations practitioners have to function in the context of this complex cultural backdrop.

The continent may be divided into six regions. Southwest Asia consists of nineteen countries, including seven nations of the Arabian Peninsula and twelve nations north and east of the peninsula with 7 percent of all Asians living in the region. Saudi Arabia is the region's largest nation; it covers about two-thirds of the Arabian Peninsula. The other nations in the peninsula are Bahrain, Kuwait, Oman, Qatar, the United Arab Emirates, and Yemen. The nations outside of the peninsula are Afghanistan, Armenia, Azerbaijan, Cyprus, Georgia, Iran, Iraq, Israel, Jordan, Lebanon, Syria, and Turkey. Even though Islam, Christianity, and Judaism originated in this region, the vast majority of the people in the region practice Islam, but Judaism *is* the religion of Israel. The region represents marked contrasts in cultural and political terms. As a Jewish society, Israel represents a European outpost with a highly developed economic, political, and cultural system. Turkey, despite being a predominantly Muslim society, historically embraced secularism, wishing to be part of the European Union. But most of the Arab nations still maintain a traditional way of living where the literacy rate is low. There is also gender segregation with limited opportunities for women in public life; authoritarian political systems dominated by kings, emirs, and authoritarian rulers; and no free press or individual freedoms.

South Asia covers about 10 percent of the continent, with India occupying about three-fourths and Pakistan about one-sixth of the region. The other nations in South Asia are Bangladesh, Bhutan, Nepal, Sri Lanka, and Maldives. South Asia is one of the world's most crowded places accounting for one-third of all Asians and one-fifth of the global population with seven times the world average. Calcutta, the capital of the states of West Bengal (a state in India), and Dhaka, the capital city in Bangladesh, have 110,000 and 74,000 residents per square mile respectively (*The World Book Encyclopedia,* 1999). India accounts for 75 percent of South Asia's population with Pakistan and Bangladesh accounting for 10 percent each. The four other countries contain the remaining 5 percent. The people of South Asia are divided along religion, language, and social class, each of which has a profound impact on the life of the people and their relationships to one other. For example, Hindus and Muslims, the two major religious groups, have frequently engaged in violent conflicts. The Indian government also changed state boundaries and created new states to give language groups their own states. In addition, each Hindu belongs to a caste, and social customs limit all forms of contact and marriage with Hindus from other castes. Quite clearly, all these conditions have grave implications for communication practitioners.

Southeast Asia consists of ten independent nations with a total population of half a billion, accounting for 9 percent of the continent's territory and 14 percent of its people. With 232 people per square mile, the region has a density of population that is three times the world average. Indonesia is the largest country in the region and is spread over thousands of islands. The other countries are Malaysia, Singapore, Brunei, Philippines, Cambodia, Laos, Mayanmar, Thailand, and Vietnam. Except for Thailand, all the countries have been subjected to European colonial rule. Buddhism is the chief religion in one-half of the Southeast Asian countries. Islam is the main religion in Indonesia, Malaysia, and Brunei, whereas Christianity is the major faith in the Philippines. The region, in general, has a high literacy rate with the exception of Cambodia and Laos.

East Asia is comprised of five nations—China, Japan, North Korea, South Korea, and Taiwan. The region also includes a small nonindependent territory called Macao. With a population density five times the world's average, these five nations account for 40 percent of all Asians and one-fourth of the globe's population. As the most populous nation in the region, China, with an ancient civilization and a history of ruling much of East Asia at different points in time, has had a deep cultural influence on the whole region. Chinese religious and philosophical beliefs, including the Confucian system of ethics, have been influential throughout the region. The two largest nations in East Asia, China, and Japan, also have different political and economic systems. China has a communist system of government, which, despite being able to achieve remarkable economic growth in recent decades, does not yet provide the civil liberties and political freedoms that Western democracies guarantee their citizens. China is a developing country with great potential for economic and social progress. Japan, however, is among the most developed countries in the world with one of the world's highest standards of living and a free-enterprise democratic system that guarantees freedoms and liberties. Ideological differences also divide China and Taiwan, and North Korea and South Korea. North Korea has a socioeconomic and political system that is based on the very rigid communist, or Stalinist, ideology. South Korea and Taiwan have emerged as powerful democratic industrial nations.

North Asia covers about 30 percent of the continent and consists entirely of Siberia, which also makes up 75 percent of Russia. Central Asia covers slightly more than one-fifth of the continent and consists of parts of Western China and six independent nations, namely, Kazakhstan, Kyrgyzstan, Mongolia, Tajikistan, Turkmenistan, and Uzbekistan. Except for Mongolia, all the other independent nations were part of the former Soviet Union until its break up in 1991. These nations have moved away from a communist system of government and formed governments that extend freedoms to citizens with varying degrees of democratic rights. The whole region is sparsely populated with a density of twenty-four people per square mile, and most make their livings by herding livestock. Most people in Central Asian countries are Muslim, but most Mongolians are followers of Lamaism.

What Is Public Relations?

Public relations has been defined in a variety of ways. A widely accepted definition states that it is the "management of communication between an organization and its publics" (Grunig, 1992, p. 4). This definition equates public relations and communication management. Quite often scholars have used public relations, communication management, and organizational communication interchangeably (Grunig, 1992). Based on a compilation of more than four hundred definitions that emphasize different elements, Harlow (1976) describes public relations as the distinctive management function that helps establish and maintain a mutual line of communication, understanding, acceptance, and cooperation between an organization and its publics. It involves the management of problems and issues and helps management stay informed about and responsive to public opinion. It defines and emphasizes the responsibility of management to serve the public interest, helps it to keep abreast of changes in public opinion, and uses it to anticipate trends. Public relations also uses research as a tool in a sound and ethical manner (Harlow, 1976).

Public relations serves all the major social institutions, such as business organizations, trade unions, government agencies, voluntary associations, foundations, hospitals, schools, colleges, and religious organizations. Each major institution in a modern society has its own mission and goals. To achieve these, each institution must develop effective lines of communication with its various publics on the basis of an understanding of the attitudes and values of the relevant publics. Public relations is not as much concerned about the general public as it is with target publics. Grunig and Rapper (1992) have identified four types of publics: Some are *active* on all issues; some are *apathetic* (i.e., inattentive and inactive on all issues); some are *single-issue* publics because they are active on a limited number of related issues; and some are *hot-issues* publics because they become active when extensive media exposure makes an issue salient to everyone.

Because in public relations identifying the target publics from among the stakeholder groups is regarded as crucial for the success of any communication program, practitioners use a number of criteria to define publics. These include geography, demographics, psychographics, covert power, position, reputation, membership, and role in the decision-making process (Cutlip, Center, & Broom, 1994). Geography indicates the boundaries within which people who need to be targeted with the desired message are available. Demographics, such as gender, income, age, education, and marital status of the target audience, may provide the basic information that public relations practitioners need in order to develop an appropriate message system for the target audience and a strategy with which to reach it. Psychographics involve clustering people based on commonalities of values, beliefs, and lifestyles (VALS) and reaching them with the appropriate message system. A public relations practitioner should also identify behind-the-scenes sources of power, that is, covert power, or individuals who may exert power over a wide range of issues without being easily observed. Conversely, there are individuals who are important from the standpoint of a program's goals and objectives because of the known positions they hold. A person's position and role make him or her a valuable part of the target public. Reputation identifies individuals as "influentials" or "opinion leaders" based on their perceived expertise, strategic location in the community, and willingness to be a bridge between groups. Membership of a certain organization or appearance on a list may also help a practitioner identify special interest groups who need to reach the target publics. The role in the decision-making process requires program planners to observe who plays the most active roles in the decision-making process so that they can be part of the targeted public as well.

Public relations managers need to be part of the "dominant coalition" of an organization, that is, the group of senior executives who make the important decisions facing the organization (Grunig, 1992). As communication specialists, they convey their views of publics to other managers, which also requires that they be in touch with the views of the public. As part of the dominant coalition in an organization, the public relations expert has to perform a range of functions. For example, a public relations practitioner has to anticipate and interpret public opinion and issues that have the potential of impacting the plans of the organization. He or she has to advise top executives concerning the ramifications of the policy decisions for the organization and its publics and remind them of the social and citizenship responsibilities of the organization. He or she also has to evaluate the impact on policies, procedures, and actions on the publics, and manage difficult issues.

A public relations practitioner also has to advise senior management on establishing new policies, procedures, and actions that are beneficial to both the organization and its publics. A public relations professional uses skills and experience that are required for opinion research, public-issues analysis, media relations, institutional advertising, publications, audio/video productions, special events, speeches, and presentations. A public relations practitioner has to maintain two-way communication between the organization and its publics, and monitor attitudes and behavior both in the internal organizational environment and in the external environment (Cutlip et al., 1994).

Public relations in economically advanced nations in North America and Europe is generally concerned with the study of how corporations in the private sector relate to their strategic publics. In most Asian countries that are underdeveloped or developing, public relations is only a part of the government developmental programs that require huge communication campaigns to mobilize people to participate in the multiplicity of socioeconomic programs to uplift the society. How public relations functions within a culture and cultural determinants needs to be considered in understanding how it works.

Cultural Determinants

Kaplan and Manners (1972) identified *techno-economics* as a basic cultural determinant. The term refers to the arrangements used by a society to apply its technical equipment and knowledge to the production, distribution, and consumption of goods and services. The technology available in a society is directly linked to the socioeconomic arrangements in the society. A person's personality may also be largely determined by his or her experiences within the family but structure may be deeply influenced by its techno-economic arrangements. In a study of attitudes, Williamson (1982) noted the following was associated with an acceptance of modernization: low kinship orientation, preference for an urban rather than agrarian lifestyle, belief in the mutability of human nature, low stratification of life chances, and universalitic norms for mobility.

Social structure has also been identified as a cultural determinant (Kaplan & Manners, 1972). Social structure refers to patterned relationships and interactions between persons and groups in a society (Stokes, 1984). The social structure of a simple, traditional society, as we would find in many Asian countries, may predominantly be a matter of kinship. The central organization that underlies such a society is based on family, lineage, and clan. In an industrial or postindustrial society, as in Japan, social structure is more complicated; groups and associations are organized around a great variety of social, economic, recreational, and other purposes. Status and role are the basic building blocks of social structure of different types. Status refers to the position occupied by an individual in a society. Individuals occupy a number of different statuses at the same time. Taken together, a person's statuses are referred to as a *status set.* Similarly, roles are the behaviors associated with particular statuses. The distinction between role and status is quite clear—individuals occupy statuses, and they play roles. An individual occupying a particular status has to play multiple roles (Stokes, 1984).

The other cultural determinants, as suggested by Kaplan and Manners (1972), are ideology and personality. Even though it is difficult to know to what extent ideology representing the values, norms, religious principles, worldviews, and ethics held by a people affect individual behavior, it is known that individuals learn cultural idiosyncrasies through the formal and informal methods of instruction that exist in the society. They also learn to use ideological constructs in various contexts as guides in structuring their social and natural worlds. In addition, once internalized, the ideological constructs may also help individuals initiate behavior (Spiro, 1966).

Cultural training and child-rearing practices in a given culture give rise to certain personality traits. Sriramesh (1996) claims that the basic personality structure determines a society's secondary institutions such as art, religion, mythology, or folklore. Scholars have attempted to place particular societies on a cultural continuum because cultural dimensions are reflected in management styles across nations (Sriramesh & White, 1992). These cultural dimensions also allow researchers to identify similarities and differences among societies. Hofstede (1980) in a study of thirty-nine nations was able to identify four cultural dimensions, the first of which was individualism-collectivism. Individualistic cultures stress individual goals and their members are expected to be more concerned about themselves and the immediate members of their families. Collectivist cultures stress group goals and the primary focus is on the welfare of the community. In this type of culture the community is assumed to take care of individuals in exchange for their loyalty to the group. Workers in collectively oriented cultures may be more attached to the organizations to which they belong. Compared to Western cultures, most of the Asian nations would easily fall more on the collectivist end of the continuum. The second dimension identified by Hofstede was power distance. This refers to the extent to which power is distributed unequally among people belonging to different strata. In clan-oriented cultures power is believed to be concentrated in the hands of those few at the top of the power structure who are known as the elite. Rank inequalities in societies manifest themselves in different ways. Bohannan (1969) mentioned three types of social inequality: caste, estate, and class. The Indian caste system has placed members of different castes at different levels of the social hierarchy. Sriramesh points out that despite the prevalence of the Indian caste system since ancient times it is the class system that is more visible in Indian organizations. Political and financial power, no longer the exclusive preserve of the upper castes, determine who exercises power in organizations and society. However, researchers found a great power distance among superiors and subordinates in Indian organizations (Hofstede, 1980; Tayeb, 1988). Tayeb also concluded that the distance in power relationships caused Indian organizations to have centralized structures.

Hofstede (1980) identified uncertainty avoidance as a cultural dimension as well. This third dimension has to do with a society's lack of tolerance for ambiguity, which leads to greater levels of anxiety. Organizations in cultures with low tolerance for ambiguity need more formal rules of conduct so that uniformity among organizational members can be ensured and risky ideas can be avoided. Hofstede's fourth cultural dimension is masculinity and femininity. In every culture certain qualities or attributes are associated with masculinity and femininity as part of an elaborate gender mythology. Even though some of these commonly held views have come to be challenged in recent decades in many Asian nations, gender roles traditionally held persist. In the Muslim Asian cultures of the Middle East, for example, despite some liberalization in recent years, strict gender segregation is practiced, and many occupations are still off limits to women. However, in other parts of the continent, such as Southeast Asia, East Asia, and South Asia, women are pursuing diverse careers and occupations, and in a number of countries women have headed governments as chief executives.

Sriramesh and White (1992) point out that organizations are influenced by culture, and linkages between culture and communication and culture and public relations are parallel. A culture of a society is determinative of the communication forms and patterns prevalent in it. Regardless of whether the public relations person wishes to serve as a mediator between an organization and its internal publics (i.e., the employers) or with external stakeholders, such as investors, consumers, and activist groups, he or she has to use various modes of communication and a variety of tools.

Characteristics for Excellence

Grunig (1992) examined if excellent organizations also have excellent communication programs. His review isolated twelve characteristics of excellent public relations departments that contribute to excellence in management. In the area of human resources, excellent organizations empower people by giving them autonomy and letting them make strategic decisions. Personal growth and quality of work life of employees are important to an organization. It also maintains a balance between teamwork and individual effort. In terms of structure, excellent organizations give people power by eliminating bureaucratic and hierarchical organizational structures. They decentralize decisions, avoid stratification of employees, and eliminate status symbols for executives that are divisive and offensive to other employees. Excellent organizations also have an innovative and entrepreneurial spirit known as entrepreneurship.

A spirit of entrepreneurship may occur if an organization develops an organic structure and cultivates human resources. It has been noted that writers on excellence do not mention the term *public relations,* yet they seem to describe communication systems of organizations as two-way symmetrical systems. This type of communication takes place through dialogue, negotiation, listening, and conflict management rather than persuasion, manipulation, and giving orders. Excellent organizations stay close to their customers, employees, and other strategic constituencies (Grunig, 1992). Excellent organizations have leaders who can cultivate and maintain a nourishing environment for personal growth. Leaders rely on networking not autocratic control, providing a shared vision for the organization, maintaining a balance between management control and team opportunity, and creating order out of the chaos that empowerment of people can create. Excellent organizations have a strong organizational culture that stresses integration, participation, and collaboration as the central values. Workers in such organizations have a sense of mission and they are integrated into the culture of the organization by its sense of strong tradition, myths, and basic beliefs. Excellent organizations also plan strategically, and good public relations departments are integrated into the process of strategic planning. Business organizations operate in societies that offer opportunities to make profits; therefore, they also have obligations to meet social responsibilities. Institutional public relations must balance the private interests of an organization with those of its publics and society. Public relations can do so through strategic planning and symmetrical communication programs.

Excellent organizations recognize the value of diversity in their workforces, employ female and minority workers, and help them move up the management ladder. Empowering women and minorities in public relations makes an organization strong and effective. In large developing countries in Asia, such as India with many ethnic, linguistic, and religious groups, minority representation is a particularly important issue. In traditional societies employment of women is directly linked with cultural and societal development. In excellent organizations total quality control is emphasized. In Imai's (1986) book, *Kaizen,* a Japanese word for continuous improvement involving both managers and workers, this management goal is explained. *Kaizen* can be contrasted with innovation. It requires improvement in processes rather than the development of new processes. It signifies small improvements made in ongoing efforts. "Innovation involves a drastic improvement in the status quo as a result of a large investment in new technology for equipment" (p. 6). Imai states that every *kaizen* program implemented in Japan has created a cooperative atmosphere and a cooperative corporate culture. Organizations with *kaizen* programs use quality circles, develop informal leaders, bring social life into the workplace, and provide workplaces in which life goals can be achieved. Excellent public relations departments need to develop internal communication programs in collaboration with managers of quality-control programs and should work with marketing departments in monitoring customer perceptions of quality.

Excellent organizations need to "develop systems and procedures to implement plans and utilize resources" (Grunig, 1992, p. 244). Public relations departments must develop internal systems for implementing and monitoring their activities.

Organizations are more effective if the societies in which they operate are more collaborative. Several authors point out the existence of a collaborative culture in Japan for its organizational effectiveness. For example, Ouchi (1984) says, "It would not be at all surprising to discover that a society must also have that combination of teamwork and competition to succeed. If there is a society that has developed a high level of teamwork across sectors of the society, it is Japan" (p. 29).

Pascale and Athos (1981) mention the importance of interdependence in Japanese culture, which is based on group harmony that includes unity, cohesiveness, and team spirit. Imai (1986) also compares Western and Japanese management by pointing out how *kaizen* works in Japan. He states "in the West cross-functional problems are often seen in terms of conflict resolution, while *kaizen* strategy has enabled Japanese management to take a systematic and collaborative approach to cross-functional problem solving. Herein lies one of the secrets of Japanese management's competitive edge" (p. xxxii). Because societal culture has an effect on organizational culture, which, in turn, has an effect on public relations, excellent management and excellent public relations can flourish only in collaborative cultures (Grunig, 1992).

Models of Public Relations

Public relations scholars have conceptualized public relations and communication management in terms of four models (Grunig & Hunt, 1984). The first is the *press agentry/publicity* model. In the evolution of models, *press agentry* is the oldest; it became prevalent in the middle of the nineteenth century in the United States. In this model the agent in a communication program attempts to gain favorable publicity for his or her client in the media. The goal of the press agent is essentially to propagandize without much concern for accuracy.

In the beginning of the twentieth century, the *public information* model developed as a reaction to attacks on large corporations and government agencies by muckraking journalists. Managers of organizations needed more than the propaganda of the press agents to counter media attacks; therefore, they hired their resident journalists to write press handouts. Even though these resident public relations practitioners focused only on good things about their organizations, they disseminated factual information with some in-depth explanations of issues and problems. Both press agentry and public information models rep-

resent one-way public relations approaches, but the goal is for the practitioner to dissemi-
te certain kinds of information about the organization to the public through the media.
The introduction of the scientific approach in public relations transformed it into *two-way* communication because practitioners made an effort to learn about and listen to key publics. But if information gathered from the publics through scientific methods is designed to be used for propaganda, persuasion, and engineering consent, Grunig and Hunt (1984) call this a two-way asymmetrical model. In a *two-way symmetrical* model the practitioner listens to the publics not necessarily to enhance persuasion but to adjust organizational behavior to serve public needs. Here, the practitioner also uses research, but the purpose is to build relationships with publics and facilitate understanding and communication.

Public Relations in Asia

It is likely that all four models of public relations are practiced in different countries and settings in Asia. However, it has to be recognized that countries in Asia differ widely in their political and economic development, educational levels, and standards of living. Therefore, issues, problems, and concerns in the public relations field also vary widely. In countries with low levels of literacy and overwhelming problems of poverty and under-development, there is little opportunity for communication experts to engage in traditional public relations activities employing Western techniques and methods of the profession. In the vast majority of Asian countries the major role of communication practitioners has been to contribute to what is known as development communication. In this form of communi-cation national governments play crucial roles because they marshal all the media and com-munication resources in their countries to achieve socioeconomic goals in planned ways. Most Asian countries in South Asia and Southeast Asia, for example, use five-year and long-term strategic economic plans to achieve specific development targets in public health, education, industrial, and agriculture sectors. Even specific targets are set in private industrial and agricultural sectors in the development plans. Various persuasive communi-cation campaigns are launched to achieve these national goals by encouraging people to participate in the national development efforts. Communication workers in government-controlled media and privately owned channels are assigned roles in the huge efforts at so-cial and human resource mobilization. Every major government agency responsible for drawing up and implementing the strategies for achieving development targets has a com-munication or public relations unit that employs communication technicians and managers. In the context of practicing development communication, public relations workers have to engage in communication activities that have strong persuasive and propaganda compo-nents. These, therefore, fall under the *asymmetric* models of communication.

Because the vast majority of Asian countries have had a colonial or semicolonial past, after achieving independence, government leaders of the countries faced the urgent task of forging nation-states with peoples divided along linguistic, religious, ethnic, and cultural lines. So most countries believed they needed to first develop plans for achiev-ing national integration by focusing on the commonalities of interests and discouraging divisive and fissiparous tendencies that existed below the surface. The government de-partments, in particular ministries of information and broadcasting, have always had the responsibility of disseminating persuasive nation-building messages. In Malaysia, the government, on gaining independence, had the difficult task of fusing the Malays, Indians, Chinese, and other groups into a coherent nation. During the emergency period from 1948 to 1960, the Department of Publicity and Printing, which included film, broadcasting, and information units, had to engage in psychological warfare against the communist guerrillas by convincing the Malaysians that the British and not the Chinese communist guerrillas had won World War II over Japan (Van Leuven & Pratt, 1996). The department then was given the task of promoting the national ideology of *Rukunegara.* This involved a public information campaign of apprising the Malaysians of the aims and objectives of the government's policies and encouraging them to participate in activities designed to achieve the goals of unity, integration, and national development. Given the low literacy rate and a largely rural population with major ethnic divisions, campaign materials were designed to "build consensus and defuse animosities" (p. 96). It was determined that interpersonal folk media would be the most effective channel, and community development specialists, also known as public relations officers, made presentations at community centers, held group discussions, and made house-to-house visits. With the launching of the Rural Development Plan in 1960, an elaborate development communication campaign was started to support road building, water supplying, and rural electrification. The larger goal was to transform the society from an agrarian to a manufacture-based industrial one. The new economic policy was put in place in 1969; its aim was to eradicate poverty and achieve educational and economic development for all races. The communication campaign at this time was specifically designed to boost food production, prevent drug abuse, discourage hoarding, encourage road safety, and improve public health, among others. Considering the ambitious development plans, it is understandable that the government employed four times as many communication workers as the private sector public relations entities.

During the 1990s, the government instituted a "Look East" policy that urged Malaysians not to be enamored of the individualism of Western societies but to look east to countries like Japan and Korea for their positive values and strong work ethic. Subsequently, the government, through its communication campaigns, encouraged people to adopt Islamic values and adapt them to developed economic and industrial life. Quite clearly, when the goal of a communication campaign is nation building through persuasion, even though feedback from receivers is important for fashioning effective communication messages, the communication is bound to be asymmetric. Malaysia and most other developing Asian countries exemplify that pattern. In the neighboring country of Singapore, which achieved independence in 1965, the government adopted an information policy as a top priority that would help create shared values and a sense of national identity among its citizens of Chinese, Malay, and Indian origin. Nair (1986) states that, after gaining independence, the government planned public relations campaigns to "educate the public, to change negative social habits and to adopt new attitudes essential for an emerging nation" (p. 11). Various campaigns were launched to eradicate some social problems and promote education, public health, and population control. For example, during the 1960s, antilitter and "Lungs for Singapore" campaigns were launched to create a clean and green environment followed by family planning, road safety, prevention of drug abuse, and safety in construction and shipbuilding campaigns. The government also promoted a "Speak Mandarin" campaign designed to reduce the use of Chinese dialects and encourage the use of Mandarin to facilitate trade and commerce with mainland China. Clearly, the government has used such persuasive campaigns to create not only a shared national culture but also a highly efficient society. Today, Singapore is one of the most successful countries in Asia with a high standard of living.

In the Philippines also it is notable that the National Congress of Public Relations in the 1990s committed itself to the "cause of economic advancement, national unity in particular, and the Philippines 2000 vision of becoming a Newly Industrializing country" (Jamias & Tuazon, 1996, p. 191). In the Philippines, public relations as a profession developed in the corporate and the government sectors, with each sector having its own professional organization of practitioners. The Public Relations Society of Philippines (PRSP), the organization of the private sector public relations professionals, for example, states in its objectives that it seeks to build public confidence in the profession by generating public support of public relations projects designed to promote general welfare. More importantly, PRSP's objectives are to assist the government in its development efforts through the adoption of projects that have socioeconomic impacts. The organization also wishes to coordinate its efforts with the government in using public relations to unify Filipino people through positive goals and projects. In the Philippines, the public relations profession consists of private and public sector practitioners, including the public relations departments of advertising agencies, public relations counselors, publicity and promotions practitioners, and government information officers (Virtusio, 1981). In recent years, publicity agents working in the entertainment industry have also wished to be accepted as legitimate practitioners.

In a government-oriented public information system there is always tension between political information in support of the government and development-oriented information. Not surprisingly, the Aquino administration in 1986, in its assessment found that political propaganda crowded out development-oriented public information. To its credit, the government attempted to maintain a balance between the two by assigning separate tasks to different government agencies. The office of the press secretary was given the task of maintaining political media relations, whereas the Philippine Information Agency was given the responsibility of dealing with development communication (Jamias & Tuazon, 1996). It has been noted that Asian countries, such as Indonesia, have the ideology of *Pancasila,* and Malaysia its *Rukunegara,* whereas Japan, Korea, and China derive their strength and unity from Confucianism, which emphasizes social harmony and the work ethic. The Philippines needed to promote entrepreneurship, industriousness, frugality, quality consciousness, and passion for excellence (Jamias & Tuazon, 1996). The assumption is that public relations practitioners can help achieve that social goal.

In Thailand the political system changed from absolute monarchy to constitutional monarchy in 1932. The new government felt the need to inform and educate the citizenry about the political system and explain government policies to them for better understanding and cooperation. Therefore, a publicity office was first created for this purpose. Subsequently, the office was upgraded to a department and renamed the Public Relations Department (Ekachai & Komolsevin, 1996). The type of public relations activities that the department engaged in could be called press agentry in that the government used the department as a "propaganda mouthpiece" to publicize its activities in a one-way asymmetric mode (p. 156). Only when the country adopted a democratic form of government was the need for a more balanced two-way symmetrical form of information exchange between the government and its people recognized. In any case, one of the duties of the department was to mobilize the public for national and rural development. In the private sector, public relations activities have grown in concert with the economy. These activities are mostly carried out within the marketing, advertising, or personnel departments of corporations under the supervision of top managers. Service industries seem to use public relations more than other industries for image building, impression management, and marketing support. Practitioners in the profession, both in public and private sectors, seem to predominantly play the role of communication technicians, largely focusing on message production and distribution.

Western-style public relations was introduced in China only in the late 1970s. Chen (1996) states that Western-style public relations in China has gone through four stages. The first stage began in 1980 and lasted until 1985, when China moved toward a commercial economy. Public relations during this stage diffused from the southern coastal regions to commercial and capital cities such as Shanghai and Beijing, and to inland cities such as Nanjing. Initially, only joint-venture manufacturing corporations practiced public relations but, subsequently, the profession spread to government institutions and other enterprises. During the second stage, between 1986 and 1989, there was an upsurge of public relations activity, and, despite confusion about the goals, roles, and practice of public relations, many practitioners learned the basics of the craft and tried to use them. The third phase began in 1989 with the prodemocracy student movement when the government felt the need to reconsider all ideas imported from the West, including public relations. It was believed that the communist party and the government must supervise public relations practices. Despite the fact that China borrowed some Western features in its public relations practices, it remains fundamentally different from the West because, as Chen (1996) suggests, "goals and features of public relations stem in part from Confucius." Confucian emphasis on "personal relationships, honest, high moral standards, and loyalty to one's group affects every aspect of individual and organizational life in China" (p. 147). Public relations practices in China emphasize the "human touch" that places personal human approaches above "business-like attitudes" in dealing with people. Because interpersonal relationships form the basis of public relations, a practitioner must build *guanxi,* a network of personal relationships. A person in a high position with more power has an advantage in building relationships. Because government-owned and -controlled media are known to be propaganda mouthpieces of the government and the party, *guanxi* is believed to be more effective as a channel of communication with key publics. Only a small percentage of the practitioners in China had work experience in the mass media prior to entering the profession, but an increasing number are receiving some formal training at various vocational schools, colleges, and universities.

In Japan public relations started when Allied occupation forces following World War II created central regional public relations offices to disseminate information and publicize their policies and programs. The Japanese government also set up similar public relations offices known as *Koho-bu.* Japan is divided into forty-seven prefectures. Even the smallest village unit performs public relations functions. All municipalities engage in public relations campaigns to educate citizens about various problems and crises. For example, the Tokyo metropolitan government in 1989 created *Gomira,* an animal character symbolizing the city's garbage crisis and the importance of recycling (Chen, 1996). The national government similarly uses information campaigns to educate the public about AIDS, drugs, and the hazards of smoking, and so on. In the private sector, public relations is concerned with investor relations, risk management, crisis management, publicity, and campaigns to establish corporate identity. However, the typical role played by a public relations practitioner is one of a technician rather than a manager.

According to Cooper-Chen (1996), public relations in Japan has tended to emphasize media relations because of the heavy use of the mass media by the Japanese and the existence of an extensive press club (*Kisha*) system that provides beat reporters who cover government and industries with physical facilities and exclusive press conferences. All reporters covering a particular industry belong to the club attached to the industry's trade association. Cooper-Chen (1996) notes a Japanese publication as saying, "Japanese society as a whole, and . . . corporations do not have the same sort of PR needs as do Western companies" (p. 224). In the Japanese workforce employees move in and out of public relations jobs as they move up the ladder in the corporate structure. Therefore, managers who are the members of the dominant coalition may have had public relations experience already. In the Japanese collectivist culture the basic concern for harmony and group welfare influences public relations practices. In the context of the Japanese value system, harmony means, as Cooper-Chen explains, that consumers do not generally engineer boycotts, the media do not investigate business practices, trust exists between employer and employees, group welfare prevails over individual desires, and clients remain loyal to the public relations agency. It is also unthinkable for an agency not to do its utmost for a client.

Japanese private sector public relations is dominated by a handful of agencies that fall into several categories—joint-ventures between Japanese and Western companies, ad agency-related public relations companies, independent niche companies that specialize in such areas as investor relations, and corporations with public relations units.

Conclusion

As the societies in Asia experience socioeconomic development and the development of information infrastructure, public and private sector public relations work is also undergoing a transformation. Clearly, as a society's emphasis changes from nation building to market development, public relations practices also shift from government settings to consultancy public relations. As various government entities are changed to public and private corporations, the scope of and opportunities for in-house public relations is increasing in South and Southeast Asian countries. Al-Enad (1990) points out that, during the nation-building phase in a developing country, a government ministry with a particular responsibility informs the public about issues of importance to persuade them to act or behave in a way consistent with achieving government developmental goals. They also wish to publicize government activities to keep the public satisfied. Typically, in most Asian countries, during the nation-building phase government ministries or agencies use information workers as extension agents or community development specialists. During this phase they may be regarded as paraprofessionals with limited mass media skills. Given the limited reach of mass media because of low literacy rates and low standards of living, information workers have to use a combination of traditional, interpersonal folk channels and some mass media in a government information campaign to reach key publics. During the market development phase there is an emergence of the middle class, which leads to a phase of trade expansion with a manufacturing base and a market for consumer goods. Multinational corporations at this stage invest in the economy and need public relations and advertising agencies. In some Southeast Asian countries government agencies turn to private consulting firms for communication and crisis management. During the market development phase, with the development of an industrial and consumer society, a different set of issues becomes important in information campaigns. One visible change that occurs is a shift from publicity in the news media to the use of special events for promoting grand openings, product launches, groundbreakings, and various other promotional activities. In Southeast Asia the third phase has been identified as one of regional-interdependence (Van Leuven & Pratt, 1996). The development of stock markets in Asia, the privatization of government-run companies, and many Asian companies seeking business and capital in international markets have necessitated corporate positioning, investor relations programs, and financial communication (Josephs, 1991). All these also require sophisticated public relations programs involving crisis communication and issues management.

Scholars seem to have certain presuppositions about the social role of public relations in society and certain worldviews relating to it. For example, there is the pragmatic social role for public relations that sees itself as a result-oriented practice. In this view, society is composed of competing groups, target audiences, and markets for commercial gain. The pragmatic social view may be common in public relations in Asia where clients determine marketing objectives without any concern for ethical considerations. It is an asymmetrical worldview where the goal of public relations may be to satisfy clients and make profits. The conservative social role of public relations supposedly defends the societal status quo and the privileges of the economically powerful. Public relations from this perspective uses various tools and weapons to neutralize opposition to its clients' positions by reaching its target audiences. The radical worldview assumes that public relations can contribute to change in society and in organizations. It can provide an outside perspective to management about the organization, but it can also provide information to the public for debate and contribute to the solution of social problems. Both the conservative and radical worldviews see public relations as a tool to be used in a war among opposing social groups (Grunig & White, 1992). The idealistic social role of public relations assumes that it serves the public interest by developing understanding between organizations and their publics through dialogue and contributes to informed debate on issues of importance in society. The neutral social role views public relations as a neutral object of study with a focus on understanding the effects of public relations, the motivations of organizations, and the objectives and goals of public relations.

Some scholars, ranging from empirical to radical Marxists, envision the role of public relations from a critical perspective. They focus on poor ethics, negative social consequences, and ineffective public relations, which is a far cry from normative theories of effective public relations. Some contend that corporations have used public relations to restrict competition, and others argue that public relations has been used to preserve the existing power structure in society. Thus, there are many views of public relations. There is no way to tell which is the predominant view in as diverse a continent as Asia. It is possible that all of these views have some bearing on understanding Asian public relations.

Discussion Questions

1. What are the diverse geographic, demographic, and cultural conditions in which communication and public relations policy makers work in Asia?

2. How is public relations commonly defined? How can one identify the relevant target publics from among the stakeholder groups? Why should public relations managers be part of the dominant coalition of an organization?

3. What are the basic cultural determinants that a public relations practitioner needs to understand in order to function effectively in various cultural contexts in Asia?

4. What are the specific characteristics of excellent public relations departments that contribute to excellence in management?

5. What are the different models within which public relations activities can be conceptualized in Asian countries?

6. What are the different approaches used in government or public sector public relations and private sector corporate public relations in Asia?

References

Al-Enad, A. (1990, Summer). Public relations roles in developing countries. *Public Relations Quarterly, 34*(2), 24–26.

Bohannan, P. (1969). *Social anthropology.* London: Holt, Rinehart and Winston.

Chen, N. (1996). Public relations in China: The introduction and development of an occupational field. In H. Culburtson and N. Chen (Eds.), *International public relations: A comparative analysis* (pp. 121–153). Mahwah, NJ: Lawrence Erlbaum Associates.

Cooper-Chen, A. (1996). Public relations practice in Japan: Beginning again for the first time. In H. Culbertson & N. Chen (Eds.), *International public relations: A comparative analysis* (pp. 223–237). Mahwah, NJ: Lawrence Erlbaum Associates.

Cutlip, S., Center, A., & Broom, G. (1994). *Effective public relations.* Upper Saddle River, NJ: Prentice Hall.

Ekachai, D., & Komolsevin, R. (1996). Public relations in Thailand: Its functions and practitioners' roles. In H. Culbertson & N. Chen (Eds.), *International public relations: A comparative analysis* (pp. 155–170). Mahwah, NJ: Lawrence Erlbaum Associates.

Grunig, J. E. (1992a). Communication, public relations, and effective organizations: An overview of the book. In J. E. Grunig (Ed.), *Excellence in public relations and communication management* (pp. 1–28). Hillsdale, NJ: Lawrence Erlbaum Associates.

Grunig, J. E. (1992b). What is excellence in management? In J. E. Grunig (Ed.), *Excellence in public relations and communication management* (pp. 219–250). Hillsdale, NJ: Lawrence Erlbaum Associates.

Grunig, J. E., & Hunt, T. (1984). *Managing public relations.* New York: Holt, Rinehart & Winston.

Grunig, J. E., & Rapper, F. (1992). Strategic management, publics, and issue. In J. E. Grunig (Ed.), *Excellence in public relations and communication management* (pp. 117–157). Hillsdale, NJ: Lawrence Erlbaum Associates.

Grunig, J. E., & White, J. (1992). The effect of worldviews on public relations theory and practice. In J. E. Grunig (Ed.), *Excellence in public relations and communication management* (pp. 31–64). Hillsdale, NJ: Lawrence Erlbaum Associates.

Harlow, R. (1976). Building a public relations definition. *Public Relations Review, 2*(4), 34–42.

Hofstede, G. (1980). *Culture's consequences.* Beverly Hills, CA: Sage.

Imai, M. (1986). *Kaizen: The key to Japan's competitive success.* New York: Random House.

Jamias, J., & Tuazon, R. (1996). Public relations in the Philippines. In H. Culbertson & N. Chen (Eds.), *International public relations: A comparative analysis* (pp. 191–206). Mahwah, NJ: Lawrence Erlbaum Associates.

Josephs, R. (1991, September). Hong Kong: Public relations capital of Asia? *Public Relations Journal,* 21–25.

Kaplan, D., & Manners, R. (1972). *Culture theory.* Englewood Cliffs, NJ: Prentice Hall.

Nair, B. (1986). *A primer of public relations in Singapore.* Singapore: Asian Mass Communication Research & Education Centre.

Ouchi, W. (1984). *The M-form society.* New York: Avon.

Pascale, R., & Athos, A. (1981). *The art of Japanese management.* New York: Penguin.

Spiro, M. (1966). Buddhism and economic action in Burma. *American Anthropologist 68,* 1163.

Sriramesh, K. (1996). Power distance and public relations: An ethnographic study of southern Indian organizations. In H. Culbertson & N. Chen (Eds.), *International public relations: A comparative analysis* (pp. 171–190). Mahwah, NJ: Lawrence Erlbaum Associates.

Sriramesh, K., & White, J. (1992). Societal culture and public relations. In J. E. Grunig (Ed.), *Excellence in public relations and communication management* (pp. 597–614). Hillsdale, NJ: Lawrence Erlbaum Associates.

Stokes, R. (1984). *Introduction to sociology.* Dubuque, IA: Wm. C. Brown.

Tayeb, M. H. (1988). *Organizations and national culture: A comparative analysis.* London: Sage.

Van Leuven, J., & Pratt, C. (1996). Public relations' role: Realities in Asia and in Africa south of the Sahara. In H. Culbertson & N. Chen (Eds.), *International public relations: A comparative analysis* (pp. 93–105). Mahwah, NJ: Lawrence Erlbaum Associates.

Virtusio, R. (1981, February). Public relations in 1980s: The social role. *Public Relations Journal,* 11–16.

Williamson, R. (1982) Attitudes accompanying modernization in advance and developing societies. In L. Adler (Ed.), *Cross cultural research at issue.* New York: Academic.

World Book Encyclopedia. (1999). Vol 1. Chicago: World Book, Inc.

17

Singapore Poised for Prominence in Public Relations among Emerging Democracies

Doug Newsom

Key Points

- Singapore, with its decision to become a paperless society, is positioned on the cutting edge of public relations—especially in international practice.
- As a trading center for centuries, Singapore excels at business-to-business (B2B) commerce.
- A solid economic climate provides a good environment for public relations; the political climate is somewhat less solid, although that seems to be changing.
- Singapore is highly dependent on foreign skilled labor and struggles to prevent "brain drain" of its own talent, but all in all it has a good pool of skilled labor.
- The Institute of Public Relations in Singapore (IPRS) and the educational institutions in Singapore are professionalizing the practice of public relations.

The global development of public relations has been breathtakingly fast, and part of the reason for this is because of the acceleration of Internet use. The Internet is the world's newest medium. Its reach and efficiency have shrunk the world. With the Internet's global reach and the dramatic effect of satellites on telecommunications, the opportunity for shared information has created more global citizens. These new publics represent a sprawling marketplace for goods, services, and ideas. As the world's newest communication tool, the Internet provides public relations practitioners with enormous resources and is an effective and efficient communication tool. Public relations activity in Singapore today is highest in the government sector, but increasingly the global importance of the city-state and its long tradition as a trading center is stepping up its outreach, especially in business-to-business public relations and its focus on tourism.

As a communication medium, the Internet has two qualities that give public relations practitioners a special advantage. First, the Internet is interactive, so public relations practitioners have opportunities to truly engage in two-way communications that are so important in building relationships with constituencies. Second, public relations practitioners have opportunities, through the use of Web sites, to present their client's or organization's side of a story directly, without media filtering. Both qualities make the Internet a good public relations servant (Newsom, 1999).

Singapore has taken full advantage of these qualities in presenting that small nation-state as a safe harbor for investments, a protected and predictable holiday choice for tourists, and a sophisticated and cosmopolitan Asian nation for business. Consider Singapore's economic status: It has the ninth-largest gross national product (GNP) per capita in the world, and in purchasing power parity, it would be fifth; it has the sixth-largest foreign exchange reserves in the world; it has the world's second-largest seaport and seventh-busiest airport; and it is the fifteenth-largest trading nation in the world (Koh, 1998).

The former British colony retains English as its language of commerce while requiring all three of its citizen groups to command their "native tongue"—Mandarin for citizens of Chinese descent, Tamil for those of East Indian ancestry, and Malay for its Malaysian population. For an inside look at all of this, visit Singapore's collection of Web sites and the nation's image is instant. This is a high-tech, high-energy place for people in the know and on the go.

Singapore is the home of the world's major advertising agencies, with forty or more in the country, and public relations firms such as Burson-Marsteller, Edelman, and Ogilvy & Mather. It also has a solid collection of homegrown public relations and advertising firms and agencies. These are populated not only with seasoned professionals, native and expatriate, but also talented groups of young adults, homegrown and educated, but polished by overseas experience often gained by study abroad during their college years. University faculty encourage students to go abroad and facilitate that experience, and they are very receptive to students from other nations coming to Singapore to study. These students are bright, business-oriented people with cell phones, palm pilots, laptops, and all of the other accouterments of the high-tech world that is Singapore. As an example, a *Straits Times* story carried a photo of a taxi driver using his palmtop computer to find the best way to an unfamiliar location (He's got the whole island, 1999).

This high-tech society, especially with its Internet access, has helped move Singapore beyond the perception of being a clean but rather rigid, restrictive place to live and work. Note the word *perception*. Singapore is changing, but its image has changed much more quickly than the reality.

The Internet, although a good public relations servant, is also an exacting master. A Web site, for example, is an unrelenting taskmaster, demanding constant updating and maintenance. Also, Web sites, like everything else on the Internet, are vulnerable to sabotage from hackers and copycat Web sites that denigrate an organization. Additionally, chat rooms on the Internet can be sources of rumor and misinformation that can precipitate crises (Newsom, 1999).

Because the Singapore government controls the nation's media, the invasion of the Internet has caused it some consternation. Although some controls seem to be relaxing in the hands of a seemingly more self-confident government, others have not. Singapore's electronic monitoring has gotten it into trouble with some of its own citizens, and their increasing sophistication has made them less tolerant of restrictive interference with this new medium. Web sites originating in Singapore are carefully monitored, but citizens have discovered they can find information of interest to them on Web sites in less restrictive societies. The government has not been as heavy handed about discouraging or actually blocking access as some other Asian nations have.

Observations about the World Wide Web

The Web's language is English, and it is the international research tool of choice for current information. Search engines can locate all sorts of information, but historical research is still limited, even with a large number of library resources on-line. This works to the advantage of emerging democracies such as Singapore.

The easy transfer of words, pictures, and sound has created a flurry of copyright lawsuits all over the world, many of which are not supportable, especially in nations that do not recognize or respect creative property. Singapore is not one of these. However, finding a place to try some cases is difficult because these are property rights in an international venue.

Whereas some nations are concerned that, because of developmental problems, their citizens will be deprived of access, Singapore is not one of these. The government has wired every home. Singapore does share the concern of some other nations, though, that its power may be eroded because of its citizens' access to the Internet. In all nations, privacy is an issue because electronic transactions all leave a "path," and there is access to much information by "unintended" recipients. In Singapore, the government has been accused by its own citizens of being too much of a "nanny," and it does watch electronic activity.

One of the problems of the Web's openness, of course, is the vulnerability of even the most secure systems to hackers. Other problems are viruses and worms that invade and sometimes destroy disk drives. Singapore authorities are vigilant, and government servers simply shut down in case of a threat, a tactic not peculiar to that nation.

The Internet has provided a new medium for news and opinion as well as advertising, and allows international discourse in "real time." It offers a place for business transactions of all kinds on a global level. The easy access creates opportunities for the homebound and facilitates learning for everyone. It gives organizations both intranet and extranet opportunities.

For a nation such as Singapore, the opportunity to share information about the country through pictures, maps, sound, and video as well as text has been an asset. Also, information can be posted in a number of different languages, a considerable advantage to a country that boasts the second-busiest seaport in the world. There are excellent opportunities for business-to-business campaigns through specialized Web sites, and Singapore's government and businesses use the intranets with great efficiency. Although the whole country has a population of slightly more than 3 million, communication still could be less efficient than it is because of the exhaustive use of intranets.

Singapore's Goal: To Become a Paperless Society

Many nations, such as Singapore, are becoming extraordinarily high-tech societies and are setting the tone for other nations. The Singapore ideal is to become a paperless society. The country is well on its way. At all government levels and in many businesses, the intranet is not simply an information system for employees, it is the only way to get anything done.

It goes without saying that paychecks go directly into the bank, and the individual finds out when the deposit was made and for how much by going to a restricted access site on the intranet. If an employee wants to claim some vacation time, that request is also filed electronically and responded to electronically. Almost all housing, at least apartment housing, is government owned but offered with 99-year leases. If a repair is needed, the request is filed electronically. Many businesses also function the same way. It is possible to call someone by phone, but the caller may then be asked to go to an electronic site to send a message. The constant sound of cell phones ringing indicates people are using the phones, but conversations are generally personal or, if business related, an "instant messaging" sort of system is used.

Although Singapore has an efficient postal system, most correspondence is by e-mail within institutions and among citizens. In all systems, service providers have access to e-mail messages. Any incorrectly addressed e-mail bounces back and a copy is sent to the mail administrator of the service provider. In most cases, in addition to the sender and receiver, at least two, maybe three others could see the message.

Singaporeans found out that their system is more carefully monitored than most when the government began invading e-mail systems to test them to determine whether they could be accessed. Some computer owners had security systems that identified the "invasion," and unhappy citizens took their complaints to the government-owned newspapers. To their credit, the papers covered the story and the government ministry apologized. For some native Singaporeans, this was an indication that the new electronic society had indeed changed the way government responded to its citizens.[1]

The situation of government intervention is significant because in the future most communication will be in an electronic medium, and it will be global, but very targeted. As a market center, Singapore is very involved in banking and investments, business-to-business (B2B) commerce, science and technology, and promoting various aspects of the city-state through global Web sites.

Investment and International Capital

Investing on-line is something everyone knows about, and some investment houses specialize in it. However, it is not really as common yet as it is likely to become, especially with the euro having focused attention on combined markets with a single currency. What is common, though, is use of the Internet to gain information and tap investment resources.

Singapore is believed to be a safe market, so it has much to offer. Its banking systems are considered reliable, and, recently, Singapore has been reaching out to the high number of expatriates employed there to participate in its retirement plan.

Singapore allows foreign workers to put their earnings into special retirement accounts. Employers used to be required to make payments into the Central Provident Fund (CPF) for all expatriate employees who were holding an Employment/Professional Visit Past. That ended in 1995, but now there is a Supplementary Retirement Scheme (SRS) that allows people working in Singapore to voluntarily contribute to their existing CPF fund accounts. And expatriates who have not been required to contribute to CPF now may put as much as 20 percent of their salaries into the system. The benefits, according to *Global Business,* are numerous (Pension schemes, 2000). First of all, corporate chief financial officers can spread out the costs of managing retirement benefits because both local and foreign workers can now put more of their earnings into retirement accounts. Second, all of the funds are available for payout beginning at age fifty-five. More important, for expatriates, the funds can be moved out of the country. Even Singapore citizens can move their funds if they take up permanent residence abroad. A third benefit is that, although employers must match the first 10 percent paid in by Singapore citizens, that is not the case with expatriate employees.

The investments are placed in privately managed banks and insurance companies and offer a guaranteed minimal return. The fund manager also must invest a portion of the funds in treasury bills and bonds, but individuals can choose to put some of their savings in higher-risk, higher-yield funds. A major benefit is that contributions to the SRS are tax free with no tax charged until the payments are withdrawn.

For Singapore, this positions the city-state for international business. The funds help the local economy by creating cheaper capital, and the city-state does not have to pay for pensions out of present income (Pension schemes, 2000). For multinational employers, such as the advertising and public relations giants in Singapore, it is an attractive incentive to expand their operations and import talent.

B2B Commerce

Although Singapore has almost no manufacturing, it is a matchmaker of incomparable skill, having been a trading center for centuries. Now that trading is manifest on the Web sites that offer information on shipping, storage, insurance, and all of the other B2B necessities, Singapore is particularly well positioned for B2B commerce.

Most tourists know Singapore as a dining and shopping paradise because of the number, size, and quality of its restaurants and malls. However, consumers are not aware of the supply side. The merchandise that comes to the consumer outlets requires intricate layers of B2B contacts and transactions.

The same is true for transportation that brings tourists and businesspeople to the island. Air and cruise lines have intricate arrangements with countries, and for Singapore, as both a tourist and business destination, that means constant contact—almost all electronic—with these global transportation systems. The reputation of Singapore as an efficient business society and trading partner is a result of enforcement of its laws and a commitment to contracts.

Science and Technology

One of the most significant development plans in some Asian nations has been science and technology parks. Singapore, along with Australia, Taiwan, Thailand, Hong Kong, and China, is one of the leaders. In building its own high-tech society, Singapore has created a pool of skilled labor. Multi-nationals are attracted to these resources. In many cases, they get top caliber scientists at lower prices. Additionally, they are likely to find science parks that emphasize research only, not business, and many are affiliated with a university (Morphy, 2000).

In Singapore, Kelvin Liu, center director of the Singapore National Science and Technology Board, explains that the goal is to adopt a new paradigm for the parks to create an environment where scientists can interact informally as well as formally. The city-state's Science Parks I and II have pedestrian and public transportation links, sidewalk cafes, and fundamentals such as broadband communications infrastructure (Morphy, 2000). High-tech business demands high-tech public relations professionals, and Singapore has not only attracted other Asians but also has developed its own high-tech public relations professionals who also find jobs there.

Strategic, Not Mass, Communication

The specialization in high tech requires strategic communication, not the kind of communication that traditionally has been used in mass media. A good example of this can be found in campaigns and the shift from mass to targeted electronic communication, much of it through the Internet.

Singapore's many ministries each have major campaign activities in addition to their ongoing day-to-day business. Although this is not unusual in that many other countries also follow this pattern, Singapore is only now beginning to get sites and launch campaigns from nongovernmental or quasi-governmental organizations.

Citizen Involvement

The anomaly for Singapore is the result of previous tight government control in a nation that has no freedom of speech or right of assembly. However, government has determined that citizen involvement can be useful. One of the first government agencies to direct efforts toward citizens was, oddly enough, the Environment Ministry. It is odd because Singapore traditionally has been very sensitive to criticism of its government on any issue, and the environment is one issue in particular. Recycling, for example, is often urged by citizens who are then reprimanded by the government. The government has conducted campaigns on many public health issues though. Perhaps the most famous, or infamous, is the government campaign against littering, known internationally for its ban on chewing gum and considerable fines for dropping anything on the ground. A government campaign against mosquitoes also is well known because residents may not have flowerpots with bases that retain water. This caused some international attention because of the punishment meted out to violators.

In 1999, the Environment Ministry decided to set up an environmental think tank of citizens, charging them with handling public education, starting with antilittering. In recognition of World Environment Day, the ministry's then public health commissioner, Daniel Wang, said the ministry was contacting people and organizations because civic groups were more effective in creating social responsibility without having to fine people. The ministry has been conducting campaigns for more than thirty years, but a survey indicated that the public, though aware of them, thought the government would take care of the problems. The effort in involving citizens was intended to encourage people to take the initiative (Nathan, 1999).

Two groups already had been put in place before 1999, the Singapore Environment Council and the Waterways Watch Society, the latter to monitor pollution in the city-state's rivers and waterways. These two, and other groups like them, will target the adult population because the government already has environmental education in the schools.

The risk the government is taking with a citizen-based initiative is opening the country to politically persuasive nonprofit groups operating in the global community, such as Greenpeace. Greenpeace is only one of a number of environmental Web sites, each with a substantive e-mail list, which makes communication and mobilization as easy as a mouse click. Historically, Singapore has strongly resisted such "invasions," though desiring to be a global player.

Many of these international nonprofit groups are very involved in attempting to affect the policies of governments. Highly visible groups in 2000 and 2001 were those opposed to biotech products. These groups tried to restrict the production and distribution of genetically engineered products, such as corn and other edibles. The policies they were trying to affect included food for both animal and human consumption, especially if the animals might become a part of the human food chain. Other high-tech developments with genes and stem cells have created yet other activist groups.

Although some of these nongovernmental organizations (NGOs) limit their activities to extensive electronic communication resulting in publicity and a few demonstrations, some groups such as Greenpeace and People for the Ethical Treatment of Animals (PETA) act out their objections in events that not only attract media attention but also impact people and property. The groups often form coalitions with other types of organizations and even with companies. One example is Global Compact, a program for protecting workers and the environment endorsed by twelve international labor unions, Amnesty International, the Human Rights Watch, and the World Wildlife Fund. Among its commercial members are DaimlerChrysler, Royal Dutch Shell, duPont, BP Amoco, Ericsson, and Novartis. However, some NGOs do not like UN support for Global Compact because they think it gives the commercial companies a marketing tool. That is true because the commercial firms use Global Compact to make environmentally friendly claims in their campaigns. The NGOs use such agreements, when endorsed, to support their own efforts and pressure other groups to accept their issues and change their policies to comply.

So, why is this international public relations effort important to Singapore? It will seriously threaten that city-state's status quo. Evidence that Singapore realizes that potential is apparent from an exhaustive project launched internally to establish its own "grassroots" activities. Instead of NGOs, what is more likely to flourish in Singapore are government-organized entities but not actually government organizations (GONGOs). GONGOs are voluntary membership organizations that serve as conduits of information to the government that affect public policy and often suggest campaigns that the government initiates or sponsors. These are different from civil society organizations (CSOs) that are primarily private but may have received government funding or partial funding for some government-endorsed activities (Ooi & Koh, 1998).

Singapore and the Electronic Global Society—The Singapore 21 Report

In 1998, Singapore's government developed what was called the Singapore 21 committee to determine how the country should respond to changes in its society and its role in global affairs (Singapore 21 Report, 1999; the full report also appeared on a Singapore government Web site: www.gov.sg/ps21, 1999).

The committee's research involved more than six thousand people who participated in some eighty forums and discussions with subcommittees of the larger body. Some of the problems addressed were primarily internal to the country but not much different from many other nations, such as an aging population and the strains it would put on resources and family responsibilities for the "sandwich" generation having to care for both children and aging parents.

Another primarily internal need, also not peculiar to Singapore but something faced by most developed and developing nations, is how to relieve stress from the 24/7 (twenty-four hours a day, seven days a week) syndrome. Of course, much of this stress is induced by a global society that knows no boundaries.

For its role in a global society, Singapore recognizes a continuing need to attract foreign talent to supplement its small population. Research for the 21 Report had shown that although Singaporeans realized the need for imported skilled labor, they also felt that foreigners got better treatment than locals and might be taking jobs that locals could fill. In response to that, the 21 Report recommended that Singapore plan for a system of lifelong learning. With this plan, when the economy is healthy, the government would pay into a fund given as dividends to every citizen—not as cash and not transferable—that could be used only for education and training.

Specifically, as a response to global society and educating Singaporeans abroad, the country is acutely aware of the risk of brain drain. Instead of developing policies and regulations that would further tie a Singaporean to the homeland, the 21 Report recommended strengthening citizens' emotional ties to their homeland.

These suggestions included preserving landmarks, setting up clubs for their expatriates abroad, providing more opportunity for feedback from expatriates, permitting citizens to vote in general elections, and having Singaporean schools with distance-learning classes. The report also recommended a reconsideration of the current ten-year rule whereby those who are out of the country ten years without returning lose their citizenship. For those returning, the report suggests a center for helping them with re-entry into Singaporean society by responding to queries, helping with paperwork, and getting children reenrolled in schools.

These suggestions seem fairly benign and doable, but the recommendation that Singaporeans have a greater say in their national affairs and more of a stake in their government is controversial in a nation that is top-down and patriarchal. The country inherited a history of top-down governance from its colonial experience, and this continued when

Harry Lee Kuan Yew became prime minister in 1959. His People's Action Party (PAP) has remained in power, largely by suppressing political opposition and media criticism. Although no longer prime minister, Lee Kuan Yew remains "the power behind the throne." Critics complain that its "democratic" government is a charade, but its political and economic stability is unique in Asia.

Another Singapore 21 suggestion, even more controversial than increased participation in government, is that women be conscripted to national service as men now are. Every male citizen has to serve the government, usually in the military, from age eighteen to twenty. This move toward recognition of equality for women is remarkable. Although women have jobs in Singapore, few are in true leadership positions especially in government, a fact confirmed by the number of those in charge of government ministries.

The report noted that Singaporeans want a greater say in national decisions and that there should be more consensus building and consultation—all this in a country that does not guarantee freedom of speech or the right of assembly. The report, quoted directly here, specifies:

- The people should be consulted both before and after a policy which affects them is decided on and implemented.
- They should be given the information to help them make decisions.
- Discussions should be held with mutual respect and trust among those involved.
- The civil service needs to be more receptive to ideas and suggestions.
- The Feedback Unit should be a people sector body, with representatives named by civil society groups, not just the Government.
- Grassroots groups should also correct the perception that they are partisan mouthpieces for disseminating government policies.
- Government Parliamentary Committees should play a bigger role in gathering feedback and passing this on to ministries.
- Ministries should publish more pre-policy discussion papers. They should also have quarterly reviews to monitor how they are dealing with public feedback.
- The media should be objective and people-oriented, with the Government intervening only where national interests are at stake.
- There should be more reports on parliamentary debates, and more discussion on government policies.
- The Out of Bounds markers for public debate should be spelt out more clearly and limited to racial and religious issues which affect social harmony and national security. Having a better understanding of this should help remove fears that those who speak up would enter a "black book."
- For their part, civic groups should not forsake national interests when pursuing their own goals.
- Civic groups should take the lead in organizing discussions and activities. The Government should review existing procedures to facilitate and encourage such civic participation. (Singapore 21 report, 1999, p. 61).

All of this is rather remarkable given that the country has a sedition law, and the government owns the newspaper in which it was published. Also, the same issue of the newspaper had two signed editorials, neither entirely positive. In many ways, the publication of the report, even the generation of it, is indicative of Singapore's increasing realization of its role as a global citizen and its image in the global community.

Implementation always was expected to be gradual, and that is the case.[2] The effects of the September 11, 2001, events in the United States impacted economic and security issues around the world. Singapore's economy began to slide with that of other market centers, with the government estimating that at least twenty thousand jobs would be lost by the end of the year. Nevertheless, the government continued its policy of recruiting foreign talent. In an unusual, for Singapore, outbreak of expressions of public opinion, Singaporeans began to protest mostly in private conversations, but some in letters to the editor and quotes reported by foreign journalists. Public questions about bringing in foreign skilled workers and professionals were raised by some members of the ruling party who realized that this would be an issue in the August 2002 elections. More than 60 percent of companies in Singapore hire foreign talent, largely in information technology, engineering, sales, and marketing. Deputy Prime Minister Lee Hsien Loong defends the government's decision by saying, in an address to PAP youth members, "What we can and should do is to tighten the criteria judiciously for skilled workers and professionals, so that we raise the quality of the foreign workers who come here to help Singapore compete for global investments" (Luh, 2001, p. B7).

In addition to investments, exports are important to Singapore, and the trade-dependent city-state has taken a rare deficit spending step for that government by announcing an 11.3 billion Singapore dollar (U.S.$6.23 billion) stimulus package with tax rebates, support for workers and small businesses, and an acceleration of infrastructure projects. Although the package cuts salaries of senior civil servants, it includes plans to issue "New Singapore Shares" to all citizens. All adult citizens will get shares valued between S$200 to S$1,700. The measure, designed to help lower-income citizens, would have cut Singapore's accumulated surpluses. Because the stimulus package was the first to be offered in twelve years, PAP opponents called it a ploy for the election of 2002. Their view is countered by many international economists who said that 2001 brought the government its worse recession, an economy expected to shrink by 3 percent caused in part the fall in the electronics industry (Day & Borsuk, 2001).

More than global economic problems face the nation trying to put its plan in place. For Singapore 21 to function effectively, the report's ideas and ideals have to be translated into policy and action through the bureaucracy of its various ministries. The first level of communication must be directly to government employees who interpret and implement policy. Written policy once promulgated with interpretation left up to the individual government employee will have to change. There is another change, too, but it already has been implemented to a large extent, in that specialized communication to employees through intranets is replacing traditional communication from management.

Public Service Strategy 21

As another part of looking to the new century, Singapore drafted a policy statement (PS21) recognizing that its economy is increasingly global and outward, rather than inward oriented, and that because of global exposures, it has a population that is demanding higher standards of service (Singapore government, 1999).

PS21 would change traditional public service from reactive to proactive by providing a framework for ideas to flow up from the workforce and by encouraging government workers to initiate change. Historically, those working in government ministries have not been encouraged to seek public opinion before putting policies in action or implementing government campaigns. Polling in Singapore is rare and generally done only to determine the results of government-directed initiatives, which is why the Singapore 21 Report is so exceptional in the first place. Public fora are held, but free expression is restricted by self-censorship in a climate set by the Internal Security Act (which restrains criticism), the Sedition Act, the Penal Code (which defines defamation), the Official Secrets Act, and the Undesirable Publications Act.

The implementation of Report 21 will take more than a government directive because most government workers do not feel secure enough to interpret policy or to stray from well-established procedures. The PS21 changes necessitate motivating public officers to be consumer oriented rather than government directed and to reward them for doing so. Traditionally, many officers were reluctant to be responsive to consumers because of fear of retribution from officials in their ministries. The changes will require a considerable switch of mind-set at the upper levels to give lower-level workers confidence. The other part of the initiative involves providing training in people skills and technology and providing a working environment where service delivery is recognized.

Another major change involves the traditional Asian evaluation of work by "face time." In a society where so much work is done electronically, Singapore, nevertheless, still values having people in view and equates that with output and quality of work. When work can be accomplished electronically from anyplace, and not necessarily in a traditional office setting, face time makes less and less sense, which makes management distinctly uncomfortable. Measuring real accomplishment—what gets done—rather than how much time an employee actually can be seen working is part of the cultural transformation, and it will be difficult. Nevertheless, PS21 is a step forward, but it is not an easy one considering the size of Singapore's government employment.

As suggested, implementation of PS21 is likely to be stymied by culture, not strategy. The government went to an inordinate amount of trouble to publicize PS21, including a S$4.5 million (Singapore dollars), five-day public service exhibition in June 1997 with the theme "Serving Singaporeans Today, Tomorrow." Exhibition visitors were exposed to what they might expect from their civil servants in the future.

A problem with this new approach is the Asian tradition of preserving "face," which includes not only personal self-respect but also respect for the entire group to which one belongs. In Singapore, one can "lose face" by criticizing someone or pointing out mistakes or errors in public (Craig, 1993). The very nature of dealing with most customer service problems involves calling attention to some mistake or error, and usually that of a higher authority.

Another form of losing face or causing someone to lose face in Singapore involves embarrassment or making someone feel insulted or humiliated. Unless handled very delicately, consumer complaints can easily do this. Reluctance or even fear of causing loss of face can impede even the airing of grievances, much less getting redress.

Yet another part of dealing with customer complaints or questions is often turning to a superior or manager for clarification. In Singapore, if an employee questions a superior, especially in public, this could cause loss of face for the person asking the question who risks being seen as "dumb" for not understanding, and loss of face for the person asked who could be viewed as not having explained the situation thoroughly initially.

Loss of face also can be associated with having to say no or refusing someone outright. This is never something anyone dealing with an unhappy consumer of goods or services wants to do, but often it is necessary. Additionally, open disagreement with a superior is cause for loss of face. When the PS21 report talks about turning public service people into activists seeking to change policy or interpretations of policy to better benefit citizens, it is difficult to imagine how this can be done to avoid some "preservation of face" problems.

Singapore Positioned on the Cutting Edge

At least three major attributes of Singapore place it on the cutting edge for prominence in public relations among emerging democracies: use of the dominant language of technology and the Internet (English), the city-state's infrastructure, and its public relations expertise.

First and foremost among its attributes is Singapore's infrastructure. Singapore works. It is one of the least dysfunctional nations in the world. Some U.S. expatriates returning home have commented on their return to a "Third World" country where services, government and commercial, often don't work or don't work right. Singapore's infrastructure is reliable. When occasional power outages occur, they are brief. If the situation is peculiar to a building, engineers are busy working on the problem almost before someone can pick up a phone to call them.

The reliability of the infrastructure is a big attraction to U.S. technology companies, among others. However, a survey showed that although these industries were aware of the nation's efficiency, two important values for high-tech companies—innovation and creativity—were not associated with Singapore. In fact, the country was seen to be somewhat stodgy.

To be sure, industry pays attention to what Singapore can offer; the country launched an estimated $1.4 million (U.S. dollars) campaign in 2000 with full-page ads in U.S. business magazines. According to the *Wall Street Journal,* "[T]he ads are part of a wider public relations effort by Singapore to shed its fuddy-duddy image and promote itself as a technology hub" (Yee, 2001, p. B13B).

The campaign's strategy was to show how similar Singapore is to the United States in its world outlook as well as lifestyle and, of course, language. The ads will provide a strong credibility test among expatriates who experienced endless campaigns on "Asian values" while working in Singapore. Another credibility test will be the government's new promises to make it easy to get work permits and permanent resident status.

A personal experience by the author illustrates this point. On reporting to the personnel office for work, two passports were surrendered, that of the employee and her spouse, because instructions from the university that had been mailed said the university would process the residents' permits for both the university employee and "wife." On the government's immigration form accompanying that instruction, where it said "wife," that line had been marked through and "spouse" written in. The male spouse had signed on the "wife" line, again marking through the word "wife" and writing "spouse." Tourist visas allowed for only a thirty-day stay, so processing papers in a timely way was important.

Ten days after that initial visit to the personnel office, the female university employee got an e-mail from personnel instructing her to come pick up her husband's passport. When his passport was retrieved, and an inquiry was made about hers, she was told that it was in the immigration office. Why? So her residency permit could be processed. The spouse, she was told, would not get a residency permit, only a social pass which would expire in fourteen days. Then what? She was told that he would have to leave the country and then return. This was quite common, it seemed, and had been tolerated by other male spouses who simply drove across the peninsula to Malaysia and returned to reprocess their papers.

This female's spouse was not as tractable. He simply announced that if Singapore did not want him, he was going home. The university's dean was so informed as was the U.S. embassy because if one went, both were going. Both the dean and the embassy went to work very effectively so that three days before the husband's tourist visa expired, the personnel office hand delivered his passport to immigration. He became "illegal" for a brief period but both were reassured that all was well, which, as it turned out, it was. However, this female employee was told she was the first to get a residency permit for her husband through the university. It probably helped that the spouse was retired and had no intention of working.

Searching for explanations for this incident, the university employee was told that the university interpreted national policy this way because native Singaporean women who worked in their country but married foreigners had the same experience. Their husbands could not get residency or work permits. Fortunately, this too changed during the author's stay in Singapore, which ended in 1999 (Newsom, 2001).

So, when Singapore says it is changing, that probably is true. For all the talk of "Asian values," Singapore is a pragmatic country. Even Singapore's senior minister, Lee Kuan Yew, is reported to have said that if developing a new economy meant social change, "so be it" (Yee, 2001, p. B13B).

The campaign to reposition Singapore shows its professionals, featured in the ads, as being very much like Americans. Mark Gordon is director of marketing at Singapore's Infocomm Development Authority (IDA), the government agency in charge of information technology policy. The IDA's campaign is running in both business and trade publications. It is interesting, too, that the newspaper report about the campaign said Singapore's Ministry of Manpower also has run spots on regional cable television showing professionals from other nations enjoying their work as well as other aspects of Singapore (Yee, 2001).

What about Asian Values?

The shift for Singapore cannot be cosmetic only. In some ways, it is difficult to see how the Asian values it has promoted for so long will be cast aside to embrace a more cosmopolitan culture. A Dutch culture researcher, the organizational anthropologist Geert Hofstede, has defined culture as mind programming to distinguish one human group's members from another (Hofstede, 1980). Hofstede used culture to refer to nations, although it generally is used to describe societies (Hofstede, 1982). And he developed five dimensions of culture: *individualism* versus *collectivism; uncertainty avoidance* or the extent to which a society can tolerate ambiguity; *masculinity* versus *femininity* or the value a society attaches to social roles based on gender; *power distance* or the extent to which wealth, power, and prestige are distributed disproportionately among people of different social strata or classes; *Confucian dynamism,* which is a long-term view of events, considered positive, versus a short-term view, considered negative, and the idea that proper human relationships are the basis for society (Hofstede, 1982).

It is this fifth dimension, *Confucianism,* that offers some principles that are known today as Asian values (Hofstede & Bond, 1988). The first principle is the stability of society based on unequal relationships between people. These rely on mutual obligations. The state exists for the people, not the other way around, and there are obligations on both parts. This applies to business too. A lower-level employee owes a senior-level employee respect but is entitled to consideration and protection in return. Second, the family represents a prototype for all social organizations, and it is the bridge between the individual and the state. Individual status and social status are developed first in the family where harmony means keeping one's place. In this tenet too is found the maintenance of an individual's "face," one's dignity, self-respect, and prestige. Third, virtuous behavior toward others consists of treating others as one would like to be treated. Fourth, virtue with regard to one's tastes in life consists of trying to gain education and skills, working hard, being patient, persevering, and not being extravagant with one's resources. The fifth principle involves respect for tradition and authority, which is seen as a way of keeping social order.

Most U.S. citizens could be comfortable with treating others as one would like to be treated; this is the familiar golden rule. The part about acquiring skills and education and working hard and persevering all sounds familiar also. There, the value similarities end. Although many U.S. citizens are conservative with their money, others see no harm in extravagance. Most people living in the United States would be uncomfortable with the acceptance of inequality, the family order being a lifetime status, and unquestioning respect for authority.

Confucianism—a philosophy developed by Confucius, a teacher of ethics—has been called a "civil religion." Singapore's society is not all Chinese, although most are people of Chinese descent. There are a significant number of Malaysians, East Indians, and expatriates from all over the world. This mix means that Singapore has a number of mosques, Hindu temples, Christian churches, and synagogues. The diversity of the country is one of its strengths. Asian values, though, are likely to be embraced also by the Malays and many of the Indians, although Indians are less conforming than other Asians. The extent to which the diversity of a steady flow of expatriates, especially Americans, is likely to change Singapore is yet to be seen.

Public Relations Practice in Singapore

As a British colony, Singapore was connected to the world's media primarily through Reuters, the British news agency. The link was mainly to strengthen the economic asset of the colony. It was after World War II, though, that organized public relations activity began in Singapore (Nair, 1986).

What was initially a British government function continued much that way when self-rule came to Singapore in 1959. The still-prevalent practice of government campaigns to affect change in society began. It was not until the late 1960s that international public relations firms began to appear to service their multinational clients (Nair, 1986). In the

1970s, as public relations in Singapore began to mature as global public relations practice, it embraced corporate social responsibility and, consequently, community relations. Local industries, especially those related to tourism, adopted public relations tactics (Nair, 1986).

The rapid growth of public relations had some negative consequences with a diffusion of focus on what public relations really was and what good public relations practice entailed. The result, though, was a positive one with the formation of the Institute of Public Relations of Singapore (IPRS) (Nair, 1986). The institute has been involved in professional practices and in education for the field so that, by the 1980s, both the public and private sector in Singapore were well-established. The first education opportunities were offered as seminars by the institute, which later were used to help develop university courses. Through the 1990s, additional attention was given to university undergraduate and graduate classes. Today, Singapore has one of the more sophisticated, securely established public relations disciplines in the world, especially considering the government limitations and restrictions that linger still.

Government Policies Restricting
Public Relations Practice Loosening?

At this point, discussion about the Singapore government is appropriate. It is essentially one party, the PAP, which, as mentioned earlier, came into power in 1959 under the direction of Harry Lee Kuan Yew and remains in power because dissent from other parties is stifled as criticism.

Despite the prevalence of many international public relations firms as well as local ones with long histories, the political environment restricts freedom of expression and association. These two freedoms seem fundamental to best practices in public relations: freedom of speech, which, of course, is demonstrated in most societies by a free press, and the right of assembly, which often is the purpose of a public relations strategy. Neither are individual or collective rights in Singapore.

The degree of freedom in both areas is a matter of interpretation. That responsibility now rests primarily with the Ministry for Information and the Arts (MITA). Prior to MITA, the responsibility belonged to the Ministry of Culture. Brigadier General George Yeo became the first to hold the MITA office in 1990. Initially, he was seen as someone who might best reflect a less restrictive government, something that had been promised by Prime Minister Goh Chok Tong (George, 1999). Yeo's successor was Lee Yock Suan, former trade and industry minister, initially regarded with some trepidation by the information community, but the evidence is always in the decisions the minister makes.

The changes Yeo instituted are attributed to "the revolution in communications technology and growing exposure to an increasingly global culture" (George, 1999, p. 42). The changes were dramatic: Available television channels went from three in 1990 to thirty and included international channels such as CNN; use of the Internet became ubiquitous, whereas before it was limited to university scholars; movies were rated, whereas previously all movies were censored for children; and museums and libraries were upgraded to a degree that visitors and patrons began to experience long lines at museum exhibits for the first time. MITA also began to attend to local artistic talent and supported its homegrown amateurs and professionals through the National Arts Council. It loosened restrictions on the performing arts so that concert programs did not require preapproval before being printed. Many of these changes were accomplished with the cooperation of other government groups such as the National Computer Board's support of the changes for libraries, now on an electronic system.

As encouraging as all of this sounds, perhaps what was not done is more telling. Political videos are banned, as are home satellite dishes. The news media are not unshackled. For example, the U.S. magazine *Cosmopolitan* still is banned. Publications that are considered to have criticized the government are "gazetted." That means their companies are served with legal documents that restrict circulation and require the posting of a bond, amounting to several thousand U.S. dollars. A local representative of the company must be appointed to receive all legal documents, rather than having these sent to the corporate headquarters outside Singapore.

The effect of this is intimidating and results in some self-censorship, which may be more restrictive than the Singapore government actually would impose. An example is the wide circulation, as late as 1999, of an incident told as a warning, and not only in academic circles. U.S. political economist Christopher Lingle in a two-year teaching contract at the National University of Singapore (NUS) wrote an opinion piece that appeared in the *International Herald Tribune* (October 7, 1994). Lingle's article was in response to a previous piece, "You May Not Like It Europe, but This Asian Medicine Could Help," by a permanent secretary to the Ministry of Foreign Affairs in Singapore, Kishore Mahbubani. In Lingle's response, he observed, "Intolerant regimes in the region revealed considerable ingenuity in suppressing dissent. Some techniques lack finesse: crushing unarmed students with tanks or imprisoning dissidents. Others are more subtle: relying upon a compliant judiciary to bankrupt opposition politicians or buying out enough of the opposition to take control 'democratically.' " That last sentence, although Singapore was not mentioned, was deemed to have "scandalized the courts" and "impugned the integrity and reputation of the nation's judiciary" (Seow, 1998, pp. 173–177).

Singapore police subsequently appeared both at Lingle's home and office and seized some documents and publications. Lingle was interrogated on at least two occasions in which the intent was to get him to admit that he meant Singapore, without naming the country. He was still in the midst of interrogations when he learned that his father was seriously ill, and he was permitted to leave the country. He did not return. Nevertheless, the case went to trial where the judiciary ruled that an ordinary reasonable reader would assume that Lingle meant Singapore, and Lingle was found liable for defamation.

The international community was unsympathetic. In fact, other Asian nations, which also could have made the same interpretation, ignored the piece, although the *International Herald Tribune,* a joint effort by the *New York Times* and the *Washington Post,* is a very prestigious paper abroad. The *Australian Financial Times* reported the views of Justice Michael Kirby, president of the New South Wales court of appeal:

> In its treatment of human rights such as free speech, Singapore was in a sort of time capsule of colonial attitudes to law, which have been captured and caught as they were when the British retreated. In this regard, Singapore has not kept up with the developments of the common law in other countries . . . punishment for scandalizing the courts hasn't been used in England for 60 years. (Seow, 1998, p. 175)

Well, perhaps that is the case. It is more likely that Singapore perceives itself more like China than many people would want to believe. There is a low tolerance for dissent in both countries, where dissent is seen as disruptive and an inducement to chaos. Perhaps it is more understandable in a tiny country such as Singapore, which is surrounded by countries where chaos occurs and is often violent.

Another suggestion is that Singapore itself is in the middle of a see-saw, so to speak, trying to keep its balance. A hint of this appears in *Straits Times* journalist Cherian George's interview with former MITA minister Yeo, who is British, educated in the United States, a native Singaporean, Chinese by descent, and Roman Catholic by faith. Yeo said, "There is a side of me which is Confucianist (and Taoist), and a side which is Christian (and Western)" (George, 1999, p. 42).

Regulations—A Restrictive Reality

Knowing which side the see-saw is likely to come down on, though, is a problem for everyone, particularly public relations practitioners. The author experienced, both personally and with her invited guest speaker from the United States, the kind of control unimaginable in many Western nations. First, the speaker had to be approved by a nationally registered organization, in this case IPRS and two universities, and then the attendance must be limited to members of those organizations and the public may not be invited. The only publicity about such events is within the organizations, and the speeches are not likely to be covered by the news media.

In May of 1999, two opposition (to PAP) politicians staged a public speech without permission from the Singapore police and were arrested. Actually, one spoke in a public park at noon and the other adjusted his microphone. The two, members of the small Singapore Democratic Party, were its head Chee Soon Juan, a neuropsychologist, and party Assistant-General Wong Hong Toy. Both were convicted for their violation, but Singapore's Supreme Court Chief Justice Yong Pung How reduced their fine and restored their eligibility to run for office, which had been removed by a lower court's ruling that fined them S$690, a sum that legally bans those fined from running for office.

An Associated Press story in the *International Herald Tribune* noted that the opposition party has no representation in Parliament, and the PAP has claimed that its tight restrictions on civic activity are necessary because emotions could get out of hand in discussions of political, religious, ethnic, and language differences due to the diversity of Singapore's 3.7 million people (Curb on speech is upheld, 1999).

Additionally, any publication by an individual or an organization must have a government license before it may be sold. Another high-profile incident in 1999 also involved Dr. Chee Soon Juan, who was waging a civil disobedience campaign against speech and press restrictions. Dr. Chee sold his book on Asian dissidents without a license from the public health commissioner. The judge rejected his request to call as witnesses the environment minister and the public health commissioner to find out how selling his book endangered the public health (Bookselling on trial, 1999).

Commenting on Chee's campaign, long before these two incidents, on the *Straits Times*'s editorial page Cherian George and Zulkifli Baharudin supported relaxing prior censorship to publication which, they noted, means licensing. They also said, "Some space needs to be opened up to allow people to speak their minds without first having to obtain permission to do so" (George & Baharudin, 1999, p. 40).

Two points need to be made here. First, the opinion piece appeared in a newspaper that is owned by the government. Second, a year, three months and six days later—April 26, 2000—the government announced the opening of a Speaker's Corner in August of that year. The idea, inspired by London's Hyde Park, is not exactly what England permitted. Instead, Singapore's Speaker's Corner is open only to Singapore citizens who first register their intention to speak at a nearby police station where they must show their identity card or passport. Approval is supposedly granted immediately. The topics are limited. Speakers must not talk about religion or any subject that could cause hatred or hostility among different racial or religious groups, and speakers must observe defamation laws, the Sedition Act, the Maintenance of Religious Harmony Act, and the penal code. Suspicious Singaporeans expressed some reluctance to accept the idea that there would be no retribution despite some reassurance from the minister of home affairs, Wong Kan Seng, who reportedly said, "If you have something to say, don't be afraid to say it. The police have a lot of better things to do than to just carry a tape recorder and tape speeches" (Webb & Borsuk, 2000, p. A22).

The *Wall Street Journal*'s article on the announcement of the corner makes a telling observation: "A general reluctance to speak out shows itself in many day-to-day situations: At conferences, few people raise questions. Public-relations officers at Singaporean companies seldom like to talk on the record, on the chance they'll say something wrong and be penalized" (Webb & Borsuk, 2000, p. A22).[3]

Changing Times? What Singaporean Scholars Say

An information technologist and a public policy think tank deputy director with a background in public relations argue that, considering its limited natural resources, Singapore had no option but to advocate an open economy, one based not only on the free flow of trade and investment but also, and more crucially, on the free flow of information. According to policy watchers Leo and Mahizhnan, Singapore is becoming an information economy with information the key factor of production as well as the product itself (1998, pp. 138–149). Their essay focuses on the impact of new technology on old concepts of censorship, including the idea that the state could unilaterally control the flow of information in and out of the country and decide what was good for its citizens and what was not. It is not that the Internet is uncontrollable, the authors contend, it is simply that only collective standards—international standards—have any chance of success for control. For Singapore, the authors argue for leaving choice to the citizen, not the state. They cite other nations where this is already the case without disastrous results: Japan, Australia, the United States, and the United Kingdom:

> Most normal adults in these countries do seem to have good moral standards and even without the state-nanny, seem to make the right choices. It would be a real irony if we, the custodians of such Asian values as communitarianism, consensus, and self-discipline somehow do not get it right when it comes to smut and politics. The irony becomes all the more acute when we consider ourselves fit to play in the first league of global economics and politics

but not fit to immunize ourselves from undesirable influences. It is about time Singaporeans resolve to wean themselves away from a state-nanny who will be increasingly powerless. (Leo & Mahizhnan, 1998, p. 145.)

Perhaps self-confidence for these emerging democracies, more than regional stability, is the issue. In an opening September 2000 speech at a Singapore conference on media
and democracy in Asia, the director of the office for regional cooperation in Southeast Asia,
Dr. Erfried Adam (2000), said:

I have the feeling that many governments should be more self-assured and allow for more
freedom. And I trust that societies in itself [sic] have the strength and ability to define their
needs and to claim what they want. (pp. 10–11)

The political climate seems to be changing, perhaps in part because of the Internet,
and, with it, public relations should emerge from its confines of media relations and safe
government-sanctioned campaigns into playing a more strategic role.

Issues to Consider

Singapore is an interesting situation to examine in light of some major issues that came to
prominence in the United States after four terrorist acts on September 11, 2001. These issues include limitations on individual privacy for the protection of the nation, government
control of media to reduce potential for chaos, restrictions on freedom of speech for national defense, and protection of national culture from Western influences. Each of these
has the potential to become a critical issue in the United States.

Limiting individual privacy always occurs when a nation is at war, but Singapore limits the privacy of its citizens on a regular basis as is evident from the discussion in this
chapter. Consider these privacy issues. Would you be comfortable having your e-mail fil-
tered by the government, the Web sites you visited checked, your book purchases reported
as well as your library check outs, your phone lines tapped? Do you think the government
should issue you an identification card that you would have to carry at all times and show
to any government official, such as a police officer, on demand?

Government control of media means that some publications would not be available
to you because the government does not allow their circulation and sale. Some broadcast
content might be deleted and some articles prohibited because the government feared
repercussions that might create domestic chaos. Are you comfortable with the government's deciding what information is available? Of course that occurs to some extent in the
United States now in that some government information is made available only to people
whose backgrounds have been checked to ensure information they get would not be considered to put the nation's security at risk. However, this does not include information generally available to citizens in other countries.

Restrictions on freedom of speech are necessary for national defense. The United
States has restricted free speech to some extent during wartime, but usually the public is simply requested to keep quiet about information that might aid the enemy. Criticizing the government is always permitted in the United States, even when some may consider it disloyal.

Protection of culture has never been much of an issue in the United States, which has such a diverse population. However, many other nations, especially those that have been colonies, believe their cultures are being chipped away by the invasion of Western culture primarily through mass media. Culture was part of the issue in the terrorist attacks on the United States. The United States has been seen as supporting despots in other countries because it was in the best business interests of the United States to do so. Critics say the leaders whom the United States has supported have not cared for their citizens and have not protected their cultures.

Conclusion

The maturity and growth of public relations in the United States is often attributed to some basic constitutional freedoms: right of free expression and assembly. Both are potentially persuasive tools used by organizations and individuals. Add to those freedoms basic stability of government despite a highly participatory democracy and the rationale becomes clear. Because Singapore is dramatically different in each of these aspects, one could ask why that small nation can be seen as an Asian PR powerhouse with increasing international stature. There are three reasons:

- Singapore's goal is to become a paperless society, and English dominates the Internet. The language of government in Singapore is English, followed by a second Asian language.

- The second reason is a strong legacy of PR practice in Singapore that counts global PR agencies as well as strong local firms in its business mix.

- Finally, the country has an infrastructure that works, albeit guided with a firm hand. The iron fist in the silk glove seems to be relaxing somewhat as the nation matures in its self confidence.

Given Singapore's historical market significance as a gateway to Asia and its accessibility and reliability, PR practice is likely to flourish even in a constrained political environment.

Notes

1. Figure 17.1 is the original apology and explanation sent from Singnet's CEO to all subscribers. After that, there is a response from an individual whose name has been blocked in this chapter but who signed a response to the Singnet mass mail announcement to its customers. (See Figure 17.1)

2. Updates are available from the Singapore Web site where fora and implementations are announced. An interesting one, PS21-MFE Forum on e-government, October 11, 2001, presented the future of e-government, an effort by Singapore to bring all of its agencies together so that its publics only have to deal with one government.

3. In teaching both a graduate and an undergraduate class at a Singapore university, the author was cautioned by faculty colleagues and professional associates. Students warned up front that the phones "probably" were tapped and the e-mail read. Because it was an employer's server, that was nothing new, and the office as well as the faculty housing was owned by the university, thus the government. Their other warnings had been heard before

FIGURE 17.1   ***Singnet Subscriber's Complaint and CEO's Response***

Doug Ann Newsom (Prof)

From:	LIM [eemailme@singnet.com.sgj]
Sent:	Monday, May 03, 1999 4:47 PM
To:	Singnet Announcement
Subject:	Re: We should have informed you first—Preventive Scanning

Dear Sir

Thanks for this piece of info (but I've read about that in today's paper already).

Though I understand that Singnet may have its subscribers' interest at heart while conducting its "operations" (and I appreciate that), we (Singnet subscribers) do hope that Singnet could be more sensitive to our concerns, needs and privacy.

As a concerned Singnet subscriber, I would like find out the following:

(1) Would you have sent us this mail had someone not discovered your "secret" activity and reported it to the press?

(2) Why was MHA asked to carry out the scanning and not NCB? I never knew that MHA is good in solving IT problems. I thought NCB or Singapore Technologies (and even Mindef IT arms) are more well known (than MHA) for their IT skills (not to mention abt the private IT companies avail).

(3) Is TAS informed of the operations before they are conducted?

(4) Would you give us the assurance that no such "measures" (or similar ones) would be carried out again without our knowledge? (If not, why even bother to apologise to us thru this mail?)

In this new Information age, I think we should continue to strive to be ethical and respect the privacy of IT users. If people lose respect and confidence in this new technology, the technology would not succeed. The same can be said about the service provider. Though in your mail you have argued that there is no invasion of privacy, I beg to differ. The mere act of scanning things not belonging to you is an invasion of privacy. Also, how could you inform those infected if you do not know who they are (as such there is no real user anonymity)?

If trojan horses and viruses are major problems (which I think they are), then did you send us e-mails about the measures to be taken before embarking on the "secret scanning" operations? (You may or (may not) have that on your web pages, but I don't recall receiving such e-mails). Previously, I had to worry about trojans and viruses (I hope and pray that I am not among the 900) . . . now I have an additional worry . . . invasion of privacy.

Finally, I hope that you do not treat this mail as a complaint but rather as some feedback that may contribute to better customer service. As a customer, I hope that my needs are served. I think that many others (includ. those who have not provided you with the feedback) feel the same.

Singnet's Response

We are aware that you may have some concerns due to the recently published "SingNet scanning computers" article in The Straits Times.

We apologise unreservedly if we have caused you any undue alarm and also regret not having informed you before we embarked on our virus-detection scanning. However, please be assured that we only had your best interests at heart when conducting the exercise.

(continued)

FIGURE 17.1   *Continued*

Why did we do it?

We have found that Internet surfers unknowingly download software, screen savers and other material that may be infected with viruses such as the "trojan horse."

The "trojan horse" virus allows the hacker to capture passwords by identifying keystrokes. With that, the hacker will be able to hack into a person's PC and get content for illegal purposes.

In order to gauge the level of "trojan horse" infection among our customers, we approached the IT Security Unit of the Ministry of Home Affairs to assist in conducting a virus-detection scan. This way, we can alert those Singnet users whose PCs are infected and advise them accordingly.

Why did we not inform you of the scanning operation?

We did not want to alert hackers of when we were conducting our scans as we did not want to give them the easy opportunity to hack into your PC during the same period. We also did not want to cause undue concern among our customers before determining the actual level of "trojan horse" infections.

In hindsight, we should have considered the impact of this exercise on you and been more sensitive to your needs. We sincerely apologise again for any alarm and anxiety that we may have caused.

How do we do the virus-detection scanning?

First, the scanning programme sends a signal to your PC. When the PC receives this signal, it sends one back. The scanning programme listens for this reply and then analyses it. Because an infected PC responds differently from an uninfected PC, by studying the way your PC responds to a scan, it is possible to know whether it contains a "trojan horse" and is therefore a potential target for hackers.

To give an analogy, the scanning programme basically knocks on the door of your PC. If your PC is virus-free, there should be no response. If there is a virus, the programme will record the infected PC's network address and the time of the incident. A network address is given to you each time you log on to your PC and changes every time you log on. No users' personal particulars such as the User ID and password are contained in this address.

The network addresses of those PCs that were identified to be vulnerable were then sent to Singnet and we looked through our records to identify the person who was using that particular address at the time of the scanning and to trace whose PC had been affected.

Has there been any invasion of privacy?

Please rest assured that we have taken special measures to safeguard your privacy before embarking on this exercise. The scanning programme used is not a hacking tool and has no ability to enter any computer system. Rather, it is a defensive measure to look for security loopholes.

Also, the programme identifies PCs by their network addresses which do not contain personal particulars. As such, user anonymity is preserved.

What are the findings so far?

As a result of the scanning conducted over just one week, we have discovered that the PCs of nearly 900 customers have been infected by the "trojan horse" virus. The presence of this virus

FIGURE 17.1 *Continued*

makes these PCs vulnerable to hacking. We will be contacting our affected subscribers over the course of the next few days and advising them on the corrective action they should take.

As a precautionary measure, we suggest that you visit Singnet's homepage at www.singnet.com.sg and click on the Anti-Trojan Horse protection banner to find out more about protection against the "trojan horse" virus.

Are the scans still being conducted?

Meanwhile, we have stopped the scanning while we seek your views on such preventive scanning measures. As a means of assuring you further, we will call upon the independent National Internet Advisory Committee to certify that our scanning exercises are not intrusive.

What can you do to safeguard your PC?

Please be aware that an important part of protecting your safety is to not download software, screen savers and other material if you are not sure where they came from.

For more information on the protection against the "trojan horse" virus, please visit Singnet's homepage at www.singnet.com.sg and click on the Anti-Trojan Horse Protection banner.

Yours Sincerely

Paul Chong
GEO
SingTel Multimedia

leaving the United States. However, in the United States, there was the warning that students probably would not get involved in class discussions that were in any way controversial. If one is teaching a fourth-level (senior) undergraduate course in issues management and crisis communication and a graduate class in public communication issues and strategies, that is rather daunting. Fortunately, that turned out not to be the case. The participation of the undergraduates, once some trust was established, was entirely open. One group handled a case that could be considered "constructive criticism" of government internship policies without any reaction except appreciation for their work. The graduate students, some of whom were diploma students rather than degree candidates, were less open, probably because most of them worked for the government.

Discussion Questions

1. Are international crises likely to cause Singapore to retract or expand margins of freedom? Either way, how would this impact public relations practice there?

2. Are Singapore's Asian values likely to tie it more to China than the United States and United Kingdom? If so, how would that affect the practice of multinational public relations firms headquartered in the United States and United Kingdom?

3. Will Singapore's public relations practitioners endorse two-way symmetry in practice and in doing so move the government toward a more open democracy?

4. Are the NGOs and GONGOs in Singapore likely to build a real grassroots constituency for public relations practitioners to tap into for campaigns?

References

Adam, E. (2000). Media and democracy in Asia. *Asian Mass Communication Bulletin, 30*(6), 10–11.

Bookselling on trial. (1999, March 31). *International Herald Tribune,* p. 4.

Craig, J. (1993). *Culture shock! A guide to customs and etiquette, Singapore.* Portland, OR: Graphic Arts.

Curb on speech is upheld, but Singapore judge reduces politician's fine. (1999, May 26). *International Herald Tribune,* p. 7.

Day, P., & Borsuk, R. (2001, October 16). Singapore needs world economy to get going. *The Wall Street Journal,* p. B11D.

George, C., (1999, May 30). B. G. Yeo's eight years at MITA, The Singaporean's split personality. *The Sunday Times,* pp. 42–43.

George, C. & Bharudin, Z. (1999, January 20). Editorial Page. *The Straits Times,* p. 40.

He's got the whole island in the palm of his hand. (1999, March 30). *The Straits Times,* p. 32.

Hofstede, G. (1980). *Culture's consequences: International differences in work-related values.* Thousand Oaks, CA: Sage.

Hofstede, G. (1982). *Culture's consequences.* (Abridged ed.). Thousand Oaks, CA: Sage.

Hofstede, G. (1984a, December 4). *National cultures and corporate cultures.* Paper presented in Helsinki. Also see Hofstede on national cultures and organizational cultures, *Journal of Management Studies, 22*(4), 347–357.

Hofstede, G. (1984b). National cultures revisited. *Behavior Science Research, 18*(4), 285–305.

Hofstede, G. (1991). *Culture and organization: Software of the mind.* London: McGraw-Hill.

Hofstede, G., & Bond, M. (1988). The Confucius connection: From cultural roots to economic growth. *Organizational Dynamics, 16*(4), 4–21.

Koh, T. (1998). Size is not destiny. In A. Mahizhnan and T. Lee (Eds.), *Singapore: Re-engineering success* (pp. 179–180). Singapore: The Institute of Policy Studies and Oxford University Press.

Leo, S. & Mahizhnan, A. (1998). Developing an intelligent island: Dilemmas of censorship. In A. Mahizhnan and T. Lee (Eds.), *Singapore: Re-engineering success* (pp. 138–149). Singapore:

The Institute of Policy Studies and Oxford University Press.

Lingle, C. (1994, October 7). The smoke over parts of Asia obscures some profound concerns. *The International Herald Tribune,* opinion page.

Luh, S. (2001, October 9). Singapore recruits foreigners despite qualms at home. *The Wall Street Journal,* p. B7.

Mahizhnan, A., & Lee, T. (Eds.). (1998). *Singapore: Re-engineering success.* Singapore: The Institute of Policy Studies and Oxford University Press.

Morphy, E. (2000, July). Asia R&D, scientific methods. *Global Business,* 66–68, 70–71.

Nair, B. (1986). *A primer on public relations practice in Singapore.* Singapore: Institute of Public Relations of Singapore and Print N Publish Pte. Ltd.

Nathan, D. (1999, June 5). Civic groups to take over campaigns. *The Straits Times,* p. 53.

Newsom, D. (1999, June). *The Internet: Servant and master.* Presentation to the Institute of Public Relations of Singapore (IPRS), Singapore.

Newsom, D. (2001, April 26). *A global marketplace? "Asian values" and business relationships.* Presentation to the Rotary Club of Austin, Texas.

Ooi, G., & Koh, G. (1998). State-society synergies: New stakes, new partnership. In A. Mahizhnan & T. Lee (Eds.), *Singapore: Re-engineering success* (p. 99). Singapore: The Institute of Policy Studies and Oxford University Press.

Pension schemes. Singapore's green pastures. (2000, July). *Global Business,* 7.

Seow, F. (1998). *The media enthralled: Singapore revisited.* Boulder, CO: Lynne Reinner.

Singapore government. (1999). PS21. [On-line]. Available: www.gov.sg/ps21,1999.

Singapore 21 report. In *Singapore 21, Together we make the difference.* (1999, May 1). *The Straits Times,* pp. 60–61.

Webb, S., & Borsuk, R. (2000, April 26). Strait talk: Creating a haven for free speech, Singapore style. *The Wall Street Journal,* p. A22.

Yee, C. (2001, March 27). Singapore sells its American attitude, ad campaign targets U.S. technology companies. *The Wall Street Journal,* p. B13B.

18

The Media and Reformasi *in Indonesia*

Public Relations Revisited

Amos Owen Thomas

Key Points

- Politics in Indonesia underwent three distinct periods: *Merdeka*—the anticolonial struggle for independence under first president Soekarno, *Orde Baru*—political stability through repression and economic development through crony capitalism under second president Soeharto, and *Reformasi*—increasing political and economic reforms under subsequent presidents Habibie and Wahid.

- The media in Indonesia has shifted from comprising only politically affiliated print and government-run public broadcasting (in the 1950s and 1960s), through being strictly licensed media controlled by business conglomerates associated with the political elite (from the 1970s to the mid-1990s), to becoming a plethora of print, broadcast, and on-line media under new, broad-based ownership and minimal regulation (in the late 1990s and into the 2000s).

- Public relations in Indonesia in the early 2000s calls for greater professionalism and specialization in order to operate in an environment of media diversity, market competition, diffused ownership, active civil society, concern for socioeconomic justice, government deregulation, and globalization of information.

- Corporations and government in Indonesia, as in all emerging democracies, need to realize that they have an ethical responsibility not only to their owners and political leaders but also to all of society, and that successful application of world-best business practices cannot be achieved without an in-depth understanding of the political, economic, social, and cultural context.

For much of Indonesia's history since independence from colonial rule, its media have been heavily controlled by government in the name of national culture and economic development. This was certainly true in the thirty-five years up until 1998, during what was called the New Order government of then-President Soeharto. However, since *Reformasi,* the political reform process that began in various grassroots movements for change in the 1990s and culminated with the toppling of that government, there has been a revolutionary change in media policy and practice. Although the same media are still operating today, they are quite transformed in content and style, and have been joined by many more new entrants. Furthermore, new media, such as the Internet and transnational satellite television, have provided alternative sources of information, in the former case with immensely greater ease of dissemination. This transformation of the media scene needs to be analyzed and understood in terms of the historical developments and social context of Indonesia. The radical change in both the quantity and character of media holds implications for the practice of public relations in this nation, as in other democracies emerging from authoritarian systems of government, both for the political left and right, at the turn of the twenty-first century.

Brief Geography and History

Located in Southeast Asia, Indonesia comprises an archipelago of about fourteen thousand islands spread over an area of almost two million square kilometers (more than seven hundred thousand square miles) straddling the equator. Significant islands are Java, Sumatra, Borneo (shared with Malaysia), Sulawesi, New Guinea (shared with Papua New Guinea), Timor (shared with East Timor), and Bali (*SBS World Guide,* 1996). The population of Indonesia as of mid-1999 was 209 million by government estimates and is projected to rise to 239 million by 2010 and to 275 million by 2025 (Johnstone & Mandryk, 2001). Although Bahasa Indonesia, a form of Malay, is the national language and lingua franca, there are fourteen major languages and more than five hundred dialects spoken by the various ethnic groups that populate the country (Department of Information, 2000). A tiny, but economically significant, Chinese minority has been a part of the territory for centuries, though their language and culture has not been officially recognized postindependence, except to place restrictions on it. Thus, it has been a challenge for the media in Indonesia to reach a nation so geographically spread out and so culturally diverse.

Colonial Era

The archipelago known today as Indonesia has a long history of being the site of a number of Hindu, Buddhist, and, later, Muslim kingdoms influenced by similar kingdoms in India from the first to the sixteenth century. Then it came increasingly under the control first of the Portuguese in the sixteenth century and of the Dutch from the seventeenth century seeking to dominate the spice trade. It became eventually the latter's colony of the East Indies, though temporarily under British administration during the Napoleonic wars of the eighteenth century. Periodic armed struggles by isolated sultanates in the East Indies were vigorously suppressed by the Dutch (Department of Information, 2000).

Modern Era

From early in the twentieth century, there were various sociopolitical movements in support of independence, which gained some impetus during the Japanese occupation during World War II. The limited vernacular press during this era were highly critical of Dutch colonialism and were dubbed *pers perjuangan* in the Indonesian language or "press of the political struggle."

Merdeka (or independence) of the Republic of Indonesia was proclaimed by the nationalist leader Soekarno after the Japanese surrender but was contested by the returning Dutch forces. The new nation was only formally recognized by the Netherlands and the world four years later in 1949 through the good offices of the United Nations and newly independent India (Department of Information, 2000). Under left-leaning nationalist Soekarno, Indonesia entered an era of anti-Western sentiment and political nonalignment in the context of the cold war. Considerable political and economic disorder saw Soekarno abandon parliamentary democracy for what he termed "guided democracy" or a form of benevolent dictatorship. From the immediate postindependence era of the 1950s to the early 1960s, the print media in Indonesia served largely as organs of political groups and other mass organizations because it was a government regulation that every newspaper or magazine belong to one such a group or organization (Hidayat, 1999). Television broadcasting commenced in Indonesia as a government-run public service, Televisi Republik Indonesia (TVRI), in a context of heightened nationalism, namely the hosting of the Asian Games in Jakarta in 1962. Even after the games, television was confined to the capital city, reaching only 65,000 sets by 1969. There was no policy or dedicated administrative structure for television under Indonesia's first president, Soekarno, a charismatic leader who saw it solely as a vehicle for his personal communication with the populace (Kitley, 1997).

A communist-led coup attempt in 1965 was put down by the armed forces led by General Soeharto, who soon replaced Soekarno as president and held that position until removed in 1998. Soeharto inaugurated an *Orde Baru* (or New Order), which concentrated power in the armed forces, propagated the socioethical code called *Pancasila* stressing national unity, favored economic liberalization, and overtly repressed communism (Speake, 1993). This New Order was instrumental in forging and perpetuating a national culture, and hence maintained a tight control over film and television, making for a form of cultural imperialism from within by the political, economic, and cultural elite (Holaday, 1996). Given the new government's perception that the ethnic Chinese minority maintained links or sympathies with communist China, all media in the Chinese language were banned. Thus, in the late 1960s under Soeharto, the mass media were uncoupled from political groups and organizations, and redesignated as partners with the government in the promotion of national development. However, the government maintained tight control of the media via the Ministry of Information. Ownership of the media soon came to rest in the hands of members and friends of the Soeharto family, their business partners, and political associates.

The agitation for *Reformasi* (or Reformation) in Indonesia, long-suppressed by the Soeharto regime, finally found its opportunity when the Asian economic crisis of 1997 adversely affected Indonesia. Student demonstrations over corruption, and violence against them by the military compelled the handover of the government by Soeharto in 1998 to his deputy, Habibie. A number of media had faced delegations from student and other protest movements that demanded changes of management personnel and content policies. During the crisis, the public had turned to television as its prime source of information for developments, although soon after there was also a burgeoning of print media to cater to the high demand for information in a new era of political freedom. As Indonesia's third president, B. J. Habibie formed a multiparty interim government and set an agenda for reform, including democratic elections for the first time since 1955. Radical changes were made also to the laws governing both broadcast and print media to allow greater freedom. Indonesia's media are not altogether ill at ease with their newfound independence because editorial staff had made the decision to drop loyalty to the Soeharto regime when it became quite evident that it would fall. As this chapter demonstrates, the process of media deregulation was continued with zeal by the government of the fourth president Wahid, who was also the first to be democratically elected in 1999. However, there seem to be indications of a possible return to government control over the media after he was replaced for alleged incompetence in 2001 by the fifth president Megawati, who is also daughter of Indonesia's first president Soekarno.

Media, Society, and Public Relations

One of the realities of public relations practice in much of Asia, as in many developing countries worldwide, is coping with media rigidly constrained by governments in the name of nation building and Asian values, which are somewhat nebulously defined as support of social harmony, political stability, national security, and economic growth (Karim, 1989). These are cynically perceived, particularly by foreign media and public relations professionals, as requiring the media and any users of it to not undermine the authority of government in power and the economic status quo. Having argued that public relations is about restoring a sense of community lost through modernization, Starck and Kruckeberg (2001) conclude that the ultimate stakeholder to whom corporations are unanswerable is society itself. Certainly, in the case of Indonesia prior to the late 1990s, there was considerable alienation between the general public and large domestic corporations, which were seen as yet another instrument of the Soeharto regime to exploit and repress. The corporate control of the media and its use of one-way, top-down communication was a confirmatory sign of their dominance.

Rationalization and domination of public discourse by professional communications organizations, such as advertising, market research, and public relations, results in what Mayhew (1997) terms the *new public*. In that context, commercial practices undermine the authenticity of social and political discourse, which ought to be grounded in constituent groups of civil society, rather than in artificial market segments purporting to represent views sympathetic to certain dominant corporations. The selective use of images and words by professional communications personnel to make arguments that are immune to critical analysis also results in their inflated influence in society. The lack of discussion of ethics in public relations is regrettable, claims L'Etang (1997), particularly when the notion of paid representation of views raises issues of lying or embellishment of the truth for the client. Despite the existence of perspectives on ethics in philosophy, sociology, and psychology, there is a tendency in public relations ethics, if it is discussed at all, to adopt a relativist view that reflects the norms of the society. This is problematic because it raises the question of whose norms are set for that society. For decades in Indonesia, for instance, it was deemed quite acceptable by business and government leadership to practice "crony capitalism" and suppress media, and much of the rest of society resigned itself to this norm.

Surveying international research on public relations, Taylor (2001) confirms that the unique economic, political, and social systems in each country affect the development of public relations. Research that Taylor cites on Malaysia and Singapore, Indonesia's nearest neighbors, indicates that public relations is used primarily for nation building by the government and for building markets and trade relations by business. However, in the Philippines, another neighbor but one with a longer tradition of media freedom, public relations is put to the service of democracy building as well as socioeconomic development. Perhaps, the practice of public relations in Indonesia is closer to that of Thailand where it is of *press agentry* and *public information.* The state of public relations practice in two transitional economies, China and Russia, is described by McElreath, Chen, Azarova, and Shadrova (2001) as being at the "rethinking" or third stage of development. In comparison, Indonesia appears to lag behind at the "upsurge" or second stage when less unethical manipulation, more accurate information dissemination, and recognition of the competitive advantage of professional public relations begins to take place.

Bemoaning the dominance of positivist perspectives on the role of public relations that emphasize a one-way mechanistic and manipulative form of communication, Mickey (1995) offers an alternative interpretive approach, seemingly based on cultural studies of communications research. Called *sociodrama,* it sees public relations as a symbolic interaction between the organization and society, which allows for dialogue in the creation of meaning and understanding. This is perhaps a more useful perspective when dealing with the complexity of environments in emerging democracies such as Indonesia, where information and research is limited, and interventions and outcomes are less predictable than they are in developed countries. Having set the historical and geographical scene, this chapter next describes the major players and plot, pre- and post-*Reformasi,* in the ongoing sociodrama of the media in Indonesia, then suggests some resolutions for public relations in the future.

Past Media Regulation

During the Soeharto regime from 1965 to 1997, the media in Indonesia were increasingly characterized by strict monitoring by the government, self-censorship by journalists, and crony capitalism in their ownership. Although this was true of all media, television and print make the most pertinent examples.

Television

Of all the media, television was recognized as an ideal means for achieving the national goals of integration, development, and political stability and consequently was incorporated in Indonesia's first five-year plan in 1969. From the beginning TVRI was governed by strict policy guidelines of the Ministry of Information and had to work in close collaboration with other government agencies for its development communications programming (Alfian & Chu, 1981). Persuaded by a U.S. multinational corporation, then-President Soeharto took the radical step in 1975 of purchasing a communication satellite, the first developing country in the world to do so (Parapak, 1990). Abruptly in 1981, television advertising in Indonesia was banned totally because the government feared that commercials raised unrealistic material expectations among the masses (McDaniel, 1994). As a result of the ban on advertising, TVRI's income was reduced significantly, private enterprise lost investment interest in television, the station became exclusively a government medium, and it declined in popularity (Kitley, 1994). During the following years there were characteristically Indonesian "polite" protests by the advertisers union, national chamber of commerce, influential businesspersons, even an Islamic political party, and a government-sponsored think tank. One of the arguments put forward was that advertising was essential for economic growth and national development (Sen, 1994). As a result of these pressures, in the late 1980s and early 1990s, the Indonesian government issued a series of decrees gradually liberalizing the television industry.

In 1987 TVRI licensed the first commercial channel, Rajawali Citra Televisi Indonesia (RCTI), to broadcast and to advertise in return for a percentage of its advertising revenue to TVRI. RCTI was jointly owned by two Indonesian conglomerates, one of them controlled by Bambang Trihatmodjo, a son of then-President Soeharto. RCTI broadcasts were initially confined by law to subscribers in the capital Jakarta and only two years later were permitted to use a domestic satellite to broadcast to the entire country, though reception would be possible only through satellite dishes. Despite these constraints imposed by government regulations, RCTI achieved market dominance through programming targeted at middle to upper classes while attracting also lower classes, perhaps by appealing to their aspirations (Thomas, 1998). In 1990 a second commercial station, Surya Citra Televisi (SCTV), was licensed by the Indonesian government for the East Java region (Suparto, 1993). A major shareholder in SCTV was believed to be Sudwikatmono, a cousin of then-President Soeharto (Sen, 1994). Other principals of the consortium that owned SCTV included a former governor of East Java, some private shareholders in common with the Bimantara group of companies that owned RCTI, and a brother of a business partner of Liem Sioe Liong who, in turn, was a close friend of then-President Soeharto (Kitley, 1994).

In 1991, the Indonesian government licensed a third nationwide broadcaster, Televisi Pendidikan Indonesia (TPI), as an educational television service operated as a private nonprofit organization. Its manifest purpose was to cater to Indonesian school students, development agencies, domestic businesses, and the wider population in support of national development. But its mandate included the provision of some commercial programs as a means of generating operating funds. Independent sources assessed educational programs to occupy only 33 percent of its airtime, with 47 percent noneducational programs and 20 percent advertising (Winton, 1991). TPI was owned by a holding company whose principal was Siti Rukmana, the elder daughter and then political heir apparent of Soeharto. Thus, it enjoyed special concessions from the government, such as the privilege of airing commercials (which continued to be banned on TVRI); the use of TVRI studios, equipment, and transmitters; and the purchase of television sets for all schools in the country (Darusman, 1991).

The fourth commercial channel, Cakrawala Andalas Televisi, operating as AnTeve, commenced broadcasting in 1993 and was available initially only in Jakarta, Bandung, Surabaya, and Medan (Lintas Indonesia, 1993). AnTeve is partly owned by the Bakrie group, a long-standing Indonesian conglomerate seen as having no ties to the New Order government, and partly owned by Agung Laksono who does have ties (Sen & Hill, 2000). After a spate of technical and marketing problems, the station was relaunched in early 1995, with a commitment to broadcasting eighteen hours daily on a national basis. Imported "Western" programming comprised 29 percent of AnTeve programming, of which eight hours per day in the afternoon and late night comprised MTV Asia programs by arrangement (Going against the grain, 1995). Permission was granted by the government in 1994 for another Indonesian conglomerate to form a joint-venture channel with TVB of Hong Kong. Known as Indosiar Visual Mandiri (IVM), it was part of the Salim Group owned by Liem Sioe Liong. It was generally believed in Indonesia that apart from his friendship with Soeharto, Liem might have found it difficult to obtain a license, being ethnic Chinese and thus a member of a politically sensitive minority. Unlike the other broadcasters, IVM was vertically integrated, producing much of its high-quality programming in-house (Lau, 1999). IVM faced a serious controversy when its Indonesian staff complained via the press of being controlled by 150 Hong Kong expatriates from TVB, but the wider issue was long-standing hostility toward the wealthy ethnic Chinese local community in the country (Kitley, 1997). See Table 18.1 for an overview of the major Indonesian commercial television stations.

In December 1996, a broadcasting law was passed by the national legislature to supersede the numerous ministerial decrees under which the media had been regulated. Similar to the previous decrees, the law sought to protect domestic broadcasters from foreign competition and extended to the Internet when it was used as a broadcast medium. Among other matters, it allowed for self-regulation by the domestic commercial broadcasters of program classification, permitted the broadcast of news programs other than those of TVRI, specified that 80 percent of programming be locally produced, and allowed TVRI itself to accept advertising (Boulestreau, 1997). However, the legislation was not signed into law by then-President Soeharto because it restricted each broadcaster to reaching no more than 50 percent of the population, a restriction with which his family members, who

TABLE 18.1 *Major Indonesian Commercial Television Stations*

Channel	Positioning
RCTI	Programming mix of local and dubbed/subtitled foreign programs; catering to an urban middle to upper class audience market
SCTV	Similar programming mix to RCTI but reputed for *telenovelas* among housewives, and for Chinese dramas and *kungfu* films
TPI	As an education-turned-family channel, its high-quality local programming includes movies, variety shows, and local serials; known for its Indonesian music programs
AnTeve	Catering to a youthful market, its programming concentrates on sports and music, including a joint venture with MTV
IVM	Broad-based broadcaster catering to upper, middle, and lower classes via local sitcoms, dramas, comic sketches, puppet shows, etc.

Source: Adapted from *Media Scene 1999–2000*

had investments in commercial television, were displeased (Sen & Hill, 2000). Toward the end of the Soeharto era in 1997, Indonesia had five privately owned commercial television stations: RCTI, SCTV, TPI, AnTeve, and IVM, all licensed to broadcast nationally. TVRI maintained the highest penetration as the sole terrestrial broadcaster. IVM and RCTI were jostling for market leadership in urban areas in the evening prime time, and TPI led during the daytime national broadcast with the help of TVRI.

Print

When the New Order government of President Soeharto rescinded the requirement of political party affiliation by print media, many partisan newspapers went out of business or were closed down by the authorities for their social activism. The media that survived were those that opted to become depoliticized and market oriented, this having implications for their organizational structure, management, and personnel. There was a new emphasis on vertical integration, capital investment, marketing strategies, promotion methods, readership research, journalistic training, impartial reporting, and so on, which had been neglected when print media were more ideologically driven. Business publications became the growth sector with such new titles as *Bisnis Indonesia, Warta Ekonomi,* and *Indonesian Business Weekly*. Some would argue, however, that their management concentrated on such directions out of fear of taking any stance on politically sensitive issues (Hidayat, 1999).

Although the 1966 Press Act, amended in 1982, guaranteed that no censorship would apply to print media, it also required all publications to obtain licenses, empowered the minister of information to revoke licenses, and allowed the government to screen personnel at print media organizations. Further decrees by the minister limited the number of publications licensed (though exceptions were made for those with political patronage) and required all journalists to belong to a single professional association. During the late 1980s and early 1990s, several newspapers and news magazines were banned, lost their licenses, or had their editors jailed—in one case for apparently investigating then-President Soeharto's wealth. Numerous other laws, decrees, and regulations forbade the inciting of hostilities, disparaging of the president, counseling of civil disobedience, and so on (Idris & Gunaratne, 2000). Ironically, hopes had been raised for change in media policy, with a senior military general calling for more participation in decision making and the government forming a commission on human rights. A government minister had also promised no more banning of newspapers and even the president had reassured the public that they need not fear expressing different views (Hidayat, 1999). As a sign of the times, print media banned in the 1980s tended to resume publication under new management and new names, whereas those banned in the 1990s tended to reappear subsequently as Web sites. As of 1995–1996, prior to the Asian economic crisis and the fall of the Soeharto regime, there were 165 newspapers with a circulation of 8.5 million, 76 of them dailies. There were also 125 magazines, 31 of them weekly, 46 fortnightly, and 37 monthly; total circulation was about 5.5 million (*Media Scene 1995–1996*).

A consequence of the New Order shift from ideological to market orientation was the growth of newspapers into media conglomerates through the assistance of government loans, tax concessions, and import duty exemptions—even if they were somewhat politically independent of the government. Thus, by the early 1990s, the *Kompas-Gramedia* and

Jawa *Post* groups comprised not only national and some regional newspapers and magazines but also book publishers, printeries, radio stations, travel agencies, hotels, supermarkets, advertising agencies, financial services, real estate, and more (Sen & Hill, 2000). Many other conglomerates had significantly greater associations with the government, then dominated by the Golkar party or the Soeharto family. Government ministers and the then-president's children controlled some conglomerates, had financial interests in many media firms, or simply lent their names to applications for licenses (Idris & Gunaratne, 2000). For instance, in 1993, the license for *Republika,* owned by a Muslim intellectuals' movement, was said to have been fast-tracked through the influence of B. J. Habibie, then the minister for research and technology in the Soeharto government (Hidayat, 1999). The publishers of the banned news magazine *Tempo* were compelled to team up with officials of the attorney general's office to publish a fortnightly magazine and later in 1997 to relinquish their share to the Bukaka Group linked to the then-minister of information, Hartono, and President Habibie. The other banned magazines were replaced by newly licensed ones: *Tiras,* part owned by the then-minister of labor; *Gatra,* financed by Soeharto confidante Bob Hasan; and *Target,* owned by Golkar leader and AnTeve part owner Agung Laksono. In 1996, the *Indonesia Observer* came under the control of the Bimantara Group associated with Soeharto's son, which also owned RCTI, as well as Peter Gontha who owned SCTV(Sen & Hill, 2000). Thus, there was considerable cross-ownership of the media in Indonesia as well as links to the interim Habibie government. Table 18.2 presents a list of the major Indonesian magazines and tabloids.

TABLE 18.2 *Major Indonesian Magazines and Tabloids*

Type	Title	Characteristics
General	*Tempo*	Reappeared after Soeharto regime ended, in-depth and controversial reporting style; middle-upper class, older, urban, white-collar readership
	Gatra	Clone of *Tempo* magazine, featuring economic, political, cultural, technological, and religious issues; appeals to male segment
	Aksi	Low-price tabloid covering sociopolitical issues; high appeal to the mass market
Business	*SWA*	Glossy, monthly business magazine covering corporate performance, finance, and banking, including profiles of executives
	Warta Ekonomi	Well-read business magazine printed on newsprint, reflecting its down-to-earth and straightforward style
Recreation	*Femina*	Targeted at urban upper and upper-middle class career women and housewives; promotes fashion, elegance, sophistication
	Nova	Leading women's medium published in inexpensive tabloid form; features fashion, recipes, news about high-profile women
	Bola	Largest weekly specializing in sports in tabloid form; provides both national and international sports news

Source: Adapted from *Media Scene 1999–2000*

*Media Scene Post-*Reformasi

The forced resignation of Soeharto as a consequence of civil unrest and economic collapse saw the installation of an interim government with elections planned for a year later. Yet almost immediately, there was a radical change of media policy, though it was largely in recognition of what was already a de facto social and business reality.

Television

The broadcasting bill that Soeharto reluctantly signed into law in 1997 in the dying days of his regime was never quite implemented by the interim government of President Habibie. Nonetheless, this bill represented a further step in the policy of deregulating the television industry in Indonesia and, when finally granted presidential assent the next year without significant revision, held promise of stimulating its growth and sophistication. One consequence was that despite the economic downturn, the Habibie government called for applications for eight new licenses to broadcast commercial television. This was interpreted as a means of deflecting concerns about the links of most existing stations with the Soeharto family and defusing pressures to revoke their licenses. In the selection of the new licensees, others saw attempts by the interim government to shore up support from sympathetic business interests for their reelection. One license went to a senior executive of *Republika* newspaper owned by a Habibie-controlled conglomerate, another to a firm owned by a former government minister, and yet another to a former top official (Asiacom, 1999). Two of the new stations were soft launched in late 2000. Metro TV has a CNN-like emphasis on news, current affairs, and documentaries, whereas another newcomer, TransTV, is challenging the major players, RCTI, SCTV, and Indosiar, in targeting the middle- to upper-class segments with broader programming. Having abandoned its educational agenda, TPI has repositioned itself as a "family" channel, catering especially to those with young children and of a lower socioeconomic status. AnTeve, which has outlived all prognosis of its demise, continues to position itself as a "youth and sports" channel (Thomas, 2001).

The 1999 inauguration of former dissident Abdurrahman Wahid as Indonesia's third president and the first to be democratically elected was soon followed by the outright abolition of the information ministry to allow for the total freedom of the media. Former officials of that ministry were subsumed under the ministry of transportation and communications, which governs technical aspects of infrastructure hardware and has no purview over content. That raised significant difficulties for the implementation of the Broadcasting Law (Panjaitan, 2000). During the *Reformasi* protests, television served as an immediate source of information on events. Reveling in their new-found freedom under Wahid, both broadcasters and audiences turned television into a medium for political discourse. One outcome has been the prevalence of news, current affairs, political forums, and talk-back programs on Indonesian television, whereas previously all commercial stations were required to relay TVRI's news bulletins and allowed only to generate their own business shows and magazine type programs. There is also greater freedom to use Chinese-language programming without dubbing but only subtitling, to broadcast non-Muslim religious programs, to produce English-language business programs, and so on (Thomas, 2001).

The economic and political crisis of the late 1990s saw all the older commercial stations in Indonesia restructured ownershipwise. Although the former majority shareholders remain, they are largely minority shareholders now and are no longer involved in management and operations. All television stations in Indonesia suffered declines in advertising revenue during the economic crisis of the late 1990s and, consequently, lacked funds to produce local programs or even to purchase new imported programs, and viewers had to resign themselves to reruns (Lau, 1999). In one way or another all existing commercial stations are currently under the control of the Indonesian Bank Restructuring Agency, because of the collapse of the banks to which they were indebted, and seeking partial foreign investment. TVRI itself is being reconstituted as a public service corporation independent of the government, but there are complications with its new legal status and its relationship with the commercial stations (Panjaitan, 2000).

Print

Following the inauguration of Habibie, the press licensing laws were significantly relaxed, and the regulation requiring journalists to join the Indonesian Journalists Association was repealed. The new minister of information was responsible for more than doubling the number of new publication permits to five hundred, among them some of the magazines banned in 1994. In late 1999 under the Wahid government, the Indonesian parliament passed a new Press Law that guaranteed noncensorship, carried penalties for those convicted of obstructing press freedoms, and permitted 49 percent ownership of news media by foreign interests (Idris & Gunaratne, 2000). Today, the leading national newspapers are *Kompas, Media Indonesia,* and *Suara Pembaruan,* and leading magazines include a range of women's, business, and sports publications, such as *Femina, Dewi, Tempo, Gatra, Warta Economi, Matra,* and *Bola* (*Media Scene 1999–2000*). A small number of Chinese-language newspapers and magazines have been established, after an almost forty-year ban on such publications. Many of the new publications are tabloids with sensationalist news on politics and sex scandals. Ongoing economic problems have forced broadsheet newspapers to reduce the number of pages or to switch to tabloid-size paper. One prediction is that 70 percent of the estimated 230 periodicals will go out of business (Idris & Gunaratne, 2000). As of 1999–2000, there are no definitive figures for the number or circulation of newspapers and magazines, except that industry sources recognize that many new players are entering and exiting the market rapidly while established players remain dominant. See Table 18.3 for an overview of major Indonesian newspapers.

Internet

When the Internet was introduced to Indonesia in 1994 through local commercial providers, a controversy arose between the Departments of Telecommunications, Information, and Transportation as to which was to regulate the industry. This was only resolved years later by the transitional Habibie government in favor of the first of these departments, though Internet service providers (ISPs) as "special broadcasters" had to obtain permits from the second. The regulation allowed ISPs to either be cooperatives, government departments, government-owned companies, or private Indonesian-owned companies. Quite flexibly, they were allowed to provide the service either to permanent subscribers or short-term users in environments such as cyber cafes. The license process for each provider took nine months, but was valid indefinitely, though subject to review by the government every

TABLE 18.3   *Major Indonesian Newspapers, Early 2000s*

Title	Characteristics
Kompas	Sole national newspaper of importance, considered credible by largely middle- and upper-class readership; covers national and international news
Suara Pembaruan	Afternoon newspaper circulated nationally through remote satellite printing; acknowledged as providing highly credible news
Republika	General news catering to its Muslim readership with an editorial ethos reflecting its ownership by an Islamic intellectual asocial
Rakyat Merdeka	Extremely popular because of its banner headlines, controversial issues, gossip, and pictures of models and actresses; enjoys high street sales but low subscription
Harian Indonesia	Chinese-language newspaper, catering largely to readership in Jakarta's Chinatown older than forty years who can still read Chinese
Jakarta Post	Sole English-language newspapers, circulated in Jakarta and Bali; catering to expatriate community though almost half of the readership is Indonesian

Source: Adapted from *Media Scene 1999–2000*

five years. As of 1999, there were forty-two licensed ISPs in Indonesia but the major impediment to growth may be the poor support services in computer hardware and software (Idris, 1999).

Thus, quite remarkably for a country that had stringent controls on broadcast and print media, there was and is little interference of Web sites or access, resulting for instance in the news magazine *Tempo* establishing a Web presence by 1996, within two years of previously having been banned. There is even a Web site called Indopubs.com, which acts as a clearinghouse for political rumors because of inadequate coverage by local media, especially toward the end of the Soeharto era. Today on-line sites are provided by most of the major newspapers and news magazines in Indonesia. Various estimates of Internet usage in Indonesia in the late 1990s range from less than 100,000 people to more than 300,000. Despite pronouncements on regulating Internet access by the Soeharto regime, no attempt was made to do so then, and the political will to do so no longer exists since *Reformasi*. Instead, the government is pressing ahead with plans to link major islands via fiber-optic cable. Together with the established satellite system, this would link Indonesia with the global information superhighway and deliver ambitious applications such as government services, electronic commerce, telecommuting, education, and banking (Idris & Gunaratne, 2000). But when the economy will turn around sufficiently to sustain the growth of the Internet into a viable medium in Indonesia remains an uncertainty.

Implications for Public Relations

In 1988, at the height of the Soeharto era, there were twenty-nine public relations agencies in Indonesia, though it was acknowledged that advertising agencies were offering public relations services as well (Karim, 1989). As of November 2000 there were twenty-eight registered with the Indonesian Association of Public Relations companies, though some have since closed. Of these, only three or four are joint ventures with international public relations consultancies. No information is publicly available on the total billings of public relations consultancies, hence it is difficult to assess whether there has been growth in the industry since *Reformasi*. By one consultant's estimate, the breakdown of expenditure is approximately 30 percent each on media relations and charity/social service, and 10 percent each on corporate advertising, financial relations, government relations, and opinion research (IPM, 2001). This distribution seems to indicate that there is still much potential for maturation and sophistication of the industry. It also reveals both opportunities and pitfalls that no public relations practitioner can afford to ignore, and yet little has been written about how they might be addressed. Following are some preliminary thoughts on the implications of the changed media environment in Indonesia for public relations practice at the turn of the twenty-first century.

Diversified Ownership, Editorial Independence

A consequence of the economic meltdown in the late 1990s is that ownership of Indonesian newspapers, magazines, television, and radio is now far more diffused. In many cases the conglomerates that previously owned various media no longer do so exclusively, and in a few cases the conglomerates themselves are no longer owned by a few key shareholders with strong political links. Through financial restructuring, such as debt-for-equity swaps, their ownership is now in the hands of multiple parties in somewhat nebulous arrangements. As a result, there is greater editorial independence for each medium and journalists and public relations executives are motivated toward greater professionalism. No longer is it taboo for journalists to criticize the activities of conglomerates, their major shareholders, or their powerful allies in government. Consequently, no longer can public relations executives take for granted that a positive spin will be given automatically to those firms, shareholders, and political leaders in these media, or that their press releases, annual reports, and corporate events will be taken at face value. The corporate image of many conglomerates in Indonesia are in dire need of repositioning as responsible corporate citizens and need incentives to professionally manage their businesses in the wake of the economic and political crises of the late 1990s and reforms of the early 2000s. Thus, community involvement needs to be designed with corporate strategic objectives clearly in mind and with the full participation of senior management in the decision (Portway, 1995).

Human Rights and Freedom of Information

Government decrees have urged human rights and freedom of information. This tendency is most potently demonstrated in the abolition of the Ministry of Information, which previously licensed, monitored, and censored the media. Immediate past-President Wahid made it clear that government-owned television was to serve the general public and not act as a propaganda vehicle of the government. Thus, journalists and editors in Indonesia in recent years have demonstrated greater courage and determination in getting to the truth of politically significant matters. Certainly, practitioners and other officials in government, particularly the military and police, will be held far more accountable for human rights and freedom of information. This places responsibility on public relations practitioners to be more astute yet candid in their handling of sensitive issues involving their own or client organizations. In the face of challenges to democracy and the power of nation-states from the rise of multinational corporations, there are few safeguards to ensure that the latter will uphold human rights or democratic principles. Public relations practitioners are uniquely placed to raise these issues with management in their roles as intermediaries between their corporations and society (Grunig, 1992). Thus, political democratization and media liberalization creates a need for the training of both journalists and public relations professionals to cope with the changed environment since *Reformasi*.

Media Choice and Diversity

As a result of liberalization, it is now easier for new publishers and broadcasters to obtain licenses; there are simply more media available. Because at this stage there has been little segmentation and competition seems to be directed toward the same mass market, public relations executives have the complex task of managing far more media vehicles than in more regulated times. As the media gain greater proficiency at targeting certain market segments, public relations professionals will have also to attain greater sophistication in evaluating media vehicles, selecting the tools, and crafting the messages to target specific publics relevant to their firm's business. Sriramesh and White (1992) have highlighted the need for analyzing the societal culture in which public relations is practiced because culture influences the pattern of communication both within the corporation and without. But an essential ingredient for success at communicating with the various publics is a thorough understanding of not only the national or societal culture but also the nuances of the myriad and evolving ethnic and socioeconomic subcultures that constitute many postcolonial countries, including Indonesia. This is particularly important in order for transnational corporations to recognize and affirm in the efforts of their local counterparts, joint venture partners, public relations consultants, and in-house executives.

Higher Audiences/Readerships and Competition

Although there are increased circulations and audiences overall as the media gains the credibility that it previously lacked, there is also greater competition for these among the much larger number of media. The temptation for each media-owner then, as happens in the developed world as well, is to seek to attract a larger readership/audience by sensationalism rather than professional reporting. There is thus the risk to firms of negative publicity being fueled by journalists as a consequence of the push for greater sales or ratings in the short term. Such practices by some media ought to be abhorred by their media peers, advertiser clients, government policy makers, and the general public, placing pressure on the offending media to change their approaches in the long run. Nonetheless, the onus in the short term is for public relations practitioners in Indonesia, as in any emerging democracy, to learn to use the media effectively and to practice public relations ethically, without giving cause for scandal. The fact that public relations and communications training and consulting are currently in demand in Indonesia implies some recognition of corporate inadequacies in these areas (IPM, 2001).

Activated Civil Society

An outcome of the reformation struggle in the late 1990s has been greater political awareness and activism among the general public. Therefore, corporations and organizations in Indonesia need to realize that there is greater accountability for its decisions, policies, and actions. Readers and audiences also have improved access to other media, all equally unrestricted, and so are able to evaluate any information from public relations sources more critically. Through transnational media—print, broadcast, and particularly, the Internet—the publics in emerging democracies are able to obtain further information and other perspectives on their government and businesses. Even though there is no longer a clear government agenda for the media to support economic development or national cultural identity, these are worthwhile values that corporations and their public relations consultants may use critically to counterbalance the pressures to crass materialism. What is needed is accountability by corporations that goes beyond financial statements to include reporting on other indices of ethical management and social contributions in quarterly and annual reports (Newson, 1989). However, government officials can no longer expect sympathetic coverage of all their activities and pronouncements. Such practices as the monitoring of media stories, opinion polls, issues management, and the training of managers/officials in public relations gain critical importance in emerging democracies with a free press.

Globalization and Pressure Groups

In an increasingly globalized world, the publics to which any corporation is accountable come from outside the country including internationally networked civil society groups and NGOs such as environmentalists, labor unions, and antiglobalization groups. With the growth of the Internet, such groups are considerably more empowered to promote their views and mobilize supporters into action, for example by initiating boycotts and protests of various sorts. Byrnes (1995) advocates opening the proverbial factory gate and going the extra mile metaphorically, offering valuable advice to governments, building trust and relationships with campaigners, providing training and skills, and so on. Public relations practitioners in Indonesia will need to scan not only their own environments but also the international environments if they are to adequately anticipate corporate communications crises. It is especially critical to have contingency strategies in place to manage such crises, whether real or contrived, and to counter misinformation with truth, candor, and transparency.

Specialization and Professionalism

Until recently in Indonesia, there was less emphasis on public relations and corporate image by businesses than on advertising and sales promotion for their products and services. Typical of many developing countries, much of the former was managed in-house by advertising agencies. Creating a corporate image is often product-related marketing public relations, and only when crisis occurs are public relations consultancies called on (IPM, 2001). In the future there will be increasing demand for greater specialization in public relations, especially as the public becomes increasingly sophisticated. Consumers will demand to know whether the businesses they patronize operate ethically as responsible corporate citizens within their country and around the world. They will seek out critical perspectives on government policies and politicians' decisions. The expertise of public relations professionals to meet these information needs is divergent and more sophisticated than those needed to advertise products and services. It calls for practitioners to have a thorough grounding in the humanities and social sciences, not only in public relations skills and techniques. Only then might they be able to resist the pressures from clients and employers for short-term private gain, which often characterizes business and government in developing countries, instead of long-term public interest. As media journalists in the post-*Reformasi* period concentrate on their fourth estate role as a watchdog for the citizenry, it is imperative to have commensurate professionalism by public relations practitioners in business and government. Otherwise, there will not be the plurality and balance in the exchange of information that ought to characterize the functioning of democratic nation-states and that oil the operations of their free-market institutions.

Conclusion

Although there is some continuity with the past, it is quite evident that the media environment in Indonesia has undergone major transformations as a result of political reform and economic crises. Until the late 1990s the print media in Indonesia were at best very guarded in their criticism of the crony capitalism and government corruption that characterized the Indonesian political economy, by virtue of their ownership and regulation. At the same time, Indonesian television was a pabulum of innocuous entertainment, bland education, and propagandist news doled out by public stations controlled by the government and commercial stations owned by the family of the president or their friends. Yet at the turn of the twenty-first century Indonesia has joined the ranks of an increasing number of emerging democracies among developing and transitional economies around the world in which political democratization has been accompanied by transformed media environments. It is imperative that public relations practitioners respond proactively and comprehensively to this greater freedom of information, diversity of media and outlets, sophistication of publics, concern for economic justice, and reassertion of political rights. Such changes nationally are taking place in the context of a world characterized by increasing globalization of business, communications, and culture, and a consequent decline in the power of nation-states to mind the activities of corporations. Responding proactively entails not only learning from the best practices of public relations professionals in the liberal–democratic nations, largely those in the developed world with the longest traditions, but also, as argued in this case on Indonesia, by adopting and adapting these best practices with sensitivity to the specific historical, economic, political, and social contexts. Yet as the situation is not altogether different for other emerging democracies, there might be some lessons for practitioners elsewhere.

Discussion Questions _____

1. Education levels and literacy in Indonesia are fairly low, as is often the case in developing countries. What public relations tools and media would you recommend for a national campaign on behalf of a foreign oil corporation extracting, refining, and marketing in the country?

2. If you were appointed as a public relations consultant by one of the media firms formerly part of a conglomerate allied to the New Order government, what would be some of your key communications objectives in the post-*Reformasi* era?

3. Nike has been accused of exploiting factory workers in Indonesia by underpaying them. Access Web sites alleging and countering this. Evaluate the efforts of Nike to manage this issue and suggest alternatives they might try for the longer term.

4. Are the implications of the media reforms in Indonesia for public relations practitioners, such as those argued in this chapter, applicable in your country or other emerging democracies around the world? Give examples of why or why not.

References

Alfian & Godwin, C. (Eds.). (1981). *Satellite television in Indonesia.* Honolulu: East–West Center.

Asiacom. (1999). Cronyism adds to existing broadcasters' worries. *Asia-Pacific TV, Cable, Satellite and Telecommunications, 5*(6). [On-line]. Available: www.batkerville.co.uk/asfp.html.

Boulestreau, E. (1997, February). Pacific Rim watch. *International Cable.*

Byrnes, B. (1995). International corporate relations. In N. Hart (Ed.), *Strategic public relations* (pp. 125–140). Basingstoke: Macmillan Press.

Darusman, T. (1991, September). Station abandons lofty objective. *Asia-Pacific Broadcasting.*

Department of Information. (2000). *Indonesia 2000: An official handbook.* Jakarta: Department of Information/National Communication and Information Board.

Grunig, J. E. (1992). Communication, public relations and effective organizations: An overview of the book. In J. E. Grunig (Ed.), *Excellence in public relations and communications management* (pp. 1–28). Hillsdale, NJ: Lawrence Erlbaum Associates.

Hidayat, D. (1999). Mass media: Between the palace and the market. In R. Baker, M. Soesastro, J. Kristiadi, & D. Ramage (Eds.), *Indonesia: The challenge of change* (pp. 179–198). Leiden: KITLV Press.

Holaday, D. (1996). Social impact of satellite TV in Indonesia: A view from the ground. *Media Asia, 23*(2).

Idris, N. (1999). Indonesia: Satellites as the backbone of telecommunications development. In A. Goonasekara & P. H. Aug (Eds.), *Information highways in ASEAN: Policy and regulations.* Singapore: Asian Media Information and Communications Centre and School of Communications Studies, Nanyang Technological University.

Idris, N., & Shelton A. (2000). Indonesia. In S. Gunaratne (Ed.), *Handbook of the media in Asia* (pp. 263–295). Thousand Oaks, CA: Sage.

IPM. (2001). Email re-PR in Indonesia. Jakarta: IPM Public Relations.

Johnstone, P., & Mandryk, J. (2001). *Operation world.* Waynesboro, GA: Paternoster.

Karim, H. (1989). Development of public relations in the Asia–Pacific region. In S. White (Ed.), *Values and Communication: Selected proceedings of the Eleventh Public Relations World Congress,* Melbourne, April 26–29, 1988.

Kitley, P. (1994). Fine tuning control: Commercial television in Indonesia. *Continuum: Australian Journal of Media and Culture, 8*(2), 103–123.

Kitley, P. (1997, July). *Deregulation and the public debate on television.* Paper presented at the Modernisation in Bali seminar, University of Wollongong.

Kitley, P. (2000). *Television, nation and culture in Indonesia.* Athens: Ohio University Center for International Studies.

Lau, T. (1999). Deregulation and commercialization of the broadcast media: Their implications for public service broadcasters—The case of Indonesia. In *Public service broadcasting in Asia* (pp. 75–83). Singapore: Asian Media Information and Communications Centre.

L'Etang, J. (1997). Public relations and the rhetorical dilemma. *Australian Journal of Communications, 24*(2), 33–53.

Lintas Indonesia. (1993). *Media guide 1993.* Jakarta: Lintas Indonesia.

Matters, N. (1995, December). Going against the grain. *Television Asia,* 101–104.

Mayhew, L. (1997). *The new public: Professional communication and the means of social influence.* Cambridge, England: Cambridge University Press.

McDaniel, D. (1994). *Broadcasting in the Malay world: Radio, television and video in Brunei, Indonesia, Malaysia and Singapore.* Norwood, NJ: Ablex.

McElreath, M., Chen, N., Azarova, L., & Shadrova, V. (2001). The development of public relations in China, Russia and the United States. In R. Heath (Ed.), *Handbook of public relations* (pp. 665–674). Thousand Oaks, CA: Sage.

Media Scene 1995–1996. Jakarta: Indonesian Association of Advertising Agencies (PPPI).

Media Scene 1999–2000. Jakarta: Indonesian Association of Advertising Agencies (PPPI).

Mickey, T. (1995). *Sociodrama: An interpretive theory for the practice of public relations.* Lanham, NY, and London: University Press of America.

Panjaitan, H. (2000, July). *The impact of the dissolution of the Department of Information on the regulation of broadcasting media in Indonesia.* Paper presented at the International Association of Mass Communication Research Conference, Singapore.

Parapak, J. (1990, July 25–27). *The progress of satellite technology and its role in the development of the Asia Pacific region—The case of Indonesia.* Paper presented at the seminar on Socio-Economic Impact of Broadcast Satellites in the Asia-Pacific region, Jakarta.

Portway, S. (1992). Corporate social responsibility: The case for active stakeholder relationship management. In N. Hart (Ed.), *Strategic public relations.* Basingstoke: Macmillan Press.

SBS World Guide. (1996). (5th ed.). Port Melbourne: Reed Reference Australia.

Sen, K. (1994). Changing horizons of television in Indonesia. *Southeast Asian Journal of Social Science,* (22).

Sen, K., & Hill, D. (2000). *Media, culture and politics in Indonesia.* Melbourne: Oxford University Press.

Speake, J. (Ed.). (1993). *The Hutchinson dictionary of world history.* Oxford: Helicon.

Sriramesh, K., & White, J. (1992). Societal culture and public relations. In J. E. Grunig, (Ed.), *Excellence in public relations and communications management.* Hillsdale, NJ: Lawrence Erlbaum Associates.

Starck, K., & Kruckeberg, D. (2001). Public relations and community: A reconstructed theory revisited. In R. Heath (Ed.), *Handbook of public relations* (pp. 51–60). Thousand Oaks, CA: Sage.

Suparto, I. (1993). *The social and cultural impact of satellite broadcasting in Indonesia.* Paper presented at the Seminar on the Social and Cultural Impact of Satellite Broadcasting in Asia. Asian Mass Communication Research and Information Centre, Singapore.

Taylor, M. (2001). International public relations: Opportunities and challenges for the twenty-first century. In R. Heath (Ed.), *Handbook of public relations* (pp. 629–638). Thousand Oaks, CA: Sage.

Thomas, A. (1998). Transnational satellite television and advertising in SE Asia. *Journal of Marketing Communications, 4*(4), 1–17.

Thomas, A. (2001). The quiet transition in Indonesian television. *Media Asia, 26*(3).

Winton, K. (1991, August). Commercial TV shakes up media scene. *Asian Advertising and Marketing, 28*(8), 6–7.

19

The Evolving Face of Public Relations in Malaysia

Anuradha Venkateswaran

Key Points

- Public relations involves mediated communication efforts between different constituents.
- The nature of the communication depends on the relationship between the constituents and can range from persuasive (one-way) to relationship building (symmetrical two-way with free give and take).
- Just as products (goods, services, and ideas) cannot be marketed in a standardized fashion throughout the world, there is no such thing as standardized international public relations.
- Public relations theories within the United States are molded within a framework of Western ideals of democracy and a free-market economy.
- Modern/international public relations theories recognize that the practice of public relations within a region is affected by complicated interrelationships among culture, communication, and technology.

Public relations is a dynamic and constantly evolving area. Controversy exists, and, consequently, articles are published on such basic issues as the definition, dimensions, and domain of public relations (Hutton, 1999). Additionally, both marketing and communications professionals claim public relations as their domain, adding to the plethora of theories and perspectives in the literature. Generally speaking, public relations involves mediated communication activities aimed at multiple publics. Public relations revolves around key constituents, such as employees, shareholders, activists/propagandists, suppliers, the media, and consumers (Taylor & Kent, 1999).

In Malaysia, public relations has evolved based on the nation's history and the nature and style of its government, which, in turn, have been impacted by the geography of the land, and the peoples in and surrounding it. A nation-building emphasis has historically played a large role in Malaysia's economic decisions, and also has influenced the nature and extent of its public relations industry. In the recent past, Malaysia has embraced advancements in technology, which, in turn, has impacted its economy and moderated (to an extent) the practice of public relations within the country. It is, therefore, helpful to gain a basic understanding of Malaysia's geography, history, government, social structure, major industries, and technological infrastructure in order to appreciate the current status and evolution of the public relations industry in the country.

Geographical and Cultural Profile

Malaysia is an independent federation located on the Malay Peninsula in Southeast Asia. Its area of 128,430 square miles slightly exceeds that of New Mexico. Malaysia is subdivided into West Malaysia, also called Peninsular Malaysia or Malaya (about 50,700 square miles), comprised of eleven states and one federal territory, Wilayah Persekutuan, which coexists with the city of Kuala Lumpur; and East Malaysia (about 77,730 square miles), comprising the states of Sabah and Sarawak (the former British colonies of North and Northwest Borneo) on the island of Borneo, and one federal territory comprising the island of Labuan. East and West Malaysia are separated by the South China Sea (www.infoplease.com/ce6/world/A0831335.html).

West Malaysia is bordered on the north by Thailand, on the east by the South China Sea, on the south by Singapore (separated only by the narrow Johore Strait), and on the west by the Strait of Malacca and the Andaman Sea. East Malaysia is bordered on the north by the South China and Sulu Seas, on the East by the Celebes Sea, and on the south and west by Kalimantan (Indonesian Borneo). Along the coast within Sarawak is the independent nation of Brunei (www.infoplease.com).

West Malaysia comprises more than 80 percent of the nation's population, despite accounting for only about 31 percent of the country's area. Of the total population, almost 60 percent are of Malay or indigenous descent, more than 25 percent are Chinese, and some 10 percent are of Indian or Pakistani descent. In East Malaysia the two largest groups are the Chinese and the Ibans (Sea Dayaks), an indigenous people, who make up about three-fifths of the total (www.infoplease.com/ce6/world/A0859445.html). Nearly all of the Malays and Pakistanis are Muslims, and Islam is the national religion. The majority of the Chinese are Buddhists, and the majority of Indians are Hindus. In addition to this diversity in culture and religion, there is a multitude of languages and dialects further complicating the situation. The official language is Bahasa Malaysia (Malay), although English is used in the legal system and in much of the media. Chinese (largely Mandarin), Tamil, and regional ethnic languages are widely spoken. Conflict between the various ethnic groups, particularly the Malays and Chinese, has played a large part in the history of Malaysia and still affects its governing priorities. The official capital and largest city is Kuala Lumpur. A new administrative capital, Putrajaya, is expected to be completed by the year 2012 (www.infoplease.com/ce6/world/A0831335.html).

History of Modern Malaysia

The early history of Malaysia dates back to the 1500s and is too extensive to detail here. Suffice it to say that its history during the 1500s to 1800s has involved the Portuguese, the Dutch, Great Britain, Siam, and Japan. In 1946, when the British took over after World War II, they first arranged a centralized colony called the Malayan Union, which included all of their peninsula possessions. This move was strongly opposed by influential Malays, who feared that the inclusion to Malayan citizenship of Pinang and Malacca, which had large Chinese and Indian populations, would weaken the special position and political power that the Malays had previously enjoyed (www.infoplease.com/ce6/world/A0859448.html). The British quickly succumbed to the pressure and (in place of the union) established the Federation of Malaya in 1948, which was headed by a British high commissioner. Pinang and Malacca were still members of this federation along with the nine Malay states, but there was no common citizenship (www.infoplease.com/ce6/world/A0859448.html). In the same year a communist uprising began that lasted for more than a decade. The communist insurrection was responsible for spurring the movement toward Malayan independence, which occurred in 1957.

The Federation of Malaya became an independent state within the Commonwealth of Nations and was admitted to the United Nations in 1957. In 1963, Singapore, Sabah, and Sarawak were added to the federation, creating the Federation of Malaysia. Malaysia retained Malaya's place in the United Nations and in the Commonwealth, and, in 1967, became one of the founding members of the Association of Southeast Asian Nations (ASEAN). Indonesia immediately waged war with the new state on the grounds that the federation was a British imperialistic subterfuge (www.infoplease.com/ce6/world/A0859448.html). The war continued until President Sukarno's fall from power in 1965. The merger with Singapore also proved problematic, owing largely to friction between Malay leaders and the Singaporean prime minister, Lee Kuan Yew, who wanted to improve the position of the Chinese minorities within the Malaysian Federation. In 1965, Singapore peacefully seceded from the Malaysia. Malaysia was also faced with nonviolent opposition from the Philippines, which claimed ownership of the state of Sabah until 1978 (www.infoplease.com/ce6/world/A0859448.html).

Government and Its Role in the Economy

Malaysia is a federal constitutional monarchy with a parliamentary democracy. The sovereign (the Yang di-Pertuan Agong) is elected every five years by, and from, the nine hereditary rulers of Perlis, Kedah, Perak, Kelantan, Terengganu, Pahang, Selangor, Negeri Sembilan, and Johor. Since 1999, the paramount ruler is His Majesty Tunku Salehuddin Abdul Aziz Shah ibni al-Marhum Hisamuddin Alam Shah (www.infoplease.com/ce6/world/A0859447.html).

The prime minister must be a member of, and have the confidence of, the House of Representatives (Dewan Ra'ayat). Since 1981, the prime minister has been Mahathir bin Mohamad. The prime minister selects the cabinet with the consent of the sovereign. Presently, the main party is the multiethnic National Front coalition, led by Prime

Minister Mahathir bin Mohamad of the United Malays National Organization (UMNO). Prime Minister Mahathir led the National Front parties to several reelection victories, the most recent in 1999. The largest opposition groups are the Chinese-dominated Democratic Action Party (DAP) and the Islamic Party of Malaysia (PAS). A formal peace treaty between the Malay Communist Party (MCP) and the Kuala Lumpur government was signed in 1989 (www.infoplease.com/ce6/world/A0859448.html). Mahathir's administration has been criticized for human rights violations and repression of Chinese and Indian minorities.

Malaysia is reported to have one of the highest standards of living in Southeast Asia as a result of its expanding industrial sector, which is predominantly concentrated in Western Malaysia. Following are relevant economic figures as of 2000 (Asia Development Bank, 2000):

Population	22.7 million
GDP growth	8.5%
Inflation	1.5%
Unemployment	3.1%
GNP per capita	$U.S.3.39

Malaysia has an enviable growth record. Its annual rate of population growth has averaged only 2.4 percent between 1994 and 2000 (World Development Indicators, 2001), a relatively low rate compared to that of some other developing countries. Projected population figures for 2010 and 2020 are 27.5 million and 31 million, respectively (World Development Indicators, 2001). Between 1973 and 1995 real average per capita income increased 2.5 times, and the poverty rate shrank from slightly more than 50 percent to 7.8 percent. This is coupled with improvements in social indicators, such as increased life expectancy and diminishing infant mortality, and increased secondary school enrollment from about 34 percent in 1970 to about 58 percent in 1996 (www.worldbank.org). The World Bank reports that these results are not only because of growth but also because of the government's strong commitment to reducing poverty levels since the 1960s. Expenditures on social services, including education, health, housing, and social assistance have averaged about 32 percent of total government expenditures. There are a variety of programs in place, including free housing; food supplements; small grants; agricultural extension programs; and aid to needy children in the form of nutritional programs, scholarships, and free textbooks (www.worldbank.org).

Unfortunately, much of these services are aimed at improving the Malays at the expense of the other ethnic minorities. As reported by Heibert (1998), Malaysia launched its New Economic Policy (NEP) in 1969 following severe ethnic rioting after a Chinese-dominated opposition claimed a significant portion of the parliamentary seats from the Malay-dominated ruling coalition. The Malays, who were the economically poorer group and who feared losing their political advantage, rioted violently, forcing the government to take action to combat the causes of the uprising. The New Economic Policy that they launched incorporates an affirmative action plan designed to help Malays through a series of government regulations, quotas, scholarships, and other privileges. As a result of this initiative, Malay's share of the national wealth jumped from 2.3 percent in 1970 to about 20.6 percent by 1995 (Heibert, 1998).

Malaysia's economic prowess is strongly linked to government control as is evidenced by the relative ease with which it appears to have weathered the Asian crisis compared to other countries in the region, such as Thailand or Indonesia. Lin (1999) reports that one of the distinguishing features of the Asian crisis was its rapid development from initial speculative currency attacks into a full-scale financial and economic crisis, with subsequent widespread contagion across the region. Although weaknesses in domestic economies was the primary cause of the crisis, instability and panic in capital markets played a key role in propagating it (Lin, 1999). Several contributing factors were identified, including massive withdrawals of foreign capital once weakness in the economies and institutions became known; globalization of financial institutions (as a result of technology); use of new financial products such as derivatives, which added to increased speculation and risk; and an increased use of leverage. Indeed, the degree of leverage used by corporations in many Asian countries was very high compared to the average in developed countries, doubling between 1991 and 1996 in Thailand and Malaysia, and increasing by one-third in Korea, commensurate with the countries' growth strategies and government policies (Lin, 1999). What is interesting is that, in contrast to other affected Asian countries, Malaysia's government, rather than following the economic prescriptions of the International Monetary Fund and World Bank, opted instead for fixed exchange rates and a series of capital controls. These administrative controls, initiated by the Malaysian government in September 1998, were the cause of much apprehension, as was reported by Malaysia's Second Minister of Finance, Dato' Mustapa Mohamed, in a report presented in Washington in October 1998 (Mohamed, 1998). Grave doubts were raised about the direction of public policy in Malaysia. The controls were seen as a step backward for Malaysia, representing a move away from a free-market mechanism and the global financial system. Mohamed emphasized that these were short-term selective administrative controls designed to allow for orderly capital inflows and to help insulate the domestic economy from external risks. He promised that the controls would be lifted once stability had returned to financial markets and once an appropriate global regulatory framework was in place. By late 1999, Malaysia was well on the road to economic recovery, and it appeared that Mahathir's economic measures were indeed working.

On a more somber note, in September 1998, Mahathir summarily sacked his deputy prime minister and finance minister, Anwar Ibrahim, after a disagreement over the best way to deal with the country's economic problems. When Anwar responded by launching a reform movement attacking the government, he was jailed and charged with what generally were believed to be trumped up charges of corruption and sex crimes (www.infoplease. com/ipa/A0107751.html). He was convicted and sentenced to fifteen years in jail. In 2001, Mahathir also assumed the role of finance minister, after Daim Zainuddin resigned from the post. Such a powerful, strong-handed role played by government is shown in subsequent sections to extend to the public relations industry as well.

Industries and Infrastructure

Malaysia's main trading partners are Singapore, Japan, and the United States. In the early 1990s, Malaysia was one of the world's largest beneficiaries of the U.S. Generalized System of Preferences (GSP) program, second only to Mexico. Under that program, Malaysia was also the United States' largest supplier of machinery, appliances, and electrical equipment (U.S. Department of Commerce, 1993). Unlike many other developing nations, Malaysia has a good logistics infrastructure to support its industrial base, with all its major cities connected by rail with Singapore and an extensive road network covering its entire west coast. Since the late 1980s the government has relaxed state control and moved to privatize several large industries, as a result of which foreign investment in manufacturing has increased tremendously (U.S. Department of Commerce, 1993). Agriculture contributes about 15 percent to the GDP, and about 20 percent of Malaysians rely on agriculture as a means of livelihood.

Under the government's seventh Malaysia plan, the telecommunications sector grew in the period from 1996 to 2000. The telecommunications sector in Malaysia is privatized, making it highly competitive. The government's ambition is to position Malaysia as the high-technology hub of Southeast Asia by creating a multimedia super corridor (MSC), analogous to the information superhighway. Massive fiber optics networks are expected to provide the necessary infrastructure to meet the demands of anticipated rapid growth and to enable value-added services, such as e-commerce, distance learning, video-on-demand, and interactive multimedia content. Within the country, Telekom Malaysia has the most extensive optical fiber network, totaling 203,000 kilometers. Malaysia is reported to be investing heavily in state-of-the-art technology and equipment (U.S. Department of Commerce, 2000).

Several relevant statistics (www.budde.com) reflect Malaysia's high-technology status among developing democracies. For instance, Telekom Malaysia launched the country's first commercial integrated services digital network (ISDN) service in 1995. ISDN had 5 percent of the market in 1995, and is expected to reach 15 percent in 2002. Fixed-line services have increased from about two million in 1990 to nearly five million by 2002, resulting in a penetration of about 20 percent. Wireless and satellite communications had reached annual growth levels of greater than 50 percent by the mid-1990s before leveling off to about 15 percent in 2000. As of March 2001, more than six million people were subscribers. The mobile market has grown from 3 million subscribers in 1999 to nearly 9 million by the end of 2002.

Malaysia's classification as an emerging democracy is misleading when considering the extent of its technological involvement. Malaysia is a member of the World Intellectual Property Organization and has one of the best intellectual property rights (IPR) regimes in Asia (Errion & Carroll, 1990). In 1986 the government passed a strong patent law and in 1987 enacted a copyright law that explicitly protects computer software. Piracy enforcement was so good that Business Software Alliance, a not-for-profit vendors' consortium, awarded Malaysia its award for vigilance in 1992. Malaysia also acceded to the Berne Convention in 1990, which significantly improves the climate for software and other related technological sales (U.S. Department of Commerce, 1993).

Media and Advertising

Media in Malaysia include newspapers, periodicals, magazines, films, television, the World Wide Web, radio, posters and billboards, and a host of other regular and casual publications. Advertising contributes significantly to the nation's economy, and three advertising associations, namely, the Association of Accredited Advertising Agents, the Malaysia Advertisers Association, and the Malaysia chapter of the International Advertising Association, have combined to promote awareness of the benefits to the economy and consumers accruing from advertising (Boon, 2001). According to ACNielson Media International (2001), total advertising expenditures in Malaysia grew by 8 percent in the first half of 2001. The growth rate was an impressive 29 percent the year before. Newspapers are the dominant advertising medium, with 63 percent of the overall market share. Television commanded a 27 percent share (having grown 2 percent). Over the same period, magazine advertising increased 52 percent, and radio advertising grew 32 percent. The leaders of growth among advertisers were reported to be department stores (37 percent), real estate (36 percent), and the banking sector (24 percent), followed by corporations and the government (12 percent), telecommunications (11 percent), and the education sector (11 percent). It is interesting to note that ACNielson Media International has classified corporations and government in the same advertising category. This "corporatization of the government" is a recurring theme when discussing Malaysia. Media usage by the government dates back to the early part of the twentieth century (Arun, 1986). Print emerged first, followed by audio, then visual media, eventually combining into audiovisual and, finally, developing into electronic and multimedia. The first radio broadcasts were aired in 1920 in Malaysia, and public TV emerged in 1962 (Arun, 1986).

In 2000–2001, consumption of videocassette disks, the Internet, and cable television rose by 43 percent, 15 percent, and 74 percent, respectively. (ACNielson Media International, 2001). Although the country did not allow private operators into the TV broadcasting market until 1995, 85 percent of Malaysian households have a television set as of April 2003. There are six free-to-air TV channels and seventy pay TV channels currently (www.budde.com/au/cat/cat106.html), including government channels TV1 and TV2. TV3, established in 1984, was Malaysia's first private channel and offers news, entertainment, and a TV guide. Nat Seven TV Sdn Bhd (ntv7) was launched in 1998 and offers current news and a program schedule (www.searchbeat.com/Regional/Asia/Malaysia/NewsandMedia/Television). Most TV channels broadcast programs in Bahasa Malaysia, as well as in English, Mandarin, and Tamil. Residents can also access ASTRO, a direct-to-viewer satellite service, and MEGA TV, a cable network (U.S. Department of State, 2001).

Major Malay newspapers (U.S. Department of State, 2001) are the *Utusan Malaysia* and *Berita Harian*. The largest Chinese newspapers are *Sin Chew Pit Poh* and *Nanyang Siang Pau*. Several English-language newspapers also exist, the largest being the *New Strait Times* and the *Star*. The primary business English publication is the *Business Times*, published by the *New Straits Times* group. Other business-oriented magazines include the *Malaysian Business, Malaysian Industry,* and the *Malaysian Investor* (U.S. Department of State, 2001). The English-literate market is generally held to be more urban-centered and affluent, but the Malay market is reported to be catching up fast (John & Damis, 2002). In addition, *Tamil* and other ethnic newspapers also exist.

Malaysia currently has some twenty radio stations (www.radio-locator.com/cgi-bin/nation?ccode=my&x=13&y=3) catering to various ethnic groups and interests. The stations offer different formats including classic rock, easy listening, adult contemporary (AC), classical, hot AC, variety, top-forty hits, Asian, and talk. The majority of them are based in Kuala Lumpur. Those featuring talk are Ikim.fm (91.5 FM), Talk Radio (101.8 FM), and RMK (97.5 FM). The first of these appears to be a government station because the e-mail address on the Web site is ikimfm@ikim.gov.my and the featured language is Malay. The second's Web listing links it to the direct-to-viewer satellite service, ASTRO. The last named offers its users community chat and a feedback forum (www.ehuha.com/radiom.html). A few of the radio channels are university based. Radio Malaysia Selangor is based at the Institute Teknologi Mara, and Radio Melaka is a campus broadcaster from the Multimedia University of Melaka (www.ehuha.com/radiom.html). Several of the stations broadcast their audio on the Internet (www.radio-locator.com/cgi-bin/nation?ccode=my&x=13&y=3).

A survey conducted by ACNielson in May and June of 2000 (Bani, 2000) revealed that nine out of ten adults on the west coast of peninsular Malaysia listen to radio and that the average time spent listening was about twenty-nine hours per week. The average audience was reported to be proportionate to the national population, that is, highest for Malays, followed by Chinese and Indian/others. Bani also reports on 1999 advertising expenditure data compiled by Dentsu, Young, and Rubicam. According to their data, radio advertising accounted for only 3 percent of total advertising expenditures. Newspapers topped the list of preferred media for advertising (58 percent) followed by TV (33 percent). This is despite the fact that radio advertising was the cheapest of the three. A lack of quality creative production, coupled with reluctance on the part of advertisers to treat radio as a medium of choice were the reasons cited. It was not reported specifically why advertisers were thus reluctant. Universiti Sains Malaysia lecturer Mohamad Md Yusoff suggests that the advertising industry is dominated by English- and Mandarin-speaking professionals, skewing ads and their placement away from the Malay media (www.adtimes.nstp.com.my/archive/2002/jan13.htm). Although Yusoff is not referring to radio per se, because most radio listeners are apparently Malays, this may well be the explanation for the comparatively low level of advertising on radio.

Role of Constituents in Public Relations

Government

Public relations as an organized practice began in Malaysia in 1945, coincident with the return of the British to Malaysia after Japan was defeated. The British established the Department of Publicity and Printing whose main task was propaganda aimed at convincing the public that it was the British who had fought and defeated the Japanese and not the Malayan Peoples' Anti-Japanese Army (MPAJA), popularly dubbed the communist guerillas. In 1946, the department was renamed the Department of Public Relations (Zain, 1986), a name that was changed in 1950 to the Department of Information (Salleh, 1986). This department played a major role in combating the subsequent communist-led War of Liberation, which began in 1948 and lasted for twelve years. The entire resources of the government's propaganda machine were put to use for this purpose, using both its Broadcasting Department and Information Department. Tools used included leaflets, popular themes, voice aircraft, signed letters of appeal to "self-renew," and information field representatives sent to work with the civilian populace. When *Merdeka* (independence) was scheduled for August 31, 1957, the government employed the phrase "Unity in Diversity" as the official motto, but the unofficial catch phrase was "nation building" (Zain, 1986), a term that guides and propels the Malaysian government's decisions even today (Salleh, 1986).

The use of what Zain (1986) terms a development-support communication program began in 1960, with the launch of the Rural Development Plan. Following the severe race riots of May 13, 1969, a new dimension was added to the development program when the New Economic Policy was introduced. At this time, the nation's basic beliefs and policies were detailed in the form of *Rukunegara,* the Malaysian national ideology promoting national integration, social equity, and progressive thought, while still maintaining cultural values. All Malaysians were required to uphold and practice these. This necessitated much supportive public relations efforts on the part of the government. Also, when the Sukarno regime threatened Malaysia in 1963, the government engaged in a massive international propaganda campaign using various psychological devices designed to garner public support at home and abroad.

In the 1980s the Mahathir and Musa administration introduced various innovative programs (Zain, 1986, p. 8) such as the "Look East" policy, aimed at getting the country to adopt the work ethics of Japan and Korea; the "Malaysian Incorporated" concept, where the government and the private sector would work together as a team in attaining economic and industrial success; "Leadership by Example" (linked to such present-day concepts as total quality management and management by objectives); and the policy of infusing Islamic values in administration. The latest in the series, dubbed "Vision 2020," premiered in 1991 and outlines the nine strategic challenges that Malaysia needs to address to achieve developed nation status by 2020. Indeed, with the advent of the multimedia super corridor project in 1995, Malaysia plans to become not only a developed society but also an informational society by the year 2020 (Jackson & Mosco, 1999).

Media and Corporations

In Malaysia the government has been reported to be the largest and the longest media user (Arun, 1986, p. 106). On a one-to-one and on an interpersonal or group basis, the government has been labeled the "largest single communicator" in the country (Arun, 1986, p. 106). Arun reported that newspapers in Malaysia carried news that was largely government oriented. A review of several of the major Malaysian dailies today shows that this is still true to a large extent.

As Salleh (1986) elaborates, in a developing country such as Malaysia, the editor has a responsibility to ensure that the newspaper helps support and further the government's efforts toward nation building, maintaining racial harmony, and fostering economic and political stability. To ensure this, public relations officers are attached to various ministers to serve as links between them and the Information Services Department. They assist in ensuring that all activities of the ministers are given full publicity by the mass media. All speeches and statements made by the ministers are distributed to more than fifty organizations in Malaysia, the local print media, radio, TV, foreign news agencies, high commissions, and embassies in Kuala Lumpur. The government controls the written press under the Malaysian Printing Presses and Publications Act of 1984 (*World Press Freedom Review,* 2001). Under this act, all printed publications are required to renew their licenses annually, although Internet sites are not required to have licenses to operate. The government has the power to shut down newspapers, withdraw publishers' licenses indefinitely, and arrest anyone who violates the act. Virtually all mainstream newspapers in Malaysia are owned or controlled by parties aligned to the National Front (*World Press Freedom Review,* 2001). According to Steven Gan, cofounder and editor-in-chief of Malaysiakini.com, an on-line news distributor, "Malaysia is an illiberal democracy. We have freedom of speech, but no freedom after speech. We have freedom of movement, but no freedom of assembly. We have a plethora of publications, but no press freedom" (*World Press Freedom Review,* 2001). Malaysiakini.com was reported to be in disfavor with Mahathir's administration because of the publication's increasing popularity, stemming from its mix of unbiased news coverage, investigative journalism, and in-depth analysis and commentary. In 2001, its reporters were officially banned from covering any government functions, supposedly on the grounds that it was an unlicensed publication (*World Press Freedom Review,* 2001). Despite the fact that Deputy Home Minister Chor Chee Heung had threatened to take unspecified action against Malaysiakini.com based on allegations of unethical funding, Gan held his ground. He stated that the allegations were without basis and added that he did not think that the government could afford to shut down the site because it had promised high-tech international investors that it would not censor the Internet (*World Press Freedom Review,* 2001).

In keeping with government control of the media, the private sector in Malaysia is expected to cooperate with the government and to pursue an enlightened public relations policy with the goal of creating an informed society while furthering the goals of economic growth, racial unity, and integration. It has been emphasized from the beginning that the private sector could not merely promote programs aimed at making profits for themselves (Salleh, 1986). According to ex-Prime Minister Hussein (1972), the private sector, under the New Economic Policy, was required to be a major motivator of social change and to help the government serve the interests of the Malaysian people by growing the economy, promoting integration, and leveling racial and social differences. He further emphasized that "corporate strategy must include recognition of the moral aspects of its strategic choice. It must be responsive to the needs of the new Malaysian society in the making" (Hussein, 1972, p. 6). This latter concept, dubbed "Corporate Social Responsibility" in business literature, has actually been emphasized only in relatively recent times in the United States.

In order to determine which constituents play major roles in Malaysian public relations, Taylor and Kent (1999) conducted a study of public relations practitioners in Kuala Lumpur in the fall of 1995. Included in this sample were an American-based public relations firm, two Malay-owned firms, a Chinese-owned conglomerate, a small business, a public relations educator/practitioner, and a newly privatized industry. Although the study contained diverse ethnic groups and represented varied business interests, as the authors themselves point out, it was by no means a random sample and certainly cannot be generalized to all public relations practitioners in Malaysia. The study, however, provides valuable information about the relative role of three key constituents—the government, the media, and the private sector.

Responsibilities reported by these public relations practitioners included writing news releases, planning communication efforts, working with marketing, and attempting to obtain favorable publicity for their clients and their organizations. The most significant aspect distinguishing the practice of public relations in Malaysia as compared to developed democracies such as the United States is the relationship between the media and government. In Malaysia, the media was reported to be government controlled, as is common in communist regimes. Journalists tended to report progovernment and probusiness news, even as industries were slowly being privatized. Newspapers lost their licenses if they dared to criticize the government. Public relations practitioners reported that, even when they did not communicate directly with government officials, "they always implicitly considered potential government response to organizational messages" (Taylor & Kent, 1999, p. 137). Government officials were routinely kept informed of organizational actions, even after the organizations were privatized. Respondents stated that this was especially true in times of organizational crisis. Government possessed the power to rescind the sale of a privatized company and to assume its daily operations. The communications director of the Chinese-owned conglomerate mentioned that the organization needed to be very careful, or else the government would make an "example of it" (Taylor & Kent, 1999, p. 138). This supports what many have characterized as the government's history of heavy-handedness and racial discrimination. Yet another practitioner noted that, although the government often hired public relations firms for contract work, it was usually the Malay-owned firms that were hired. Moreover, the government reportedly retained public relations firms that were owned and operated by Malays. The overwhelming consensus among the diverse public relations practitioners was that the government had "the ability and inclination to influence the practice of public relations" (Taylor & Kent, 1999, p. 138). Thus, firms had to be "vigilant" about keeping up-to-date on government initiatives and positions. According to Taylor and Kent (1999), in Malaysia "personal influence often counts for more than good business practices," and "public relations may be best understood as government relations" (p. 140). This emphasis on "personal influence" and on cultivating relationships with governmental publics is by no means unique to Malaysia. As pointed out by Sriramesh (1996), it is common in many developing nations, including India, which is interesting given that India has a different structure of democracy from Malaysia.

Consumers

In Malaysia the consumer movement traces its origin to December 1964, when the Penang Consumers' Association was formed as a result of a high level of public discontent with retail price fluctuations on essential items such as food (Adnan, 1986). Although the association became defunct only three months later because of the lack of a clear and sustained program, its founding inspired the formation of another consumer group—the Selangor Consumer Association (SCA) in January 1965. The latter survived because its founders recognized right from the start that there was a need to maintain a continuous and sustained public interest, as well as a need to develop a large membership. SCA was the first consumer association to recognize the importance of "brand consciousness or brand identity." In order to develop this, the group participated in a number of fairs and exhibitions, attempting to come in direct contact with the public, rather than merely appearing in a secondhand fashion through occasional mentions in news releases (Adnan, 1986). Surprisingly, the then-federal government was one of the first to encourage them, giving them a $5,000 "no strings attached" grant (Adnan, 1986, p. 28). It was the success of the SCA that led to other states in Malaysia forming their own consumer associations. In June 1973, the Federation of Malaysian Consumers' Associations (FOMCA) was formed, "with a view to providing the consumer movement in Malaysia with a national stature, and also, in order to act as a coordinating and consultative agency by, and through which, consumers' associations could exchange views and information, take collective decisions, and authorize action on matters of mutual importance" (Adnan, 1986, p. 31). In addition to the various state and independent district, and national organizations, there is also the International Organization of Consumers Unions (IOCU) with a regional office in Penang. Apart from tabloids, magazines, and newsletters, consumers' associations in Malaysia have produced books, leaflets, pamphlets, posters, and films dealing with consumer, environmental, and education issues (Adnan, 1986).

Despite the existence of all these consumer groups for so long, Man (2001) claims that the majority of Malaysian consumers are ignorant of the existence of relevant laws and facilities available to them, and also of the proper procedure for registering a complaint. This does not speak well of the effectiveness of public relations efforts on the part of the consumers associations. They are also reported (Man, 2001) to have trouble maintaining their memberships these days because many consumers join to help settle their particular problems and immediately drop out once they have been addressed.

As regards the procedure for redress, the government plays a large role again. The Ministry of Domestic Trade and Consumer Affairs arranges for settlements through the Consumer Claims Tribunal, an independent agency created under the Consumer Protection Act of 1999 (Man, 2001). The tribunal is present in every state and holds sessions on an as-required basis. Each side has to argue its case (lawyers are not allowed), and the judge rules on the decision, which is binding (Man, 2001). The good news is that awareness of this course of remedy appears to be spreading. All in all, 1,040 claims were filed in 2001, of which 744 were claims on goods and 296 cases pertained to services. Of these, 800 had been settled by the Consumer Claims Tribunal as of December 7, 2001 (Consumer claims, 2001). In contrast, there were only 291 total cases for 2000. The bad news is that because of the complicated procedure involved even those who may be aware of consumer protection laws sometimes cannot be bothered to take action. This is a far cry from the ease with which consumers in the United States can return unwanted/defective goods. Man (2001) states that there is no law that mandates a money-back clause and that firms are only required to offer a warranty or guarantee to repair or replace items within one year of purchase. Companies dealing with direct selling, however, are required to offer a ten-working-day cooling-off period, within which period the buyer can return goods for a refund. As of August 2001, the government was trying to formulate a new law aimed at promoting fair trade and fair competition. The Domestic Trade and Consumer Affairs Minister, Tan Sri Muhyiddin Yassin, hoped that the "to be enacted" law would help curb indiscriminate price increases (Bernama, 2001).

It appears as though there is a significant need in Malaysia for targeted public relations efforts aimed at consumer education and lobbying to make the process more consumer friendly. All in all, consumerism in Malaysia has a long way to go, and consumers are not at present a dominant player in Malaysia's public relations industry.

Public Relations and Higher Education

Malaysia has eleven public universities and colleges with a total enrollment of some 150,000 students as of 1999 (Ayob & Yaakub, 1999). Of these, ten use Bahasa Melayu, the national language, as the medium of instruction, except at the postgraduate level, where there is more flexibility. The eleventh, Kolej Tunku Abdul Rahman (KTAR), was established by the Malaysian Chinese Association, and uses mainly English as the instructional medium. The government guides the focus of the curricula, as well the policy and admission requirements at these public institutions, as is obvious from a study of the Web sites of some of these institutions. For example, the Universiti Sains Malaysia (www.bio.usm.my), which is advanced enough to have a distance learning program, nevertheless, requires candidates who want to do research in Malaysia to first seek permission from the Socio-Economic Research Unit of the Prime Minister's Department. It also states that application for admission to the undergraduate program is not direct and is processed together with the other local universities by the central processing unit, Higher Education Department, at the Ministry of Education. A review of the Web site of Universiti Utara Malaysia (www.uum.edu.my), linking to the faculty Web page of Professor Dr. Mohammad Haji Alias, reveals his list of research and consultancy projects. These clearly show that economic and rural development and information technology are priorities, in keeping with the government's priorities. Indeed, many of these projects are funded by government agencies. The stated mission on the Universiti Putra Malaysia's (UPM) Web site is "To be a leading center of learning and research, contributing not only towards human advancement and discovery of knowledge but also to the creation of wealth and nation building." Curricula at these public universities are geared toward accountancy and business management, information technology, and science and engineering. No evidence of public relations courses was found on the various (English-language) Web sites visited, although some material may conceivably be presented under the general heading of marketing. The exception is the Universiti Sains Malaysia in Penang (www.ips.usm.my/schoolsandcentres.html) whose School of Communication offers undergraduate as well as postgraduate studies in communications. Its bachelor of communication degree program allows for specialization in journalism, film, and broadcasting, or in persuasive communication. The persuasive communication major requires a variety of courses among which are public relations, advertising, media planning, campaign planning and evaluation, organizational communication, corporate communication, and a nine-credit persuasive communication package course in the final semester. According to the details provided on the Web site (www.comn.usm.my/Courses.htm), students registering for this last course are given the opportunity to plan, implement, and evaluate campaigns. Texts listed for these courses include popular Western texts as well as Malaysian ones.

Some of the universities are advanced enough to have an on-site business center or quality management center. For instance, the Universiti Putra Malaysia's University Business Centre (UBC) was established in July 1996 and is featured as the "investment arm" of the university; it is associated with UPM's commitment to commercializing technology and to assisting its academia into moving technology, capabilities, and expertise into the industry. University Utara Malaysia, which has the specific mission of providing education and research programs in the field of management, established a centre for quality management in 1991, which was upgraded to the Quality Management Institute in 1993 (www.uum.edu). The institute is charged with conducting research in problem areas of quality management and also with maintaining a database on quality and productivity movement in the country, with particular emphasis on the government's quality enhancement initiatives, ISO 9000 certification, and quality control circles (www.uum.edu). It is interesting to note, once again, the "corporatization of government" and vice versa, not to mention the strange dichotomy between advanced "Western" modes of operation and business models, coupled with fairly rigid government control. Malaysian public universities were corporatized in 1997, and many corporate figures have been appointed as directors to the management boards of these universities. However, the government's national policies, programs, and priorities still guide curricula and entrance requirements. Quality control at all universities (public and private) is being implemented through a National Accreditation Board (LAN) established by the government in 1997 and charged with scrutinizing all curriculum for accreditation and ranking purposes (Ayob & Yaakub, 1999).

Malaysia's affirmative action plan embodied in its New Economic Policy requires a quota system whereby some 55 percent of openings in public universities are reserved for *bumiputras,* or indigenous Malays. It was mainly because of the quota system that KTAR was founded to stem the outflow of qualified Chinese students to foreign universities. Until now, outspoken critics of the Malay quota policy have faced the possibility of being charged with sedition by the government (Cohen, 2001). Only recently, does it appear to have been brought home to the Mahathir administration that this "brain drain" of highly qualified Chinese is inconsistent with its efforts to position Malaysia as a high-tech giant in the South Asian region. What may be precipitating a relaxation in this regard is the fact that the top 560 scorers in the 2001 SPM examinations (Malaysian equivalent of O-levels) all failed to get seats at local universities. Without exception, all of them were Chinese (Cohen, 2001). Following this incident, in May 2001, the Malaysian government asked the nation's eleven national universities to make public their policies for granting admission to Chinese students.

Rapid economic growth, the quota system, and the rapid growth of information technology have been important contributing factors to the establishment and growth of about six hundred private higher education institutions in Malaysia. Several of these have "twinning" arrangements with foreign universities. Others have started collaborating with local public universities through a franchising program (Ayob & Yaakub, 1999). At the height of the economic boom in the mid-1990s, there was a need to speed up the production of skilled graduates, which spurred the Malaysian Parliament to pass the Private Higher Educational Institutions Act in 1996, thus allowing the private sector to enter the higher education market in an expanded, yet regulated, fashion. The act empowers the minister of education to approve or disapprove the setting up of private colleges and also to invite select corporations to start some. Along with this act, a new post-Registrar General of Private Higher Educational Institutions was created within the Ministry of Education, charged with the responsibility of "supervising" and "regulating" the operation of these "private" institutions. As pointed out by Ayob and Yaakub (1999), there are several in the business who regard it as a "highly regulated" industry, despite being corporatized or privatized. Thus, just as with the public colleges, the pure liberal arts such as history or literature are shunned even at the private institutions. Enrollment in the private universities totaled about one hundred thousand in 1999, with about 95 percent of these being non-*bumiputras.* Ironically, the Asian crisis and the resultant devaluation of the Malaysian ringgit also played a large role in increasing enrollment in these private universities because previously many such students had traveled overseas for education.

As a result of the competition in higher education, there has been an increase in aggressive and differentiated advertising, largely in the English-language print media. The *Star* carries the most advertisements for private higher education institutions and also runs education feature articles regularly (Ayob & Yaakub, 1999). Even though the products being promoted are essentially the same, for example, a degree in computer science, the fact that a college may be "twinning" with a specific foreign partner provides much of the rationale for the differentiation. Two examples offered by Ayob and Yaakub (1999) illustrate the point—a "HELP" Institute ad emphasizes that it is "more than a degree—it's an American experience," and RIMI College in Penang notes that it offers "a part-time American degree for busy people." Advertisements, however, have to be careful to comply with Article 75 of the 1996 act, outlawing false or misleading advertisements in promoting a private higher educational institution (Ayob & Yakub, 1999).

In the context of higher education in public relations, special mention must be made of the Institute of Public Relations Malaysia (IPRM), whose constitution was adopted by founding members in March 1962 (Goh, 1986). IPRM is the national professional body championing the cause of public relations and promoting it widely nationally and regionally. For example, IPRM played a key role in establishing the Federation of Asian Public Relations Organizations (FAPRO) in October 1977. The institute was formally incorporated as a company under the Companies Act 1965, with the registered name of Institut Perhubungan Raya Malaysia. It currently has about five hundred members, per its Web site (www.itm.edu.my/iprm). It is a nonprofit organization and the only institute that regulates the professional conduct of public relations practitioners in the country (Goh, 1986). These practitioners include full-time staff officials on the organization's payroll, a small number of consultancies (some of them branches of international public relations firms), and advertising agencies with specialized public relations departments. In addition to regulating professional conduct, the institute also is charged with interpreting public relations as a tool in nation building (Goh, 1986). It acts as an examining body for public relations examinations and promotes career development in public relations (www.itm.edu.my/iprm).

The institute's Education and Training Committee is charged with the responsibility of designing and conducting suitable courses to help practitioners, especially in the private sector. Professional courses in public relations offered by IPRM are listed under three modules: theory and evolution of public relations, skills and tools of communication in public relations, and public relations in practice (www.paac.edu.my). To cater to the needs of those who cannot take on-site classes, the Education and Training Committee initiated the distance learning programme (DLP), originally a correspondence course, in early 1984 (Goh, 1986).

IPRM also has a student association (IPRMSA). Its objectives (www.geocities.com/Athens/Sparta/9616/page5.html) include:

- Encouraging participation in public relations activities among students and academics from local universities and private colleges;
- Enhancing the image of the profession and the status and potential of the students through the activities held by the association;

- Cultivating mutual understanding and forging a closer relationship among IPRM professional public relations practitioners and student members; and
- Encouraging networking among students of all public relations programs of institutes of higher learning in Malaysia.

Public Relations Evolution— Where Does Malaysia Stand?

Van Leuven (1996) has identified a framework wherein a nation progresses from largely nation building, to market development, to establishing and maintaining regional interdependence. Concurrently, the practice of public relations is gradually expected to morph from one-way communication aimed largely at persuasion and education, to two-way communication ultimately emphasizing relationship building. As cautioned by Van Leuven (1996), the aforementioned three-stage development model need not have discrete starting and stopping points. Practices associated with the nation-building phase can exist concurrently with practices associated with the market-development phase, and also with the regional interdependence phase.

Has Malaysia made the transition from a government-dominated economy to a free-market economy? It has done so to an extent, as far as has been allowed by government. The case can be made that both before and after the Asian crisis, whenever market-controlled forces appeared to be acting in a manner detrimental to Malaysia's economic growth, the government stepped in and implemented short-term controls. Similarly, although the major industries and higher education in Malaysia are privatized, as in a free-market society, government controls are firmly in place through licensing, entry quotas, the accreditation process, approval of curricula, the necessity of complying with national acts, and the like. As for press freedom, there is little doubt that the media, other than the Internet, is still subject to government control.

According to Grunig and White (1992), two-way symmetrical communication has its basis in equality, autonomy, innovation, decentralized management, conflict resolution, and interest group liberalism. In Malaysia, the current relationship between the government and its constituents, such as the private sector, media, or consumers, still reflects a highly unequal status, thus inhibiting effective two-way symmetrical communication. As Taylor and Kent (1999) opine, "power distance" and "personal influence" seem to be more accurate frameworks for the practice of much of the public relations in Malaysia (and in other newly industrializing countries), given the cultural and linguistic conditions, minimal power of the media, and lack of consumer activism. Whereas the media are slowly beginning to deviate from this model, especially given the rising influence of Internet and Web-related, unregulated communications, activism and true consumer power lag severely behind that of developed democracies.

However, it can be argued that comprehensive campaign planning; use of outside consultants; and a four-stage approach to communication planning, involving research, action, communication, and evaluation, imply a transition into the market-development phase (Van Leuven, 1996). Furthermore, the extent of privatization of key industries (such as the telecommunications industry), the use of regional satellite and cable services, the relaxation of Bahasa Malay as the medium of instruction in private universities, the opening up and allowing of foreign universities to partner with Malaysian ones, and the move toward interactive media technologies all reflect a degree of regional interdependence, the third and final stage of development. Certainly, the World Wide Web is an important communications tool (Hill & White, 2000), and Web sites can be used to keep stakeholders up-to-date, provide information to media, gather information about publics, strengthen corporate "brand identity," as well as conduct e-commerce. Web sites in the United States tend to be highly interactive, and those of all major corporations are geared toward e-commerce. In contrast, e-commerce is in its formative phase in Malaysia. Although several firms have progressed beyond providing mere information, or "brochureware," into the "interactions phase," very few have reached the e-commerce phase, although many are planning to do so (Le & Koh, 2002).

According to Khattab (2001), media in Malaysia have been transformed from mainstream, mechanical modes of transmission to passive audiences, to multifaceted, multimedia, interactive communication channels with an active interpretive audience. Khattab also argues that there is increased activism and consumerism in Malaysia. One should note, however, that this is probably relative to the way Malaysia society was in the mid- to late 1990s.

Two items are worth mentioning in this regard. One is the increasing push toward retail loyalty programs in Malaysia. Ganesan (2001) reported that, as of June 2001, about 2.5 million individuals held some sort of loyalty card, as the battle among retailers for customers heated up. The obvious advantage of such programs for retailers, apart from retaining customers, is that it facilitates database compilation of relevant demographic and purchase pattern information. Eventually, this could help propel Malaysia into the relationship management stage via micromarketing. The second trend is the increasing use of credit. Ganesan (2002) reported that, according to Bank Negara Malaysia, plastic money transactions in 2001 were at RM 17.99 billion, which represents an increase of 25.79 percent over credit card transactions in 2000. The point could be made that increasing use of credit with its resultant "paper trail" may make it easier to substantiate claims for returns and exchanges. At present however, the level of consumerism and two-way interaction still lags far behind that of established democracies.

Strategic management is a four-stage process involving planning, implementation, standard setting and performance measurement, and feedback. That the Malaysian government has been long aware of this is evident in an excerpt from a speech in 1972 by then-Prime Minister Hussein (1972):

> Effective communication has to go beyond just keeping the public informed of the reasons behind government policy decisions. . . . Most important, it must have an effective system of feedback. The government must be able to check its performance to see if it has not gone off track. . . . Our communication must be able to produce adaptive behavior. It must be able to help us constantly to refine our performance in the interest of our national survival.

Relationship management, however, implies effective communication, mutual adaptation, mutual dependency, shared values, and above all, trust and commitment. Each transaction contact with the public is treated as a step toward fostering a long-term relationship.

Needless to say, public relations, neither in the public nor the private sector, in Malaysia has attained this level. It appears as though Malaysian public relations at the present time can best be characterized as concurrently having layers or aspects of nation building, market development, and regional interdependence. Communication still tends to be largely asymmetric, reflecting centralized management on the part of government. As opined by Taylor and Kent (1999), the lack of consumer activism in Malaysia makes the practice of public relations less crisis driven than in the West because the Malaysian public does not actively question organizational policy. They further point out that the converse, therefore, holds true too, that is, organizations in Malaysia do not need to waste their scarce resources communicating with the general public to the extent that their counterparts in the United States do, although they certainly do need to communicate with government.

Even consumer advocates in Malaysia seem to acquiesce to government leadership. For instance, Datuk Anwar Fazal, a consumer advocate, counsels Malaysians that "when something is wrong, don't let it go or let it be" (Emmanuel, 2002). However, at the same time he argues that more action needs to be initiated at the *government* level. He specifically proposes the following:

- A Center for Consumer Studies that can contribute systematically to the intellectual and utilitarian aspects of the consumer movement;
- An annual "State of the Consumer Report" to be debated on World Consumer Rights Day;
- A guaranteed budget for the Center for Consumer Studies and the Annual State of the Consumer Report through a tax on advertising;
- Systematic training of consumer professionals; and
- A consumer complaints page in every newspaper.

Prime Minister Mahathir recently noted in the *Star Online* (Leoi, 2002):

Malaysia is an Asian country. We do not reject all Western values but where we think Asian values are better, we should be allowed to retain our values. . . . We believe that only peace can bring about prosperity. In the maintenance of peace, sacrifices must be made and we are prepared to make these because we do not believe in being beholden to ideology (of democracy) to the point of destroying ourselves. . . . We regard it as wrong for individuals and minorities to exercise their rights in a disruptive way. The exercise of human rights must be accompanied by responsibility towards the community and towards maintaining stability and peace. If anyone shows a lack of this responsibility, then he must forfeit his rights.

On June 25, 2002, only a few months after delivering the preceding statements, Dr. Mahathir announced his resignation from office, taking everybody by surprise. On being pleaded with (by party officials and cabinet members) to reconsider, he agreed to hold office until October 25, 2003, to allow for a smooth transition of power to his successor Abdullah Ahmad Badawi, currently the deputy prime minister (Bonner, 2002).

Conclusion

In Malaysia, excellence in public relations is still slowly emerging as is democracy itself. Given that U.S. public relations theories have as their basis democracy and capitalism (Pearson, 1990), will Malaysian public relations ever attain these so-called Western ideals? Will the advent of the multimedia super corridor and accelerated thrust into the Internet and a Web-based information age foster more open, two-way interaction in society, and thus tilt the balance away from Malaysia's particular brand of "Asian democracy" toward more conventionally understood and accepted Western norms of democracy? The point is arguable. Indeed, the majority of Malaysia's people, and certainly its government, may not even aspire to attaining such Western ideals either in governance or in public relations.

Discussion Questions

1. Singapore and Malaysia are close neighbors and trade partners. Compare and contrast the present status of the evolution of their public relations industries.

2. Use major search engines, such as Google, Askjeeves, Lycos, or Infoseek, to locate five major Malaysian university Web sites. Surf them and gauge their level of interactivity. What can you conclude about their course offerings? Repeat the same exercise with five moderately large U.S. universities. What are the differences (if any) with regard to Web site construction, curricula, and level of interactivity? How do you explain the differences?

3. How important are social and cultural values (including language and religion) in shaping the way public relations is conducted in a country? The majority of Malays are Muslims. Would this impact public relations practices? If so, how?

4. Discuss what is meant by consumerism. Research on-line some recent editions of major newspapers in the following countries: England, Malaysia, India, Singapore, and Indonesia. What is the extent and nature of consumerism in these countries? Are there distinct differences? How do you explain them?

5. How would you define democracy? Access several different sources for reference. Is there only one generally accepted definition or can you find several? If several, do you think the differences lie in the semantics of the wording or more in the interpretation and implementation? Discuss. How do you think the "state of democracy" of a country would affect its public relations practices? Again, elaborate.

References

ACNielson Media International. (2001, September 21). Newspapers retain lead, Ad. Expenditure Survey 2001. *The Malay Mail.* [On-line]. Available: adtimes.nstp.com.my/archive/2001/sep21.htm

Adnan, M. (1986). Public relations for consumers associations. In B. Morais & H. Adnan (Eds.), *The Malaysian experience* (pp. 26–46). Kuala Lumpur: Institut Perhubungan Raya Malaysia, Federal Publications Sdn. Bhd.

Arun, K. (1986). Media relations. In B. Morais & H. Adnan (Eds.), *The Malaysian experience* (pp. 106–107). Kuala Lumpur: Institut Perhubungan Raya Malaysia, Federal Publications Sdn. Bhd.

Asia Development Bank. (2000). [On-line]. Available: http://europa.eu.int/comm/external_relations/malaysia/intro/index

Ayob, A., & Yaakub, N. (1999, December 6–8). *Business of higher education in Malaysia: Development and prospects in the new millenium.* Presented at the ASAIHL conference, The Auckland Institute of Technology, New Zealand.

Bani, E. (2000, August 16). Survey shows increase of radio listeners. *Business Times,* Media and Services, p. 7.

Bernama (2001, August 17). Ministry drafting new law to protect consumers: Muhyiddin. *Business Times,* Nation. [On-line]. Available: http://adtimes.nstp. com.my/archive/2001/aug17a.htm

Bonner, R. (2002, June 26). Malaysia's prime minister to step down after two decades. *The New York Times.* [On-line]. Available: www.nytimes.com/2002/06/ 26/international/asia/26MALA.html

Boon, K. (2001, May 9). Advertising a dynamic force behind healthy economies. *Business Times,* Nation, p. 2.

Cohen, D. (2001, May 3). Malayan universities rejecting Chinese students. *Education Guardian Co.,* U.K. [On-line]. Available: http://education.guardian.co. uk/Distribution/Redirect_Artifact/0,4678,0-483781, 00.html

Consumer claims tribunal solves 800 cases, says Muhyiddin-Nation. (2001, December 7). *Business Times.* [On-line]. Available: http://adtimes.nstp.com.my/archive/ 2001/dec7a.htm

Emmanuel, M. (2002, March 14). World Consumer Rights Day. *New Straits Times,* Focus. [On-line]. Available: http://adtimes.nstp.com.my/archive/2002/mac14. htm

Errion, L., & Carroll, P. (1990, October). Marketing in Malaysia. Overseas Business Reports (Report No. OBR 90-11). U.S. Department of Commerce, International Trade Administration.

Ganesan, V. (2001, June 27). More Malaysians join retail loyalty programmes. *Business Times,* Companies. [On-line]. Available: http://adtimes.nstp.com.my/ archive/2001/jun27.htm

Ganesan, V. (2002, February 5). Malaysians keen on using credit card. *Business Times,* Nation. [On-line]. Available: http://adtimes.nstp.com.my/archive/ 2002/feb5a.htm

Goh, S. (1986). History of IPRM. In B. Morais & H. Adnan (Eds.), *The Malaysian experience* (pp. 193–203). Kuala Lumpur: Institut Perhubungan Raya Malaysia, Federal Publications Sdn. Bhd.

Grunig, J. E., & White, J. (1992). The effect of workviews on public relations theory and practice. In J. E. Grunig (Ed.), *Excellence in public relations and communication management* (pp. 31–64). Hillsdale, NJ: Lawrence Erlbaum Associates.

Heibert, M. (1998, May 28). Lessons from Malaysia. *Far Eastern Economic Review.* [On-line]. Available: www.worldbank.org/eapsocial/countries/malay/ pov1.htm

Hill, L., & White, C. (2000). Public relations practitioners' perception of the World Wide Web as a communications tool. *Public Relations Review, 26*(1), 31–51.

Hussein, T. (1972, September 8). *Motivating the people: The role of public relations in the implementation of the new economic policy.* Presentation at Dewan Tunku Abdul Rahman, Kuala Lumpur.

Hutton, J. (1999). The definition, dimensions, and domain of public relations. *Public Relations Review, 25*(2), 199–214.

Jackson, S., & Mosco, V. (1999). The political economy of new technological spaces: Malaysia's multimedia super corridor. *Journal of International Communication, 6*(1), 23–40.

John, E., & Damis, A. (2002, January 13). Advertisers beginning to eye Malay market. *New Straits Times,* p. 2.

Khattab, U. (2001, September 7). Where is public relations and where is it going? *New Straits Times.* [On-line]. Available: http://adtimes.nstp.com.my/ archive/2001/sep7a.htm

Le T., & Koh, A. (2002). A managerial perspective on electronic commerce development in Malaysia. *Electronic Commerce Research, 2,* 7–29.

Leoi, S. (2002, April 12). Dr. M: Malaysia has the right to do things its way. *The Star Online,* Nation. [On-line]. Available: www.thestar.com.my/news/story. asp?file=/2002/4/12/nation/11william&sec=nation

Lin, J. (1999, November). *The Asian financial and economic crisis: Causes and long-term implications.* Paper presented at the Manila Social Forum: The New Social Agenda for East and Southeast Asia, Manila, Philippines. [On-line]. Available: www. worldbank.org/eapsocial/manila99

Man, P. (2001, December 10). Asserting consumer rights. *New Straits Times,* Life and Times, p. 2.

Mohamed, D. (1998, October 4). *Malaysia: Measures for economic recovery.* Presented to the International Monetary Fund, World Bank Group, Washington, DC.

Pearson, R. (1990). Perspectives on public relations history. *Public Relations Review, 16,* 27–38.

Salleh, M. (1986). Government public relations. In B. Morais & H. Adnan (Eds.), *The Malaysian experience* (pp. 77–85). Kuala Lumpur: Institut Perhubungan Raya Malaysia, Federal Publications Sdn. Bhd.

Sriramesh, K. (1996). Power distance and public relations: An ethnographic study of Southern Indian organizations. In H. Culbertson & N. Chen (Eds.), *International public relations: A comparative analysis* (pp. 171–190). Mahwah, NJ: Lawrence Erlbaum Associates.

Taylor, M., & Kent, M. (1999). Challenging assumptions of international public relations: When government is the most important public. *Public Relations Review, 25*(2), 131–144.

Universiti Sains Malaysia. Available: www.bio.usm.my

Universiti Utara Malaysia's Quality Management Institut. Available: www.uum.edu.my/ipq/i_about.html

U.S. Department of Commerce International Trade Administration. (1993, May). *Foreign economic trends and their implications for the United States—Malaysia.* (FET 93-07).

U.S. Department of Commerce Office of Telecommunication Technologies. (2000). [On-line]. Available: www.corporateinformation.com/mysector/Telecommunications.html

U.S. Department of State. (2001). *Country commercial guide (2001).* [On-line]. Available: www.corporate-information.com/mysector/Media.html

Van Leuven, J. (1996). Public relations in South East Asia from nation-building campaigns to regional interdependence. In H. Culbertson & N. Chen (Eds.), *International public relations: A comparative analysis* (pp. 207–222). Mahwah, NJ: Lawrence Erlbaum Associates.

World Development Indicators. (2001). [On-line]. Available: http://devdata.worldbank.org/hnstats/files/MYS_pop.xls.

World Press Freedom Review (2001). [On-line]. Available: www.freemedia.at/wpfr/Asia/malaysia.htm

Zain, D. (1986). Public relations practice in Malaysia: An overview. In B. Morais & H. Adnan (Eds.), *The Malaysian experience* (pp. 4–6). Kuala Lumpur: Institut Perhubungan Raya Malaysia, Federal Publications Sdn. Bhd.

Index